THE EARLY YEARS

1756–1781

Mozart

THE EARLY YEARS
1756–1781

Stanley Sadie

Foreword by Neal Zaslaw

OXFORD
UNIVERSITY PRESS

OXFORD

UNIVERSITY PRESS

Great Clarendon Street, Oxford OX2 6DP

Oxford University Press is a department of the University of Oxford.
It furthers the University's objective of excellence in research, scholarship,
and education by publishing worldwide in

Oxford New York

Auckland Cape Town Dar es Salaam Hong Kong Karachi
Kuala Lumpur Madrid Melbourne Mexico City Nairobi
New Delhi Shanghai Taipei Toronto

With offices in

Argentina Austria Brazil Chile Czech Republic France Greece
Guatemala Hungary Italy Japan Poland Portugal Singapore
South Korea Switzerland Thailand Turkey Ukraine Vietnam

Oxford is a registered trade mark of Oxford University Press
in the UK and in certain other countries

British Library Cataloguing in Publication Data
Data available

Library of Congress Cataloging in Publication Data
Sadie, Stanley.
Mozart : the early years, 1756–1781 / Stanley Sadie.—1st ed.
p. cm.
Includes bibliographical references (p.) and index.
1. Mozart, Wolfgang Amadeus, 1756–1791.
2. Composers—Austria—Biography. I. Title.
ML410.M9S153 2006
780'.92—dc22
[B]
2005018637

Typeset by SPI Publisher Services, Pondicherry, India
Printed in Great Britain by
Ashford Colour Press Ltd, Gosport, Hampshire

ISBN 978–0–19–816529–3 (Hbk.)   978–0–19–921475–4 (Pbk.)

1 3 5 7 9 10 8 6 4 2

This book is dedicated by the publisher to Julie Anne Sadie
and to the memory of Stanley Sadie

CONTENTS

ILLUSTRATIONS

FOREWORD
BY NEAL ZASLAW

IT WAS MANY years ago that Stanley Sadie revealed to me his desire to write a 'big book' about Mozart's life, times and music. I came to understand that by 'big book' he meant something general as well as something personal—'general' in the sense that no single book has ever managed to occupy the position long held by Otto Jahn's path-breaking four-volume biography of 1856–9, written simultaneously and in conjunction with Ludwig Köchel's similarly path-breaking catalogue of Mozart's works. These two scholars jointly established the historical landscape in which subsequent writing about Mozart would be placed. Jahn's pioneering study was as comprehensive and as reliable in its details as the then-current state of knowledge about Mozart permitted. Jahn created a sympathetic, coherent portrait of a cultural hero for German lands, a portrait that satisfied many generations of music lovers. His vision is with us still—in sublimated form—in thousands of program notes, recording notes, popular essays and books.

Jahn's work was revised several times before Hermann Abert thoroughly reworked it in 1919–21, taking advantage of seventy additional years of research and adjusting Jahn's tone and opinions to post–World War I European sensibilities. Subsequently, Abert's version of Jahn itself went through revisions. The flood of Central European performers, critics and musicologists fleeing Nazism to Great Britain, North America, Australia and New Zealand in the 1930s and 40s ensured that the Jahn-Abert image of Mozart was transplanted to the musical and academic cultures of the English-speaking world.

The absence of a replacement for Jahn has not been for lack of trying. Books about Mozart number in the hundreds. Yet even though a few of them are outstanding contributions, no author has succeeded in creating a Mozart for our times in quite the way that Jahn created the Mozart for his times and Abert for his. The person who came closest for the Anglophone world was Alfred Einstein, one of those who fled to the United States in the 1930s. In his books, articles and revisions of Köchel's catalogue, Einstein dominated post–World War II thinking about Mozart. He modified but did not replace Jahn-Abert.

For a number of reasons, no one has been able to occupy the position once held by Jahn. Certainly, the world of high culture is a more fractured, fractious place than it once was, and we are less inclined to accept spurious 'official' or totalizing views of the world. The daunting amount of historical material now available to document Mozart's life, works and times, combined, paradoxically, with the certainty that no amount of evidence could suffice to answer all questions, leaves open endless possibilities for more or less convincing interpretations. Recent valuable biographies in English have been produced by Maynard Solomon, Ruth Halliwell, and Stanley Sadie himself (see below).

The failure of most authors to alter the obsolete aspects of the Jahn–Abert–Einstein take on Mozart is due at least in part to their political or cultural aspirations (not that Jahn, Abert or Einstein lacked such aspirations!). Mozart's music, his prestige and his persona have been, and continue to be, contested cultural property. Many biographies, especially but not exclusively popular books of *haute vulgarisation*, made him a supernatural phenomenon—more god than man—a brilliant meteor that flashed across the skies of the dying *ancien régime* and burnt out in a blaze of glory. Polyanna-ish good-old-days biographies made him a kind of royalist. Biographies from Germany and Austria during the Nazi era represented him as a Germanic nationalist, whereas books from other countries needed to see him as a cosmopolitan lover of mankind in general, the best of Germanic culture before it took a grievously wrong turn. Biographies from Eastern Europe (and occasionally elsewhere) wanted to see Mozart as a people's composer—a proponent of Socialist Realism *avant la lettre*. And not surprisingly, many of the intellectual trends of the late twentieth century have been applied to Mozart biography: he has of course been the subject of social history, the history of ideas and histories of musical style. He has also been put on the psychoanalytical couch, acquired status as a New Age guru, and made into a pink-haired punk. He has been constructed, deconstructed and reconstructed.

Because of the complexity of Mozart's person, music and times, and given the vast amount of extant documentation about all these aspects, almost any approach to writing about him can be supported by at least some evidence, and often by a great deal of it. The difficult task that Stanley seemed to have in mind was to consider all of these approaches but allow none to hijack the narrative. Thus the 'general' picture.

On the personal side Stanley was, I suspect, thinking about the way his career had gone. Despite his prolific contributions as a music critic, broadcaster, reviewer, essayist, author and editor (detailed in *Words About Mozart*, a 2005 festschrift in his honor), and especially in his crowning achievement of creating nearly from scratch *The New Grove Dictionary of Music and Musicians*, arguably the finest music encyclopedia ever conceived, Stanley longed to have the leisure to make a different type of original contribution to scholarship. He loved Mozart's music and knew it well, having written about it on many occasions. He himself wrote the Mozart article for *The New Grove*, which then enjoyed success as a separate publication. But even a relatively long encyclopedia article must be compact and factual, lacking adequate space to explore complex or contentious issues, to limn the background, to take time to dwell on the many fascinating elements that would comprise a fully nuanced telling. Stanley wanted to have a go at our culture's portrayal of Mozart, painting it in his own way on a large canvas.

Stanley was one of the hardest-working people I ever met. He often had several projects under way at once, pursuing them with fierce determination and lucid organization. It was those qualities, along with an extraordinary memory for details (decades after a year I had spent in London, he still could summon up my phone number there, which I myself had long forgotten), that enabled him to create *The New Grove*, which involved coordinating unimaginable amounts of information, dealing with numerous contributors from every continent—some of them temperamental, others tardy in meeting their deadlines—and then choosing, training and supervising a staff to high levels of competence. His journalistic and broadcast assignments had given him the opportunity to hone his prose style, which was elegant and clear without being patronizing. His work on *The New Grove* had turned him into a generalist who could deal with arcane details without losing track of larger contexts. These were the skills he brought to his desire to write a big book about Mozart.

I suspect that Stanley thought about this book as he commuted to and from work or lay awake at night, but his seemingly endless rounds of other assignments meant that he had trouble finding uninterrupted time for a project of such scope. A research fellowship at Sidney Sussex College of the University of Cambridge gave him some weeks of calm, during which he was able to outline the book and write drafts of some chapters. But then a horrific automobile accident in the Ukrainian-Russian outback, while researching *Calling on the Composer*, a book on composers' homes written with his wife, Julie Anne, proved to be a major setback. Fortunately he was flown to London by a rescue service, miraculously brought back from death's door and reassembled by skillful surgeons. Soon he was back to other work, and the big book had to be put aside.

Finally, Stanley left his beloved London and retreated to the bucolic splendor of the Manor House at Cossington. There he and

Julie founded a concert series, tended their garden, and entertained visiting family, friends and colleagues; and he began to finish what he had begun at Cambridge. But disaster struck again, this time in the form of a wasting illness that slowly sapped Stanley's strength. With the tenacity that had characterized all his endeavors, he succeeded in finishing the first half of his Mozart biography, working at it until almost his last day.

Reading Stanley's account of the early years of Mozart's life, I experience many emotions. Sorrow at having lost a valued friend and colleague. Admiration for the book and for the doggedness that enabled him to finish it even as his life ebbed away. Pleasure at the idea that he was able to finish it. Enjoyment of an old story well told with many a new twist. Regret at never being able to read his take on the final ten years of Mozart's life.

Stanley's book has many virtues, resulting in part from his command of the vast Mozart literature, of which he somehow kept abreast until the end. This factual basis undergirds his companionable prose style, an obvious passion for the task at hand, his ability to deal with controversial issues in an even-handed manner, and perhaps most strikingly, his gift for conveying a sense of time and place. Stanley had visited most of the cities, villages, courts and monasteries that the widely traveled Mozart had frequented, walking in and around the surviving houses, theaters and palaces where Mozart had walked. His words have the ability almost to make you feel the cobblestones underfoot, smell the inns and horses, and hear the music. Stanley's Mozart is not an idealized archetype but a flesh-and-blood—if exceptionally gifted—human being trying to live his life. It is perhaps no longer possible to write a single Mozart for our fractious times, but Stanley Sadie has come perhaps as close as anyone could.

Cornell University
June 2005

PREFACE

I MAKE NO APOLOGY for adding to the voluminous Mozart literature. Abundant as it is, it still has several conspicuous lacunae, of which the most obvious and perhaps the most surprising is an up-to-date study in English of Mozart's life and works. The present book is designed to remedy that situation. It is the first of two volumes, chronologically organized; the second will cover Mozart's Vienna years, 1781–1791. [*The author did not, unfortunately, live to complete the second volume.—Ed.*]

There are of course other biographies in English, and more are to be published in the 250th anniversary year of 2006. My book, how-ever, is designed on a rather larger scale than most and is intended to be as near to comprehensive as such a book can reasonably be. No event in Mozart's life is ignored. No major work and very few minor ones are passed over without discussion in terms both of context and of the music itself. By context I mean two things: first, the reason Mozart composed the work when he did (for Mozart, a professional of his time, never wrote a piece of music simply because he felt like it or because of some 'inner need' but virtually always because it was in some sense a requirement[1]); and secondly, the reason for writing the work *as* he did—that is, its relation to other works of the kind, for we cannot begin to understand Mozart unless we are able to distinguish what is unique to him. These are ambitious aims and I do not often achieve them, the first for dearth of specific information, the second because it is impossible to know enough of the music that he knew, or to hear it as he heard it.

In any case, the 'facts' are always changing about anyone who is the subject of as much intensive research as Mozart. A great deal of new material has come to light in recent decades—not discoveries of unknown works (some unimportant ones apart), but information gleaned in new ways from existing material. The sketches (now for the first time completely published, by Ulrich Konrad) and the autograph manuscripts (now meticulously analysed for their handwriting, by Wolfgang Plath, and the papers on which they are written, by Alan Tyson) have yielded new information on Mozart's methods of composition and on the dates of many of his works—and no doubt the fresh cataloguing of his works (by Neal Zaslaw) will also be productive. Some of this information carries significant biographical ramifications. It does not solve all the mysteries and sometimes substitutes new ones for old. I have tried to digest and interpret all such information and to inch closer to the truth. Similarly as regards the circumstances of his life: new work has modified our view of his career, both in Salzburg (Cliff Eisen, Ruth Halliwell, Ernst Hintermaier, Manfred H. Schmid) and in Vienna (Viktor Braunbehrens, Dexter Edge, Dorothea Link, Mary Sue Morrow, H.C. Robbins Landon).

The most important source for the events of Mozart's life is, of course, the family correspondence. Since 1975 this has been available, in the original German, in a complete critical edition with detailed commentary (edited by Wilhelm A. Bauer, Otto Erich Deutsch and J.H. Eibl). The standard English edition is that of 1938, the translation by Emily Anderson, which includes all the letters then known that were written by Mozart himself (one paragraph excepted) but excludes because of space constraints large sections of the letters written by Leopold Mozart. Anderson stated that all material directly concerning Mozart himself is included, and in a narrow sense that is generally true. More broadly, however, Leopold's letters are seriously misrepresented by the exclusions, which lead to a false idea of his (and indeed Wolfgang's) interests and priorities and often present remarks or passing references in Wolfgang's responses that seem arbitrary and hard to understand. These have frequently drawn unwary Mozart biographers into traps that I hope I have been able generally to avoid. On the basis of the letters, it is not possible to understand the family's concerns, their attitudes to the Salzburg court and their friends and colleagues in the city, or for example their feelings on medical matters or religious ones—both of which bulk large—without looking at the correspondence in its totality. In quoting the letters, I have often drawn on Anderson's translations but have usually modified them in the hope of conveying more clearly Mozart's meaning and something too of his use of language.[2] (References in the notes to both the English [LMF] and the German [MBA] editions of the letters are by letter number, not by page.)

The excepted paragraph referred to above, written on 13 October 1781, instructs Leopold on the remedial value of a packet of wagon-grease carried on his chest and of a vealbone in his pocket. It may not be very important, but it does tell us something about Mozart. I cite this as a warning, lest we feel too readily that we can identify with the Mozart family and its world. This applies not only to areas in which there has been scientific progress. Writing to his sister from Milan in 1771, Mozart comments on having just seen a group of rascals hanged in the Piazza del Duomo: 'they hang them here just as they do in Lyons'. The Mozarts had been in Lyons in 1766, when their parents took the ten-year-old Wolfgang and fifteen-year-old Nannerl for a jolly treat one free afternoon.

The new Romantic age that broke just at the time of Mozart's death had a profound influence on attitudes to Mozart and his music. The Romanticization of Mozart biography affected the reading of his letters: early biographers were predisposed to think that the fact of Mozart's genius meant that he must be trusted and that he always told the truth. This idea was accepted by most modern commentators, although there have been questioning voices among English-language writers and, since Hildesheimer, German ones too. Recent Mozart literature has demonstrated, many times over, that not everything in the letters can be taken at face value. The Mozarts, like everybody else, wrote letters designed to convey something more complex than simple factual information, especially at times of family crisis or disagreement. Romantic biography—fed by all manner of tales, from the childhood anecdotes retailed in his obituary to the idea that he could conceive entire works without writing anything down and died haunted at the idea of composing his own Requiem—had an enduring effect on the Mozart literature and one that the modern biographer has to take into account.

There is, inevitably, a certain amount of technical musical terminology used in this book: for this I apologize to those who find it difficult to cope with. It is, however, unavoidable in the kind of book that aims to consider, at least at some level, how Mozart put his music together. Terms relating to musical forms are used as defined in *The New Grove Dictionary of Music and Musicians*, which is to say in only their traditional sense, which any dictionary of music will explain (I use 'rounded binary' for what is essentially a sonata-form movement that lacks a tonic recapitulation of the first subject).

Money

Financial matters, inevitably, are often mentioned in this book. The basic unit of money for the Mozart family was the gulden or florin. Leopold Mozart's annual salary in Salzburg during Mozart's youth was generally between 350 and 450 gulden. There were 60 kreuzers to the gulden and, in Salzburg, $4^1/_2$ gulden to the ducat (in some areas of the Habsburg empire the ducat held a slightly different value). Most of the Mozart family references to money matters are conducted in gulden and I have followed that as a general procedure. But many other currencies are mentioned in the correspondence, among them the French louis d'or, which during the time under discussion was usually worth about 11 gulden, the Italian cigliato, about one ducat, and the English guinea (£1.1s.), about 10 gulden. Direct comparisons however are often misleading, because of the wide differences of living costs between countries or even within a single country, and other arrangements left unspecified: Haydn's salary in the Esterházy establishment, for example, included a certain amount of payment in kind (straw, firewood, wine, medical services etc.).

K.

Mozart's works are identified in this book, as everywhere else, by their K. or Köchel numbers (or in German, KV), as they have been since the publication of the first edition of Ludwig von Köchel's chronological thematic catalogue, *Chronologisch-thematisches Verzeichnis sämtlicher Tonwerke Wolfgang Amadé Mozarts* (Leipzig, 1862). A second edition, edited by Paul, Graf von Waldersee, was published in 1905, and a heavily revised third, edited by Alfred Einstein, in 1937, with a supplement in 1947. The so-called fourth and fifth editions are simply reprints; the next true edition was the sixth, edited by Franz Giegling, Alexander Weinmann and Gerd Sievers (Wiesbaden, 1964; subsequently numbered editions are also unchanged reprints). A new edition, scheduled for publication in 2006, edited by Neal Zaslaw and others, is in preparation; it will have no further number changes. The chronological numbering ran from 1 to 626 in the first two editions. Einstein's and later the sixth edition's redating of many works, as well as their addition of works rediscovered or newly considered authentic and the rejection of others regarded as unauthentic, involved shifting works to, from and between appendices and much renumbering, which was done by the introduction of letters auxiliary to the numbers: for example, K.204 became K.213*a* (meaning that it was now thought to have been composed immediately after K.213) and K.364 became K.320*d*. Sometimes capital letters had also to be introduced, for example for works thought to fall between K.173*d* and K.173*e* (K.182 and 183 became K.173*dA* and 173*dB*). Because the traditional ones are so familiar, such numberings are usually given in double form, generally as K.204/213*a* (the form used in this book), K.204=213*a* or K.204 (213*a*). The redatings resulting from more recent research in fact mean that even the numberings of the sixth edition correspond uncertainly with the actual chronology. Where it is necessary to refer to specific editions of the Köchel catalogue, the forms K^1, K^3 and K^6 are used for the first, third and sixth editions. For full bibliographic descriptions of these and of the standard scholarly edition of Mozart's works, familiarly known as the 'Neue Mozart-Ausgabe' [NMA], see the table of abbreviations preceding the notes, pages 549–50.

Acknowledgments

I am grateful to Sidney Sussex College, Cambridge, for granting me a Visiting Fellowship that enabled me to get this book started. I should like to thank Peter Adcock for his work on the music examples and Bruce Cooper Clarke for reading over the entire manuscript.

Stanley Sadie
London
27 January 2005

The issue in paperback of Stanley's book provided an opportunity to make small editorial corrections. I am pleased to acknowledge here the generous assistance of Peter Adcock, William Cowdery, and Bonna Boettcher (Music Librarian of Cornell University).

Julie Anne Sadie
Cossington
26 April 2007

Publisher's Acknowledgments

The publisher wishes to acknowledge the generous assistance of the late author's wife, Julie Anne Sadie, who stepped in under extraordinarily difficult circmstances to become a vital team member in helping to guide this book on its path to publication. We also wish to express our overwhelming gratitude to Neal Zaslaw, who read the entire manuscript, made many important suggestions, and wrote a valuable foreword. Also, we are grateful to Robert Levin, who contributed numerous significant, last-minute corrections and improvements.

Mozart

THE EARLY YEARS

1756–1781

1

Salzburg and the Mozart Family

RANTED THE SCALE of Mozart's genius, we can still see that much of Mozart's destiny as a composer was determined by the place and time of his birth and the family into which he was born. Of his father, Leopold Mozart, by far the most formative and most powerful influence on his character and his career, much more will emerge as the story of Mozart's life unfolds. But first it may be best to sketch the significance of his birthplace, Salzburg, as a centre, political and ecclesiastical—which matters determined to a large extent its musical life—along with its geography, its size and its social make-up.

Salzburg, a city at the north-eastern extreme of the Alps on the river Salzach, now in Austria close to the Bavarian border, began its modern development at the end of the seventh century with the foundation of a Benedictine abbey (St Peter's, the oldest monastery in the German lands) and a cathedral shortly thereafter.[1] It then became an archbishopric. It fell within the Holy Roman Empire of the German Nation established under Charlemagne in 800, a fairly loose league of independently ruled states, which until its dissolution during the Napoleonic wars extended through all the German-speaking lands as well as present Belgium, the Czech Republic, part of Poland, Slovenia and Croatia. In the thirteenth century the emperor (a Habsburg, as the emperors normally were) appointed the Salzburg archbishops as princes within the empire, so that they were temporal as well as spiritual rulers.

The Salzburg archdiocese, which extended across much of Upper and Lower Austria and Styria and even into present-day Bavaria, was one of the largest and most powerful of the church states of central Europe, and its archbishop was 'Primas Germaniae', the highest-ranking archbishop of the empire. As early as the twelfth century musicians, instrument makers and bellfounders were working in the city and in the thirteenth a position of Kantor (teacher of singing) was created at the cathedral. The supposed first German poet-musician, known simply as the Monk of Salzburg, worked there in the fourteenth century, and a school for choirboys was established in the fifteenth, when three churches had Kantors and there is evidence of musical life among the rich families. Heinrich Finck and Paul Hofhaimer, two of the leading German composers of their time, were among the musicians working in the court musical establishment (or Kapelle) in the early sixteenth century, and in the 1590s the music there was put on a firmer basis by the reformist archbishop Wolf Dietrich, who also did much to give the city its present architectural character.

The cathedral had burnt down in 1589; a new one was inaugurated in 1628, with a *Te Deum* for twelve choirs, sung from the marble galleries around the cathedral, by the Italian composer Stefano Bernardi. The first opera performances outside Italy, of an *Orfeo* sometimes claimed as Monteverdi's, had been given in Salzburg in 1614, and a school (1617) and university (1622) had been established under the Benedictine order, for whom drama with music was a method of pedagogy, sometimes with an element of moral indoctrination (Salzburg was ecclesiastically conservative; in the late fifteenth century the Jews were expelled, and in 1731–2 some 30,000 Protestants migrated to Prussia after a period of severe persecution). The most distinguished composers working in Salzburg during the seventeenth century, who contributed to the repertory include Heinrich Biber, a Bohemian, active in Salzburg (for 20 years as Kapellmeister) from 1670–71 until his death in 1704, and the Alsatian Georg Muffat, court organist from 1678 to 1690, as well as such local musicians as Andreas Hofer, a member of the Kapelle for 30 years from 1654, ultimately as Kapellmeister. The celebrations of the 1100th anniversary of the founding of the archbishopric, in 1682, may have been the occasion when the famous 53-voice *Missa salisburgensis*, composed by Biber, was performed. In the years from 1716 to 1727 dramatic music was supplied to the court by the Italian composer Antonio Caldara, who paid regular visits from Vienna (where he was court vice-Kapellmeister) to stage his operas and direct his oratorios.

Salzburg was always an attractive and reasonably prosperous city. It lay on several important trade routes, from parts of Germany to Italy and to the east from both France (through Switzerland) and southern Germany (through Munich). The main part of the city lay on the south-west side of the river Salzach, shallow but fast-flowing, and curling to the south as it flowed eastwards beyond the centre of the city. Salzburg was dominated then, as it still is, by the fortress, Hohensalzburg, towering over the curve in the river. Built on the end of a long ridge, the Mönchsberg, then effectively the southern boundary of the city, it dates back to the eleventh century, though it was completed only in the seventeenth. On the north-east side are more hills, hemming the city in, or (in early times) setting its boundaries, with the central one, the Kapuzinerberg, site of a Capuchin church, protruding almost to the river. The cathedral, modelled on St Peter's in Rome, stands across a square at the northern foot of the hill below the fortress, with further spacious squares to the north (with the archbishop's Residence and the famous bell tower or Glockenspiel) and the west, the cathedral square, close to which there is an agglomeration of churches and other ecclesiastical buildings. More than most, Salzburg was a city of churches. St Peter's Abbey, a Renaissance building but with florid Baroque decoration, lies between the cathedral and the Mönchsberg, with the fifteenth-century Franciscan church close by. Moving towards the river, there is the collegiate church by the university, just behind the Getreidegasse, the busy commercial street running parallel to the river one double row of buildings away from it, in which the Mozarts were to live. Across the wooden bridge, on the north-east side of the Salzach, were more churches (including the Trinity Church, incorporating a school for boys of the upper levels of society, and a little to the north, St Sebastian's), and houses, among them several of the residences of the minor Salzburg nobility, and also the Schloss Mirabell, the archbishop's summer palace, with its ornamental gardens. The population at this time was about 16,000.

Salzburg, and the region governed from the city, was in effect under the personal rule of its prince-archbishop, with a cathedral chapter of 24 canons, most of them members of local noble families. His court exercised great power. It supervised every aspect of the city's life and employed vast numbers of people—numerous churchmen, legal and administrative staff, army personnel, and controllers of all the important local industries such as forestry and salt (the original basis of the city's wealth), as well as day-to-day functionaries such

View of Salzburg: engraving by A. Amon after F. von Naumann, 1791 (*Museum Carolino Augusteum, Salzburg*)

as secretaries, grooms, valets and maidservants. This of course included the musicians. It watched over the personal lives of all its employees. There was little alternative employment: Salzburg had few of the older noble families, though there were several families of the minor, newer aristocracy—and all had close links with the court.

In 1737 Leopold Mozart moved to the city, and in 1743 he took up a position, initially unpaid, as violinist in the court orchestra. Among his colleagues the two most important, both from nearby Bavarian towns, were Johann Ernst Eberlin, an admired composer of church music, court organist from 1726 and Kapellmeister from 1750, and Anton Cajetan Adlgasser, initially a chorister and then Eberlin's successor as organist. These musicians, and from the next generation Michael Haydn, from Lower Austria—Joseph's younger brother, who took up a post in 1762—were to exercise some influence on the boy Mozart and indeed on the mature composer too. Salzburg's situation as the centre of an archdiocese, with its rulers primarily men of the church, inevitably meant that its strongest traditions were in the realm of religious music of one kind or another, chiefly masses and other liturgical items but also including Benedictine dramas composed for the university. Sacred works by Salzburg composers were widely disseminated in the churches, the monasteries and the other ecclesiastical establishments of the surrounding region. A tradition of symphony composition existed too, somewhat later, and the works of Leopold Mozart and Michael Haydn were to achieve some circulation beyond the city. But they show no clearly identifiable Salzburg style: it typifies the situation of Salzburg, geographical as well as musical, that there are influences from all directions.[2] One genre however was unique to Salzburg, and the creation of specific circumstances there. It was the custom at the Benedictine University to celebrate the end of the academic year and certain other festive occasions with a serenade (called 'Finalmusik' if at the end of the year[3]) and Salzburg composers seem to have developed a particular type, beginning and ending with marches with some eight movements between, two or three with instrumental solo parts. The full work was rather akin to a symphony with an interpolated concerto. Both Mozarts, father and son, wrote such works, and so did Michael Haydn and other local composers.

In 1757, a Berlin music journal published an anonymous 'Report on the Present State of the Musical Establishment at the Court of His Serene Highness the archbishop of Salzburg';[4] its author is generally, and surely correctly, taken to be Leopold Mozart, who had been in correspondence with the editor, Friedrich Wilhelm Marpurg (the lengthy and detailed entry on Leopold himself, the longest by far, anyway betrays his hand). The report lists the members of the musical establishment, describing their individual skills and outlining the careers of the more important members. He names first the directors, Eberlin, his deputy Giuseppe Francesco Lolli (later to succeed Eberlin as Kapellmeister) and the three court composers (Caspar Cristelli, Leopold himself and Ferdinand Seidl). Second, the instrumentalists: eight violinists, two each of violists, cellists and double-bassists, two keyboard players, three oboists or flautists, four bassoonists, two hornists and a trombonist (these are the players' first instruments only; as most of them have alternative instruments, some of them several, the list makes no statement about the actual disposition of the players or balance of the orchestra). Then follow the solo singers—a court chaplain, one soprano (and three vacancies), two tenors and two basses. Next, the choir, divided into three groups, the gentlemen (three altos, two of them named as falsettists, nine tenors and nine basses), the hymn singers (an alto, three tenors and four basses) and the fifteen choirboys (who normally enter court service soon after their voices break), with three trombonists in addition, supplied by the town waits. Lastly, a group of ten trumpeters (plus two vacancies) and two kettledrummers, for ceremonial occasions; they also 'play well' on string instruments and are required to do so in large-scale performances. There are two instrument makers, required to be in constant attendance, and three servants. Leopold computes this as a musical establishment of 99 people in all—an impressive total for a court of quite modest size. These numbers reflect the strength of Salzburg's musical traditions, as well as the enthusiasm of the current archbishop, Siegmund Christoph, Count von Schrattenbach, who indeed had sent some of his musicians to Italy for further training and was to permit (that is, in effect, subsidize) most of the Mozart family's tours. Leopold names the origins of most of the adult musicians, which gives an indication of the area on which Salzburg could draw: 22 are Salzburgers, 19 Bavarians and nine Swabians (including Leopold himself, from Augsburg), ten are from the Czech lands, nine from Vienna or other parts of Austria, four from the Palatinate (the Mannheim region), three from Silesia, two from Italy and one from Hungary.

Leopold Mozart's original reason for moving to Salzburg had been to enter the university.[5] Born in 1719, he was just 18 when he enrolled as a student of philosophy and jurisprudence, and he was the first member of his family to undergo university education. The eldest of three sons, he had been intended by his father, who had died in 1736, and his godfather Johann Georg Grabner for the priesthood, and it seems that this remained his ambition for a time. He had received a thorough education at the Gymnasium and at the Lyceum attached to a private Jesuit school, St Salvator's, in his native Augsburg, leaving with a certificate of distinction. He had also been trained as a violinist and organist and was a choirboy at the monasteries of Heiligkreuz and St Ulrich's. At the Salzburg Benedictine University he studied for the Bachelor of Philosophy degree, which he took in 1738, but the next year he was expelled for poor attendance at certain classes.

Possibly by now Leopold had already been seduced by music, or perhaps, having met his future wife, he had decided that a celibate life was unacceptable. At any rate, in 1740 he took a position as valet-musician to the count of Thurn-Valsassina and Taxis, a Salzburg cathedral chapter member, with a traditional mixture of musical and domestic duties. Three years later he was granted a right of candidature to an appointment in the court musical establishment, and after holding various minor posts he was appointed in 1747 to a court position, serving as a violinist and later as violin teacher to the choirboys. He and Maria Anna were married later that year (just after his marriage, Leopold wrote to the Augsburg authorities, seeking to maintain his right to citizenship there, and accordingly asking permission to marry; his letter contains an extraordinary and seemingly pointless series of falsehoods).[6] In 1757, the year of the report for Marpurg, he became a court composer, in 1758 second violinist and in 1763 deputy Kapellmeister. His preoccupations thereafter, as we shall see, precluded further advancement. His report lists his areas of activity as a composer, which are numerous. He names only a single publication, a set of trio sonatas which he engraved himself and dedicated to count Thurn, but much in manuscript—a 'great number' of symphonies, more than 30 serenades, a variety of concertos, chamber and occasional pieces, twelve oratorios, theatre music and of course 'numerous' pieces of church music. A singular feature of his music is its inclusion of humorous and illustrative works, such as pieces depicting a peasant wedding, a sleigh-ride or a hunt. Leopold was, however, chiefly famous in his day as the author of the *Versuch einer gründlichen Violinschule* ('Treatise on the Fundamental Art of Violin Playing'), published in the year of Wolfgang's birth, 1756, but even before its publication he was widely respected among writers on music. In 1755 he was invited to apply for membership of Lorenz Mizler's Societät der Musicalischen Wissenschaften, a corresponding society of learned musicians (in fact he seems never to have joined), and, as we have seen, he was in touch with Marpurg. The *Violinschule* was warmly received by reviewers and had several later editions, including an expanded one and Dutch and French translations. Though deeply indebted to Tartini, it is generally acknowledged as the central textbook on violin playing in the mid-eighteenth century.

The background of the family has of course been the subject of much research.[7] Leopold (in full, Johann Georg Leopold) came from a family of bookbinders, a trade pursued by his brothers. His father, Johann Georg Mozart (1679–1736), had in 1708 married his master's widow, acquiring his business in the traditional way. On her death ten years later he was speedily remarried, to Anna Maria Sulzer

Leopold Mozart: pencil drawing, attributed to Franz Lactanz Count Firmian, c1762 (*Internationale Stiftung Mozarteum, Salzburg*)

(1696–1766), who bore him nine children. Leopold was the eldest. Johann Georg was a master bookbinder who produced some refined work.[8] Anna Maria's father, Christian Sulzer (c1663–1744), a master weaver, had come from Baden-Baden and in 1695 married Maria Dorothea Baur (1672–1742), from Augsburg, daughter of Michael

Baur (1652–1685), also a master weaver, and Anna Khien (1637–1684), from Biburg.

Johann Georg's father, Mozart's great-grandfather Franz Mozart (1649–1694), was a master mason (which could also signify an architect) who probably worked for the Fugger family and who in 1678 married Anna Hairer or Härrer (*c*1653–1716), from Obernbuch am Buchrain, where her father was a 'Tagwerker', a labourer paid by the day. Franz's father was David Mozart (*c*1620–1685), from the village of Pfersee, a master builder, architect and master mason who married Maria Negeler (*c*1622–1697), from nearby Lechhausen, in 1643. At this point the trail cools in the absence of secure documentation. David's father and mother may have been another David (*d* 1625–6), from Leitershofen, a builder in Pfersee, and Anna Langenegk, who was the daughter of an Augsburg carpenter Balthas Langenegk (originating from the Ottobeuren region) and Anna Hering (from Waalhaupten). Going back further becomes increasingly conjectural, although a paternal ancestry of seven more generations has been hazily traced (Peter Motzhart, carpenter and soldier in Leitershofen, *d* 1619; Lienhard Motzhart, *c*1525–1591, a mercenary in Leitershofen; Hannss Motzhart, *c*1500–1560, also a mercenary there; then to Hannss's supposed grandfather, Ändris Motzhart, a builder in Aretsreid-Heimberg; and his father, of the same name, place and occupation). In the absence of wives' family names, only the male line is open to investigation.

The name Mozart (in one form or another) is found in this region—the countryside west of Augsburg, in such villages as Fischach and Heimberg—as early as 1331. There was one musician of the name, Johann Mozart (*c*1592–1668), who sang in Augsburg Cathedral, where he was a pupil of Erbach, and he was later prior of the Heiligkreuz monastery, but he cannot be linked with the known line to Wolfgang. Nor can the painters Christoph Mozart (1541–*c*1590) and his gifted son Anton Mozart (1573–1625). But other artistic talent in the family can be linked with Wolfgang's line, at least collaterally: his great-grandfather Franz's brother Michael

(1655–1718) was a sculptor in Vienna, and his grandfather Johann Georg's brother Franz (1681–1732) was a sculptor in Strasbourg.

Mozart's mother's family, the Pertls, has been less fully investigated, perhaps on the assumption that his musical inheritance came exclusively from one side. The clumsy orthography and limited expression of Maria Anna's letters have sometimes been taken to suggest that her background was inferior to Leopold's, though more allowance might reasonably have been made for the relatively meagre education accorded to girls. Maria Anna Walpurga Pertl (to follow the form she used, in preference to Anna Maria Walpurga, the form in which she was baptized, on Christmas Day, 1720) was in fact the daughter of a lawyer. Wolfgang Nikolaus Pertl (1667–1724), educated at the Benedictine University, sang and taught singing at St Peter's and then worked at the Salzburg court before becoming assistant *Pfleger* or general administrator of, first, St Andrä, where he was unsuccessful, and in 1716 of Hüttenstein and St Gilgen. In 1712 he had married Mozart's maternal grandmother, Eva Rosina Barbara Puxbaum, *née* Altmann (1681–1755), a widow aged 31, from Stein an der Donau. Her father, Dominik Altmann (*c*1635–*c*1702), was also a lawyer, and a finance officer, from Krems-Stein but of Viennese birth; both his father, Jakob Altmann (*d* 1639), and the father of his mother, Maria Oeller, were gardeners in Vienna. Eva Rosina (or Euphrosina) was a child of the third of his four marriages, to Anna Sophia Zalner (1651–1685), daughter of a market tally-clerk from Hallstatt, Hans Wolfgang Zaller, and his wife Regina Pöckl, from St Wolfgang, where her father was a baker of gingerbread. Mozart's mother's paternal grandfather, Johannes Pertl (1607–1698), was a cloth maker and gardener in Salzburg, where he married Magdalena Zachner (*c*1632–1681) from Kirchheim, daughter of a carpenter. Johannes's father, Bartholomäus (*d* 1601), was a personal coachman in Salzburg; his mother, Ursula Schmidt, was from Lamprechtshausen, just north of the city. Mozart's grandfather Pertl seems to have had persistent poor health, possibly mental as well as physical. At St Andrä he had been unable to manage his administrative responsibilities for the St Gilgen area, where he failed to collect the necessary dues (taxes, fines and the like, from which his own income was meant to be drawn), and he died in 1724 leaving the district in confusion and his wife and two daughters deeply in debt. His widow moved to Salzburg and seems to have subsisted on a small pension perhaps augmented by occasional earnings from sewing or lace-making.

Geographically, then, Mozart came from stock originating over a swathe of southern Germany and northern Austria, ranging as far west as Baden-Baden and as far east as Vienna, but predominantly from the area of Augsburg and the villages to its west and south, and from that of Salzburg and the villages to its north and east. His paternal inheritance, it seems, included elements of artistic creativity, though primarily in the visual arts; socially, this side of the family had been of the middle classes for a century at least. His maternal inheritance shows fewer hints of artistic susceptibility, except just possibly among the gardeners, depending upon exactly what the term then signified. Clearly, however, most of the family had moved up in the world from humbler occupations to the level of skilled artisans or the professions. In the last resort, little of this is particularly revealing, although attitudes towards matters of social class certainly played a part in determining Mozart's and his father's behaviour in many of the situations they were to face. The level of Mozart's musical genius, however, is not something that any aspect of his heritage can even begin to explain.

2

Childhood and First Travels

L EOPOLD MOZART AND Maria Anna Pertl were married in Salzburg on 21 November 1747; he was just 28, she nearly 27. He recalled the event in a letter from Italy, 25 years later:

> Today is the anniversary of our wedding day. It was 25 years ago, I believe, when we had the sensible idea of getting married—though we'd had such thoughts for some time before. Good things are worth waiting for![1]

In the *liber matrimonialis* of Salzburg Cathedral Leopold is described as 'Chelista' (violinist) to the court; one of the vicars-choral and a court chamberlain stood as witnesses. Leopold and his wife, a family friend wrote many years later, were considered 'the handsomest couple in Salzburg'.[2] Their first three children, a son and two daughters, born in August 1748, the next June and the May following, lived respectively nearly six months, six days and eleven weeks. The fourth, a girl, Maria Anna Walburgia Ignatia, was born on 30–31 July 1751, and survived: this was Mozart's sister, known as Nannerl (the name to be used here, to avoid confusion with her mother). Two more children followed, a boy born in November 1752, who lived for three months, and a girl, born in May 1754, who survived seven weeks. The mortality rate was not unusual for the time.

The next child, happily, survived: born on 27 January 1756, at eight o'clock in the evening, in the family home on the third floor of no. 9 Getreidegasse. The Mozarts had lived since their marriage in this tall stone-built house in the centre of the city, dating from the twelfth century and owned since 1713 by the Hagenauer family, who ran a business in groceries and spices on the ground floor (the building was acquired by the Internationale Stiftung Mozarteum in 1917 and has been a Mozart museum since then). The baby was baptized at half past ten the same evening in the names Joannes Chrysost[omus] Wolfgangus Theophilus. The names Johann and Chrysostom, to give them their vernacular form, commemorated the boy's birth on that saint's day. The Theophilus ('beloved of God')—which Leopold gave as Gottlieb in a letter a few days later—recorded the godfather, Joannes Theophilus Pergmayr, a Salzburg town councillor and businessman; he or Maria Cordula Pergmayr (widow of his late employer, whom he married, inheriting the business) stood as godparents to all the Mozart children. The Pergmayrs were good friends of the Mozarts, and in later years absent members of the family often sent them greetings (as the 'Götten', or godparents). The name Wolfgang presumably commemorated his maternal grandfather. Later, Mozart virtually never used the first two names. As to the others, he was flexible. He often signed himself as 'Wolfgang Amadé' as a young man; later he normally favoured 'Wolfgang Amadè' (sometimes 'Amade', not 'Amadeus'). Occasionally he used 'Wolfgang Gottlieb', plain 'Wolfgang', 'W.A.', or simply 'Mozart', 'WMZT' or 'MZT', and when he was in Italy he sometimes wrote 'Wolfgango Amadeo'. In formal announcements, reports and advertisements, the predominant forms are 'W.A. Mozart', 'Wolfgang Mozart' and 'Wolfgang Amade Mozart'. The form 'Wolfgang Amadeus Mozart' is not unknown in his lifetime but is exceedingly rare. His pet names as a child were the diminutives 'Wolfgangerl' or 'Woferl'.

It is in the nature of early childhood that it is unlikely to be

The house of Mozart's birth (left centre), in the Getreidegasse: lithograph by C. Czichna after J.A. Wenzl, 1831 (*Mozart-Gemeinde Augsburg*)

dependably documented. It was not in fact until after Mozart's death that most of the familiar anecdotes of his first years were written down. At the beginning of 1792, the obituarist Friedrich Schlichtegroll, of Gotha, wrote to Albert von Mölk, member of a Salzburg family of ecclesiastical administrators who were friends of the Mozarts, for information on his early years. Mölk approached the only surviving person who was close to Mozart at the time, his sister, then living at St Gilgen, near Salzburg.[3] He put to her a series of specific questions from Schlichtegroll. Nannerl responded and also sent a brief article about her brother, an account of the early years and the family travels, including (drawn from family letters in her possession) material on some of the journeys during which she had remained at home. On the period after about 1772 her replies are relatively cursory, and for information on Mozart's later life she refers Schlichtegroll to Viennese sources (she was not, it seems, even aware of how many children her brother had left). Mölk sent this material on to Schlichtegroll, with what seems to be an addendum of his own, including a remark—which has often, probably mistakenly, been taken to represent Nannerl's view—that is critical of Mozart and his marriage. Any information retailed after 30 years needs to be treated with a little reserve, especially when memories have not only become clouded by time but may also have been coloured in retrospect by events since. Dependable or otherwise, this is the only information we have on Mozart's earliest years. Nannerl tells (in the third person) how Wolfgang's gifts first became apparent as a result of her harpsichord lessons:

> The son was at the time three years old when the father began instructing the seven-year-old daughter on the clavier.
>
> The boy immediately showed his extraordinary, God-given talent. He often spent long periods at the clavier, picking out thirds, and his pleasure showed that they sounded good to him.
>
> When he was four years old, his father, as if for a game, taught him some minuets and other pieces at the clavier. It went so well and was so effortless that he had easily learnt a piece in one hour and a minuet in half an hour, so that he could play them without mistakes and with the utmost delicacy. He made such progress that when he was five years old he was composing little pieces, which he would play to his father who would write them down.

Nannerl may actually have remembered these events, but she was able to refresh her memory from the so-called 'Notenbuch für Nannerl', the musical commonplace book that Leopold put together from 1759 onwards for teaching his daughter, which was still in her possession and intact when she wrote these words.[4] In it Leopold noted against some of the pieces the dates and even the hours of the day when Wolfgang learnt them (there were several around the time of his fifth birthday, the earliest being a Scherzo by Wagenseil, 'learnt by

Wolfgangerl on 24 January 1761, three days before his fifth birthday, between 9.00 and 9.30 in the evening'), or in the case of Wolfgang's own pieces their dates of composition, sometimes exactly, sometimes approximately. Of these, the earliest are the works numbered 1*a* and 1*b* in K[6], said to have been composed during the first three months after his fifth birthday, that is, early 1761.

Nannerl not only responded to Schlichtegroll herself but, in response to further queries, wrote to Johann Andreas Schachtner, in Salzburg, passing on to him questions about her brother's early childhood. Schachtner was a court trumpeter—he is among those listed in Leopold's 1757 report for Marpurg—and an accomplished violinist and a cellist. He was also a skilled poet and translator: he wrote several texts for Mozart, including the unfinished opera *Zaide*, and provided the German text for the libretto of *Idomeneo* in 1781. Schachtner had fond and vivid recollections of events from Mozart's early childhood, which he duly retailed.[5]

Notenbuch für Nannerl Mozart, first page of no. 20, Allegro in C K.9*a*/5*a*, in Mozart's hand, 1764 (*Internationale Stiftung Mozarteum, Salzburg*)

. . . To your first question: what were your late brother's favourite pastimes in his childhood, besides his preoccupation with music.

This question cannot be answered: for as soon as he occupied himself with music he had no interest in other occupations, they were dead to him, and even childish nonsense and games with toys had to have a musical accompaniment if they were to hold his attention; when we, he and I, were carrying his playthings and toys from one room to another, the one of us who was empty-handed had to sing a march, or play on the fiddle, as we did so. But before then, when he had not begun music, he was ready for any piece of nonsense as long as it was spiced with a little joke, and he would forget about food, drink and everything else. As you know, he and I saw a lot of each other, and he grew very fond of me, and would often ask me ten times over in a day whether I loved him, and when for a joke I sometimes said No, bright tears would well up in his eyes, so sweet and so affectionate was his good little heart.

Second question: you ask how he behaved as a child when great people expressed their wonderment at his musical talent and art.

In all truth, he betrayed nothing less than pride or ambition: and there was no better way to satisfy these than by playing to people who understood little or nothing of music, but he did not want to play unless his audience were very knowledgeable about music, or he had to be a little deceived into thinking they were.

Third question: what kind of studies did he like the best?

Answer: he was easily led in this, for it did not matter what he was given to learn, he only wanted to learn and left the choice to his greatly loved father as to what field he should work in—it seemed as if he understood that he could not have found in the whole world a teacher, still less a guide, to match his unforgettable father.

Fourth question: what peculiarities, maxims, routines, idiosyncrasies and leanings towards good and bad did he have?

Answer: he was full of fire, his attention to any topic was very slender; I think that if he had not had so good an upbringing he could have become a wicked villain, so susceptible was he to every temptation before he could examine its goodness or badness.

A few curious points worthy of wonderment
from when he was four or five years old,
the truth of which I would swear to.

I once went back to the house with your honoured father, after Thursday service, when we came upon the four-year-old Wolfgang busy with his pen.

Papa: What are you writing?

Wolfgang: A clavier concerto, the first movement is nearly finished.

Papa: Let me see.

Wolfgang: It's not ready yet.

Papa: Let me see: it must be quite something.

His father took it away and showed me a smear of notes, most of them written over rubbed-out inkblots. (NB: not knowing any better, little Wolfgangerl had dipped the pen to the bottom of the inkwell each time, so when he put it to the paper a drop of ink was bound to fall off, but he could deal with this by drawing the palm of his hand across it, wiping it away, and then writing straight on.) We began to laugh at this obvious gallimaufry, but then your father began to give attention to the chief question, the notes and their composition and, after looking at the sheet for some time, he began to shed tears, tears of wonderment and joy. Have a look, Herr Schachtner, he said, see how correctly and properly it is written, but it is really no use as it is so extraordinarily difficult that no-one could play it. Then Wolfgangerl said: That's why it's a concerto, you must practise for a long time to get it right, you see, that's how it goes. He played, and managed to get just enough out of it for us to know what he wanted. He had the idea at that time that to play a concerto and work a miracle were one and the same thing.

Mozart's first known appearance in public was in a play at the university theatre, given in September 1761 to celebrate the archbishop's nameday, when he was among the dancers in a school drama *Sigismundus Hungariae Rex*, with music by Eberlin. His first appearance as a child prodigy may have been four months later. According to Nannerl's recollection, 30 years later, the family made a journey in January 1762, when Leopold took both children—Nannerl was hardly less gifted a player than her brother—to the court at Munich, where they remained for three weeks and played before the Elector of Bavaria, Maximilian III Joseph. There is no independent documentation of this journey, nor any later reference to it. When in 1763 Leopold mentioned meeting the Elector, the conversation he reported seems to imply that they had not recently met, and others of his remarks suggest that Mozart had no previous experience of performing there.[6] There must be considerable doubt as to whether the visit did in fact take place or whether Nannerl's memory was confused.

For the remainder of the family journeys, and indeed Mozart's solitary ones up to his last years, there exist letters from Leopold, Mozart himself and occasionally his mother and his sister, providing a source of incomparable richness to the biographer and the student of the times. These letters were written by highly intelligent and observant people, often with great candour, and with little or no thought (as motivated the letters of composers a couple of generations later) of image or posterity. Leopold did preserve the letters carefully, however, primarily with thoughts of writing a biography of his son. When the family was divided, and the correspondence was between Mozart's parents or between father and son, it speaks eloquently of family affections and tensions; when, as in most of the earliest travels, the whole family was together and the letters were directed to a Salzburg friend, it provides endlessly fascinating information on their central activities.

From the first journey of this kind (the brief and dubious Munich one apart), nine letters survive from Leopold to Lorenz Hagenauer, his friend and landlord at Getreidegasse 9. A wealthy merchant, with wide international connections, Hagenauer was probably in effect Leopold's banker, or the central figure in a group that financed his tours.[7] The family set out for Vienna on 18 September 1762, taking with them a servant, the copyist and bassoonist Joseph Richard Estlinger, and arrived home on 5 January 1763. On these tours, Leopold had one objective: to show off his children, in this case before the royal and imperial family at the Viennese court, for which they could expect ample rewards, in money or in gifts, as well as the kind of attention that could secure them future patronage. But he would expect to take any other opportunity that might present itself for additional earnings, both en route and in the imperial capital, where noblemen from the Habsburg domains and other parts of the Holy Roman Empire had their city houses to which they went in the season, making Vienna a flourishing centre of musical patronage. On the journeys this meant, above all, pausing near the seat of any rich nobleman and offering to perform for him; a gift of money or, more often, some trinket, would ensue. There were however disadvantages: if they offered to play, and the reply was long delayed or only a vague promise issued, they would have no choice but to wait nearby, perhaps for a considerable time, at their own expense (usually at an inn, sometimes in private lodgings or, if only Leopold and Wolfgang were travelling, occasionally in rooms at a monastery). Sometimes, if a definite but unscheduled invitation was received from a powerful nobleman, they would be obliged to stay, awaiting his pleasure. There was no true public musical life in most of central Europe, but the Mozarts could sometimes organize a concert themselves, although this was financially risky and again subject to the whim of a local nobleman or other authority.

On this first journey to Vienna, in fact, they had to wait five days in Passau, probably staying at an inn, either Zum roten Krebs or the Goldene Sonne.[8] Eventually, Wolfgang played for the prince-bishop, receiving just over four gulden, and Leopold complained that he lost 80 gulden as a result. In Linz they stayed in the Zur Dreifaltigkeit inn for a week, giving some kind of performance there or in the Land-haus, and travelled on down the Danube, pausing at Ybbs, where Wolfgang played the organ 'so well that some Franciscan monks . . . rushed to the choir and were almost struck dead with amazement':[9] the first of countless such reports. They reached Vienna on 6 October, having had their passage through the customs eased when Wolf-gang showed his travelling clavichord to the officer and played him a minuet on his violin. They probably stayed for about a week at the inn Zum weissen Ochsen in the Fleischmarkt, then moved to lodg-ings with the Ditscher family in Tiefer Graben—a first-floor room, '1000 paces long, 1 pace wide', partitioned in two, with Leopold and Wolfgang sharing one bed and Maria Anna and Nannerl the other (Leopold complained of the children's wriggling).

Once in Vienna, they wasted little time; Leopold had spread word ahead about the visit and used his Salzburg connections to secure invitations from noble patrons. They arrived on a Wednesday. On the Saturday the children played privately at the palace of Count Collalto (a building of 1671, still standing in central Vienna), where the other performers included the singer Marianna Bianchi, who had created the role of Gluck's Eurydice in *Orfeo ed Euridice* at the court theatre, the Burgtheater, only four days before. Among those present was Johann Karl Count Zinzendorf, a councillor at the Treasury who later held various high offices in Vienna (ultimately prime minister, 1808–9) and who for more than 50 years kept a diary in which he recorded daily his activities and his impressions, many of them to do with the musical events he regularly attended.[10] On this occasion he noted that 'Bianchi sang and a little boy, said to be only five-and-a-half years old, played the harpsichord'; Mozart was actually just under six-and-three-quarters. On the Sunday the Mozarts played at the palace, near the Michaelerplatz (and again still in existence), of Count Wilczek, another civil servant, like most of the Viennese nobility. Afterwards Leopold went to see *Orfeo* at the opera, where he overheard the Archduke Leopold talking about the boy visiting Vienna who played so brilliantly on the clavier. On the Monday there was an event in the palace of the Imperial Vice-Chancellor, Rudolph Joseph, Count Colloredo, in the presence of 'leading ministers and members of the imperial court', including the Hungarian and Bohemian chancellors, Counts Pálffy and Chotek. All the ladies, Leopold wrote, were in love with his little boy.

Even before they had sent formal notification of their presence in Vienna, the Mozarts were invited to appear at court. Word had arrived through the younger Count Pálffy, who had heard them in Linz and told the Archduke Joseph (soon to be Emperor Joseph II) about the talented boy. This was the famous occasion where Wolfgang, received with such 'extraordinary graciousness', jumped up on to the lap of the Empress Maria Theresa, 'put his arms round her neck and kissed her heartily'. They were in the royal presence for three hours, during which time, according to Nannerl's recollection, the Emperor Francis teased Wolfgang by saying there was no skill in playing with all one's fingers and that it would be clever only if the keyboard were covered, whereupon he played with one finger, and then with the keyboard covered so that he could not see it. At one point, when the emperor came to turn the pages for him, Wolfgang said: 'Isn't Herr Wagenseil here? He should come, as he understands'. The emperor yielded his place to Wagenseil, a court composer, to whom Wolfgang said: 'I'm going to play a concerto of yours, so you should turn the pages for me'.[11] The young Archduchess Joanna showed Wolfgang over Schönbrunn, the splendid and spacious royal palace on the southern outskirts of Vienna, which Maria Theresa preferred to the Hofburg palace as her residence. Then they went on to the Rofrano (later Auersperg) Palace to play to the prince of Saxe-Hildburghausen, an important musical patron who had employed Gluck and Dittersdorf, and they earned six ducats there. The next day too there were two engagements, for Countess Kinsky, at her palace in the Freyung (a building no longer standing, smaller than the present one, which it adjoined), and Count Ulfeld, Lord High Steward, in the Minoriten-platz. The next day the empress sent the Mozarts, through her Privy Pay-master, sets of full-dress court clothes for the children, discards from a young archduchess and archduke, for them to wear on court occasions. These are the clothes worn in the paintings of Nannerl

Mozart and Nannerl in gala clothes: oil paintings by Pietro Antonio Lorenzoni, 1763 (*Internationale Stiftung Mozarteum, Salzburg*)

and Wolfgang made the next year, the earliest known of the children, probably by the Salzburg painter Pietro Antonio Lorenzoni, show-ing Nannerl in plum-coloured taffeta appliquéd with sheer white lace, Wolfgang in a lilac jacket and matching, brocaded lilac waist-coat, with a great deal of gold braid, gold buttons and tassels, white lace collar and cuffs and white stockings; he is holding a black hat, probably a tricorne, and wearing a sword. He is standing in front of a keyboard instrument, his left hand tucked into his waistcoat, with a charmingly serene expression, perhaps a shade doll-like. The painter used a standard model for the figure and background of Nannerl's portrait.[12]

Concert activity continued, though some of it was probably more a matter of providing entertainment during a social gathering than actually giving a recital. On 15 October they were at one house by

2.30, were picked up at 3.45 by Count Hardegg's coach and transported to play to 'a lady', then collected at 5.30 and taken to play for the chancellor, Count (later Prince) Kaunitz, remaining in his palace in the Gumpendorf area until 9.00; the next day, they played at 2.30 for the two young archdukes, Ferdinand and Maximilian Franz, probably at the Hofburg, and at 4.00 for Nicolaus Count Pálffy at his Renaissance palace in the Josefplatz (part of which is still used for concerts); and on the next, a Sunday, they played for Count Thurn or Thun, on Zinzendorf's ambiguously decipherable testimony (he goes on: 'the little child from Salzburg and his sister played the harpsichord. The poor little boy plays marvellously, he is a child of spirit, lively and charming, his sister's playing is masterly and he applauded her. Mlle de Gudenus, who plays the harpsichord well, gave him a kiss, and he wiped his face . . .').

On 19 October the court paymaster brought a request to them to prolong their stay in Vienna and to make a further court appearance, with 100 ducats to sweeten it; this meant that Leopold would need to request an extension of his leave from Salzburg, which he duly did in late October or early November. He was tempted to use some of the money to buy a coach, to allow the children to travel in less discomfort and to save having to be collected each time by their hosts. Later that day the children played for the French ambassador, the count of Châtelet-Lomont, and they performed twice the following

day, for a Count Harrach and for 'a certain rich nobleman' at a concert where all the greatest virtuosos in Vienna were to play (the
reward was six ducats). On 21 October they played again at Schönbrunn, but then Wolfgang was taken ill, with large, raised red spots,
back pain and a fever; it was thought to be a form of scarlet fever, but
Leopold's clear description permits a more accurate modern diagnosis, *erythema nodosum*, a rash probably caused by a streptococcal infection.[13] There were no more performances for a time (one arranged
for the Postmaster-General, Count Wenzel Paar, had to be cancelled);
the next, on 5 November, was at the house in Tiefer Graben of the
doctor, Johann Anton von Bernhard, for him and his friends, in gratitude for his advice on Wolfgang's treatment during his illness.
Leopold requested six masses to be said in Salzburg in thanks for
Wolfgang's recovery. Wolfgang's nameday, 31 October, passed while
he was unwell; it is usually said that Leopold presented him with a
music book similar to Nannerl's on the occasion, but the so-called
'Wolfgang Notenbuch' has been proved to be a forgery.[14]

In his letters to Hagenauer from the end of October, Leopold
asked his friend to enquire as to whether he might expect to be
appointed to the position of vice-Kapellmeister at the Salzburg court,
now vacant, and in one letter he asked Hagenauer to press his claims
with court officials. It is clear from the context of his remarks that he
was contemplating the possibility of seeking a post in Vienna if promotion was not forthcoming. Like his son twenty years later, he was
attracted by the possibilities offered by this large city with its pool of
patronage and (in his own words) 'became confused' when he compared Salzburg with Vienna. He was made the more sensitive over the
issue of the Kapellmeistership by the way some of the Viennese
(including the emperor himself) talked of him as 'the Kapellmeister
from Salzburg'—the term was often used loosely of a senior musician—when he had no right to the title.

The children gave (as far as we know) only one more performance, for Vincenzia, Marchesa Pacheco, in the house of Joseph
Windischgrätz in the Bankgasse. On that occasion Count Collalto

distributed a poem, which a few days later was printed, in praise of Mozart, in particular expressing the hope that, unlike another famous child prodigy of the time (a boy from Lübeck who at six could speak several languages), he would not die young. The poem is by one Pufendorf, possibly the Baron Pufendorf whom Mozart knew many years later. Little is known of what the Mozarts were doing in Vienna during the next month. They attended, as spectators, two state banquets, lunched with various friends including the court Kapellmeister, Georg Reutter, and went once to the opera with Dr Bernhard. Then they were persuaded by members of the Hungarian nobility to visit Pressburg (now Bratislava), the headquarters of Hungarian government. They were there from 11 to 24 December, but nothing is known of any concerts they may have given. Back in Vienna, they attended a banquet given by Countess Kinsky on 27 December, and on 31 December they left for Salzburg, where they arrived on 5 January 1763. Mozart was ill on their return home, with a fever and pains in his legs and feet, and spent a time in bed. Leopold feared smallpox, and he might too have had cause to fear typhus, of which the Archduchess Joanna (whom Mozart met) had just died, but the actual complaint seems to have been rheumatism or rheumatic fever.[15]

Another group of Schachtner's anecdotes of Mozart's prodigious childhood, told to Nannerl, belongs to the period after the family's return from Vienna:[16]

Honoured lady! you will remember that I had a very good violin which the late Wolfgangerl, on account of its soft and full tone, always called 'butter-violin'. Once, soon after your return from Vienna, he played it, and could not praise my violin enough; a day or two later I came to see him, and found him entertaining himself on his own fiddle. 'How's your butter-violin?', he asked, going on playing at his fantasia. Then he looked thoughtful and said to me: 'Herr Schachtner, your violin is tuned half a quarter-tone lower than mine'. At first I laughed, but your papa, knowing the child's extraordinary sense of pitch and his memory, asked me to fetch my violin to see if he was right—I did so, and indeed he was.

Another time, a few days after your return from Vienna, and Wolfgang had a little violin that he had got as a present there, our former very good violinist, the late Herr Wenzel [Hebelt], came. He was a beginner in composition and brought with him a set of six trios that he had written while your honoured papa was away; he wanted papa's views on them. We played the trios, your papa taking the bass part on his viola, Wenzel was the first violin and I was to play the second. Wolfgang had asked if he could play the second violin, but his papa refused this foolish request as he had not yet had any instruction in the violin and, your papa thought, could not possibly play anything. Wolfgang said that to play the second violin you don't have to have studied, and when your papa said he should go away and not disturb us any more, Wolfgang began to weep bitterly and stamped off with his little violin. I asked if he might be allowed to play along with me, and papa eventually said: Play along with Herr Schachtner, but so softly that no-one can hear you, otherwise you'll have to go: and so it was. Wolfgang played with me, and soon I realized with astonishment that I was wholly superfluous, so I put my violin aside, and looked across at your honoured papa, to see tears of wonderment and solace flowing down his cheeks: and thus he played all six trios. When we finished, Wolfgang was emboldened by our applause to assert that he could play the first violin part. For a joke we tried this experiment, and we almost died for laughing when he played this too, with completely wrong and irregular positioning, though never quite broke down.

Lastly: about the gentleness and fineness of his hearing. Nearly to his tenth year he had a terrible fear of the trumpet, when it was played alone, without other instruments; pointing a trumpet towards him was just like putting a pistol to his heart. Papa wanted to cure him of this childish fear and once asked me, despite his reluctance, to play [my trumpet] towards him, but, my God! I should never have been persuaded to do it, for when Wolfgangerl heard the blaring sound, he went pale and began to faint, and if I had gone on any longer he would surely have had a fit. . . .

To your third question.

Whenever he was given something to learn, it occupied him so completely that everything else, even music, would be set aside; for example, when he was doing sums, the table, the chair, the walls and even the floor would be covered with chalked numbers.

Soon after the family's return to Salzburg, Leopold was promoted to vice-Kapellmeister, succeeding Giuseppe Lolli, who moved into the full Kapellmeistership succeeding Eberlin, who had died the previous June. The announcement was made on 28 February 1763, the archbishop's birthday, which was further celebrated—not with a party but with a musical event in which the performers included, as reported in the Salzburg court chronicles, 'to everyone's astonishment, the new vice-Kapellmeister's little son, aged seven, and daughter, aged ten; they played on the harpsichord, the son also on the violin, as well as anyone could ever have hoped'. Three months later, on 19 May, a report appeared in the *Augsburgischer Intelligenz-Zettl*, under the heading 'Merkwürdigkeiten' ('Curiosities'), in which a paragraph on German ascendancy in music is followed by a letter from an anonymous correspondent in Vienna reporting on the children's accomplishments: the girl of eleven can play 'the most difficult sonatas and concertos . . . most accurately . . . in the very best taste', and the boy of six (by now he was in fact seven) can play in a manly way, including 'fantasizing out of his own head, with the best of ideas in the modern taste', accompanying at sight, playing just as well with a cloth covering the keyboard, and naming correctly notes played to him. The correspondent had also heard of Mozart's latest performances, of a solo and concertos on the violin, in Salzburg. It is not impossible that the report was inspired by Leopold.

It was clear to Leopold that his son's gifts should not be concealed from the wider world, and in June 1763 he embarked on a tour that was to last more than three years.

3

The Road to Paris

I T IS EASY to criticize Leopold Mozart for his readiness to
'exploit' the talent of his children. It is also misguided. The notion
that it could in some way be damaging to the children to be
exhibited as they were is a wholly modern one, representing attitudes
to upbringing and to child psychology that would have been incom-
prehensible to a man of the mid-eighteenth century. It could not have
occurred to Leopold that the programme of touring and concert-
giving into which he plunged his family might interfere with his son's
development into a stable and responsible adult; and certainly any
claim that it had an adverse effect on Mozart's development as a
musician can scarcely be taken seriously. In fact, Leopold saw it as
something of a duty—particularly, he would undoubtedly have said,
as a Catholic and a German—to show his children to the world. In a
letter he wrote to Lorenz Hagenauer during a later visit to Vienna, in
1768, he explained his position, talking of the duty he felt to his
prince, his country and God to

> . . . proclaim to the world a miracle, which God allowed to be
> born in Salzburg. I owe this act to Almighty God, otherwise
> I would be the most ungrateful creature: *and if ever I have an*
> *obligation to convince the world of this miracle, it is precisely now,*

*when people ridicule anything that is called a miracle and deny the
existence of miracles.* Accordingly, people must be convinced of
it: and was it not a great joy and a great victory for me to hear
a Voltairian [Friedrich Melchior von Grimm] say to me, in
astonishment: *Now for once in my life I have seen a miracle: this
is the first!*[1]

A reader of today might suspect a hint of hypocrisy and self-
justification here. Yet in the light of what we know about him there
is no reason to think that Leopold was other than perfectly sincere.
This letter, we shall later see, was written in anger—a long-nurtured
scheme for his son's advancement had just been frustrated by
intrigues, he believed—but his attitudes were consistent and he saw
no contradiction between his almost evangelistic religious attitude
and his worldly hopes for his son and the family. Nor need he have
done: none then considered it improper to turn their natural gifts to
financial advantage, nor do they now unless there is an element of
excessive or damaging exploitation. Indeed the full development of a
God-given genius must have seemed to Leopold self-evidently a
sacred obligation, a trust imposed upon him by a benevolent deity—
and indeed a sign that this deity had approved or even guided his
decision not to enter the priesthood but rather to take up music and
start a family. Whether, at a later stage, he may have damaged his son
or impeded his development into manhood from motives that were
partly selfish, or in some way short-sighted, is another matter.

Another issue is the question of Nannerl, her musicianship and her
relationship with Wolfgang. In Vienna, and on the travels of these following years, she had played a considerable part in the show put on
by the family. But her role was decidedly that of second fiddle. She
was a fine keyboard player ('one of the most skilful in Europe', in her
father's view[2]), but although nearly five years younger Wolfgang
could perform the same feats and more, and he understandably
inspired greater wonder. Possibly, in a different age, when it was
thought appropriate to develop women's gifts and their opportunities

more nearly matched those open to men, Nannerl might have been as fully and professionally trained as her brother was, and have developed into a considerable composer. But it is clear that the family, living in a socially conservative environment, always took it for granted that a girl's only destiny was marriage, and there is no indication that Nannerl ever nurtured other ambitions. As far as we can judge from the family correspondence and from their later relations, she never felt any jealousy towards Wolfgang, recognized his superior abilities and always took great pride in his success.

It is in this context, then, that Leopold's decision to take his family on an extended tour of western Europe needs to be seen. His planned route, through his native country of southern Germany, along the Rhine and up to Brussels in the Austrian Netherlands, then to Paris (the excursion to London represented a change of plan), then back through Paris, eastern France, Switzerland and southern Germany, or perhaps an extension to north Italy, was sagely devised to take in a large number of princely courts in the fragmented German lands and one (and ultimately both) of the largest, richest and busiest cities in the world. He naturally wasted little time over setting off: the children were growing up and, however rapid their development, the younger they were, the more spectacular would be their gifts. The archbishop, Siegmund Christoph, Count von Schrattenbach, was ready to give Leopold paid leave: the Mozarts' successes could only conduce to the glory of Salzburg and its rulers and of God. Lorenz Hagenauer clearly had some role in its financing, and so almost certainly did other Salzburg business people. The omnipresent theme of money in Leopold's letters—how much the Mozarts were having to spend, how much they might (or did) earn—suggests that Hagenauer, and probably his friends, regarded the tour in the light of an investment and expected to reap some of the rewards of its success. Those could be considerable: an evening's takings in a large city could well amount to double Leopold's annual salary of 354 gulden. This would certainly explain why Leopold so often seems to have felt bound to justify his decisions and his expenses. It is also possible that

Leopold's 36 letters to Hagenauer, sent about monthly (rather less frequently in 1765–6), and the travel diary he maintained, were part of a specific obligation to supply people in Salzburg with potentially useful information about conditions in other countries. Even apart from any commercial value, first-hand reports on travel and foreign countries were read eagerly in this enlightened age, as the numerous travel books of the time testify. The letters may also have served to keep the archbishop informed about what his absent employee was doing.[3]

In a letter written many years later, Leopold instructed his son how to proceed when on tour.[4] It gives a clear picture, allowing for circumstances, of how Leopold organized concerts during the early family travels:

> This is the way to do it. Ask your host who is the Kapellmeister or musical director of the town; or, if there isn't one, who is the best-known musician. Ask to be taken to him, or, according to his standing, ask him to come to you, and speak to him; that way you will quickly know whether the cost of putting on a concert is too great, whether you can obtain a decent keyboard instrument—whether an orchestra can be got together, whether there are music-lovers—you might even find whether there is anyone who out of a love of music would play some part in the undertaking etc.: in short, one would quickly discover the truth, whether something can be done or not—and this should be done in travelling clothes, without even unpacking: just put on a couple of fine rings or something, in case when you call you find a keyboard instrument there and are asked to perform.

On 9 June 1763 the family set off. There were several different modes of carriage travel in Europe, the traveller's choice depending on cost, the degrees of comfort and speed required, and the quantity of baggage to be carried. The richest travellers would use their own carriage, with their own horses; more often horses would be hired, stage by stage. Alternatively, a carriage could be hired, either with horses or with changes of horses; or there were two public services— the stage-coach, with accommodation and food provided at established stops, or (the fastest option) the post-coach. There were two basic types of carriage: the closed, wooden, four-wheel carriage, leather-topped and suspended by leather braces and steel springs, with two seats (facing each other) each taking two or three passengers, sometimes with baskets for passengers or luggage; and the two-wheel type, the chaise or (in Italy) the *sedia*, essentially a large sedan chair for two passengers.

For the Mozarts, undertaking a long series of journeys with a servant, initially their valet Sebastian Winter, it was clearly an economy to use a carriage of their own. They were quickly made uncomfortably aware of the hazards of travel when on the first day a wheel broke, just short of Wasserburg in Bavaria. Speedy help provided a wheel but of slightly the wrong size, so Leopold and Winter walked for two hours so as not to strain the ailing carriage, to which the valuable iron from the old wheel had prudently been strapped, and an extra night had to be spent at the inn, Zum goldenen Stern. While the carriage was being repaired, and the other back wheel replaced as a precaution, Leopold took Wolfgang to the church and explained to him the use of the organ pedalboard (presumably none was available in Salzburg). Wolfgang tried it *stante pede* ('standing'), pushed the stool away and played with the pedals 'as if he had been studying it for several months. Everyone was astonished; this is a new sign of God's grace'.

On 12 June they moved on to Munich, staying at Zum goldenen Hirschen in the Theatinerstrasse. On their first day they went to Nymphenburg, the palace outside the city, where by chance they encountered the Palatine Count Friedrich Michael of Birkenfeld-Zweibrücken-Rappolstein, whom they had met in Vienna. He told the Elector Maximilian III Joseph of their presence and they were summoned to the concert that evening, where Wolfgang played on the violin and the keyboard and improvised. The two following evenings they played to Duke Clemens August, Elector of Bavaria. 'Now', wrote Leopold, 'it is a question of how we will get away from here, as the charming custom is to keep people waiting for their presents' (one musician of his acquaintance, Haydn's Eszterháza colleague Luigi Tommasini, had waited three weeks). Further, when the Mozarts were in attendance during a gala luncheon, the Elector twice said that he also wanted to hear Nannerl play, leaving Leopold no option but to offer to stay longer. Eventually Nannerl played, to warm applause, and Leopold received 100 gulden from the Elector and 75 from the duke. Leopold's report of his conversation with the Elector, as we have seen, makes no reference to any visit by the Mozarts to Munich the previous year; the Elector merely said he and Leopold were old acquaintances and had met 19 years before. Nannerl noted in her travel diary visits to Nymphenburg and the four castles, Amalienburg ('the most beautiful, where the fine bed is and the kitchen where the electress herself has cooked'), Badenburg ('the largest . . . with a bath of marble'), Bagotenburg ('the smallest, with walls of majolica') and the Ermitage ('where the chapel of shells is').[5]

The next stop was Augsburg, where the Mozarts lodged from 22 June to 6 July at the fine Zu den drei Mohren inn in the central square (not, as one might have expected, with his family; presumably they visited his mother and his brothers). There was no court or resident nobility, and they were able to give three concerts, at the inn, where almost all the audience, in a city divided roughly equally between Catholics and Protestants, Leopold noted, were Lutheran. They called on the eminent maker of keyboard instruments Johann Andreas Stein, from whom Leopold bought a clavichord small enough to be carried on their travels.[6] On 7 July they reached Ulm, staying at Zum goldenen Rad. Leopold expressed his dislike of this 'loathsome, old-fashioned, tastelessly built' city; medieval architecture had little charm for him. But they went to the minster to see, and presumably play, the organ. The plan had been to go next to Stuttgart, to the Württemberg court, but en route Leopold had learnt that the duke, Carl Eugen, was away at his hunting-lodge, so they went instead

to the summer residence, Ludwigsburg, taking rooms at Zum goldenen Waldhorn. He did not in fact catch the elusive duke, whose reputation for slowness, both in granting a hearing and in paying for it,
was anyway enough to put him off. But Leopold heard a play at the
French theatre and met two of the leading musicians, the violinist
Pietro Nardini, whose pure tone and singing style he admired while
noting that he played 'rather lightly', and the Kapellmeister, the eminent Italian opera composer Niccolò Jommelli. He regarded Jommelli with some suspicion, however, believing that he was trying to
oust the German musicians in favour of Italians—and what is more
he enjoyed an income of 4000 gulden with allowances, more than ten
times Leopold's own. Jommelli's Italian friends were heard expressing
their wonderment at the notion of a German child having such
genius for music. Leopold commented on the excessive militarization
of Ludwigsburg (Carl Eugen was famous for his military preoccupations): 'Soldiers rather than hedges or garden trellises form the walls
of this town. Should you spit, it's into an officer's pocket or a soldier's
cartridge box . . . and you see nothing but arms, drums and war materials'. The sergeant-majors, he noted, received 40 gulden a month. In
a letter written after he had left the town—he did not dare write it
while he was still there, for the post might be subject to censorship—
he added that there were twelve to fifteen thousand soldiers, 'who
strut around dressed up to the nines but can hardly walk for their
tight gaiters and breeches of fine linen'.

They left on 12 July, pausing at Bruchsal, where they lodged at the
Zum Riesen inn, admired the elegant new Residenz built in the
1720s, and arrived at Schwetzingen, summer residence of the
Mannheim court, on 14 July. There they stayed at Das rote Haus.
Musically, Mannheim was the most distinguished and most famous of
the western German courts, where under the patronage of the Elector Carl Theodor (who had acceded in 1742) and the musical direction first of Johann Stamitz and then, after his death in 1757,
Christian Cannabich, an orchestra of renowned virtuosity had been
built up. Mannheim drew for its musicians on Bohemia and much of

southern Germany, as well as Italy, and it had close connections with Paris musical life too. The highly disciplined style developed there had given rise to new types of orchestral writing, with brilliant violin passages, powerful and uniform attack and rich expressive nuance; the 'Mannheim symphony' quickly became a distinctive genre while the concerto, the sinfonia concertante (in effect a concerto with two or more soloists) and the opera, both Italian and later German, all underwent critical development at the Mannheim court during the 1760s and 70s. Many of the musicians were themselves composers, as Charles Burney's famous remark about the orchestra, 'an army of generals, equally fit to plan a battle as to fight it', reflects.[7]

Leopold, as usual, came to Schwetzingen well armed with letters of recommendation: he had two from Vienna, including one from Count Friedrich Michael and one from Duke Clemens August of Bavaria. A concert was promptly organized for the Mozarts, on 18 July; among the musicians he heard Leopold singled out the flautist Johann Baptist Wendling in a letter to Hagenauer (19 July; others, including the Toeschi brothers, Cannabich and Fränzl, are named in his travel notes). He described the orchestra as of 'people who are young and of good character, not tipplers, gamblers or dissolute fellows'—a commentary, perhaps, on the generality of orchestral players. He added that his children's performance set Schwetzingen in a spin and the Elector (who was to play a role in Mozart's later life) and Electress were amazed.

Leopold's letters disclose a number of preoccupations during these months of travel. First, of course, are his children's welfare (his wife, incidentally, is almost never mentioned), their health and their successes. Secondly, money matters bulk large: the fees or rewards he is given—as they were wholly discretionary they varied a great deal—and the cost of food and lodgings. He often commented, too, on exchange rates and currencies. Religious matters constantly interested him: in the Palatinate area, for example, he refers to the presence of four religions, Catholic, Lutheran, Calvinist and Jewish, and the absence of holy water stoups and crucifixes in the inns, as well as the serving of meat on fast days. He also sometimes commented on the layout of cities and their architecture, his taste being characteristically of his time in favouring the recent over the ancient. He noted sometimes the ravages of war, notably in Worms and Heidelberg, which had been affected by the fighting following Louis XIV's claim to the Palatinate. He seems to have viewed the journey as improving and educational—Nannerl's travel notes were presumably made at his instigation, or at least after his example—as well as potentially profitable, and occasionally the family took diversions to visit tourist sights, such as the great tun (which could hold 221,726 litres of beer) and the castle at Heidelberg.

The Mozarts arrived in Heidelberg on 19 July, where they stayed at the Zu den drei Königen. Wolfgang played on the organ at the Heilig-Geist-Kirche to such effect that a local official had his name and details of the event inscribed on a plate on the organ as a permanent record; the organ is gone, the inscription apparently with it. They went back to Schwetzingen, then on to Mannheim, lodging at the Prinz Friedrich: since the court was at Schwetzingen, this three-day visit was purely for sightseeing, and Leopold and Nannerl noted the castle, the opera house, the art gallery, the library and the treasure room. Then they moved on to Worms, staying at the Zum Schwan, and through Oppenheim to Mainz, this last stretch a particularly pleasant journey by the Rhine, Leopold wrote, with fields, villages, gardens and vineyards. The exact timing of these journeys is unrecorded, but the Mozarts reached Mainz on 3 August and remained there initially about a week, returning for two further weeks at the end of the month. They stayed at the König von England inn.[8]

Mainz had an electoral court, but the Elector was ill and there could be no appearance before him. They gave a concert in the hall of the Zum römischen König inn; recollecting the visit fourteen years later in an irate letter to his son, Leopold mentioned three concerts and takings of 200 gulden.[9] One, possibly two, of the concerts took place on their return there in September. Notes in Leopold's travel diary record that they met in the city the famous soprano Anna de Amicis, with her family entourage, on the way from London, and many of the local musicians (who would have assisted at the concerts). They also met a violinist from Kassel, Karl Michael Esser. Leopold does not mention him in his diary, but nearly twenty years later he reminded Wolfgang of what, as a highly precocious seven-year-old, he had said: 'he plays well but adds too many notes, and ought to play the music as it is written'.[10] He records seeing numerous churches and other sights in what he described as a 'narrow, closely-built town', and refers to visiting neighbouring towns, Biberich, Wiesbaden and Kostheim. Probably those journeys were made only after the family's return from Frankfurt, where they went on the market boat down the Rhine about 10 August, leaving some luggage and their carriage in Mainz. In Frankfurt they stayed for a night or two at the Zum goldenen Löwen and then apparently took lodgings in Bendergasse where, on a window, Leopold scratched: 'Mozart / maitre de la musique / de la chapelle de Salzbourg / avec Sa Famile le 12 Août / 1763' (the glass is preserved in the Frankfurt Historisches Museum). Frankfurt was already an important commercial centre and Leopold's letters contain much about business matters. There was no court, and the Mozarts gave four or five public concerts in the city, on 18, 22, 25 and/or 26 and 30 August. Goethe, present at the first of them as a boy of fourteen, remembered many years later 'the little fellow with his wig and his sword'. The paucity of information about what was actually performed at these concerts is relieved here by an advertisement:[11]

> Tuesday 30 August, in Scharf's Room on the Liebfrauenberg, at 6.00 in the evening . . . where the girl, in her twelfth year, and the boy, in his seventh [they were in fact already 12 and 7], will not only play on the harpsichord or the fortepiano, the former playing the most difficult pieces by the greatest masters, but the boy will also play a concerto on the violin, accompany symphonies on the keyboard, and play with the

keyboard completely covered by a cloth as well as though he could see the keyboard; he will also name, most accurately, from a distance, any note that may be sounded for him, singly or in chords on the keyboard, or on any conceivable instrument, including bells, glasses or clocks. Finally, he will improvise out of his head, not only on the fortepiano but also on the organ (for as long as anyone wants to listen, and in all the keys, even the most difficult, that he may be asked) . . .

For these events, Leopold must have engaged groups of local musicians to provide the orchestra; a selection of different types of music was the normal concert fare, and the full programme would normally have included a variety of orchestral items and probably some arias, as well as the pieces in which the children took part.

The Mozarts duly returned to Mainz on 31 August. The concerts, Leopold reported, had gone splendidly and Wolfgang was 'extraordinarily cheerful', although one morning he had woken up weeping because he could not see his Salzburg friends (he names adults, mainly musicians, rather than children, which perhaps is not surprising), and Nannerl, he wrote on 20 August, 'now no longer suffers by comparison with the boy, as she is playing so well that everyone is talking of her and admiring her skill'. They remained nearly two weeks in Mainz, at the same inn. We know only that they gave 'another concert for the nobles', which presumably, as there were three in all, was preceded by a first 'for the nobles'. It may have been referred to on the lost opening page of Leopold's next letter, of 26 September, an immensely long one. In it he gives a detailed account of a yacht ('Jacht') journey down the Rhine to Coblenz in weather so appallingly stormy that the yacht had several times to put in at villages on the way and the journey took nearly four days instead of just one. He also reports on various new acquaintances (notably the family of Baron von Kerpen, privy councillor in Coblenz), the state of buildings in the town, the prices of beef, butter and other foods in various of the towns they have been through and the exact costs of their accommodation at each inn on the journey. He writes as well about carriage repairs and horses—he mentions the need to travel in good style, 'nobl oder cavaglierment', for the reputation of his court and his family's health, and adds that they have associated only with a better class of travelling companion. Once in Coblenz, as usual, he has something to say about local religious dispositions and customs.

They had reached Coblenz on 17 September and stayed at the Zu den drei Reichskronen. Introductions through noblemen who had been with them on the boat journey down the Rhine—an imperial envoy and a kinsman of the Elector's—procured them a speedy hearing at court: they played on 18 September before the Elector of Trier, resident in the Philippsburg Castle in Coblenz, who rewarded them, through his chamber director, with ten louis d'or. Three days later they gave a public concert, not very profitable but with modest expenses. As Wolfgang had a cold, doubtless a consequence of the wet and windy river journey, Leopold delayed their departure for Bonn until 27 September, and this time they travelled by private boat. The Elector of Cologne, normally resident there, was away, so after one night (at Zum goldenen Karpfen) they went on to Brühl. There too they spent a single night (at Zum englischen Gruss), visiting the castle and the hunting-lodge Falkenslust, completed as a summer residence for Duke Clemens August of Bavaria only in the 1740s. Leopold reported with enthusiasm on the pheasant preserve, the Indian houses and the 'so-called snail-house', as well as the collections of jewellery, paintings, statues and clocks, and in the large hall the 'most beautiful' black marble tables, inlaid to give the impression of having engravings resting on them.

This stage of the journey, then, was partly tourism, but with Leopold continuing to make copious notes about the places they visited, the people (especially musicians) they met, the inns at which they stayed and anything else that seemed to him interesting or potentially useful. At Cologne, where they lodged at the Zum heiligen Geist inn, he was not much impressed by the cathedral and still less by its music (the choirboys screaming 'like rascals from the alleys' at the tops of their voices). From Cologne, on 30 September, to Aachen, where Princess Amalie, sister of Frederick the Great of Prussia, was staying, apparently with something like a mobile hospital to sustain her. The children were presented but rewarded only with kisses, as she had no money, 'but neither the innkeeper nor the postmaster can be paid in kisses'. Amalie tried to persuade Leopold to take the family to Berlin rather than Paris and made him various offers in inducement, that were evidently too extravagant to be taken seriously or even written down ('I shall not write them down as no-one would believe them; I did not believe them myself'). They lodged at Zum goldenen Drachen. Nannerl's reference in 1792 to a concert in Aachen is probably to the appearance before Amalie rather than some other event, which there would not have been time to prepare or advertise. Early on 2 October they set out, reaching Liège ('large, populous and productive') that evening and staying at Zum schwarzen Adler; the previous day's travel had been on a wretched road and they had trouble with the iron hoop on one of the front wheels. Three hours after they set out next morning, part of the hoop snapped in another front wheel and they had to have a prolonged peasant lunch—meat and root vegetables cooked in a large hotpot, with the door left open and grunting pigs 'honouring them' with visits—while repairs were done. Leopold found the people 'the most malicious in the world'. However, they reached Tirlemont in the evening, admiring the ruined fortress and the fine town square, and arrived in Louvain early enough the next day to do some sightseeing. There they went to Zum wilden Mann, the best inn in the city, where they lunched (referred to in a later letter[12]) and may have stayed overnight. Leopold noted that the priceless paintings of the Netherlanders began to be found in this area, and also the beautiful black and white marble altars. He clearly partook of his family's ancestral feeling for art: 'I stood transfixed before a Last Supper' (a triptych in St Peter's, by Dieric Bouts), he wrote, and later, in Brussels: 'Day and night I have before my eyes the Rubens picture of Christ giving Peter the keys in front of the apostles'.

The Mozarts reached Brussels, the centre of government of the Austrian Netherlands (equivalent to modern Belgium and Luxembourg), on 4 or 5 October 1763. The governor-general, before whom they hoped to play, was Prince Carl Alexander of Lorraine, brother to Emperor Francis I. They had to remain in the city, however, for nearly six weeks. Leopold's report to Hagenauer, in a private note to him of 4 November appended to a long letter dated 17 October—the note, which incidentally confirms that Leopold's letters were in general intended for wider circulation, deals chiefly with financial arrangements Leopold needed to have made against his forthcoming spell in Paris—expresses a characteristic predicament. Prince Carl has expressed his intention of hearing the children but told Leopold that he cannot give a public concert without permission, and accordingly the Mozarts have no option but to wait, as the prince (busy with hunting, eating and drinking) ignored them. Their indebtedness to the Hôtel d'Angleterre steadily mounted. They spent some time in sightseeing, and Leopold wrote warmly about the fine, hilly city, its lively canal-borne trade, its great town hall and its numerous fine paintings. On 14 October Wolfgang composed a fairly substantial Allegro for harpsichord, copied by Leopold into Nannerl's Music Book (and to be used later in the sonata K.6). There is no documentation of any performance by the children until 7 November, when they gave a concert in Prince Carl's presence, but Wolfgang was given 'two magnifique swords', one by the archbishop of Mechelen, Count von Frankenberg, and one by General Count De Ferraris, which suggests that they did make some private appearances. There were other gifts too from courtiers, including clothes for both children and trinkets.

The Mozarts were able to move on from Brussels on 15 November; to Paris it was a four-day journey, with overnight stops in Mons, Bonavis and Gournay-sur-Aronde (Leopold observed that the rates for hiring horses here were astonishingly high). They arrived in Paris on the afternoon of 18 November and went straight to the palace of Count van Eyck, the Bavarian minister in the city. There they were warmly welcomed and offered accommodation, in a room in which the countess's harpsichord stood, for their entire visit (that is, until the following April). Leopold was thus enabled to cancel, at moderate cost, the arrangement he had made in advance to take rooms in the house in the rue St Honoré of the notary Le Noir where the composer J.G. Eckard and a friend Christian von Mechel, an engraver and art dealer, lived. The countess was a member of the Arco family, from Salzburg. The palace, the Hôtel de Beauvais, was in central Paris, near the present Hôtel de Ville in what is now the rue de François-Miron.[13]

PARIS WAS THE most important musical centre in Europe. With Versailles, it was the home of the court of Louis XV, of great wealth and power, and it was beyond competition as an intellectual centre. It was the capital city of the largest true European nation, and numerous rich noblemen with houses there were patrons of the arts. It had a lavish court opera house and a rival one that was giving rise to a new type of repertory, the genre coming to be known as *opéra comique*, wider in appeal than the traditional classical *tragédie*. Its flourishing music-publishing industry attested to the presence of a substantial body of active lovers and practitioners of music. Its public concert life, however, was modest. The dominant organization was the Concert Spirituel, but it gave only some 25 concerts each year, most of these in Lent or Easter and otherwise scattered throughout the year by the exigencies of the church calendar.

Leopold's hopes in Paris devolved chiefly on appearances at court and at the houses of the nobility. His first letter to Hagenauer (8 December) refers—along with the usual discussions of financial matters, local prices, their lodgings and the like—to engagements at two noble houses, those of the Marquis of Villeroi and the Countess Lillibonne, in a way that implies these were just two of many. A recent death in the royal family precluded appearances at court for the moment. However, Leopold's travel notes from December show how energetically he had pursued acquaintances, both colleagues and patrons. Among those listed are five composers, the pianists Eckard and Johann Schobert, the violinist Pierre Gaviniès, the cellist J.-P. Duport and the harpist Christian Hochbrucker, as well as the amateur composer and violinist Baron de Bagge. There are also such aristocrats as the Princes of Conti, Condé, Turenne and Rohan, the Princess of Robecque, the Duchesses of Mazarin and Aiguillon, and many more, as well as Friedrich Melchior von Grimm, an eminent German intellectual and diplomat, secretary to the Duke of Orléans, who was associated with the Encyclopedists and became their firm supporter.[14] A much later letter of Leopold's, sent to Mozart when he was visiting Paris in 1778, fills in detail on some of the Parisian musicians and patrons.[15]

Grimm's manuscript journal, *Correspondance littéraire, philosophique et critique*, included on 1 December 1763 one of the earliest serious appreciations of Mozart's abilities. Grimm writes not only of the boy's playing pieces but of his improvising for an hour or more and 'giving rein to the inspiration of his genius and to a mass of enchanting ideas'; 'the most consummate Kapellmeister could not be more profound in the science of harmony and modulation'. He mentions some of Mozart's usual feats and goes on to describe new ones: Grimm asked a woman to sing the boy an aria he had not heard before, which he accompanied correctly after a single hearing and then accompanied in different styles several times over.[16]

On 24 December the Mozarts went to Versailles, staying there for two weeks in lodgings with a landlord Cormier in the rue des Bons Enfans. A note home written from Versailles, accompanying what was probably a new year's greeting to the archbishop, mentions gifts for the children from the Countess of Tessé (a lady-in-waiting to the Dauphine and intimate of the Prince of Conti, a leading musical patron) and the Princess Carignan, widow of the Prince of Savoy. By this time they must have played to a number of courtiers; these and others are named in the travel notes for these two weeks. The royal family dined publicly, or at least in the presence of people of distinction, on special occasions such as the new year's banquet or *grand cou-*

vert; the Mozarts had been present and Wolfgang was singled out for the privilege of standing close to the table, being allowed to kiss the hand of the queen (who unlike Louis XV spoke German) and given morsels to eat. He and Leopold went several times to the royal chapel to hear the motets. Leopold, brought up in a wholly different musical tradition, was contemptuous of the solo sections ('empty, frozen and wretched') but admired the choruses. In referring to instrumental music, however, he was more sweeping: 'the whole of French music is worth nothing', and he stresses the growing pre-eminence of German keyboard composers, in particular, in Paris. There is no specific report in any of Leopold's letters, or in any other source, of the children's playing before the royal family until an issue on 5 March 1764 of the *Avant-courier* (believed to be the work of Grimm, and similar to his earlier report), but a gift of 50 louis d'or and a gold snuffbox was sent from the Menus plaisirs du roi (the office in charge of royal entertainments) during February in respect of their appearances.

The Mozarts moved out of the van Eyck house early in March. At the end of January the countess had suddenly been taken ill, and to everyone's shock and dismay she had died on 6 February. Mozart himself was unwell, probably with tonsillitis, in mid-February; a German doctor prescribed Vienna laxative water and he soon recovered. Baron Grimm—described by Leopold as our best friend, 'to whom I owe everything here . . . a man of learning and a great friend of humanity' (letter of 1 April)—provided accommodation in the rue de Luxembourg for the remainder of the Mozarts' stay. Their servant and *friseur* from Salzburg, Sebastian Winter, left them at the beginning of March to take up a post at the Donaueschingen court, and they engaged Jean-Pierre Potivin, an Alsatian. Leopold continued, as his travel notes show, to enlarge his Paris acquaintanceship: those listed include the harpsichordist and composer Le Grand (probably Louis-Alexandre), the famous *haute-contre* singer Pierre de Jélyotte and the soprano Marie Fel, the harpist-composer Philippe-Jacques Meyer, the noted *opéra comique* composer Egidio Duni and the composers Antoine Mahaut and Josef Kohaut, the violinist Le Duc (probably

Simon), the painters Carmontelle (Louis Carrogis) and Vanloo, and many officials and members of the aristocracy.[17]

On 10 March the family gave the first of two concerts (the second was on 9 April), in a private theatre owned by a M Félix in the rue et Porte St Honoré. This, Leopold explained, infringed the royal privileges for musical performances (which were forbidden except under royal licence) and thus involved applications for permission, which needed to be supported by various noble patrons. Tickets, which had to be bought in advance, cost the equivalent of a quarter of a louis d'or, and as the takings amounted to 112 louis d'or the attendance would seem to have been about 450, a surprisingly high figure. There would have been attendant expenses, including fees for other musicians (some of the miscellaneous ones, for example for lighting, were borne by Grimm, who also helped distribute 320 tickets, done by passing blocks of tickets to ladies, whose importuning would be hard to refuse). At the second concert Gaviniès and a singer are known to have taken part. Grimm and Leopold arranged for the family to be painted, in watercolours, by Louis Carrogis de Carmontelle, one of a series of stylized musical pictures, with Wolfgang at the keyboard, Nannerl behind it singing and Leopold with his violin. There are several slightly different versions of it, and an engraving based on it by Jean Baptiste Delafosse.

The family left for London the day after their second concert. But the other important event of these months in Paris was the engraving and publication of four sonatas for harpsichord and violin by Mozart, K.6–9. The first two were dedicated to Madame Victoire de France, second daughter of the king, and issued as Opus I, by J.G. Wolfgang Mozart of Salzburg, aged seven years (he was eight by the date of publication but six or seven at the time of composition); the second pair were dedicated to the countess of Tessé, as Opus II. The flowery, flattering dedications were supplied by Grimm: apparently he at first overstepped the mark with Op.II and the countess required the dedication to be revised in less extravagant terms, causing, to Leopold's anxiety, some delay in publication.

Leopold Mozart and his children: engraving by J.B. Delafosse after the watercolour by L.C. de Carmontelle (*Mozart-Gedenkstätte, Augsburg*)

MOZART HAD BEEN trying to write notes on music paper since he was four, no doubt in emulation of his father. Not all the pieces he wrote as a child, of course, have come down to us (nothing is known of the scribbled concerto reported by Schachtner, for example), but Leopold had every reason to preserve whatever he could, and some very early efforts are to be found in the pages of Nannerl's Music Book. Again, however, it is impossible to be sure that these are his own unaided work, especially as Leopold usually copied the pieces out and, as his composition teacher, is likely to have made corrections or improvements; many emendations in Leopold's hand can be seen on Wolfgang's early autographs. This must apply to much of his music of the early years, even beyond the date when Wolfgang's technique in general overtook his father's. Indeed, as late as 1780 Leopold still made suggestions to his son about ways of managing particular effects (see Chapter 20)—and Wolfgang still accepted some of them.

Nannerl's Music Book[18] was given to her in the summer of 1759, on her nameday or birthday (they are very close, 26 and 30 or 31 July). It originally consisted, almost certainly, of 48 leaves of eight-staff paper, of which twelve are missing from the book as it now stands; it is clear that several were removed (Nannerl is known to have given some of them away), but eight of those can be accounted for. Nevertheless, we are missing the originals of certain known early compositions by Wolfgang (these can be restored on the basis of texts in Nissen's biography of Mozart)[19] and possibly also some unknown ones. In its fullest possible reconstructed form, the book contains 64 pieces, including some exercises and incomplete ones. Seventeen of these are by Wolfgang, six of them early versions, for keyboard without violin, of movements he included in the sonatas published in Paris. The book begins with nineteen short minuets, many of them sixteen bars long; all are anonymous but one is known to be by Leopold. A mixture of pieces follows—allegros, marches, andantes, more minuets. Of other composers whose work is identified in the book the first is G.C. Wagenseil (a Scherzo, no. 31), a Presto by J.N.

Tischer (no. 43) and an Allegro by J.J.Agrell (no. 45). No other composers are named. Leopold copied 35 of the pieces and Wolfgang
four, with the remainder written by Salzburg copyists. Clearly the
book was put together over some years, from 1759 to at least 1764,
and the choice of repertory was dictated simply by the kinds of music
Leopold thought it appropriate for his daughter to play.

The minuets at the beginning are all quite easy, calling for few and
only simple chords. Mozart, Leopold noted, learnt the first eight and
no.19 in his fourth (meaning fifth) year, and the long (40-bar) no.11
on the eve of his fifth birthday, which took him half an hour. A couple of them require octave stretches that must then have been beyond
him. At that time he also learnt nos. 31, 32 (with crossing hands) and
a bright little Allegro no. 41. Some of the technically more demanding pieces, with continuous passage-work requiring a degree of
agility, were presumably intended for Nannerl in the first place.
Clearly these well-formed, *galant* little pieces by up-to-date composers were garnered by Leopold from a variety of sources as appropriate for early keyboard instruction, but clearly, too, they were
prominent among Wolfgang's first composition models. What is supposedly his earliest piece, K.1*a* (the original K.1 is renumbered to 1*e*
and *f*), is an odd little Andante, half in 3/4 time and half in 2/4. Neither this nor K.1*b*, a brief 2/4 Allegro beginning with notes in alternate hands and ending with a cadence emphatic enough to round off
a piece ten times the length, has obvious models in the Music Book.
K.1*c* looks like a jolly south German folkdance, twelve bars long, with
the last four bars the same as the first four. This piece and K.1*d*, a minuet in 8 + 12 bars (the second part unrelated to the first except at the
cadence), were written on 11 and 16 December 1761. All these survive only in Leopold's hand. K.2, according to Nissen dating from
January 1762, is the Minuet in F familiar to most embryo pianists, a
much more closely organized piece in which the opening motif is
used throughout. K.3, from March 1762, is a 30-bar Allegro in what
might almost be called sonata form (its first half cadences in the dom-

inant, its ideas are then 'developed', and there is a recapitulation ending in the home key). The minuet K.4, of May 1762, follows just the
same scheme, and the K.5 minuet, of July, uses a similar one, with no
recapitulation of the opening but passage-work patterns that reflect
the boy's pleasure in the keyboard. (The second minuet used in the
K.6 sonata, also from July 1762, uses this scheme too; it is however an
arrangement, in idiomatic keyboard terms, of the trio of the first
minuet of a serenata by Leopold.[20]) If the dating is dependable, these
little pieces already show a developing awareness of musical resources
and musical coherence.

Most of the other pieces by Mozart in the Music Book date from
the time in Brussels and Paris, that is, between October 1763 and
April 1764. Five are in fact first versions for keyboard alone of movements used in the Paris accompanied sonatas. The accompanied
sonata, normally for keyboard (as the principal instrument) and violin (the accompanying one) was a popular genre at this period, above
all in the large commercial centres, such as Paris, London and Amsterdam, where it was *par excellence* the genre for amateur music-
making in a context where young women were expected to play a
keyboard instrument to a moderate level of proficiency and men the
violin (occasionally the flute) to a more modest one. In answer to a
particular social need, this type of sonata developed in the third quarter of the eighteenth century, with the melodic role assigned almost
exclusively to the keyboard and the violin restricted to sustained
notes, accompanying figures, filling-in phrases and lines shadowing
the keyboard a third or a sixth below.[21] It was no doubt plain to the
Mozarts, or explained to them by their Paris publisher, Vendôme, that
this type of sonata was commercially more viable and to be preferred
to that for keyboard alone. Best of all was to publish sonatas with an
optional violin part, and that is what Mozart did. The title-pages read:
Sonates pour le clavecin qui peuvent se jouer avec l'accompagnement de violon.

It would seem, then, that Mozart, when it was decided that he
should prepare two pairs of sonatas for publication in Paris, drew on
pieces that he had already written as keyboard solos for three move-

ments of K.6 and one each of K.7 and K.8. It was child's play, literally, to add a secondary violin part. K.6 in C begins with an Allegro from the Music Book (no. 46), a movement on virtually the same scale as his adult contemporaries were writing; as well as adding the violin part Mozart added some chords and some embellishment to the existing keyboard part. As in the smaller pieces, Mozart is inclined to use a short motif many times over, in sequence patterns, as his main mode of construction, and in this movement several are used this way, one in effect for each section of the exposition, with the left hand perpetually in 'Alberti bass' figuration (as in all but the most sophisticated examples of the genre at this date). Echoes of phrases by Eckard (his op.1 no.1 sonata) have been noted here, although there must be some doubt as to whether Mozart could have seen the Eckard work, published in Paris in 1763, when he wrote the first version of K.6.[22] The Andante, too, is a more polished version of a piece (no. 25) in the Music Book, probably written the previous autumn, employing a single motif almost throughout; it has a remarkable chromatic twist in its second half and a delicately managed recapitulatory section. The third movement consists of a pair of minuets from the Music Book (nos. 26 and 48, the latter arranged from Wolfgang's version of July 1762 of a movement by Leopold), but the fourth is new, and may take its inspiration from a sonata (op.1 no.2) by Schobert, with which it has figuration in common. With its lesser dependency on sequence and incessant Alberti bass, it generates energy through the freshness and pleasing flow of ideas across its 115 bars—a long movement for a child composer to handle.

The other three sonatas, more conventionally, are in only three movements. K.7 begins with the kind of brilliant writing common in its key, D major, with arpeggio figures passing between the hands; its finale is a minuet, partly based on no. 47 in the Music Book. The central Adagio is Mozart's earliest attempt at a type of movement he later handled particularly happily, the slow movement with a long-breathed melody unwinding above a soft and warm texture. Here the melody is too fragmented and at times awkward in line for the move-

Title-page of Mozart's first published music, the sonatas K.6 and 7 (*Internationale Stiftung Mozarteum, Salzburg*)

ment to be wholly successful. The next sonata, K.8 in B flat, starts with a bustling Allegro (Music Book, no. 24) begun soon after the Mozarts reached Paris, music of momentum and vitality even if its ideas are rather mechanical. There is a 3/4 Andante grazioso of a certain formal grace, based on a single theme that is developed and recapitulated, and finally a crisp, four-square minuet, recalling the first movement in its thematic outline and with a trio in the rare key of B flat minor where forceful unisons are set against harmonized phrases. K.9 in G, the final sonata, has a spacious opening movement, sectional in plan. It begins with an early-*galant* formality and moves into a passage with chromatically rising patterns, which in turn leads into faster-moving second-group material (the left hand echoing the right in inversion). The opening material dominates a long development, in which a rising (and then falling) chromatic line in the bass draws the earlier ideas together. Contrasts between *piano* harmonized phrases and *forte* unison ones supply the main material of the Andante, but for once the effect is rather childish and naïve, and the ideas in the minuets again reflect the boy composer's occupation with keyboard patterns and sonorities too strongly to possess much interest for the listener.

Mozart's models here are clear, but it would be mistaken to argue that these sonatas are simply the work of a clever mimic. Their technique is astonishingly sure, their line of thinking ('filo', the thread, as Leopold later called it[23]) is clear and smooth and their formal balance is beyond reproach—in all these respects Mozart already surpassed many of his lesser contemporaries. Leopold Mozart's preference for German keyboard music, in particular that of Eckard (like himself, a native of Augsburg, and a friend) and Schobert (far more talented a composer, although Leopold mistrusted him personally), is reflected in their material and their textures. But the influence, and the occasional help over detail that his father provided, as the autographs show and a remark in a later letter bears out,[24] do nothing to diminish the extraordinary achievement that these sonatas represent for a composer of just eight years old.

4

Playing for the English Court

LONDON, THE LARGEST and richest city in the world, and one in which many musicians had sought and a few had made their fortunes, was an obvious place for Leopold Mozart to take his children. Like Paris, it was a great publishing centre, supported by a substantial public drawn from the middle classes, newly enriched by the country's commercial and industrial development; and unlike Paris it had a flourishing concert life, public and private, largely untrammelled by governmental or courtly regulation. It had not originally been part of Leopold's intention to venture so far, but he seems to have been encouraged by acquaintances in Paris.

The family set out from Paris on 10 April 1764, in their own coach, leaving some of their luggage in the care of their Parisian banker, Hummel, but prudently taking an extra servant with experience in crossing the English Channel, an Italian called Porta. They left their coach at Calais and hired a boat, for five louis d'or (saving two of these by taking on four passengers); the boat accommodated fourteen. The Mozarts had never seen the sea before, and Nannerl noted with wonderment its tidal ebb and flow in her travel diary. It must have been a rough crossing. Leopold reports on the discomfort of the journey with so many people on board, adding that they made a

heavy contribution to the Channel by vomiting—but characteristically, self-mockingly noted that at least they had saved money on
emetics. On arrival at Dover they were transferred to a small boat for
going ashore and then were surrounded by 30 or 40 would-be
porters touting for work, calling out 'your most obedient servant'. No
details of the journeys between Paris and Calais or Dover and London were recorded by the Mozarts, but Leopold's letters indicate that
they stayed one night in Dover. They arrived in London on 23 April,
lodging for their first night at the White Bear in Piccadilly, the main
terminal inn for travellers from the Channel ports and certain other
parts of the country.[1]

The Mozarts found lodgings in Cecil Court, by St Martin's Lane,
in a house above a barber's shop owned by a John Cousins. Leopold's
letters of introduction must have served him well, for he quickly
made contact with the court: they appeared at Buckingham House,
the recently established royal residence in the area of St James's Park
and more modest predecessor of Buckingham Palace, on the evening
of 27 April, playing before George III and Queen Charlotte (who
was of German birth). Leopold reported that the graciousness with
which they were received was beyond description.

> To put it briefly, their unpretentious manner and friendly
> ways made one forget that we were with the King and
> Queen of England. At all courts we have been courteously
> received, but here our welcome surpassed all others. A week
> later we were in St James's Park when the King and Queen
> rode by, and although we were wearing different clothes they
> recognized us, greeted us, and what is more the King opened
> the window, saluting us cheerfully, especially our Master
> Wolfgang, nodding his head and waving his hand.[2]

Leopold was slightly less content with the reward, 24 guineas, but at
least it was handed to them immediately; and in the same letter he
reports that a further 24-guinea fee was forthcoming on their return

visit, on 19 May, when the brothers of the King and Queen were also present:

> The King had [Wolfgang] play not only pieces by Wagenseil but also ones by [J.C.] Bach, Abel and Handel, and he sightread them all fluently. He played the King's organ in such style that they value his organ playing even above his harpsichord playing. Then he accompanied the Queen when she sang an aria, and a flautist who played a solo. Lastly, he took the bass part of some Handel arias, which happened to be lying there, and above this plain bass he improvised the most beautiful melody, in such a manner that everyone was astonished.

Leopold commented too on his son's nostalgia for home and its mixture with his musical ambitions:

> Not a day passes without Wolfgang's talking at least thirty times about Salzburg and his and our friends and patrons. He is thinking all the time about an opera that he would like to perform there with a number of young people.

A story related in 1777 by the famous 'bluestocking', Samuel Johnson's friend Mrs Thrale, about Mozart's appearance before the King is charming but probably confused. When, she wrote, Mozart began with a slow movement, the King took it for bashfulness: 'don't be afraid, my little Fellow says he, don't be afraid I say', and Mozart responded 'Afraid! why I have played before the Emperor'. This seems to be a corruption of a story told elsewhere about an appearance of Mozart's at a German court.[3]

The Mozarts' arrival in London was not happily timed for public performances; the main part of the season was over and the richer people were drifting off to their country houses. There had been plans for him to play in a concert organized by the cellist and composer Carlo Graziani, on 17 May, advertised on 9 May ('Concerto on the Harpsichord by Master Mozart, who is a real Prodigy of Nature; he is but Seven Years of Age, plays any thing at first Sight, and composes amazingly well'). It was then postponed until 22 May, as the musicians of the opera orchestra were busy that night, but a repeat advertisement on 21 May notes that 'as [Mr Mozard] is sick I cannot promise he will play'.[4] He had played two days before at Buckingham House. Leopold nowhere mentions that he was unwell, and it could be that the illness was diplomatic, actuated by his reluctance for Wolfgang to anticipate his own benefit event, only a few days off, by appearing elsewhere sooner.

Wolfgang eventually made his public London début in a concert at the Great Room in Spring Garden, St James's, on 5 June—this was one of the general-purpose halls in London, used for auctions and dancing schools as well as concerts, 62 feet long and 52 wide.[5] Leopold chose a date when some of the nobility would be in town for celebrations of the King's birthday, calculating that 600 tickets, at half a guinea (ten shillings and sixpence), might be sold, against expenses of 40 guineas. Also engaged were several eminent London musicians, François-Hippolyte Barthélemon as the leading violinist, playing a solo, Giovanni Battista Cirri as the cellist, playing a concerto, and two singers from the opera house to sing arias. (He cites the more detailed costs: half a guinea for hiring a keyboard instrument, five or six for a singer's services, three for the leader or up to five if a solo or concerto is to be played, half a guinea for a rank-and-file orchestral musician, and five for the hire of the hall, without lighting, and the music stands. Several of the musicians in fact declined any fees.) In the event, only some 200 came ('not only all the ambassadors, but the principal families in England attended'), but expenses were only about twenty guineas, so there was a reasonable profit, of some 90 guineas. Now Leopold accepted a request that Wolfgang should appear at a benefit concert, on 29 June, in aid of a new lying-in hospital, to play an organ concerto, as an act of enlightened self-interest:

... so to perform the act of an English patriot who, so far as he can, seeks to further the usefulness of this hospital, established *pro bono publico*; this, you see, is a way of winning the affection of this very exceptional nation.

The event was advertised:

> ... the celebrated and astonishing Master MOZART, lately arrived, a Child of 7 Years of Age, will perform several fine select Pieces of his own Composition on the Harpsichord and on the Organ, which has already given the highest Pleasure, Delight, and Surprize to the greatest Judges of Music in England or Italy and is justly esteemed the most extraordinary Prodigy, and most amazing Genius, that has appeared in any Age.[6]

That concert was at the Ranelagh Pleasure Gardens, one of three principal gardens in London where music was performed during the summer. In a letter (28 June), Leopold describes Ranelagh, by the Thames at Chelsea, and its three-hour concerts, held from 7.00 to 10.00 in the great Rotunda, illuminated by numerous chandeliers, lamps and wall lights, and followed from 11.00 to 12.00 by music for wind band. He was impressed by the facilities for sitting at tables in the alcoves or in loggias at an upper level, drinking tea or coffee and eating bread and butter, all included in the 2s 6d entrance charge, and he was struck by the number of people, 2000 to 4500, of all classes, who visited there.

But he was still more amazed by the famous and much larger Vauxhall, describing it with an air of wonderment, or rather by saying it was impossible to describe—akin to the Elysian Fields, with night transformed to brilliant day by no fewer than a thousand lamps in the most beautiful glass holders illuminating the avenues, with floodlit pyramids and arches, pavilions and a fine concert hall with organs, trumpets, drums and other music, with thousands of people paying only a shilling for entrance (though much more if they needed refreshment) and the noblemen and common folk mixing happily.

Leopold was clearly overwhelmed by the sheer size of London. His letters of these months culminate in one, written in November, which draws on a published, detailed statistical survey of every aspect of the city, down to the number of street lamps (55,435) and the quantity of cheese consumed annually (21,660,000 lbs, excluding imports). Other letters comment on such matters as the cost of living and the local eating and drinking habits. Leopold admired English meat and produce generally as the best in the world, was struck by the custom of keeping a kettle on the boil to serve visitors tea with bread and butter, noted the different types of beer and punch and mentioned that noblemen never dined until after midnight. He also remarked on the women's fashions and the materials used, the fine horses, the building styles, the habit among Oxford students of cutting their hair short so that its growth did not impede their intellects, the urchins in the streets who shouted at foreigners (he may not correctly have understood their cries of 'Buger French!') and of course the weather.

The English weather, however, nearly caused Leopold's downfall. On 8 July, he related in two letters (3–9 August and 13 September), they were playing at the house of the Earl of Thanet in Grosvenor Square (no doubt this was only one of many such engagements in private houses which are unreported). It was a fine day, and a Sunday, so all the carriages were booked. Leopold accordingly hired a sedan chair for the children and walked beside it. But the bearers moved so quickly that Leopold found himself overheated and perspiring, and as the evening grew cooler, with the windows open, he caught a 'kind of native complaint, which is called a *cold*'. This, Leopold wrote, can become dangerous and turn to consumption; that is why many English have to go abroad to recover their health. Leopold took his illness seriously: 'Prepare your heart to hear one of the saddest events', he began the first letter to Hagenauer, with perhaps exaggerated drama, though in those times he may indeed have had some reason to wonder, as he did, whether he was close to death's door. In fact, about a week after the chilling, a fever and a throat infection had developed. He had medical treatment (he gave Hagenauer full details of the prescriptions), but then violent gastric pain on 22 and 23 July. So he consulted another doctor, the cousin of their friend the cellist Siprutini, a Portuguese Jew, was given different medication and was, he said, 'clystered, purged and bled' (in exchange, Leopold tried to convert him to Christianity). Of his London acquaintances only Giordani—presumably the opera composer Tommaso Giordani— came to visit him during his illness, twice daily. By 29 July he was well enough to take a sedan chair to St James's Park, for an airing.

On 5 August, after some rainy days, he could go by sedan chair to Chelsea to arrange to take rooms for the main part of the summer in a house there, where the pure air and the country atmosphere would aid his convalescence. A planned visit to Tunbridge Wells, presumably to give concerts at that popular watering-place, was abandoned, and the family moved on 6 August to accommodation in a house owned by a George Randal in Ebury Row (sometimes called Five Fields Row). Now 180 Ebury Street, Victoria, the house still stands—a plain Georgian building, at the end of a terrace, with three storeys and a basement. In Cecil Court the family's food had to be brought in; here they tried the same arrangement but the food was unsatisfactory and, as the accommodation evidently included kitchen facilities, Maria Anna cooked it herself. Leopold was delighted with the country views, 'nothing but gardens and the finest mansions in the distance'. Several times in the correspondence he asked Hagenauer to arrange for masses to be said at churches in or near Salzburg; this time, under-standably, he requested no fewer than 22, at specific churches which he considered relevant to his and his family's situation.

It is usually supposed that it was during the time at Ebury Row that Mozart composed his first symphonies and perhaps the keyboard pieces in the so-called London Sketchbook. That does not square with the facts about Leopold's illness and Nannerl's oft-quoted accounts:[7]

In London, when our father lay ill and close to death, we were not allowed to touch the clavier. So, to occupy himself, Mozart composed his first symphony with all the instruments, above all with trumpets and drums. I had to sit by him and copy it out. As he composed, and I copied, he said to me: 'Remind me to give the horn something worthwhile to do' . . .

On 5 August, they had to rent a country house, outside London, in Chelsea, so that the father could recover from a dangerous throat illness, which almost brought him to the brink of death.

By the time the family was in Chelsea—Ebury Row was in fact not in Chelsea but in the City of Westminster, just east of the Chelsea boundary and some way from Chelsea village—Leopold was recovered, and there was no need for silence; clearly the symphony had been composed in Cecil Court. At Ebury Row they were not far from Ranelagh, Chelsea Royal Hospital for pensioners (which a note in Nannerl's diary suggests they once visited) or the Chelsea waterworks (a famous sight, where water was extracted from the Thames; it too is noted in Nannerl's diary). There were views across gardens, fields or farmland to Kensington and Westminster. It may be from here that the Mozarts went on excursions to the royal gardens at Kensington, to Richmond (where Nannerl particularly admired the views) and to the gardens at Kew. At some stage they also visited the Tower of London (where the roar of the lions frightened Wolfgang) and the hospital and park at Greenwich.

About 24 September the Mozarts moved back into London, in good time for the beginning of the season, which would normally be in November. They took lodgings in Thrift (now Frith) Street, Soho, in the house of a Thomas Williamson, corset maker, on the site of no. 20, on the east side (not, as is usually stated, no. 21). The house, built of brick in the 1720s, three or four storeys high, is no longer standing, and its site is occupied by the back of the Prince Edward

Theatre.[8] (Mozart's periods of residence here and at 180 Ebury Street are commemorated with blue plaques.) The situation was a particularly convenient one, close to a number of concert rooms, to the street where J.C. Bach and C.F. Abel lived and to two Catholic churches, one of them the so-called Bavarian chapel. Johann Christian Bach (youngest son of J.S. Bach), who had come to London in 1762, was composer to the opera house, music master to the Queen and organizer of a concert series with Carl Friedrich Abel (an acquaintance of the Bachs from Cöthen and Leipzig, talented composer and player of the viola da gamba). Curiously, Bach is little mentioned in Leopold's letters; there is simply a statement that they knew him. But Nannerl refers in her recollections to an occasion when Bach took Mozart

> ... between his knees, the former played a few bars, and then the other continued, and in this way they played a whole sonata and anyone not watching would have thought it was played by one person alone.

This may be the same occasion as the one described by the English composer and organist William Jackson, of Exeter, in his memoirs:

> When [Mozart] was a mere infant (I think under six years of age) he was exhibited as a great performer on the harpsichord, and an extraordinary genius for music. John Bach took the child between his knees and began a subject on that instrument, which he left, and Mozart continued—each led the other into very abstruse harmonies, and extraneous modulations, in which the child beat the man. We were afterwards looking over Bach's famous song 'Se spiego' in *Zanaida*. The score was inverted to Mozart, who was rolling on the table. He pointed out a note which he said was wrong. It was so, whether of the composer or copyist I cannot now recollect, but it was an instance of extraordinary discernment and readiness in a mere infant.[9]

Johann Christian Bach: oil portrait by Thomas Gainsborough (*Civico Museo Bibliografico Musicale, Bologna*)

J.C. Bach, by all reports a much-loved figure, seems to have had a warm relationship with the Mozarts; musically, he was to prove a considerable influence on the boy and in some degree the grown man. His opera *Adriano in Siria* had its première while the Mozarts were in London and they would certainly have gone to see it. Several pasticcios and two new operas by Vento and one by Arne were also given at the King's Theatre in the winter and the spring of 1765, while at Covent Garden Arne's much admired *Artaxerxes*—a serious English opera in the Italian style—was in the repertory, along with a season of Handel oratorios (in the tradition established by Handel himself) in February and March.[10] Again, the Mozarts are likely to have attended performances.

Leopold, his finances suffering from his spell of illness and from the high cost of living in London, had hopes of making 'some thousands of gulden' during the London season. He had told Hagenauer:

I am in a city that no-one from our Salzburg court has yet dared visit and to which perhaps no-one ever will go in the future. *Aut Caesar, aut nihil*:[11] we have reached our long journey's end and once I leave England I shall never again see guineas. So we must make the most of our opportunity.

It was a setback, then, when he found that the recall of Parliament was postponed until 10 January 1765, because of the tension between King and Government (George III had attempted to appoint his own nominees to political power and had been the victim of ferocious personal attacks by the MP and journalist John Wilkes). This, he said (8 February), dealt a severe blow to the arts and sciences, because a large proportion of the potential patrons would remain out of town until then. The Mozarts did in fact visit Buckingham House, for the third and last time, on 25 October 1764, and it may have been then that the Queen asked to have a set of sonatas by Wolfgang dedicated to her (as Leopold reports). It is not clear whether the sonatas, K.10–15, already existed or were composed at her request. The dedication itself, an embarrassingly arch and flowery effusion, going to the very limits of the exaggerated flattery usual in dedications of this period, was printed in the conventional French and no doubt written by a professional in this pseudo-literary field. It is dated 18 January 1765, implying that the sonatas had lately been delivered to the engraver (Leopold had to meet the cost of the engraving and printing). They were published on 20 March and elicited 50 guineas from the Queen. Meanwhile, Leopold arranged for a batch of copies of the Paris sonatas to be sent for sale in Salzburg, Frankfurt, Augsburg and Nuremberg, as well as having them reissued in London. Some were no doubt heard at an event at the Salzburg court on 3 January, reported in the court diaries, when a 'small Cammer-Musique, which the young son of Mozart, the resident vice-Kapellmeister, had composed, was given'.[12]

Concert life began early in the new year with the opening, on 23 January, of the first of the Bach-Abel concerts, an important and highly fashionable subscription series, held in Carlisle House, Soho Square, owned and organized by the somewhat notorious Theresa Cornelys, former opera singer and courtesan. Leopold had apparently nurtured a scheme for a similar series there, or so he told Baron Grimm in Paris.[13] It is uncertain whether he contemplated a series of his own, or some link with Bach and Abel, or possibly an arrangement with Gioacchino Cocchi, an Italian composer who had been involved in running concerts in London and whom the Mozarts had met (or so the entry in the travel notes suggests) on the same day as Mrs Cornelys. But there could be no competing with musicians of the stature of Bach and Abel, whose series, in which the best and most recent music from various parts of Europe was performed, continued for sixteen years up to the time of Bach's death. Leopold had underestimated the difficulty of making money as a musician in a city as large and as active musically as London, where there were many established series and numerous musicians trying to make a living.

The Mozarts' next public appearance was set instead for 15 February, then postponed for three days because it clashed with an oratorio performance to be given by Thomas Arne (their meeting him is recorded in the travel notes), and then for a further three. The final advertisement for the event, which was at the Little Theatre in the Haymarket (immediately opposite the opera house, the King's Theatre), includes a note that 'all the Overtures will be from the Composition of these astonishing Composers, only eight Years old' (the plural was of course a mistake). 'Overtures'—the term is interchangeable at this date, in England, with 'symphonies'—would normally begin and end the programme. Leopold took some 130 guineas, against expenses of 27 guineas, but the concert was less well attended than he had hoped (at the usual half-guinea for admission, the takings imply an attendance of only 260). He told Hagenauer that he had to copy all the music himself for the orchestral parts of Wolfgang's symphonies, because of the high cost in London ('our Estlinger would laugh', he adds, alluding to his regular Salzburg copyist). It would, a Salzburg friend recorded after Leopold's return home, have been cheaper to send all the music to Salzburg for copying and have the parts sent back again than have them copied in London.[14] Although the event on 21 February clashed with a concert in the

Bach-Abel series—as Leopold knew, for he set his concert in the early evening so that it would 'not hinder the Nobility and Gentry from meeting in other Assemblies the same Evening'[15]—he suspected that the poor attendance had another cause:[16]

> But I know the reason that we have not been treated with more generosity (although since we arrived here we have made a few hundred guineas). I have not accepted a proposition that has been made to me. But there is no point in talking about this matter, on which, after careful thought, and many a sleepless night, I have now put behind me, as I shall not bring up my children in so dangerous a place (where most of the people have no religion and where there are nothing but evil examples before one's eyes). You would be astonished at the way children are brought up here. Of other matters to do with religion nothing need be said.

The idea that audiences shunned his concert, in some massive conspiracy or gesture of disapproval, because he had declined to accept a position in England—his remark can mean nothing else—seems absurd, even paranoid. It is hard to avoid feeling that the Mozarts had overstayed their welcome. The family gave one further public concert, rather late in the season, on 13 May 1765, at the popular concert room close by their lodgings, Hickford's Great Room in Brewer Street (where the appearance at Graziani's concert was to have been, a year before). As in their very first concert, the assisting artists were Barthélemon and Cirri, who previously had played a violin solo and a cello concerto; this time it was a violin concerto and a cello solo. The advertisement promised, too, 'all the OVERTURES of this little Boy's own Composition' and 'Concerto on the Harpsichord by the little Composer and his Sister, each single and both together'. Tickets this time were at the modest price of five shillings. Surprisingly, Leopold nowhere mentions the event in his letters. Perhaps the takings were poor; the concert fell at a bad moment, when there were riots and marches by unemployed weavers, with the army keeping order and conflict between King and Government.

The reference to the children's playing 'both together' raises some questions. This performance is usually thought to be of a sonata by Mozart for four hands, a three-movement work in C, K.19d, supposed to have been written in London. Indeed, according to Nissen's biography of Mozart, Leopold wrote in his letter of 9 July to Hagenauer that 'In London Wolfgangerl wrote his first piece for four hands. Until that time no sonata for four hands had ever been composed'.[17] This passage is not however in the only surviving source for that letter, which is a copy rather than the original, and as Nissen occasionally confused his sources or interpolated material from other letters its authority is doubtful. It is not inconceivable that Nissen was reproducing a later annotation of Leopold's own (hence the retrospective-sounding 'In London', which he would hardly have written at the time), but a list of his son's works made by Leopold in 1768 includes no such sonata.[18] In any case there is no reason to think that a two-keyboard or four-hand sonata by Mozart was played at this concert. The advertisement specifies a concerto rather than a sonata and does not claim Mozart as its composer. There is evidence that the Mozarts owned the music of at least one two-keyboard concerto by Wagenseil (they had probably played one at their Spring Garden concert nearly a year before; a letter of Leopold's refers to the cost of hiring two instruments for such a piece). The earliest known

For the Benefit of Mifs MOZART of Thirteen, and Mafter MOZART of Eight Years of Age, Prodigies of Nature. HICKFORD's Great Room in Brewer Street, This Day, May 13, will be A CONCERT of VOCAL and INSTRUMENTAL MUSIC. With all the OVERTURES of this little Boy's own Compofition. The Vocal Part by Sig. Cremonini; Concerto on the Violin Mr. Bartholemon; Solo on the Violoncello, Sig. Cirii; Concerto on the Harpfichord by the little Compofer and his Sifter, each fingle and both together, &c. Tickets at 5 s. each, to be had of Mr. Mozart, at Mr. Williamfon's, in Thrift-ftreet, Soho.

Notice from 'The Public Advertiser', London, 13 May 1765 (*British Library*)

source for K.19*d* is a French edition of 1788, with no claim to authority. In the absence of any authentic source, and several features in the music that point to a later style (among them a finale theme that seems to echo that of Mozart's wind serenade K.361/370*a* of the early 1780s), it must be highly doubtful whether Mozart had anything to do with the work.[19] Mozart's priority as a performer of keyboard duets, at least in the late eighteenth century (there are isolated precedents from early seventeenth-century England), is not however challenged and was acknowledged by a writer in *The European Magazine and London Review* in 1784:[20]

> The first instance of two persons performing on one instrument in this kingdom, was exhibited in the year 1765, by little Mozart and his sister; and the first musick of this nature presented as duettos, was composed by the ingenious Dr. Burney.

In their final months in London the Mozart children also played privately for paying visitors. For several weeks between April and June 1765 Leopold invited callers to their lodgings 'every Day in the Week from Twelve to Two [later One to Three] o'Clock', where those paying five shillings or buying a copy of the sonatas for ten shillings and sixpence could 'have an opportunity of putting [Mozart's] Talents to a more Particular Proof, by giving him any Thing to play at Sight, or any Music without a Bass, which he will write upon the Spot without recurring to his Harpsichord'. For a week in July he took a room at the Swan and Hoop tavern in Cornhill, in the City, from midday to three o'clock, where 'he will give an Opportunity to the Curious to hear these two young Prodigies perform', this time for a mere two shillings and sixpence. These were Leopold's last, desperate effort to extract guineas from the English public, and the place and time were well chosen to attract men working in the world of commerce.[21]

In London, according to a report in a Salzburg paper, the *Europäische Zeitung*, the children used (presumably for their last public concerts) a new harpsichord, built for Frederick the Great of Prussia by the Swiss-born maker Burkat Shudi (or Tschudi), with pedal-controlled stops. The report continues:[22]

> It was truly enchanting to hear the fourteen-year-old sister of the little virtuoso playing the most difficult sonatas on the keyboard with amazing dexterity and her brother at another keyboard improvising an accompaniment.

It is of course possible that this report was placed in the Salzburg publication by Leopold or his friends, perhaps even written by him. Shudi was a near neighbour, in Pulteney Street in Soho, and he and three other leading makers of keyboard instruments, Jacob Kirckman, Johannes Zumpe and Frederic Neubauer, are among the acquaintances listed in Leopold's travel notes. Among the musicians listed are Bach and Abel (at the head, preceded only by the King and Queen), the composers Mattia Vento, Thomas Arne and his son Michael, Samuel Arnold, Thomas Mazzinghi, Antonín Kammel, Domenico Paradies and the pianist John Burton, as well as several others already mentioned (Giordani, Giardini, Cirri, Siprutini, Barthélemon and Graziani), and a number of singers, including the castratos Giovanni Manzuoli and G.F. Tenducci, the sopranos Charlotte Brent, Miss Young (probably Polly, who married Barthélemon) and Regina Mingotti, now retired and lately manager of the opera. This group represents a selection of the more cosmopolitan part of London musical life, understandably biased towards the opera house and concert hall rather than the more traditional spheres of the native composers, the church and the pleasure gardens.

Other people listed by Leopold include John Zoffany (a Zoffany painting of a boy from this time is widely believed to be of Mozart), the ambassadors from France, Denmark, the Austrian Empire, Bavaria and Naples, and many noblemen and women, most of them connected with the court. They include the Duchesses of Ancaster and Hamilton, the Earls of Eglinton, March and Thanet, Lord Fitzmaurice, Lady Effingham, Lady Clive and Lady Harrington. No doubt the Mozarts played at the houses of some of these potential patrons. Lady Effingham was related to the Beckford family, who (the reclusive writer and musician William Beckford later claimed) invited the Mozarts to their house and their country estate at Fonthill, Wiltshire, so that Wolfgang could give him lessons (he was four years Mozart's junior). They met too his cousin, also William Beckford (of Somerly), an acquaintance they renewed in Rome in 1770.[23] At the house in Berkeley Square of Lady Clive, wife of Clive of India, the Mozarts probably took part in a concert with Manzuoli on 13 March 1765.[24] Lady Clive, a keen operagoer, music collector and amateur musician, and a friend and pupil of the blind organist John Stanley, wrote to her husband the previous day:

> Tomorrow I shall have a great deal of Company indeed all the people of quality etc I am on an intimate footing with, or that like me and music, to hear Manz[u]oli sing here, accompanied by Mr Burton on the harpsichord, on which the Mozarts, the boy aged 8 the girl 12 will also play most completely well and this together with two good Fidlers and a Bass will be all the concert I shall have . . .

This may be the occasion on which the Mozarts first met Manzuoli, who was enjoying great success on the opera stage, and was to become a firm friend. The music performed is likely to have included sonatas from Mozart's recently published K.10–15 set, of which Lady Clive's own copy, which includes the rare cello part, survives.[25]

There were also numerous tradespeople, including music publishers and business men with whom Leopold had dealings. Curiously, the name of the music historian Charles Burney is absent from the letters as well as the travel notes, although Burney later recorded having seen Mozart. He commented on Master Mozart's playing 'on my knee, on subjects I gave him',[26] and that he heard Mozart at his lodgings and at Mr Frank's (a member of a prominent Jewish mercantile family whose name is listed by Leopold as 'Frenck', one of several 'Juden' they met). Burney noted Mozart's accomplishments:[27]

> Extempore & sight Playing, Composing a Treble to a given Base & a Base to a Treble, as well as both on a given Subject, as well as finishing a Composition began by another. his fondness for Manz[u]oli—his imitations of the several Styles of Singing of each of the then Opera Singers, as well as of their Songs in an Extemporary opera to nonsense words—to which were [added] an overture of 3 Movem[ts] Recitative—Graziosa, Bravura & Pathetic Airs together with Several accomp[d] Recitatives, all full of Taste [and] imagination, with good Harmony, Melody & Modulation. after w[ch] he played at Marbles, in the true Childish Way of one who knows Nothing.

It was perhaps to be expected that in England, where the spirit of scientific enquiry was so strong, there would be interest in an objective test of Mozart's abilities. In June 1765 the Hon. Daines Barrington, whose father Viscount Barrington was a member of the government and who was himself a scientist, lawyer and music lover, put Mozart through a series of tests, the results of which he presented four years later in a published report to the secretary of the Royal Society, of which he had been elected a Fellow in 1767.[28] It begins:

> If I was to send you a well attested account of a boy who measured seven feet in height, when he was not more than eight years of age, it might be considered as not undeserving the notice of the Royal Society. The instance which I now desire you will communicate to that learned body, of as early an exertion of most extraordinary musical talents, seems perhaps equally to claim their attention.

Barrington's essay of some two thousand words, supported by a verification of his date of birth from the Salzburg register (it is actually wrong by ten days), is couched in terms appropriate to non-musicians, with a number of explanations and analogies to clarify the nature of the tasks he set Mozart and the significance of the boy's responses to them. They included showing him a duet, a setting by 'an gentleman of some favourite words in Metastasio's opera of Demofoonte' (a libretto familiar to operagoers, but the setting would obviously be unknown), with two violin parts and a bass, with the voices notated in the '*Contralto* cliff'. The intention was to 'have an irrefragable proof of his abilities'. Mozart

> began to play the symphony [the opening ritornello] in a most masterly manner . . . in the time and stile which corresponded with the intention of the composer. . . . The symphony ended, he took the upper part, leaving the under one to his father. His voice . . . was thin and infantine, but nothing could exceed the masterly manner in which he sung. . . . His father, who took the under part in this duet, was once or twice out . . . on which occasions the son looked back with some anger pointing out to him his mistakes, and setting him right. He not only however did complete justice to the duet, by singing his own part in the truest taste, and with the greatest precision: he also threw in the accompaniments of the two violins, wherever they were most necessary, and produced the best effects.

Barrington explained the significance of this feat by analogy with the reading of a Shakespeare speech and at the same time conveying the essence of three commentaries, in Greek, Hebrew and Etruscan. The next test was to ask him to extemporize a love song, such as his friend Manzuoli might sing in an opera.

> The boy on this . . . looked back with much archness, and immediately began with five or six lines of a jargon recitative proper to introduce a love song. He then played a symphony

which might correspond with an air composed to the single word, *Affetto*. It had a first and a second part [i.e. it conformed with the standard pattern for an opera aria], which, together with the symphonies, was of the length that opera songs generally last: if this extemporary composition was not amazingly capital, yet it was really above mediocrity, and shewed most extraordinary readiness of invention.

Barrington followed up this with a request for a Song of Rage, which Mozart similarly provided: in the middle, 'he had worked himself up to such a pitch, that he beat his harpsichord like a person possessed', and this time he focussed on the word 'perfido'. Barrington went on to hear a newly composed harpsichord piece, then requiring Mozart to add a bass to a given treble 'which, when tried, had very good effect', and he praised Mozart's command of modulation and his ability to play the harpsichord with the keys covered. Barrington 'could not help suspecting his father imposed with regard to the real age of the boy', in spite of some childish behaviour ('a favourite cat came in, upon which he immediately left his harpsichord, nor could we bring him back for a considerable time. He would also run about the room with a stick between his legs by way of a horse'). So he made enquiries about his age and, on being told the date of his birth, concluded that Leopold 'did not impose'. That is surprising. Most of the announcements do in fact appear to present Wolfgang as one year younger than his actual age. Barrington however writes that a 1764 portrait of him, marked 'agé de sept ans', is correct as he was in his eighth year, and that at his tests, in June 1765, 'the boy was only eight years and five months old'. This, for a scientist knowing that Mozart was born in January 1756, would seem a curious way of reckoning the years in a paper to the Royal Society, but it is at least consistent with Leopold's own reckoning. Leopold does seem to have used 'in his eighth year' in the sense 'when he was eight', rather than in the modern sense. Barrington, writing in 1769, ends his report by noting Mozart's more recent achievements and by comparing him with another child prodigy (John Barratier, an accomplished linguist at nine) and with Handel.

There was another acknowledgment of Mozart by the English learned world in 1765 when, in June or July, the family (or at least Leopold and the children; Maria Anna often seems to have been left at home) visited the British Museum, although children were officially forbidden there.[29] A name, that of the Rev. Thomas Birch, in Leopold's travel notes may give an indication of how his contact with the Museum came about. Leopold also mentions Birch in a letter as a friend who had lost horses and carriages in a fire (one of two he vividly describes: 9 July 1765). Birch, an antiquarian and literary man, was a trustee of the British Museum and in that capacity could have initiated the Museum's request to the Mozarts, which was for copies of the printed sonatas, a portrait and musical manuscripts of Wolfgang's. The Museum had no music collection and had hitherto shown no interest in music. Another contact at the Museum was the Rev. Andrew Planta, an assistant librarian of Swiss and German origins who as a German speaker is likely to have shown the Mozarts over the Museum during their visit, on which Nannerl records their having seen 'antiquities, all sorts of birds, fishes, insects and fruits . . . '; 'the Rev. Mr Planta and his family' too appear in the travel notes. The gift was received on 19 July and entered in the minutes of the Standing Committee, and a formal printed acknowledgment form was sent thanking Leopold for the 'present of the musical performances of your very ingenious son' (those words were written in). The manuscript music was a brief piece for four voices, Mozart's only setting of an English text, *God is our Refuge* K.20. There may have been other items too (the Nissen report refers to 'some original manuscripts', in the plural), but if so they are lost, and in fact *God is our Refuge* was unearthed by Vincent Novello in 1832 only 'after a very long search'. The title, the heading and the date, and probably some of the braces and the words, were written by Leopold, but the notes and the first line of words are in Wolfgang's hand.

During the Mozarts' time in London, the Hagenauers had performed various chores for them—besides arranging for masses to be said—in Salzburg. Leopold had sent home copies of Wolfgang's publications and engravings of the Paris family portrait, for sale there and through other music sellers in southern Germany, and for presentation to the archbishop, and he also asked Hagenauer to circulate news of the Mozarts' doings through the Salzburg newspaper. In turn, Hagenauer (and his son Johann Lorenz Jr., whose apparently voluminous letters to the Mozarts do not survive) kept Leopold informed about what was going on at home, especially in the musical establishment. Leopold was prepared to take a great deal of trouble for his friends and made various purchases for them in London of objects, including cloth and English watches, of a quality or character not available in Salzburg, as well as souvenirs.

So packing for the journey was a long and laborious business ('The very sight of the luggage we have to pack makes me sweat', Leopold had written in April). Leopold instructed that six masses should be said in Salzburg for their safety on the Channel crossing. They set out on 24 July 1765 for Dover, pausing at Canterbury. There they had an invitation to stay at Bourn Place, a nearby country house owned by Sir Horace Mann, British Ambassador in Florence and correspondent of the author and wit Horace Walpole (a son of the former prime minister Sir Robert Walpole) but currently used by his nephew and heir, Horace Mann. Part of the intention was to attend the local race meeting, another part was to give a concert. It was traditional in rural England for concerts, assemblies and other such social events to take place when the leading people in the neighbourhood were gathered together for such occasions as an assize week or a race week. Leopold advertised a concert for eleven o'clock on the morning of 25 July. Whether it actually took place is uncertain: the family cannot have arrived until late the previous evening and it would have been difficult to prepare for it. The event is nowhere recorded, but nor would one expect it to be, and though in his next letter Leopold states that they spent a day in Canterbury before going to Bourn Place, without mentioning any concert, the lack of a reference in a letter of

Leopold's is not, as we have seen, in itself significant.[30] They bade a slightly lingering farewell to England, taking the boat from Dover to Calais on 1 August 1765, at ten in the morning. With a favourable wind and smooth crossing they reached Calais three-and-a-half hours later 'and took our midday meal with a healthy stomach'.

MOZART'S OUTPUT IN London falls into four groups. In the first group are the keyboard pieces, some of them miniatures, some more substantial, in the so-called London Sketchbook, which can be seen as a continuation and an extension of the kinds of piece he contributed to the Nannerl Music Book. Secondly, there are the symphonies he wrote during and perhaps after Leopold's illness in the summer of 1764. Thirdly, there are the six accompanied sonatas dedicated to the Queen, which may well belong to the weeks following the 25 October audience. Lastly, there are some vocal pieces, including *God is our Refuge*, from June or July 1765, and a number of arias, of which only one survives—Mozart could have composed it after hearing a version of Handel's *Ezio* (the source of the text) at the opera house, or could have intended it for a concert or, more fancifully, might have been provoked to write it by the Barrington test in June 1765.

The London Sketchbook was given to Wolfgang by his father when he was eight, the same age at which Nannerl received her notebook. This book however fulfilled a different function, as its title indicates. It was less a collection of pieces for a young player than a jottings book for a young composer. Mozart, now able to write down his pieces himself rather than play them and leave the writing to his father, used it exclusively, and Leopold's writing is nowhere found in it. The book contains 43 pieces, a few of them incomplete. No material from them appears in any other work. They are numbered K.15*a* to 15*z* and 15*aa* to 15*ss* (excluding *j* and *jj*). Most are for keyboard, although several have textures implying that they are sketches of orchestral pieces. It has in fact been suggested that Mozart's first symphony, the one whose genesis is discussed by Nannerl, might be a work now to be found only in keyboard–sketch form in these pages.[31] The invention in these pieces is decidedly uneven, and there is considerable variation in style. The gavotte rhythm and keyboard manner of the second piece, for example, show a marked French influence, while another (K.15*g*) consists of a series of chords for arpeggiation followed by a brief contrapuntal section, akin to a Baroque toccata and in some respects an English organ voluntary. The next piece seems like a little exercise in elementary imitative writing.

As in the Nannerl Music Book, there are several attractive minuets and other dance–like pieces (notably K.15*a*, in passepied rhythm, two gigues and a couple of pieces in undefinable folkdance patterns). Some seem quite clumsy, especially K.15*n*, where the rhythms go awry and the barlines end up in the wrong places. One (K.15*o*) is a charming *perpetuum mobile*. This is followed by a dynamic and extended G minor 3/4 movement, which foreshadows two later movements (the Allegro of the K.379/373*a* piano and violin sonata and the Allegro for piano K.312/590*d*) while also picking up a phrase from a work of Gluck's that Mozart is likely to have come across when he was in Vienna, his *Don Juan* ballet (a dance that recurs in the Paris *Orphée*, for the Furies). This movement, with its distant modulations, imaginatively controlled, is Mozart's most remarkable piece to date. Followed by a B flat slow movement and a G minor quick one, it must surely have been envisaged as the first movement of a keyboard sonata (K.15*p*, *q* and *r*) or indeed, in the light of the implied textures, an orchestral work. A similar three–movement group starts with K.15*t*, again an extended 3/4 movement (98 bars long), and this too could well have been conceived for orchestra. More unambiguously orchestral pieces come later in the book (the music from K.15*cc* onwards is written in ink, the earlier part in pencil). The disposition of chords in K.15*cc*, unsatisfactory on the keyboard, implies a transcription of an orchestral conception, as too does K.15*kk* with its throbbing triplet inner voices, an effect Mozart was to use many times later. The vigour of the writing in the best of these pieces and the command of the processes that lead to satisfactory sonata form or rounded binary form movements is well beyond that shown in the Nannerl Music Book.

Seven symphonies have at one time or another been ascribed to Mozart's London years. One, in E flat, K.18, has long been identified as a work of C.F. Abel's, his op.7 no.6, though the manuscript copy that Mozart made in London for study purposes (symphonies were not usually available in score) was taken, by Köchel and the editors of the original complete edition, as a work of his own. Another is a symphony in B flat, K.17, taken into the canon on thin evidence by the early publisher and Mozart authority Johann André, though already viewed with suspicion by Köchel. There is little doubt that this is a work of Leopold's.[32] A third is a symphony in A minor numbered 16*a* by Einstein, in the third edition of Köchel, on the strength of the incipit alone, which appeared in a manuscript catalogue formerly owned by the publishing house Breitkopf & Härtel.[33] When the symphony came to light in 1982 in Odense, Denmark, it quickly became clear that its style and its procedures were remote from Mozart's and that the attribution was groundless.[34] Lastly, there is another incipit identifying a symphony in C ascribed to Mozart in the Breitkopf catalogue, which Einstein accepted and assigned the number K.19*b*. In the manner of J.C. Bach, it seems plausible, and there is evidence that Mozart wrote a symphony in C in London, but without more music than the opening two-and-a-half bars there is little more that can be said. Of precisely the same status as K.19*b* are a further five symphonies—works attributed to Mozart in the Breitkopf catalogue, where their incipits are quoted, but otherwise unknown (K.19*b* is differently situated only because Einstein thought its opening suggested an early, London work). These are K.Anh.215/66*c* in D, K.Anh.217/66*d* in B flat, K.Anh.218/66*e* in B flat, and two spurious works, K.Anh.223/C11.07 in D and K.Anh.223/C11.08 in F.

That leaves three surviving symphonies that might have been composed by Mozart in London. K.16 in E flat has traditionally been regarded as the first, although there are no trumpets and drums as specified by Nannerl—unless, as is not uncommon, the parts for those instruments were separately written out—and there is little evidence that Mozart gave the horn 'something worthwhile'. The symphony begins with a common-chord fanfare in unison, immediately dropping to *piano* for a contrasting phrase (a feature much used by J.C. Bach and his Italian models), which is simply a series of harmonies with suspensions to maintain the tension. A tutti carries the music to the dominant for the secondary material, most of which is a sturdy tutti. Here, the autograph shows, Mozart originally wanted the violins following each other in close imitation, but Leopold wisely simplified the passage—the effect would have been confused and the line unclear—and had the violins doubling (see the last three bars in the illustration on page 85). The four-bar phrase to which this belongs is repeated at pitch in the exposition; but in the recapitulation, where it is in the home key of E flat and so could appear either a fourth higher or a fifth lower, he has it first in the upper octave, then in the lower. A small point: but the octave displacement (in whichever direction) has a significant effect, one that Mozart later habitually exploited, and it seems that he already had some idea of its potential at the tender age of eight.

If this movement, especially in its chordal passages such as the *piano* response to the opening phrase, seems to evoke the boy at the keyboard exploring harmonic patterns, so too does the Andante, with its repeated triplets in the upper strings and, characteristically (as we saw in the last chapter), a much-repeated motif below. Conceivably, the four-note horn phrase beginning in bar 14 could be a consequence of the reminder from Nannerl; this pattern (in C major, C–D–F–E) is heavy with significance for the later Mozart, most famously in his last symphony but elsewhere as well (see p. 147). The finale, a rondo with its first episode repeated (though not so shown in the NMA score), adopts a typical lively triple rhythm, with short (3/8) bars, evoking the jig or the hunt with its fanfarish phrases.

K.16 is written on paper obtained in London, the same paper as he used for *God is our Refuge*.[35] There can be no doubt that it was composed there. Mozart's autographs for the next two symphonies are lost, and the earliest sources are orchestral parts made by Leopold on papers from France and the Netherlands. These papers were readily available in England, and while there is no strong reason to doubt that the parts we have are those that Leopold was referring to when he complained of the high cost of copying in London, it is not possible to say with certainty that these symphonies belong to the London months. An annotation on the wrapper of K.19—it was first used for a symphony in F (presumably K.19a), then one in C (perhaps the lost K.19b) and ultimately the one in D—may well imply that they were composed in that order.[36] The F major work, K.19a, long known from its incipit, which appears both on the wrapper of the D major and in the Breitkopf catalogue, was rediscovered only in 1981, in the Bayerische Staatsbibliothek, Munich. The music of the first movement is rather sectional, as if made up of modules rather than composed as an evolving whole; one passage uses simple imitative writing in a way particularly favoured by J.C. Bach. But the Andante is a real step forward with the tenderness of its melodic line and its feeling for orchestral resource (for example in the flickering viola figure that so happily animates the texture). The finale is again a 'hunting' rondo, a genre Mozart already handles with some wit in his repeated phrases and his echoes. The D major work, K.19, is the most confident of this group, already hinting at the brilliance and swagger that mark Mozart's later symphonies in the key. J.C. Bach's manner seems very evident at the opening, in the handling of the first movement's form and especially in the graceful and shapely invention of the Andante, but the expressive slip into the minor mode at bar 30 in the first movement is a device foreign to Bach and Abel and characteristic of Leopold Mozart, Eberlin and composers of the Salzburg symphonic tradition, which remains Mozart's fundamental model.[37] The shock A sharp at the beginning of the first movement development however seems a wholly individual gesture, indeed an operatic one. The finale, in the usual rhythm, is a binary movement, its motifs thoroughly worked.

Folio 1^v from the autograph manuscript of Symphony in E flat K.16: note the deletion of the imitative passage between the violins in favour of a unison, with Leopold Mozart's handwritten annotation (*Bärenreiter-Verlag, Kassel*)

The group of sonatas dedicated to Queen Charlotte was presumably completed about the end of 1764. The Queen requested them on 25 October, on 27 November Leopold was contemplating the expense of their engraving, and on 18 January the dedication was completed (implying that the sonatas were now in the engraver's hands). It is of course possible that some were composed earlier. These, again, are keyboard music with accompaniments. The title originally read: *Six Sonates pour le Clavecin qui peuvent se jouer avec l'accompagnement de Violon ou Flaute* [sic] *Traversiere Très humblement dediées A Sa Majesté Charlotte Reine de la Grande Bretagne Composées par I. G. Wolfgang Mozart Agé de huit ans.* Some copies, however, show that the title-page was later adjusted, for the words 'et d'un Violoncelle' are added after 'Traversiere'. The cello accompaniment thus seems to be an afterthought—to please the royal cellist, George III, perhaps, or to increase the sonatas' commercial viability. The option of a flute was certainly offered with that purpose; the violin part often goes too low for a flute and includes multiple stops. Indeed the violin part itself is no more than optional, and almost certainly a *post facto* addition. Occasionally it enlivens the texture, particularly with shreds of imitative writing, but it virtually nowhere adds to the musical sense and sometimes confuses it. The original publication is, in the customary way, in the form of a keyboard and violin score, with no separate violin part (the violinist was expected to look over the keyboard player's shoulder; Leopold provided a manuscript part himself with the royal presentation copy). There is a printed cello part, which simply doubles the principal notes in the keyboard left hand.

The sonatas represent some advance on the Paris ones; Mozart must, in the meantime, have seen the polished op.2 sonatas of J.C. Bach for the same combination. Mozart's sonatas again have long stretches of unrelieved Alberti bass, notably in the first movement of K.10, but the keyboard writing is generally more varied and the ideas are more freely treated. In the Andante of K.10, for example, when the main secondary theme is recapitulated its outline is preserved but not its original pitch scheme or placing in the octave, and it acquires a stronger sense of finality. This sonata and three others are in three movements, the last a pair of minuets. The first minuet of K.13 is oddly based on chromatic scales, and the second of K.14 is headed 'en carillon', with the keyboard in its top register and the violin *pizzicato* (like the traditional funeral bells of the Lutheran cantata). There are several other movements of particular character: in K.11, the opening Andante, a sonata-form miniature with some delicately ornamental keyboard writing, and the second movement, where a minor-mode minuet serves as 'trio' to a sprightly 2/4 Allegro; in K.12, the elaborate Andante, where a lively rhythmic figure in the left hand is echoed by the violin and comes to dominate the right hand too; in K.13, the smooth F minor Andante, in spite of some repetitive and inconsequential invention; in K.14, the first movement with its arresting and ingenious opening and the insistently worked second; and in the final sonata, the extraordinarily pompous first movement, an Andante maestoso—the only movement where the violin part could be thought to contribute to the musical sense. This last movement is the only one with dynamic markings, which, though often carelessly omitted, are placed in such a way that a harpsichordist could change manuals for contrasting passages; they do not imply that the music was imagined for the new fortepiano. A sketch survives of the beginning of another sonata, in C like K.14, which Mozart crossed through and abandoned after eleven bars. He kept the sheet of manuscript paper and used the other side many years later, probably about 1782, for the beginning of a fugue, also abandoned.[38]

Mozart's solitary vocal works in London were some arias and *God is our Refuge*, which has variously been described as a motet, an anthem, an introit, a fugue, a sacred madrigal and a chorus (the NMA groups it among the partsongs).[39] It is a setting for four voices of the first verse of Psalm 47 (Revised Standard Version), beginning in imitative style though not strictly and soon moving into homophony, with one very odd chord (bar 20). It would be over-assessing the piece to seek its models or influences—which could lie in English church music but just as well in Austrian—since it was written for a specific purpose, which did not include performance, and is *sui generis*. 'Va, dal furor portata' K.21/19c is by contrast an attempt to replicate a particular style, that of Italian opera, which it does with the young Mozart's characteristic skill. It may be the sole survivor of several arias: Leopold later said that Wolfgang wrote fifteen in London and The Hague, but only four from this period have come down to us. A setting of 'Quel destrier, che all'albergo è vicino', which Mozart's widow owned in 1799, probably dates from the London months. The words come from Metastasio's *L'olimpiade*, which the Mozarts might have heard at the opera house in Arne's new setting. The text of 'Va, dal furor portata' is also by Pietro Metastasio, the imperial court poet in Vienna, whose librettos had long been regarded as representing a standard of excellence to which others could only aspire, even if by now they were old-fashioned. It comes from his *Ezio*, a pasticcio version of which had more performances while the Mozarts were in London than any other opera, between November 1764 and May 1765. The Mozarts had met the singer, Ercole Ciprandi, who took the role to which the aria belongs, but it is hardly likely that it would have been written for inclusion in an actual performance (Leopold would certainly have mentioned it in a letter if it were). Two scores exist, one showing some small refinements by Leopold in the orchestral writing. It is a shortened *da capo* aria (that is, with the opening ritornello omitted second time) for tenor. Following the standard key scheme, it conveys something of the 'furor' expressed in the words, offers the singer a grateful vocal line with a brief and appropriate opportunity for virtuosity, and has an effectively varied texture in the middle section.

Mozart may be forgiven if at the age of eight or nine he did not yet disclose his full potential as a composer of operatic arias. But the London visit was important for the contact it offered him with a different musical culture and in particular the music of such men as Abel and especially J.C. Bach, whose cosmopolitanism—an Italian fluency and clarity grafted on to a solidly German technique—must have struck a chord in Mozart, whose own music was to move in similar directions. Bach's personal influence may in the past have been exaggerated, but few composers, Leopold Mozart apart, exercised a comparable one on the boy or indeed the man.

5

The Homeward Journey

WHEN THE MOZARTS set out from London, their intention had been to go direct to Paris and then homeward to Salzburg. But shortly before they left, the Dutch envoy in London had tried to persuade them to go to The Hague, to play before Princess Caroline of Nassau-Weilburg, and when on 24 July 1765 he called at their lodgings to renew his appeals and found they had just departed he pursued them to Canterbury. Leopold, who more than a year before had firmly said he would not go to Holland, felt unable to refuse the envoy's entreaties, and by the time they reached Calais he had changed his plans. He was now back in travelling mode. In Calais, where they arrived on 1 August and stayed at the Hôtel d'Angleterre, he made contact with a couple of potential patrons, the Prince of Croy and the Duchess of Montmorency, no doubt in the hope of playing to them, and with the local organist, perhaps with a concert in view, but whether any such hopes were realized we do not know. Having collected the family carriage, the Mozarts set out not for Paris but eastwards along the coast to Dunkirk. Here too Leopold met the organist and other local worthies, including the local Commandant, M de Mezières, who pressed him to go through Lille. After a night or two in Dunkirk, at the Hôtel à St Catharine, and sufficient sightseeing to note the damage done in recent wars between England and France and the demolition of the fortifications, as well as the fine square and large houses, they continued through Bergues and arrived at Lille about 5 August.[1]

They remained a month in Lille, at the Hôtel de Bourbon in the Grande Place, but not from choice. First, Mozart was taken ill, with a 'strong catarrh', probably a heavy cold or tonsillitis, and then Leopold succumbed, with sickness and dizziness. They apparently gave no concert there but made contact with several musicians, and they may have played to some of the leading local people. Leopold was still not fully recovered when, about 4 September, they moved on to Ghent, where Mozart played the organ at the Bernardines chapel[2] and they lodged at the Hôtel St Sébastien. They went to view the town from the municipal tower, where they saw the famous 52-bell carillon. Next on to Antwerp, where as it was Sunday they took an extra day, staying at the Hôtel à la Poste in a square by the cathedral. Wolfgang played the cathedral organ and met the organist, Van Bosch. Leopold thought the Rubens *Descent from the Cross* 'surpassed anything one could imagine', also admiring other paintings and, again, the black and white marble. Nannerl noted the several churches they went to see, as well as the Town Hall, and the views of the city from the towers. They left their carriage in Antwerp and travelled on 9 September to Rotterdam by post-coach, pausing overnight and going on by water to The Hague, where after a few days at La Ville de Paris, 'une tres mauvaise auberge' ('a very bad inn'), Leopold noted, they found lodgings at the house of a watchmaker, by name Eskes. Leopold now had no regrets at having undertaken the Dutch part of the trip: 'I should have been sorry not to have seen Holland . . . the Dutch villages and towns are quite unlike any others in Europe . . . I must mention that I greatly appreciate their cleanliness (which to many of us seems overdone)'.[3]

During their first eight days in The Hague, Mozart and his father appeared at court twice before Princess Caroline, and on 18 September and during the following week before her brother, the Prince of

Orange. Leopold provides no details about their performances or their rewards (except to say that the journey was in effect paid for), but mentions that further visits were planned when Nannerl had recovered from the cold that so far had prevented her from appearing. A public concert advertised for the Oude Doelen hall for 30 September, where all the symphonies in the programme were to be by Mozart, may have been postponed, but on 1 October Mozart played at the residence of the British ambassador.[4]

The Mozarts had contemplated a brief stay, so that they could reach Paris early in November. If winter conditions made travel difficult, it was important for them to be in a large city and a centre for patronage. In the event they did not finally leave The Hague for six months. Again, illness intervened. Nannerl's cold developed into a fever, almost certainly typhoid.[5] Over the next month Leopold despaired. He and Maria Anna prepared her 'to resign herself to the will of God' and talked to her of the world's vanity and the happiness of the death of children, and on 21 October she received the last sacrament. That day, the royal physician Professor Thomas Schwenke, sent by the princess, visited her, overturned the diagnosis of the previous doctor (who had been recommended by various ambassadors) and changed the treatment (as before, Leopold gives full details in his letters of all the medication). In little more than two weeks she was recovering.

But then Wolfgang fell victim to the same infection. 'In four weeks', Leopold wrote on 12 December, 'it made him so wretched that he has become absolutely unrecognizable, nothing but tender skin and little bones; for five days he had to be carried from his bed to a chair'. By this date however Wolfgang was already able to walk a little, and Leopold had been heartened by Nannerl's quick recovery. Hagenauer was asked to arrange for masses to be said in thanks at various Salzburg churches.

The letters of these final months are fewer. Leopold's briefer account of this last part of their journey, as they turned towards home, betrays a degree of weariness—they would soon, anyway, be able to relate their adventures and impressions by word of mouth. But those he sent show his mind turning anxiously back towards Salzburg. He kept Hagenauer informed over his baggage plans. A chest had been sent by sea from London through Hamburg, another went from the Netherlands, and more would follow from Paris, and his two big coffers, his clothes-bag and even the compartments under the seats of the carriage were already full. He asked Hagenauer to have a new cupboard or desk made (he preferred the English style, with smooth surfaces, as easier to keep clean) and told him where to put it, and enquired whether Hagenauer might build new rooms on to the house as the accommodation was becoming inadequate: Nannerl will need somewhere to sleep and Wolfgang must have a room of his own for all the studying he will need to do. He enquired too about the state of his harpsichord and the number of broken strings—should Egedacher, the local instrument maker, be called in to work on it?—and about the new Salzburg city gate (an entry to the city through the Mönchsberg mountain was under construction).

On 22 January 1766 the Mozarts, all now restored to health, gave a concert at the Oude Doelen hall. The advertisement took almost exactly the same form as the one in September (three months are added to Mozart's age, but a year is still subtracted). The performance was their first or their second public event in The Hague. The family probably left their lodgings about the time of Wolfgang's tenth birthday, for by 29 January they were in Amsterdam, staying at De gouden Leeuw and giving a concert at the Salle du Manège (Riding School), at which 'all the overtures will be the work of the little composer'. At a second concert in the same hall, on 26 February, the children, it was advertised, would play 'not only concertos together on the different harpsichords but also on the same one with four hands, and finally the boy will play on the organ his own caprices, fugues and other pieces of the most profound music'. The 'caprices' are a group of pieces (K.15a–15ss) in the London Sketchbook—Constanze Mozart referred to them a number of times by that name in her correspondence with music publishers after Mozart's death.[6] In Amsterdam

Leopold was much troubled by meeting an old Salzburg acquaintance (whom he does not name) who had embraced Calvinism, and he spent much time and energy trying to draw him back into the Catholic fold, as he related at length to Hagenauer.

Early in March the Mozarts returned to The Hague, where on 11 March they took part in a festive event on Prince William of Orange's reaching the age of 18, which meant that he was able to take up the office of Stadholder. The occasion gave rise to at least nine works of Wolfgang's. According to Leopold his first set of keyboard variations, on a Dutch song in celebration of the event by the court Kapellmeister, Christian Ernst Graaf (or Graf), 'Laat ons juichen, Batavieren!' ('Let us rejoice, Batavians!'), was written for the prince's installation; Wolfgang also 'dashed off hurriedly' another set, on a song, 'Willem van Nassau', that 'everyone all over Holland is singing, playing and whistling'. These, K.24 and 25, were quickly published, in Amsterdam and The Hague respectively. He was also asked to write a set of six more accompanied sonatas, here again the preferred genre, for Princess Caroline (K.26–31), and composed 'arias for the princess'. Three arias from this period survive, settings of words from Metastasio's *Artaserse* (of which the Mozarts had probably seen Arne's English setting in London). Leopold further refers to Wolfgang's composing 'something for the prince's concert'. As Nannerl's later recollections confirm, the work was the *Gallimathias musicum*, which Leopold entered in the catalogue he later prepared of Wolfgang's works as 'Composed for the Prince of Orange'; it ends with a fugue on 'Willem van Nassau'. Mozart had also written two symphonies, and conceivably as many as four: K.22 and K.45a (the so-called 'Old Lambach', formerly K.Anh.221) and the two discussed in the previous chapter (K.19 and 19a). Leopold could take pleasure in an accomplishment of his own, when a beautiful, newly printed Dutch edition of his *Violinschule* was presented to the prince, in his presence, in the course of the festivities.

Leopold was given a copy of the new publication a few days later, when the Mozarts, finally leaving The Hague at the end of March on

their way back to Amsterdam, paused in Haarlem. There the publisher, Joannes Entschedé, brought it to him at their inn, Het gulden
Vlies, and he also brought with him the organist of St Bavo's Church,
who invited Wolfgang to play on the organ there, one of the largest
in the country, with 68 stops. In Amsterdam, although it was a season
when concerts were forbidden, they secured permission on the
grounds that a concert by Wolfgang was a demonstration of God's
bounty. It was again at the Riding School, on 16 April, and consisted
only of his instrumental music, with the children playing together
both on one harpsichord and on two. While they were in Amsterdam,
the new sonatas were published. Two days later they left for Utrecht,
where they lodged in the Plaets-Royal and gave a concert at the
Vreeburg on 21 April with the local Collegium Musicum. That was
their final appearance in the Netherlands.

Leopold's annotations in his travel diaries include the usual selection of names, local nobles, several ambassadors, doctors and other
professional people, music dealers (notably the Hummel brothers in
The Hague and Amsterdam, who published Wolfgang's music),
bankers and other business men, and various musicians. Few of the
musicians are well known. Among them in The Hague are the cellist-
composer J.G.C. Schetky from Darmstadt (later a leading figure in
Edinburgh), the admired oboist J.C. Fischer (his name will recur) and
Jean-Joseph Boutmy (a keyboard composer), but none in Amsterdam
is of wider repute, and the unfortunate musicians named in Utrecht
are collectively immortalized by Leopold with the epithet 'Capital
Esel' ('prize asses'). No report survives of the Utrecht concert, and it
may not have been wholly successful.

The Mozarts' route took them to Rotterdam and back into the
Austrian Netherlands, present-day Belgium. Their first stop, for three
days, was at Antwerp, where they gave a concert at the Bourse, with
all the symphonies by Wolfgang.[7] They must also have resumed possession of their carriage. They passed through Mechelen, calling on
the archbishop, Count von Frankenberg, whom they had met before,
and thence to Brussels, where they spent a night (8 May). At Valenci-

ennes they saw the automatic clock at the Town Hall and visited Marie-Thérèse Geoffrin, a leading salon figure in Paris who later wrote a letter of introduction for them. The only other port of call on the journey to Paris, apparently, was Cambrai, where they visited the tomb of François de la Motte Fénelon, whose *Télémaque* (1699) and other writings Leopold much admired. They arrived in Paris on the evening of 10 May, going to lodgings in the house of one Brie, a proprietor of baths, in the rue Traversière (now rue Molière, close to the Comédie Française), which Grimm had arranged.

They remained in Paris for just two months, with a few days at the end of May at Versailles (in their old lodgings, chez Cormier). Little is known of what they did in Paris. Mozart composed one piece, at least, the Kyrie K.33, his first known setting of words from the Mass. The painting by Michel-Barthélemy Ollivier of a party in the Prince of Conti's drawing-room, with Wolfgang visible (though small) at the harpsichord, accompanying the singer Jélyotte, is believed to date from this time. Mozart was evidently heard by Grimm, who reported on the family's recent travels and on the children's progress:[8]

> Mlle Mozart, now thirteen [actually nearly fifteen], and moreover much prettier, has the finest and most brilliant execution on the harpsichord. No-one but her brother can rob her of her supremacy. This marvellous child is now nine [actually ten] years old. He has hardly grown; but he has made prodigious progress in music. . . . He has composed symphonies for full orchestra, which have been played and universally applauded here. He has also written several Italian arias and I do not doubt that, by the time he is twelve, he will have had an opera given at some theatre in Italy. Having heard Manzuoli in London during a whole winter, he has profited so well that, although his voice is excessively weak, he can sing with as much taste as expression. But what is beyond comprehension is his profound grasp of harmony and its most recondite progressions that he possesses to a supreme

degree, and which caused the hereditary Prince of Brunswick
. . . to say that many Kapellmeisters who have attained the
peak of their art will die without knowing what this boy
knows at the age of nine. We have seen him withstand, for an
hour and a half on end, the assaults of musicians who have
sweated blood and undergone agonies to keep up with a
child who leaves the battle without a sign of being tired. I
have seen him at the organ, disconcerting and silencing
organists who considered themselves highly skilled. In London, Bach took him between his knees and they improvised
alternately on the same harpsichord for two hours on end in
the presence of the King and the Queen. Here he underwent
the same test with M Raupach, an able musician who spent
a long time in St Petersburg, and who improvises in a very
superior way. One could go on talking about this singular
phenomenon. What is more, he is one of the most loveable
creatures one could meet, putting wit and spirit into everything he says and does with all the charm and sweetness of a
child of his age. Further, his gaiety reassures one against the
fear that so early ripening a fruit might fall before it comes to
maturity. If these children live, they will not remain at
Salzburg. Monarchs will soon be disputing as to who should
have them . . .

It may be deduced from these words that there was in fact some performance of Mozart's music—certainly his symphonies—during
these weeks in Paris, and that he underwent tests, with Hermann
Friedrich Raupach and other musicians. Possibly something of the
kind had been arranged by Grimm in advance. The visit of the Prince
of Brunswick, himself a violinist, is recorded in one of Leopold's letters. No doubt there were other occasions comparable with the
Conti party at which Mozart performed. Leopold would not have
chosen to return through Paris, an expensive city to live in, had not
there been good financial reasons for doing so. Among the Parisian

contacts Leopold noted on this visit were a number of musicians: Cannabich, from Mannheim, Leontzi Honauer (whom he had met before), Ignaz von Beecke (a noted keyboard player) and François-André Danican Philidor, a leading composer of *opéra comique*, with his brother-in-law the tenor L.-A. Richer. Before they left Paris, Leopold had much to arrange, in packing and forwarding luggage, dealing with business matters, and having new clothes made for all the family.

On the evening of 9 July, at about eight o'clock, the homeward journey began, with six post-horses (and presumably the family carriage). It was to take nearly six months. The first stop was Dijon, where they had been invited by the Prince of Condé on the Burgundian assembly's triennial meeting; they probably arrived about 12 July.[9] They were in the city about two weeks, and among those they met was Charles de Brosses, the writer and man of learning who was president of the court of the Dijon parliament. Their concert was on 18 July in the assembly room at the Town Hall. The advertisement took the now usual form, promising concertos on two harpsichords and duets on one, with the symphonies by Wolfgang, who was also prepared to sightread any music submitted to him. There was however one novelty in that Wolfgang would 'sing an air of his own composition'. A minute of the event tells how the prince refused to sit on a special throne set up for him in solitary splendour, had it removed, and instead sat with the ladies. Regrettably, it says nothing about the concert itself, but that may not have been an outstanding event. Leopold, in the last of his travel notes, wrote the names of some of the musicians, with comments: against the name of the leader, 'très mediocre', the second violinist 'un miserable italien detestable', against the next three 'asini tutti' ('all asses'), and the viola 'un racleur' ('a scratcher'), while the two cellos are 'miserable', the two oboes 'rotten'.

The Mozarts arrived in Lyons about 26 July and took part in a concert on 13 August, given in a regular Wednesday evening series in a hall in the Place des Cordeliers. The main items were dramatic works by Bernard de Bury and Rameau. Mozart and his sister played

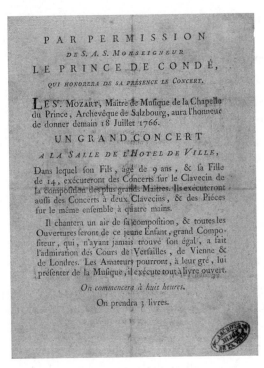

Concert notice, Dijon, 18 July 1766 (*Archives Municipales, Dijon*)

harpsichord pieces ('les plus difficiles') and 'all the symphonies played were of the composition of this little virtuoso . . . he preluded for an hour and a quarter with the most capable master here, yielding to him in nothing'.[10] While they were there they went to see a public hanging.[11] At Lyons Leopold had to decide whether to indulge the hope he had nurtured of going on to Italy at this stage, to be at Venice for the Ascension festival. He had also been urged to go to Bordeaux and Marseilles. But he had promised to return home, no doubt pressed by Hagenauer and worrying about his reception after so long an absence, and turned his route towards Switzerland, though not without some show of feeling hard done by:[12]

> Do you not think it a very heroic and magnanimous decision
> to abandon a trip to Turin, which lies almost in front of our
> noses? don't you think that our proximity, our situation, the

general encouragement we have received, our own interest and love of travel should have induced us to follow our noses and go to Italy, returning home, after seeing the Ascension festival in Venice, through the Tyrol? is this not the right time, when the youth of the children arouses everyone to wonderment? Well, my decision is already made; I have said I shall go home and I shall keep my word.

The next call, then, was Geneva, where they arrived about 20 August.[13] As Leopold had given Hagenauer a correspondence address in Geneva 'chez Mr Huber', it seems that he may have stayed with the artist and writer Jean Huber, at his house near the cathedral, if they were not (as is usually supposed) at the Hôtel Balance. He commented on Voltaire's presence at Ferney, his château nearby, but in the light of Leopold's beliefs it is perhaps unlikely that he made any effort to see him, although it seems that both Mme d'Épinay, Grimm's mistress, and the encyclopedist Étienne-Noël Damilaville, had written to introduce them. Voltaire was in fact ill at the time, as he told Mme d'Épinay ('Your little Mazar, madam, chose, I fear, an unfavourable time to bring harmony into the temple of Discord . . . I was very ill when this phenomenon shone on the black horizons of Geneva').[14] The Mozarts gave two concerts at the Town Hall, as a draft letter from the French Resident in the city, Pierre-Michel Hennin, in response to one of recommendation from Grimm makes clear:[15] 'were it not the season', he continues, 'when the number of inhabitants in Geneva is much diminished, they would have had to have been as pleased with this town as with those capitals where they were best received'. Mozart was also heard by Gabriel Cramer, Voltaire's publisher ('he plays the harpsichord as it has never been played . . . he composes instantly on every possible theme'),[16] and, presumably in a private house, by the composer André-Ernest-Modeste Grétry:[17]

I once met in Geneva a child who could play anything at sight. His father said to me in front of the assembled company: 'So that there can be no doubt about my son's talent, write for him, for tomorrow, a very difficult sonata movement'. I wrote for him an Allegro in E flat, difficult but without pretension; he played it, and everyone, except myself, thought it was a miracle. The child had never broken off; but following the modulations, he had substituted a number of passages for those I had written.

Grétry does not mention Mozart's name, but there can be no doubt whom he meant. While the tale, told only after Mozart's death, may seem to be tinted by professional envy, it should be recognized that Mozart might well sometimes have improvised when confronted by passages he could not manage. No-one else called upon to test him, however, seems to have commented in this sense.

'If one wants to visit Berne one must also pass through Lausanne', wrote Leopold.[18] When they arrived in Lausanne, probably on 13 or 14 September, intending to stay for half a day, the Mozarts were met by servants of Prince Ludwig of Württemberg and other 'distinguished personages' in the city and prevailed upon to spend five days there. Some flute pieces Mozart wrote for Prince Ludwig are now lost. Contemporary diaries and accounts show that the Mozarts gave a concert at the Town Hall on 15 September, attended by 70 people at 40 sous per head, and a second three days later.[19] They spent eight days in Berne but there is no record of a concert. Leopold however mentions that they 'had opportunities of getting to know men of learning' there (the only known contact is a musician and music dealer, Johann Andreas Seul) and in Zürich, where they arrived in the last days of September and stayed for two weeks. The principal men of learning they met in Zürich were the poet Salomon Gessner, who presented them with an inscribed copy of a new collection of his works, and his brother the scientist Johannes. Nothing is known of the success of the concerts they gave at the City Hall with the local Collegium Musicum on 7 and 9 October, or of anything else they did in the city, though the autograph manuscript of a little keyboard piece, K.33B (now in the Zürich Zentralbibliothek), presumably preserves Wolfgang's new contribution to the concerts. About 12 October they left Zürich, passing through Winterthur, for the medieval city of Schaffhausen, where they spent four days: a pleasant stay, Leopold reports, without mentioning any performance there, although a notice about their passing through had lately appeared in the local newspaper,[20] suggesting that Leopold had been hoping to draw public attention to their arrival.

The Mozarts then crossed into Germany, reaching Donaueschingen about 20 October, to be welcomed by the Salzburg singer, their friend Joseph Meissner, who helped them and their luggage out of the carriage and no doubt gave Leopold the latest news of events in the Salzburg musical establishment. Their former servant, Sebastian Winter, was there too. They already knew the Prince of Fürstenberg, a noted music-lover, who invited them to court through his director of music, Franz Anton Martelli. They were in Donaueschingen for twelve days, during which they spent nine evenings, from five until nine o'clock, making music for the prince. 'Each evening', Leopold wrote, 'we played something different', including some cello pieces newly written by Wolfgang for the prince (K.33b, now lost) and probably the *Gallimathias musicum*, as the copies of the performing parts in the princely archives imply. Departure was accompanied by liberal tears, on both sides, and gifts from the prince of 24 louis d'or and diamond rings for the children. After that the Mozarts travelled 'head over heels' through Messkirch, Ulm and Günzburg, to reach Dillingen on 4 November. There they spent two days and played at the court of the Landgrave of Hesse (who was also Prince-Bishop of Augsburg), picking up two more rings. There were brief stops at Biberach, where Wolfgang competed on the organ with another gifted child, Siegmund Bachmann, two years Mozart's senior, each acquitting himself with honour,[21] and after a day in Augsburg— where they again stayed at the Drei Mohren and presumably Leopold visited his brothers and his elderly mother (she died little more than a month later, on 11 December)—the Mozarts reached Munich on 8 November, again lodging at Zum goldenen Hirschen.

It was to have been a brief visit to Munich. On their first day in the city Mozart played before the Elector, composing a piece on a melody that the Elector himself hummed to him. That night, however, he was taken ill, with leg pains and a fever, rheumatic fever seems the likeliest. A journey to Regensburg, in response to the requests of various noblemen, had to be called off, with the winter weather closing in, and Wolfgang was barely recovered when on 22 November he and Nannerl were required to play again at the Munich court. Leopold wrote three letters from Munich. It is clear that he was growing increasingly anxious about what awaited him in Salzburg, and about the family's cramped living accommodation; the servant they were bringing back with them would have to live out (and might get into bad company). But he hoped they could look forward to a warm reception. It was probably on 27 November that at last they set out for home. They arrived in Salzburg on 29 November, just ten days short of three-and-a-half years since they had left home. Mozart had been a little less than seven-and-a-half when they left; he would be eleven in two months' time.

UNDERSTANDABLY, HEAVY TRAVELLING was not conducive to composition. Since leaving the Netherlands, Mozart had written only the Paris *Kyrie* and a few trifles for various occasions en route, of which the sole survivor is the little keyboard piece from Zürich. The works from The Hague or Amsterdam consist of the three items written at the time of the Orange festivities (two sets of variations and the *Gallimathias*), six accompanied sonatas, probably two symphonies and a group of arias.

The keyboard variations follow a simple pattern, basically the standard type of variation pattern that Mozart was to use throughout his life. In the 'Laat ons juichen' variations, the right hand simply moves a little faster at each variation, as the note values halve and triplets and dotted rhythms are introduced; then there is an Adagio variation, and finally the theme is repeated with a busy left-hand accompaniment. It is precisely the kind of piece that Mozart might have improvised, with a clear formula for each section. The 'Willem van Nassau' set is equally formulaic, though the Adagio here is not the last but is followed by a brilliant-sounding figurative variation, with the same kind of final one as before.

The *Gallimathias musicum*—the title means the same as 'quodlibet', a piece using well-known melodies—is to some degree a joint composition of Mozart and his father. Manuscripts survive showing Mozart's hand and his father's reworkings and other changes, but the copy made in Donaueschingen under their joint supervision is the only definitive text. There are seventeen movements, all but the last very brief. Few of the sources can readily be identified: they will have meant more to audiences in The Hague, or Salzburg, than they do today. Among the movements is a Pastorella (no. 4), with a musette-like drone, possibly drawing on a Swabian folksong (the first version had another Pastorella that quoted a Christmas carol, 'Joseph, lieber Joseph mein', as heard on a carillon in Salzburg). One brief piece (no. 8) has a text underlaid, presumably a popular song. Several movements give prominence to the wind instruments, especially the horns, and in one rather odd Andante a single phrase passes from one instrument to another. Nos. 10 and 15, one an inversion (roughly) of the other, come from organ versets by Eberlin. One (no. 11) takes its opening bars from a symphony by Leopold. No. 13 is for keyboard, and no. 14 a minuet orchestrated from no. 19 in Nannerl's Music Book. The piece ends with a fugue on 'Willem van Nassau', worked at excessive length, with a good deal of contrapuntal artifice, and here Leopold made many cuts in his son's original working.[22]

The Symphony in B flat K.22 was composed, according to a note on the manuscript, in December 1765, and almost certainly intended for performance at the January concert in The Hague. It is formally a good deal more sophisticated than the symphonies discussed in the previous chapter. Its opening theme, with its *forte–piano* contrasts, is quickly adapted to lead into a climax, with a 'Mannheim crescendo' (the type of protracted crescendo, a device relatively new in orchestral music, habitually used by Mannheim composers). This theme follows directly at the end of the exposition, that is, the beginning of the next section, in the new key, the dominant. After some purposeful development, the recapitulation follows, on the rounded binary form model, but at the end the music continues as it did after the exposition, leading in fact to a reappearance of the opening theme in the home key. The formal usages are not quite as easily defined as textbooks are apt to imply, since this is in effect a 'reversed recapitulation', although it is reached only by the music's continuing as before. There is also a resemblance, historically not coincidental, with the ritornello form of the late Baroque concerto. Whatever way this usage is defined, its rhetorical force is considerable, as Mozart evidently understood even before his tenth birthday. The slow movement, with its naive punctuation points, is less advanced, although the expressive imitation between the violins and the constantly interesting string textures show imagination and technique in happy conjunction. The rondo finale is another cheerful romp in 3/8, sharing a cliché opening theme with a J.C. Bach movement (in a piano concerto, op.1 no.6, which Mozart must have known)—a cliché that later found a place in the Act 2 finale of *Le nozze di Figaro*.

The other symphony written during the Dutch months was K.45*a* in G, long known as the 'Lambach' Symphony because its only known source was a manuscript at the Austrian monastery of that name. It was presented to the monastery in 1769, along with a symphony of Leopold's in the same key. It was for a time suspected that the symphonies had become confused and that the attributions were reversed: K.45*a* came to be known as the 'Old Lambach' and the other work as the 'New'. In 1982, however, a set of parts of K.45*a* came to light, not only confirming the original attribution but also making clear, through Leopold's title-page annotation and the actual paper on which it was written, that the work was composed in The

Hague in 1766.[23] It is a sturdy piece, less adventurous than K.22 in the form of its first movement but using the motifs that make up its principal theme and much else in the movement in a way wholly typical of Mozart at this stage. The Andante, however, shows something quite new in its exquisite melodic line for muted first violins, with a soft accompaniment of pizzicato basses, gentle 'Alberti'-type writing for the inner strings and sustained horns. The finale, the last in this group in 3/8 metre, has a happily light touch in texture and content alike. The work, incidentally, underwent a certain amount of revision in its detail, especially the indications of articulation, between its composition in 1766 and its presentation to Lambach three years later.

The accompanied sonatas K.26–31 mark a considerable advance in technique and ideas since the Paris and London sets, though the violin part clearly remains an afterthought and optional. Mozart puts a distinct best foot forward in the first of the set, as composers often did, with the only three-movement work, leading off with an energetic triple-metre Allegro molto (two of his three later sonatas in this key, E flat, for these instruments also begin with 3/4 movements; patterns are set young). The slow movement in C minor, Adagio poco andante, has an expressive line of some originality. The first movement of K.28 in C, with its persistent Alberti bass, is more in the old manner, with more brilliance than content. In the tradition of the *galant* two-movement sonata, some begin with slow movements: K.27 in G and 30 in F, each with constant left-hand triplets, are of this type, the one with an expressively detailed line, the other with effective and (even in an Adagio) acrobatic hand-crossing for a dialogue between a fragmented melodic line and a bass. The remaining two, K.29 in D and 31 in B flat, have more conventional first movements. All follow the rounded binary pattern. The finales are mostly rondos or minuets, some with *minore* episodes. That of K.30 is a rondo-minuet, with a brief and telling appearance of its principal theme in a chromatic version in F minor, Poco Adagio, while that of the final sonata is a minuet with a set of variations along the usual formulaic lines. Significantly, these were Mozart's last accompanied sonatas until the time of his next journey northwards and westwards from Salzburg, in 1777. The genre was not favoured at home.

Of the vocal music, the Paris *Kyrie* K.33 is a piece of only 42 bars, for four voices and strings, mainly homophonic but with a little imitation in paired voices. According to Leopold's 1768 list of his son's works, a short *Stabat mater* setting for four voices, without instruments (which may mean only continuo organ), dates from these months, and a setting is referred to by Nannerl in a later letter,[24] but no such work is known. Not on Leopold's list at all is the offertory *Scande coeli limina* K.34, which is said to have been written at the Benedictine monastery of Seeon when the Mozarts were travelling through on their way home from Paris. The family did not in fact pass through Seeon, as they took a more northerly route. The local legend—that Wolfgang, learning during dinner from the prelate that the monastery had no offertory for the coming St Benedict's day, slipped out of the room and instantly provided one—must be in doubt. A shade less improbably, the work could have been written, or delivered, on an excursion to Seeon after the family's return but before St Benedict's day, 21 March. Or it may not belong to that period at all; or it may not be by Mozart. It consists of a soprano aria, graceful and of greater harmonic subtlety than most of Mozart's music of this date, and a chorus of little distinction.

The three arias dating from this time are all settings from Metastasio's popular *Artaserse*, a readily available text, which, as we have seen, Mozart probably encountered in London. 'Conservati fedele' K.23, composed October 1765, is a simple Andante grazioso setting of the opening number in the opera, as Mandane bids her lover farewell. It consists almost wholly of two-bar phrases: Mozart seems unconcerned with avoiding the rather rigid rhythmic structure that comes of such direct setting of the words. Two versions survive, one in Mozart's autograph and in a copy by Leopold, the other in a further autograph, now lost and known only from a transcription, but thought to represent a reworking, probably from January 1766. Yet the supposed earlier version (in the main NMA text) carries the more refined dynamic and articulation marks that one might expect in a revision, and the more poetic and imaginative treatment of the cadential climaxes in this version, with a brief orchestral intervention and a sharper vocal flourish, argue the opposite way. It also seems likelier that Leopold would have copied a final version than a superseded one.

That aria is in *da capo* form, with a brief middle section, while for the two others Mozart set only the first section. These were long believed to date from his Italian journey, as their Köchel numbers (including the revised ones) reflect. But handwriting and paper studies have established the earlier date;[25] in any case, a false start for one of them, separately entered in K[6] as K.73D, is found on the autograph of the *Gallimathias musicum*. 'Per pietà, bell'idol mio' K.78/73*b* is Mozart's first (known) aria of the *aria d'affetto* type, expressive pieces in slow or moderate tempo and often in E flat major. This one has an eloquent, spacious opening, but Mozart was not yet skilled at sustaining such a mood through coloratura writing, and the ensuing passages cannot quite escape triteness. 'Per quel paterno amplesso' K.79/73*d* is preceded by Mozart's first (known) orchestral recitative, music that shows him to have taken in the traditional musical gestures of the genre. The aria itself is again somewhat constricted in rhythm, with Mozart's direct setting leading to four-square patterns and a good deal of solid motion, and the coloratura writing is of modest interest. Perhaps, if designed for the princess in The Hague, it suited the purpose very adequately.

6

The Eleven-Year-Old in Salzburg

THE LUXURIANT ARRAY of sources of information for Mozart's life when he was touring—the newspaper reports and advertisements, the opinions of those who heard him, above all the streams of words from Leopold's pen (and later his own)—dries up almost entirely when he is at home in Salzburg. It is in the nature of a normal domestic existence, or even the less normal one that a genius might expect to live, that it leaves few traces. Nor even is there ready scope for inference, for the everyday concerns of childhood and family life at home are not the stuff on which correspondents wax poetic or indeed have the opportunity to do so. Accordingly, the sources for Mozart's activities between his return to Salzburg, on 29 November 1766, and the beginning of his next journey just over nine months later, are few and slender: except, that is, for the actual music that he produced.

Nannerl, in her later memoir of her brother, published in the *Allgemeine musikalische Zeitung*, touches on other areas of his childhood personality:[1]

> Even in his childhood years, when in ordinary men it is still dormant, Mozart's over-rich imagination was so alive and so

vivid, and perfected whatever it took hold of, to such a degree that one cannot visualize anything more singular, and in some ways more moving, than its multitude of creations— which, because the little man knew so little of the real world, were as distant from it as the heavens. Here is just one example: as the journeys we used to make (he and I, his sister), took him to different lands, so, as we travelled from one town to another, he would think out a kingdom for himself, and he called this the Kingdom of Back [*Königreich Rücken*]—I can no longer remember why it had that name. This kingdom and its inhabitants were given everything that would make them good and happy children. He was the king of this land, and this idea so gripped him, and he pursued it so far, that our servant, who could draw a little, had to make a map of it, and he would dictate to him the names of the cities, the market towns and the villages.

He had so tender a love for his parents, especially his father, that he composed a melody that he would sing, daily, at bedtime, for which his father had to put him up on a chair. Father always had to sing the second part, and after this ceremony, which could never be omitted, he kissed his father with the greatest tenderness and then went to bed, peaceful and contented. This piece of fun continued until his tenth year.

The Salzburg diarist Beda Hübner, librarian of St Peter's Abbey, reported in some detail on the return of the 'world-famous' vice-Kapellmeister Leopold Mozart and his family, 'to the solace and joy of the whole city'.[2] Parts of his entries reflect the local, and in some respects the wider, reaction to the phenomenon of the children. His first, immediately on their return, is primarily an account of where they went and how they were received, but it also adds some detail to the picture as otherwise shown.

The two children, the boy as well as the girl, both play the instrument, or the keyboard, the girl more artfully, and more fluently, than her little brother, but the boy with much greater refinement and with more imaginative ideas, and with the most beautiful harmonic inspirations . . . the boy Wolfgangl has not grown very much during this journey, but Nannerl has become quite tall and is already almost marriageable. There are strong rumours that the Mozart family will not be staying here long but are to visit the whole of Scandinavia and the whole of Russia, and perhaps even travel to China, which would be a very great journey and a formidable undertaking . . . The journey they have made is said to have cost them about 20,000 gulden, which I can well believe; but how much money will they have taken?

A few days later, Hübner 'unexpectedly found himself' at the Mozart family's and reported further and at length on Wolfgang's accomplishment, in the terms now becoming familiar—'there is none in the whole continent of Europe that is his equal . . . in art, rapidity, exquisite ideas and wondrous manipulations', he can play anything, 'even more excellently and artfully than it is written down, through the use of his own inventions and adjustments', and all this in spite of the fact that 'his little hands are still too small to span an octave on the keyboard and he has always to spread [i.e. break] it'. He also lists the gifts the children received—nine gold watches, twelve gold snuffboxes, more gold rings with precious stones than he can count, earrings, necklaces, knives with gold blades, bottle-holders, pens and writing-pads, toothpick boxes and various other gewgaws, to a value (Hübner guessed) of 12,000 gulden, including a snuffbox filled with coins from Louis XV that the king would buy back for 1000 gulden should Leopold wish to sell it.

Hübner reports too that a symphony of Mozart's had been performed that day (8 December) in High Mass at the cathedral, 'with great approbation from the court musicians'. This no doubt was a symphony that he had written in London or The Hague, not one of the single-movement epistle sonatas, none of which he had yet composed (there is ample evidence, both circumstantial and internal, that symphonies were often used in church, within the Mass and at other times).[3] The first item we know him to have composed after his return was an aria, K.36/33i, given as a *licenza*—a tribute to a patron being honoured on a festive occasion, in this case the anniversary on 21 December of the archbishop's consecration. This is a setting for tenor of words—'Tali e cotanti sono di Sigismondo i merti'—no doubt written or adapted by a local poet for Siegmund ('Sigismondo') von Schrattenbach. Preceded by a lengthy accompanied recitative in appropriately pompous style ('Or che il dover'), it is a melodically rather bland *da capo* aria in D major, a popular key for ceremonial music, with trumpets and drums—Mozart's first use of them, as far as we know, for his previous works with orchestra had been content with strings, oboes and horns and occasionally bassoons, the standard orchestra of the time. It is amusing to note a curious error of Mozart's here. The text, it seems, was given to him with the abbreviation 'Riv°' for 'riverendo', and, although the scanning of the verse demands otherwise, he set it as a single syllable throughout, so that some rewriting of the rhythms is necessary to accommodate the extra syllables. Works that may belong to 1766 include a group of keyboard sonatas, K.33d–g, sent by Nannerl to the publisher Breitkopf & Härtel in 1800 and subsequently listed in their manuscript catalogue but now lost.

During the period that Mozart was at home he was presumably receiving some kind of education. There is no evidence that he ever underwent formal schooling, except possibly in a religious context. Schachtner's remark about his father as teacher (quoted on p. 20) seems to suggest that he had no other teacher than Leopold and probably no attendance at a school. As we have seen, Leopold had earlier talked of the studying Wolfgang would need to do, in a quiet room of his own, and it seems clear that he was conscious that the boy's broader education had been set aside as a consequence of his musical gifts. He had learnt Latin when young, as a Catholic child of his social position would be expected to do, and probably studied

Siegmund Christoph von Schrattenbach, Prince-Archbishop of Salzburg, 1753–71: anonymous pastel (*Internationale Stiftung Mozarteum, Salzburg*)

Italian, up to a point, if only in order to be able to set it appropriately. Later he learnt French and, much later, some English, of which he may have picked up a smattering on his travels. Schachtner comments on the boy's love of arithmetic, and there is evidence of this in the number games scrawled on some of his later manuscripts. As to musical education, we have no evidence of formal harmony or counterpoint teaching at this period, but he must have had lessons in key-board and violin playing: no exercises survive, although we know that Leopold owned copies of standard theoretical and didactic works, including the most famous, Fux's *Gradus ad Parnassum* (1725). It is reasonable to infer that Mozart's later teaching methods reflect his own tuition, and that involved strict counterpoint *à la* Fux as well as adding basses to melodies and similar exercises—all things that Mozart by this date could do with his eyes closed at a cloth-covered keyboard in front of an audience. Among the lost music of this period are a number of fugues, the composition of which, then as now, was considered apt training. But Mozart did not need exercises. His tech-nique was already of an order where there was nothing that Leopold, or perhaps anyone else, could teach him, and he could best learn, and had already learnt, the procedures of composition by studying and lis-tening to other composers' music. What he needed now was matu-rity and experience, and that could come only with time.

Mozart wrote a number of works for use at the Salzburg court during the winter and spring of 1767. There was, first, another *licenza* aria, this time for the archbishop's birthday, 28 February (the per-formance was the next day). An opera, *Vologeso* (probably Sarti's, in its revised version recently heard in Venice), had been given at the end of 1765 and was to be revived for the occasion, and Mozart's soprano aria 'Sol nascente' K.70/61*c*, to understandably anonymous words, was presumably added at the end as a tribute. The text of the prefa-tory recitative, 'A Berenice e Vologeso sposi', refers to the happy final union of the lovers in the opera, and goes on to speak of honouring Sigismondo on this auspicious day. The 'newborn sun' of the aria, symbolizing the prince-archbishop, is represented by a rising melodic line, but the topic does not seem to have acted as an inspiration to Mozart, although the coloratura writing here is more imaginative than in the previous *licenza*.

Another new, and more substantial, work by Mozart was heard on 12 March as part of a *geistliches Singspiel* (a sacred sung drama), which the court had commissioned for Lent for performance in the Rittersaal at the Residenz. Leopold headed the work 'Oratorium' and dated it, surely mistakenly rather than deceptively, March 1766. It was usual in Salzburg to divide the composition of such works between several composers. Mozart wrote Part I, which was performed on 12 March and repeated on 2 April. Parts II and III, by Michael Haydn (Joseph's younger brother, who had become Konzertmeister at the court in 1763) and Cajetan Adlgasser, were given on 19 and (probably) 26 March.[4] The text for this work, *Die Schuldigkeit des ersten Gebotes* ('The Obligation of the First Commandment') K.35, was supplied by Ignaz Anton von Weiser, a prominent figure in Salzburg, where he was a textile merchant and city councillor and was later (in 1772) to become mayor; he was an old friend of Leopold's (Leopold had set cantata texts that he had written) and a half-brother of Hagenauer's wife. *Die Schuldigkeit* belongs in the tradition, well established in Salzburg, of Catholic schooldrama, for which the words were usually written by Benedictine instructors. The 'characters' and their original singers are as follows:

Die göttliche Gerechtigkeit (Divine Justice)	Maria Anna Braunhofer (*soprano*)
Die göttliche Barmherzigkeit (Divine Mercy)	Maria Magdalena Lipp (*soprano*)
Der Welt-Geist (The Worldly Spirit)	Maria Anna Fesemayr (*soprano*)
Der Christien-Geist (The Spirit of Christianity)	Franz Anton Spitzeder (*tenor*)
Ein lauer und hinnach eifriger Christ (An Indifferent, then Zealous Christian)	Joseph Meissner (*tenor*)

The act composed by Mozart begins with the Christian Spirit inviting Justice and Mercy to help him impress on erring mankind the importance of the First Commandment. Each expresses his view of mankind's situation; Worldly Spirit offers an alternative view. A Christian, awakening with anxieties about ultimate judgment, is persuaded by Worldly Spirit of the importance of worldly pleasures. Christian Spirit, in the guise of a doctor, advises him of the necessary treatment, but he turns to Worldly Spirit, and Christian Spirit, Mercy and Justice resolve to pursue the rescuing of lost souls.

The work is set in the normal manner of an oratorio, or a serious opera, of the 1760s, with extended arias linked by lengthy recitatives. The text has few dramatic qualities—the work was almost certainly designed for concert rather than stage performance—but most of the arias allow opportunity for illustrative or expressive writing of a kind not beyond Mozart at this stage. It has as overture a symphonic Allegro in C major, a lively piece, somewhat childish in its short-breathed, over-emphatic cadences. A point of interest, however, is Mozart's use of the opening theme, in adjusted form (with a chromatic inflexion and a simplified continuation) as a main part of the secondary material. In a movement in rounded binary form, the return of this theme thus has something of the sense of a sonata-form 'double return' recapitulation (tonic key and opening theme). The tumbling figure in the ritornello of Christian Spirit's first aria seems to represent the downfall of souls, coupled in invertible counterpoint with what may stand for the rising force of those who would save them. Figures from it permeate the texture of the aria, the voice often sustaining a new line against it. This is a full *da capo* aria, as are five of the seven; its central section has the change of tempo and metre usual at this period, with graphic violin writing to represent the 'overflowing rivers that froth and flood', the metaphor for man's sensuality. Mercy's aria, which follows, talks of the angry lion roaring in the forest and the torpor of the huntsman, with busy forest murmurs in the strings and horns evoking the hunt—obligatory if naive imagery. Here the lengthy E flat first part, with a 28-bar ritornello and a good deal of florid vocal writing, ends in the dominant key, and after the slower section (C minor to G minor) the return of the opening is akin to a rounded binary recapitulation in the home key. Following, however, we find a second slower section, extended and vocally elaborated (A flat to E flat), with an orchestral coda on material from the main section. No doubt Mozart had models for arias of this kind, yet his control of these expansive forms and the complex relation between key-scheme and material is impressive. If the music seems leisurely in pace, that is a commentary less on Mozart's handling of the material than on the local tradition for works of this kind.

After a turbulent accompanied recitative with highly dissonant writing portraying Christian Spirit's state of mind, an aria from Justice calls Christian to wakefulness, a gentle Andante in A major; in the short middle section hell and death are briefly and more forcefully evoked. He awakens to a vision in accompanied recitative, at first a soft-textured C major, perhaps recalling the Elysian Fields of Gluck's *Orfeo*, until images of hell and death intervene, and a *pianissimo* phrase from the trombone (the German for 'last trumpet' being 'letzte Posaune', or 'last trombone') serves as a reminder of mortality and judgment. Worldly Spirit offers an aria, minuet-like in rhythm, with sprightly ritornello and accompaniment figures and lively coloratura, a series of musical metaphors for frivolity. But Christian remains troubled: the role of the trombone, sombrely scored with divided violas, and Mozart's use of ominous diminished-seventh harmony to colour his opening words ('the strength of those thunder-words') reflect his state of mind. Further arias, with only generalized expression of the text, follow from Worldly Spirit (on the pattern of Mercy's) and Christian Spirit, and lastly there is a terzet, gracefully written.

The various types of expression of words, or of moods, in *Die Schuldigkeit* are not of course new. Some are hallowed by long tradition, such as the diminished seventh chord, which is a modern counterpart to many an example of Renaissance or Baroque word-painting. They are remarkable only because they show Mozart, now eleven, absorbing and using with imagination and fluency an increasing repertory of techniques. *Die Schuldigkeit*, his first dramatic work, is scarcely touched by the new developments in dramatic music of the 1750s and early 60s that for us are most clearly seen in Gluck's *Orfeo*, but it is an astonishingly accomplished work of its time, pol-

ished in technique and with as acute a sense of general musical character as all but the most progressive and intellectual among professional composers of the time. Its score, now in the Royal Library at
Windsor Castle, is fluently written, but with many small changes and
corrections in Leopold's hand. It is of course likely that Leopold suggested many of the illustrative and other special features in the musical treatment; if he was still (as we shall see) doing so at the time of
Idomeneo, in 1780, he was surely doing so in 1767. Yet it was Mozart
himself who executed them with such skill. There is no reason to
think, on the basis of Leopold's music, that his own musical ideas will
have intruded more than marginally into Wolfgang's music of this
date or after.

Two more dramatic works followed within a few weeks. First was
probably the *Grabmusik* ('Grave Music') K.42/35*a*, a Passion cantata
noted by Leopold on his 1768 list as composed in 1767, and almost
certainly the subject of one of the most famous anecdotes about
Mozart's childhood. It originates with Daines Barrington:[5]

> I have made frequent inquiries with regard to this very
> extraordinary genius since he left England, and was told last
> summer [presumably 1767 or 1769], that he was then at
> Saltzbourg, where he had composed several oratorios, which
> were much admired.
>
>   I am also informed, that the prince of Saltzbourg, not
> crediting that such masterly compositions were really those of
> a child, shut him up for a week, during which he was not
> permitted to see any one, and was left only with music paper,
> and the words of an oratorio.
>
>   During this time he composed a very capital oratorio,
> which was most highly approved of upon being performed.

It was long supposed that the 'oratorio' referred to was *Die Schuldigkeit*, as the only work properly so described. But the score, of 201
pages, could hardly have been written in a week, and it bears more

signs of intervention on Leopold's part, in the course of composition, than would be compatible with the story. The only other work that seems to answer the circumstances—assuming the story's truth—is the *Grabmusik*. This work was presumably composed for Easter; if the archbishop's scepticism was brought about by *Die Schuldigkeit*, the week's confinement might have been between its first hearing on 12 March and the onset of Easter (Good Friday fell on 17 April). The *Grabmusik*, probably performed at a representation of Christ's grave in a Salzburg church, possibly the cathedral, consisted originally of two arias, for the Soul and an Angel, and a duet, with introductory and linking recitative. The first aria, for a baritone, is an extended piece to a text about the splitting rocks and terrible tremors at the crucifix-ion. The music, however, in spite of some sharply alternating *forte* and *piano* markings and string tremolandos, is essentially untroubled, and the vocal coloratura, in dialogue with the violins, carries little dra-matic force. There is a stormier middle section ('Brüllt, ihr Donner!') with rushing string scales and then carefully indicated diminuendos to illustrate a world struck by lightning and flames, with some rapid and startling modulations; a sequence D–E flat–C minor–E flat–G minor–C minor–E minor within 30 bars leads directly into a very abbreviated *da capo*. The second aria, for a soprano Angel, is a short contemplation in G minor, with a string accompaniment enriched by divided violas. A brief accompanied recitative leads to the duet, a flowing, minuet-like Andante of repentance, gracefully rococo in manner, which ends the work in its original form. Some four years later Mozart added a substantial, affirmative final chorus.

It may have been the success of *Die Schuldigkeit* that produced another commission for a dramatic work, though more probably the commission had come earlier. At any rate, by the end of April the industrious Wolfgang must have been near to completing a miniature opera, the work nowadays known as *Apollo et Hyacinthus* K.38, by then already under rehearsal. It originally was nameless, called by Leopold simply 'Eine Musik zu einer lateinischen Comoedie' ('Music for a Latin Comedy') in his 1768 list, but in 1799, to identify it unambiguously, Nannerl annotated the list 'Apollo und Hyacinth'; for a Latin work a Latin title is to be preferred. *Apollo et Hyacinthus* was composed as an *intermedium*, to be performed at the university, by a youthful cast, between the acts of a more serious work, a five-act Latin tragedy *Clementia Croesi* ('The Clemency of Croesus').[6]

There was a longstanding tradition of performing Latin plays at the Benedictine University in Salzburg, and indeed more widely in southern Germany and other parts of central Europe (primarily the Catholic countries). At Salzburg, the main event was at the end of the academic year, usually in August, but individual classes sometimes gave performances at other times. This particular event was organized by one of the Gymnasium classes, the third-year class known as the 'Syntaxists', who followed the 'Poetae' and the 'Rhetores'. Their professor was Rufinus Widl, a Benedictine monk formerly at the monastery at Seeon who had come to Salzburg in 1763 to teach the 'Rudimentisten', ascending with his class, now at the 'Syntaxisten' level; the next year he became professor of philosophy. His five-act mythological play, based on Herodotus, deals at length with the question whether King Croesus of Lydia should forgive the prince Adrastus, a visitor at his court and tutor to his son Atys, for killing Atys in a hunting accident. As in the larger theatrical and operatic world, it was common to incorporate within, or alongside, the performance of a tragedy a lighter work that might reflect its main theme in a different way and perhaps put it in another light. For the supporting work here, Widl used as a basis the mythological story of Apollo and Hyacinth, from Euripides and, more particularly, from Ovid's *Metamorphoses*. In its original form the tale of the jealousy of Zephyr of the love of Apollo and Hyacinth, and his murder of Hyacinth, would not serve, partly because of its homoerotic theme and partly because the analogy with the main play was too thin. Accordingly, Widl added two other characters from neighbouring myths, Hyacinth's sister Melia, as the object of the two men's love, and Oebalus, Hyacinth's father. The cast for the first performance was as follows:

Oebalus, *king of Lacedaemonia*	Matthias Stadler (*tenor*)
Melia, *his daughter*	Felix Fuchs (*treble*)
Hyacinthus, *his son*	Christian Enzinger (*treble*)
Apollo, *visitor to Oebalus's court*	Johann Ernst (*alto*)
Zephyrus, *friend of Hyacinthus*	Joseph Vonderthon (*alto*)
Two Priests of Apollo	Joseph Bründl, Jakob Moser

All the principals except Stadler, a university student in moral theology and canon law, and later a tenor and violinist in the court music, were Gymnasium pupils whose voices had not broken. The three youngest were choirboys in the Kapelle. Enzinger (in the Rudiments class) and Ernst were each twelve, Fuchs (in the Grammar class) was fifteen and Vonderthon seventeen (a Syntaxist; they were permitted to draw on students from other classes). There is no solo music for the priests, but presumably they joined in the chorus, which, if sung only by the assembled soloists, would mean that one was a bass: Bründl (in the Poetry class) was eighteen and Moser (another Syntaxist) sixteen.

The work is in three parts, 'Prologus' (given before the play), Chorus I (after the second act) and Chorus II (before the fifth and last act). Each part has three vocal numbers. The overture (or Intrada) is a brief and lively piece, neatly put together from conventional tags rather than true themes, a common procedure for Mozart in this key, D major, throughout his life. In Apollo's temple, Zephyr talks to Hyacinth in the opening recitative of a love for his friend that surpasses that for Apollo; it seems to carry more than a hint of the original plot. A short chorus, with a central prayer from Oebalus, invokes Apollo, but lightning destroys the altar, and Hyacinth and Zephyr are concerned that their exchange may have drawn the god's wrath. Hyacinth's aria, designed to dismiss fear, takes advantage of the words ('rident et iocantur', 'they laugh and they jest') to justify some coloratura writing as representational. It is a full *da capo* aria; Mozart made concessions only selectively to his youthful singers. When Apollo enters, instantly capturing the hearts of Melia and Hyacinth (to Zephyr's perturbation), he sings an aria of conventional cut, in two sections, rounded off by the ritornello of the first.

Melia's aria 'Laetari, iocari', however, in which at the beginning of Act 2 she welcomes the prospect of marriage to Apollo, is a brilliant representation of jubilance, with its trumpet-like arpeggio phrases and its coloratura setting of 'gaudia dat' ('gives rejoicing'). But Zephyr enters to report—falsely, as he confesses aside—that Apollo has killed Hyacinth with a discus during their sport, and in a short aria pleads with Melia to marry him instead. Apollo however enters and exercises his divine powers to have Zephyr transformed into a wind. The duet for Melia and Apollo that follows is of altogether greater interest for Mozart's imaginative handling, simultaneously, of her indignant, dismissive music with its short, exclamatory phrases and his gentle pleas and protests. It is a *da capo* duet, of which the middle section, for Apollo alone, portrays his tortured state of mind with highly chromatic music, as he resolves to remain in spite of her dismissal.

The last act begins with an orchestral recitative for the dying Hyacinth and his father: we hear enough of this touchingly composed death scene to know that Oebalus is telling the truth in saying that it is Zephyr, not Apollo, who is guilty of Hyacinth's death. But before then he not only completes a stormy recitative but sings an extended *da capo* aria. This is a simile aria, of the traditional type associated with the Metastasian *opera seria*, involving a comparison that allows for vivid musical imagery. Here Oebalus compares the surges of bile in his breast with the raging seas on which a ship might be tossed, and Mozart rises to it with turbulent music—darting themes, rushing violin figures, sharp dynamic contrasts. An experienced composer might have found more to do in raising the emotional temperature with its rhythms and its harmonies, but it remains an effective piece and a climactic moment in the score. Another climax of a different kind follows: Melia, learning the truth, joins her father in mourning Hyacinth's death and the god's departure in a delectable duet, with a touching melody for the muted first violins accompanied by *pizzicato* second violins and basses, with a soft harmonic accompaniment from the violas with sustaining horns. Mozart later used this movement in a symphony, K.43. Apollo now returns, in an accompanied recitative, to turn Hyacinth's grave into a bed of flowers. All is explained and set right, he marries Melia, and they and Oebalus join in a joyous terzet.

School performances of this kind were evidently taken seriously by the authorities. Towards the end of April rehearsals began, and a number of classes were postponed 'because of the coming comedy'. The Great Hall (the Aula) of the university was converted into a theatre by 1 May, and the usual daily celebration of Mass there was moved to the university church. But the decorations had been hired to a visiting Italian troupe who would not return them until threats of legal action were issued, and when they did they were in wretched condition. Towards the date of the performance rehearsal became intensive, with a daily 'proba musica' from Sunday 10 May. When it was given, on 13 May 1767, the performance 'pleased everybody',

Salzburg University (right) and the university or collegiate church (the houses in the distant left back on to Getreidegasse): engraving by K. Rembshart after F.A. Danreiter, c1730 (*Staats- und Stadt-Bibliothek, Augsburg*)

and in the evening, after the performance, Mozart played the harpsi-chord, 'giving us notable examples of his musical art'.[7]

What did he play? Possibly his first 'piano concerto'. For if April 1767 was the momentous month in which Mozart wrote his first opera, it was also the month of his first attempt at another genre in which he was to be especially distinguished. As we saw in Chapter 3, Leopold was much impressed when the family was in Paris with the music of the German composers' colony there: the names of Eckard, Schobert, Honauer and Raupach all occur in his letters and his travel notes, Eckard's many times (he was a friend), Schobert's several (no friend, Leopold suspected), Raupach's in the story related by Grimm (p. 97), Honauer's as someone the Mozarts met. It seems, however, that Leopold brought back from Paris music by all these composers, possibly even then with a particular use in mind—of adapting them as concertos.

Whether the primary purpose was practical or didactic is uncer-tain, probably the former. But it was by using movements from sonatas by these composers that Mozart first learnt how to cope with the special structural problems raised by concerto form, at least in the context of actual concerto composition. That rider is necessary, for he had already written a fair number of arias—possibly the fifteen Leopold claimed, as well as the two *licenze* and those in *Die Schuldigkeit*, the *Grabmusik* and now *Apollo et Hyacinthus*—where the forms were essentially the same or very similar. Leopold, however, had devised (the idea must surely have been his) a way of making concerto composition easy by allowing the young Wolfgang to solve its problems one at a time. Essentially, then, Leopold, or probably Leopold and Wolfgang together, planned out a series of four concer-tos made out of sonata movements mostly by other composers, which they no doubt felt would be useful performance material for the future. The idea, which seems obvious enough, seems not to have occurred to any other composer of the time. K.37, the first of these pasticcio concertos, as the Mozarts themselves called them, was writ-ten in April 1767, as noted on the score by Leopold; the second, K.39, in June, and the third and fourth, K.40 and 41, in July.[8] Leopold's exclusion of them from his 1768 list signifies that he did not regard them as true compositions of his son. The works are as follows:

K.37 in F	i Allegro	Raupach: op.1 no.5.i (Allegro di molto)
	ii Andante	probably by Mozart
	iii Rondo	Honauer: op.2 no.3.i (Allegro)
K.39 in B flat	i Allegro spiritoso	Raupach: op.1 no.1.i (Allegro moderato)
	ii Andante	Schobert: op.17 no.2.i (Andante poco allegro)
	iii Molto Allegro	Raupach: op.1 no.1.iii (Allegro assai)
K.40 in D	i Allegro maestoso	Honauer: op.2 no.1.i (Allegro pomposo)
	ii Andante	Eckard: op.1 no.4.i (Andantino)
	iii Presto	C.P.E. Bach: 'La Boehmer' WQ117/26, H81 (Prestissimo)
K.41 in G	i Allegro	Honauer: op.1 no.1.i
	ii Andante	Raupach: op.1 no.1.ii (Andantino)
	iii Molto Allegro	Honauer: op.1 no.1.iii (Allegro assai).

The autographs of these four works are joint products of Leopold and Wolfgang, though K.41 is mainly in Leopold's hand. The principle Mozart followed is simple. He retained the sonata, in most cases virtually as it stood, to form the solo keyboard part, and round it he wrote orchestral ritornellos and accompaniments. It may be worth looking at one of the movements quite closely.

The first movement of K.37 begins with a 25-bar ritornello, using the principal theme for the opening four bars—in the form in which it appeared on the 'accompanying' violin in Raupach's original. For the continuation, Mozart devised orchestral ideas compatible harmonically with Raupach's original keyboard continuation (as yet unheard), and then moved on to a half-cadence with four bars of new material. Then follows a statement, still in the tonic key, of a secondary idea, this being Raupach's original second subject (which the keyboard will later announce in the dominant key), and a flourish of conventional scalic passages leads to a cadence. Then the keyboard enters, playing Raupach's music. After the soloist has presented the secondary idea in the dominant key and another rather slight theme made up of scale passages, he reaches what in the sonata original was the central double bar, where there is a short orchestral tutti in the dominant, beginning and ending like the opening ritornello but telescoped to eleven bars. The soloist moves on to a development, expanding Raupach's laconic one into sixteen bars, then leading to a recapitulation of the solo opening followed by a developmental diversion to minor keys before leading back to the tonic. A four-bar tutti enables the orchestra to replay its original opening before the soloist resumes, with his additional secondary theme. Mozart added extra keyboard flourishes to supply a touch of virtuosity apt to a concerto before a tutti of eight bars (incorporating the first secondary theme) ends the movement. This movement, presumably the first to be written, departs more from the sonata model than any other in the series. The finale, for example, is much simpler, partly because Mozart retained the central double bar: there is a 27-bar tutti at the beginning, a twelve-bar one to open the second half, and a ten-bar one to end with—and Mozart had to invent no new material as the original supplied a sufficiency of cadential ideas for him to draw upon. Throughout the solo music the orchestra provides unobtrusive support, sustained notes, harmonic filling-in, pointing-up of cadences and occasionally an echo phrase.

The Andante is another matter. Any source has resisted identification, and although the movement could be based on a work in manuscript, now otherwise lost, the possibility of its being original should not be ruled out. The warmth of style may be akin to Schobert,[9] but it is also characteristic of Mozart himself. Moreover, at three points in the movement there are substantial alterations to the keyboard part, made by Leopold, and if the music were simply a copy of another composer's work he might have been less ready to intervene, as indeed the other eleven movements demonstrate. The only comparable changes, in one bar of left-hand figuration in the first movement of K.37 and in the final flourish in the first of K.39, are in passages Mozart inserted.

The pattern of treatment becomes fairly consistent. Most movements have added tuttis at the beginning, the end of the exposition and the end of the recapitulation (either side of the cadenza, of which there is one in all but two of the outer movements); some also have a brief tutti to introduce the recapitulation. There are other minor adjustments by Mozart, for example the repetition of a phrase in the K.41 Andante to make the cadence points match, which they did not in the Raupach original. Movements of particular interest include the second of K.39, after Schobert, by far the most talented of the composer models, with its throbbing triplets, powerful basses and singing lines, and the graceful Eckard Andante of K.40. Honauer's movements tend to rely on brilliance of keyboard figuration. The C.P.E. Bach piece was not published; possibly the Mozarts had encountered it during their travels. Schobert's op.17 was not in print until the end of 1767, and the Mozarts must have acquired a manuscript copy in Paris.

The importance of these pasticcio concertos lies in Mozart's deft management of the tuttis—his translation of keyboard ideas into idiomatic orchestral writing and his handling of this material so as to create links across the movement—and his early assimilation of the essentials of what was to be his mature concerto form and style. The structure of the great piano concertos of the 1780s is already there, in all essentials, in these prentice works that are not even wholly his own. There are some puzzles: why did he choose these particular pieces? why did he not retain Raupach's op.1 no.1 whole rather than divide it? what practical purpose, if any, did they serve? Once again, however, Leopold's canniness in having him put these pasticcio concertos together, and his own adeptness at rising to the special challenges they offered, compel admiration.

7

Disappointment in Vienna

HERE ARE GOOD reasons to believe that, from the moment the Mozart family arrived back in Salzburg at the end of 1766, Leopold was contemplating a further journey. Principally, it was a matter of capitalizing on the children while they were still young enough to arouse wonderment—Wolfgang was nearly eleven, Nannerl now sixteen—but his letters also hint that he felt Salzburg to be too small, too provincial, too limiting to be a suitable place for his preternaturally gifted son to see through even the rest of his childhood. Thoughts of Italy had been with him a long time, but in fact his next journey was not across the Alps but to Vienna, where an opportunity seemed to present itself. In the autumn of 1767 a wedding was in prospect in the imperial family: the Archduchess Maria Josepha, sister of Joseph II, was to be married to King Ferdinand I of Naples (Ferdinand IV of the Two Sicilies). Although smallpox was currently prevalent in the capital (Joseph's wife, Maria, had died of it in May), the festivities that traditionally surrounded such events would draw in all the noble families of Austria, Hungary and Bohemia, many of them patrons and connoisseurs of music. Clearly, this would be a good moment to be in Vienna. Several other Salzburg musicians, including Michael Haydn, were going too.

As before, Leopold sent regular letters throughout his absence, which turned out to be considerably longer than had originally been contemplated, to Lorenz Hagenauer in Salzburg, at first weekly, later roughly every three or four weeks. These again provide our chief source of information about the family's activities.[1] Possibly the continuation of this arrangement implies that Hagenauer and his friends had again invested in some way in the Mozarts' journey, which in turn implies that the previous investment had been well rewarded.

The Mozarts, with their servant Bernhard, left Salzburg in the family carriage on 11 September 1767. The route to Vienna was one they had followed before and would again. On the first night they stayed at Vöcklabruck, and by lunchtime the next day they were at Lambach, where they took their midday meal at the monastery. By the evening they had reached Linz, where they lodged at Zum grünen Baum, on the edge of the city close to the palace of the prelate of Lambach, whom Leopold immediately informed of their arrival; the prelate invited them to lunch the next day and presumably heard the children play. They then travelled through the hilly Strengberg country, staying overnight at the town. The following day they reached Melk, where they saw round the famous monastery and, without announcing who they were, had 'Wolfgangganggangerl' (as Leopold wrote) play unannounced, then hurried out to their carriage, leaving the organist and the monks to guess who their visitor had been. They reached St Pölten that evening and went on through Purkersdorf to Vienna the next morning. They took lodgings in Vienna on the second floor of the house of a goldsmith, Gottfried Johann Schmalecker, in the Weihburggasse. Already, it seems, the city was in festive mood: in his first letter Leopold comments on the nightly performances of operas and plays and on balls, illuminations and fireworks in the Liechtenstein gardens and at the Neapolitan embassy.

By the time of his second letter, 29 September, Leopold had been to see *Partenope*, the new opera commissioned for the festivities. The work treated a Neapolitan theme, apt to the occasion, and boasted a new libretto (several older ones existed) written by the court poet,

Metastasio, and set by Johann Adolf Hasse. Born near Hamburg but wholly Italian in his orientation, Hasse had held positions in Naples and Venice, at the Dresden court and in Vienna, and was the senior, most respected and most admired *opera seria* composer of the time. *Partenope*, first given at the Burgtheater on 9 September and strictly a *festa teatrale* (as indeed was Gluck's *Orfeo*), was described as 'beautiful' by Leopold, though he thought the occasion might have merited a less ordinary cast of singers, among whom he mentions only three, the tenor Giuseppe Tibaldi, the castrato Venanzio Rauzzini and the soprano Elisabeth Teyber.

On 7 October Leopold wrote to Hagenauer to say that the princess-bride was unwell: she had smallpox and the court was in total confusion. He enlarged on this a week later. Although taken ill on 3 October, on one of the next two days (the Sunday or St Francis's day) she had been with her mother to the Franciscan Capuchin Church, where the Habsburg family were buried, for a three-hour service, and by 6 October the smallpox rash had appeared. In his next letter, on 17 October: 'The princess-bride has become the bride of the heavenly bridegroom'—and Leopold relates the various rumours of her illness, her supposed recovery and her final sinking. This, he points out, was the second archduchess the king of Naples had lost, since Joanna, his previous promised bride, had died in 1762. Another extraordinary coincidence, he adds: the second festival opera, given on the late Emperor Francis's nameday, 5 October, was *Amore e Psiche* by Florian Gassmann, in which the beautiful, virtuous and innocent bride, Psyche, is killed—and now, in real life, the beautiful, virtuous and innocent bride, the Archduchess Maria Josepha, had died. Operas for wedding festivities were expected to have allegorical significance, but this one was hardly intended to be so close. Leopold had another interpretation: the coincidence of opera subject, the onset of Josepha's illness on her father's nameday and her death on her mother's all indicated divine planning.

The royal death meant not only that the planned festivities would be cancelled but that the court would go into mourning. The theatres would close for six weeks, then it would be Advent, and all would be quiet in Vienna until the end of the year. There was little point in the Mozarts' being in Vienna, and indeed it was a bad place to be with smallpox taking its toll. One of their landlord's children had the disease, but the Mozarts had not been told until he had recovered, by which time two other children of the family had caught it. 'You can well imagine how I felt', Leopold wrote, and his situation was made the more difficult by the fact that the emperor had expressed a wish to hear the children play and was liable to summon them at any moment. For the moment, all he could do was take Wolfgang out of the infected house, and that he did, lodging with a friend and leaving his wife and Nannerl there for the time being, with the servant (they suspected, wrongly, that Nannerl had already had smallpox as a child and so was in less danger). When he heard that another of the young archduchesses had contracted the disease—their acquaintances included the imperial physician, Louis-Alexandre Laugier or L'Augier, for whom Domenico Scarlatti had written some sonatas many years before—Leopold felt himself freed of any obligation to remain in Vienna. The nearest sanctuary he could seek, it seems, was in Moravia, where he had various connections through noble families in Salzburg. It was evidently far enough away to escape the likelihood of pursuit by the epidemic, but also close enough for him to be able to return when the epidemic was over and the city ready to listen again to music.

On 23 October the family left Vienna for Brünn.[2] There Count Franz Anton von Schrattenbach, brother of the archbishop of Salzburg, had a palace, and he and his daughter Countess von Herberstein took them in and talked of arranging a concert in the city. But then Leopold, moved (he wrote) by an instinctive inner conviction that he could not get out of his head, decided that he must move on to Olmütz. The count agreed, and they postponed the concert until the return journey. On 26 October they packed and left, reaching Olmütz rather later than intended because of a three-hour break for carriage repairs at Wischkau. In Olmütz they went to the inn

Zum schwarzen Adler, where they were not comfortable: the room was damp, and the stove brought in to heat it smoked and made their eyes smart. They moved the next morning to better rooms, but by now Wolfgang had a fever and was delirious that day and the next. On 28 October Leopold went after church to see the dean of the cathedral and rector of the university, Leopold Anton, Count Podstatsky, who was an old Salzburg acquaintance, and told him of his suspicion that Wolfgang had smallpox. Podstatsky at once offered to take the family into his house: he had his steward prepare rooms, and sent a doctor to the inn (this was Joseph Wolff, who came to Salzburg eleven years later; Leopold remembered that Wolfgang had written a song for his young daughter, but the piece is apparently lost).[3] Wrapped in leather and furs, the feverish boy was taken to the cathedral deanery. His eyes, as was usual during smallpox, were painful and had to be rested; Nannerl later said that he could not see for nine days. Nor could he write or compose, but he rapidly learnt card tricks from the bishop's chaplain, Johann Leopold Hay (later Bishop of Königgrätz).[4] Some small red spots appeared on 29 October and during the next two days the smallpox broke out fully and the fever diminished; by 9 November the spots began to disappear and the swelling declined. Leopold was profoundly grateful to Count Podstatsky for his generosity and kindness in accommodating them: 'this deed', he wrote, 'will do him no small honour in the biography of our little one that in due time I shall have printed'.

His remaining anxiety was, of course, that Nannerl might also catch smallpox, as she duly did, but hers was a milder case and according to Leopold left no pockmarks. Wolfgang, on the other hand, looked at himself in the mirror and said 'Now I am like little Mayr', referring to the son of a member of the Salzburg orchestra, similarly marked. Leopold told Hagenauer that Wolfgang had only a few pockmarks, but Nannerl, many years later, said that he was a handsome child until he was disfigured by the disease.[5] With this crisis behind him, Leopold could return to normal correspondence, and from Olmütz at the end of November he told Hagenauer about his plans, about meeting Michael Haydn's lady friend in Vienna (daughter of a hosier, a neat person, medium height, a good figure, fair complexion, the most beautiful teeth—but he does not think he should bring her to Salzburg, which in fact he did not), about the preponderance of priests and soldiers in Olmütz, and about the prayers being said because of a plague of worms and mice that was damaging the crops and ravaging the granaries in Moravia and making the cows ill in Silesia.

The Mozarts remained in Olmütz until 23 December. They were in Brünn from 24 December until 9 January, staying at Schrattenbach's palace, and played in a concert arranged by Schrattenbach in the Taverne on 30 December, with the town waits, local professional musicians, leading a group that probably comprised mostly amateurs. Mozart 'could not bear the trumpets which were incapable of playing in tune with one another', though his playing 'excited the admiration of all'.[6] It was a difficult and costly journey back to Vienna, Leopold reported, in deep and drifting snow which had caused the post-coaches to be heavily delayed or even unable to run. Travelling with four post-horses, through a snowstorm, by six in the evening they reached Poysdorf, where they spent a night, and with six horses, leaving at eight o'clock, they were back in Vienna by five on the evening of 10 January. They took lodgings at Zum roten Säbel in the Hohe Brücke (now the Wipplingerstraße). On 19 January they at last had their hoped-for audience with the imperial family. Leopold says nothing in his letters about the music they played, but was delighted at the warmth of the welcome they received from Joseph II (now emperor and co-regent of the Austrian Monarchy), the Empress Maria Theresa, Duke Albert of Saxe-Teschen and the archduchesses. Maria Theresa talked to Maria Anna Mozart about the children's smallpox and their grand tour, and Joseph to Wolfgang and Leopold about music and other things 'which made Nannerl blush'. Whether all this would mean a good fee Leopold was unsure; and in the event it was only the condescension that was generous, for they were given nothing but a medal.

Leopold discussed the situation at length in his next letter, in fairly but understandably cynical terms. The Viennese public, he says, want only comic theatre, clowning and magic, and nothing sensible or serious; the royal family are friendly and gracious, but cheeseparing; the other Viennese nobles, following the imperial example, are cutting down their expenses; Prince Kaunitz, the powerful Chancellor, has avoided the Mozarts because he is so terrified of smallpox that he hates to see anyone with even residual signs of it; no audience of noblemen can be assembled as it is carnival time; and now, he hears, there is such professional jealousy from other musicians—with the honourable exception of Wagenseil, who however is ill—that their progress is likely to be hindered. Having refused to hear Wolfgang, he adds, other musicians can deny the possibility that his talents are what they are claimed to be. Leopold's anger and resentment misled him into ill-advised action. The fault was partly the emperor's. At their audience, Joseph twice asked the boy, Leopold reports, whether he would like to compose and direct an opera. Wolfgang, naturally, said that he would. Whether Joseph meant this seriously must be doubtful. In any case, the decision as to whether an opera of his would actually be given did not rest wholly with the emperor but rather with the lessee and impresario of the court theatres, Giuseppe Affligio (or Afflisio), who although subject to the emperor's will was himself commercially liable and could not be expected to put on an opera that he thought would be a failure.

The suggestion that Wolfgang might write an opera had given Leopold a tempting glimpse of fame and riches far beyond anything he had envisaged and, coupled with the frustration caused by the debacle of the autumn, led him to put aside his usual caution and act precipitately, in a way that could not have failed to alienate many people who might otherwise have been friendly and helpful, or at least neutral. There was one immediate and important example, Christoph Willibald Gluck. 'I have even', Leopold writes, 'won Gluck over to our side, even if, I admit, only to the extent that, though he is not whole-hearted, he will not dare let it be noticed as our patrons are also his'. Evidently Leopold, in a grievous and far-reaching lapse of judgment, had attempted to importune the doyen of Viennese opera composers, a man of formidable intellect, whose *Don Juan* ballet in 1761, his *Orfeo ed Euridice* in 1762, and his *Alceste* only three weeks before (on 26 December 1767) had begun a revolution, to put it only a little too strongly, in the world of musical drama. Was Leopold so blind to realities and to human nature as to imagine that Gluck would support the notion of an opera by a twelve-year-old, and would be able or willing to conceal his reservations about it? The very notion of an 'innocent' writing an opera negated all that Gluck stood for.

Well, at least it was to be only a comic opera. 'It is not an *opera seria*, as there is no more *opera seria* here now, and people do not like them', Leopold wrote. Joseph was already encouraging the abandonment of the old, courtly type of opera, even if partly because *opera buffa* was much less costly. Affligio went along with the plans, at least for the moment, and gave Mozart his new text: the opera was to be *La finta semplice* ('The feigned simpleton'), a full-length work of two-and-a-half to three hours (according to Leopold), for which the court theatre poet Marco Coltellini adapted an existing text by the acknowledged leading writer of comic librettos, the veteran Carlo Goldoni. Mozart worked steadily on the setting of it, and on 30 March Leopold could report that he was making good progress.

By that date, Leopold's pay from Salzburg had been stopped, along with that of two other absentee members of the musical establishment. This was less a reprimand than simply a reminder that he could not be expected to be paid indefinitely when he was away. That was perfectly acceptable to him. He could, he later wrote, have obtained that part of his salary that was specific to violin teaching, but 'in fairness and honour' was disinclined to ask for something he was not earning, and felt his position for applying for future leave—Italy was at the forefront of his mind—would be the stronger if he would willingly forgo his salary. There is no record of how long a leave he had originally applied for, but it is clear from his letters that he had by now overstayed it, and with the opera in prospect he was tied to Vienna for some weeks or months more.

La finta semplice was originally to have been produced soon after Easter, but as further changes had to be made in the libretto it was not yet ready, and in any case Joseph II went in April on a tour to Temesvar and the Banat, postponed from the previous year because of the smallpox epidemic. So no performance would be possible until his return in June. By May, Leopold had realized that they would still be in Vienna at least to the end of July, and as it was embarrassing, in the warmer weather, to turn up in cloth at their hosts' houses, he asked Hagenauer to have various additional clothes sent (including the ladies' Persian silk dresses, his own silk suit from Lyons and Wolfgang's grey camlet suit, as well as patching material for various of their suits). There is no record of the hosts they were visiting during these months except for one event, on 24 March, a concert at the residence of the Russian ambassador, Prince Golitsïn. Leopold was also concerned about this time with his *Violinschule*, contemplating having it translated into Italian, no doubt in readiness for a visit to Italy before long.

At some stage during the spring, probably early in June, the first rehearsal for Act 1 of *La finta semplice* took place. It was a disaster, and an intentional one. Leopold, as he later reported to the emperor in a petition or (as he headed it) 'Species facti',[7] had earlier shown the Act 1 arias to three of the principals and obtained their enthusiastic approval ('questa opera anderà alle stelle! è una maraviglia!'—'this opera will make the heavens ring! it's a marvel!'). But there had been no keyboard rehearsals with the singers, as there ought to have been at this stage, to ensure that they knew their parts and understood how the finale ensembles were to go; at the rehearsal, everything, understandably, was confused, in the presence of the orchestra. 'No-one who was present can recall the rehearsal without blushing', Leopold later wrote to the emperor. As a result a number of changes were made, as required by the singers, at Affligio's request. Affligio reassured Leopold and said that, with these relatively minor changes, the opera would be given in four to six weeks' time, soon after the emperor's return. The alterations were duly made, including the composition of two new arias for Act 1. Meanwhile, another opera was running at the theatre. To protect their reputation from the inevitable gossip, Leopold had Wolfgang play over the entire work, at the keyboard, at the house of Baron Gottfried van Swieten, a leading patron of music (later to play an important role in Mozart's career), in the presence of several connoisseurs.

At the end of June, however, it was clear that the situation was no better. 'I could tell you', he wrote to Hagenauer, 'of an oppressive quantity of all sorts of contriving schemers and spiteful persecutions, but I am weary of going over all this in my mind and it will be better to tell you of them in conversation, which will be following shortly'. It was probably in July that yet another opera was put into production. When Leopold complained, Affligio assured him that Wolfgang's would soon follow, but that he had to have other operas in reserve in case Mozart's failed. Leopold, though conscious of the expense of the prolonged stay in Vienna, had to agree. More adjustments were made to some of the arias.

By the end of July he knew he would not, after all, be seeing Hagenauer soon, and was ready to give him a full account. He begins by explaining that his stay in Vienna had to be prolonged for the sake of his and Wolfgang's honour and reputation:

> Would you like everyone in Vienna to say that Wolfgang had not been able to compose an opera? or that it turned out so poorly that it could not be performed? or that he could not write it himself, but his father etc.?

He goes on to explain the limitations of the emperor's control over the theatre in the light of Affligio's financial responsibility, but that on the emperor's instructions Affligio had issued a contract for the opera, for a hundred ducats (or 450 gulden, the usual fee at the time, and nearly a hundred more than Leopold's annual salary). Leopold tells the story:[8]

The opera was to be performed at Easter. But first the poet obstructed this, for on the pretext of making a few necessary changes here and there he kept on postponing, so that by Easter only the first two of the amended arias had been received from him. Then the opera was scheduled for Whitsuntide, and then for the emperor's return from Hungary. At this point, the mask fell from the face.

For in the meantime all the composers, among whom Gluck is a leading figure, undermined everything to prevent the opera's success. The singers were spoken to, the orchestra was stirred up, and every means was used to impede the production of the opera. The singers, who hardly knew a note of it, and some of whom have to learn their parts by ear, were now told to say that their arias were unsingable, even when they had previously heard them in our room and approved and applauded them and said they were suitable for them. The orchestra would now say they did not want to be directed by a boy, and a hundred similar things. Meanwhile, several people spread word that the music wasn't worth a blue devil; others said the music didn't match the words and didn't fit the metre, and that the boy didn't understand enough Italian.

As soon as I heard all this, I demonstrated in the most eminent places that Hasse, the very father of music, and the great Metastasio themselves had made it clear that any slanderers who spread these tales should go to them and hear from their own mouths that thirty operas have been given in Vienna that in no way approach the opera of this boy which both of them marvel at in the highest degree. Then they say that not the boy but the father has written it.

Here again the credit of the slanderers falls. For they go *ab uno extremo ad aliud* [from one extreme to another] and in either case find themselves in hot water. I asked someone to take any part of the works of Metastasio, open the book, and put the first aria he sees in Wolfgang's hands. He took up his pen and wrote, with astonishing speed, in the presence of several people of distinction, the music for the aria with many instruments. He did this at the houses of Kapellmeister Bonno, Abbate Metastasio, Hasse, the Duke of Braganza and Prince Kaunitz. During this time, arrangements were made for another opera, and as no further objections can be raised Wolfgang's will be performed immediately after it.

Soon after he wrote that letter, however, Leopold heard that the copyist had not been given the revised arias to copy. He complained once more to Affligio, to be assured that copying would now begin and rehearsal would start in two weeks' time. But on the very same day the copyist, he discovered, had in fact been instructed to stop work, and a few days later the singers had told Affligio that the opera, although 'composed incomparably well', was untheatrical and could not be performed. After many representations and recriminations, it seems, Affligio warned Leopold that if he insisted on a performance 'he would see to it that the opera would be laughed to scorn and hissed'.

In his letter to Hagenauer Leopold goes on, as we have seen (p. 33), to argue the importance, indeed the sacred duty, of convincing the world, to the greater glory of God, of the 'miracle whom God allowed to be born in Salzburg'. He also explains something of Affligio's complex position in relation to the emperor, Kaunitz and the French company currently playing, not very successfully, in Vienna— they are performing at Kaunitz's wish but Affligio's expense, and no-one is going as the emperor doesn't care to. All of this conspires to 'persuade Affligio to reject little Wolfgang's opera and keep his hundred ducats in his pocket'.

Leopold was indeed faced by a dilemma. If he simply went away it would have seemed like an admission that the opera was inadequate, and if he stayed in hopes of a performance there might be still more humiliation and certainly more expense. The dilemma was in no way lessened by being largely of his own making, because of his excessive and unrealistic ambition—for opera commissions were few and coveted by composers, who could hardly be expected to accept with equanimity the notion of one going to a twelve-year-old from outside Vienna with a pushy father. The Mozarts remained in the city, still hoping that *La finta semplice* would reach the stage, but Affligio's frank warning about a wretched performance and an arranged fiasco brought his hopes to an end. What long-term effects this episode may have had on Mozart's career, and further on his attitudes to his fellow men and fellow composers, can only be conjectured.

The composition of *La finta semplice* had, of course, been Mozart's primary task between, probably, February and April and more sporadically up to June. It was a large score, much larger than any other he had written, amounting to 558 pages. At some stage, probably when it was finished or nearly finished, Mozart wrote another opera, much shorter and slighter, *Bastien und Bastienne*, for private performance. Tradition, going back to Nissen's biography, has it that the work was first given in the garden theatre of the famous medical experimenter, early hypnotist and father of 'animal magnetism' (to be parodied in *Così fan tutte*) Franz Anton Mesmer, himself a keen musician, a tenor, cellist and harpsichordist who also played the glass harmonica. It is in fact doubtful whether the theatre had been built by the summer or autumn of 1768: some years later Leopold Mozart described it in a letter to his wife, which must imply that she had not seen it before. If the work was written for performance *chez* Mesmer, it could have been given in his house at any time in the latter part of 1768.[9] With no prospect now of a Viennese performance of *La finta semplice*, the Mozarts might simply have gone home. But Leopold was too incensed to let the matter drop and during September he drew up his 'Species facti' for submission to the emperor. His account of *La finta semplice*'s suppression, while slightly more sober in tone than the account he had given to Hagenauer, was still deeply indignant. He took care not to mention Joseph's own role in the initiation of the work.

There is no reason to doubt the basic truth of what he says, much of which Joseph could have checked; his interpretation and reporting, however, need to be understood as any evidence in a dispute must be. Joseph did nothing. There is no record of payment of the promised fee, nor of any recompense for Leopold's heavy expenses (which he estimated at 160 ducats, or 720 gulden). But Joseph did find a way of rescuing the Mozarts' honour—the damage to which was characteristically presented as the central issue in Leopold's petition—and sending them home reasonably contented. A new church was to be consecrated shortly at the orphanage (Waisenhaus) in the Rennweg; Wolfgang was invited to provide the music for the ceremony and to direct its performance before the entire court. The Mozarts had earlier met the Jesuit priest there, Father Ignaz Parhammer, who had worked in Salzburg some years before and was confessor to Joseph. This event duly took place on 7 December 1768, in the presence of Maria Theresa and two of the archdukes, Ferdinand and Maximilian. The *Wienerisches Diarium* reported on the general applause and admiration and on Wolfgang's accurate conducting and singing in the motets.[10] His music consisted of a mass, K.139/47a, an offertory and a trumpet concerto (the last for one of the boy pupils at the orphanage to play), but only the mass survives.

The Mozarts set out for home at the end of December and were at Melk Abbey on 28 December, where they were entertained for luncheon and dinner.[11] They passed again through Linz, and must have stopped at the Lambach monastery: there are presentation copies there of symphonies by the Mozarts, father and son, annotated 'Dono authoris 4ta Jan.769'. They arrived home in Salzburg on 5 January 1769, after an absence of sixteen months.

A BY-PRODUCT of Leopold Mozart's anger over *La finta semplice* was a list of compositions, to date, by his son, which he submitted along with the petition. This document, or more probably a copy of the original, remained in Nannerl's possession until 1799, when she sent it to Breitkopf & Härtel to help them sort out the early manuscripts. Unlike many of the documents held by Breitkopf, it survives, and it is now in the Bibliothèque Nationale, Paris.[12] Most but not all of the list can easily be squared with our knowledge of his compositions thus far. The four sets of published sonatas (K.6–15, 26–31) are listed, and the two of variations (K.24 and 25). So are the *Gallimathias* (K.32) and the three Salzburg dramatic works, *Die Schuldigkeit* (K.35), the *Grabmusik* (K.42/35a) and *Apollo et Hyacinthus* (K.38). Leopold says there are fifteen Italian arias, composed partly in London and partly in The Hague, which must imply 'as well as in Salzburg'. We have a total of six—one from London (K.21/19c), three from The Hague (K.23, 78/73b and 79/73d) and two from Salzburg (K.36/33i and 70/61c)—and nine are lost (though one, 'Quel destrier', is identifiable). There are rather more puzzles surrounding his figure of thirteen for the symphonies (discussed below).

The catalogue is a useful tool for stocktaking at this point. Lost works (the Köchel number is given where they are included in the catalogue, which in its successive editions has followed no consistent policy over the inclusion or numbering of lost works) are the Paris *Stabat mater* (K.33c), six four-part divertimentos for various combinations for 'violin, trumpet, horn, flute, bassoon, trombone, viola, cello etc.' (K.41a), six trio sonatas, solos (i.e. sonatas with continuo) for the violin, the cello (K.33b), the viola da gamba and the flute (K.33a), and pieces for trumpets (including processionals, with drums), for horns and for basset-horns (all K.41b), three sets of marches, one each for orchestra, wind band and string group (all K.41c) and minuets for 'all sorts of instruments' (41d). The violin solos however could include two surviving two-movement pieces (K.46d and e), composed in Vienna and dated 1 September 1768, even though they are not of the type usually embraced by the term 'solo'. There are the two books of keyboard pieces—the London Sketchbook (K.15a–15ss) and Nannerl's Music Book—a couple of lost fugues, one for keyboard (K.41e) and one for voices (K.41f), and then the Viennese works—the two operas, *La finta semplice* (K.51/46a) and *Bastien und Bastienne* (K.50/46b), and a group of sacred works, two masses (K.49/47d and 139/47a), the lost offertory (K.47b) and a *Veni Sancte Spiritus* (K.47).

As to the symphonies, most but not all can be firmly identified. The only certain ones from before the Vienna journey are K.16, K.19, K.19a, K.22 and K.45a, with the addition of a lost C major work, probably K.19b; during his time in Vienna Mozart composed K.43, K.45 and K.48. This last postdates Leopold's drawing-up of this list, but so do some of the sacred works, which indicate that he must have supplemented the surviving copy after the original submission in September (though he did not add the trumpet concerto written for the orphanage church, nor a song thought to date from late 1768). There are several other known symphonies that may make up the missing four or five to complete Leopold's thirteen. These include K.45b and the two works known only by their incipits (already mentioned), as well as three more from the Breitkopf catalogue numbered in K³ as 66c, d and e (which Einstein, on the slender basis of their incipits, thought were later), though all these must be clouded by doubts about date and authenticity. There are also the pieces in the London Sketchbook which, as we have seen, could be reductions or first versions of symphonies. Leopold may also have taken into his reckoning some of the overtures to dramatic works.

THE FIRST WORK known to have been written during the Viennese journey of 1767–8 is the Symphony in F K.43. The autograph is in fact dated 'Vienna 1767', but at some stage Leopold also wrote on it 'a Olmutz 1767', though that was later struck out. There is every reason to think that it would first have been heard at the Brünn concert on 30 December 1767. It is written on Salzburg paper so may have been begun at home, or perhaps the Mozarts carried a supply with them. This is the first of his symphonies that needs no kind of apology on account of his youth. It begins with a fanfare-like figure, a cliché of the period, but used here with great spirit and then developed after the first tutti by the basses, below 'scrubbing' violins, to draw the music to the dominant for a lighter, contrasting theme; then follows a rousing and emphatic tutti. The development, with the fanfare theme in the bass, is simply a nine-bar passage heard twice over, the second time a step lower. With a deft use of music from the exposition, in an adjusted order, Mozart leads to the lighter theme (now in the tonic) with every semblance of logic and, to lend it the finality it now needs, he provides a brief extension and a new harmonic, melodic and rhythmic twist. Nothing sounds illogical or irregular about this movement, yet its phrases, including three-bar, five-bar, seven-bar, nine-bar and eleven-bar ones, avoid the fearful symmetry that can so easily deaden the music of lesser composers. The Andante is based on the duet from *Apollo et Hyacinthus*. It is not a direct transcription: the themes are the same but the music is reworked to provide a binary structure suitable to the new context, with a stronger pointing-up of the cadential structure and no ritornello-style repetition, while there are subtle changes to the orchestral texture—the violas, formerly accompanying in slurred pairs of notes, are now staccato, the horns have quite different sustained music (they are horns in C in the opera, in F here, so cannot play the same notes), and a pair of flutes is added, providing a gentle halo to the texture. The movement, following up the manner of that of the Andante of the K.45a symphony, has a fragrant charm of its own. The minuet—this is a four-movement symphony, written for a city where symphonies with minuets were favoured—is short and sturdy, the finale a gigue-like 6/8 movement, a neatly worked-out example of the binary type with witty interplay between first and second violins.

It is hard to imagine that within weeks of writing this polished little masterpiece Mozart would have composed another symphony, in the same key, also in four movements, substantially inferior in imagination and technique. K.76/42a is assigned to this period by many scholars, though later by some and earlier by others.[13] No autograph is known, and the attribution hangs tenuously on a set of manuscript parts passed by Nannerl to Breitkopf and entered as 'Mozart' in their manuscript catalogue. The confusion is symptomatic, for the symphony has little in common with Mozart's music of any date. Its weakness is not as such an argument for its expulsion from the canon, for Mozart could nod, but the first movement's thick, unrelieved wind writing and its often dense string textures, its four-square phrase structures and the discontinuity of its invention are quite uncharacteristic. The pizzicatos of the Andante, again clumsy in its harmonies and rhythms, and the awkward harmonic rhythms of the minuet, speak too against Mozart's authorship; and the finale, with what has been imaginatively identified as an allusion to a Rameau gavotte (from *La temple de la gloire*),[14] is scarcely closer to any authentic example of Mozart's style, at this date or any other. It is a failure of the critical and stylistic aspects of Mozart scholarship that this symphony has not long since been rejected as unauthentic. A case has been argued that the 'Mozart' attribution is correct but that the composer is in fact Leopold Mozart.[15]

The Mozarts were back in Vienna, after the Brünn–Olmütz excursion, on 10 January 1768. Six days later Mozart had another symphony ready, K.45. This, in D, immediately strikes what is already becoming a specific D major manner, using light textures and orchestral figuration of a brilliant and effective type, with ideas of an altogether less thematic character, sharply alternating *piano* and *forte* effects and brief arpeggio-based patterns. The music is effective and vivacious. One tutti closely echoes the opening of K.45a with its tremolando violins above a dotted figure in the basses. For the first time, there are trumpets and drums in the orchestra. Whether the opening movement also ranks as Mozart's first in a symphony in full sonata form is a nice point: there is a 'double return' (tonic key and opening theme), but speedily side-stepped after just one bar of recapitulation. A brief but graceful Andante is followed by a sturdily Viennese minuet, a sonata-form in miniature with attractively extended phrase-lengths to its main theme. The finale, in the rhythm of a contredanse that keeps breaking, gigue-like, into triplets, draws on a traditional contredanse theme that Leopold had quoted in his famous 'Schlittenfahrt' ('Sleighride'); the theme is enterprisingly used in the bass in the tuttis of this light and witty piece. Mozart later adapted this symphony as the overture to *La finta semplice*.

Another symphony that may belong to this period is K.45*b* in B flat, one of the symphonies known only from an incipit in the Breit-kopf catalogue until a rather later set of parts was discovered supporting the attribution (though whether the support was independent is uncertain). There is however no strong reason to question the symphony's authenticity, though its scale is modest and the ascription to the Viennese period is based on little more than the presence of a minuet in a style very like those of K.43 and K.45. Its triple-metre opening movement resembles, rather, that of K.22 (see pp. 104–5): the opening theme is modified to provide the closure of the exposition, and when the rounded binary recapitulation arrives at this point, the opening recurs—but now in its original form, providing a 'reversed recapitulation'. Later, as we shall see, Mozart uses this device a good deal more purposefully and dramatically. Another device used here that was to become much more significant is the famous four-note phrase (in C major, C–D–F–E), most famous from the finale of the 'Jupiter' Symphony K.551, but occurring in several other contexts, such as the K.16 Symphony and the Credos of the K.192 and K.257 masses; here it happens to form a natural bass line to the main secondary theme, and it would be ill-advised to read any greater significance into its appearance. Both the Andante and the finale here are sonata-form movements, the latter an extended and vigorous piece with features (the staggered start to the tutti, the use of chromaticism) that foreshadow Mozart's later modes of thought.

The last of these Viennese symphonies is dated 13 December 1768. If it was written for a concert—and Leopold talks in a letter of their being detained in Vienna for some reason beyond the orphanage ceremony on 7 December—we have no record of it. It would have been a substantial event, for the symphony, K.48 in D, calls for trumpets and drums as well as the usual oboes, horns and strings (oboists could normally play the flute too, and were often asked to use flutes in a slow movement, as for example in K.43). In it Mozart shows he has learnt some Viennese lessons. The first movement, though in D major, is not in the lightish, Italianate vein of K.45, written nearly a year before, but in a more solid manner, with fuller textures, bustling string tuttis (a favourite style in the Gloria and Credo movements of the Viennese masses that Mozart must have heard), and most tellingly of all with a longer development section than he had ever written before and a formal, carefully prepared return of the opening theme. Curiously, however, there is no recapitulation of the main secondary material—a *sine qua non* for sonata form as generally understood. The *galant* device of *Trommelbass* ('drum-bass') with its constant pounding notes from the lower instruments persists virtually unbroken, but this much criticized device sustains a sense of urgency. The Andante's simple surface, an almost childlike violin melody with note-by-note accompaniment, conceals a subtle rhythmic structure, a six-bar theme with a continuation whose overlapping phrases seem to defy conventional parsing. The pompous, rather formal minuet is followed by a strongly directed gigue-style finale with a characteristic mixture of wit and purposefulness, and with a sophisticatedly epigrammatic ending. Mozart's symphonic learning days were over. He was nearly thirteen.

HIS OPERATIC LEARNING DAYS, however, were just beginning. Mozart's first opera for the real operatic world, as opposed to a Salzburg school, was to have been *La finta semplice*, for the main court theatre in Vienna, the Burgtheater. An Italian opera, of course: opera in Vienna at this date meant Italian opera. German opera, or Singspiel, was soon to come into prominence, as we shall later see, but German theatre in the city was at this date confined to broad comedy. Italian opera was the central tradition, going back to the early seventeenth century and had been more or less regularly performed since the time of Leopold I, who had come to the throne in 1658. The Austrian Empire extended, of course, to northern Italy, including Milan and Florence, and Italian composers had been recruited for many years to supply Viennese theatrical music, among them Cesti (composer of the famously spectacular *Il pomo d'oro* of 1668, written to celebrate Leopold I's marriage and to vie with Louis XIV's wedding opera), Antonio Draghi, Antonio Caldara and many more. Italian singers, designers and librettists were also employed by the court, these last including the most eminent and still living in Vienna, Pietro Metastasio.

Metastasio, more than anyone, had created or at least codified the systems of serious opera, lending it a method and a philosophy uniquely suited to the values and the political priorities of the Catholic church and the Habsburg court. Italian opera had been suppressed in Vienna in the 1750s, partly because of its heavy cost, partly because of the political needs of the moment and the inclinations of those in charge of opera, and French opera—modern *opéra comique*, not the great *tragédies* of Rameau and his generation—had enjoyed a brief period of favour, partly under Gluck, which continued up to the mid-1760s. Italian opera had found its way back, but the accession of Joseph II as emperor (of the Holy Roman Empire) and co-regent (of the Austrian Monarchy) in 1764, with authority over the court theatres, had introduced an era of change. Metastasian *opera seria* was no longer much wanted, as representative of an older era and a regime of a kind Joseph did not favour; in any case, its singers and its settings were much more costly than those for *opera buffa*. Some serious operas, notably those of Gluck (which anyway departed radically from the Metastasian model, seeking a more 'enlightened', French-influenced approach) and Hasse, were still given, particularly for court celebrations. In fact, the court theatre poet, Marco Coltellini, who was charged with preparing the libretto for Mozart's opera, had written only one comic work before and otherwise only *opere serie* and *feste teatrali*. He was born in Livorno, became an *abate* but later married (the soprano Celeste Coltellini was his daughter). A disciple of his fellow-Livornese Ranieri de' Calzabigi, Gluck's 'reform' librettist, in 1763 he had written a notable *Ifigenia in Tauride*, markedly French-influenced and in the Gluckian sense progressive, which was successfully set by Tommaso Traetta. Coltellini had worked in Vienna from the early 1760s.

The original libretto of *La finta semplice* had been written by Goldoni for production in Venice in 1764, with music by the little-known Salvatore Perillo. Its model was French, P.N. Destouches' *La fausse Agnès ou Le poète campagnard* (1734). We know little about the process of its composition. For a serious opera, a composer would be required to listen to the singers for whom he was writing and would then draft the principal arias and submit them to the singers for approval, with the understanding that they could be adjusted or rewritten as needed. Operas were written for a series of immediate performances, not for posterity, and a central part of the composer's role was to show the voices to best advantage. This was considerably less exigent a task in comic opera, not only because the music was vocally less florid and less demanding, and less dependent for its effectiveness on the singing as such, but because as much responsibility lay in the management of the comedy to suit the capacities of the company as to exploit the voices.

La finta semplice was not, as we have seen, performed in Vienna. But it was written for a particular Viennese cast, to suit their voices. Their names are shown here, with those of the cast who may have sung the work in Salzburg in 1769 below, indicated by (S):

Rosina, *a Hungarian baroness, sister of Fracasso*	Clementina Poggi (*soprano*) Maria Magdalena Haydn [*née* Lipp] (S)
Don Cassandro, *a rich misogynist*	Francesco Carattoli (*buffo bass*) Joseph Hornung (S)
Don Polidoro, *his younger brother*	Gioacchino Caribaldi (*buffo tenor*) Franz Anton Spitzeder (S)
Giacinta, *their sister*	Teresa Eberhardi (*contralto*) Maria Anna Braunhofer (S)
Ninetta, *their chambermaid*	Antonia Bernasconi (*soprano*) Maria Anna Fesemayr (S)

Fracasso, *captain of a Hungarian troop*	Filippo Laschi (*buffo tenor*)
	Joseph Nikolaus Meissner (S)
Simone, *his sergeant*	Domenico Poggi (*bass*)
	Felix Winter (S)

Instead of composing a new overture to the opera, Mozart used his latest symphony, K.45, which happened to be in an appropriate key and of an appropriate character for an *opera buffa*; he revised three movements, omitting, of course, the minuet. The revisions, presumably made some three months after the original composition, are partly a matter of orchestration: the opera orchestra evidently had flutes and bassoons, but not, at least for this work, trumpets or drums. The musical content is unaltered, but the texture is slightly filled out with extra woodwind, the articulation is made more specific, and in the first movement a couple of extra bars are added to give better point to the main cadences; in the Andante the melody is adjusted so that even notes become dotted rhythms. Many of the changes have to do more with precision of notation (so perhaps designed as an aid to efficient rehearsal in the opera house) rather than musical content.

The plot is of a familiar Goldonian type, drawing on *commedia dell'arte* traditions, with the lively young people outwitting the stupid or older ones so that the right pairs of lovers are finally united. Here the protagonist, Rosina, the 'feigned simpleton' of the title, exercises her wiles in the household of the rich brothers Cassandro and Polidoro, the one misogynistic, dominant and good-looking, the other timid and inept, to secure Cassandro for herself and their sister Giacinta for her soldier brother Fracasso, who is billeted on them; she also makes possible the marriage of the servants, which the brothers had forbidden.

Mozart's first Italian opera is, essentially, written in the *opera buffa* style of the day, the manner of such composers as Giovanni Paisiello or Niccolò Piccinni. The arias are lightly scored (especially those for the servants and the other secondary characters) and nearly all are fairly brief, with touches of sentiment, especially in the amorous music for the central characters. A good number of lively arias on such standard topics as the war of the sexes, masters and servants, food and drink, money, military matters and the like are mostly set in predictable fashion: they include graceful minuet arias for the ladies (two for Ninetta); a vigorous 6/8 tirade against marriage; a drunken song for Cassandro, with three- and four-bar phrases tumbling over one another (this is the main *basso buffo* role, the centre of the opera's comic interest); and for Simone (the secondary *basso buffo*) plenty of rapid articulation, as well as a touch of sentiment in his final aria, as he comes to take love more seriously. For Polidoro's first aria Mozart plundered *Die Schuldigkeit*: to music originally composed for the Christian Spirit, Polidoro sings of the confusion that women arouse in him; the aria's sustained and more serious manner is perhaps not quite of a piece with the rest of *La finta semplice*, even allowing for the characterization it is presumably intended to bear. Polidoro's role is more lyrical than that for the other tenor, Fracasso (sung by the father of the singer who was later to create the Countess in *Le nozze di Figaro*). He has short arias in the first two acts—Mozart rewrote the first, replacing what was a striking two-tempo aria with a much simpler setting—but ends with the most extended aria in the opera, a swaggering military piece in *opera seria* style, with a middle section in minuet tempo (added, doubtless at Laschi's request to the original single-tempo version). That aria is a response to Giacinta's final one, a C minor outburst (the only minor-key number) with dramatic tremolandos, forceful accents and rushing scales in the orchestra portraying her panic. But the fullest musical characterization is reserved for Rosina. Two of her arias present her as a simpleton, but the two central ones say more: 'Senti l'eco', in E flat and almost a traditional *aria d'affetto*, is an Andante un poco adagio with a minuet-like middle section, using a solo oboe (to sound the echoes) and two English horns in accompaniment, with sweetly murmuring violins at her word 'sussurrar'; the E major 'Amoretti' also incorporates orchestral murmurs, this time violins and bassoons, with textures softened by divided violas and violin triplets portraying the flying Cupids of the text.

There are numbers in *La finta semplice* where Mozart is apt to fall into pattern-making in the accompaniments and routine repetition of figuration, but many too where there are artfully devised textures to indicate something of the character or the sense—the delicate flute writing and the high viola part, for example, in Giacinta's 'Se a maritarmi arrivo', or the interweaving of violins and divided violas in Fracasso's 'In voi belle'. And already Mozart uses, several times (and notably in 'Senti l'eco'), a device that he later developed individually and tellingly: when, in a recapitulated section, the music lies in a different register and cannot be literally repeated, he devises a new phrase, different in contour yet unmistakably recapitulatory and at the same time expressively heightened.

It was Goldoni, especially when working with his chief collaborator, Baldassare Galuppi, who is primarily responsible for the development of the 'chain finale' in *opera buffa*—an 'action ensemble' in which a series of movements, usually in different keys, different tempos and different metres, allied to a changing verse structure, reflects events on the stage. Here the action ensemble begins, in D, 2/4, and as a rather slow Allegro, when Rosina expresses her shock at Polidoro's approaching her room (she is supported by Fracasso, with Ninetta). When Cassandro enters the music moves to G, and a faster 3/8, with shorter lines of verse; he pours scorn on his brother. Now the tempo changes to Andante, the metre back to 2/4, the key to C and then to G, and the verse to seven-syllable lines, as Polidoro offers Rosina a gift. Rosina asks Cassandro for his ring as a token of affection, and he gives it to her as the music stabilizes for a cadence in G. As Simone enters the verse reverts to short lines, the rhythm to 3/8, and the tempo accelerates. Cassandro, to keep control of his ring, invites all present to a meal with him and, as the music moves to the home key of D and the verse reverts to longer lines, all sing their acceptance. The shorter second finale, largely in G major, the key in which the act began, uses alternating patterns of metre, 2/4 and 3/8, before settling to an ensemble in 3/4. The third finale opens in G major with a duet, in 2/4 and then 3/8, for Rosina and Polidoro, which Cassandro interrupts to an acceleration of tempo. Their trio reaches a climax as the music moves to D, and the rest of the cast enter in a 3/8 Allegro. Then as Giacinta and Ninetta, who had taken flight with the brothers' riches, plead for forgiveness and to be permitted to marry their lovers, the tempo changes to Un poco adagio, the metre to 3/4 and the key to G—a typical softening in such a situation. Cassandro agrees, and now Rosina, in an Andantino in A major, again in 3/4, tells him of her love. The *finta semplice* is revealed: the brothers accept the situation in a 2/4 Allegro, and all celebrate in a lively 3/8.

The techniques here described are not, of course, Mozart's personal invention. They are standard ones, used in *opera buffa* during the 1760s across most of Europe. Comparing them with those he applied in, for example, *Le nozze di Figaro* is in itself without meaning; both require a context in practices of their time if we are to understand Mozart's individuality and his particular powers of expression. *Opera buffa* itself changed hugely over the eighteen years that separate these works, although many of these techniques remained a part of the composer's expressive repertory and indeed came to be used in increasingly complex, subtle and adventurous ways. *La finta semplice* is a fairly typical *opera buffa* of its time, perhaps unsurely proportioned, in some respects too elaborately composed, probably not ideally written for its singers, and certainly not always a comfortable setting of the Italian text. It might well have provided Mozart with a humiliating failure had it been produced in such a city as Vienna and found to be doubtfully suited to the singers and theatrically ineffective. Certainly the weak, perfunctory endings to several arias that Mozart revised and some of the inferior discarded versions of others show a composer with a half-formed theatrical technique. It does Mozart's genius no service if we unthinkingly join Leopold in his vociferous protests against what may have been well-judged criticism and sensible deferment of his son's Viennese operatic début, painful and costly though the experience must have been.

Mozart did in fact have an opera staged in Vienna in 1768, *Bastien und Bastienne,* but not in a public theatre.[16] The origins of the libretto used by Mozart lie in a pastoral *intermède* by Jean-Jacques Rousseau, *Le devin du village*, given at Fontainebleau in 1752 and Paris early the next year. This work arose out of Rousseau's championship of Italian *opera buffa* against the courtly French tradition, and did much to establish *opéra comique* as well as its preoccupation with rustic virtue as opposed to aristocratic corruption. It was quickly parodied for the popular theatre, with a tougher and more realistic tone, by the Favarts, Charles-Simon and his wife Marie-Justine-Benoîte, and Harney de Guerville, under the title *Les amours de Bastienne et Bastien*, given in September 1753 at the Comédie-Italienne. During the ascendancy of French *opéra comique* in Vienna in the 1750s it was heard there, and in 1764 a German version was prepared by Friedrich Wilhelm Weiskern, a comic actor and writer at the Kärntnertortheater (which, of the two court theatres, put on the more popular pieces). Johann Heinrich Friedrich Müller provided texts for three numbers (nos. 11–13). Rousseau's version had fourteen lyrical numbers. The parody had many more, as there was no recitative. In the German version, there was spoken dialogue and the number of lyrical pieces happens again to be fourteen (their correspondence with the original is not exact).

There were no real models for light German opera in Vienna or southern Germany, although one was beginning to develop in the north. A popular tradition of comic plays existed, a Viennese reinterpretation of the *commedia dell'arte* with such characters as Bernardon (the creation of the dramatist and singer Joseph Felix von Kurz) and Hanswurst. Some of the songs for such plays from the 1750s survive in a collection under the title *Teutsche Comoedie Arien*.[17] Weiskern's texts for the songs in *Bastien und Bastienne*, translations from the loosely structured, parodied French version and new texts of his own, follow the traditions of the *Teutsche Comoedie Arien*, with their predominance of arias and their varied verse structures,[18] and lack the implications for musical form of Italian verse of the time, or indeed French *opéra comique* verse. They tend to be long and conversational in style (half the arias have more than the conventional two quat-

rains), in a way that precludes or inhibits more formal musical treatment, as well as irregular in metre. The manner of the *Teutsche
Comoedie Arien*, which are mostly through-composed with little or
no musical repetition, may have provided Mozart with a model, if
one was not already implicit in the words he had to set. The work is
written for a modest orchestra of strings, with oboes (or flutes) and
horns, and a cast of three—the lovers Bastienne, a shepherdess
(soprano; in Rousseau, Colette), and Bastien (tenor; Colin), whose tiff
is settled by Colas (bass), the village soothsayer or 'cunning-man' (to
use the title of Charles Burney's English version), who advises Bastienne to feign indifference. As the brevity of the arias and the unam-
bitious nature of the solo parts show, with much conjunct writing for
the lovers and no coloratura, Mozart must have had amateur performers in mind, or perhaps a youthful cast such as those of a travelling company or of the kind for which *Apollo et Hyacinthus* had been
composed.

Bastien und Bastienne begins with a brief, monothematic 'intrada' in
G major, on a phrase whose resemblance to the main theme of the
first movement of Beethoven's 'Eroica' Symphony is bound to strike
the modern listener. Bastienne is musically the best served of the
characters, with five arias, of which four are in two tempos; Bastien
and Colas have only single-tempo arias, three and two respectively.
The lovers share one aria, taking stanzas in turn. Several numbers are
firmly anchored to almost exclusively four-bar phrases. These are
generally settings of new words by Weiskern rather than translated
texts, and in the case of the early numbers for Bastienne may be an
attempt to convey an image of rustic simplicity, as may the prevalence
of moderate tempos and a 3/4 metre. Faced, however, with the
uneven metric structure of a text designed to accommodate existing
music (set to a different language), Mozart often shows considerable
ingenuity in devising rhythmic patterns that bring coherence to the
setting and effectively vary the pace of the words and the musical
phrase structure,[19] although at several points his setting matches
accent and stress uncertainly. Few of the arias possess a formal struc-

ture, even to the degree of a phrase of recapitulation or an echoed cadence, which is apt to lend the music a certain looseness; only Colas's first aria and the last for each of the lovers (a full modified ternary for Bastienne) involves the recurrence of thematic material. Colas's second aria is a mock incantation of the powers of darkness, in C minor, with tremolando strings and nonsense words. The duets are essentially settings of dialogue, and largely unstructured, though the final one, a lovers' tiff and reconciliation, is an impressive piece of rhetoric. The opening is largely dialogue, as accusations are exchanged (with skilful use of modulation, especially to the minor, to reflect the sense). When an agreement to disagree is reached, the voices are together; they then exchange apologies separately, and finally join for a full reconciliation, in the traditional manner of love duets. The opera ends with a terzet, in two tempos, each beginning in D major but 'recapitulated' in G, the home key of the opera.

The Mozarts' Salzburg friend J.A. Schachtner is usually cited along with Weiskern and Müller as an author of the text of *Bastien und Bastienne*. It had long been thought that Mozart might have begun the composition in Salzburg, for in 1766 the Berner children's theatre troupe had visited the city and they had in their repertory the Favart version, translated by Weiskern and with extra music by J.B. Savio. Had Mozart decided to set it then, Schachtner might have played a part in the preparation of the libretto. But the existence of a copy of Mozart's opera showing only Weiskern's text, and the recent rediscovery of the autograph, on which it can be seen that the revisions to accommodate Schachtner's changes represent a second layer of work (and it is anyway written on Viennese paper), have made it clear that it was the Weiskern-Müller text, with spoken dialogue, that Mozart initially set.[20] Only after the Mozarts' return to Salzburg at the beginning of 1769 did Schachtner work on the opera, adjusting the text in various ways and versifying the dialogue so that Mozart could convert it into recitative. Whether it was performed at Salzburg in that form is unknown, but it seems unlikely that the work of altering it would have been undertaken unless a performance had been in prospect, although Mozart's incomplete setting of Schachter's recitatives may indicate that the project was abandoned.

A small by-product of *Bastien und Bastienne* is a song entitled 'Daphne, deine Rosenwangen' K.52/46c. This is merely an arrangement by Leopold of Bastien's aria, no. 11, 'Meine Liebsten schöne Wangen', with keyboard accompaniment; on ten-staff manuscript paper, it will have been made in Salzburg, probably in 1769. There are two other secular vocal items with little more call on our attention. One is a fragmentary duet of 31 bars for two sopranos with no accompanying part, 'Ach, was müssen wir erfahren!' K.Anh.24a/43a, with words continuing 'Wie? Josepha lebt nicht mehr!', suggesting that the piece would have been written, perhaps for Nannerl and Wolfgang, on the archduchess's death, to be accompanied by Wolfgang himself. The other, 'An die Freude' K.53/47e (K³.47c), was for a time imagined to be the song written for the daughter of the Olmütz doctor who saw Wolfgang through smallpox, but as it is a setting of words by Johann Peter Uz, published only in 1768, that is unlikely, unless Mozart somehow obtained the text earlier. More probably it was written some time later in 1768; it was printed, along with 'Daphne, deine Rosenwagen', in a collection *Neue Sammlung zum Vergnügen und Unterricht* issued in Vienna by Rudolf Gräffer at the end of the year. (The suggestion that the recently rediscovered 'Cara, se le mie pene' may have been the piece for the doctor's daughter may also be ruled out, on the grounds that Mozart is hardly likely to have composed for her an Italian coloratura aria in full *da capo* form requiring strings and horns.) There are also two brief, two-movement works dated 1 September 1768 and usually classified as sonatas for violin and bass, K.46d in C and K.46e in F. Each consists of a short Allegro (20 and 24 bars respectively) followed by a pair of minuets. The autographs bear corrections in Leopold's hand. The style and especially the texture of the lower part imply that they are duets for violin and cello rather than violin sonatas; neither is particularly appealing and the first is rather clumsily written, though not inferior to the generality of such pieces. Presumably they were composed for some particular purpose.

The remaining Viennese works of 1768 are sacred music. The *Veni Sancte Spiritus* K.47, mentioned in Leopold's list, is a jubilant choral setting with trumpets and drums in C major, the first movement a vigorous 3/4 Allegro, beginning with a rising arpeggio figure on the violins; the style is homophonic, with a few brief and simple imitative points. It breaks into 2/4 and Presto for the 'Alleluia', which has some powerful unison exclamations and short paired solo passages for the upper, then the lower, voices. It would be a curious piece to have been written without reason: perhaps it was heard in a Viennese church during 1768.

The *Missa brevis* in G K.49/47*a*, too, was presumably more than an exercise. It is a short setting, of the type used for ordinary Sunday celebration of the Mass in churches possessed of a choir and string orchestra, as opposed to the *missa longa* or *missa solemnis* for a feast day, a more extended 'cantata' setting with each section broken up into several separate movements. Clearly a prentice work, its interest is modest. The words are hastily despatched in a largely homophonic and often four-square setting, against violin figuration or repeated notes, and the conventional requirements of the Austrian tradition are observed—fugal endings to the Gloria (on a theme drawn from its opening) and the Credo, a slowing-down and refinement at the 'Et incarnatus', and (more Mozart's common preference than a firm tradition) a Benedictus assigned to the soloists. There is one solo aria, a setting for bass of 'Et in Spiritum Sanctum'.

When it came to the commission for a mass on the consecration of the Waisenhauskirche, the orphanage church in the Rennweg, Mozart was clearly on his mettle, particularly in view of the prestige he had to recover after the incidents surrounding *La finta semplice*. The identity of the mass written for the occasion has been a matter of dispute, particularly since Köchel dated the C minor work (numbered K.139) to the end of 1772 and Einstein, initially, to about a year earlier (numbered 114*a* in K³), so the *Waisenhaus-Messe* was assumed to be lost. In fact, the paper used for K.139 was bought in Vienna in 1768: one of the paper-types appearing in it was used in *Bastien und Bastienne* and another in a replacement aria in *La finta semplice*.²¹ A dating of between autumn 1768 and mid-1769 (as in the NMA) may be duly cautious, but the circumstantial evidence in favour of the identification of this grandly ceremonial piece as the *Waisenhaus-Messe*, and justifying its K⁶ number of 47*a*, is now overwhelming.

Always listed as a C minor mass, it is in reality and in its expressive world a C major one, and indeed the use of four trumpets (two of them specified as 'clarini', the term used for high trumpet parts) puts beyond doubt its festive and ceremonial nature. It begins with twelve bars, Adagio, of C minor, solemn choral exclamations alternating with gestures on the violins and trombones, but then plunges, or leaps, into a C major Kyrie, Allegro, in energetic triple metre, as jubilant as the occasion of its première called for. There is a 'Christe eleison', slower and in F major, for the soloists, and a *da capo* of the 'Kyrie eleison'. In the Gloria, choruses alternate with solo numbers: an imposing C major Allegro with busy violins is followed by a graceful 'Laudamus te' for the two upper voices, an imposing 'Gratias' for chorus by a 'Domine Deus' for the tenor and bass, and an Adagio 'Qui tollis' in a sustained F minor by a vivacious 'Quoniam' for soprano. Finally comes a fugue on 'Cum Sancto Spiritu'—not merely a fugal exposition as had served in K.49, but a fully worked out, academic one, of the kind favoured in the Salzburg tradition, with a countersubject, middle entries in the proper range of keys, a four-voice stretto and a dominant pedal. The Credo begins with an extended choral statement of the opening lines, in a vigorous C major, which breaks off for a duet setting, an Andante for soprano and alto of 'Et incarnatus est'; the 'Crucifixus', in C minor, is introduced with subdued fanfares on muted trumpets, a favoured effect in Viennese church music but also one used in Leopold Mozart's Mass in C (Seiffert 4.1, clearly one of Wolfgang's models for K.139), and the 'Et resurrexit' borrows even more obviously from Leopold's, beginning with a dramatic, rising running passage for solo voice before the choir enters. The Credo ends with another fugue on 'Et vitam venturi', a double fugue, rather less formally worked out but still embodying some stretto treatment. The Benedictus takes an unusual form, with a solo soprano phrase followed, each time, by choral Hosannas. While the opening of the Agnus Dei is set in C minor, for tenor with a solo alto trombone, a spirited 'Dona nobis pacem' in C major, an Allegro in 3/4, ends this festive mass as the Kyrie began it. Its triumphal notes must have had a special resonance in the Mozart family's ears as they left for Salzburg at the end of their difficult year in the imperial capital.

8

Salzburg, 1769

FTER THE MOZARTS REACHED home in January 1769, they spent most of the year in Salzburg. But Leopold had long been intending to take his children to Italy and had already begun to lay plans, with the intention of leaving in October, possibly even earlier, though in the event they were at home until December.[1] As we have seen, information on their activities when they were at home is thin. Leopold returned to his duties at court. He petitioned for the restoration of some of his docked salary on the grounds that the family was delayed in Vienna against his will and to his disadvantage, pleading moreover that he and his son had composed music for the church, and in particular for use in the cathedral. In March he was paid for January and February when, but for a few days, he had anyway been present.[2]

We do not know what music Leopold was referring to as composed for the cathedral: perhaps there are works now lost, or perhaps he was alluding to music written in Vienna and now given in Salzburg. But possibly one of the works in his mind was Wolfgang's newest mass setting, K.65/61a, a *missa brevis* in D minor, completed on 14 January. It is usually supposed that this was the work heard at

Salzburg Cathedral: oil painting on wood by Karl Schneeweiss, 1790. (*Museum Carolino Augusteum, Salzburg/ akg-images*)

the collegiate (university) church, in the archbishop's presence, on 5 February, at the beginning of a forty-hour prayer, but that occasion may have required a larger-scale, *solemnis* setting, in which case Mozart's K.139 mass could have been the one used, or possibly some other work that has not survived.[3]

Leopold must also have asked that a hearing should be allowed to the unperformed *La finta semplice*, and this was granted, at least in principle. A libretto was printed, showing the cast (listed above, pp. 150–51) and stating that the work was being given by order of the archbishop. It has generally been assumed that the performance took place on 1 May 1769, the archbishop's nameday, but as Schrattenbach was away at the time that is unlikely. Furthermore, no firm evidence of any performance, from court records, diaries or elsewhere, has ever come to light, and although it has been widely accepted that Mozart was awarded the consolation prize of a Salzburg performance there can be no certainty that one actually took place. If it did, it could well have been in concert form rather than fully staged. The cast, all local

St Peter's Abbey, Salzburg: engraving by S.I. Klauber after F.X. Kinnig, 1772
(*Mozart-Gedenkstätte, Augsburg*)

singers, would hardly have provided a performance on the level
Mozart could have expected from the Italian opera-house singers in
Vienna.

Mozart himself, we may suppose, returned to some kind of educational activities under his father's supervision. Now thirteen, he had
as yet no formal standing as a court musician, but he played the violin in at least some court performances and clearly he was ready to
write music as required. He was also used by the secular arm, specifically the university and the Gymnasium.

As we have already seen (p. 7), the university end-of-year ceremonies in Salzburg involved performances of what was locally
known as Finalmusik.[4] The composition of instrumental serenades
flourished at several courts in southern Germany and Austria, in particular those at Munich, Regensburg and Wallerstein. Each centre had

its own traditions, arising from local ceremonial and social circumstances. The principal tradition in Salzburg was based on the university. Since the 1740s, perhaps going back still earlier, and up to at least the mid-1780s, each of the two university philosophical faculties, the Logic class and the Physic (or natural sciences) class, performed a large-scale orchestral serenade in August to celebrate the end of the academic year. The works were played by an orchestra of students, with other local musicians, first for the archbishop at his summer palace, the Mirabell, then the other side of the river, outside the university, to honour the professors (the archbishop's precedence of rank demanded that he be serenaded first). The marches associated with the individual serenades were used for processing to and from each site or were played on arrival and before departure. Playing marches on the move presents obvious difficulties with some of the instruments, though cellos were not normally included in the Salzburg serenade orchestra. In one of Mozart's first works of this type, K.99, the music of the last movement leads direct into a *da capo* of the march, perhaps indicating that the marches were simply used to round off the performance and had nothing to do with actual marching. Leopold Mozart, according to the report published by Marpurg in 1757, had written as many as thirty such 'grand serenades, in which are introduced solos for various instruments'. Other composers who contributed to the repertory include Michael Haydn and Joseph Hafeneder.

Often, it seems, Finalmusik serenades were freshly commissioned and paid for by students from prominent local families or the families themselves. Earlier examples may simply have been made up from pre-existing works. Concerto-type music, with 'solos for various instruments', were popular in the earlier decades, and by the time Mozart was old enough to be composing Finalmusik, some movements were purely orchestral and others were in a concerto-like style. These Finalmusik performances were not, of course, the only serenade-type performances in Salzburg; the local nobility often commissioned serenades, or smaller-scale divertimentos of a similar character, for their private entertainments. But the local tradition of works in six or more movements, with some of them in concerto style, also affected works for use outside the university.

Mozart's first serenade-type works for the university were written in the summer of 1769. He and his father used the title 'Cassation' for some of these works, a term used in Austrian and southern Germany and generally thought to derive from 'Gasse', a street or alley, and 'gassaten', 'to prowl the streets'; it was thus a piece for playing out of doors and possibly on the move. One was provided for the Logic class, one for the Physic class: the performances, reported as 'ab adolescentulo lectissimo Wolfg. Mozart' ('by the most learned youngster . . .') and 'ab eodem adolescentulo facta' ('done by the same youngster') in the minutes of the Gymnasium, were on 6 and 8 August respectively, and were noted too by Cajetan Hagenauer, the son of the family's landlord, in his diary.[5] It would be guesswork to assign any one of the works from this period specifically to either occasion. We know only that Mozart composed two works in six movements, the Cassations K.63 in G and K.99/63a in B flat, and one in eight, the Serenade or Cassation in D K.100/62a, each with an associated march. (There is no certain evidence that K.100, whose march has a separate K. number, 62, was written before 1770, although Mozart's handwriting suggests 1769; he listed the incipits of all three in a letter of 4 August 1770 to Nannerl, apparently in response to a query.[6] A reference in a letter of Leopold's two years later to Wolfgang's 'little Cassation in C' has led to speculation that there was a fourth work, now lost. Of course, Leopold may have erred over the key, or the work might have been composed at some other date.[7]

Later in 1769 Mozart wrote two shorter church works, possibly for use at the cathedral. A further mass followed in the autumn, given on 15 October at St Peter's for the first celebration of Mass by Cajetan Hagenauer, who had taken holy orders and was now Father Dominic (hence the *Dominicus-Messe* K.66). Hagenauer recorded in his diary that afterwards Mozart played the organ for half-an-hour to 'to everyone's amazement'; and the next day, when the mass was repeated at the Nonnberg church, Hagenauer entertained the local ecclesiastical establishment to dinner at the house he owned in the Nonntal district of Salzburg, at which Mozart played and sang in a concert organized by his father.[8]

In October, the Mozarts were given permission to go to Italy and, more than that, they were given a financial allowance for doing so, 120 ducats or 600 gulden. This seems generous, but it had long been a tradition that noblemen would pay for their employees to travel, especially when it could be expected to result in the improvement of their professional skills. No doubt Leopold's earlier restraint was now reaping its reward. Furthermore, in November Mozart was formally appointed 'Concert-Maister' at the court, with no salary as yet but a promise of one on his return. The title covered a variety of possible roles, and a court the size of Salzburg's would employ more than one musician with this title. The leading violinist would be entitled 'Konzertmeister', and so too would a keyboard player who (by himself or in conjunction with the violinist) directed performances. Mozart was sufficiently accomplished on both instruments to undertake either of those roles, but the evidence suggests that at this stage he mainly played the violin in the Salzburg orchestra. From this time onwards, his name appears in the annual listing of the Hofkapelle; in the 1770 edition it is found in the Konzertmeister list alongside those of Ferdinand Seidl and Michael Haydn.[9]

IF MOZART'S TREATMENT of the Mass text seems perfunctory in such *missa brevis* settings as K.65, it should be realized that he was subject to severe constraints over the time allowed for a Mass in Salzburg Cathedral. Later, in a famous letter to Padre Martini,[10] his complaints about these constraints may seem to imply that they were connected with the warmly hated Hieronymus Colloredo, who had become archbishop in 1772, but they existed earlier too. In the present mass, intended for use in Salzburg and accordingly more compressed even than the brief K.49 setting, the entire Kyrie is 40 bars long, a direct, homophonic setting (making, incidentally, occasional use of a violin

figure that must have stuck in his mind from the Kyrie of K.139/47d),
and the Gloria, with its lengthy text, has fewer than 50 bars of music,
including a fugal exposition on 'Cum Sancto Spiritu'. In the Credo
the text is telescoped further with overlapping phrases for the solo
voices, a procedure traditionally discouraged by the church, but there
is an Adagio setting of 'Et incarnatus' and a fugal exposition at 'Et
vitam venturi'. Some of the most carefully worked music in what is
one of Mozart's simplest mass settings comes in the Benedictus. The
survival of three drafts[11] affords a glimpse into Mozart's workshop—
his first two versions, for four soloists and then soprano alone, are very
brief (nine and eight bars respectively), and in the first he misman-
ages the key (it needs to move from G minor to the dominant of D
minor for the *da capo* of the Hosanna). He then embarked on a duet
version for soprano and alto, in 13 bars, which he finally elaborated,
adding an accompaniment figure that echoes phrases in the 'Et vitam
venturi' fugue and the accompaniment of the Sanctus and another
foreshadowing a phrase in the Agnus. These may be fortuitous, or
unconscious reminiscences, or deliberate: such things happen from
time to time in Mozart's works. The mass is scored for strings without violas, which were not normally used in the cathedral, with three
trombones doubling the lower voices, in the accepted practice in
Salzburg and elsewhere.

The 'Dominicus Mass' is on an altogether different scale, a substantial and spaciously written *missa solemnis* in the festive key of C major.
Mozart wrote the score in the first place with clarino trumpets and
strings, but then he and Leopold prepared additional parts, before the
first performance, for oboes (doubling flutes), horns, ordinary trumpets and timpani. The solemn twelve-bar introduction that proclaims
its scale leads to a brilliant, binary Allegro in triple metre, a 'Kyrie
eleison' with the 'Christe eleison' beginning at the middle point in
the formal scheme, and a secondary theme for the soloists in longer
notes with an accompaniment in what is now the rhythm of a Viennese waltz. The Gloria has seven movements, choral and solo in alternation. Of the latter the most original is the 'Laudamus te', in the

manner of a symphony slow movement for flutes and strings that would seem virtually complete in itself without the almost incidental contributions from the soprano and alto; there is a nobly impressive G minor 'Qui tollis', with a string ostinato phrase (akin to that of the Agnus Dei of the *Requiem*) heard against solemn, homophonic declamation from the chorus, and a fugal 'Cum Sancto Spiritu' on a typically austere, academic subject, duly worked out. In the Credo, also in seven sections, Mozart sets the 'Et incarnatus est' as a graceful Adagio for the soloists, making the usual gesture towards wonderment at the mystery of the incarnation but without imbuing it with any deeper expression. His scope at this stage did however extend to an impressively sombre C minor 'Crucifixus', beginning starkly with the choir in bare octaves, and with muttering trumpets and ostinato strings—a strong piece of musical imagery, matched by the vivid rising scales of the 'Et resurrexit', although this is in fact a recapitulation of the music of the 'Patrem omnipotentem'. The 'Et vitam' fugue makes less obeisance to the academic manner, with no pedal or stretto. The Austrian 'rushing violins' are heard briefly at the beginning of the Gloria, the kind of movement in which they typically appear; here, unusually, they are busy again in the Benedictus, accompanying the quartet of soloists.

Of the two shorter sacred works of 1769, the offertory *Benedictus sit Deus* K.117/66a has been claimed as the lost offertory written in 1768 for the Waisenhauskirche and, more plausibly, as the offertory for Father Dominicus's first celebration. It is written on Salzburg paper, the same paper as Mozart used for most of his other works of this period.[12] It is akin to a small symphony, with its three fairly short movements—two choral ones embracing a slower soprano aria in F major with flutes and horns. In the final chorus the voices declaim a line of their words to a psalm-tone (in turn trebles, tenors, basses and altos), accompanied only by rushing figuration, a device Mozart probably drew from a motet of his father's, *Convertentur sedentes*. For the *Te Deum*, a setting by Michael Haydn written in Grosswardein in 1760 provided a close model.[13] Michael Haydn was one of the composers—others were Eberlin and Georg Reutter, and of course his own father—whose works, especially for the church, Mozart spent time copying, at many stages in his career and well into his mature years. In times when music was not available in score for study, this was a normal step on the way to technical polish (it has incidentally led in the past to several misattributions). The *Te Deum* is a vigorous piece, with clarinos, trumpets, timpani and strings. The imposing first movement, in choral homophony with bold gestures in the violin part, is followed after a brief Adagio by a 3/4 Allegro and then a dou-

Michael Haydn: engraving by J.F. Schröter the elder (*Mozart-Gedenkstätte, Augsburg*)

ble fugue, worked out at some length while the violins busy themselves with running passage-work; the stretto that threatens turns
soon to homophony and a jubilant ending.

The three serenades, two of which certainly come from the summer months, belong in the Salzburg Finalmusik tradition. A specific
style came to develop for this type of work, close to that of the symphony but lighter and freer in texture and thematic material, and
more four-square in its themes, with, at least at this stage, shorter
movements, little thematic working and generally more exact recapitulations. The slow movements tended to be largely melodic, with
a 'sentimental' (in the eighteenth-century sense) tinge to the line and
often with a softly textured accompaniment, and the minuets sturdy
and regular in rhythm. Most serenades included movements in concerto style; otherwise, between the fast outer movements, minuets
(with one trio or two) generally alternated with slower movements.
The plans of the three 1769 works are shown in the following table:

K.63	K.99/63a	K.100/62a
March	March	March K.62
1 Allegro	1 Allegro molto	1 Allegro
2 Andante	2 Andante	2 Andante★
3 Menuet	3 Menuet	3 Menuetto★
4 Adagio★	4 Andante	4 Allegro★
5 Menuet	5 Menuet	5 Menuetto
6 Allegro assai	6 Allegro/Andante	6 Andante
March	March	7 Menuetto
		8 Allegro
		March

★ With solo music

In numbering Mozart's works, Köchel reckoned the march as part
of the work in the first two cassations, although this represents a difference in the sources rather than any generic distinction. All

Mozart's later orchestral serenades are in D major, an ideal key, at least in Mozart's mind and his father's, for the kinds of orchestral writing, usually with trumpets and drums, apt to these occasions. K.100 is in D, but K.63 is in G and K.99 in B flat. These last two are scored with oboes, horns and strings, with the slow movements mostly for strings alone—the first of K.63 is a melodious Andante with pizzicato accompaniment, the second an Adagio exquisitely scored for solo violin, initially with a throbbing accompaniment on muted violins supported by sustained, divided violas, though the texture simplifies as the solo part grows more dramatic. The minuet between them is in strict canon, the bass following the first violins a bar later (there are examples of similar procedures by Joseph Haydn and others). The finale reverts to the 'hunting' rhythms of the earliest symphonies. The first movement of K.99 is more energetically argued; in the Andante Mozart again establishes an appealing texture, this time with flowing inner strings, muted, above a pizzicato bass, in support of an expressive melody above. Here the finale, initially a 2/4 Allegro, subsides into a slower tempo and 6/8 for its secondary material, and the popular nature of the 6/8 theme suggests that it may have been familiar to Mozart's audience.

The greater length and more elaborate character of K.100, with its scoring for trumpets and possibly drums and its attendant march K.62, hint at a different kind of occasion for the work's genesis. The march, marked 'Maestoso', is double the length of the other two and with its crisp military rhythms has an air of pomp absent from the others. Mozart used it the following year in his Milan opera *Mitridate*. The first movement, with its typical D major brilliance, has nothing that could be called a theme, but it is nevertheless effectively written. The next three movements demonstrate the beginnings of the concerto within a serenade. The Andante has prominent parts, though not in full concerto style, for a solo oboe and solo horn, including joint cadenzas at the close of each half; in the trio of the first minuet they again have solo passages. The Allegro that follows is a true concerto movement, on a miniature scale, with an opening ritornello.

This scheme—a fast movement and a slow movement, and a minuet with solo writing in the trio—was to become Mozart's standard one for a concerto within a serenade. In the second slow movement he again exploits the delicate textures offered by muted strings, this time with flutes and pizzicato basses. The finale is an extended 3/8 rondo, much in the manner of the early symphonies.

The only other music that can be firmly ascribed to 1769 is a set of minuets, composed at the beginning of the year (26 January, the eve of his birthday), for two violins and bass, K.65a/61b: intended for actual dancing, they necessarily conform to a fairly rigid rhythmic structure, usually in eight- or sixteen-bar sections. Characteristically, Mozart had already found ways of creating variety within them, with the occasional offbeat accent or unexpected melodic turn.

QUESTIONS ABOUT THE DATE of composition of certain of Mozart's works have already arisen several times and will do so again, so it may be useful to outline some of the problems of chronology and some of the solutions that have been found.

Many of Mozart's works are easy to date. Often, specific works can be linked with documented events in his life, and in many cases the surviving autographs are dated—rarely by Mozart himself, but often by his father and sometimes, posthumously, by others who could speak with authority. Most of the dates on his works are demonstrably accurate and there is no reason to doubt most of the others, but a few are open to question, and for a small number of works the original date has, for some curious reason, been rendered illegible. Very few of his works after February 1784 are in dispute because from that date he kept a catalogue (not always quite accurately or comprehensively, but even so the questions are few). There are however many undated earlier works where additional clues need to be sought. Until recently, scholars have placed a good deal of weight on musical style as a means of dating (particularly Einstein in his 1937 edition of the Köchel catalogue), but stylistic analysis is notoriously undependable and open to disagreement, and methods of a more objective kind have been needed.

During the second half of the last century two scholars worked on the Mozart chronology from different standpoints, neither of them using a method that could be regarded as wholly secure, but the results of their research have coincided to a degree that must inspire a good deal of confidence. Wolfgang Plath's studies were devoted to the minutiae of Mozart's handwriting, in which he traced, on the basis of his close reading of manuscripts that can be securely dated for external reasons, the gradual changes that took place in his musical script and in the ancillary instructions. He also carefully analysed Leopold Mozart's writing, which had often been confused with his son's and which appears in Wolfgang's manuscripts up to the time of his finally leaving Salzburg.[14] Plath analysed the forms Mozart used, for example, for treble and bass clef signs, for abbreviations, for individual letters, for *piano* and *forte* indications (the slope and the curl in the tail of the *p* or *f* are highly significant), for natural signs, for rests and for actual note-stems and note-heads. Mozart's changes are remarkably consistent and can often be very precisely dated, which means that careful scrutiny of otherwise undatable manuscripts can often lead to the establishment of their probable date. By about 1780, however, when he was 24, Mozart's adult handwriting was virtually fully formed—as it is for most adults in their early-middle twenties—and from the early 1780s onwards the handwriting offers fewer and less dependable clues.

Alan Tyson's analysis is based on the manuscript paper Mozart used. Paper of this period is handmade and it mostly bears a distinctive watermark. Batches of paper are identifiable not only by their watermark but by their staff-rulings, which were executed in a number of different ways involving multi-nibbed pens (or rastra) and machines that determined the exact placing and spacing of the lines. The batches of paper used by Mozart can usually be identified first by watermark and secondly by the dimensions and other features of the staff-rulings.[15] This method could be totally dependable for dating only if Mozart had used up each batch of paper before he bought the next, which of course he did not do, but it is nevertheless often clear when or where a composition was begun or completed. Many types of paper can be traced to particular mills that supplied different cities, indicating where and therefore when Mozart is likely to have bought them. And when, for example, leaves from a paper known to have been used at one date also appear in a much later work, or when supposedly early works are written on paper known to have been used for late ones, the dates at which such works were begun may come into question. These are only a few typical instances of the kinds of question that may be raised by paper-type analysis.

9

Italy without Nannerl

EOPOLD MOZART HAD now finally decided to take his
son to Italy. This time it was not exclusively a matter of
exhibiting him to the world, to convince sceptics of the continuing existence of God-given miracles and to capitalize on his abilities; it was also a part of Mozart's musical education. Italy, for two
centuries and more, had been a Mecca for musicians, the *fons et origo*
of all that was new in musical style, the home of church music and,
above all, of opera. The opportunities to hear the latest music in
Venice and Rome and Naples were ones that the young Mozart
needed to equip him for life around the opera houses of Europe,
which were the late eighteenth-century composers' honeypots, offering riches far beyond those even of the respectable court appointment that Leopold knew his son ought to obtain. There was another,
longer-term objective too: making a reputation in Italy might open
up possibilities of a position for Wolfgang, and perhaps for Leopold
himself too, at one of the north Italian courts ruled by the Habsburg
family.

It was now too late to take Nannerl as well. She was eighteen in
the summer of 1769; in effect an adult, she would be judged by adult
standards and was no longer suitable for exhibition as a child wonder.

It was therefore sensible, and economical, for her and her mother to stay at home—which they understandably resented, as the correspondence later makes clear[1]—and Leopold and Wolfgang went alone. The letters they were to write are thus rather different in tone and in content from those sent to Lorenz Hagenauer during the previous journeys. They still deal with financial matters, of course, though not relative commodity prices but domestic ones. Often Leopold sent instructions to Maria Anna on business matters, including the management of the sales of his *Violinschule* through various agencies outside Salzburg. They also touch from time to time on plans for Wolfgang's career, which clearly had been much discussed before they left. And the servicing of friendships with influential members of the Salzburg court, some of whom had links with Italy, was one of Maria Anna's tasks in Leopold's absence. But essentially these letters are family communications, and they read more personally and intimately, with much detail about the way father and son are living, about the people they meet, about the doings of their friends in Salzburg, about their feelings and their health: in fact, the common matter of lively and affectionate family intercourse (once Leopold tartly pointed out that the women had sent him no nameday greeting, but he withdrew when the greeting arrived by the next post; Wolfgang had been concerned that his sharp tone would have hurt his mother and sister). Naturally, there is a different kind of vividness and vitality to Leopold's writing, as he tries to share his experiences with his wife and daughter, from that in the Hagenauer letters.

Wolfgang now regularly added postscripts, usually addressed to Nannerl in particular, mostly about local events and people that he wanted to describe as well as his own activities, and often too with messages for and enquiries about Salzburg friends. Usually his comments are high-spirited and jocular. He never wrote to his mother, nor did Leopold to Nannerl, but clearly the letters were all shared within the family. Sometimes, especially later, after Archbishop Schrattenbach's death and the succession of Colloredo in 1772, there are passages in a special family code, a simple substitution cipher easy for Maria Anna to read but presumably too difficult for the censors in Salzburg to be likely to bother with (all mail was subject to scrutiny, and anything subversive would be reported to the archbishop's representatives). These passages usually refer to gossip about Salzburg and the archbishop, the Mozarts' career plans, and occasionally scraps of scandal or reports of international news.

The family letters—those sent home by Leopold and Wolfgang, that is, not the responses—were assiduously collected and kept in the family archive; not a single letter known to have been written during this period went astray or was mislaid. Leopold's determination that they would be saved and used for a biography of his son, even if never fulfilled in the terms he contemplated, has earned the gratitude of later biographers and will no doubt long continue to do so. His plans for their retention and later use must have affected from time to time what he wrote, partly by inducing him to be more comprehensive in his reporting but also by inclining him to put actions and events in their best possible light with a view to the favourable judgment of posterity.

While Leopold was certainly hoping from the outset to secure his son an opera commission (or *scrittura*) in Italy, an important part of his intention remained, of course, to exhibit Wolfgang before a new series of patrons and audiences, and with that in mind to travel to all the main centres of the north and as far south as Rome and Naples. In Lombardy in particular, part of the Austrian monarchy, and in Tuscany, a Habsburg archduchy, they could expect to meet patrons favourably disposed and no doubt well prepared by letters of introduction and recommendation from relatives, friends and colleagues in Austria. As we have seen, Leopold also procured introductory letters from Hasse, whose recommendation would carry weight in musical circles. Hasse sent two letters to his friend in Venice, the Abbate Giovanni Maria Ortes, who was influential in operatic circles—a short one for Leopold to take with him, asking him to assist them, and a longer one sent by post. In the latter he said:[2]

[The son], who cannot be more than twelve or thirteen years old, is already a composer and a master of music. I have seen the compositions that must be his, and they are certainly not bad and I detect in them no signs of a boy of twelve . . . I administered to him a variety of tests on the harpsichord, in which he let me hear things that are remarkable for a boy of his age and would be admirable too in a fully-grown man. . . . The said Signor Mozard [Leopold] is a very polite and civil man, and his children are very well brought up. The boy, further, is attractive, vivacious, graceful and very well-mannered, and, knowing him, it would be difficult not to love him. It is certain that, if he develops in due accordance with his years, he will be a prodigy, provided, perhaps, that his father does not pamper him too much, or spoil him with excessive eulogies, which is my only cause for fear.

Leopold and Wolfgang set out on Wednesday 13 December 1769, seven weeks later than they had originally intended, not in their own carriage but in a hired one, with a coachman engaged for the beginning of the journey (Leopold in fact told his wife, a little later, that she should sell the family carriage, and the horse they apparently owned; they contemplated no more long journeys).[3] On the road to Innsbruck, they stopped for lunch (pickled veal and beer) at the Kaitl Inn in Reichenhall, and spent the night at Lofer, where they ordered a meal at the inn but were then invited to stay at the prefecture (the prefect's brother was a Salzburg acquaintance)—so they took their meal along with them. The next day they reached St Johann at lunchtime and stopped overnight at Wörgl, where the vicar was a friend. Wolfgang added notes to his mother and sister in Leopold's first letter, saying that he was enjoying the journey, that it was warm in the carriage and that the coachman was a fine fellow who went very fast (they had covered nearly 100 km in the first two days).[4] The next day they reached Schwaz at midday and in the late afternoon arrived at Innsbruck, where they lodged at Zum weissen Kreuz, a fifteenth-century inn, which still survives. Innsbruck, a former Habsburg capital city, was still an important centre of government in the Tyrol and there were potential patrons there; one was the governor, Johann Nepomuk Count Spaur, whose brother was in the Salzburg Cathedral chapter. He welcomed the Mozarts, lent them a carriage in which they could call on acquaintances, and organized a concert for the Sunday afternoon at the palace of the Lord High Steward of the region, Leopold Franz Count Künigl. The Mozarts were given twelve ducats. The local newspaper reported the arrival of the boy 'who since his sixth year has become famous for his extraordinary musical knowledge' and his performance at a concert organized by the leading nobility, 'at which he gave the finest proofs of his quite outstanding skill'.[5]

The Mozarts left Innsbruck on 19 December. With Wolfgang's help, Leopold resumed his old system of keeping travel diaries, usually noting where they stayed and the names of people they met.[6] These diaries show that they travelled on the first day to Steinach, the next through Sterzing (at lunchtime) to Brixen (or Bressanone) overnight, and then through Atzwang to Bozen (Bolzano), where they lodged two nights at the Zur Sonne in the central square. They had friends there, including a violinist, Kurzweil, and were twice entertained. Notes of introduction from Salzburg led them to invitations and meals, one of them (from the Stockhammer family, whose house still stands) very lavish; presumably Wolfgang played to their hosts. They hastened on to Neumarkt (Egna) for the next night, then Trient (Trento) at midday on the Sunday and then to Rovereto, where they arrived on 24 December and stayed, at the inn Zur Rose—or Rosa d'Oro, for they were now in Italian-speaking country—for three nights.

Here they were immediately greeted by the brother of the Lord Lieutenant of the district, Nicolaus Cristani, who many years before had been a violin pupil of Leopold's and had heard that they were on the way. Also in Rovereto were members of the Lodron family, prominent in Salzburg. Other eminent local people included the mayor, Baron Giovanni Battista Todeschi, whom they had previously met in Vienna and at whose house a concert for the nobles was quickly organized for 25 December (Christmas did not occasion any special holiday). On that day they had 'a merry midday meal' with the Cristani family and on their second 'again a cheerful table' with the Cosmi family. It was arranged that Wolfgang then would play to six or eight leading people on the organ of the main church, San Marco, but word had got around and 'all of Rovereto had assembled' to hear him; it took some strapping young men to push the crowd aside to let them through. Leopold described Rovereto as formerly a wretched place, but improved by the industry of the inhabitants in winemaking and the silk trade, and the people were polite to strangers.[7] During all their travels, especially in southern Germany and northern Italy, the Mozarts met many friends and acquaintances, or simply families with whom they were in some way connected. The network of leading families, the degree of mobility for such people between the main cities, and the important role assigned to musical activities provided between them a series of strands that could readily be exploited in the social fabric of the time.

On 27 December the Mozarts travelled on to Verona, where they remained for two weeks, staying at the inn Delle due Torri (a fourteenth-century building, formerly a guest house for a leading Veronese family, now a modern hotel). Here again Leopold was soon in touch with the leading noblemen, who lunched them and arranged for Wolfgang to give a concert with the local Accademia Filarmonica. It could not however take place until 5 January, as at this time of year, the beginning of the carnival, there was an opera performance every night. The event was reported in the *Gazzetta di Mantova* a week later:[8]

> . . . In the company of several distinguished professionals he was able, first, to produce a beautiful overture of his own composition, which merited all its applause. Then he played

splendidly, at sight, a harpsichord concerto, and successively other sonatas that were wholly new to him. Then, on four verses submitted to him, he composed an aria in the best of taste while actually singing it. A subject and a finale were put to him, and on these he improvised marvellously in accordance with the best rules of the art. Then, at sight, he played very well a trio by Boccherini. He set excellently in score an idea put to him on the violin by a professional musician.

Mozart himself clearly enjoyed Verona, to judge by the high spirits of the letter, much the longest he had yet written, that he subjoined to his father's. It is written half in German, half in Italian. There is no word about Verona itself, the Roman arena, the city that was birthplace of Dante and the setting of the story of Romeo and Juliet. He tells Nannerl about their visits to the opera (they had been given the key to the Marchese Carlotti's box): but typically of his time he scarcely refers to the music and does not even name the composer. The opera, he says, is *Ruggiero*; it was in fact by Pietro Alessandro Guglielmi, a leading opera composer of the time, to words by Caterino Mazzolà, with whom Mozart was to collaborate more than twenty years later. He tells scraps of the story in disjointed fashion, and criticizes the singers: a baritone, forced when he sings falsetto, a soprano with a passable voice and good figure but 'out of tune like the devil', a castrato who 'sings somewhat in the manner of Manzuoli and has a very beautiful strong voice and is already old, he is fifty-five and he has a flexible throat', a woman singer who 'has a very beautiful voice but there is so much whispering in the theatre that you can hear nothing', while another woman 'has a muffled voice and is always a semiquaver late'. These comments, from a musician, may serve to help us understand something of how audiences of the time approached opera. For even if Mozart, as he must surely have done, was taking in what was happening musically, it is not that but the singing (and the dancing, on which he also reports briefly) that he thought appropriate to describe to his sister. It comes as a salutary reminder of changing attitudes and values.

One of the Veronese notables much concerned with the Mozarts during their visit was Pietro Lugiati, a well-known patron and financial director of the province, who arranged to have Mozart's portrait painted. Mozart had sittings on 6 and 7 January (the second clashing

Mozart: oil painting, Verona, 1770, probably by Saverio dalla Rosa (*Internationale Stiftung Mozarteum, Salzburg*)

embarrassingly with a lunch invitation from the Bishop of Verona). The painter was for a time thought to be one of the Felice brothers, and then Giambettino Cignaroli (who according to their travel notes the Mozarts met), but Saverio dalla Rosa, a nephew of Cignaroli and a distant relative of Lugiati, is now generally credited with this appealing likeness. Mozart is painted at the keyboard of a Celestinus harpsichord dated 1583. On the stand is a piece of music, a Molto Allegro in G major, otherwise unknown but understandably accepted as a work of Mozart's that survives only in this incomplete form (it is assigned the Köchel number 72a). After the second sitting, Mozart went to the church of S Tommaso, a fifteenth-century stone and terracotta building in a mixture of Romanesque and Gothic styles, to play the two organs there; as in Rovereto, a huge crowd gathered to hear him and afterwards to see him. While he was in Verona two flowery, fanciful eulogistic poems were presented to him, and the local *maestro di cappella*, Daniel Dal Barba, improvised a setting of 'beautiful verses' about him. On 8 January the Mozarts saw the Roman amphitheatre and other local sights, and on 10 January they moved on to Mantua.

There they arrived at five in the evening, and within an hour they were at the opera. Again, Mozart gave his sister an amusing account of the singers' characteristics ('the seconda donna looks like a grenadier and has a powerful voice too'), but as to the music, a setting of Metastasio's *Demetrio*,[9] he said nothing, though he called the evening as a whole 'charming'. The Mozarts spent nine days in Mantua, lodging at the Croce Verde. Once more, there were family connections to tap: Francesco Eugenio Count Arco was related to the Arco family from the Tyrol, of which there were members at the Salzburg court, and the Lodron family from Salzburg. Leopold came duly armed with letters. They were courteously treated at the Arco palace, but when he tried to call on a member of the Thurn und Taxis family, also Lodron relatives, he was at first put off, and then, when he followed them from church, was told by an embarrassed servant that the prince was too busy and inferred that he had 'no great desire' to see them. The weather was bitterly cold and their rooms were unheated; Leopold had earlier talked of their hands going black, blue and red, and in Mantua Wolfgang became flushed and sore because of the cold and the open fires and needed a skin salve for his hands. Here again they gave a concert with the local Accademia Filarmonica, in the Teatro Scientifico, which Leopold described as the most beautiful of its kind he had ever seen, built like an opera house with audience boxes and a platform for the orchestra. The concert, which the Accademia moved from its usual date to 16 January in order to accommodate the Mozarts as they passed through the town, was a long one; the programme survives (in slightly different forms, printed and manuscript programmes and a manuscript invitation; additional information from the manuscripts is bracketed):[10]

1   Symphony by Mozart [1st and 2nd movements]
2   Harpsichord Concerto, played by Mozart at sight
3   Aria [sung by Uttini, the opera tenor]
4   Harpsichord Sonata, played at sight by Mozart, and Variations extemporized by him and then played in another key
5   Violin Concerto [Angelo Orsi]
6   Aria composed and sung at the same time by Mozart, with accompaniment on the harpsichord, to words he had not previously seen
7   Another Harpsichord Sonata, composed and performed by Mozart, on a theme supplied by the first violinist
8   Aria [and Cantata, sung by Signorina Angiola Galliani]
9   Oboe Concerto [Luigi Livraghi]
10   Fugue, composed and played by Mozart on the harpsichord, brought to a proper conclusion according to the laws of counterpoint, on a theme submitted to him
11   Symphony by Mozart, to be played by him with all the parts on the harpsichord from a single violin part, submitted to him extempore
12   Duet [sung by Signorina Leonora Ambreville and Uttini]

13   Trio, in which Mozart improvises a part on the violin
14   Symphony [last movement]

The programme was clearly designed to put Mozart through a variety of tests but it did not include much of his actual music; most of his items were sightread or improvised. It is sometimes said that three symphonies were given (they have even been identified, as specific lost works, an exercise in sheer fantasy), but in fact it was only one; no. 11 was not Mozart's, and nos. 1 and 14 are the same work—it was customary to begin a concert with part of a symphony and end it with the finale. The review in the *Gazzetta di Mantova* describes the event and mentions that Mozart, 'gracefully coupling' the two themes given to him for sonatas (nos. 4 and 7), reached in his fugue 'so masterly a harmonic interweaving of all the voices and so bold a resolution as to leave the audience dumbfounded', besides playing the violin 'marvellously well' in the trio; he seemed 'to be born to confound all the experts in the art' and was 'a miracle in music, one of those freaks that Nature causes to be born'.[11] The Mozarts did not, however, make much money out of these successes in Italy. The concerts in Verona were free to the nobles who promoted them, and in Mantua they were free to a wider audience, including too the military and leading citizens, as they were in effect subsidized by the empress. Leopold expected little profit from this journey but hoped to cover travel expenses, though 'even if you live *a pasto* [pay per meal] and hardly ever lunch at home', Italy was a costly place, he said.

The Mozarts, now carrying another poetic eulogy (by Signora Sartoretti, who had supplied the hand salve), left Mantua on 19 January. They reached Bozzolo that night, staying at the Della Posta inn. They arrived at six o'clock and were at once taken off by a local priest-musician, Carlo Saragozzi, to sightread and undergo other tests, including playing the harpsichord part of a trio by Giuseppe Saragozzi, 'giving unspeakable pleasure and satisfaction to the military and political authorities and many other gentlemen'.[12] The next day they arrived at Cremona, where they immediately saw *La clemenza di*

Invitation to the concert at Mantua, 16 January 1770 (*Marchese d'Arco, Mantua*)

Tito, in a setting of the Metastasio libretto by Michelangelo Valentini, originally written in 1753 and lately revised: once again, Mozart comments on some of the singers but mentions neither the music nor the name of the composer. There is no record of where they stayed or when they left, but we know that they arrived in Milan at noon on 23 January. The lists of people they met in the principal centres resumes, with the predictable patrons and a number of musicians though few in these lesser cities who ever gained wider fame; Luigi Gatti, *maestro di cappella* in Mantua, however, was later to go as Kapellmeister to Salzburg.

Milan was the centre of Austrian government in north Italy, and although its musical history over recent decades had been less significant than that of Venice, Naples or Rome, it was becoming an important intellectual and artistic centre and a focal point for the Enlightenment in Italy. An Accademia Filarmonica had lately been established, under one of the leading Italian instrumental composers,

Giovanni Battista Sammartini, and its opera house, the Teatro Regio Ducal , was steadily gaining in prestige. It was soon to overtake all its rivals when, rebuilt in 1778 after a fire, it staged under its new name, La Scala, some of the most forward-looking Italian operas of the time.

The Mozarts spent more than seven weeks in the city, where they lodged not at an inn but an Augustinian monastery—not free, Leopold hastened to point out, but comfortable, safe and close to Count Firmian. Carl Joseph Count Firmian, governor-general of Lombardy, was noted for his learning and his broad cultural sympathies. The family, again, had links with Salzburg (an uncle of his had been archbishop there when Leopold joined the court, and he himself had studied in the city), and Leopold must again have been well armed with letters of recommendation; moreover, he could reasonably expect Firmian, from an Austrian (specifically Tyrolese) family, to be particularly favourably inclined towards him and his son. It is unclear whether the Mozarts saw the first carnival opera, a setting of Metastasio's *Didone abbandonata* by the minor Turinese composer Ignazio Celeonati, which was succeeded at the end of the month by *Cesare in Egitto* by the prolific Niccolò Piccinni. The Mozarts met Piccinni, whose opera Leopold described as excellent. The only other significant news in Leopold's early letters from Milan is that Mozart was composing, for two young castratos with whom he was friendly, a couple of motets (if these were ever written, they are lost)[13], and that Firmian, after entertaining them to lunch, had presented Wolfgang with a set of the Turin edition of Metastasio's writings (begun in 1757, nine volumes to date)—an essential part of the professional equipment of a composer with operatic aspirations, and given to him with a clear purpose. By this time they had met Sammartini, whom Mozart had duly impressed. Other composers they met included G.A. Fioroni, G.B. Lampugnani and Carlo Monza. Possibly Mozart wrote a symphony, K.84/73q, while he was in Milan.

Leopold's plan was that they would be in Rome for Holy Week, travelling through Bologna and Florence. If time permitted they would also visit Turin, but that could be postponed. Gossip in their letters includes the news that the Marchese Litta (formerly a patron of J.C. Bach's), to his family's irritation, had died during carnival instead of waiting until Lent. He complains that the church services consist merely of music and adornment, and 'apart from this, the most abominable licentiousness prevails'. It shocked him too that the Milanese, following the local church usage (the Ambrosian Use), began Lent four days late, eating meat on Ash Wednesday and the Thursday and holding balls on the Saturday. With the jollifications at the end of carnival coming, Leopold and Wolfgang had to buy cloaks and cowls, amid grumbles at 'taking part in this tomfoolery' at his age; his consolation was that the material could afterwards be used for linings or kitchen cloths. He also complained that Maria Anna and Nannerl neglected to write letters, and urged Nannerl to practise the harpsichord. Mozart continues to add postscripts to his father's letters, addressed to 'Cara sorella mia' ('My dear sister'), describing the carnival festivities, mentioning that they had been to the opera six or seven times (probably to the same opera, or two operas) and with eager enquiries, as usual, after their Salzburg acquaintances, and sometimes with a little gentle teasing of his sister about possible men friends.

On 18 February there was a concert at the Firmians' palace for the Duke of Modena and his daughter, Maria d'Este, who was betrothed to the Archduke Ferdinand, one of Joseph II's brothers. After it they went to the opera and a ball. The Mozarts' principal concert, open (unlike most in Italy) to the public, took place five days later; Leopold offers no description as it went off 'just as all our concerts have done everywhere'. The takings in Italy, however, would be modest: 'admiration and bravos' would have to serve as payment. A final concert, in Firmian's house (probably the Palazzo Melzi rather than his official residence, the Palazzo Reale near the cathedral), to be given for a select audience of 150, was set for 12 March. This concert was in fact by way of an audition, to discover whether Mozart was capable of undertaking the composition of a serious opera for the Teatro Regio Ducal.[14] He was required, it seems, to set three texts, one of them with a prefatory orchestral recitative, which he (or someone else)

selected from Metastasio's *Demofoönte*, a libretto particularly praised in
the preface to the edition Mozart had just been given. One was for
the *prima donna*, one for the *primo uomo* and one for the *primo tenore*,
respectively 'Se tutti i mali miei' K.83/73*p*, 'Misero me . . . Misero
pargoletto' K.77/73*e* and 'Ah più tremar' K.71. They were almost certainly sung by three of the singers who would be expected to take
part in the opera, Antonia Bernasconi, Giuseppe Aprile and
Guglielmo d'Ettore. Mozart himself later made it clear that he was
being tested for his capacity for writing for the theatre.[15] He evidently passed, for within two days a *scrittura*, or contract—for which
Leopold had been hoping and possibly negotiating since their arrival
in Milan—was issued. He was to compose the first opera for the carnival season next year, 1771, that is, to be produced on 26 December
1770 (in Milan the first carnival opera carried less prestige than the
second, and a more modest fee; it was appropriate for a young and
relatively little-known composer).

So when, on 15 March, the Mozarts left Milan, it was in the
knowledge that, subject to the formality of the archbishop of
Salzburg's permission, they would be back again in the autumn for
the composition and the production of the opera. A timetable had
been worked out and incorporated in the contract, and some of the
singers had been engaged. They now travelled south, armed with letters of introduction given to them by Firmian at a farewell dinner (he
also gave Wolfgang a snuffbox set in gold containing twenty cigliati,
the same value as twenty ducats). Their first overnight stop was Lodi,
not mentioned in the Mozarts' letters or travel notes, but recorded on
the manuscript as the place of composition, on 15 March, of a string
quartet, Mozart's first (K.80/73*f*). They spent a few days in Parma,
presenting a letter from Firmian to a local patron of the arts,
Guglielmo du Tillot, Marquess of Felino, and calling on the imperial
ambassador, Franz Philipp, Baron Knebel.[16] They also met the
soprano Lucrezia Aguiari, known as La Bastardella or Bastardina,
famous for her acting and the beauty, agility, refinement and compass
of her voice, who astonished the Mozarts with her trills and her

extraordinarily high notes, which father and son both reported (Wolfgang copied down, for Nannerl, some of the high passages);[17] they met too the composer Giuseppe Colla, whom Aguiari later married. It was not all work: they saw tightrope walkers with dogs, and one night at the inn were entertained by a troupe of comedians.

On 24 March they arrived at Bologna and took a room at the Pellegrino, the best hostelry in the city, where (in Leopold's characteristically ironic turn of phrase) they 'had the honour' of paying a ducat a day.[18] This city, as Leopold said, was the centre for 'masters, artists and scholars', and he was anxious that Wolfgang should have a hearing there. Firmian had directed them to Giovanni Luca Count Pallavicini-Centurioni, an elderly nobleman and a field-marshal who was a noted patron of the arts. When Leopold went to see him, the day after their arrival, Pallavicini at once arranged a concert for the following evening, at his palace, for some 150 members of the local nobility. Two distinguished castratos, Giuseppe Aprile and Giuseppe Cicognani, sang, and Mozart played in a programme that lasted from about half-past seven until half-past eleven. Mozart was given 205 lire and Leopold 20 zecchini (a zecchino was the equivalent of a ducat). Among the guests were the son of the Austrian chancellor, Joseph Clemens Count Kaunitz, and Giovanni Battista Martini. Padre Martini, universally recognized as the leading musical theorist of his day, was now in retirement, working on his monumental *Storia della musica* (the second volume was on the point of publication; only three of the planned five were to be completed) and his two-volume counterpoint manual, *Esemplare ossia Saggio fondamentale pratico di contrapunto sopra il canto fermo*, and conducting a voluminous correspondence with musicians who had technical queries. He rarely attended concerts. The Mozarts twice visited him, and Wolfgang wrote fugues on subjects he provided. They visited too another musician of distinction, the most famous of all the castratos, Farinelli (Carlo Broschi), at the luxurious villa on the estate outside Bologna to which he had retired in 1759 after a career on the stage and at the Spanish court. Other musicians they met in Bologna include several singers, the

Bohemian composer Josef Mysliveœk, whose opera *La Nitteti* was staged about this time at the Teatro Comunale, and Vincenzo Man-fredini, a leading local composer whose *Armida* was in preparation. They also visited the Istituto, where there were statues by Johann Baptist Hagenauer, the Salzburg court sculptor, and a scientific exhi-bition that 'surpasses the British Museum'.[19] Before they left, they equipped themselves with a series of recommendation letters from Pallavicini, including one to his distant kinsman who was a cardinal and secretary of state in Rome, Lazaro Opizio Count Pallavicini.

The Mozarts left Bologna on 29 March and arrived in Florence the next day, staying for a week at the Aquila. After a free day, occa-sioned by Wolfgang's having a cold, they went to see Franz Xaver Wolf Count Orsini Rosenberg, a senior administrator at the Tuscan court (who was to play an even more significant role in Mozart's life in the 1780s), and on the strength of Firmian's and Kaunitz's recom-mendations were at once granted an audience in spite of a waiting crowd. They were soon sent on to the grand duke, Leopold, one of Maria Theresa's sons and a future emperor, who had heard Mozart as a small child and would be in contact with him again close to the ends of both their lives. The grand duke talked with them at the Pitti Palace for a quarter of an hour and the following evening had them brought to Poggio Imperiale, his summer palace outside Florence, where they remained until ten o'clock and 'everything went off as usual'. The fee was just over 333 lire.[20] Those present included Euge-nio Marquess of Ligniville, the ducal director of music, who had a reputation as a learned contrapuntist and gave Wolfgang difficult themes to work, 'which', wrote Leopold, 'he threw off and worked out as others might eat a piece of bread'.[21] The next day they met their old friend the singer Manzuoli and the English boy violinist Thomas Linley, a pupil of Pietro Nardini. Leopold was clearly much touched by the warmth of the friendship that sprang up between the two boys, of the same age and size; they played duets on their violins the whole evening, 'constantly embracing each other', then again at the Mozarts' rooms the following day, and at the house of the general administrator to the grand duke, Gavard des Pivets, the day after. Leopold thought Linley a charming boy who played 'most beautifully'. The boys parted with tears, embraces and the presentation by Linley of a sonnet to Mozart, written for him by the court poet Maddalena Morilla-Fernandez ('Corilla Olimpica'). Linley followed the Mozarts' coach to the city gate. They never met again; Linley, son of a composer of the same name, and a pupil of William Boyce in London, had a brief career as violinist and composer but in 1778 he was drowned in a boating accident.

Their arrival carefully timed for Holy Week, the Mozarts now moved on to Rome, an unpleasant five-day journey in rainy and windy weather, across uncultivated country, pausing at 'disgusting, filthy inns where there was nothing to eat', at least until they reached Viterbo.[22] As they approached Rome, on Ash Wednesday, 11 April, there was lightning and thunder; they felt, Leopold wrote, like great men being welcomed by the firing of salutes. On arrival, they had lunch, passing by the German College (where they called on a friend, Albert von Mölk, son of the Salzburg chancellor and a student there)[23] and went to St Peter's and to Mass. The next day they saw the pope, Clement XIV, serving the poor. Leopold pushed their way through the crowd, getting his servant to order the Swiss guards to stand aside for them, using his German and allowing them to think, he said, that Wolfgang was a German courtier, perhaps a prince, and he his tutor. They reached the cardinals' table:

One of them gave Wolfgang a sign and said to him: *Would you be so good as to tell me, in confidence, who you are?* Wolfgang told him. The cardinal answered him with the greatest surprise, saying: *Ah, so you are the famous boy, about whom so many people have written to me.* On that, Wolfgang asked him: *Are you not Cardinal Pallavicini?*—The Cardinal answered: *Yes, I am he, and why do you ask?*—On which Wolfgang said *that we had letters*

to deliver to his Eminence and were going to pay our respects to him.
The Cardinal seemed delighted at that and said that Wolfgang
spoke Italian very well . . .

Leopold goes on to tell the famous tale of Gregorio Allegri's *Miserere*,
the showpiece of the Sistine Chapel choir, and 'so greatly prized that
the singers in the chapel are forbidden on pain of excommunication
to take away a single voice-part, copy it or give it to anyone. However, *we have it already*. Wolfgang has written it down'. It in no way
lessens Wolfgang's feat of memory to point out that the *Miserere* was
nowhere near as secret as Leopold thought; many copies were in existence. Leopold himself soon came to realize this, as a letter he wrote
from Naples, mentioning that even the pope knew that Mozart had
written it out, makes clear.[24]

The Mozarts spent four weeks in Rome on this first visit. At first
they stayed in a private lodging found for them, with one room and
only one bed: 'Mamma can well imagine that I get no sleep', Wolfgang wrote. They moved after three days to the more spacious house
of a papal courier, Steffano Uslenghi, who was away; his wife and
daughter vied in waiting on them and treated Leopold as master of
the house. On 16 April they began to deliver their numerous letters
from Count Pallavicini; several of the acknowledgments sent to
Pallavicini are preserved.[25] On 19 April they played for Prince San
Angelo, of Naples, and the next day for Prince Agostino Chigi, in the
presence of Pallavicini, Baron Saint-Odîle (the Tuscan ambassador)
and Charles Edward Stuart, Pretender to the English throne (they
met several Englishmen in Rome, some of them old acquaintances
from their London days). Others before whom Mozart played
include Princess Barberini, about 26 April, the ambassador of the
Maltese order of St John (probably the pope's *maestro di cappella*,
Giuseppe Santarelli) on 28 April, and Baldassare Odescalchi, duke of
Bracciano and Geri, who invited them to a concert the next day
being given by Giuseppe Maria Altemps, duke of Gallese. On 30
April he played at the Augustinian monastery. The next day was free

and they visited a country estate (at Mass in the morning, however, they had met an old friend, their former servant Porta, who offered his services again: Leopold, who thought him an adventurer, declined).[26] On 2 May Wolfgang played at the German College and on 3 May at the Doria Pamphili palace: at the former, after performing lengthy harpsichord improvisations on supplied themes and accompanying the Salzburg singer Joseph Meissner in some arias, he played the organ too.[27] Probably Mozart's last performance on this visit was on 7 May, when he was heard by Kraft Ernst, the young Count Öttingen-Wallerstein, at the residence of the Venetian ambassador. There may have been more appearances, but not at this stage before the pope, although Count Pallavicini had suggested that to Cardinal Pallavicini ('I would dare to propose to your Eminence that you let him be heard by our Lord . . . I flatter myself that he would meet with His Holiness's entire satisfaction').[28]

During all the frenzied activity in Rome Mozart, to judge by his letters and postscripts, seems to have been in high spirits. He is full of jocular remarks, often self-deprecatory, calling himself a dunce and bewailing his smallness (he had to be lifted up to kiss the feet of St Peter's statue), and teasing his family with observations about how they would like the 'regular' features of some of the Roman architecture: he seems to be echoing, in fun, comments made during previous travels. He asks Nannerl to send him 'arithmetical tables'; from a later letter it seems that he was referring to mathematical puzzles of some sort.[29] He mentions a number of compositions, but it is not always certain which works he is referring to. Among those definitely identifiable are a contredanse K.123/73g, sent home from Rome with some instructions for its choreography (Mozart and Leopold were much concerned that the dance should reflect the musical structure, ideally with five couples dancing to match the five solo sections), and an aria K.82/73o.[30] He also writes of soon finishing one symphony and of another he has already finished, which his father was copying as they were afraid to send it out: the copyists would make another, illicit copy and sell it, the Mozarts would lose control over the distribution of the music, and the work would diminish in value through its loss of uniqueness. (The identity of the symphonies written in Italy is discussed at the end of this chapter.)

On 8 May the Mozarts left Rome for Naples, the furthest south they were ever to travel. They had been anxious about the journey because of highwaymen, but after a recent incident the police and the 'bloodthirsty papal soldiery' had been sent out and the robbers killed or dispersed (and some police killed too). They travelled, in company with some Augustinian monks, in a convoy of four *sedie* (a *sedia* was a small, two-wheeled carriage taking two passengers). Leopold reports stopping at several Augustinian monasteries: on the first day at Marino, where they had a light lunch; on the third day at Sessa, where they were well fed at an evening meal; and on 12 May at Capua. There they waited overnight, at the request of one of their companions, to observe a ceremony the next day at which a lady took the veil, a 'very magnificent' occasion, with three or four coachloads of musicians to begin the proceedings with symphonies and a *Salve regina*.

They arrived at Naples on 14 May and spent their first two nights in a house owned by the Augustinians before moving into modestly-priced lodgings. Once again armed with recommendations, they went to Portici to call on 18 May on the prime minister, Bernardo Marquess Tanucci (who had initiated the excavations at Pompeii and Herculaneum), and later that day they visited the British ambassador, William Hamilton, whom they had met in London and whose first wife, Catherine, was an admired keyboard player (she trembled to play in front of Wolfgang). There were two London acquaintances there; the Mozarts kept meeting old friends from their earlier travels, among them a Dutchman, Simon Donker, and a merchant from Lyons, J.G. Meurikofer, with whom they went to see an *opera buffa* on 21 May. On 19 May they first visited the imperial ambassador, Ernst Christoph Count of Kaunitz-Rietberg, on whose wife they called again three days later. There was another journey to Portici on 20 May, but their programme in Naples was not arduous. The imperial ambassador was one of the organizers of the concert they gave on 28 May, the central event of their stay in Naples, for which the ambassador's wife joined forces with Mrs Hamilton and members of the local aristocracy; Leopold expected to make 150 zecchini out of it. A portrait, of unknown authorship but Neapolitan provenance, showing a boy at the harpsichord in a crowded room, has been said to represent that occasion, but there is no supporting evidence.

Two days later the court was fully back in town for the king's nameday, and the first performance of Jommelli's opera *Armida abbandonata* at the Teatro San Carlo, the principal (and royal) opera house, at which serious operas were given (as opposed to the several others devoted to performances of comic operas more popular in appeal). The title role was taken by the much admired soprano Anna Lucia de Amicis, the role of Rinaldo by Aprile, who both 'sang amazingly well', Mozart told Nannerl. This time his comments were not exclusively about the singing: after a rehearsal he wrote that he truly liked the work and that it was well composed, though after the performance he felt that, 'though beautiful, it is too old-fashioned and serious for the theatre'. Such remarks have to be weighed in the context of serious opera of the time and the controversies surrounding Jommelli's somewhat complex manner of composition ('a learned and ingenious Music . . . full of harmony and contrivance', according to one critic[31]) and his attempts to adapt it for the Neapolitan taste. Mozart was not opposed to serious opera as such—he was just about to compose one himself—or indeed to elaborate harmony or contrivance, and his views are best understood as a general comment on style and dramatic pace. The Mozarts visited Jommelli's house and met there the San Carlo impresario, who invited him to write an opera, but the date would have clashed with the one to which he was committed in Milan. As the impresario observed, the length of the journey would not be justified by a single commission; should Wolfgang be invited to compose an opera for Bologna or Rome, he said, he would then send him a *scrittura*.

The Mozarts' concert-giving in Naples was now nearly finished.

There was a summons to the Princess of Francavilla on 29 May,
rewarded with a 'beautiful present', but for the rest it was social activities with friends, as well as a ball at the French embassy to mark the
betrothal of the future Louis XVI and Marie Antoinette. Leopold
hoped to leave in mid-June, but this depended on some factor left
unexplained in his letters: either they leave then, or they will have to
remain five months—until, that is, too close to the time when they
needed to be in Milan. It may have been a matter of receiving
another, expected invitation, or it could have been connected with
the hoped-for, but never received, summons to play before the king
of Naples (the Mozarts note they were acknowledged by the king
and the queen at gatherings, but that is all). They had mixed feelings
about the city. The inhabitants they found almost as rude as those of
London, but they admired the rare variety of fruits, vegetables and
flowers, the lively atmosphere and the many beautiful sights, including the daily *passeggio*, the parade of a few hundred nobles in their
coaches in the afternoon (illuminated with countless flambeaux as
twilight descended), though not the filth, the beggars, the godlessness
or 'the disgraceful way in which children were brought up'. Leopold
was appalled by their superstition and idolatry, which affected not
only the common people but also those of distinction. Nannerl, many
years later, related a tale that Wolfgang must have told her back in
Salzburg. When her brother was playing at the Della Pietà conservatory (an event not otherwise recorded), a rumour circulated that his
skill was connected with a magic ring he was wearing; only when he
removed it was the audience duly astonished.[32] Naples was however
an incomparably musical city: the Mozarts' acquaintance in Rome, to
judge by the list in their travel notes, included only two musicians of
any significance (the *maestri di cappella* Aurisicchio and Costanzi), but
in Naples, besides several singers, there were Abos, Jommelli, Cafaro,
the two De Majo (father and son: Wolfgang thought a piece of
church music by Gian Francesco 'bellissima'), Manna, Paisiello, Bar-
bella and Doll, nearly all natives or at least Neapolitan-trained.

By 9 June Leopold had decided to leave Naples as soon as he

could, possibly travelling with the imperial ambassador, Count Kaunitz. But he was an earnest tourist and would not miss the important sights around the city. On 13 June he and Wolfgang went to Pozzuoli and took ship to Baia, where they saw the Roman baths associated with Nero, various temples and subterranean rooms and Virgil's grave, and on 18 and 19 June they made a two-day excursion to Vesuvius, Pompeii, Herculaneum, Caserta and Capodimonte. They finally set out on 25 June, not waiting for Kaunitz; and Leopold decided to make it a speedy journey, using the post-coach, without overnight stops—27 hours instead of four-and-a-half days. His journey was made the faster because he told the innkeepers and officials that he was steward to the Imperial ambassador, ensuring good horses and speedy service. During the journey they slept little and ate only four roast chickens; when they reached Rome, they were grateful to Signora Uslenghi for giving them lightly boiled eggs and rice—but Wolfgang sat down, 'at once began to snore' and had to be undressed and put to bed. The speedy journey had its price. Close to Rome, the postillion continually lashed the horse supporting the carriage and eventually it reared, stuck in the mud and fell, pulling the carriage over. Leopold, in holding Wolfgang back to prevent his falling out, gashed his right shin deeply on the dashboard. The wound, 'the width of a finger', caused him considerable pain and trouble over the ensuing months.

During the two days after their arrival, however, the Mozarts went to the public celebrations, with fireworks and a service at St Peter's, of the annual ceremony of the handing-over of a tribute from Naples as a papal fief. They soon called on Cardinal Pallavicini, lunching with him on 5 July and the next day with Baron Saint Odîle. Before going to Pallavicini's they learnt the particular reason for this invitation: they were to be told that Wolfgang was to be awarded a papal knighthood—he would be entitled to wear a gold cross and to be called 'Signor Cavaliere'. The Renaissance composer Orlande de Lassus and Gluck held similar awards; Mozart's, like Lassus's, was a knighthood of the first order ('of the Golden Spur'). Pallavicini bestowed it on him at his residence in the Quirinale palace on 5 July, and three days later he was received by the pope, at the Santa Maria Maggiore palace (the necessary witness may have been the Bishop of Gurk, Hieronymus Colloredo). In a note to his sister on 7 July Mozart signed himself 'Chevalier de Mozart'; this was also the first of his letters to include 'lavatory humour' (a note to say: 'Shit in your bed and make a mess of it'). An anonymous 1777 portrait of him wearing the insignia sent to Padre Martini hangs in the Conservatorio di Musica in Bologna.

The Mozarts left Rome on 10 July. It was still more than three months before they needed to be in Milan and they had apparently been invited to spend some of the summer, at least, at Count Pallavicini's estate near Bologna. They took a circuitous route so as to visit pilgrimage sites, and travelled initially by night.[33] Setting out from Rome at six in the evening, they travelled until five the next morning, when they reached Città Castellana; they were bitterly cold, although wearing their furs over their coats, and had a drink of hot chocolate. They then slept until ten, when they went to Mass, after which Wolfgang played the organ, and they slept again until their departure at five in the afternoon. This peculiar schedule was so designed that they could avoid travel during the hot central part of the day, and specifically to reduce the likelihood of their contracting malaria, which was prevalent. There is a great deal in Leopold's letters about the weather and the discomforts and anxieties it caused. On other days, their schedule was less strange: they travelled from three or four in the morning until nine, then rested during the hottest part of the day and continued from four in the afternoon until eight or nine in the evening. The journey was nevertheless very tiring, according to Leopold, with their sleep badly disturbed and flies and other insects constantly troubling them. Understandably, his injured leg, now swollen and with the wound reopened, was worrying him, though in his letters home he spared Maria Anna anxieties by remaining cheerful and optimistic about it. Their route took them through Terni, Spoleto and Foligno to Loreto, where they arrived on

16 July; the Santa Casa was the central objective of their journey. They passed through Ancona, Senigaglia (where they went to a fair), Pesaro, Rimini, Forlì and Imola. Leopold reported that the whole coast, from Loreto to Rimini, was swarming with soldiers and police to protect travellers who had lately been the object of sorties from the pirates off the coast.

They reached Bologna on the evening of 20 July and lodged at the San Marco inn, where they stayed for three weeks; further travel was out of the question, for Leopold now needed to rest his leg, and in fact he remained in his room, in bed or with his foot on a chair, for more than two weeks, his troubles exacerbated by what seems to have been gout in his other foot. The libretto and cast-list for Wolfgang's new opera to be composed for Milan, *Mitridate, rè di Ponto*, were sent to them there, arriving on 27 July (presumably Leopold had informed the Milan authorities of their whereabouts). Leopold had been told in Rome that the opera was to be *La Nitetti*;[34] they had come across Myslivecek's setting of the same Metastasio libretto in Bologna in March (in fact a version of *Nitetti*, set by Carlo Monza, was the second carnival opera). They were called on by Myslivecek and by two other composers, Manfredini and Schmid (not certainly identifiable). Wolfgang adds his usual postscripts to letters home, mostly devoted to messages, queries and observation—now of course often seeming cryptic because we know too little of their frame of reference (many mention Salzburg friends)—and telling Nannerl what he has been doing. In one letter from Bologna he answers his mother's question as to whether he has been playing the violin: presumably he had not, as he has now had it restrung and is playing daily. He gives his sister the incipits of his three 1769 cassations at her request, as she thought someone in Salzburg had been trying to pass them off as his own. His sole occupation at the moment is 'dancing English steps, pirouetting and cutting capers', but 'Italy is a sleepy country; I am always drowsy'. In the meantime, he adds, he has composed four Italian symphonies, five or six arias and one motet.

IT IS HARDLY likely that, when the Mozarts set out for Italy, they would have had no symphonies in their baggage. The symphony, as we have seen, was standard fare for the opening item of a concert, and often for the closing item; one might also be used at some other point. It would have been improvident and uncharacteristic for Leopold to risk their being caught short. For one of the Salzburg cassations, K.100, a 'symphony' version exists—a set of parts in the family's possession preserving a four-movement work, the first Allegro and the three final movements. They could well have taken this with them. Another work that may belong to Mozart's last weeks in Salzburg or the beginning of the Italian journey is the Symphony in C K.73 (numbered 75a in K^3 but restored to 73 in K^6). This work is particularly difficult to date. It is written on Salzburg paper of a kind Mozart used from 1769 to 1772. The handwriting suggests a date no later than 1769–70, demonstrated in particular by the form of the treble clef that Mozart used.[35] The autograph bears the date 1769, possibly in Leopold's hand, possibly a later one. A jotting of a theme from the work appears on a set of minuets (K.103/61d) belonging to 1772; and a few bars from the bass part were noted by Leopold on a sheet bearing some workings of a puzzle canon that appears in the second volume of Padre Martini's *Storia della musica*, which the Mozarts could have seen in March 1770 but could have obtained only in October. It is of course impossible to know which was written first. Circumstances can be imagined to explain most of these scraps of information, but the only one not susceptible of alternative explanation, and accordingly the one that has to take precedence, is that of handwriting, for as we have seen Mozart's handwriting was changing fast and consistently at this period. The work is therefore best treated as belonging to the early part of the Italian journey or just before.

This, then, is the first of Mozart's surviving C major symphonies, a distinguished and distinctive series within a series, to be marvellously crowned nearly twenty years later with the 'Jupiter' Symphony K.551. Characteristics of the breed are the use of trumpets and drums and a spacious, ceremonial manner, often martial in tone, weightier and less dashing than the symphonies in D. The first movement here opens with a spirited flourish around the common chord of C, then sets against it a couple of bars of counterpoint of an almost Corellian formality. There is no secondary material that could be described as a theme, and indeed there is hardly anything truly thematic in a movement made up largely of noisy tuttis full of busy violin tremolandos. The Andante, like the first movement in full sonata form, is of the now familiar type in which a single line of melody unfolds continuously above a regular accompaniment; here the melody is largely doubled, and sometimes texturally glossed, by a pair of flutes (with one moment where a flute briefly enters into dialogue). The brass are silent here but return for the rather pompous minuet (with a typically docile trio) and for the finale, a lively piece in the form and the manner of a *contredanse en rondeau*, formally *A-B-A-C-A-D-A*, with the last episode a witty minor-key one with the violins in octaves and pizzicato basses.

The style here is not truly Italian in the sense that it is in several of the other symphonies that belong, or may belong, to 1770. Mozart was not, regrettably, very explicit in his sundry remarks about symphonies in his letters home. There were two, one nearly finished, in Rome; in Bologna, four—which we should probably take to include the two mentioned in Rome, but perhaps not K.73 if it had been started in Salzburg, as Nannerl would already have known about it. More may have followed. In any case, what did he mean by 'Italian symphonies'? Symphonies composed in Italy? or symphonies in some particularly Italian manner? or three-movement symphonies? or some combination of these?

One unmistakably Italian symphony, in all senses, is K.74 in G, which is in the form of an Italian overture—that is, a work in three movements, without normal movement breaks (and often with the outer movements based on the same material). Further, it is written on Italian manuscript paper of a type that Mozart otherwise used only for the aria *Se ardire*, composed in Rome. This, then, may be one of the two Roman symphonies he referred to in a letter of 25 April

1770. Here again we have themes that are not much more than fragments of figuration succeeding one another in two- or four-bar
phrases, often repeated, relieved by a secondary theme offering a brief
touch of lyricism. Such comments, however, need to be viewed more
as description than as negative criticism, for the movement is spirited
and effective on its own terms. Again both the first movement and
the somewhat unassuming second, into which it leads, are in sonata
form, with nugatory development sections. The finale is another *contredanse en rondeau*, a witty and resourceful movement beginning
piano, for the violins alone, a device Mozart was to use many years on,
in Paris, to compel attention. Here again the last episode (this time
the second, not the third) is a minor-key one with unusual textures.

Four more symphonies, all in D major, have claims to be considered as belonging to these months in Italy: K.81/73*l*, K.84/73*q*,
K.95/73*n* and K.97/73*m*. Neither their spacing in K^1 nor their
bunching by Einstein in K^3 is based on firm evidence; no autographs
are known, nor any copies with dependable authentication. For K.81,
a set of parts survives marked 'Rome, 25 April 1770', but the thematic
catalogue issued annually by Breitkopf includes it in 1775 as a work
of Leopold's. There is no way, beyond the hazardous grounds of style
criticism, of determining its authorship. K.84 is also attributed to
Leopold in one manuscript, but to Dittersdorf in another, as well as
to Mozart in a third and in the Breitkopf manuscript catalogue (with
however a marginal note about its uncertain authenticity). Here
detailed analysis has led to the conclusion that it is more likely to be
by Mozart than the other composers, a conclusion supported by stylistic impression.[36] The manuscript with the attribution to Mozart is
twice inscribed: 'In Milano, il Carnovale 1770 / Overtura' and 'Del
Sig[re] Cavaliere Wolfgango Amadeo Mozart a Bologna, nel mese del
Luglio, 1770'. This probably indicates that the work was composed in
Milan in January or February and revised in Bologna in July (or perhaps begun at carnival time and completed later). K.95 is known only
from a manuscript copy, now destroyed but once owned by Breitkopf
and ascribed to Mozart, as is K.97, though in this case there seems

also to have been a copy owned by Nannerl. If all these four are authentic, we may end up with more symphonies than we know to have been written, or to have been written at this time, but Mozart could of course have produced more after writing the Bologna letter. Here, in fact, we are in no better a position to provide confident answers than in the case of the symphonies in Leopold's 1768 list: again there are works of unprovable authenticity along with information from the Mozarts that can be understood in different ways.

The weakest and perhaps the most dubious of the group is K.95, for which a date as early as 1767 has been suggested.[37] It is scored, uniquely, with oboes and trumpets but no horns, its second movement follows its first without a break, and it has a minuet, as also has K.97. Italian symphonies with a minuet as the third of four movements, in the Austrian manner, were rare. Rather, there might be an extended minuet finale—as was in Mozart's mind, as well as the dance music he was specifically referring to when he wrote: 'We wish we could introduce the German style of minuet here in Italy, where the minuets are so long that they last nearly the length of a whole symphony'[38] (the short 'German minuet' he was referring to was typically of 8 + 16 bars, occasionally 10 or 12 in the first section). It has been conjectured that these minuets might be later additions.[39] Yet in general style K.95 is much closer to these D major works than to the earlier symphonies.

These four symphonies have enough in common stylistically—and in common too with Mozart's overtures to *Mitridate* and *Ascanio in Alba*, which are certainly authentic—to encourage the notion that he might well have written most or all of them, and written them at roughly the same time. Their thematic matter, more figurative than melodic, tends to fall into neat, symmetrical patterns, and leads to a rhythmic structure more four-square than most of Mozart's music of the time, as well as inviting static harmony and regular tonic–dominant alternation. They are unadventurous in texture, depending largely for their interest on the first violin line, with the wind instruments doing little more than sustaining in the tuttis. The development sections in the first movements are mostly modest: a brief interlude on a dominant pedal in K.81 and 84, in K.97 a rather more dramatic section with sharp dynamic contrasts and chromaticisms, and only in the K.95, a rounded binary movement, is there allusion to the opening material. Yet for all the absence of such traditional sources of interest, these are remarkably brilliant and spirited pieces, deftly written in imitation of the symphonies or opera overtures of such composers as Piccinni, Paisiello or Sarti, and intended for the audiences that relished their music. And with his command of instrumental cliché, his clarity of form and his ready, *opera buffa*-like wit—in the perky secondary theme in the finale of K.81 or the scurrying triplets in that of K.84, but perhaps at its subtlest in the opening movement of that symphony—Mozart (if Mozart it is) surpassed his models.

The other instrumental works of Mozart's first months in Italy—the vocal ones must await discussion in the next chapter—are dances and his first string quartet. Dance music was clearly important to Mozart; there are many references to it in his letters, not only his own dances but other composers'. He sent Nannerl from Italy a dance he had heard at the opera, and she sent him copies of minuets by Michael Haydn, on which he commented ('you have set the bass to it exceedingly well, without the slightest mistake, and I urge you to try such things more often': in spite of her five years' seniority, his authority was clearly taken for granted by both of them). The contredanse with five solos K.123/73g is a lively, elegant little piece, with five contrasting eight-bar phrases for two violins each repeated by the whole band (oboes, horns, two violins and bass: violas were not normally used in dance music). A short minuet K.122/73t followed, probably written soon after the Mozarts' arrival in Bologna.

The string quartet K.80/73f, composed at seven o'clock in the evening in an inn at Lodi, as a note on the autograph states, and as Mozart remembered many years later,[40] is a remarkably polished piece, clearly written in emulation of the quartets of Sammartini and his Milanese colleagues that Mozart must have seen or heard in Milan, and not unaffected too in its movement layout and some aspects of its melodic style and its texture by the music of Boccherini that he had played there.[41] The actual melodic character is conservatively *galant*, and the texture is often close to that of the trio sonata, with the violins exchanging material, a static bass and the viola often merely filling in. Yet it shows too a sure instinct for the sound of the string quartet, as opposed to the orchestra, with its intimacy of expression and its poetic sustained notes emerging from the texture in the opening movement, an Adagio (which, incidentally, begins with a melodic cliché that Mozart was to use many times in expressive contexts: it may be dubbed the 'Porgi Amor' theme after its most famous use). The second movement is an energetic Allegro, more in a symphonic manner, and there is a final minuet, more a short German than a long Italian one. But a three-movement work ending in a minuet would not do outside Italy, and some years later Mozart added a short Rondeau in gavotte rhythm.

10

Mitridate at Milan

FTER THREE WEEKS at the San Marco inn in Bologna, the Mozarts moved, on 10 August 1770, to the country house of Field-Marshal Count Pallavicini, Alla Croce del Biacco, a short distance outside the city. Leopold's recovery was much hastened by the life they now led, with 'sheets of linen finer than many a nobleman's shirt', silver bedroom sets, a servant sleeping in the ante-room to attend their every want and to dress Wolfgang's hair, meals in the terrace room, drives with the Pallavicini family, Mass on the premises, and the finest figs, melons and peaches.[1] The intention was still to leave Bologna at the end of the month, and travel through Pisa, Lucca, Livorno and Genoa, then again to Florence, a city Leopold especially loved. But in the event Leopold's recovery was slow, and the Mozarts stayed at Alla Croce del Biacco until the end of September. Mozart wrote to his womenfolk on 25 August about one of their companions:

> We have the honour to go around with a certain Dominican, who is said to be a holy man, but I don't think that is right, for at breakfast he often takes a cup of chocolate and then at once a good glass of strong Spanish wine, and I myself have

had the honour of lunching with this holy man who at table drank a whole decanter and ended up with a full glass of strong wine, a couple of good slices of melon, peaches, pears, five cups of coffee, a whole dish of birds and two saucers of milk and lemon; he may be following some sort of diet, but I think not . . .

Meanwhile, Leopold could report, Wolfgang, now fourteen-and-a-half, was growing and his clothes needed altering; moreover, his voice had now broken—'he has neither a deep voice nor a high one, not even five pure notes; he is very cross about this as he can no longer sing his own compositions, which he would sometimes like to do'.

On 30 August Pallavicini took the Mozarts to the Accademia Filarmonica performance of Mass and Vespers at San Giovanni in Monte, where by tradition each section of the Mass and each Vesper hymn was set by a different member of this exclusive academy. There they met Charles Burney, from London, in Italy during his journeys for collecting material towards his history of music. Burney noted the meeting in his travel journal:[2]

> I went to S. Giovanni in Monti to hear the Philharmonic performances . . . who should I spy there but the celebrated little German Mozart who 3 or 4 years ago surprised every-body in London so much by his premature musical talents. I had a great deal of talk with his father. . . . The little man is grown a good deal but still a little man. He is engaged to compose an opera for Milan. His father has been ill here these 5 or 6 weeks. The pope has knighted the little great wonder.

For the published version of his diary Burney adjusted the wording somewhat, adding that Mozart had been much admired in Rome and Naples and that the Milan opera was for the next carnival. In this later version he added that Mozart 'astonished the Italian musicians wherever he stopt' and that the Milan opera was to be given 'on occasion of the marriage of the Principessina of Modena, with one of the Arch-Dukes of Austria'. Mozart was indeed to write a work for that occasion, but it had not been commissioned at the date to which the diary entry applied, though it could have been under discussion. It is unclear whether, writing somewhat after the event, Burney was confusing one commission with another, or whether he was bringing his information up to date. He adds:

> There are to be 3 new operas composed on this occasion. I know not yet who are his concurrents; but shall be curious to know how this extraordinary boy acquits himself in setting a language not his own. But there is no musical excellence I do not expect from the extraordinary quickness and talents, under the guidance of so able a musician and intelligent a man as his father.

Nothing is known of the Mozarts' activities during the main part of September. But by now they had the libretto and cast list for the Milan opera, *Mitridate, rè di Ponto*, and Wolfgang must have begun planning it. A remark in one of his letters indicates that he and Leopold sometimes played to entertain Countess Pallavicini. He wrote to Thomas Linley expressing his regrets that they could not revisit Florence as they had hoped because of the delay caused by Leopold's injury and because, out of season, they would be unable to recover their expenses.

At the beginning of October the Mozarts moved back to Bologna and on 4 October they attended the festival at San Petronio in honour of the patron saint: 'they had to fetch trumpeters from Lucca for the fanfare, but they played atrociously', Wolfgang wrote. Two days later he played one of the organs at San Domenico. Then, on 9 October, he went to the Accademia Filarmonica and took the test for membership of that august body. A plainsong antiphon was chosen, in the presence of all the members, with the princeps accademiae and two censores, and he was required to set it, in a locked room, in the 'strict style', adding three contrapuntal voices above the given bass. He was allowed three hours; Leopold wrote that he took half-an-hour and the academy records say 'less than an hour'. His first manuscript of this piece, *Quaerite primum regnum Dei* K.86/73v, shows lines and harmonies that go beyond the conventions of the style he was meant to be using, and distributes the interest unevenly between the added voices. Another version survives in Padre Martini's hand, presumably reworked to show Mozart more closely what was wanted, with a copy in Mozart's. This version, using little of Mozart's own material once past the first bar, is more homogeneous in texture and allows the tenor to cross with the given bass, which it seems that Mozart had thought was not permitted (it would have made the task easier). Mozart's copy of the Martini working—they may of course have composed it jointly—was submitted; the examiners all produced their white balls and he was duly admitted as a foreign member in the rank of composer. The usual provisions, for a minimum age of twenty and a year's study in the junior class, were waived; Martini paid the admission fee on his behalf and supplied the testimonial to his abilities.

It is generally supposed that while he was in Bologna Mozart studied with Martini, but there is no reference in the correspondence or elsewhere to any lessons. The existence of Mozart's *Miserere* K.85/73s, a short setting done in Bologna, probably in July or August, of the odd-numbered verses from the *Miserere* for three voices in an antique, partly polyphonic style, though not without some modern harmonic inflections (the even verses were left, presumably to be sung in chant), may hint at some kind of contact with old *maestro*, or at least preparation for the test. Leopold mentions that they visited Martini's house daily and 'had long discussions about the history of music'; he gave Martini a copy of his *Violinschule* and Martini gave the Mozarts the first two volumes (the second newly published) of his *Storia della musica*. Leopold wrote to Martini, in warmly respectful terms, later in the year, and Wolfgang did so six years later, sending him a copy of a work he thought Martini would particularly approve.

The time to be in Milan was now approaching. On 29 September Mozart began work on the recitatives for *Mitridate*.[3] They probably left Bologna on 13 October, and travelled to Parma, where they were delayed by heavy rain and a threat of flooding (in the damp, Leopold was troubled by his chronic rheumatism). They eventually reached Milan on 18 October, where they took up their assigned lodgings near the theatre, a large room with three windows and a balcony, and a bedroom of equal size with a nine-foot bed and two windows but no fireplace ('so if we do not freeze to death we shall be sure not to smell, for we have plenty of air', Leopold wryly wrote). Two days later Wolfgang reported that his fingers were aching from writing the *Mitridate* recitatives.

MITRIDATE IS DESCRIBED in the original libretto as a *dramma per musica*, the most common description of any opera over the preceding century and a half. It is nowadays generally called an *opera seria*, a term almost never used at the time but adopted since for the kind of heroic opera that took shape, in Naples, Rome, Venice and Vienna, in response to a particular set of circumstances, political and social, religious and intellectual. Serious opera reached a 'classical' era in the operas set to the texts of Pietro Metastasio, the enormously influential imperial court poet in Vienna, universally admired and recognized as the supreme master of the genre, from the late 1720s onwards.

Serious opera was primarily a court entertainment, and it was expected to harmonize in its content with the philosophy of the court; it had to embody some degree of moral purpose and allegorical meaning. Many of the stories used for opera had tragic endings, but that would not do for the orderly ethical system that needed to be propagated: the world was fair and just, and good behaviour would meet its due rewards—in this world, not just the next, in this secular age. The *lieto fine*, the happy ending that came about not through divine intervention but because in a rational, enlightened age virtue must triumph and be seen to do so, was virtually obligatory. Usually

the central figures in the plot would be placed, because of the decep-
tions or the evildoings of others, in some kind of moral dilemma,
commonly involving a conflict between private emotion and public
duty, in which they would ultimately make the 'right' decision.

The poetic and musical pattern for this form was a regular and
highly rational one. The action of the plot was conducted in dialogue,
or recitative, which moved at a normal conversational pace and in
which the musical treatment did no more than gently heighten the
ordinary cadences of discourse and dialogue; the light, punctuating
accompaniment permitted the words to be clearly heard. In each tract
of recitative the plot would take a further step forward and information would be disclosed that affected one or more of the characters.
The climax to each scene was an aria in which, as it were, the action
was frozen while the character expressed his or her emotions in the
light of the latest situation, either generally or to another character.
After that there was nothing more to be said; the scene ended and the
singer left the stage—hence the notion of the 'exit aria'.

Most arias in the heyday of *opera seria*, the second quarter of the
century, took the *da capo* design, with the first part repeated after a
shorter middle section. This gave singers the opportunity to provide
'improvised' ornamentation in the repeated material, to show their
technical skill and their ability to apply it to the expression of the
words (it was not, in the hands or the throats of accomplished singers,
merely a licence for vocal gymnastics). There were occasionally
shorter arias, or cavatinas, and usually one or two orchestrally accompanied recitatives at dramatic highpoints for the principals. Most *opere
serie* included a duet, generally late in the work and for the central
couple, either when they are supposedly bidding each other a last
farewell or when they are finally reunited, or occasionally both. Further ensembles were uncommon, but often there was a final *coro*, celebrating the triumph of right over wrong and drawing a moral, for
the principals (including those representing characters who had been
killed in the action earlier on; there was not normally a chorus in the
modern sense).

The opera house itself was a social centre. Most of the boxes were owned or rented by the leading families in the area: the noblest families were on the first floor, the *piano nobile*, with the social standing of each family embodied in its degree of proximity to that level. They would attend most of the performances, including repeats of the same work; they were not expected to give a performance their concentrated attention, especially when the lesser singers were on the stage, and they would move freely in and out of the theatre, and converse, eat, gamble or play cards at their pleasure. Printed librettos were sold at the theatre (bilingual if the opera was not in the audience's native tongue) so that they could follow the plot, and the theatre lighting, with individual candles by the seats, made it possible to do so. Burney's description of the Teatro Regio Ducal at Milan conveys something of this:[4]

> The theatre here is very large and splendid; it has five rows of boxes on each side, one hundred in each row; and parallel to

Teatro Regio Ducal, Milan: engraving by M.A. dal Re (*Civica Raccolta Stampe Bertarelli, Milan*)

these runs a broad gallery . . . as an avenue to every row of boxes: each box will contain six persons, who sit at the sides, facing each other. Across the gallery of communications is a complete room to every box, with a fireplace in it, and all conveniences for refreshments and cards. In the fourth row is a *pharo* table [for gambling at cards], on each side of the house, which is used during the performance of the opera. There is in front a very large box . . . set apart for the . . . governor of Milan . . . In the highest storey the people sit in front; and those for whom there are no seats, stand behind in the gallery . . .

Part of the librettist's task was to balance the principal roles so that the singers each had a number of arias appropriate to their importance—four or five for the *prima donna* and the *primo uomo* (the leading castrato, usually at mezzo-soprano pitch), three or four for the *seconda donna* and the *secondo uomo*, about four for the tenor (who was rarely a heroic figure and more often an older man, sometimes a king), and one or two each for the confidants, generals and the like (often mezzo-sopranos and basses). These last were usually placed soon after an interval, where they could readily be missed by those returning late or obscured by the clink of spoons as the audience ate their sorbets (the *aria di sorbetto* tradition was sustained well into the next century). The *primo uomo* was traditionally considered the most important, and was the highest paid, of the singers, though by Mozart's time the decline of the castrato had already begun (he would be almost eliminated by Rossini's time), and the leading soprano might be paid half as much again as the *primo uomo*.[5] Each character's arias, above all those of the principals, needed to show a wide variety of feeling so that the singers could display their voices in different expressive contexts. Various devices were employed to make this easier, among them the 'simile aria', in which the character would parallel his or her situation with, for example, that of a bird, or a ship tossed in a stormy sea and seeking a haven, or a mountain stream, which provided the composer with opportunities for attractive and varied musical imagery. Although the *opera seria* genre drew on artifice of this kind, it was not, by the canons of its own time, inherently undramatic. Its creators and their audiences thought of it no less as a *Gesamtkunstwerk*—a purposeful alliance of music, poetry, dance, gesture and stage design—than did Wagner more than a hundred years later.

By the time that Mozart came to write *Mitridate*, the patterns of *opera seria* were already loosening in the hands of a new generation of 'enlightened' patrons, librettists and composers—in that order of precedence, for it was the patron who called the tune, and the intellectual instigator of change would be the poet rather than the composer. The changes were local, not universal. In the 1750s Jommelli at Stuttgart and Traetta at Parma, both progressive and French-influenced courts, had begun to break down the formal schemes with different types of aria, ensemble and chorus and programmatic orchestral writing; Gluck, in Vienna, went still further in *Orfeo ed Euridice* (1762). Such developments were known to Mozart, who was familiar with Gluck's *Orfeo* and *Alceste*, but they probably did not seem relevant either to the libretto he was required to set in Milan or to the taste of the court there. It must also be uncertain whether he was temperamentally attuned to the thinking behind opera 'reform' or, at this stage, mature enough to deal with the issues it raised.

On receiving a libretto, a composer's first step at this period was, after reading it carefully, to plan the key structure, aria by aria (according to an account by Salieri of his own procedure, which he detailed in his memoirs).[6] There were certain traditions Salieri would normally observe, such as setting the heroine's chief expressive aria in E flat and the love duets in A major, and he would take care that successive numbers were related in a way that accorded with their dramatic significance. Then he could compose the linking recitative, ensuring that each section ended in a key that led smoothly into the next item. Normally he would next write any choruses and ensembles, and the overture. The overture and the act finales would normally be set in a key in which trumpets could be used (this generally meant C, D or E flat). By this time he would need to be in the city where the opera was to be produced, and the singers contracted to take part would be arriving to learn their music, normally with the lowest paid, singing the minor parts, coming first. As each singer arrived, the composer would listen to his or her voice and tailor the arias to suit it (the image of 'fitting the costume to the figure' was one that Leopold and Wolfgang used, as did others).[7] The singers would try their arias over and, depending in some degree on their status (and the composer's), would have the right—indeed the obligation—to reject or demand modifications in arias with which they were uncomfortable or which they felt did not suit their voice. An opera was designed not for posterity but for a single run of performances, and had to be composed effectively for the cast actually taking part; should it later be revived, it could easily be revised to suit the new cast.

THE FIRST REPORT we have on the progress of the composition of *Mitridate*, apart from Mozart's comment on his aching fingers, comes in a letter of 10 November 1770, when Leopold reports on their 'first battle'. Someone had given the *prima donna*, the well-known soprano Antonia Bernasconi (who had created Gluck's Alcestis and had been in the provisional cast for *La finta semplice*), a complete set of arias for the opera and tried to persuade her to sing them instead of Mozart's. The libretto was originally the work of Vittorio Amedeo Cigna-Santi, a scholar and poet from Turin, after Racine's *Mithridate*. It had been set in 1767 by the Turin Cathedral *maestro di cappella* and court chamber composer Quirino Gasparini—although there are several texts set by Mozart that seem to be substitutes for ones set by Gasparini, which may be the work of the Milan house poet Giuseppe Parini rather than Cigna-Santi's (whose name, perhaps significantly, is not printed on the libretto). Choosing a libretto that had recently been set by a reputable composer was clearly a sensible precaution: it meant that Gasparini's arias could be used if Mozart's failed to satisfy the singers. Leopold saw the proposed replacement arias and at first thought they were new; only later did he learn that they were Gasparini's. But he could report that Bernasconi was 'beside herself with delight' at Mozart's settings, as too was her *maestro*, Lampugnani, who 'cannot sufficiently praise them'. Leopold however saw further battles on the horizon. He asked that the letters from home be as entertaining as possible to Wolfgang, as he was 'now busy with serious matters and is therefore very serious himself'. Mozart, it seems, did most of his composing in the mornings; Leopold tried to keep him from having to work after the midday meal unless absolutely necessary.

On 17 November they went to the country for the weekend, staying at the house of Leopold Troger, a court official who was the Mozarts' main contact with Firmian and whose sister lived in Salzburg. A week later, Leopold was more anxious at the non-arrival of the *primo uomo*, the castrato Pietro Benedetti: Wolfgang had written one of his arias but was reluctant to go any further—he 'refuses to do the work twice over and prefers to await his arrival so as to fit the costume to his figure'. Another week further on: 'If you think the opera is ready, you are very much mistaken. Had it depended solely on us, two operas would have been written by now. But in Italy everything is quite crazy'. Most of the singers must by now have learnt their parts, for rehearsals were about to begin. This was the rehearsal schedule:

5/6 December	recitatives (1)
8 December	recitatives (2)
12 December	with small orchestra
17 December	with full orchestra
19 December	theatre rehearsal (1)
21 December	recitatives (3)
22 December	theatre rehearsal (2)
24 December	dress rehearsal
26 December	first performance

The first instrumental rehearsal was designed mainly to prove the copying, but it served too, Leopold wrote, to confound those who had predicted the opera's failure on the grounds of Wolfgang's immaturity and his inability to handle the '*chiaro ed oscuro* needed in the theatre' (the light and shade, the subtlety of colouring). The full orchestra numbered 60, Leopold said, then provided figures that add up to 56: strings consisting of fourteen each of first and second violins, six violas, two cellos and six double-basses, pairs of flutes, oboes and bassoons, four horns and two trumpets (there must also have been a timpanist) and two harpsichords. The delight of the copyist, which he reported on 15 December, was a particularly good omen: opera-house copyists prospered when operas succeeded as they personally were paid for making copies of the arias (they could even do better than the composer, Leopold notes). The singers were all satisfied, he adds, especially the *prima donna* and the *primo uomo*, 'who are enchanted with their duet'. The latter told Leopold he would let himself be castrated again if it was a failure.

Leopold was not in fact telling the whole truth; as so often, he paints a slightly rosy picture to spare the womenfolk's anxieties. All the principal singers had at some stage been discontent with their music, as the surviving alternative versions of their arias testify. One of them, possibly two, remained so, to the degree of insisting on the substitution of Gasparini's arias. That was certainly the case with the tenor, Guglielmo Ettore (or d'Ettore), Sicilian-born, about thirty years old, an admired court singer at Munich, thought by Burney 'the best singer of his kind on the operatic stage' and himself a composer and a papal knight. In a letter many years later Leopold reminded his son of the unpleasantness surrounding their dealings with d'Ettore.[8] There exist five versions of his opening aria, all but the final one drafts or incomplete, indicating that he must have rejected four attempts,[9] and in Act 3 he evidently sang an aria of Gasparini's (with modifications by Mozart) which has continued to be sung in modern revivals—it is erroneously printed as if Mozart's own in all published scores, with Mozart's original setting relegated to an appendix.[10] The final version, for which Mozart drew some ideas from Gasparini, is an outstandingly graceful piece, and allows d'Ettore several of the large vocal leaps on which he evidently prided himself. In three of his other four arias, Mozart set only part of the text; all are rather short, which suggests that d'Ettore already had physical limits. For the *prima donna*, Bernasconi, two arias were rewritten. One aria each for the *seconda donna* and the *secondo uomo* were rewritten, and so was one of the *primo uomo*'s, which was then adjusted again to accommodate a new solo part for a horn (Mozart left the voice part as it was, but some ingenious expansion of the ritornellos allows for the horn solos). Even the 'enchanting' duet was a second version.

It is instructive to compare the rejected versions with the accepted ones. The duet, more than any other item, represents a change of view. This is the climactic number, the Act 2 finale, where the two principals bid each other a (supposed) final farewell. Mozart first set it in the traditionally expressive key of E flat, with warm and eloquently amorous lines in the Adagio sections and impassioned raging at fate in the fast ones. The revised version, in the traditional love-duet key of A major, is shorter, lighter and more graceful, with no recurrence of the slow section. Probably Mozart had written the original before he heard Benedetti, the *primo uomo*. Bernasconi may well have rejected her first aria as making an indifferent initial impression; the replacement, a noble and spacious piece, certainly offers more scope to her voice. The rejected Adagio section of her Act 2 'Nel grave tormento' embodies some unusually enterprising orchestral writing, using flutes and oboes much as Mozart did ten years later in the temple scene of *Idomeneo*, but the long, sustained lines of the revised setting may have been more to her taste. The *seconda donna*'s rejected aria, also her first in the opera, was probably insufficiently showy and too low in tessitura, the *secondo uomo*'s simply too long—Mozart changed what was in effect an Allegro aria with a slow introduction and interlude into an aria half the length with an equal balance of slow and fast. It is easy to be critical and indignant on Mozart's behalf, but that is beside the point. It was his job to provide arias in which the cast felt they could shine, for it was only through their shining that the opera could be a success.

Mozart's autograph score of the final version does not survive, but autograph material for the rejected numbers is in Paris (the Bibliothèque Nationale, Conservatoire collection). The early copies of the final version there and in Lisbon (the Biblioteca Ajuda) are likely to have been made after rehearsals and the première and would therefore show the text as it was actually performed. The Lisbon score is doubtless the one Mozart referred to in a letter of 2 January 1771 as being copied for the court there. Leopold later reported that four more were made, two for Vienna, one for the Duchess of Parma and one for the theatre management; one of those could be the Paris copy, but otherwise their fate is unknown.

This was the cast:

Mitridate [Mithridates], *king of Pontus and other kingdoms, in love with Aspasia*	Guglielmo d'Ettore (*tenor*)
Aspasia, *Mitridate's betrothed, already proclaimed queen*	Antonia Bernasconi (*soprano*)
Sifare [Xiphares], *younger son of Mitridate, in love with Aspasia*	Pietro Benedetti (*soprano*)
Farnace [Pharnaces], *elder son of Mitridate, in love with Aspasia*	Giuseppe Cicognani (*alto*)
Ismene, *daughter of the Parthian king, in love with Farnace*	Anna Francesca Varese (*soprano*)
Marzio [Martius], *Roman tribune*	Gasparo Bassano (*tenor*)
Arbate [Arbates], *governor of Nymphaeum*	Pietro Muschietti (*bass*)

The Mozarts went to the first night, on 26 December 1770, anxious at the opera's prospects. They had lately heard from Naples that Jommelli, though so widely esteemed, even revered, had just had a spectacular failure there with his *Demofoonte* (his fourth setting of the admired Metastasio libretto). Three days after Mozart's première, however, Leopold could report its success. One of the *prima donna*'s arias had been encored, unprecedented on a first night; and after almost all the arias ('except a few at the end') there were cries of 'Evviva il maestro! evviva il maestrino!' The next night two of the *prima donna*'s arias had to be repeated, and the duet would have been too had not the management discouraged encores. In any case, the opera lasted six hours, Leopold wrote, including two hours of dancing (there were ballets, composed by Francesco Caselli, on the Judgment of Paris between the first two acts, on The Triumph of Virtue over Love between the second two, and at the end a celebration of the marriages in the opera; these, he wrote, would be shortened). Leopold was triumphant: various enemies, he told both his wife and Padre Martini, had circulated malicious rumours about the opera as 'barbarous German' music, but they had been proved wrong. Mozart himself directed the first three performances, in the accepted way, from the first harpsichord, with the theatre *maestro* Lampugnani at the second; thereafter Lampugnani took over the direction, with Chiesa at the second harpsichord. Leopold wrote:[11]

> If, about fifteen or eighteen years ago, when Lampugnani had already composed so much in England and Melchior Chiesa in Italy, and I had seen their opera arias and symphonies, someone had told me that these masters would serve in the performance of my son's composition, and, when he left the harpsichord, would have to sit down and accompany his music, I should have told him he was crazy and fit for the madhouse.

The opera had 22 performances, a good number for a first carnival opera. The *Gazzetta di Milano* said that it satisfied the public 'as much for the good taste of the stage designs as for the excellence of the music and the ability of the actors . . . The young *maestro di cappella*, who is not yet fifteen years of age, studies the beauties of nature, and represents them adorned with the rarest musical graces'.[12] The stage settings were the work of the Galliari brothers, Bernardino, Fabrizio and Giovanni Antonio, admired across much of Europe and dominant in Milanese stage design at the time. They had also been responsible for the designs for Gasparini's version.[13] While they would not have used the same designs again, the settings for Mozart's opera would have followed the same general style with its graceful, idealized realism.

The opera is set in Pontus, in Asia Minor, where the historical Mithridates VII Eupator had long resisted the Romans during a reign that ended in 65 B.C.E. Racine's play, and the opera that roughly follows it, draws only sparingly on historical fact. Here the elderly

Mitridate, rè di Ponto: libretto and dramatis personae (*Staatsbibliothek, Preussischer Kulturbesitz, Berlin*)

Mitridate has two sons, the faithful Sifare and the traitorous Farnace, the latter in league with the Romans. Both sons love their father's betrothed, Aspasia, who reciprocates Sifare's love; Farnace is loved by the Parthian princess Ismene. Mitridate lays a trap for his sons by sending news of his death in battle and then returning home; both, ultimately, are condemned to death. But Sifare earns his father's forgiveness by coming to his aid in battle, and so finally does Farnace, who undergoes a double change of heart, renouncing Aspasia and then turning on his Roman allies. In the battle Mitridate is mortally wounded, so the way is open for the obligatory happy resolution. It was less important for a plot to be convincing in realistic terms than to supply opportunities for the display of a wide range of human feeling.

Mozart made use of several different kinds of structure for his arias, choosing them according to their position in the opera and their dramatic function, and also making due allowance for the ranking of the singer. The longest arias are of the *dal segno* type, akin to the Baroque *da capo* aria but recapitulating, after a central section, not from the head (*capo*) but, to avoid excessive length, from a sign (*segno*) placed at some point in the course of the principal section.[14] Often the central section is set in a contrasting tempo and metre, particularly where the words carry a different sense. In *Mitridate* all the principals introduce themselves with an aria of this sort, except for the tenor; there are four in the first act, two each in Acts 2 and 3. Arias of this type, with long ritornellos, taken up and further supplemented by the singer (forming what is sometimes misleadingly called a 'double exposition'), have close links with Mozart's later concerto forms. The pattern to be used in his mature piano concerto first movements, a concerto or aria variant of what was becoming the standard sonata-style procedure, is already there in its essentials: an orchestral ritornello with two main themes, both in the tonic key; an entry for the soloist with the opening theme, then a modulation to the dominant for a different version of the second; after a ritornello, a solo passage with free modulation; then a return of the basic material (often only the secondary themes) in the tonic key. After a contrasting central section, normally in a related key (usually subdominant or relative minor), the *segno* indicates a repeat of some of the first section: it may be just the 'recapitulation' material or even only part of it, but sometimes it includes the preceding section too. Where there is a middle section, the second stanza of verse is reserved for it; otherwise the second stanza is usually set in the section following the central ritornello. Arias of this type usually offer scope for both expansive singing and for virtuoso passage-work, which Mozart supplied in a variety of patterns to suit the singers' diverse capabilities.

The faster or moderate-tempo arias of this type, whose formality was not particularly conducive to naturalness of expression, often tend in *Mitridate* to a rather generalized vocal virtuosity. Sometimes they are a singer's first aria, before any situation calling for strong emotional feeling has been established. That may be said of all four examples in Act 1, excepting possibly Farnace's defiant 'Venga pur'. Also rather pedestrian are Ismene's Act 2 aria and the single aria assigned, in the last act, to Martius (both, typically for arias for a secondary character, are scored for strings alone). But this extended type is also used for the principal slow arias for the *primo* and *secondo uomo*—Sifare's moving farewell to Aspasia in Act 2, 'Lungi da te', and Farnace's final aria of repentance, although its middle section and repeat are omitted in the Lisbon source, which probably reflects the Milan performances. Mozart's changes to 'Lungi da te'—adding the obbligato horn part to the already rewritten aria, adjusting the first violin line or an inner detail, extending a ritornello—are an object lesson in ingenuity and economy. The aria shows a clear debt, in its melodic line (especially in its first version) and its textures, to an aria in Myslivecek's *La Nitteti*, which Mozart must have come across in Bologna.[15]

There are also several two-tempo arias, still basically following a sonata-style pattern but simpler in structure, a useful form where the words invite, or permit, a change of mood to correspond with the change in tempo: Sifare's second aria, for example, begins with a solemn statement of resolve which in Mozart's setting turns into a call for action, with a change from a slow tempo to Allegro. Aspasia's Act 2 aria, similarly, begins with an Adagio as she talks of her torment and moves to a fiery Allegro as she confronts it. (Mozart's initial working of the Adagio, which he abandoned, is more elaborate and implies a larger aria, perhaps of the *dal segno* type.) The best motivated examples are Mitridate's first Act 2 aria, where he addresses the loyal Sifare in an Adagio and then rounds on Aspasia ('tu, ingrata') in an Allegro, and Farnace's first admission of guilt, 'Son reo, l'error confesso', which begins Adagio maestoso but moves on, when he turns to denounce his brother and Aspasia for crimes supposedly still more heinous, to an Allegro. (Here Mozart's first version, essentially the same music, had included repetition of the opening words within the Allegro, effectively set but weakening the link between music and sense.)

The music for Mitridate himself, however, stands slightly apart, not only because he was the sole principal with a true male voice but also because his arias seem to have been deliberately kept short. There are five of them, more than are allotted to the *prima donna* or the *primo uomo* (who however sing a duet too). Perhaps d'Ettore had physical difficulties that precluded his undertaking a full-length aria. They did not preclude very high notes, up to a top C, but he evidently could not cope with the usual kind of rapid *fioritura*. Mozart's struggles over his first aria, seen in the four surviving drafts, would seem likely to be the products of the 'storm' Leopold reported, as by then weathered, on 17 November. The result however seems to have been worth the trouble, for this one-section aria or cavata, 'Se di lauri il crine adorno', has a melodic line of exceptional grace, ideally suited to a high lyrical tenor, and is arguably the most appealing number in the opera. Here Mozart set the usual two stanzas, using a sonata-form scheme that he followed in six of the arias altogether. In three of the other four for Mitridate only a single stanza is set. The libretto shows that his opening aria, a sonata-form Allegro that ends Act 1, was originally to have had a second stanza, but both the two-tempo aria and 'Vado incontro' (whether in Gasparini's setting or Mozart's) were originally single-stanza arias. The former shows a fifteen-bar cut in the Lisbon score.

It has often been suggested that Mozart had access to Gasparini's score when composing his own and that he drew on its procedures from time to time, especially in the orchestral recitatives. We know that Bernasconi had copies of Aspasia's arias, and d'Ettore, who had sung the title-role at Turin, had copies of at least some of those for Mitridate. Certain obvious types of resemblance may be accounted for simply by the fact of two composers working in the same tradition and setting the same text—for example, in the handling of some of the accompanied recitatives, and the alternation of slow and fast tempos in Mitridate's 'Tu che fedel' and the first setting of the duet (there the key structure is also the same, but in his second version Mozart inserted two lines of text, which altered the nature of the passionate outburst from anger to grief). Another point of resemblance comes in the design and treatment of Farnace's aria at the beginning of Act 2, where there is a musical link between their settings of the second stanza, less a matter of influence than of Mozart's seeing no objection to allowing the occasional echo of an apt phrase. In one important procedure they usually differ. Gasparini generally favours recapitulating from the beginning of each aria, as in the traditional *da capo*, but then making a large cut to shorten the *da capo* section. Mozart prefers to enter the final section at a later juncture, which tends to soften the formal outlines of the movement. But the most obvious difference between the two scores lies simply in the level of invention: next to Mozart's score, Gasparini's textures seem thin, his harmonic vocabulary limited and his dramatic invention routine.

In what respects, then, does *Mitridate* foreshadow the musical dramatist of *Idomeneo* or the later operas? It would be mistaken to expect the resource or originality of such works in an opera by a boy of fourteen designed to meet the requirements of the Milan opera house and its audiences. Mozart differs from his Italian contemporaries in his rich scoring and in the sheer length of some of the numbers; Italians, though not the italianate J.C. Bach, tended to write more briefly and to permit less instrumental competition with the voice ('in Germany we rather like length', Mozart wrote in a letter from Paris in 1778).[16] His dramatic powers—his matching of music to situation and feeling—are seen here in the management of some of the two-tempo arias noted above (especially 'Lungi da te' and 'Son reo'), in the often vivid accompanied recitatives, and perhaps particularly in the music that portrays Aspasia's emotional states. The agitation of 'Nel sen mi palpita' in Act 1, set in the traditional key for agitation, G minor, with its urgent opening (without ritornello), its string tremolandos, its chromaticisms and its expression of breathlessness in the vocal line, represents something more than a gifted boy's clever imitation of his models. Much the same applies to the parallel number in the last act, in C minor, for Sifare ('Se il rigor d'ingrata sorte'), and again to Aspasia's *scena* in Act 3, where two accompanied recitatives embrace an *andante* cavatina, 'Pallid' ombre', whose spacious line and broad declamatory manner recall similar scenes in the Gluck operas that Mozart knew. The cavatina is dramatically interrupted by recitative—a rapid violin scale, then a throbbing accompaniment (marked, exceptionally, 'tremolo', as her hand, she says, freezes and her mind grows turbulent as she is required to take poison). This view of Aspasia's music is not just a modern one: the report of the opera in the *Gazzetta di Milano* quoted above, which was contributed by Giuseppe Parini, commented only on the arias sung by Bernasconi, which 'vividly expressed the passions and touched the heart'.

THE MOZARTS WERE able to relax after the first three performances of *Mitridate*. There is no hint, in Leopold's remarks, that Wolfgang would have preferred to continue directing, and it is clear that father and son enjoyed listening from various parts of the house, walking about during performances wherever they chose and meeting and talking to members of the audience. As they were always hungry after the performance they were rarely in bed until 1.30 or 2.00 a.m. Clearly they were in a festive mood. They were entertained by vari-

ous friends—Leopold reports that on 3 January Madame von Aste-
burg, daughter of the Trogers, gave Wolfgang liver dumplings and
sauerkraut at his request, as well as a capon and a pheasant, and on the
next day they appeared at a concert at Count Firmian's, where Wolfgang played a new, difficult but beautiful concerto (the composer is
not identified), and where they dined on 5 January. A few days later
they heard that on that date Wolfgang had been granted membership
of the Accademia Filarmonica of Verona; the nomination document
is a fulsome tribute to his skills and reports on his triumphs in the city
the year before when he 'wonderfully and with the highest mastery
and to the astonishment of all this noble gathering underwent the
most demanding musical tests'.

   On 14 January 1771 the Mozarts set off for Turin, one of the cities
Leopold had been keen to visit. It was the capital of the Sardinian
monarchy and the main city of Piedmont, with two opera houses and
a long tradition of string playing. Among the musicians they met
there was the leading violinist Gaetano Pugnani, one of whose pupils,
a few months older than Mozart, was G.B. Viotti. They also met several of the court musicians, including Gasparini, the wind-playing
Besozzi brothers, the court *maestro di cappella* F.S. Giai (son of a more
famous father), the composer Ignazio Celoniati, the cellist Chabran
and several singers, as well as Giovanni Paisiello, who was in the city
for the première of his opera *Annibale in Torino* at the principal theatre, the Teatro Regio, on 16 January; this was almost certainly the
'magnificent' opera that Leopold reported their hearing. They stayed
in Turin at the Dogana Nova inn. Leopold's travel notes name a number of local noblemen whom they met and before whom, presumably, they played during their two weeks in the city. Their
acquaintance with so many court musicians suggests that they might
also have played at court. On 31 January they returned to Milan. They
lunched with Count Firmian on 2 February and left two days later,
for Venice, on the first part of their journey home.

   Because of wretched weather and 'astonishing' winds, it took the
Mozarts a full week to reach Venice. They spent their first night in

Canonica and passed through Brescia, Verona, Vicenza and Padua—the intention had been to see the operas being given in those cities, Leopold said, when he gave their itinerary in an earlier letter, though we know only that they heard an *opera buffa* in Brescia.[17] They took lodgings in the Casa Ceseletti, a private house by the Ponte dei Barcaroli, central and on the water (the house, still standing, bears a plaque), but they spent a good deal of time with the former Salzburg family of Johannes Wider, a business colleague of Hagenauer's. Wider was apparently the father of six beautiful daughters, referred to by Mozart in letters to Nannerl and Johann Hagenauer Jr. (their landlord's son, who had stayed with them in Venice) as 'pearls'. The six pearls and their mother evidently attempted, in vain, to put Mozart through the *attacco*, the ritual of 'becoming a true Venetian', which entailed his being held on the ground and having his bottom spanked ('but they couldn't get me on to the floor'); they also gave the Mozarts gifts and serviced their clothes.

There was serious business too. On 5 March the Mozarts gave what Leopold described as a 'fine concert'; nothing is known of where it was given or what they played. They went to the opera, hearing the admired soprano Anna de Amicis, probably in G.B. Borghi's *Siroe* (at the San Moisè) and Antonio Boroni's *Le contadine furlane* (at the San Benedetto). Leopold mentions that the performance began at two o'clock and finished at seven. It may not have been possible for them to go more than once as Lent began just after their arrival.

Leopold must have come to Venice armed with introductions, as he soon reported that they were regularly lunching with members of the nobility, such as the Cornaro, Grimani, Mocenigo and Dolfino families, who would send their private gondolas to collect them and would personally accompany them back afterwards. They also lunched with Count Giacomo Durazzo, now the imperial ambassador, but formerly the highly influential opera intendant in Vienna, responsible for the production of Gluck's 'reform' operas there. It may be through the Grimanis, who had built and until 1766 owned the San Benedetto theatre, that the Mozarts negotiated with the company that ran that theatre, small but distinguished and the principal one devoted to *opera seria*, for a contract for Wolfgang to compose an opera for production there. The contract materialized, the following August, for the second carnival opera for 1773, probably to reach the stage in January that year, but the opera did not, for as we shall see Mozart was obliged to be in Milan at the time he would have been needed in Venice.

Leopold's letters suggest that they were generously fêted, but a letter to Hasse in Vienna from his friend Giovanni Maria Ortes, a priest and writer, says, perhaps reflecting Hasse's earlier remarks to him:[18]

> I do not believe that they (the Mozarts) find themselves very pleased with this city, where they probably thought that, as elsewhere, others would seek after them rather than they after others . . . It is a curious thing that the boy regards this difference as a matter of no concern, while the father seems a shade piqued.

Hasse responded:

> The young Mozard is certainly wonderful for his age, and indeed I love him infinitely. The father, as I see the man, is equally discontent everywhere, for here too he made the same lamentations. He idolizes his son a little too much, and thus does all he can to spoil him; but I have so good an opinion of the boy's natural good sense that I hope he will not, in spite of the father's flattery, be spoilt, but will grow into a fine man.

Only one Venetian musician of any significance is named in their travel notes, the composer Ferdinando Bertoni, *maestro* at one of the orphanage-conservatories for which Venice was well known and a leading opera composer, though a 'Schulz di Prussia Cembalista' named by Mozart (both he and his father made lists) may be J.A.P. Schulz from Lüneburg, later to be eminent.

They set out for home on 12 March, travelling by boat ('Borcello') on the Brenta to Padua, accompanied by part of the Wider family and Abbate Ortes, picnicking on board. In Padua they stayed in the *palazzo* of the Pesaro family and did as much sight-seeing as was possible in a single day, during which they also visited the renowned theorist and church composer F.A.Vallotti at the basilica of San Antonio (known as 'Il Santo'). There Wolfgang played the organ, as he did too at Santa Giustina, as well as playing the harpsichord at the house of the composer Giovanni Ferrandini. In the course of the day they also acquired a commission, from Don Giuseppe Ximenes, Prince of Aragon, for Wolfgang to write an oratorio to be given in the city. The next two days were spent, still with their friends from Venice, at Vicenza, as guests of the bishop, a member of the Cornaro family— 'not without good reason', Leopold adds, presumably meaning that they expected to be well rewarded for Wolfgang's playing there. On 16 March they reached Verona, where they stayed at the house of Pietro Lugiati, a financial official for the province; the next day they played for his guests. There Leopold received a letter from Milan, telling him news of another commission he was to receive, in Salzburg, from Vienna; he does not disclose its contents except to say that it would bring their son 'imperishable honour'. This, clearly, was news of the forthcoming commission, to be issued from the imperial court, for a wedding serenata to be given in Milan in the autumn when Maria Theresa's son, the Archduke Ferdinand, was to marry Beatrice, Princess of Modena. There was also 'another very pleasing piece of news' in the letter, possibly about the commission from Milan for another carnival opera, to be given at the end of 1772. The contract had presumably been negotiated when they were still there and was formally issued on 4 March, offering a fee of 130 gigliati as opposed to the 100 for *Mitridate*. Evidently Leopold had not at this point understood that because of the clash of dates acceptance of the Milanese commission would preclude Mozart's undertaking the Venetian one.

So the Mozarts departed across the Alps on the final part of their journey—Leopold had all along been determined to get home by Easter at the latest—with three or four substantial commissions for Italy in prospect, likely to involve two return journeys within the next two years. Leopold had hoped to take a different route back, through Carinthia ('I have already seen the Tyrol, and there is no pleasure in taking the same route twice, in the manner of dogs'). But in the event the need for speed prevailed, and they travelled again through Rovereto and Brixen and over the Brenner Pass to Innsbruck, arriving in a violent gale and bitterly cold weather and pausing there for a day. After an absence of more than fifteen months, they reached home in Salzburg on Maundy Thursday, 28 March 1771.

11

Success in Milan

MOZART AND HIS FATHER were in Salzburg for less than five months. Life there was not ideally comfortable for the family. Their apartment was now so cramped that Leopold, and perhaps his wife too, took a room at a nearby lodging-house to sleep in. A letter Leopold had sent from Venice asks Maria Anna which of three she preferred (with the Sailerwirt family, close by in Getreidegasse; at the Sternbräu, further down the same street; or the Saulentzl, at a butcher's shop in Goldgasse. He also suggested for himself the 'Löchl', in the Löchlplatz immediately opposite).[1] 'The way we now sleep together, like soldiers, is no longer possible', he added, 'Wolfgang is no longer seven years old'. Mozart was in fact fifteen, and Nannerl nearly twenty. Clearly they had outgrown their apartment; presumably, it was uncertainty about their longer-term future in Salzburg that made him disinclined to undertake the commitment of a move to a larger house.

Not a single document survives from these months to tell us what Mozart was doing—apart, that is, from composing. There is however one letter from Leopold Mozart, sent in July 1771 to Count Pallavicini in Bologna, primarily to inform him of their plans for further visits to Italy for the two Milan commissions.[2] In it he also refers to the Paduan oratorio, *La Betulia liberata*. They proposed, he said, to send the score to Padua for copying as they passed through Verona, en route to Milan, and then to return through Padua to rehearse and probably to perform it; presumably the performance was scheduled for the autumn, perhaps at Advent (Lent would have been more usual for an oratorio). It is clear that Mozart must already have received instruction, presumably from Ferrandini when they were previously in Padua, about the singers and their capabilities. The work, a setting of a popular libretto by Metastasio, was composed during the months in Salzburg. The wedding serenata for Milan, *Ascanio in Alba*, could not be begun because the words had yet to be written, 'by a certain Abbate Porini', Leopold wrote. Giuseppe Parini, Professor of Rhetoric at Milan and house poet at the opera, was a significant Enlightenment figure, who, as critic for the *Gazzetta di Milano*, had written warmly about *Mithridate*.[3] The text had also to be approved by the court in Vienna, as the wedding to be celebrated was that of an imperial archduke, the seventeen-year-old Ferdinand, son of Maria Theresa, who was to marry Princess Maria Beatrice Ricciarda d'Este of Modena, a lady (as Leopold later noted) known to be 'friendly, agreeable and virtuous' if not beautiful. Mozart would not in any case expect to compose it until he had met and heard the singers, although the *primo uomo* was to be an old and dear friend, his one-time singing teacher Giovanni Manzuoli.

There was probably another commission awaiting Mozart when he arrived back from Italy, or it may have arrived soon thereafter: a serenata in honour of the archbishop, Siegmund von Schrattenbach. Each 21 December the anniversary of his consecration was celebrated in Salzburg. As Mozart could not expect to be back from Milan until shortly before that date, the work would have to be written during the summer. The commission—no document survives—might how-ever have been for a different celebration; Schrattenbach would have been in the service of the church for fifty years on 10 January 1772, and his next birthday would fall on 28 February. All were events that called for local festivities, but works intended for the later dates, the

February one in particular, would probably not have needed to be completed so much in advance. Another product of this summer, then, was an allegorical work, again to a Metastasio text, *Il sogno di Scipione*, composed in Schrattenbach's honour—but in the event never to be heard by him.

There were also more routine commissions for the archbishop's Kapelle. Among the works of these months is a setting of the *Litaniae lauretanae* text (K.109/74*e*), which Mozart simply dated 'May'. The Litany of Loreto, a series of Marian invocations, each with the response 'ora pro nobis' ('pray for us'), dates back to medieval times and acquired official status in the sixteenth century; it was probably then that it became associated with the Santa Casa at Loreto. Mozart was to make two settings each of this and the sacramental litany text, the *Litaniae de venerabili altaris sacramento*.[4] Litany settings, used for festivals and other special occasions, often with processions, were particularly popular in south Germany and Austria. There are examples by many leading composers of the generation immediately before Mozart's, including Caldara, Fux and the younger Reutter in Vienna and Eberlin, Adlgasser, Leopold Mozart and Michael Haydn in Salzburg, where the tradition goes even further back, at least to Biber. The local church calendar for 1772 specified the performance of litany settings in the extended forty-hour prayer session beginning on Palm Sunday and in connection with certain saints' days, including St Nepomuk's in May.

Mozart's first setting of the Litany of Loreto text is modest in scale, related to the later ones much as a *missa brevis* is to a *missa solemnis*. It may have been intended for a small-scale performance in the chapel of the Schloss Mirabell rather than some more formal occasion in Salzburg Cathedral, probably about the time of St Nepomuk's day (16 May). Set with two violins, bass and organ continuo, with trombones doubling the lower choral parts in the usual manner, it is modelled on Leopold's setting in F (now in the Salzburg Cathedral archive) in its choice of tempo and metre for each movement. It begins with a direct, homophonic choral setting of the 'Kyrie', a 4/4 Allegro in the work's basic key, B flat. The 'Sancta Maria' follows, a 3/4 Andante in F major, consisting of a succession of brief solos in a generalized expressive style, each line ending 'ora pro nobis', with the echo of the words sometimes taken up in the music; this leads into a short chorus and then a further group of solos. Following the precedent of earlier settings, and indeed the natural way of treating its more solemn words, Mozart set the beginning of the 'Salus infirmorum' as an Adagio in a minor key (D minor, 4/4), for chorus in a simple note-against-note style, but it soon brightens into B flat and Allegro moderato. 'Regina angelorum', a 2/4 Vivace in E flat, is however a series of solos, some of which recall at 'ora pro nobis' the cadences of the 'Sancta Maria', though probably only because this is a natural setting of the phrase. Lastly there is a 3/4 Andante 'Agnus Dei', a short chorus with solos, showing no interest at the 'miserere nobis' response in paralleling the setting of those words at the end of the 'Kyrie'.

Composed about the same time was a four-movement setting in C major of the *Regina coeli* K.108/74d; with oboes, horns, trumpets and drums, and a full string band including violas (often divided), it was clearly intended for some more ceremonial occasion, where a large band would have been available. Its outer movements are choral, embracing a pair of soprano arias, the first with choral 'alleluia' sections, the second a setting of 'Ora pro nobis Deum' as an A minor Adagio un poco andante, delicately accompanied and with expressive chromaticisms; each has some coloratura writing. But the general inventive level, here and perhaps especially in the concluding choral 'Alleluia', rarely rises above routine. These outer movements are cast in the same formal pattern that Mozart used for his opera arias, with primary and secondary material heard in a ritornello and then from the chorus, with a move to the dominant, and later a tonic recapitulation of some or all of the original material. The sonata-style procedures, part of Mozart's natural musical language, applied as much in choral music as elsewhere. His only other sacred work of these months, probably composed a little later, is a single-movement choral setting of *Inter natos mulierum* K.72/74f, an 'Offertorium de S. Joanne

Baptista'. This is for smaller forces but is written with considerable ingenuity (exceptionally, the orchestra and choir present the same pair of ideas in the primary material, in opposite sequence) and carefully detailed working of motifs and contrapuntal patterns in the interests of varied and attractive choral textures and apt expression of the words. The additional closing chorus for the *Grabmusik* K.42/35a may also have been a product of these months.

Of the three major works of 1771, *Il sogno di Scipione* was probably the first to be written; Mozart used mostly the same types of paper as for the litany, which implies that it was chiefly composed during the spring months. *La Betulia liberata* is uniformly on a different paper-type, suggesting that it was written in a single spell, probably in the summer. The third work, the wedding serenata *Ascanio in Alba*, was not written until Mozart reached Milan, as the paper on which it is written, bought in Italy, indicates.

Ascanio in Alba, however, was the first and possibly the only one of the three to be performed. Mozart and his father obtained leave for the journey to Italy (Count Firmian approached his brother, Chief Steward at the Salzburg court, and the archbishop agreed but decided to suspend Leopold's salary; through an oversight it was in fact paid up to October). They set out on 13 August. The archducal wedding was to be in mid-October. They took the same route as before, pausing on the first day for lunch at the Kaitel Inn (boiled beef with strong beer, while the horses ate hay), soup and sherbet at Waidring and supper at St Johann; on the next day, lunch at Kundl and supper at Innsbruck; on the third lunch at Steinach and supper at Brixen; and on the fourth lunch at Bozen and supper at Trento. This was exceptionally speedy travel: some 68 km the first day, nearly 90 the second, over 80 the third (across the Brenner Pass) and virtually 100 the fourth. The Mozarts were travelling long hours and by nine the next morning they were in Rovereto, 24 km on. But there they met friends, Baron Piccini (or Pizzini), the keyboard player and business man G.A. Bridi and the violinist Antonio Lolli. With peasant carts slowing them down on the narrow roads they abandoned their hope of reaching Verona (another 70 km) that night and stopped at Ala, where they could visit more friends, two further members of the Pizzini family, making music for them and going to church. Leopold wrote from Verona the following day, asking his wife to send on some music he had forgotten to pack for a friend in Milan: piano trios by Joseph Haydn, Wagenseil and Adlgasser, sonatas by Rutini (these can be identified as op.6 nos.2 and 6) and Wolfgang's 'little Cassation in C', the work, otherwise unknown (unless C is an error for G), referred to on p. 166.[5] In Verona, as on previous visits, they stayed with their friend Pietro Lugiati, remaining for two nights, then going on to a friend of Lugiati's in Brescia and reaching Milan on the evening of 21 August.

In Milan the Mozarts took the same lodgings as they did at the time of *Mitridate* (this can be deduced from Mozart's reference, in a letter to Nannerl, to his having perfected sign language: the son of the house was deaf). They were not ideal in that violinists lived above and below and a singing-master and an oboist in neighbouring rooms: 'This is delightful for composing!', Mozart wrote, 'it gives you plenty of ideas'. The libretto for *Ascanio in Alba* had not yet arrived from Vienna, and when it did Parini spent a couple of days making emendations.

By 31 August work was under way: Mozart had written the three-movement overture, a 'rather long' Allegro, an Andante decidedly Gluckian in manner for dancing by a small group (later it turned out to be eleven, graces and goddesses) and as finale 'a kind of con-tredanse and chorus, to be sung and danced' (with a chorus of 32 and sixteen dancers). He next wrote the choruses and recitatives,[6] and probably the ballets, to be danced at the end of each act (this was exceptional, since usually the ballets were left to another, specialist composer: they are now lost). These were done by the middle of September. Mozart added postscripts to most of his father's letters home, short ones, because he had a heavy cold and his fingers were aching from composing, but usually with some family joke, a message to friends in Salzburg and sometimes a cryptic remark to Nannerl about girls there (clearly puberty was now under way). Leopold kept his

womenfolk informed about the festivities in Milan, commenting on
the refurbishment of the theatre, the decorations and the foregather-
ing of people in the city, among them their friends the Davies sisters,
Marianne, an armonica player, and Cecilia, a soprano, who was to sing
in the opera by Hasse, *Ruggiero*, the main festal work (the further
commissioning of Mozart's serenata had been an afterthought). Hasse
himself had of course arrived earlier, and the Mozarts soon paid a
courtesy call on him.

By 21 September Mozart could report that he had only two more
arias to compose, and two days later he was finished. Rehearsals for
the dances had begun more than a week before. The full rehearsal
schedules cannot be established, as Leopold's letters give incomplete
information and do not always distinguish one kind of rehearsal from
another, but we know that recitative rehearsals began on 23 September, choral ones the next day and orchestral ones on 28 September.
On 11 October the serenata had its fourth rehearsal (presumably a
full one, in the theatre), and the last was three days later. The première
was on 17 October, the evening after that of the Hasse opera. This
was the cast:

Venere [Venus]	Geltrude Falchini (*soprano*)
Ascanio [Ascanius]	Giovanni Manzuoli (*castrato mezzo-soprano*)
Silvia, *a nymph, of Hercules' line*	Antonia Maria Girelli Aguilar (*mezzo-soprano*)
Aceste [Acestes], *priest*	Giuseppe Tibaldi (*tenor*)
Fauno [Faunus], *a leading shepherd*	Adamo Solzi (*castrato soprano*)
Chorus of Genies, Shepherds and Shepherdesses	

The serenata, given four repeat performances, on 19, 24, 27 and 28
October,[7] was evidently a success, much more so than Hasse's *Ruggiero*, the product of a librettist aged 73 and a composer a year
younger. Metastasio, writing his last heroic libretto, to a plot after

Ariosto, was aware that he was straining to repeat his earlier successes, and Hasse knew himself to be out of touch, and out of sympathy, with the latest Italian theatrical taste. The aged Maria Theresa, not surprisingly, expressed her pleasure in the opera, but otherwise it seems to have come a poor second to *Ascanio*. 'It truly distresses me greatly', Leopold wrote, deceiving no-one, 'but Wolfgang's serenata has killed Hasse's opera'. His verdict is borne out by a report in the Florence paper, the *Notizie del mondo*: 'The opera has not met with success . . . the serenata has however received great applause, both for the text and for the music'.[8] The setting, a representation of an altar in a glade of oak trees, with a smiling countryside and distant mountains behind, was again the work of the Galliari brothers; the ballets were by Le Picq and Favier.

Ascanio in Alba is described in its libretto as a *festa teatrale*, one of the several generic terms used more or less interchangeably for semi-theatrical works in the Habsburg domains.[9] As Leopold himself said,

Johann Adolf Hasse: miniature oil portrait by Felicita Sartori Hoffman, *c*1740 (*Gemäldegalerie alter Meister, Dresden / Lebrecht Music and Arts*)

it is really a short opera (at one point he calls it an *azione teatrale*, at another a cantata), but of an undramatic kind and with a strong allegorical element apt to a royal marriage. It refers to the Trojan prince Ascanio, son of Aeneas and of Venus (who, as the chorus's opening tribute makes clear, had anyone doubted it, symbolizes Maria Theresa, mother of the bridegroom). In this mythological fantasy Ascanio is betrothed to the nymph Silvia, a descendant of Hercules (Ercole was a popular name in the Este family and that of the bride's father). Silvia falls in love with a dream image of Ascanio, and he falls in love with her but is not allowed to declare himself. This prohibition allows each to have a scene of anguish before, their virtue duly tested and proved, they can be happily united. The creation of the city of Alba, founded by Ascanio in the twelfth century B.C.E., near Rome, probably on the site of the modern Castel Gandolfo (the Albanians are said to have been transported from there by Hercules), is predicted and takes place in the course of the work. The names for the secondary characters, Fauno and Aceste, were drawn by Parini in the traditional way from related myths.

The first part of *Ascanio* is fairly conventional music, apt to the conventional text and its modest emotional range. All but two of the arias follow roughly the same pattern: a ritornello with two ideas, the second of which, with a new gloss from the soloist, becomes the secondary material in the dominant key; then after a brief section in a nearby key (usually the subdominant) a recapitulation with the secondary material in the tonic. Mozart was now finding varied and imaginative ways of glossing the secondary material in arias of this type, using themes in the opening ritornellos that later serve in a variety of attractive ways as counter-subjects to the new vocal line. The entry aria for the prima donna, Silvia, is a simple cavatina, which is immediately succeeded by an expansive aria (embodying one of Mozart's characteristic effects, offbeat string figures to represent the words 'va palpitando il cor': 'makes the heart race'). Ascanio's response is an aria whose structure reflects his passion: the primary material is

Adagio and the ensuing section fast, with a central Andante in a different metre.

In the second part, with stronger emotions to be conveyed and the focus more firmly on the principals, to whom four of the six arias fall, Mozart's handling is less stereotyped. The unusual verse structure of Ascanio's first aria gives rise to an ingenious two-tempo treatment (the fiery last two lines of a five-line stanza recapitulated after a four-line one). In the principals' second arias, each in two tempos, the recapitulation of the opening slow section gains in intensity through Mozart's free handling of the material, avoiding anything like orthodox recapitulation. Silvia's is accompanied with rich string textures, with divided violas (popular in Salzburg, rare in Italy), and Ascanio's, much of it in three-bar phrases, is lusciously scored with flutes, English horns, bassoons and horns. The two are finally joined by the High Priest in a terzet. The chorus plays a prominent role throughout the work with brief, recurring choral (and dance) numbers interspersed, for male and female choruses separately and together; the effect, presumably of Parini's devising rather than Mozart's, is charming and unusual.

If the arias and ensembles of *Ascanio* do not go beyond those of *Mitridate*, in terms of technique or expressive scope, its accompanied recitatives touch on a new note. Those of *Mitridate* and, broadly speaking, of the various earlier concert arias, deal aptly enough with the standard declamatory style, with gestures from the strings to match the singer's verbal gestures. But here, spurred on by an imaginative libretto, Mozart does more, having the orchestra (mostly just the strings) mirror the singer's feelings, often before they are verbally expressed, touching on tender as well as forceful emotion. The recitatives preceding Ascanio's first aria and Silvia's last particularly lend depth to the quicksilver changes in the character's emotional state.

The marriage festivities, or at least the musical part of them, continued into the beginning of November, in spite of an accident at the *Ascanio* performance on 24 October when scaffolding collapsed and many people were killed or injured. Hasse's opera was given on 2 November, but the Mozarts did not go (Wolfgang wrote that he could hear and see it in his head as he knew nearly all the arias by heart). Meanwhile, Leopold had been making further operatic plans for the following year. He wrote to Pallavicini in Bologna on 30 October to say that Wolfgang was to write the first carnival opera for Milan at the end of 1772 and the second for the San Benedetto theatre in Venice immediately thereafter[10] (in the event, the over-ambitious plan had to be dropped and the Venice commission foregone—to write two operas for the same carnival season, even different parts of it, would have required Mozart to be in two places at once). On 8 November they and Hasse lunched with Count Firmian; Hasse was given a snuffbox and Mozart a watch set with diamonds. By then Leopold was expecting daily to leave for home. The intention was still to travel through Verona with the possibility of a few days in Padua.[11] Clearly they had in mind rehearsing and possibly performing the new oratorio, *La Betulia liberata*, which they had planned to post to Padua when they passed through Verona at the end of August. It is not hard to conjecture, however, why they remained considerably longer in Milan. In the following week's letter Leopold reported that he 'had more to think about' than his wife could imagine, and that the success of the serenata would probably not secure an appointment for Wolfgang were one to be vacant. Another week later he wrote that he was to see the archduke, at the moment away in Varese, on 30 November. He presumably enquired about a post, or more probably posts for both himself and his son, and Ferdinand must have asked him to wait for an answer (Leopold wrote, a few days later, that 'the affair is not without hope', presumably referring to this)[12] and then passed on the request to Vienna. Maria Theresa's notorious letter to him about the Mozarts was dated 12 December:

Vous me demandez de prendre a votre service le jeune Salzburgois je ne sais comme quoi ne croiant pas que vous

ayez besoing d'un compositeur ou des gens inutils si cela
pourtant vous serais plaisir je ne veux vous l'empecher ce que
je dis est pour ne vous charger des gens inutils et jamais de
titres a ces sortes des gens comme a votre service cela avilit le
service quand ces gens courent le monde comme des gueux
il a outre cela un grand famille.[13]

(You ask me about taking the young Salzburger into your
service. I do not know why, believing that you have no need
for a composer or useless people. If however it would give
you pleasure I would not hinder you. What I say is so that you
do not burden yourself with useless people and ever giving
titles to people of that sort. If in your service, this debases the
service when such people go around the world like beggars.
Furthermore, he has a large family.)

The archduke did not offer the Mozarts employment. Beyond
that, however, the content of Maria Theresa's letter raises questions,
with wider ramifications than those of the immediate situation in
1771, about Mozart's standing and the effect on patrons in the longer
term of Leopold's carrying him around Europe. Maria Theresa had
never been anything but friendly to the Mozarts on the surface, and
indeed must have assented in person to the commissioning of *Ascanio
in Alba*. Her basic advice may have been sound, in that Ferdinand did
not need him, and the employing of a German composer in an Italian city might anyway have been ill-advised as far as the smooth running of Ferdinand's establishment was concerned. But the gratuitous
comments about the debasement of the service—certainly Leopold
felt they were bringing nothing but credit and honour to the archbishop of Salzburg's employment by appearing with distinction as
members of his Kapelle—and the mistaken or misleading remark
about the 'large family' are puzzling. Her comments would have
caused Leopold much anger and distress had he known of them, and

they would certainly have turned his future hopes for Wolfgang's career in different directions. No other observation by Maria Theresa about the Mozarts is recorded.

The Mozarts' last letter from Milan was sent on 30 November: Leopold expected that they would leave in three or four days' time and be home a week later. In the same letter Mozart noted that they had seen four rascals hanged in the Piazza del Duomo, and that it was done there in just the same way as they had seen in Lyons; clearly they regarded such events as not to be missed. It is salutary to be reminded that we should not impute modern humane ideals to Mozart. They finally left for home on 5 December, following their usual route, pausing at Ala with the Pizzinis and at Brixen with Count Spaur, the bishop there, where they made music with his nephew Canon Ignaz Spaur on 11 and 12 December.[14] They reached home on 15 December.

It seems clear that the long wait in Milan must have precluded a visit to Padua, or at any rate delayed it beyond any appropriate date. In fact, it is unclear whether the Padua oratorio *Betulia liberata* was given at all. As there is no known record of a performance, no libretto for the occasion survives, and the work is never alluded to again in the family correspondence (not, that is, until 1784, when Mozart thought he might draw on it for an oratorio commission in Vienna),[15] it has usually been assumed that it was simply set aside. That may not be the true situation. Two printed librettos do in fact survive for settings of *Betulia liberata* heard in Padua in 1771; the named composers are Mysliveček and a local figure, Giuseppe Calegari, whose name however is struck through in the sole surviving copy.[16] It is scarcely plausible that three settings of the same libretto would have been commissioned in the same year. Nor is any setting by Mysliveček known to have existed; had he been engaged on one, there would surely have been some reference to it in Leopold's letters, especially when he comments on their meeting Mysliveček in Milan during November (his 1771 oratorio for Padua is usually taken to be *Giuseppe riconosciuto*). Mozart's setting may have been received and for some reason rejected, but it is also conceivable that it was performed, possibly without a specially prepared libretto, or with one that names the composer incorrectly, or indeed with a normal libretto of which no copy survives. It could have been performed in November or December, or during the following Lent on the visit of a prominent patron, Maria Antonia Walpurgis. No cast can be named, but these are the characters and the voices:

Ozìa [Ozias], *Prince of Betulia*	(*tenor*)
Giuditta [Judith], *widow of Manasses*	(*contralto*)
Amital, *Israelite noblewoman*	(*soprano*)
Achior, *prince of the Ammonites*	(*bass*)
Cabri [Chabris], *leader of the people*	(*soprano*)
Carmi [Charmis], *leader of the people*	(*soprano*)
People of Bethulia	

Mozart could not have composed *Betulia liberata* in ignorance of the singers who were to perform it, and presumably he had been briefed on their qualities during his meeting with Ferrandini the previous March. In any case, 'suiting the clothes to the figure' was somewhat less important in an oratorio than in an opera. The singers would be local men (castratos, not women, in the high roles), church singers rather than visiting virtuosos whose special qualities needed to be exhibited. But the text itself—Mozart would already have had a copy in the collection of Metastasio's writings given him by Count Firmian early in 1770—follows much the same pattern as that of an opera, with alternating recitatives and arias, and some simple choruses, principally to end the acts. The Handelian type of oratorio, with its more central role for the chorus, was virtually unknown outside England. The story, from the Apocrypha, of Judith and Holofernes and the liberation of the city of Bethulia from the besieging Assyrian army was an immensely popular one and even before Metastasio's time had been used more than 60 times for oratorios. Metastasio had written his text for the Viennese composer Georg

Reutter in 1734, and Mozart's setting was probably about the eighteenth of nearly 50 made during the eighteenth century. In Metastasio's treatment it is not a dramatic, operatic story: Holofernes never appears, and in the classical tradition the lurid scene of his death is not enacted or represented but related. Judith herself tells it on her return to the Israelites' camp bearing his severed head. Metastasio's primary concern is to draw moral messages from the characters' diverse stances and reactions to their situation.

Metastasio's polished libretto offered opportunities and challenges with its varied versification, its elegant diction and its suggestive imagery. Mozart took the composition of *Betulia liberata*, as a sacred work, seriously. Certain of its arias, like movements in some of his early masses, are scarcely different in manner from those he was composing for operas, and at best tenuously expressive of the words. Such cheerful, showy and expansive arias as the opening one for Ozias, where he exhorts the besieged Israelites to have faith, or two of those for the Israelite noblewoman Amital—one where she talks of the pitiable lamentations of the doomed Israelites, one where she draws a simile between the pilot about to founder or the invalid about to die and Bethulia on the brink of catastrophe—are obvious examples. But several numbers catch a tone of quiet gravity rare in the young Mozart.

The overture is at once remarkable, not only for its key, D minor, but for its fiery gestures, its terse structure and its hint of cyclic form: the first of its three continuous movements, a mere 61 bars unrelenting in impulse, is a sonata miniature (the secondary material nothing more than a half-dozen bars of tutti, the 'development' a mere thirteen bars), and the finale is based on a figure clearly linked to that of the opening (see the example following). The first act includes a pair of brief lamentations in C minor for Ozias and the chorus (using pizzicato strings, no doubt to symbolize funeral bells, a tradition that goes back to J.S. Bach's cantatas and beyond). Between them Judith enters—the recitative accompaniment turns to a halo of strings, akin to that traditionally used for Christ in Passion music—to sing, after

rebuking those present for their lack of faith, an aria embodying a rather tortuous Metastasian simile: as the river banks are equally barren in flood or drought, so are excessive hope and excessive fear equally damaging. Mozart does not take up the watery simile in his setting, but this aria, in moderate tempo and with its orchestral colouring softened by flutes, is graceful and at times warm in expression, especially at its secondary theme:

At the parallel point in her second aria, a brilliant and vigorous G major Allegro in which Judith asserts her determination and faith, this theme recurs (to 'vo per l'ombre, e l'orror non ho': 'I go through the darkness and have no horror'):

A musical cross-reference of this kind between independent numbers is rare in Mozart, and the change of sense implied by the change in

mode and rhythm is clearly intentional. Judith's third aria, an Adagio in D major following her account in an accompanied recitative of her killing of the drunken and somnolent Holofernes, also shines out in this uneven score, for its loftiness, its sense of dignity and steadfastness of faith: Mozart did not fail to catch Metastasio's central moral message. That is caught too in the characterization of the Ammonite chief, Achior, who falls captive to the Israelites. He first sings a blustery aria describing Holofernes ('Terribile d'aspetto'), but is converted by the events portrayed to the God of the Israelites in time to sing a tender Andante, 'Te solo adoro'. In a remarkable sequence of arias, however, this is capped by the final one for the once-proud Amital, who expresses her penitence in a two-tempo aria (both slow, Andante and Adagio) of singular beauty, with soft and solitary violin phrases, where the tempo slows, to convey her self-abasement in prayer.

In all these arias the primary material tends to be conventional but the secondary carries considerable emotional weight. Mozart's ingenuity in handling the secondary material is happily seen here in Amital's 'Quel nocchier', where the vocal counter-subject to the orchestral theme is given a new twist on its reappearance in the home key. He uses the standard sonata-ritornello pattern[17] with considerable flexibility; in particular, the final *dal segno* may go back to the 'development' section, to the recurrence of the opening material (so seeming more like a true *da capo*) or simply to the restatement of the secondary material in the tonic, according to the scale of the piece and the effect he was seeking. Mozart never heard *La Betulia liberata*; unless new documents come to light, we shall never know whether anybody did during his lifetime.

MOZART DID NOT waste the time he spent waiting in Milan for Archduke Ferdinand's decision. A divertimento, a symphony and a symphony movement belong to his weeks in the city, almost certainly to the waiting period, for until then he was otherwise occupied. The months in Salzburg in 1771 also produced at least one symphony, K.110/75*b* in G, which Mozart dated July 1771, and two others that have been assigned to that summer, K.75 in F and the work best called K.74*g*. No autograph or other authentic source survives for either. K.75 is known only from nineteenth-century transcriptions of a set of parts once in the Breitkopf archives but now lost, while K.74*g* is another of those symphonies listed by its incipit in a Breitkopf catalogue (hence its original assignment to the Köchel appendix, as Anh.216) and then identified with a set of parts, found in Berlin but now missing; it was printed in a rare supplement to the old complete edition in 1910 but has never quite established a place in the canon.[18] This symphony was admitted to K^3 as 74*g* but then ejected, somewhat arbitrarily, by the editors of K^6 (they retained in the main body of the catalogue several other symphonies with exactly equivalent claims to authenticity) and relegated to an appendix with the number C11.03; similarly, in the NMA it is separated from its fellow symphonies and confined to a volume of works of uncertain authenticity.

There is in fact no certainty that either this work or K.75 is by Mozart, but the attributions are not implausible. Nor are there strong stylistic grounds for arguing against the dating of both to 1771. In the case of K.74*g*, it was supposed hints of Italian influence that led to the suggestion, implied by its K. number, that it belonged to this period. But it could well be earlier: features in common with K.48 (a triple-metre first movement with a wide-ranging opening theme, one note to a bar, and *forte–piano* alternations) as well as divided violas might indicate a Viennese work of the late 1760s.[19] It has a vigorous sonata-form first movement, with a typically Viennese recurrence of first-subject material in the second, but slender textures and themes that are little more than violinistic tags in the manner of the Italian symphonies discussed at the end of Chapter 10. The Andante has some charm but is somewhat trite in its handling of cadences. There is a minuet, rather four-square in rhythm, and a spirited finale marred by a clumsy handling of sequences in the development section. Its place in the canon must be suspect. K.75 is more secure. It too begins with a 3/4 movement, embodying some novel and imaginative treatment of texture, with the wind group prominent in the primary material and lively imitation in the strings in the secondary, as well as a graceful if miniature development section. It seems to be a symphony written with particular relish: witness the polished minuet (exceptionally, placed second), with no hint of Austrian rumbustiousness but smoothly and economically written (minuet and trio are each built around a single phrase, subtly varied); the nicely detailed Andantino with muted violins and carefully worked accompaniments; and the jolly 3/8 finale in sonata form, with the cadence of its main theme delayed by a rhythmic hiccup that converts the phrase from a conventional eight bars to a teasing nine.

That work sits convincingly as a companion piece to the one symphony we know for certain to come from the summer of 1771. K.110/75*b* again starts with a triple-metre movement, this time of a powerful impulse that carries it forward for 36 bars before there is a *piano* respite for the main secondary theme, after which the tutti resumes, with a restatement of the opening theme. The passage following the double bar is interludial in character, but there is some true development within the recapitulation when the violins break into dialogue on a snatch from the linking material. With this Haydn-like device, the almost unrelieved tutti scoring and the unflagging momentum, the work seems markedly Viennese, much in the manner of K.48 as well as K.75. The first movement calls for oboes and horns. For the slow movement the oboists take up their flutes, the horns rest and two bassoonists (hitherto unspecified, and so doubling the cellos) take obbligato roles. The content is modest but the sound is lent a surface bloom. Haydn is recalled again by the minuet, where the basses follow the violins in exact canon a twelfth below (as, for example, in his Symphony no. 44); this severe music contrasts with an E minor trio with chromatic writing in string-quartet-like textures. The finale is a rondo in the contredanse pattern, similar to that of K.73 (see p. 203), if less extended, and again with a minor-mode episode.

The symphonies written in Italy (written on the same paper as *Ascanio in Alba*) are K.112 in F and a work compounded of the first two movements of the *Ascanio* overture (K.111) and a new finale, K.120/111*a*. The latter was the first of several symphonies that Mozart was to make up by adding a movement or two to the overture of a dramatic work, as he did too by extracting movements from serenades; clearly there was a constant demand for new or fairly new symphonies. This finale is a slight but energetic 3/8 Presto. Another symphony, K.96/111*b*, with no verifiable source and surviving only in a set of parts once in the Breitkopf library, is sometimes assigned to these weeks. It has to be regarded as suspect. In the heavily pompous C major manner, with trumpets and drums, its first movement depends on fanfarish effects and a surface busy-ness of texture, and embodies some eccentric harmonic progressions and an oddly perfunctory, ill-balanced handling of form; there is little attractive music here. The sombre Andante, in C minor, is in the manner of a Baroque *siciliano*, with *forte* and *piano* markings to alternate notes. It is suggested by Zaslaw that a resemblance to the opening aria of *Il rè pastore* (1775) might indicate a later date[20] and lend support to the claim to authenticity, but the compositional solecisms would seem to belie that. Nor do the minuet and the finale, energetic and conventional, encourage a belief in the work's authenticity.

Certainly K.96 seems impoverished alongside K.112, which Mozart signed and dated (2 November 1771) in Milan, and which is a small masterpiece. Its first movement has the rhythmic swing of Mozart's best triple-metre music, and although most of its themes are in themselves clichés, their conjunction and presentation is full of wit and ingenuity; the shape of the exposition is articulated by the conjunction of emphatic or spirited material with gentler, more lyrical music. The B flat Andante for strings is simple and song-like, with figured accompaniments giving way at the end of each half to one of Mozart's favourite expressive textures, the violins in octaves with the violas a third below the second violins. The symphony continues with a hearty minuet (copied in the autograph in Leopold's hand, so presumably composed earlier than the rest) and a gentle trio with some textural subtleties, and it is rounded off by a Molto Allegro finale, a 3/8 rondo, much the kind of finale he had written in his childhood days but now with more shapeliness and refinement to its detail.

During November, probably after he had finished the symphony, Mozart wrote a 'Concerto ò sia divertimento' in E flat, K.113, for strings with pairs of clarinets and horns. This was his first use of clarinets in a composition of his own (they are called for in the Abel symphony he had copied in London); the work may have been given in a concert on 22 or 23 November.[21] In four movements, it is written in a curious style, designed perhaps for some particular set of physical circumstances or simply to contrast the wind pointedly with the strings: the pairs of clarinets and horns are used not as part of a collective orchestra but rather for solo passages, taking up the argument where the violins leave off. The effect is slightly fragmented, but the invention is attractively designed in terms of a special kind of antiphonal performance. Clarinets were not regular members of the orchestra at this date but were the principal wind instruments in many military bands; composers tended to use only their upper register, as Mozart does here. Later, probably early in 1773, Mozart wrote an extra score for the work giving only parts for pairs of oboes, English horns and bassoons. Probably it was designed less to supplement the original (the clarinet parts are duplicated, largely by the oboes, occasionally by the English horns) than to adapt it for use in Salzburg where clarinets may not have been available, or at least to present a number of options in performance.[22]

The last work of the year, written two weeks after the Mozarts' arrival back in Salzburg, was another symphony, K.114. This was Mozart's first symphony in A major, a key that tended to impose a special colour on the music. The horn used in Mozart's day, before valves made it a fully chromatic instrument, could play only a limited number of notes, those of the harmonic series (and sometimes notes immediately neighbouring them). To make the instrument serve in any particular piece, a crook (a length of tubing) was fitted to the main body of the instrument to enable its selection of notes to fall usefully in the key of the piece. In A major the horns had to be pitched higher than usual, thereby inducing composers to consider including flutes in preference to oboes, as the natural coupling of woodwind and horns would press oboes to an uncomfortably high register. Music in A, accordingly, often has a softer and warmer tone than music in other keys (that is why it was traditionally favoured for love duets). In K.114, then, Mozart reversed the common procedure of using oboes in the fast movements and flutes in the slow. The symphony starts however with violins alone, *piano*, in a rather unconventional theme, which is developed in the ensuing tutti. The secondary theme, with its repeated notes and expressive appoggiaturas and particularly its touch of imitative writing,

recalls the J.C. Bach–influenced writing in the symphonies of Mozart's childhood, but is now much more expressively handled. The 'development' section presents only new material. The Andante too, again begun by violins alone, has a graceful development section at best remotely related to the movement's thematic material. Mozart struck through his first attempt at the minuet (a rather perfunctory and four-square piece, which possibly he rejected because it too closely resembled the Andante), then wrote a more interesting and original one, enlivened by emphatic chromatic gestures, with a witty trio (a near-monotone melody accompanied by running triplets). The finale again uses new ideas where development of old ones might be expected. Did the application of this procedure, to all three sonata-form movements, represent a conscious decision by Mozart? or was his reluctance to refer to his stated themes connected with their more motivic character and the developmental procedures he was using in their presentation? At any rate, this spirited, light-textured work stands at the beginning of a prolific and fascinating period in Mozart's development as a symphonist.

12

Working for the Prince-Archbishop

O N 16 DECEMBER 1771, the day after the Mozarts returned from Italy, their employer the prince-archbishop of Salzburg, Count Siegmund von Schrattenbach, died. Schrattenbach had been a generally tolerant and generous patron to them. He seems to have been aware that, father and son, they stood somewhat apart from the generality of Salzburg musicians, in their ambitions beyond the court, their social aspirations within Salzburg and outside it, and their unwillingness to conform readily to court expectations by composing predominantly church music.

It was in the nature of an archiepiscopal court that church music should lie firmly at the centre of the Salzburg tradition. In fact, the court musicians at Salzburg were not at this date specifically required to compose music for use in the cathedral. The system dictated that three directors shared, on a weekly rotating basis, the charge of music-making there, and they were free to perform whatever music they chose—though no doubt it was duly observed and noted if they were lazy or conservative in their selection and did not go to the trouble of producing novelties. Several, notably Eberlin, Adlgasser (at least up to the early 1760s) and Michael Haydn, were prolific composers for the church and not particularly productive in secular fields.

The Mozarts however directed more of their energies towards orchestral music, for which the demand at court was relatively modest, and in any case much of their output was intended for use outside the court, to earn money and favour from other members of the Salzburg nobility. It would be naive to suppose that the attitude represented by the Mozarts' orientation away from the court would have escaped Schrattenbach, still less their colleagues in the Kapelle. Schrattenbach, clearly, was not wholly unsympathetic, but the injustice Leopold felt he suffered when, in spite of his wider eminence, he was never promoted beyond the rank of deputy Kapellmeister may well have been of his own causing. His obituary, by the family friend Dominikus Hagenauer, said that he was 'always persecuted' in Salzburg and favoured there less than he was in other places.[1] If his fortune at home was poor, that was partly at least because he sought it so assiduously elsewhere.

It is unlikely that the Mozarts saw Schrattenbach's death as a particular setback. The general expectation in Salzburg was that he would be succeeded by another scion of one of the local aristocratic families, with which the Mozarts had good relations. One candidate was Count Saurau, a canon of the cathedral and a particular friend of the Mozarts, and another was the dean, Count Waldburg-Zeil. In the event, however, larger-scale politics entered into it. The imperial court in Vienna intervened in the election; pressure was brought to bear on the canons, and after many ballots Hieronymus Joseph Franz de Paula, Count of Colloredo, since 1761 Bishop of Gurk, was chosen, on 14 March 1772.[2] Born in 1732, Colloredo came of an eminent family (their name derives from the site of their castle, in the Friuli, in Italy). His father, whom the Mozarts had met on their earliest visit to Vienna, was Vice-Chancellor of Austria, his mother was from the equally well-known Starhemberg family, his elder brother later became Vice-Chancellor and his uncle was commander of the Austrian section of the Teutonic Order. Colloredo, as we shall see, was a reformist ruler and churchman, well attuned to the outlook of

Hieronymus, Count Colloredo, Prince-Archbishop of Salzburg, 1772–1803, oil painting by J.M. Greiter (*Museum Carolino Augusteum, Salzburg*)

Joseph II, and was never very popular with the Salzburgers, least of all the Mozarts.

One of Colloredo's earliest actions, however, was to take Wolfgang formally into court employment, and to grant him a salary. From 9 July, at the age of sixteen, Mozart received 150 gulden a year (one third of what his father earned) as Konzertmeister, the post he had occupied on an honorary basis. His main role was to play the violin in the orchestra, with some degree of responsibility for leading, though the presence of other, senior violinists suggests that he was rarely required to exercise it. The new archbishop was no enemy to music, although his ideas on its use in worship were those of the Enlightenment. According to a letter of November 1772 to Charles Burney from the English diplomat Louis de Visme, Colloredo 'plays well on the Fiddle. He takes pains to reform his Band, which, like others, is too harsh. He has put Fischietti at the head of it . . . Young Mozhart too is of the Band'. Visme heard the Mozarts at their house, noting that Nannerl was 'at her summit which is not marvellous', but he may not have been a sound judge, for he also wrote that Wolfgang was 'one further instance of early Fruit, which is more extraordinary than excellent'.[3]

One of Leopold's first actions on hearing of Schrattenbach's death, apparently, was to petition the cathedral chapter for the portion of his salary withheld during his absence. The salary had inadvertently been paid for a month and a half, and it seems to have been taken for granted that he would retain that sum, but when told of their success in Milan Schrattenbach had evidently agreed to restore the remaining missing sum, 59 gulden. That was granted. Of course, any plans to perform *Il sogno di Scipione* in his honour during December or January were now abandoned, but Mozart made some small changes, substituting 'Girolamo' (the equivalent of Hieronymus) for 'Sigismondo', so that it could be used for the celebrations on Colloredo's installation. Colloredo took up residence at the end of April. There is no firm evidence that the work was ever performed, apart from the internal evidence of Mozart's adjustments, but reports of the festivities on 29 April 1772, when Colloredo formally took up residence, include reference to the performance of a cantata at a grand dinner given that evening for 160 people in the Marcus-Sitticus-Saal and the Kaiser-Saal at the archbishop's residence. *Il sogno*, given in concert form, as serenatas normally were, could well have been so described and may have been the work given.

Il sogno di Scipione is an allegorical serenata in one act. A Metastasio libretto written in 1735, it had been set by Luca Antonio Predieri
in honour of Charles VI (the original tribute had been to 'Carlo') and
several times since. Metastasio based his text on Cicero's *Somnium Sci-*
pionis, in which Scipio—the Roman consul Scipio Aemilianus
Africanus, adopted son of Publius Cornelius Scipio, son of Scipio
Africanus—is visited in a dream by Virtus (Virtue) and Voluptas (Pleasure) and is required to choose between them. In the Italianized version, Metastasio has his Scipio, and by allegory the ruler to whom the
conceit is addressed, choose between Costanza (Constancy) and Fortuna (Fortune); his adoptive father and his true one proffer advice but
leave the choice to him. None of the original singers can be identified, though a Salzburg cast would probably have included at least
some of those who took part in *Die Schuldigkeit* in 1767 and *La finta*
semplice in 1769. These are the voices called for:

Scipione [Scipio]	(*tenor*)
Costanza	(*soprano*)
Fortuna	(*soprano*)
Publio [Publius], *Scipio's adoptive father*	(*tenor*)
Emilio [Aemilianus], *Scipio's father*	(*tenor*)
Chorus of Heroes	

Il sogno di Scipione consists of ten arias with linking recitatives and
with brief choruses near the middle and at the end. The vocal palette
is limited, with no bass and no low female voice, and not even a castrato (there were apparently no good castratos in Salzburg at this date)
to provide variety of timbre. Scipio is addressed by the two rival suitors, then (after a chorus) by his fathers, then again by the suitors. He
finally makes his choice, in the work's single orchestral recitative, first
stormy, then contemplative, and after a recitative commenting on the
virtues, parallel to Scipio's, possessed by Girolamo, a *licenza* aria follows in tribute to him. In the spring of 1772 Mozart made a second
setting of the *licenza* text, more expansive and more solemn, in slow

and fast tempos, perhaps apter to the occasion; the two arias, although so different, follow the same unusual structure, ritornello-binary.

The work is essentially an occasional piece, decorative in nature, touching on no great depths of feeling but nevertheless composed with considerable polish and subtlety. Mozart responds to the very varied structure of Metastasio's verse with unusual rhythmic patterns, for example in the first aria for Costanza where the triple-metre setting of seven-syllable lines leads to three-bar phrases. Scipio's opening aria artfully suggests his perplexity, in his short and wandering chromatic phrases to 'confusa la mente, che oppressa si sente' ('confuse the mind, oppress the feelings'). Fortuna's first aria is in a bold and brilliant C major; under its spacious lines runs of rapid notes in the second violins depict the fickle winds with which she compares herself. Several arias use such graphic effects, for example Emilio's with its chromatic writing for a child's tears at 'piange' and Publio's, where a sturdy oak withstanding the winds is represented in violin tremolandos and sharp accents. It is the vigorous and extended final aria for Costanza, another graphic piece of writing with rushing violin passages standing for the sea that batters the steadfast rocks, that finally convinces Scipio to reject Fortuna. He does so in an aria with slow introductory sections and much vivid bravura in its fast music.

There is also ample variety in Mozart's treatment of musical forms. The arias, most of which include a good deal of florid writing, nearly all follow the same fundamental pattern, with a two-theme opening ritornello, an 'exposition' with the voice, a brief 'development' and a recapitulation, usually only of the secondary material in the tonic (and so analogous to the rounded binary model). Then follows a middle section, and a *dal segno*, the placing of which again varies. Sometimes the recapitulation is of the secondary material alone, although more often the development is also included, while sometimes it is of both primary and secondary material, and once (in Costanza's final aria) it comprises the development as well as both thematic groups. This range of formal options enabled Mozart to scale the arias in a variety of proportions according to their importance in the drama. 'Drama', however, is not the right word for a work that is essentially static, for even if the music does in some degree characterize the rival suitors—Fortuna capricious but seductive, Costanza warm and stead-fast—there is no serious attempt in either text or music to portray any internal conflict. The conclusion is pre-destined and the mean-ing entirely symbolic. By its own quite modest canons *Il sogno di Scipione*, however, is a successful and attractive occasional piece, gracefully and imaginatively composed.

From about the time of *Il sogno* comes a group of three diverti-mentos for strings, K.136–8/125a–c. They are undated but are writ-ten in a hand of early 1772 on the same twelve-staff manuscript paper (obviously preferable, for four-part music, to the usual ten-staff Salzburg ruling) as Mozart used for the choral numbers in *Il sogno*. These delightfully fluent and popular pieces—the earliest of his music to hold a firm place in the repertory—stand curiously apart from any of his stylistic mainstreams. It is unclear for what purpose they were composed and in particular whether they were intended as solo or orchestral music. Mozart himself headed them 'divertimento', a term that in Austria tended, at least from this time onwards, to sig-nify one player to a part. Features that hint at solo performance include rapid running passages, which are not comfortable with a larger group, finely detailed inner accompaniment patterns, the figu-rative complexity of the textures and the general absence of the sim-ple types of accompaniment that abound in his other occasional works for larger groups of around this period. But nor is the manner that of his string quartets. Mozart had not, of course, composed quar-tets in Salzburg, and was never to do so there. His first had been writ-ten in Italy, as his next six were to be, and six under Viennese influence followed later; so there is no secure basis for comparison. If the extravert style and the three-movement form, fast–slow–fast (or in one case slow–fast–fast), are uncharacteristic of the string quartet, the three-movement pattern is scarcely more typical of the orchestral divertimento. Nor, although they are sometimes known as the 'Salzburg symphonies', are they wind-less symphonies: their manner is entirely different from that of Mozart's true symphonies of the time. It has been proposed that they were symphonies written for the next Italian journey, with the wind parts to be added as needed, but why that should be necessary when he already had a portfolio full of freshly composed symphonies, including wind parts, is unexplained.[4] Much shorter, less serious and purposive than his symphonies of the time, less refined than his chamber music, distinct in layout from the divertimentos or serenades, and unparalleled in the works of other Salzburg composers, they have to be regarded as *sui generis*.

The autograph manuscript of the divertimentos shows the two upper staves jointly marked 'Violini', the third staff 'Viole' and the bottom one 'Basso'. The implication that there should be more than a single viola (the part is never in fact divided, as the viola part often is in Salzburg music) might be taken to imply orchestral performance. Mozart was not dependably careful with his indications, but there are numerous examples of his correct use of the singular. 'Basso', though singular, means only 'the bass part'. This was Mozart's normal usage, and it could stand for any one instrument or combination of instruments. It is worth considering whether this part, distinctly less athletic than the others, was intended for double-bass, especially in view of the comparatively modest use of the cello in Salzburg and the preference for the deeper instrument in several of Mozart's later Salzburg works (for example K.203 or K.247), but the part calls for the full cello range, often dipping characteristically to low D or C, which would argue against that.[5] In February 1772 Leopold wrote to the publisher Breitkopf in Leipzig that his son could provide keyboard works, string trios or quartets or symphonies, or anything else to order.[6] This declaration has been taken to imply that Mozart had composed some string quartets, and as there are no others it has been proposed that these divertimentos are the works referred to, but it is in fact clear that Leopold was itemizing music that could be supplied rather than works that already existed. (Breitkopf, incidentally, was apparently not interested; he published nothing of Mozart's during his lifetime.)

Whatever their purpose, these three short works are full of a kind of spirited invention otherwise unfamiliar in Mozart at this time. The opening movement of the first, in D major, is typical with its repeated figures, its snatches of dialogue on quite improbable ideas, its witty accompaniments (note the *minore* section of the development, where the murmuring passages of shorter notes in the second violin and the alternate pizzicatos in the viola and the bass give the lie to the first violin's implied seriousness). The wit in the finale is even more palpable, with its staccato *piano* phrases echoed or answered *forte* and its mock-serious contrapuntal development. The thematic link between its outer movements, of a kind not uncommon in Mozart, has often been remarked. The slow movements of all three works strike a particular kind of tenderness and warmth of expression without infringing the limits of the divertimento style, though the poignant dissonances of the Andante of the F major work come close to them before their tension is characteristically dissolved in a '*galant* cadence' (marked *x*):

The finale here, with the elaborate near-counterpoint of the accompaniment to its principal theme and the uncomplicatedly witty eight-bar episodes, encapsulates the quartet-symphony dualism of the series.

Once again, for the main part of 1772, there is a total dearth of information about Mozart's activities except those relating to composition. He wrote a number of canons (K.89/73k, K.89aI/73i and K.89aII/73r), in a variety of styles and dispositions, which suggests that he spent some time working on his contrapuntal technique (these have sometimes been ascribed to the first Italian journey, but the paper-type and handwriting argue composition in Salzburg in 1772). As regards 'real' composition, it seems to have been a spring and summer of fairly steady work, principally on church music and symphonies. In March he wrote a substantial work for the church, doubtless for use at Easter, a setting of the *Litaniae de venerabili altaris sacramento*. The first of his two Eucharist litanies, K.125 in B flat, this has long been recognized as modelled on his father's setting in D major of 1762,[7] much more closely than was the *Litaniae lauretanae* K.109/74e discussed in the previous chapter. The points of similarity and departure reflect the younger man's greater originality and superior command of structure. Leopold begins his opening movement with a choral 'Kyrie', Adagio maestoso, which after twelve bars gives way to a symphonic Allegro, with a ritornello before the chorus re-enter. Wolfgang begins his with an orchestral ritornello, which breaks off for a solemn six-bar Adagio 'Kyrie' and then resumes the Allegro with the chorus; the material is broadly similar in its disposition in relation to the musical form, although Wolfgang uses solo voices for the secondary material ('Christe eleison'), which Leopold does not. Each setting has a 3/4 'Panis vivus' for soprano, Wolfgang's much the more varied in texture and warmer in expression, and a brief, slow setting of 'Verbum caro factum'. Wolfgang's 'Hostia sancta' is the movement most closely related to the model, although Leopold's setting is an Adagio, with persistent, repetitive violin figuration (which by 1772 would have seemed distinctly old-fashioned) and Wolfgang's a lively Allegro. Wolfgang's principal theme derives directly from

Leopold's, and several other ideas in the movement follow Leopold exactly—the disposition of the words among the solo voices, the sustained longer notes at the first 'miserere nobis', the use of chromatic harmony at particular points. Each leads into a brief, minor-key 'Tremendum' with repeated rapid notes in triplets in the strings and alternations of *forte* and *piano*, moving to Allegro for 'ac vivificum sacramentum'. The two 'Panis omnipotentia' settings are each tenor solos in triple metre, with almost identical handling of the word setting. Wolfgang's fugue to 'Pignus futurae gloriae', 226 bars in its original form, is even more extended than his father's, and harmonically perhaps duller because constrained by the repeated notes and octaves of its subject, although some well devised rising sequences help sustain the interest. His 'Agnus Dei' is a soprano solo, Un poco adagio, leading into a short concluding chorus on the same musical material; Leopold's is a setting for all the soloists and chorus with, again, constant violin figuration. Why Mozart drew in this way on his father's setting is unclear; there do not seem to be other examples of this kind of close modelling. Perhaps it was to save time, perhaps to test his ingenuity and his use of more modern techniques within a similar framework.

The litany's relatively large scale and the size of the forces used (oboes, horns, clarino trumpets, strings including violas) suggest performance in the cathedral. It was not forgotten. No doubt it was heard again in Salzburg; it was almost certainly given in Munich, when Leopold sent home for it (and his own setting in D), referring to it as Wolfgang's 'grosse Litaney', with a view to performance on New Year's Day 1775. He also requested, a few days later, a sheet indicating cuts (three, totalling 46 bars) to produce a shorter version of the 'Pignus' fugue, which is understandable.[8] In 1778, Leopold sent copies to the Heiligkreuz monastery at Augsburg, where this and Mozart's later sacramental litany were performed on 10 and 11 May in conjunction with processions.[9]

A *Regina coeli* setting, K.127 in B flat, followed in May. The occasion for it is unknown, but the solo soprano for whom it was composed was Maria Magdalena Lipp, the wife of Michael Haydn (Leopold referred to it many years later as composed for her).[10] It speaks well for her voice and her agility. The opening movement is a chorus, in Mozart's usual sonata-ritornello form, with some spirited and even witty invention to match the jubilant text. Second is a graceful Andante in F for soprano, with chorus to round off each verse with alleluias and the orchestra softened by flutes and horns. It leads directly into the 'Ora pro nobis', set in E flat, and the heart of the work, a passionate plea from the soprano with a line of increasing floridity and large, dramatic leaps as the cadences are approached. The soprano also leads off each section of the final chorus, a 3/8 'Alleluia'.

A sub-genre of sacred music was the epistle sonata. Mozart's first three examples date from near the beginning of 1772: they are not in fact dated, but the handwriting evidence is decisive, although the paper on which they were written was used at various dates between 1768 and 1784. Epistle sonatas were performed at or after the reading or intoning of the epistle; there was a long tradition of music at this point in the celebration of Mass, after the Credo, sometimes for organ alone, often for strings. The use of a single fast movement for a small string group of first and second violins and bass instruments, with organ continuo—the form taken by most of Mozart's seventeen pieces in the genre—seems to have been unique to Salzburg. A few of Mozart's later examples use wind instruments, and some have fully written-out organ parts with solo passages. Only one, the first, K.67/41h in E flat, seems to be a slow movement; it has no tempo indication but is usually interpreted as an Andante. It is an appealing sonata-form miniature of just 44 bars, within which Mozart finds space for a good deal of graceful, expressive sentiment, including in the secondary material some surprising chromatic writing. The second and third sonatas, K.68/41i and 69/41k, in B flat and D respectively, are clearly quick movements, in the manner of miniature symphonic Allegros. Though only about 60 bars long, they find room for a little development, snatches of imitative writing proper to the church (K.68) and brilliant italianate violin figuration (K.69), as well as secondary themes that adjust subtly and expressively on recapitulation in a different register. None of these three earlier sonatas can be linked with any particular liturgical event, or with the use of specific mass settings; with later ones, the choice of key and instrumentation sometimes offers hints. They may well have been used within another composer's mass settings.

With the experience he had by now acquired in composing instrumental music, it seems at least curious that, during the spring of 1772,[11] Mozart should have reverted to arranging other composers' sonatas as concertos, just as he had done with movements by Schobert, Honauer and others five years before. Leopold copied out three keyboard sonatas by J.C. Bach, op.5 nos.2, 3 and 4, and to these Mozart added string ritornellos and accompaniments, for two violins and bass instruments, to turn them into 'concertos'. It has been suggested that he came across these sonatas in London and wrote his concerto conversions then (hence the Köchel-Einstein number 21b, as opposed to the original 107, to which K⁶ reverts). But the sonatas were not in fact published until 1766 and, though it would have been possible, it is hardly likely that the Mozarts would have made manuscript copies before publication. Accepting, then, that these works were put together in 1772 (as the handwriting in the manuscripts shows), we are left with no plausible cause for their existence. Might Mozart have prepared them, in the spring, for use in Italy during his planned visit in the autumn and winter? might they have been intended as an exercise in concerto composition, in anticipation of writing some original works? No answer is particularly convincing. Whatever the case, these pieces are decidedly superior in musical quality to the earlier group, though the credit for that belongs less to Mozart than to J.C. Bach. These three concertos were never included, as the earlier four were, in the traditional numbering of Mozart's keyboard concertos, nor is there any logic in the three works being required to share a single Köchel number when the others had one apiece. The first of them is in three movements, with a particularly attractive central Andante in J.C. Bach's quite individual melodic style. The others are in only two, the E flat work, the third, being specially appealing for its spacious opening movement and its wistfully graceful minuet.

The year 1772 was Mozart's most prolific as a symphonist. In February he composed one, K.124 in G, then between May and August came a further half-dozen (these seven are nos.15 to 21 in the traditional reckoning). K.124 is a decidedly jolly piece for one composed, and possibly performed, during Lent, with the vigorously swinging triple-metre rhythms and *opera buffa*-like figurations of its opening movement (beginning with the same pattern as the previous symphony). It does however have a longer development section, 36 bars, than Mozart had customarily been writing, even if much of it is only thinly related to the thematic material already heard. The Andante, a sonata-form miniature, is pleasantly melodic in manner, with phrase extensions to create variety and secondary material with dialogue between wind (oboes and horns) and strings. After a minuet of an oddly stop-and-start character, the rondo finale carries its *buffo* style into what is surely a jocular coda, where for bars on end almost nothing happens.

An outburst of creativity in May was perhaps provoked by the arrival of a violinist archbishop. The first of the May symphonies, K.128 in C, again has a triple-metre first movement, although here the predominant triplet motion curtails the energy (the Allegro is qualified with 'maestoso'). The secondary material, however, manifests a different kind of energy in its spacious, striding theme and its modulating development, where again Mozart's invention ranges freely. One of Mozart's favourite later habits in a recapitulation was to carry the primary material towards the subdominant, then back again, so that the material immediately before the cadence is presented exactly as it was in the exposition. The adjusted tonal equilibrium in the listener's mind ensures that the tonic statement of the secondary material seems a natural and properly balanced outcome. Mozart uses this procedure in the present movement, shortening the restatement of the primary material, then passing through F major and A minor before returning, extending the music by only one bar (eleven instead of ten) but creating an effective tonal balance. The Andante grazioso, in the dominant, G, rather than the usual subdominant, is in a more chamber musical style, with imitative writing and refined detail. The finale (this symphony and the next have no minuets) is a noisy, hearty jig-rondo with fanfaring horns to round it off.

Mozart had begun composing the next symphony, K.129 in G, on the paper he used for the main part of *Il sogno di Scipione* and the K.109 litany; his handwriting at the beginning bears out a rather earlier date.[12] Presumably he had set it aside and went back to it during May. There is a rich mixture of styles to this movement: an opening in a manner akin to J.C. Bach, a standard Italianate tutti, a delicately imitative secondary theme derived from the opening:

and a prototype Mannheim crescendo, and a well-shaped development makes effective use of the primary theme. A song-like Andante,
built of gracefully handled clichés, and a jig-finale, binary but worked
out thoroughly and at unusual length, complete this ingeniously
composed piece.

The third and last of the May crop of symphonies, K.130 in F, is
scored with flutes rather than oboes, and with four horns. Mozart
began composing for the usual two horns, but when working on the
third movement decided to add the second pair and wrote an extra
staff on each page of the earlier movements to accommodate them.
Possibly he did so to supply music for the family friend Joseph Leutgeb, the local virtuoso, recently returned from a tour, but there was
anyway a ready supply of hornists from the court band. In all movements except the second the extra horns are keyed in high C, that is,
written at sounding pitch and strenuous for the players, and Mozart
was cautiously sparing of the higher notes for them. At the start of
the symphony the music is close to the world of *opera buffa* with its
vivacious snapped rhythms, and the main secondary idea is full of
spirited trills (echoed by the second violins when repeated) and
triplets. A return of a version of the opening material, used imita-
tively, to serve as codetta, and its use again in the quite brief but purposeful development, show the deepening of Mozart's involvement in
composing shapely and well unified movements.

Compositional curiosity of another sort informs the Andantino,
with its three-bar phrases: the pattern is two threes followed by a four.
At the beginning of the second half of the movement, however, the
theme is inverted and extended to normal four-bar phrases. The coda
here is another oddity, perhaps in some way allusive for contemporary hearers: the horns and flutes in turn present some rather banal
ideas, and then the main theme is stated, first *piano*, then (with the
violin mutes removed) *forte* by the whole orchestra in unison. The
minuet is one of those where the basses imitate the violins, more or
less in canon, with a folksy tone added by a middle part, violas or second violins, on a kind of wobbling drone. The curious trio has a

strangely shapeless melody, in pairs of three-bar phrases and with per-
ilously high horn writing. The finale's main eccentricity lies in its
scale and its symphonic weight, coupled with a vigour that welds a
diversity of quite ordinary, direct themes into a unity with an impression of taut and purposeful organization. The work as a whole seems
to herald in Mozart the move, which was affecting other composers
at the same time, towards assigning greater substance to a finale, coun-
terbalancing the intellectual weight traditional to a first movement.
This retreat from the idea that the prime function of later movements
was to supply light relief after the opening Allegro and the slow
movement has significant implications about the way composers, and
audiences, were beginning to think about music and listening to it.

This symphony was speedily followed by another with unusual
features and, musically, perhaps more attractive. K.132 is in E flat,
Mozart's first use of the key for a symphony since his very earliest
essays (unless others in between are lost). This again calls for four hornists, and here Leutgeb and his colleague would have had to stretch
their lips still further, for except in the slow movement the additional
pair is keyed in high E flat, a type of horn otherwise unknown—
again, Mozart runs no risks with their upper register, never writing
above the ninth harmonic, notated d''.[13] The flourish that begins the
symphony is one that Mozart used repeatedly in his E flat works, in
identical or similar form. It heralds a movement that is unexceptional,
though sturdy and well-proportioned, with a witty secondary theme
(even more wittily varied, characteristically, when recapitulated in a
different register) and a development that alludes only marginally to
the movement's material.

Mozart composed two slow movements, both in the dominant
key, B flat. The one appearing at the usual point in the autograph
score is a 3/8 Andante, of unusual length, whose opening melody
echoes, inexactly but very obviously, the Gregorian plainsong for
'Credo in unum Deum'. An Austrian Christmas song, 'Joseph, lieber
Joseph mein', familiar to Salzburgers as it was played on their local
carillon, is also incorporated in the second violin part later in the

movement. There is however no particular reason to think that such features imply an ecclesiastical provenance for the work, which is only one of many Austrian symphonies to embody readily recognizable quotations of this kind (Haydn's 'Lamentation' Symphony, no. 26, is another).[14] The alternative movement, a 2/4 Andantino grazioso appearing at the end of the autograph score, is beautifully textured, with divided violas often coupled with the oboes, graceful accompaniment figures and some charming pre-imitations of the first violin melody by the violas. The main part of the minuet is again largely canonic, the second violins in pursuit of the first, with the basses joining in; while the trio is another bizarre piece of writing, a melody largely of two notes, as if a parody of a psalm-tone, or perhaps some private or local allusion. The symphony ends with a rumbustious *contredanse en rondeau* with three episodes, the central C minor one again mildly eccentric in its invention.

If this group of symphonies is marked by its oddities, at least the last two, dating from July and August, are more regular in their behaviour. K.133 in D, scored with trumpets, is in the usual brilliant style associated with that key, with a spacious crescendo at the opening (not specified, but the intention is unmistakable), bustling tuttis and themes of a fairly conventional cut. It is however a strong and finely proportioned movement, with a short but purposeful development that leads directly into the intermediate tutti of the exposition, bypassing the opening material—which, embodying the lengthy crescendo, would anyway have been impossible to introduce at this point. Having worked to the apparent end of the recapitulation, Mozart then brings back the opening material, which can be read either as a coda or as a 'reversed recapitulation'. This is a device that he and others often used in the later 1770s. Whatever it may be called, and whatever its historical origins (the kinship with ritornello form is obvious), in such a context as this its rhetorical force, as opposed to any real sense of recapitulation that it conveys, is considerable. (The 'reversed recapitulation' was little used by Salzburg composers, although there is an example in a symphony by Michael

Haydn which Mozart is likely to have heard just before writing K.133.[15]) The Andante, in the dominant, A, is a beguiling piece for solo flute, with muted violins, a ticking viola accompaniment and pizzicato basses. The hefty, peasant ring and the four-bar phrases of the minuet are offset by a trio in softer, part-contrapuntal textures; and the symphony ends with a jig-like finale which, drawing on Mozart's growing technical arsenal, uses touches of counterpoint and interchanges between strings and wind to add force and momentum to the invention.

Like the symphonies of 1771, this group ends with an A major work, K.134, written in August, and again one that requires flutes rather than oboes (in all movements; K.114 reverts to oboes in the Andante). The first movement is the most densely worked of Mozart's symphony movements to date, with its vigorous opening motif used in a variety of ways and senses—in a *piano* echo, as bass to a loud tutti, to accompany a closing-section figure and then to appear again, *piano*, at the end of the exposition. Mozart's persistent use of it in the development effectively precludes his presenting it to open the recapitulation, for further repetition so soon would have been otiose, but with a careful juggling of the order of events he introduces it at a later point, alongside a *minore* variant of the secondary theme, and in this context the final, simple *piano* return acquires something of the character of a reversed recapitulation. The movement exemplifies Mozart's readiness to manipulate structures to accommodate new types of idea and the treatment they invite.

The Andante of K.134 is also exceptional among the symphony movements of this period for its sensuous warmth, close to the world of the serenades, and its richness of texture. Its principal theme is the 'Porgi Amor' idea (as it was to become, fourteen years on), one that always held strong expressive resonances for Mozart. Here it is heard against a gentle 'Alberti'-type accompaniment, with restrained comments from the violas and flutes between phrases. The 'development' section here seems oddly irrelevant to what has passed. There is a minuet, along the now usual pattern of a boisterous first section and a more docile, almost inactive trio. The finale is bubbling with high spirits in its witty rhythmic figures, syncopations and mock counterpoint, but even the jocular Mozart composed closely and carefully, and the re-use of material from the principal theme within the codetta couples happy ingenuity with formal concision.

Mozart had another, more obvious outlet for his musical wit during the summer months of 1772, in the serenade K.131, dated June. There is no reference to this work in any known document or letter. The time of year of its composition implies that it was intended as university Finalmusik (though no introductory march survives, as it does for other, documented works of the kind), but it could have been designed for some other festive use in Salzburg, conceivably one connected with Colloredo's installation. It is usually described as a divertimento, on the strength of the heading in the score, but the handwriting there is not Mozart's, and the work is closer to the serenade or cassation pattern of the 1769 works and those of 1773 onwards than to that of any true divertimento. It is in six movements, the second and fourth slow, the third and fifth minuets. The *concertante* element here is handled rather differently from how it is in most of the serenades, no doubt partly because of the unusual forces Mozart seems to have had at his command that particular summer. K.131 calls for only a single flute, oboe and bassoon, and four horns. In the first movement, which is loosely composed compared with the symphonies of the time, the secondary material involves solo passages for the woodwind, and the horns, in true four-part writing, add fullness to the tutti textures. The first slow movement is a typical serenade Adagio for strings with an expressive cantilena for the first violins, the second a graceful gavotte-like Allegretto with prominent flute writing. It is in the minuets that the horn ensemble comes into its own. The first has a principal section for strings alone, then three trios— one for the horns, one for the three woodwind and one for all the wind, with a number of stopped notes (non-harmonic or chromatic) for the horns to allow for harmonic variety. In the second minuet the first and the last eight bars are for the horns alone, with an eight-bar passage in between; in the trios the flute and oboe each have solo music. Lastly there is a coda in which the horns' eight solo bars are emphatically repeated by a tutti. The humour may not be subtle, but writing acceptable music for four horns, with their limited array of available notes, is testing, and Mozart carries it off with due skill. The horns introduce the finale, too, with a sombre slow introduction, which is followed by a bustling Allegro molto (with some solo writing for the flute and brief episodes for the horns) and lastly a 3/8 Allegro assai, forming in effect a double movement.

A handful of other instrumental works belong to the spring and summer months of 1772. There are a number of minuets, presumably designed for dancing. These include a collection of twenty, K.103/61*d*, made up of a group of twelve (which also survive in a keyboard version) and a group of eight, which Mozart rearranged as a set of nineteen (some lacked trios, so could be combined). The orchestral settings are for two violins and bass, mostly with two oboes (or in some cases flutes) and two horns (occasionally clarinos). They are along the usual pattern, with each strain eight bars, sometimes extended to ten or twelve. A further group of six minuets, K.164/130*a*, written in June, call for two oboes in the main sections and a single flute in the trios; the first three require clarinos, the last three horns. Lastly, Mozart may have written, or at least begun, a keyboard duet sonata in the latter part of 1772, K.381/123*a*; this will be discussed in Chapter 14.

It was probably not until the autumn that Mozart began work on the opera commissioned for the Milan carnival, *Lucio Silla* K.135. The libretto, this time a new one, by Giovanni De Gamerra, had been sent to the Mozarts in advance so that Wolfgang could begin work on the recitatives, which the contract had specified should be delivered during October. On 24 October 1772 father and son duly set out, on their third and final Italian journey.[16] They took their usual route, reaching St Johann on the first day and Innsbruck at 10.00 p.m. on the second (a Sunday: they had to make a late start, 7.00 a.m., as the earliest mass was at 6.00, Leopold reported). At Innsbruck they stayed at the fourteenth-century Zum goldenen Adler (the inn still exists; it was the post-stop, to which Leopold had his mail sent on the return journey) and paid a visit to the royal convent at Hall, where they were shown round by Countess Lodron, sister-in-law of the Salzburg chief steward, and Mozart played the organ. The next day they reached Brixen and the day after Bozen, or Bolzano ('this gloomy town'), where they visited a friend in the Dominican monastery. They paused there, as it was pouring with rain. At the inn, Leopold wrote, Wolfgang whiled away the time by composing a string quartet—probably K.155/134*a* (it is curious that his only string quartets so far were written in Italian inns)—and he also wrote an uncomplimentary rhyme about Bozen in a postscript to his father's letter. Then to Rovereto, and on 30 October to Ala, where they spent an extra day, Wolfgang's nameday, with their friends the Pizzini brothers. They also spent an extra day at Verona, where again they saw friends, and they went to an *opera buffa*. After a night in Brescia, or the nearby town of Montirone, where their host Count Fausto Lecchi had a villa, they reached Milan on 4 November and stayed close to their friends the d'Aste family.

Mozart himself wrote the first letter home from Milan, giving two reasons—Papa simply could not find time to write, as he and their hosts had so much to talk about, and he was too lazy. Leopold wrote a week later, on 14 November, mentioning that the singers for *Lucio Silla* had still not arrived in Milan, except those singing the *secondo uomo* and the secondary tenor role. In the meantime, Wolfgang was busy with composing three choral numbers and adjusting and rewriting the few recitatives that he had written in Salzburg. De Gamerra had sent a copy of his text to Metastasio himself, in Vienna, who had now returned it with corrections and changes, and with a whole scene added in Act 2; Metastasio's approbation and help were fulsomely acknowledged in the printed wordbook. De Gamerra was a young man, at the beginning of his career. A Livornese, he had taken minor orders, studied law at Pisa, and served in the Imperial army before turning to writing. He had an *Armida* text to his credit, of which no setting (nor any of any other libretto by him to date) is known, but he went on to make a considerable reputation, serving from 1771 as poet to the Teatro Regio Ducal in Milan, working in Vienna as a court poet in the mid-1770s and the 1790s and attempting to reform the Neapolitan theatres; his political views, initially progressive, caused him some difficulties. In his 'Osservazioni sull'opera in musica', published in 1771 with his *Armida* text, he argued for the revival of the spectacular element in opera, but he was chiefly reputed as the leading Italian exponent of the *comédie larmoyante* (or *dramma lacrimoso*) type of play or opera.

By the time of the next letter, written on Leopold and Maria Anna's twenty-fifth wedding anniversary, as Leopold affectionately notes, the *primo uomo*, Venanzio Rauzzini, had arrived; Rauzzini, only 26, was a musician of some ability, a harpsichordist and composer, who later had a considerable career in London and Bath. A week later Leopold could report that Mozart had composed the first of his arias, which is 'incomparable', and Rauzzini 'sings it like an angel'. But there was not much else to report, Leopold says, in response to his wife's plea for more news. He tells of his health, and that they eat only once a day, at two in the afternoon, having an apple, a slice of bread and a glass of wine in the evening. By 5 December, with just three weeks to the première, the *prima donna*, Anna Lucia de Amicis-Buonsollazzi, had only just arrived, after delays on the road from Venice because of mud and flooding. The tenor who was to have sung the title-role was ill and a substitute was hastily being sought (the secretary of the theatre had gone to Turin and a courier to Bologna, a traditional singers' market, for the purpose). Mozart added a note to say that he still had fourteen numbers to write, including presumably all four of the arias for De Amicis (he had heard her before, in Jommelli's *Armida* in Naples, but would not expect to compose her music until she was present) and the planned four for the tenor, as well as the ensembles ending the first and second acts.

An early Italian biographer of Mozart, Folchino Schizzi, writing 45 years after the event, tells an anecdote about the composition of

De Amicis's arias that may have some truth in it.[17] Surprised that so young and inexperienced a composer was to write the opera in which she was to appear,

> she took Mozart gently by the hand and asked him to tell her what his ideas were concerning the arias and scenes in which she was to sing, adding that she would take care of the composition herself. Mozart laughed to himself at her pride and answered that he would do as she wished. A few days later Mozart presented himself at the rehearsal and apologized to Buonsollazzi for having completely written the first aria. The singer took this composition in her hands, gave it a quick look, and, taken aback by its many beauties and the mastery with which it was composed, could not stop praising the boy, and reproaching herself. Mozart told her with a smile that if she did not like the aria, he could present her with a completely different one, composed especially for her; and that if the second was not pleasing to her, he could submit a third.

Schizzi goes on to tell a tale about Mozart's competing in an improvisation contest with a sceptical *maestro*, at the Passione church, and playing 'in a way that can only be described as divine'.

Those events took place, if Schizzi's account is true, in the week before 12 December, when Leopold reported that three of the arias for the *prima donna* were written and that she was pleased with them. In her main aria, he writes, 'Wolfgang has introduced passages that are new, very special and astonishingly difficult' which she sings amazingly well—he is referring to her first aria in Act 2, 'Ah se il crudel periglio', which has florid passages of a very fanciful and brilliant kind. Rehearsals had now begun, without the tenor, who was a church singer from the small town of Lodi, had little stage experience, and arrived only on 17 December. The next evening, Leopold reported, Mozart had written two of his arias, and contemplated composing two more, but in the event it was decided, no doubt in view of the singer's limitations and the short learning time now available, that just the two would be sufficient. The rehearsal programme was as follows:

12 December	recitatives (1)
?13–17 December	recitatives (2, 3)
19 December	in theatre, with orchestra (1)
20 December	with orchestra (2)
22 December	with orchestra (3)
23 December	dress rehearsal
26 December	first performance

In spite of all the pressures on the Mozarts, they pursued a busy social life too: on 18 December they dined with Therese and Ferdinando Germani, court officials, the next day they lunched with Albert Michael von Mayr, a paymaster to the court, and on the evenings of 21, 22 and 23 December they were in attendance at 'great parties' given by Count Firmian, with numerous nobles present and music from 5.00 until 11.00 p.m. Wolfgang performed each evening, in particular the third. The celebrations were partly in honour of Firmian's brother, the Bishop of Passau, who had just been created cardinal.

When Mozart arrived in Milan, with some of the recitatives, he would also have brought his plan for the opera, showing its intended key structure, which he would have followed while composing the recitatives.[18] But he did not stick to it. For nine of the 18 arias and one of the ensembles, the autograph score shows adjustments in the recitatives' final bars and their cadences, so that they end in keys different from those he had originally intended. Moreover, some of the links between recitative and aria in other numbers, often the less important ones, for minor characters, are unorthodox and uncomfortable, and inconsistent with Mozart's usual practices—which implies that he did not have time to make all the changes he would have wanted, leaving those where the effect would at least be passable. Clearly Mozart was compelled, for some reason, to change his tonal plan. This might have happened at an early stage (one adjustment falls where an aria for Silla was cut and so must have been made before the decision to omit it). He may have become discontent with his original scheme, or may have realized that it led to some of the cast having to sing in keys they did not like. Possibly Metastasio's changes had something to do with it. There is reason to think, from the nature of certain of the changes, that he might have set some of the music at a pitch the singers did not find comfortable: the adjustments before Giunia's and Cecilio's arias suggest he needed to transpose their music down, and the links with Celia's indicate that these may have been put up. But such miscalculations are rare for Mozart, even at this age, and there is no surviving sketch or draft to lend support to the theory.

This was the cast:

Lucio Silla [Lucius Cornelius Sulla], *Roman emperor*	Bassano Morgnoni (*tenor*)
Giunia [Junia], *daughter of Caius Marius, betrothed to . . .*	Anna de Amicis (*soprano*)
Cecilio [Cecilius], *proscribed senator*	Venanzio Rauzzini (*soprano*)
Lucio Cinna [Lucius Cinna], *patrician, friend of Cecilius, secret enemy of Silla*	Felicità Suardi (*soprano*)
Celia, *sister of Silla, in love with Cinna*	Daniella Mienci (*soprano*)
Aufidio [Aufidius], *tribune, friend of Silla*	Giuseppe Onofrio (*tenor*)
Guards, Senators, Soldiers, the People, Maidens	

Mozart's last letter before the première, sent on 18 December, shows him in high spirits, writing jocular nonsense to his sister (and with alternate lines upside-down) of a kind that seems typical of someone both tired and elated. Leopold's written after the première, on 2 January 1773, deserves to be given at length for the glimpse it affords of contemporary operatic life:

The opera is happily launched, although on the first night various very distressing incidents took place. The first problem was that the opera, normally due to begin *one hour after the Angelus*, started three hours after the Angelus, that is, about eight o'clock German time and it went on until two hours after midnight. The archduke rose from his midday meal just after the Angelus, and then had to write five letters of New Year greetings in his own hand to their majesties the emperor and the empress, and NB he writes very slowly etc.

Imagine now, the whole theatre was by half-past five so full that no-one more could get in. The singers, on a first night, are always very nervous at having to perform before so distinguished an audience. The anxious singers, the orchestra and the entire public, many of them standing, had to wait three hours, impatiently in the overheated atmosphere, for the opera to begin.

Second, you should know that the tenor, an emergency substitute, is a church singer from Lodi who has never before acted on so large a stage, has only appeared about twice as principal tenor in Lodi and was engaged only about a week before the performance. Where, in her first aria, the *prima donna* had to wait for a sign of anger from him, he exaggerated the angry gesture so much that it seemed he was going to box her ears and hit her on the nose with his fist, and this made the audience laugh. Signora de Amicis, wrapped up in her own singing, did not at once realize why the public were laughing, and became disconcerted, thinking that she was being laughed at but not knowing why, and she did not sing well for the rest of the evening; moreover she was jealous because, as soon as the *primo uomo* came on to the stage, the clapping of hands was heard from the archduchess. This was a trick on the part of the castrato, who had arranged that the archduchess be told that he would be too nervous to sing, to make sure that the court would give him courage by applauding him. To console De Amicis their royal highnesses summoned her to court about noon the following day, and had an audience lasting a whole hour with them, and only after that did the opera begin to go well, and though with a first opera the theatre is usually very empty, at the first six performances (today's is the seventh) it was so full that no-one could squeeze in, and the *prima donna* has the upper hand and her arias have to be repeated.

The opera ran for no fewer than 26 performances, of which Mozart, in the usual way, directed the first three. Like those for *Mitridate*, the settings were the work of the Galliari brothers, some of whose drawings survive.[19] Also in the usual way, there were three ballets, *Le gelosie del serraglio* after Act 1, *La scuola di negromanzìa* after Act 2 and *La giaccona* at the end, the work of the two distinguished choreographers Charles Le Picq and Giuseppe Salomoni. The last would almost certainly have been nothing more than a dance to Mozart's final chorus, which is in the French chaconne style. The other two, neither of them new ballets, would have been to music by other composers. It was at one time thought that Mozart had written the first ballet, and he may have contemplated at least arranging it; he did in fact note down some themes and make some sketches, under the heading *Le gelosie del serraglio*, but some of the music has been identified as the work of the Viennese ballet composer Joseph Starzer, and one movement is linked to the original 1758 setting (by François Granier) of *Les jalousies du sérail*.[20] No press reports or criticisms of the opera appeared; and after this the opera was never again performed in Mozart's lifetime (that was the normal fate of an opera at the time). The libretto was re-used: there are settings by Anfossi (1774), J.C. Bach (1775, for Mannheim, with the text adjusted by Mattia Verazi; Mozart later saw and admired the score) and Mortellari (1779).

Drawing by Fabrizio Galliari for the opening scene of *Lucio Silla*: 'A deserted place with scattered trees and ruins of buildings, by the bank of the Tiber; there is a distant view of Mount Quirinale with a small temple at the summit' (*Pinacoteca Brera, Milan*)

Mozart did not forget his music and made use of a couple of the arias for Giunia on later occasions.

Lucio Silla was not quite the work it was intended to be. In the original libretto a central role falls to Silla himself, who is virtually as important a member of the cast as Giunia or Cecilio. But the withdrawal of the original tenor, Arcangelo Cortoni, and the substitution of an inexperienced, second-rate performer in a role that demanded not only a good singer but also (as Leopold wrote) 'a first-rate actor with a handsome presence' inevitably involved the curtailing of the part and a significant shift in the dramatic balance. The historic Lucius Sulla (103–78 B.C.E.) was a great military man (among those he fought was Mithridates, king of Pontus) and a constitutional reformer but a bloodthirsty and vindictive dictator. Among his enemies may have been Cecilius Metellus, presumably the source of the name

Cecilio in the opera. The historical Aufidio was one of Silla's friends, and Cinna was also a historical figure; the name Celia may have been suggested by that of one of Silla's wives, Clelia. The behaviour of Silla at the end of the opera is apparently quite out of character for the man himself but it represents, of course, the magnanimity of rulers that it was customary, indeed obligatory, to laud in operas of the eighteenth century. De Gamerra was not particularly successful in providing motivation for his *volte face*, but since Silla's actions at the end of his career continue to baffle classical historians he is not perhaps to be blamed. The love interest, and the link between Giunia and Silla's predecessor, were De Gamerra's invention. His main historic source was Plutarch.

At the beginning of the opera, Cecilio, though proscribed, has returned in secret to Rome, where he meets Cinna. He learns that his betrothed, Giunia, has been told he is dead and is being pursued by Silla. After warnings from Cinna he decides to see Giunia only when she is alone, and at the end of the first act he surprises her at her father's tomb. Giunia has refused Silla's importunities, and does so again in Act 2; when nevertheless he announces in public his plans to wed her she rejects him, and the impetuous Cecilio enters, sword drawn, to be arrested and sentenced to death. Act 3 begins with Cecilio in prison; Giunia is ready to die with him. Cinna's plot to kill Silla has failed. But Silla decides to be merciful: he spares Cecilio and Giunia, telling them to marry, and forgives Cinna his plot and gives him his beloved, Celia. And finally he renounces his throne and restores freedom.

The traditional *opera seria* allowed limited scope to De Gamerra's interest in the spectacular and still less to his penchant for the pathetic. He ingeniously managed to combine the two in the finale of Act 1, which is a 'scene complex' of a style becoming increasingly popular in serious opera of the time; it is also of the genre known as an '*ombra* scene', even though the *ombra* (shade) is not a 'real' one (Giunia also has an *ombra* scene in Act 3 where again she imagines her husband dead, speaking to her as a ghost). Silla has just stormed out after a forceful D major aria, with trumpets and drums, speaking of vengeance and death. A brief Andante, no doubt to allow time for the scene change, carries the music to A minor, with dark chromatic inflections, as we see Cecilio in a dimly-lit atrium, leading to the catacombs, with monuments to Roman heroes. He reflects on death and destiny, to sustained string accompaniments. Then the music becomes agitated as, hearing the approach of Giunia with her maidens and some noblemen, he conceals himself behind the urn containing the remains of her father, Marius. The music has been moving between C major and E flat, where it settles for a chorus for Giunia's attendants, in two sections, the first sombre (a *lugubre canto*, according to the libretto, surely indebted to the opening chorus of Gluck's *Orfeo*), the second vigorous; between them Giunia calls on her father's shade (in G minor, with muted violins and *pizzicato* violas, perhaps again a symbol for funeral bells). As she addresses the spirits of her father and her husband in a recitative, Cecilio emerges, and she takes him to be a ghost (her tremors are heard in the orchestra). She still does so as they join in a duet, originally to have been in C major, rounding out the tonal pattern of the scene, but adjusted to A major. It begins as an eloquent Andante and, at the point where she recognizes that he is indeed alive, uses phrases that Mozart was later to remember, in *Così fan tutte*. Finally there is a jubilant Molto allegro with much singing in thirds and sixths and rapid passage-work, symbolizing in the music their oneness of purpose. This is the most powerful scene in the opera, with a grandeur of conception that hints at Mozart's much later works, although the handling of keys lacks the purposefulness that became an important part of his musico-dramatic armoury. It moves quite rapidly between tonal centres remote from one another with less dramatic justification than he would later have permitted himself.

The musical and vocal skills of Anna de Amicis, coupled with a friendliness to the Mozarts that gave much pleasure to Leopold ('De Amicis is our best friend. She sings and acts like an angel . . . ', he wrote on the day of the première), drew the finest of the opera's music from Wolfgang. The aria with the specially original passage-work, 'Ah se il crudel periglio', is a splendid showpiece, with its coloratura writing carrying real force, but all three of her other arias are of greater depth and originality. In 'Dalla sponda tenebrosa', sung in Act 1 in defiance of Silla, she has nobly spacious slow music to mourn her father and her brother, fast music to swear vengeance upon the tyrant, with a quicker, still more impassioned coda. The second of her Act 2 arias is a vivid representation of her state of breathlessness and alarm, 'Parto, m'affretto', with broken phrases in the voice, offbeat rhythms in the string accompaniment, and vocal divisions with a hint of hysteria. For her last aria, 'Fra i pensier', as she looks forward only to death, Mozart forsakes the usual forms to provide a simple two-part structure, slow-fast (anticipating the rondò type, to become so popular for a final, climactic aria in the later 1770s). The music passes from C minor to E flat and back again, with a style of declamation in the Andante above throbbing string triplets and pizzicato basses that is closer to Gluck than anything else in Mozart and partly dictated by the verse, with its long decasyllabic lines in place of the seven-syllable ones that prevail in this work.

Rauzzini too must have been well pleased with his music. His heroic first aria gave him ample opportunity to show the Milanese his beauty of tone and his *messa di voce* (gradual swelling) on long, sustained notes, his capacity for wide leaps and the brilliance of his divisions. His second, an outburst of passion, begins without an orchestral ritornello (confounding the audience's expectation in this way was a traditional means of conveying the stress of a character, unable to stand around at the orchestra's pleasure before expressing himself); it is a D major 'military' aria, an expression of defiance, complete with trumpets and drums and violin tremolandos. His third is the only true slow aria in the opera—an *aria d'affetto* in E flat, richly scored even though only with oboes, horns and strings. While this is an aria to show Rauzzini in a grandly expressive vein, with its broad lines and, again, many wide leaps and long held notes, his final one—Cecilio's (supposedly) last farewell to his beloved as he goes to his death—is an expression of personal anguish, in a more intimate manner. A gentle, tenderly flowing minuet, it hints at his despair with the rise and fall of its melodic line (in two-bar patterns, then intensifying with single-bar ones) accompanied only by strings, and exceptionally is in a simple rondo form.

The other roles are relatively blandly drawn. Cinna has three arias, all long ones of a generalized heroic character, stressing the singer's upper-middle register and occasionally demanding virtuosity in the passage-work. When it came to writing Silla's part, clearly Mozart was severely circumscribed by the capacities of Morgnoni, the church singer from Lodi. His two arias, again both Allegros, are modest in the compass, the technique and the expressive resources they predicate, and the result is a somewhat puny dictator, although there is some effective blustering—from the orchestra rather than the voice—in the D major aria in Act 1. Aufidio is a one-aria minor role, singing immediately after the first interval when no-one would be seriously listening. Only Celia seems to have caught Mozart's fancy: he introduces her with a Grazioso minuet aria of considerable charm and intimacy (again, with a strings-only accompaniment), including some high staccato passages, continues with a delicately scored aria with flutes and another with strings only in the second act, the latter calling for more high staccato, and ends with her only formal aria, a short one with oboes, horns and trumpets (sparingly used, never against the voice). It is easy to tell from these arias precisely the kind of voice Mienci possessed.

Lucio Silla is curiously proportioned, and not solely because of the curtailment of Silla's role. Besides the chorus in each of the acts, the first contains only five arias and one ensemble, whereas the second has nine and an ensemble and the third only four (under the original plan there would have been ten in Act 2 and five in Act 3). As in *Mitridate* and the intervening semi-dramatic works, Mozart uses the standard ritornello-sonata form for nearly all the arias, but in several different ways. In Cecilio's first aria, for example, the main part, leading to the first tonic close, is in effect in 'rounded binary' form, but after the middle section the repeat provides a full tonic recapitulation. The succeeding number, for Celia, has no true recapitulation (the secondary material does not reappear) before the first tonic close, but after the contrasting section the secondary material is recapitulated. Giunia's short aria near the end of Act 2 consists, in effect, of an exposition, a contrasting section, and a recapitulation of only the secondary material: this heavily abbreviated form reflects the urgency of the dramatic situation. A similar pattern is used in Celia's Act 3 aria, again where a long disquisition would be unsuited to the situation. In Silla's first aria, Mozart uses the shortest possible form of recapitulation as he can, of the secondary material alone, to close the aria satisfactorily: here the reasons for his choice would probably have been more practical than aesthetic.

In the two years that elapsed between *Mitridate* and *Lucio Silla* Mozart's invention and technical resource had developed. As in *Mitridate*, the arias are lengthy—substantially longer than those of the generality of Italian operas of the date[21]—and they are also richer in their scoring. Although several, as we have seen, call for strings alone, and others use the traditional orchestra of strings with oboes and horns, more than half require trumpets as well as horns, and several need divided violas. Italian composers of the time tended to score their music more lightly and make it easier for the voice to predominate. The music of *Lucio Silla* is more imaginatively characterized than that of the earlier work, and fewer numbers are of a bland or routine quality. During his travels in Italy in the interim Mozart had enlarged his experience of opera. His orchestral recitatives in particular are better focussed: by using figurative or thematic ideas in sequences, usually ascending, he is able to regulate (usually to increase) the dramatic tension, for example in those preceding Silla's second aria, and particularly before Giunia's final aria, where a figure in thirds for oboes with divided violas an octave below is used intermittently in the recitative and achieves its ultimate form only when it introduces the aria.

ALTHOUGH AT THIS period the continuing run of an opera cannot be taken as certain evidence of its success, nor a short one of its failure (it could mean that the next opera was unready, or contractual factors might be involved), it seems clear from Leopold's letters that the run of 26 performances did in fact represent a response to the opera's reception. The second carnival opera, Paisiello's *Sismano nel Mogol*, also to a libretto by De Gamerra, was not given until 30 January, which meant that it would have a rather shorter run, as the season had to end at the beginning of Lent (28 February). The Mozarts went to the première, but neither Paisiello's name nor the opera's title is mentioned in their letters. Wolfgang had earlier reported, after the first orchestral rehearsal, that as there were to be 24 horses and a great crowd of people on the stage some accident was bound to happen. Leopold commented on the lavishness and costliness of the staging.

Leopold however was busy investigating other possibilities. Prospects in Salzburg looked bleak. The court seems to have had almost a tradition of making arbitrary appointments, promotions and salary increases, and the naming as Kapellmeister of Domenico Fischietti (a Neapolitan who had enjoyed brief success with some Goldoni *opere buffe* in the late 1750s but had done little since), on a three-year contract starting in 1772, a post to which Leopold was at least entitled to aspire, can only have spurred him to further efforts. A message added at the foot of his letter of 9 January, ciphered in the family code, mentions that the grand duke in Florence had received his letter and was considering it sympathetically. Leopold was seeking employment there, certainly for Wolfgang and possibly for himself too. In his next letter he refers less hopefully to the situation; a letter from Florence to his Milan friend Leopold Troger, Firmian's secretary and chaplain, indicates there is little likelihood of work there. He adds that he begrudges every kreuzer he spends in Salzburg as he needs to save for future journeys. Leopold had of course been looking for openings in Italy for some time, but this is the first indication of the discontent he felt under the new archbishop.

Mozart himself seems to have been relatively untroubled by such matters. He added a preposterous postscript to his father's letter of 9 January, asking Nannerl to deliver his greetings to various friends who were in Milan and sending greetings to her from others in Salzburg. He was however very much occupied with composition. The string quartet he had been working on during the journey to Italy was the first of a series of six he completed in Italy. He also wrote a motet for Rauzzini to sing in the Theatine Church in Milan, as he mentioned in a note to his sister (with the words all written, a typical piece of jocularity, in a higgledy-piggledy order).

The motet is the famous *Exsultate, jubilate* K.165/158a, a three-movement piece, almost a concerto for the voice. It begins with an Allegro in the manner of a short operatic aria, with oboes and horns in the orchestra and a spacious ritornello, duly taken up by the soloist, whose gloss on the secondary material—in its orchestral form a series of little flourishes by the oboes with string punctuation, now with a sustained line added—is particularly felicitous, as is the representation of 'psallant aethera cum me' with its vocal flourishes. After a brief recitative, a slower movement in triple metre, 'Tu virginum corona', follows, this time a complete ritornello-sonata movement in A major, its lines full of graceful appoggiaturas and with suave octave doublings in the strings; it leads into the final 'Alleluia', back in the original key of F major. This is a jewel of a piece, with its high spirits and its wit: note the redistribution of the Latin accentuation, '*Alleluia, alleluia*' (somewhat akin to the humour of Mozart's postscripts), the mischievous offbeat themes, the little excursions into virtuoso divisions, the harmonic surprises that cast a momentary cloud. The motet is like no other piece of Mozart's; its music speaks unmistakably of his relaxed high spirits at the time he wrote it and of the elation and confidence that his opera-house success had brought him. Though operatic in style and approach, to the point of a marked *amoroso* flavour in its central movement and drama in its finale, it is still essentially couched in terms of the chaste passions of church music.

The six string quartets written in Milan have been assigned to various fairly specific times during Mozart's months in the city, but that is guesswork. The first of them, K.155/134*a*, begun in Bozen, is no doubt correctly taken to belong to October and November, but it is scarcely possible to be sure of the order in which the others followed or just when they were written. The order in which they stand has more to do with the assembling of the six separate manuscripts in key sequence—D, G, C, F, B flat, E flat—than with chronology. All the autographs are on the same type of paper, one that he presumably obtained in Bozen or shortly before he arrived there (it is used in no earlier works): it has a ten-staff ruling, not ideal for string quartets, and appears also in *Exsultate, jubilate*, also making up an odd page of *Lucio Silla* and serving for the sketches for the ballet in that opera. The first of the quartets is still in the manner of the Salzburg group, K.136–8, a direct and untroubled style in which the first violin carries almost the entire musical interest and the lower strings do little more than accompany, often in repeated notes. In the brief development of the first movement there are a few bars of imitative writing, and occasionally there are snatches of dialogue between the violins, but the textures are predominantly divertimento-like. The outer movements of the last quartet, K.160/159*a* in E flat, are also somewhat in this manner, and much of the music could pass for orchestral but for one or two ventures into higher positions for the first violin than Mozart used in orchestral music and occasional cello writing that departs from the prevailing repeated notes (or 'Trommelbass', 'drum bass').

In K.155 Mozart again wrote 'Viole' and 'Basso' against the lower string voices but later corrected them to 'Viola' and 'Violoncello'. His 'viole' in K.158 and 159 led the K[6] editors to label these two quartets, and K.155, as 'Quartett [Divertimento]'. That is not justified, however, either by his orthographic slip nor by their musical content: for the later quartets in the set move, astonishingly rapidly, towards a more integrated style in which Mozart grasps and exploits the unique qualities of the quartet medium. Here he uses it certainly no less fully than did Joseph Haydn in his op.17 set, his fourth collection, composed in 1771 and published in 1772 (though it is unlikely that Mozart would have come across those by the time he was writing his own). A good deal of Mozart's four-part writing, however, is harmonically in three voices, with the violins (or occasionally first violin and viola) in octaves and with the middle parts in thirds; the silky sound of strings in octaves, rare in Haydn, clearly had a special attraction for him.

The work in G, K.156/134*b*, begins with a spirited Presto, with a development section sustained by an ostinato figure, initially on the second violin against a dialogue, then tossed around within the texture to become a dominant pedal on the cello. Mozart composed an E minor Adagio as second movement, a dull piece, with a simple violin line that is rhythmically rather static and a throbbing inner accompaniment. He then scrapped it and wrote another Adagio in the same key, more colourful and imaginative, with *forte* and *piano* alternations, faster and more varied harmonic movement and much more elaborate inner parts, with exchanges of line to vary the texture. This quartet and K.158 in F end with substantial minuets, in the Italian style to which Mozart had alluded in letters during his first visit to Italy.[22] Each has a minor-key trio. The use of the minor mode, rare in instrumental music at this date (Mozart had yet to write a minor-key symphony), is a feature of these quartets: four have minor-key middle movements. K.157 in C is an expansive work, with a spacious first movement using rather bland material, although its perky secondary ideas lend themselves well to development. Its finale is Mozart's earliest true sonata-rondo, following the scheme *A-B-A-C-A-B-A* (where the first *B* is in the dominant and the second a tonic recapitulation of it). The rondo of K.159, on a brief, witty yet graceful theme (a mere eight bars), has no fewer than four episodes, taking the unusual pattern *A-B-A-C-A-D-A-E-A* (for an extended rondo Mozart later preferred to use a theme that itself was ternary, repeating only its main section between episodes).

This quartet, K.159 in B flat, the most original of the set, begins with an Andante at whose opening Mozart delays the entry of the first violin so that, when it does enter with the principal theme, it poetically turns it in a new direction, towards the dominant key; in the recapitulation its entry, again delayed but one bar earlier, carries the music towards the subdominant. The Allegro here is a fiery, triple-time G minor movement, markedly similar in type to two later movements (in the piano and violin sonata K.379 and the piano Allegro K.312/590*d*), with forceful unisons and a pounding pulse. A minor-key sonata form movement raised issues Mozart had not met before in the handling of key relationships in an Allegro. In the recapitulation, the music would need to remain in the minor at the point equivalent to where previously it had moved to the relative major. He adjusted the linking passages, generally preserving their lines but shifting their registers and often their key relation to neighbouring passages, at the same time exploiting the new harmonic possibilities offered by the minor mode. Parts of the bridge section are in G minor, but others are in C minor, thus providing a new way for Mozart to lean—as he usually does at this point—towards the sub-dominant side, and additionally allowing a passage formerly heard in G-string colouring to retain that colour by changing its pitch only one degree. The effect is striking and lends the movement an uncompromising character—the result of the replay in the minor of music first heard in the major—that we shall often find in Mozart's minor-key works (and more rarely in other composers'). Another particularly original movement among these quartets is the central one, in A minor, of the F major work K.158, where following a lightly scored Allegro the actual invention is dictated by the four-part imitative writing for the four instruments, as an array of counterthemes piles up. Yet another is the A flat Un poco adagio of the last quartet, starting (after the preceding movement's close in E flat) on a dominant seventh of B flat minor, which makes the famous dissonant beginning in a foreign key of Beethoven's First Symphony, nearly 30 years later, seem quite modest in its unorthodoxy.

THE MOZARTS REMAINED in Milan throughout February. Leopold had written that he was suffering severe pain from rheumatism in the cold weather and could not travel. But he added a note in the family cipher saying that this was written only to provide a reason for his extended absence, of which his wife was to inform the court officials, and in fact he was perfectly well (Maria Anna was to cut off the scrap of paper bearing the note but did not do so). Then he claimed to be delayed because of the ice in the Tyrolean mountains. Meanwhile he was still waiting for word from Florence. It had evidently arrived by 27 February, when he told his wife that there was nothing to be done. They had been visited earlier in the month by Joseph Leutgeb, their hornist friend from Salzburg. Wolfgang had been prepared, had he arrived in time, to write a horn obbligato into an aria in *Lucio Silla* for him (possibly this was a jocular reference to the horn obbligato he had been required to add, at the last moment, to an aria in *Mitridate*; Leutgeb would surely have been told about this).

About 4 March, they set out for home. No letters survive from the return journey, but it is clear from those of the outward journey that they expected to take the same route and visit some of the same friends or patrons, including Count Lecchi in Brescia, and as Leopold asked for mail to be sent to Zum goldenen Adler in Innsbruck we know they again stayed or at least called there. It is perhaps ironic that they planned to reach home, from this last journey to Italy, on the evening of 13 March 1773, in time to join in the celebrations on the anniversary of Colloredo's election to the Salzburg archbishopric.

13

Vain Hopes in Vienna

O NCE AGAIN, FOR a period during which the Mozarts were quietly at home *en famille*, the dearth of documentation about their activities leaves us largely ignorant of what they were doing. This time Leopold and Wolfgang were in Salzburg for no more than four months, between the middle of March and the middle of July. No word about them is to be found in the surviving court archives during this period; if there was any correspondence, it is lost. All we have, in fact, is music. These months produced from Wolfgang yet another group of symphonies, probably four divertimentos, a mass and probably a violin concerto.

Two of the divertimentos—the title is not Mozart's own but is perfectly apposite—are for pairs of oboes, English horns, clarinets, bassoons and horns. This combination is not known to have been used in Salzburg or indeed anywhere else (English horns were occasionally used in wind bands, for example Prince Schwarzenberg's in Vienna, but in place of clarinets rather than in addition to them).[1] One of the divertimentos, K.186/159*d* in B flat, is undated; the other, K.166/159*d* in E flat, bears the date 24 March 1773 and so must be one of the first pieces he composed on his return. It is written on paper of a size and shape that Köchel, and all writers on the subject since, have called *Klein-Querformat*, or small oblong (it measures about 170 × 225 mm, giving the vertical measurement first; Mozart's usual papers are about 225 × 305 mm).[2] Mozart had occasionally used a small oblong paper in 1769–70, but K.166 inaugurates a period of some four years when he used it predominantly for his music, instrumental and sacred. K.186, written partly on the same paper as the Milan string quartets, and partly on a Salzburg paper Mozart had used occasionally since 1771, is usually reckoned to date from the end of the Mozarts' stay in Milan, partly on the grounds that clarinets were available in Milan but not in Salzburg. But he certainly composed K.166 at home, and these ten-instrument works are clearly a pair, which are overwhelmingly likely to have been written together, for the same purpose and the same group of players; in any case, clarinets had in fact been available in Salzburg since 1769.[3] One must suppose that these pieces were intended for some special use on an occasion otherwise unrecorded. It must surely be relevant that the second version of the K.113 divertimento (see Chapter 11), originally composed with clarinets and now rescored to include oboes, English horns and bassoons, also dates from these months.

Wherever they may have been written, there is something curious about these two works which might be explained if we knew more about the circumstances for which they were composed. Each is in five movements, along the same, unorthodox plan: an Allegro, a minuet, an Andante and then a brief Adagio before the final Allegro. The opening movement of K.186 is a mere 62 bars, mostly in eight-bar phrases and devoid of real musical content. There is a brief minuet, a 26-bar Andante and a 24-bar Adagio, and then a rondo finale of more normal proportions, whose principal theme is one of those Mozart had noted in Milan in connection with the ballet *Le gelosie del serraglio*, in *Lucio Silla*. The scoring is curious, too. The clarinet parts are not essential in terms of musical content: they merely add brilliance to the tuttis and could be omitted without leaving any gap, just as in the fully scored second version of K.113 where, it has been suggested, the new parts for the double-reed instruments could well have been intended to replace rather than supplement the clarinets. The two bassoons double throughout K.186, as they also do in K.166. The invention in the two opening movements of K.166 is fairly thin and unsubtle, but the work is on a more normal scale. Here the clarinet parts though still modest are essential, with scraps of solo writing, and the textural possibilities offered by the presence of English horns are more enterprisingly exploited (in both works they chiefly double the oboes an octave below, enriching the tuttis, and occasionally entering into dialogue with them in the quieter music). The Andante here is not original but based on a movement from a symphony by Giovanni Paisiello, used in at least one of his opera overtures and, according to a note on the autograph, composed only in 1772.[4] Mozart simply rescored the movement, simplified a repeated passage, added four bars and modified the ending. He could well have come across the piece in Milan, where he would have met Paisiello at the opera house during the rehearsals and performance of *Sismano nel Mogol*. Here again one movement, the Adagio, corresponds with one of the incipits of *Le gelosie del serraglio*. To what extent these movements as a whole might duplicate those in the lost ballet must of course be uncertain, just as is their authorship.

Probably there is some link between these two divertimentos and another pair, K.187/159c/Anh.C17.12 and 188/240b, dating from the same period. These are for the extraordinary combination of two flutes, five trumpets and four timpani, no doubt again dictated by circumstances. The combination suggests some sort of military or state occasion, or that the band was intended to mimic the famous Salzburg *Hornwerk* (the open-air mechanical organ in the tower of the Salzburg castle). The Salzburg establishment included a dozen trumpeters, who had ceremonial and military duties and were also, according to Leopold's 1757 report, good musicians who also played the violin; the best of them were outstanding trumpeters, and the Mozart's family friend Johann Andreas Schachtner was among them. As the number in the K^6 appendix indicates, K.187 is not authentic: it is an arrangement of dances by Gluck and Starzer,[5] all but two in

Leopold's hand, the remaining two (one of which is lost) in Wolf-gang's hand. Some of the ballet pieces in *Le gelosie* are also by Starzer, which would seem to support any argument that these works have something in common, especially as they belong, most probably, to the same period as the ten-instrument works and could have been designed for the same occasion or a similar one.[6] The music of K.188—the autograph survives, and there is no reason to doubt that it is Mozart's own composition—is in itself of little consequence, but the ingenuity Mozart put into the writing for this odd ensemble compels admiration. Three of the five trumpets are in C and two in D (with the timpani tuned, to match, G-C and A-D). Between the two groups, each able to play only the natural harmonic series, he was able to devise ways in which they could supply some of the support-ing harmony to the flutes and outline some simple melodic ideas of their own, even when the music changed key. There are six short movements, including two minuets without trios, an ingenious, mod-estly expressive Andante in G major and an imaginatively composed final gavotte.

Before March was finished, Mozart had composed a new sym-phony, and three more followed in the next seven weeks. Leopold, in his usual way, wrote the dates of these symphonies in the top right-hand corner of the first page of the scores, but they were virtually obliterated, with thick and heavy overscorings, by someone else. This was most probably done, after Mozart's death, by his wife and those helping her to obtain the best possible price for his manuscripts, which would be the more valuable if a buyer could be led to think that they were works of his mature years. It is however possible that the defacement was done by Mozart himself, during his Viennese years, in the hope of selling them to a patron without disclosing that they were old pieces. Of the four symphonies he wrote during the spring of 1773, it is fairly clear that the first belongs to 30 March and the last to 19 May; the ones between seem to date from 10 (or per-haps 16) April and 29 (possibly 19) April.

The first of this group of symphonies, K.184/161*a* in E flat (166*a* in K³, no. 26 in the traditional numbering), is the most remarkable: it is scored with flutes as well as oboes and bassoons, and trumpets as well as horns, and its three movements are played without a break. This last point has led commentators to suppose that it may have been written for the theatre, for the continuous three-movement form had been associated with the Italian opera overture since the time of Alessandro Scarlatti. It would however be imposing too rigid a schematicism on Mozart and his contemporaries to suggest that a continuous work was necessarily theatrical, or conversely that a work in separate movements was not: the overtures to *La finta semplice*, *Mitridate* and *Lucio Silla* are all in separate movements, and several of the early symphonies have linked ones. An argument in favour of theatrical origins, however, is Mozart's use of so large a wind contingent, on a scale that would be more usual in a theatre than elsewhere.[7] As we have seen, trumpets rarely have a place in the Salzburg symphonies, and pairs of flautists and oboists were not generally available (or, rather, the oboists often relinquished their instruments in favour of flutes, sometimes for a whole work, sometimes for a single movement). But it can be inferred from the existence of the ten-instrument divertimentos, and the four-horn symphonies of the previous year, that additional wind players were sometimes available in Salzburg.

In fact, K.184 was later used theatrically—by the travelling troupe directed by Mozart's friend Johann Böhm—which says more about the music itself than about the movement structure or the instrumentation. It served at the end of the 1770s as overture to a drama, *Lanassa*, an adaptation by Karl Martin Plümicke of a French tragedy by Antoine-Marin Lemierre about a Hindu widow who dies on her husband's funeral pyre. The symphony begins with pounding chords in a martial rhythm, typical (as we saw in K.132) of Mozart's E flat openings, and typically with a violin arpeggio figure in response. The tuttis involve sudden changes to the minor mode, forceful unison writing, urgent syncopated rhythms and *forte–piano* alternations, and the opening idea returns to serve ambiguously either to close the exposition or to open the development. At each appearance the E flat chords are repeated one step higher; on their final recurrence, at the end of the recapitulation, Mozart screws them up another step, providing a dramatic twist to the lead into C minor for the Andante. The Andante is a brief movement, but on a new level of expressive power for a Mozart symphony. Its main idea is a five-note motif, worked in a variety of ways, tossed between first and second violins, then between violins and the wind ensemble, all against rather weightier textures than he usually favoured, and with a secondary theme that rises to a climax of some passion. This theme is tellingly adjusted in the recapitulation (now in C minor), to allow the violins to remain in their most effective register and to leave the appoggiatura figure demanding resolution and thereby adding power to the eventual C minor close; the passages are shown in parallel in this example:

The finale, in 3/8, is by no means a throwback to the traditional hunting-type movement, though it embodies elements of it; rather, it is a fully worked-out sonata-form piece, 236 bars long, with a development far bolder in its counterpoint and lines than anything in Mozart's earlier symphonies and indeed of the type that Mozart was to use in later and larger works. The unusually rich wind ensemble, used structurally rather than decoratively, plays a central part in the dialogues of the development.

If that symphony seems to represent a step forward, into a larger expressive world, the three that follow it to some extent retreat. The first of the April symphonies, K.199/161*b* in G (162*a* in K³; no. 27), begins with a triple-time movement of some vitality but notable primarily for its touches of wit—the *piano* echo of a pompous tutti, the graceful interlude that serves between exposition and recapitulation. The Andantino grazioso (Mozart used this marking for the next three symphony slow movements) is easygoing, unassuming music, the violins largely in thirds in the main theme, until the secondary theme comes to an end with a striking interrupted cadence, glancing at distant keys and darkened by sustained wind and low-pitched divided violas; but the cloud soon passes. Like K.184, this symphony keeps some of its surprises for the finale (again a long movement, this time 323 bars), whose principal theme is a piece of skittish two-part counterpoint:

It takes on a different character, however, to serve as secondary theme, a charming piece of humour, economy and ingenuity:

The relation of its outline to the main theme of the first movement

seems unlikely to be intentional—if Mozart did this regularly, or more than very rarely, one might suspect otherwise—but it can justifiably be regarded as more than coincidental. The contrapuntal idea from the opening is used not in the development, as one would expect (this comes from an energetic working of a note-pattern taken, characteristically, from the last bars of the exposition), but at the beginning of the recapitulation, where it is used to apply the element of subdominant tonality, so important to Mozart in establishing the proper tonal balance for the return of the secondary material in the tonic.

The second of the April symphonies, K.162 in C (no. 22), in no way consolidates the territory explored in the two preceding, which may seem surprising, at least to the cultural historian predisposed to concepts of progress and deepening. This is only one of numerous moments in Mozart's career when we need to remind ourselves that our ideas of progress, or indeed of merit, may not correspond at all with those (insofar as they existed at all) of Mozart himself and his contemporaries. The C major work, like some of the Italian symphonies discussed in Chapter 9, consists largely of figuration. Although neatly, even wittily put together, its first movement is little more than a collection of clichés. A curious feature is the elision of the brief (twelve-bar) development with the recapitulation, which begins at the point corresponding to the thirteenth bar of the exposition, with only a brief reference at the end (as at the end of the exposition) to the opening material. The Andantino grazioso is enriched by divided violas and some concertante writing for the oboes and horns but remains thematically conventional, as does the jig finale. This work and the May symphony, K.181/162*b* in D (no. 23), both include trumpets. Mozart calls them 'trombe lunghe' here, the more usual 'clarini' in K.181 (and simply 'trombe' in K.184), but there is no indication that the terms indicate any distinction beyond the physical shape of the instruments—long or straight trumpets, as opposed to the normal curled type. The name is not specific to the key of the trumpets: Mozart calls for 'trombe lunghe' in D in several works, such as the overture to *Ascanio in Alba*.

The D major work, K.181, which like K.184 has no breaks between movements, is another with little thematic character, but with its juxtaposing of various types of cliché passage it does achieve a certain grandeur of scale. Its first movement is in fact Mozart's longest to date in a symphony, at 181 bars (it was soon to be exceeded), and it is not unreasonable to imagine, in the light of the unusual 'building-block' element in the structure and the careful management of the harmonic and rhythmic tensions that propel the various unrelated sections that make up the exposition, that Mozart was consciously trying to expand the scale of his thinking. As in K.162, there is only a brief interlude between the exposition and the recapitulation, which again avoids the formal 'double return' by omitting the exposition's opening gesture. The slow movement, if musically unexceptional, is structurally curious: a twelve-bar theme for strings, followed by an extended elaboration of it in the dominant for oboe, in *siciliano* style, soon followed by a recapitulation with the primary theme unaltered but the oboe version recast for its tonic-key appearance, allowing the oboe to remain in its most effective register. This duly leads into a sonata-rondo finale in quick *contredanse* rhythm. The use of trumpets, the slender musical character and the brevity of these last two symphonies—each takes some nine minutes in performance, about half the length of the more substantial symphonies of 1772 or indeed of K.199—imply that they may have been composed for a specific function that required shorter, lighter and noisier pieces.

At a time when he was so actively writing symphonies and divertimentos on his return from Italy, it may seem unlikely that Mozart would also have composed a violin concerto, his first independent work of that genre. Until recently it had been presumed that all five of his violin concertos (K.207, 211, 216, 218 and 219) were written in 1775. The autographs are dated: each shows the exact day and month, but the year is less clear, for here again the dates have been tampered with. Most seem to have been adjusted to 1780 and then changed back again; where the corrected date is unclear it has been added separately, alongside. With the first concerto, K.207, composed on 14 April, the second annotator, unable to restore the messy date to legibility, has added '1775', the same date as on the other manuscripts, just below. But 1775 may not in this case have been the original, obliterated date. According to Wolfgang Plath's carefully observed *Schriftchronologie*, the autograph shows features that are earlier than that, in particular in Mozart's *piano* indications. By 1775 Mozart always wrote the initial *p* with a double hook, a small upwards movement before his pen descended to the lowest point of the main upward stroke. In K.207 there is only a single hook, made by a clear, straight, downward stroke forming an angle of some 30° or 40° to the main upward stroke; this, the style he generally used up to the end of 1774, combined with other features, suggests an earlier date for this concerto. Evidence from the paper is indecisive. K.207 is written on the small oblong paper that Mozart used for a few works in the spring of 1773 (see pp. 297–8) and many more from later in the year and from 1774 and 1775; half of the second of the violin concertos is written on this paper, half on the paper principally used for the other three. It is certainly plausible that he would have used the same paper for four works dated 24 March, 10 (or 16) April, 14 April and 19 (or 29) April. Further, in March and April 1775 he was heavily occupied in the composition of *Il rè pastore* and is unlikely to have been in a position to put it aside to write a violin concerto. The arguments in favour of 1773 consequently seem strong.[8]

It is not certain for whom, or for what purpose, the K.207 concerto was written. Some years later, Leopold referred in a letter to Wolfgang to a violinist friend, named Kolb, playing the concerto Wolfgang had written for him;[9] if K.207 was written separately from the other four it would be the likeliest candidate. There were several members of the Kolb family in Salzburg, and it is uncertain which of them was the violinist, for although 'Herr Kolb' is often referred to in Leopold's letters his first name is never mentioned. Probably it was Franz Xaver Kolb, an administrative officer, or just possibly one of the sons of the businessman and local official Johann Anton Kolb, Andrä or Joachim. Whichever it was, he was an amateur musician who organized concerts and was good enough to teach the violin and to win Leopold's praise.[10] When Mozart composed K.207, he had still to find the freedom of voice in this new genre that allowed the violin a fully idiomatic means of expression in a concerto context; his invention may have been inhibited by Kolb's limitations as a player (if the work was indeed for him). But the sustained, expressive line in the Adagio speaks to the particular capacities of the interpreter. In the outer movements the violin part tends to depend on a fairly anonymous kind of passage-work, at least by comparison with the later concertos. Nevertheless, there is plenty of lively interplay between soloist and orchestra, especially in the Presto finale. This is an extended movement with some ingenious deployment and development of themes and some hints of the principle of 'open-ended' sections— ones that can be turned in different directions on successive appearances—which were to be a hallmark of the mature piano concertos.

Mozart's only other substantial work during the spring and early summer of 1773 was a mass setting, K.167 in C, marked 'in honorem SS:^mae Trinitatis'. A mass so marked and dated in the month of June, as this is, is likely to have been written for Trinity Sunday (5 June, in 1773) and possibly for use in the Trinity Church, a fine building by

Fischer von Erlach in the Hannibal-Platz, across the river from the old city. It calls for an orchestra of strings without violas, two oboes, four trumpets and timpani (the trumpets are two clarini and two in low C, written in the bass clef: this seems to be simply a conventional notation, akin to the one for horns, with an octave transposition, rather than a true part for the very rare bass trumpet). The usual doubling trombones are not specified. This is Mozart's only wholly choral mass setting, with no solo vocal writing. That and other departures from his usual style would support the idea that K.167 was not composed for Salzburg Cathedral.

The Kyrie is a single sonata-form movement, with its main musical thread in the violin parts, which are full of interesting detail; the chorus carry what is often, as it were, a solidified version of the violin line. The Gloria too is a single movement, a typical triple-time Allegro with 'rushing violins'; the 'Qui tollis' and 'Miserere nobis' texts are underlined by augmented seconds, strangely unvocal intervals, in the treble part. Fully one-third of the Gloria is devoted to a fugal setting of the last line, 'Cum Sancto Spiritu', with new music for the chorus against which the strings maintain the figuration used earlier. The Credo hurtles through the words up to 'descendit de caelis', which is set in the usual illustrative way to a series of descending phrases, heralding a short Adagio 'Et incarnatus est'; 'Et resurrexit' serves as recapitulation. But there is also a separate, gracefully *galant*, minuet-like setting of 'Et in Spiritum Sanctum', and a brief recurrence of the opening music (at 'Et unam sanctam catholicam ecclesiam') before, again, a fugal setting of the final line ('Et vitam venturi'). With 136 bars of four-square, academic fugal writing culminating in a stretto (the voices entering in closer succession), this seems generously proportioned to the rest of the movement, but it certainly provides a powerfully assertive 'Amen'. After the Sanctus there is an appealing Benedictus, again a movement where the interest falls primarily on the string parts, with the violins weaving almost in trio-sonata fashion, to which the rather duller choral parts seem almost supernumerary. Lastly, an Adagio setting of Agnus Dei introduces yet another fugue, 'Dona nobis pacem', on a wide-spanning, ungainly subject, something of a schoolbook effort; but Mozart finally renounces counterpoint to supply a confident homophonic ending.

COMPOSING MUSIC FOR Salzburg residents independently of the archiepiscopal court seems to have become increasingly important to Mozart about this time. Leopold, who would have probably have solicited the commissions, was clearly planning to augment the family's income and to increase his son's reputation while ingratiating himself and his family with the most influential families in the city, who might at some time be valuable to them should Wolfgang (or indeed Leopold himself) come to be seeking posts elsewhere. The Mozarts' orientation was less exclusively towards the court and its music than was that of the other court musicians, and the development of other contacts must have seemed increasingly important to Leopold when working for an archbishop whom he did not much like or trust.

Most of the potential Salzburg patrons were, of course, connected with the court in some way. Certainly one work of the summer months, for example, and possibly a second, is connected with the family of Johann Ernst von Antretter (or Andretter), court military councillor and district chancellor. This is the serenade K.185/167a, which apparently was commissioned in the early summer of 1773. Mozart had not quite finished it when he and his father left Salzburg for Vienna on 14 July; with their first letter home, a week later, they sent 'the beginning of the Finalmusik' to 'young Herr von Andretter', and by 12 August Leopold was acknowledging the news of the work's success in Salzburg.[11] The 'beginning', in these circumstances, must surely mean nothing more than the introductory march, K.189/167b, since it is hardly conceivable that Mozart would have left the composition of the first movement to so late a stage. The 'young Herr von Antretter' was Johann Ernst's eldest son, Judas Thaddäus, who was to graduate at the end-of-year degree ceremonies in Salzburg, and it seems that the Antretters had commissioned the work or at least were much involved in its performance. The other work of this period often associated with the Antretters, though perhaps less securely, is the divertimento K.205/167*A* (173*a* in K³); this is usually taken to be the work Leopold Mozart referred to, in a letter four years later, as the 'Andretterin-Musik'—that is, the music written for a female member of the Antretter family.¹² The case for associating this work with the family, though thin, is plausible. The handwriting indicates a date of 1773¹³ and the paper-type is consistent with that. Its style and its modest instrumentation suggest a domestic celebratory work. Maria Anna Elisabeth von Antretter's nameday fell on 26 July, which invites the speculation, in the absence of any other known reason why Mozart might have written the work, that it was intended for that occasion.¹⁴ That the march usually linked with the divertimento, K.290/167*AB* (173*b* in K³), seems to be written in a slightly earlier hand, and on a paper of a type Mozart used little in 1773, is probably of no real significance; the link between the works is supported by the similarity and the uniqueness of the instrumentation and the identity of key.

The divertimento, which Mozart must have completed before the middle of July, is for three solo string instruments, violin, viola and double-bass, with the pair of horns usual in this kind of work, where they can add fullness to the tuttis and venture the occasional slightly bucolic solo, and also a bassoon. This last may have been an afterthought, for it is clear from the autograph that the words 'Fagotto e' were squeezed in above the word 'Basso', which had already been written against the bass line. Its addition reflects the availability of a player on the occasion for which it was intended rather than any artistic purpose, for the bassoon part is in no sense characteristic and it is not independent of the bass. Indeed, the bassoon, which is not indicated in the march, is silent in the central Adagio, a serenade-type movement in which the violin (and briefly the viola) draws an elaborate solo line, wide in span and warm and graceful in expression, above a light accompaniment. The Adagio is framed by two minuets, each with an original and entertaining trio: in the first the violin echoes the viola as it recapitulates the principal theme, one beat behind (and thus often in dissonance with it), while the second is based on a cheerful fanfare for the horns. The outer movements too are of a lively and often witty character, offering support to the idea that the work was intended for some sort of celebration, such as that for Frau von Antretter's nameday. The same applies to the march, clearly a jocular piece.

The autograph of the serenade K.185[15] shows another of the scratched-out dates, probably decipherable as 'nell'agosto 1773'; the evidence of handwriting and to some extent paper-type (less decisive, as Mozart used this paper over three years) support that date, and help confirm that this is the work given as Finalmusik that summer. The Salzburg performance, in the early days of August, after the degree ceremony, was directed by the Mozarts' friend Joseph Meissner, the bass singer. This is the first of the larger-scale serenades of the

First page of Mozart's autograph score of the Serenade in D K.185/167a (*present whereabouts unknown; reproduced from a microfilm courtesy of Dan Leeson*)

Salzburg type discussed in Chapter 8, which essentially consist of a symphony with a concerto embedded in it. K.185 begins, after the march (K.189), with a symphonic Allegro in D; then follow an Andante and Allegro, both in F, with solo violin, after which the music returns to D for a minuet, an Andante (in A), a further minuet and a finale. Later, Mozart found ways of relating the first minuet to the concerto-type movements. Here the concerto consists of only the second and third movements, while the symphony comprises the first and the last three or four. The incipits of the first and third movements appear in the Breitkopf manuscript catalogue, as a symphony and a concerto, so the music must have had some circulation, possibly after Mozart's time, as two separate works.

The dichotomy between the 'serious' style of the symphony and the more relaxed manner of the serenade—entertainment music more to be heard than to be listened to—is manifest in a number of ways. The music of K.185 is cheerful, simpler in style and texture and more direct in its thematic material than that of Mozart's symphonies of the time, and also less subtle in manner than that of the more chamber-musical K.205. The first movement has a heavy predominance of four-bar phrases and is built around a motto-like theme, used somewhat repetitively, of stark simplicity (Einstein, under the impression that the serenade was written for a wedding, thought it embodied 'all too clear' erotic symbolism).[16] The slow movement of the concerto is cast in a sonata–ritornello form, on a modest scale, and uses a typical aria device, the soloist's long note set against the orchestra, gradually swelling and assuming the foreground—a device Mozart was later to use with increasing variety and subtlety. The fast movement is a rondo, with the orchestra assigned the main theme and the soloist episodes of increasing virtuosity.

Mozart's later practice in the minuet was to provide an orchestral principal section and a trio with solo violin music. The trio of the first minuet is a solo for flute and viola with accompaniment for second viola and bass; the second minuet has two trios, one for the solo violin with accompaniment for upper strings, the other with prominent oboes and horns. Mozart often took the opportunities offered by trio sections for some fanciful kind of orchestral layout, and in his serenades even the slow movements tended towards a more concertante manner than he normally permitted himself in his symphonies, as can be seen in the oboe and horn writing here. A deeper note is momentarily struck by the slow introduction to the finale, though it soon dissolves in a lively 6/8 Allegro which is however longer and more elaborately developed than one might have expected.

THERE CAN BE only one reason why Leopold Mozart should have decided to take his son to Vienna in the summer of 1773: to seek for Wolfgang a post or some other kind of advancement there, or elsewhere in the Habsburg domains controlled from there. He may, in the light of Wolfgang's operatic successes in Italy, have been seeking an opera commission, to set right belatedly the indignity they had suffered over *La finta semplice* five years before. Had he known of the Empress Maria Theresa's disdain of his family and its activities over previous years, as expressed in her letter to her son in Milan at the end of 1771 advising against their employment (see pp. 244–5), he might not have troubled. He had been nurturing plans of this kind since at least the time of *Lucio Silla*, and had referred to them in passing in a letter from Milan—in cipher, as he did not want his thoughts known to the archbishop.[17] But the situation had altered. First, he must have asked for leave of absence, and have given a reason for it. It is clear from the petition that Mozart wrote to Colloredo four years later[18] that the archbishop had specifically told Mozart he 'had nothing to hope for in Salzburg and would do better to seek [his] fortune elsewhere', although Leopold's letters make it clear that, to protect his own and the family's position, he was anxious not to arouse suspicion of any disloyalty or lack of commitment on his own part to the Salzburg establishment. Colloredo was perfectly well aware of what was going on, and in fact he visited Vienna while the Mozarts were there and agreed to a request from Leopold that their leave be extended. The prominent Viennese Kapellmeister Florian Gassmann was ill (he died at the beginning of the next year), apparently giving rise to rumours in Salzburg of specific ambitions that Leopold was nurturing on Wolfgang's behalf. Leopold dismissed them as foolish gossip,[19] but his denial is belied by his own remark in the same letter that Gassmann's reported recovery might affect the plans for their stay in Vienna. He may not have aspired on Wolfgang's behalf to Gassmann's own position, but the death of a Kapellmeister would surely have led to promotions and vacancies at a lower level.

The Mozarts, father and son, left Salzburg about 14 July and probably arrived in Vienna on 16 July.[20] They had written to some old friends, the Fischer family (the father, who had died in 1759, had been a chief cook at the court; the son-in-law, also named Fischer, was a coppersmith), to ask if they could lodge with them at their apartment in the Tiefer Graben, in the inner city. The letter had lain unopened, as the daughter to whom it was addressed was away in Baden, but they were welcomed by the old lady. As usual, Leopold embarked on a social round, no doubt a purposeful one. They spent a good deal of time with the Mesmer family, not only the well-known doctor and 'animal magnetist' Franz Anton, at his fine house in the Landstrasse suburb, but also Franz's relative Joseph Conrad, who was director of the school at St Stephen's Cathedral. Others they met included Franz Reinhard Heufeld, director of the German theatre company, the dramatist and actor Gottlieb Stephanie, the court composer Giuseppe Bonno and his family, the composer Marianne Martinez and hers (she was daughter of the papal nuncio in Vienna, an acquaintance of Metastasio, Haydn and others), the court violinist Matthäus Teyber (his daughter Therese became a well-known singer), a member of the Mölk family from Salzburg, two doctors (their old friend Laugier and the Dr Bernhard who had treated Wolfgang in 1762) and a university mathematics professor Wilhelm Bauer; one day they ate with a former servant of theirs, Porta.

By 12 August Leopold could report on his audience with the empress: she was gracious, but no more. On 7 August, St Cajetan's day, the Mozart's were invited to the eponymous monastery to lunch and to the service. Because the organ was not good enough, Mozart had (in Leopold's words) the cheek to play a concerto on a violin borrowed from Teyber—perhaps his own, K.207 (he could not have had the new concerto movements of K.185 to hand). The next day Leopold directed a performance of Mozart's 'Dominicus' Mass K.66 at the Jesuit church. There was also a concert in the Mesmer family's theatre in the garden at the Landstrasse. Leopold talked in his letters of returning to Salzburg as early as 16 August, but if not he would remain at least to the end of the month; clearly he had further business in the offing, presumably the investigation of more potential openings for Wolfgang. Nothing however is known of what they might have been. He and Wolfgang apparently had no more musical engagements, as far as we know. They took an excursion to Baden, the spa south of the city, with the Fischers and the Teybers, and later another to the Mesmers' country house at Rothmühle, south-east of Vienna, near Schwechat. They also met during these weeks the painter Rosa Hagenauer-Barducci, a Salzburg friend (with a slightly questionable sexual reputation) who was married to a relative of their landlord, and the well-known ballet-master Jean-Georges Noverre, who had worked with Gluck on *Alceste* and whom the Mozarts already knew.

Understandably, Maria Anna Mozart seems to have resented being left behind in Salzburg. Her letters are lost, but Leopold's responses speak for themselves: she and Nannerl could have come, and their friends would happily have accommodated them, but the journey would have been inconvenient, it would have made an undesirable sensation in Salzburg, it would have strained their finances, but above all anything that might have attracted attention or provoked suspicion, and given their enemies opportunity to catch them out, had to be avoided. Leopold did however buy various fripperies ('corselets, caps and so on') for Nannerl, who was eager to know the latest Viennese fashion. He reported in his letters on the suppression of the Jesuits in Austria, quoting various opinions and discussing the consequences but offering no view of his own. He also wrote lengthily and with much distress about the death of a Salzburg friend, Dr Niderl von Aichegg, who underwent an operation in Vienna and died under it the following day. The Mozarts evidently had to stay in Vienna until about 24 September, for reasons unknown to us since Leopold decided that he would explain them only on his arrival home. He planned to travel back to Salzburg by a slightly different route, through Mariazell, St Wolfgang (where Mozart could see the church of his patron saint) and St Gilgen (Mozart's mother's birthplace), though in the event they took the quickest route, through Linz and Lambach.

Mozart himself added postscripts to some of his father's letters, in his most high-spirited and youthfully preposterous vein. Some are in mixed languages, one is mock high-flown rhetoric, and there is also one in semi-nonsense verse to a Salzburg friend, Heinrich von Hefner. Another is signed 'Gnagflow Trazom' (his name spelt backwards). 'Wolfgang is composing eagerly', wrote Leopold at the end of his letter of 18 September. That is the sole reference to his composing in Vienna. The only works known to date from these weeks, the completion of the Antretter Finalmusik apart, are the six string quartets K.168–73, a set of piano variations and some incidental music for a drama by Baron Tobias Philipp von Gebler, *Thamos, König in Ägypten*. The surviving sources for this music date from much later, partly 1776 and partly 1779, and its composition history is obscure,[21] but Gebler himself referred in a letter of December 1773 to the original score of music to *Thamos* 'set not long ago by a certain Sigr. Mozzart', of which the first chorus was 'very fine'.[22] Mozart must therefore have written at least two choruses, or the three as in the final version; these were performed when the play was given at the Kärntnerthortheater in Vienna on 4 April 1774. Mozart's music was admired as 'beautifully written' but it was apparently poorly sung. It was also praised by the poet Christoph Martin Wieland when Gebler sent it to him—he reported that the composer Anton Schweitzer, then at Weimar, thought there were many fine things in it but discerned that the composer must be a beginner.[22] Probably the *Thamos* music that survives represents a revised and augmented version of what was composed in 1773 (the work is discussed in Chapter 19).

The piano variations K.180/173c are generally taken to date from the Viennese weeks. Mozart would probably have come across the theme in the imperial capital rather than elsewhere: an aria from the admired masked-ball scene in Act 2 of Salieri's *La fiera di Venezia*, first given in Vienna early in 1772 and subsequently in Mannheim, Bonn and other cities. The pattern of the variations and the treatment is entirely conventional, with six variations in all, the penultimate an Adagio and the last in altered metre. They were published in Paris in 1778, with other sets; no autograph survives to confirm (or contradict) the dating.

The autographs of the quartets K.168–173 are on Salzburg paper. Either Mozart had begun the set before he left or, more probably, he took with him an ample supply. The traditional view is that these works were provoked by contact, in Vienna, with the music of Haydn, and in particular Haydn's latest string quartets, the three sets published as opp.9, 17 and 20. This needs to be carefully weighed. First, as we have twice seen, Mozart evidently found the string quartet a congenial genre on which to work when he was away from home. Secondly, there is no evidence that Mozart played string quartets in Vienna (he did not have his violin with him), had any particular contact with string quartet performance or studied string quartets. Thirdly, there must be considerable doubt as to whether he could actually have had access to all three of Haydn's recent sets of string quartets: op.9 had been published in 1769–70 and op.17 in 1772, but op.20, composed in 1772, was not yet in print (it appeared only in 1774, an unauthorized edition issued in Paris), and there is little likelihood that manuscript copies would have been in circulation or available to him. In short, tempting as it is to see the quartets as inspired by contact with the music of Mozart's greatest contemporary, any question of specific influence needs to be carefully and critically considered.[24]

If Mozart was indeed attempting to emulate Haydn, he had yet to acquire the boldness of invention and the command of large-scale structure that are to be seen in the older composer's op.17. Mozart's first quartet, K.168 in F, bears an obvious superficial resemblance to Haydn's work in the same key, op.17 no.2.[25] Its opening movement shows experimentation with unusual phrase lengths (the opening theme is made up 3 + 2 + 4) and has some neatly worked imitative writing in transitional passages and in the development (using the final tag of the opening theme), but its sectional structure seems primitive and tame alongside Haydn's work, with its bold textures and adventurous lines and its subtle use of unifying figuration. If Mozart's movement were a response to Haydn's, it would seem to represent a rejection of it in favour of the more refined and formal manner that he was used to. Further evidence for Haydn's influence has been discovered in the theme of the Andante here, which uses a figure common in contrapuntal music earlier in the century and used by Haydn as a fugue subject in op.20 no.5. Mozart's handling of it is canonic, initially but briefly in four voices, in a movement that for all its chromaticisms has more than a whiff of the academy.

Above all, the finale of K.168 is cited as evidence of indebtedness to Haydn. Like the finales of three of Haydn's op.20 quartets, it is a fugue—not, as in certain finales in Mozart's mature music, a sonata-form movement embodying fugal writing but a fugue pure and simple, in which he slips into a more *galant* manner only in a couple of brief passages. On a spirited, fast-moving subject of a fairly conventional and impersonal kind, the fugue is fully developed, with a regular series of middle entries in related keys, stretto (some of it with the theme inverted) and a unison statement of the subject to end with. Mozart was of course already experienced in writing fugues, of a rather different kind though using essentially the same techniques, in his church music. The decision to write fugues in string quartets seems sure to have been provoked by contact with other examples. In the unlikely event of Mozart's having known Haydn's op.20, the fugues there could have been his model, although one whose taut, economical writing and powerful structure he was not equipped to match, perhaps not even to understand. But Haydn's were by no means the only models available to him, for there was a long tradition of fugal writing in pre-classical chamber music, with examples in the quartets of such Viennese and central European composers as Gassmann, Monn, Ordonez, Richter and Wagenseil, many of which could have been accessible to him.[26]

The second quartet, K.169 in A, partly reverts to the divertimento-like manner of K.136–138 and two of the Milan quartets, particularly in its opening movement but also in the Andante, with its four-square rhythms, and in the finale, a gavotte-like rondo in 2/4 metre. This is the first of several elegant Rococo-style dances in this set, of which the next is the finale of K.170 in C. That quartet, like Haydn's op.17 no.3, begins with a set of variations, in 2/4 metre, of a simple, figurative kind, the manner of each variation set in its first bars (such as a melodic elaboration, or a rhythmic patterning). The slow movement, Un poco adagio, is a simple violin cantilena with even simpler accompaniment. This manner serves too for the Adagio of K.172 in B flat, but here—the 'Porgi Amor' theme again—the music is more deeply felt, with the accompaniment subtly interwoven and some telling touches in both harmony and melodic line. The violin line here, as in these quartets generally, is in itself unadventurous, rarely calling for anything higher than third position and thus more in Mozart's orchestral style than the much freer violin parts in his solo divertimentos or his concerto writing. Perhaps this reflects his composing for a less specific purpose, as opposed to writing for players whose capabilities he knew. K.172 continues with a minuet involving canonic and other imitative writing, confined to the upper three voices, and there is more in the development of the finale, a spirited piece written with a sophisticated grasp of quartet textures.

The most original quartets of the set, however, are the fourth and the sixth, K.171 in E flat and K.173 in D minor. K.171 has an unorthodox first movement, of a type for which there are various precedents in Viennese music, by Haydn (for example Symphony no.

6), Wagenseil and others.[27] It has an Adagio introduction which returns as coda; initially it leads to the dominant, but finally, in recapitulatory style, to the tonic. In between is an Allegro assai in triple metre, an exposition and recapitulation with no development. After a minuet with a trio embodying imitation for the first violin and viola, the C minor Andante, with strings muted (including, exceptionally, the cello's), is a solemn piece, much of it in two-part contrapuntal passages, heard either on the first violin and the cello or the two middle instruments, but blossoming at the ends of the three sections of this sonata-form miniature into four-part writing, still partly contrapuntal in character. The finale, in 3/8, is more in the divertimento style, or even that of a symphony finale with oboes and horns.

The first movement of the final quartet, K.173—the first of Mozart's two quartets in a minor key, both D minor—is marked (in Leopold's hand, like many of the tempo directions in these quartets) 'Allegro ma molto moderato', an exceptional instruction for music of exceptional character. A tone new to Mozart is struck in its austere textures (some contrapuntal, some in bare octaves), the downward slope of its main theme, the syncopated accompaniment in the tuttis, and the passionate repeated-note motif used to destabilize the tonality; at the secondary group, this quickly departs from the dominant, going further afield to E minor, thence to G minor and to uncertain regions around D minor at the end of the exposition. The slow movement, in D major, is another stylized gavotte, slower and more graceful than those Mozart had used in finales. The minuet returns to the passionate D minor tone of the first movement and is conspicuously longer, more developed and more irregular in its metric structure than any other in the set (even the trio departs from the eight-bar norm for its first strain). But it is the finale, another fugue, that has always excited most attention. The fugue subject is one hallowed by long use, essentially a descending chromatic scale, which lends itself readily to ingenious and varied stretto treatment. Entries of the three-bar subject occur at first two bars apart, later with closer overlaps (including one-and-a-half bars, with alternate appearances of the subject inverted), then at half-bar intervals with mixtures, and lastly there is a set of one-bar entries. For his final version Mozart extended his original by 14 bars, much improving the shape of the end of the movement by adding material that made it more than simply a parade of stretto technique. In the handling of strettos, and in the patterns of motivic treatment, the music is much closer to ecclesiastical models than are Haydn's fugues in his op.20, which are altogether more idiomatic to the string quartet. But in spite of a certain self-consciousness (and by this date most fugues, including Haydn's, partake of that), Mozart's movement has a structural balance that makes it an effective finale to a work of an unorthodox cast and one that heralds important developments in his creative personality.

14

A Stable Period at the Salzburg Court

FROM THE AUTUMN of 1773, when Mozart and his father returned home from Vienna, their ambitions in the imperial capital—whatever they may have been—unrealized, the family remained in Salzburg for four years, apart from a few weeks in Munich at the beginning of 1775. Wolfgang resumed his role as a Konzertmeister, playing the violin in the court orchestra (the principal Konzertmeister was Michael Haydn and the elderly Friedrich Seidl was another), Leopold his as a vice-Kapellmeister. Wolfgang's post was officially half-time, and his salary was commensurate with that. With the family at home and undivided, there is of course no correspondence from these years; their day-to-day activities leave few documentary traces, and those chiefly in occasional diary references. There is little to tell us what the Mozarts were doing or thinking over most of this period.

Soon after their arrival back in Salzburg, the Mozart family moved house. Leopold's letters from as far back as the time of the 'grand tour' make it clear that he was dissatisfied with their apartment in the Hagenauer premises in the Getreidegasse, which was becoming increasingly cramped as the children grew up. He had returned to the point more recently at the end of the first visit to Italy.[1] Nannerl was now 22, Wolfgang nearly 18, and presumably the family were still 'sleeping like soldiers'. It is possible that Hagenauer had made more space available since their return in 1766, although there is no sign that any extra room had been built on, as Leopold had suggested. In fact the family had been together in Salzburg during rather less than half of the time that had elapsed since then (just over 39 months of the 82), with no prolonged periods for all of them at home, so perhaps they had not felt the need for a move too pressingly; nor could they have thought that one was opportune if, as they hoped, they might even be leaving Salzburg for good reasonably soon. The return from Vienna, with any residual hopes of a court appointment there abandoned, seems to have provided the moment for Leopold to reconcile himself to remaining in Salzburg, or at least to making the best of an inescapable situation.

So during the autumn of 1773 the family finally left the apartment in which they had lived since Leopold and Maria Anna's marriage. For more than a year, Leopold had been contemplating a move to the building known as the Tanzmeisterhaus, the Dancing Master's House, in the Hannibal-Platz. He apparently discussed the possibility during the previous autumn before he and Wolfgang had left for Milan, for *Lucio Silla*. In a letter sent from Milan on 6 February[2] he told his wife to ask 'Jungfrau Tanzmeister Mitzerl', Anna Maria Raab, from whom he was planning to lease a floor of the house, to be patient until he arrived home. He presumably had to ask for even longer forbearance on her part if he was not prepared to commit himself until the following autumn, after the journey to Vienna.

The house, which had stood at least since the early seventeenth century, had at one time been owned by a dancing-master from France who had married into a Salzburg family and had taught dancing, which included etiquette and courtly manners. Raab had inherited the house in 1767 from her cousin, the dancing-master Franz Carl Gottlieb Speckner. One room was still employed for balls and another had been used by Salzburg University students and their tutors.[3] The Mozarts rented a flat on the first floor, with eight rooms:

The Mozart family house in Hannibal-Platz, 1773–87: lithograph after J. Pezold, *c*1840 (*Museum Carolino Augusteum, Salzburg*)

a large flat for a family of four, with their servants, but it offered them the opportunity of taking in resident pupils (both Leopold and Nannerl did so, though possibly not in their earlier years in the house) and of demonstrating and selling musical instruments on the premises, which Leopold did on a commission basis. Their landlady seems to have become a firm friend, and many letters include greetings to 'Jungfer Mitzerl'. (In one, of December 1774, Mozart refers to his imagining her in her charming negligée—that is, with her hair undressed—talking of her beauty and his undying love: but this was no more than a coarse, boyish piece of irony, for she was then about 65.)

The Hannibal-Platz, now the Makart-Platz, is on the northern and eastern side of the river Salzach, opposite the oldest part of the city, with the cathedral, the principal churches and court buildings and the university, where the family had previously lived. The new accommodation was on the first floor and had a garden in which the family and their friends could play games, such as skittles and airgun shooting at painted targets. The large Tanzmeistersaal, or ballroom, was used by the Mozarts for rehearsals and concerts. It had a musicians' gallery for dances and was also used for family games, including shooting, as well as for showing the instruments in which Leopold traded and displaying published anthologies containing some of Leopold's music, his violin treatise, his son's publications, and other odds and ends.

This more spacious part of the city was favoured by many members of the Salzburg nobility, some of whose houses occupied other parts of the square. Near to the Mozarts' house was Holy Trinity Church, and close by was the town theatre, in a building that had once been the property of the archbishopric. The palace belonging to the Lodron family, one of the most influential in Salzburg, linked with the Thun, Arco and Firmian families, was in the same square: former Lodrons included an archbishop, and the current countess was particularly influential at Colloredo's court. The Mirabell Palace and its gardens were not far away, on the same side of the river. The Mozarts' parish church was now St Sebastian's.

Their new situation must have been congenial. The move represented a step upward, socially speaking. Leopold remained in the house until his death, when it reverted to the Raab family. In 1856, on Mozart's centenary, a sign 'Mozart's Wohnhaus' was put up (modified in 1905 by the addition of 'L.' at the beginning, because Mozart himself had lived there for only a relatively short time). The Internationale Stiftung Mozarteum attempted to buy it in the 1930s, but the purchase was not fully completed before World War II, during which much of the building was destroyed. The Tanzmeistersaal itself (though not its musicians' gallery, which was not later restored) survived; it was acquired by the Stiftung in 1955 and was used from the next year for chamber concerts. In 1981 it became a small museum, and in 1991 the rest of the site (which had been rebuilt after the war as the premises of an insurance company) was finally acquired, to be restored to its original exterior form and developed as a more substantial museum, which opened in 1996, taking over the rare treasures from the nearby Mozarteum, which holds the central library and archive of the Stiftung.

The period of nearly four years, from fall 1773 until September 1777, which Mozart spent almost wholly in Salzburg, was the most stable part of his entire career. His output during these years was not particularly large: apart from two operatic works in 1775, he wrote some dozen pieces each year. Circumstances were not stimulating, and the requirements of his post were quite modest. The Salzburg system still made no regular or specific demands upon him, and there is no distinct pattern to his output at this time. There was a brief energetic spell in the spring and summer of 1774 when he composed four sacred works, with two further masses the next year and another group of three and a substantial litany in 1776. The only instrumental works certainly intended for use in connection with the Salzburg court authorities were a pair of Finalmusik serenades, in 1774 and 1775, and a group of small-scale wind divertimentos. Otherwise he wrote pieces for the Salzburg nobility, no doubt to commission, and in 1773–4 a handful of symphonies—and he now began to take up the concerto, first for violin and then for keyboard. His earliest surviving solo keyboard sonatas belong to the last months of 1774 or the early ones of 1775.

The first works Mozart completed on his return from Vienna were in fact symphonies. He arrived home about 26 September 1773; a week later, on 3 October, one was completed, and another followed two days later. The dates at the head of each work, like all those in the nine-symphony manuscript collection later assembled by Leopold,[4] are heavily overscored but can be deciphered as 'il 3 d'ottobre' for the B flat work K.182/173dA (166c in K³) and 'il 5 ottobre' for the G minor K.183/173dB. It seems that Mozart composed these pieces at a great pace immediately on his return, although the possibility cannot be excluded that they may have been begun in Vienna or even in Salzburg several months before. They are written on the same small oblong Salzburg paper that he had used since his return from Italy, but so too were the Viennese string quartets and the symphonies composed earlier in the year, so that tells us little. If they and the ensuing symphonies were given at Salzburg court concerts, they would have been played by an orchestra of probably 21 violins and violas, one cello, three violones, two oboists who doubled flute

as needed, two bassoons and two horns, with two trumpets and timpani as needed. That is the official complement of the musicians in
the 1773 court calendar (with the number of violinists augmented by
the ten ceremonial trumpeters who doubled as string players): additional players were always available as required from the cathedral and
elsewhere if the music so demanded.[5]

The B flat work shows Mozart seemingly untouched by any Viennese musical experiences. With its brisk dialogues of *forte* and *piano*,
its elegant use of conventional figuration and the vivacious Scotch
snaps (or Lombardic rhythms) of its secondary material, the first
movement breathes the atmosphere of *opera buffa*, though it is flawed
by its interludial development, which after a lively contrapuntal start
resorts to sequences and banal gestures. For the Andantino grazioso,
a miniature rondo that can also be construed as sonata form, Mozart
calls for flutes—unusual in E flat, but clearly the inspiration of the
principal theme, in which they charmingly double the muted violins
in the octave, later conversing with them. The world of *opera buffa*
returns for the last movement, the last and one of the most entertaining of Mozart's 3/8 finales.

The G minor symphony—sometimes called the 'Little G minor'
to distinguish it from the famous work of 1788, K.550—is Mozart's
first symphony in a minor key (unless the partly programmatic, or
illustrative, D minor overture to *Betulia liberata* be reckoned a symphony). It may also be claimed as his first 'great' work, his earliest, it
seems to twentieth-century listeners, to enter the realms of serious
human feeling. Biographers and critics of Mozart's music have always
regarded it as a landmark in his development, not only as composer
but also as man. Why should he have elected to compose a symphony
in the minor mode, still quite rare for symphonies, which were
regarded as primarily grand and festive compositions, and in so
impassioned a tone? Einstein writes of Mozart's 'personal suffering'
(as opposed to the depiction of suffering in the minor-key Passion
symphonies of the time).[6] Wyzewa and Saint-Foix discuss his 'passion
romantique' (which they had earlier noted apropos *Lucio Silla*) and

link the symphony with the *Sturm and Drang* movement of the mid-1770s in German literature.[7] This is also much discussed by Landon,[8] in particular with reference to the 'romantic crisis' in Austrian music at the time and the minor-key symphonies of the late 1760s and early 1770s that Mozart might have encountered in Vienna, among them several of Haydn's (especially nos. 26, 39 in G minor, which like Mozart's calls for four horns, 49 and perhaps 52) and one of Vanhal's (also in G minor). By contrast, Larsen saw no particular personal expression in the work or any deeper psychological significance to its content, but rather that Mozart felt it was appropriate to 'try his hand' at a minor-key symphony (the controversial nature of that view is underlined by the footnoted comments of Larsen's editors).[9] Whoever is right, we have to be on guard against any facile assumption that Mozart and his contemporaries brought the same emotional associations to such music as we do today.

Passionate minor-key music was not something new to Mozart in the autumn of 1773; there are plenty of examples of it in his operas and his sacred works. What is more unusual is the application to instrumental music, and particularly to the symphony, of techniques and styles more usually reserved for operatic heroines *in extremis*, although instances in the instrumental music of other composers are likely, as usual, to have spurred him to emulation. The quality and the emotional force of the music of the G minor symphony speak for themselves, but no differently in kind, though certainly in degree, from the music at the climax of *Lucio Silla*. Mozart's symphony has features in common with other works of the time in the same key, notably the Vanhal symphony, a quartet by Gassmann,[10] the G minor symphony (op.6 no.6, published in 1770) of J.C. Bach and Haydn's no. 39. He may have heard these works, or have seen the scores, but to a considerable extent the ideas are the common coin of impassioned expression in the 1770s—syncopated repeated notes, snapped rhythms, tremolandos, large leaps, urgently repeated phrases and forceful orchestral unison passages.

The symphony begins with a *forte* unison statement, with agitated syncopations in the upper strings and a dramatic falling diminished seventh, followed by leaping arpeggio figures, enhanced by the clanging chords of four horns (two are keyed in B flat and two in G, to maximize the available notes and enrich the textures). This sort of opening is worlds away from the formal, courtly beginnings of most of his symphonies to date. When the music cools, at the end of the primary group, it immediately takes fire again with the secondary material, where the bass instruments imitate the violin figure. Though there is a more *opera buffa*-like theme in B flat major to come, even this, repeated *forte*, acquires weight and tension; and when, in the recapitulation, it recurs in the minor, there is little of the *buffa* about it. This of course is a consequence of normal sonata-form structure in a minor-key movement: the presentation in the minor of a theme first heard in the major is bound to lend the music a pessimistic slant. Exceptionally, Mozart specified repeats of both halves of the movement, and he supplied an extra coda with a dramatic final restatement of the opening theme, just as he had in several other symphonies of 1773.

The Andante too, in E flat, is different in manner from most of Mozart's slow movements of the time. Its principal idea is not a melody with accompaniment but a three-note figure, which is echoed on the bassoons (their first use as independent instruments in a Mozart symphony) and, twisted into various patterns, dominates the movement; the secondary idea, a warm-textured four-bar tutti, is the only relief. This figure, with its middle note often a dissonant appoggiatura, winds through the brief development, and the patterns it takes there recur within the recapitulation. Once again Mozart expands the linking material between subject groups to give the final part of the movement a stronger focus by reinforcing the sense of tonal homecoming when the secondary material is reached. The minuet is back in G minor, with austere unisons and pleading chromaticisms, and the notion of an idealized dance is far away. The trio shifts to G major and to the wind sonorities of the Salzburg divertimento—two each of oboes, bassoons and horns, an arrangement that

Mozart was to use several times in the ensuing years—but the bassoons, after their prominence in the Andante and the trio, soon revert to their role of optional doubling of the bass line. For the finale the stormy manner of the first movement returns, with an urgent, *piano* unison opening and agitated syncopations in the tutti that follows. The lyricism of the secondary material, its suave tone reinforced by Mozart's carefully selective octave doubling of the violins with the violas, is quickly overtaken by a further vigorous tutti. The principal ideas are not used in the development, for which Mozart takes a figure in the last bar of the exposition as the starting-point. Again, the recapitulation's unbending allegiance to G minor contributes to the severity, and so does the alarmingly abrupt coda. As in the first movement, each half is directed to be repeated.

MOZART'S SOLITARY CHAMBER WORK of these Salzburg years was a string quintet, K.174. As a genre, the string quintet, for two violins, two violas and a lower instrument, was not as firmly established as the quartet, but there did exist a distinct Austrian tradition of quintet composition, particularly among monastic composers.[11] Mozart may have come across string quintets in the course of his travels, but almost certainly the works that provoked him into trying the genre himself were two by Michael Haydn, both from 1773, one written in February and the other in December.[12] These, in common with examples by other composers, were entitled 'Notturno', and the lowest part is named 'Basso', for which an instrument sounding an octave below written pitch is needed, a violone or a double-bass. That too is the case with other composers' works, and indeed with some of Michael Haydn's own later quintets, two of which are seven-movement divertimentos. Mozart also used the word 'Basso', but it is clear from the compass of the part and its occasional athleticism that in K.174 the cello is the intended instrument. It is often suggested that Mozart began the work early in 1773, under the impact of Michael Haydn's first quintet, then returned to it in December, to replace the trio of the minuet and rewrite the finale, after he had heard Haydn's second quintet. But there is no particular evidence to support that: the entire work was written on the same batch of paper, and there are already enough attested compositions to fill the period between his return from Italy and his journey to Vienna. There is no convincing reason to question the applicability of the date on the autograph, December 1773, to the work as a whole.

Like both the Haydn works, and Mozart's own quartets of the autumn months, the quintet K.174 is in the regular four-movement form expected in a chamber work. Writing for five voices poses special problems to a composer whose normal harmonic language is four-part (or even three-part): what is to be done with the extra instrument? Mozart's answers are ingenious. One, following Michael Haydn, is to use the first viola as a kind of tenor counterpart to the soprano first violin. Mozart does this in inspired fashion in the later quintets, but even here, on the opening page of K.174, the first viola takes up the theme given out by the first violin and re-presents it in altered register and softened colours. Then there are such devices as treating the violins and the violas as pairs above a neutral bass, or dividing the ensemble into two harmonically self-sufficient groups, one high in pitch and one low. Sometimes Mozart simply uses the fifth instrument to enrich the texture, frequently with one of his favoured octave doublings. The invention in the opening movement of K.174 is often subtle. The curious metric structure at the beginning, for example, gives rise to a theme eleven bars long, and there is a moment of mystery in the secondary material as the two lowest instruments, *piano*, sound a harmonically disorientating chromatic phrase. The movement also has something of the playful, extravert character and careless abundance of Mozart's more casual works, yet the development, consisting of an energetic instrumental dialogue on a cadential idea—no more than a descending scale in triplets—is tightly argued among the five voices.

The Adagio is remarkably original. Two bars of bare octaves at the beginning—pianissimo and muted—establish, like a Baroque ground bass, a solemn, hieratic atmosphere that leaves its mark, even though the octave theme does not persist through the elaborate and expressive dialogue that ensues for the first violin and first viola. The minuet, with its hint of a drone and its four-square metric pattern, represents a typical courtly presentation of a peasant idiom, analogous perhaps to Marie Antoinette's pseudo-rural frolics. The trio abandoned by Mozart continued in unimaginative four-bar phrases. His new version largely preserves four-bar structure but breaks it up with echo effects between two string trios, the second violin and viola echoing, literally, a phrase (or the end of one) just played by first violin and viola—three bars echoed by one, four by the entire four, two by two, with a variant after the double bar. The effect is elegantly witty. Mozart wrote a substantial finale of 255 bars, beginning with a *moto perpetuo* theme. Then he replaced it with another, retaining however his original main theme (with a significant adjustment) but changing its status by making it secondary to a new opening idea. A partly contrapuntal dialogue on this theme forms the development section in the original version but only a half of it in the much expanded revision. Mozart's subtler working of the secondary material is also fascinating, in particular his elimination of three distinct thematic ideas in the closing section, which greatly tightens the structure and divests the movement of its former empty bravura writing.

Mozart's first true keyboard concerto, as opposed to concertos that are sonatas (by other composers) with added ritornellos, dates from immediately after the visit to Vienna. The occasion that called forth this work, K.175 in D, is unknown, but Mozart's use here of trumpets and drums as well as the usual oboes, horns and strings implies that it was intended for some special purpose, perhaps a concert during the Lent season. The work remained a favourite: Mozart took it with him to Munich in 1774 and to Mannheim and Paris in 1777–8, and played it even in his Vienna years, writing in 1782 that it was particularly liked there.[13] It was among the few of his piano concertos to be published in his lifetime. That does not necessarily mean that he ranked it above others but rather that it was easy enough for amateurs to play, and therefore saleable, and that he had no reason to retain it for his exclusive use. The original text of the concerto does not survive. The only authentic source is a Salzburg copy made after the composition of K.382, the new finale, in 1782. Mozart made some minor revisions to the oboe and first horn parts in 1778.[14]

A great deal has been written about the formal schemes of Mozart's piano concerto first movements.[15] Later they vary a good deal, within certain close limits, but they are always most readily understood in terms of their historical origin, which lies in the aria form, considered earlier in the context of Mozart's operas and other vocal works. This form was modified, as indeed was the aria itself, by the sonata principle that underlies virtually all the music of the classical era, and enhanced by the astute referential use of orchestral tutti material. In this particular concerto the opening ritornello presents two main thematic ideas, in the same key. These are heard again, from the soloist, on his entry, but between them the music moves to the dominant key for the presentation of the second idea (which is also extended and supplemented, presaging Mozart's later procedures). Here the piano is supported by strings on its first entry: in most of the early concerto arrangements (all but the last two), and in all Mozart's later piano concertos, the piano's opening music is presented without orchestra, allowing the soloist a modicum of freedom. After the central section—quite short, and never moving far from the home key—the two main ideas are recapitulated, both in the tonic, in standard sonata-form procedure. The material itself is simple and conventional, with no strong thematic character, although the question-and-answer formula of the main secondary theme is very typical. There is a lot of busy Alberti bass in the left hand and decorative passage-work in the right.

The slow movement, a heartfelt piece where the usual 'Andante' is significantly qualified by 'ma un poco adagio', is characterized by its uneven phrase patterns, with a predominance of three-bar phrases. The movement is cast in the same general formal scheme as the first. But Mozart's method of treating the solo line already presages his later techniques—the piano, taking up music already heard from the orchestra, sometimes adds expressive flourishes and sometimes interrupts its rhythmic patterns by elaborated repetition or other insertion, so adding a new rhetorical element. At the end of the cadenza the piano cadence leads not to the expected tutti entry but, poetically, to a phrase (from the opening tutti) for the violins in octaves alone before the full entry. The finale, which Mozart later dropped in favour of a movement that modern taste unanimously finds inferior, is another ritornello-style movement with a witty pseudo-contrapuntal undertone to the principal theme. More remarkable here, perhaps, are the portents of Mozart's later concerto style with its dialogues and interchanges between solo and orchestra: while the orchestra insists on the opening idea of the movement, the piano is intent on brilliant passage-work, and the piano then takes up the harmonic scheme of the secondary theme and adds a bravura gloss to it.

Two more concertos followed in the spring of 1774; again, we know nothing of what provoked them. First, dated 31 May, is the Concertone K.190 (renumbered 166b for K^3, when the scratched-out date on the autograph was misread to 1773, then restored as far as 186E in K^6). 'Concertone'—Mozart wrote the word himself on the autograph, and he and his father always used it to refer to the work—simply means 'large concerto'; whether it relates to the length of K.190 or its multiple soloists is uncertain, but the latter seems more likely. The term 'sinfonia concertante', used for such a work in Italy (or 'symphonie concertante' in France), seems not to have been a part of the Mozarts' musical vocabulary at this date. The word 'concertone' appears in letters of Leopold Mozart's in 1777 and 1778, referring to works commissioned by the Salzburg archbishop from Mysliveček.[16] Clearly Mozart thought well of the work: in 1777–8 he took it on his journey to Mannheim and Paris, the two cities where the sinfonia concertante genre was particularly popular, although he never actually played it other than on the piano to friends. Johann Baptist Wendling, the Mannheim flautist, adjudged it well suited to current Paris fashions; Baron Bagge, visiting Mannheim from Paris, was 'quite beside himself' over it.[17]

Although usually listed as for two solo violins, K.190 also has solo roles for oboe and cello. Its relaxed and leisurely style is closely akin to that of the sinfonie concertanti that J.C. Bach was composing in London, but which Mozart is unlikely to have known. The format is in some degree dictated by the necessity of providing solo music for several players, as opposed to the single soloist of the concerto proper. But even the opening tutti, with its martial rhythms, broad lines and slow harmonic tempo, proclaims its expansiveness and its ceremonial character. The first solo music shows Mozart beguiled, perhaps distracted, by the colourful possibilities of his musical palette: duetting violins in canon, followed by violas in thirds and sixths, then a sustaining oboe against a dialogue with modest thematic content between solo violins, orchestral violins and violas; later there is solo music for the leading cellist. It is almost a concerto for orchestra. This manner prevails for the whole movement. Similar decorative writing, warmly and gracefully executed, marks the Andantino, which departs from the norm by using new, lyrical material for the initial solo entries (though the departure has no effect on the movement's broad structure). Mozart's cadenza, for all four soloists, neatly draws the strands together. The finale is an extended minuet, akin to the kind used in Italian symphony finales and described by Mozart to his sister[18] (J.C. Bach used this type in some of his sinfonia concertante-type works). In substance it is an orchestral minuet with a trio section, thematically unrelated, for the soloists, after which there is the usual *da capo*, and in that respect it is similar to the type of minuet used in the concerto sections of Mozart's Finalmusik serenades. There are festive trumpets in the score, so perhaps the work was intended for some other occasion of the kind for which the serenades were composed. But its particular and endearing style is unique in Mozart's output.

It has long been supposed that Mozart's single surviving bassoon concerto, K.191/186e, was composed for the amateur bassoonist Thaddäus Freiherr von Dürnitz of Munich, to whom he dedicated a piano sonata in 1775, but the work was completed on 4 June 1774 (five days after the Concertone), and as far as we know Mozart did not meet Dürnitz before the end of the year. Whether he wrote other bassoon concertos for Dürnitz, or anyone else, remains uncertain. Four more have at various times been claimed for him, two in B flat and one each in F and C, but all that survives is an incipit for one in F, K.196d, in a manuscript catalogue drawn up by the publisher Breitkopf, and that looks so uncharacteristic, and so ill-written for the bassoon, as to test the credulity. Another concerto sometimes ascribed to Mozart clearly has nothing to do with him and has tentatively been attributed to Devienne.[19]

Mozart's concerto, then, is likely to have been written for one of the Salzburg bassoonists, of whom we know nothing beyond their names, Melchior Sandmayr and Johann Heinrich Schulz. Composing a concerto for the bassoon poses special problems because of the instrument's compass and its reticent voice in an orchestral context, and Mozart had few if any models. Vivaldi of course composed bassoon concertos, as did some of his contemporaries, but even had Mozart known them the relationship between soloist and orchestra in a Baroque concerto would have had no significance for him. Mozart's solutions are ingenious. First, he elected to write in B flat, not only a good key for the bassoon of his time but also one that enabled him to use high-pitched horns, which give the orchestral music a particular colour and can avoid the register chiefly inhabited by the bassoon. He then devised a series of themes distinct from those in others of his works: a wide-spanning opening melody and a secondary theme with pronounced staccatos. The bassoon's entry with a melody using wide leaps, of a kind both easy and effective on the instrument, immediately stamps a particular character on the music. The staccato secondary theme, falling in an inappropriate register when heard (as it first is) in F major, remains the property of the violins, but it acquires a bassoon countermelody, and the material is exchanged in the recapitulation. Effective passage-work using rapid repeated notes, scales and leaps shows Mozart's ready grasp of the instrument's special capacities.

The slow movement, marked (uniquely) Andante ma adagio and with muted strings, touches on an aspect of the bassoon relatively little used in the eighteenth century—its expansive, potentially pathetic lyrical vein. Mozart once again uses the 'Porgi Amor' figure, as in the K.134 symphony and the K.80 and K.172 string quartets, and here he approaches more closely what was to be its ultimate expressive context. The line is indeed operatic, using sighing appoggiaturas and large leaps of the kind that suit singers as much as bassoonists. The finale is a rondo, marked 'Tempo di Menuetto' (as in the Concertone, though with the qualification 'Vivace'). It is something of a frolic: an orchestral statement of a broad, four-square minuet theme is followed by three episodes (the central one an impish G minor bassoon solo) and, finally, by a full restatement of the theme, led off by the bassoon, which then breaks away to cavort around the orchestra. A tonic recapitulation of material from the first episode rectifies the tonal balance. This unpretentious work embodies a degree of mastery scarcely less remarkable than that of the larger and more obviously original works of these years.

Of those, the finest is certainly the Symphony in A K.201/186a, no. 29, dated 6 April 1774, a work on the same plane of mastery as the G minor and like that symphony long since granted a firm place in the standard repertory. No less personal in tone, and arguably more so in that its expression of passion is less tied to the conventional language of the time, K.201 is intimate and refined in expression and closer to chamber music in its techniques. Its opening bars, unlike any other symphony of Mozart's, or anyone else's, quietly state a simple idea, scarcely a 'theme'—a dipping octave and an appoggiatura figure, in a series of rising sequences (see the example following). But repeated, *forte*, in octaves, and with imitations, it acquires an unexpected drama and intensity. The secondary themes include a lyrical one, with a proliferation of other ideas following from it, but the

development does not allude to material already heard, no doubt because the principal theme is self-developing. As in the G minor work, a forceful coda based on the opening idea follows the orthodox recapitulation, and one can now see Mozart's earlier ventures with reversed recapitulations as directed towards this kind of dramatic and powerful climax.

The Andante, in D, with muted violins, consists for the most part of a flowing violin melody, sometimes with a gloss added by the firsts when the seconds take over, sometimes with the line shared in dialogue. The type is familiar but the depth of feeling is new. Again ideas are abundant, and again the development is independent of them. Mozart extends the principal theme in the recapitulation, carrying it to G major to establish the balance of tonalities, heightening the intensity with sharp, *forte* exclamations between *piano* phrases. As in the first movement, there is a coda with a rhetorical restatement of the opening theme, which Mozart strengthens by having the violins remove their mutes. The minuet is marked by its predominant dotted rhythms, with punctuation provided by fanfare-like echoes on the oboes and horns; this sets off a lyrical trio with telling chromatic touches, which Mozart carefully indicates are to be stressed. The finale, almost manically spirited, draws on the manner of the old hunting-style finales in 6/8, but now urgent and vigorous rather than

simply ebullient, because of the nature of the ideas, the astute management of harmonic pace that steers the music decisively towards its
cadence points, and its sturdy and well-directed development (this
time based on the opening idea). The upward-rushing, unaccompa-
nied violin scales that mark out each formal juncture are a remarkable and arresting feature. Yet again there is a coda with a dramatic
reminder of the opening of the movement.

In another month, by 5 May, Mozart had written his next symphony. As with the G minor symphony, an impassioned, highly original work lies adjacent to a more conventional one. Symphony no. 30
in D K.202/186b is a festive piece in nature, close to the serenade tradition (it calls for trumpets as well as oboes and horns). But the material of its opening movement, some of it motivic, is thoroughly
worked out and tries some new effects: there is imitation between
violins and basses in some of the tuttis, and in another the violins
declaim a line at the top of a texture while the rest of the orchestra
is in imitation on a trill figure. The 'development' again is on new
material, persistently argued, and in the coda it is this rather than the
opening material (whose reappearance would have been an inaptly
dramatic gesture) that returns. After a graceful Andantino for strings,
more sophisticated than earlier movements of this type in its treatment of the lower voices, which is not often contrapuntal but always
interesting, the minuet is close to the serenade manner. So too is the
finale with its martial rhythms, its contrasts of the outspoken with the
hushed and the slightly facile sequences of its secondary theme. But
there is wit here that Mozart would not have ventured in the more
casual music of the development, with its dialogues on a simple
dotted-rhythm figure. Formally, the pattern is the conservative one
with two repeats and a coda quoting the opening. That opening has
a marked resemblance to the opening of the first movement—a
descending arpeggio in dotted rhythm—but there is little reason to
think this was intentional: no other Mozart symphony shows anything of the sort, and the ideas themselves are common coin of the
period.

The last symphony Mozart was to compose until 1778, when he was in Paris, is probably no. 28 in C K.200/189*k*. The autograph bears a date, in Mozart's hand or his father's, but so thoroughly has it been obliterated that it is impossible to be certain whether the day, in November, is 12 or 17, or (more crucially) that the year is 1774—just possibly it is 1773. Nor is there paper evidence to help (it is on a paper-type Mozart used for several years), still less any circumstantial information. The marshy grounds of stylistic argument would probably support the later date: the symphony has a certain compactness and ease of manner that suggests an extra hint of maturity. Like that of K.202, its first movement is in triple metre. It is formally very clear-cut, with a development built almost exclusively on the principal idea, a motif incorporating a trill, which once more recurs in the coda. But this time the idea returns before the repeat mark (both halves of the movement are repeated, as they are also in the slow movement and the finale), so that with a nicely epigrammatic air it leads first back to the development and then on to the movement's conclusion. The Andante, with violins muted, is another appealing example of a sonata-form movement made up of continuous cantilena. The minuet derives a particular charm from its juxtaposition of the sturdy and the lyrical, which are linked (twice, in different ways) by a phrase for the horns. Anyone bent on seeking connections between movements might point to the trill figure that forms the principal idea of the finale, a Presto in a helter-skelter manner. It scarcely pauses for breath, not even in the development, which is wittily elided into a recapitulation that Mozart allows to steal in unheralded. Yet again the coda provides a final, emphatic reappearance of the music that began the movement.

Whether or not these symphonies were used at court or in the cathedral in Salzburg we do not know, but there must have been some continuing demand for new works during 1774. We saw in Chapter 11 that Mozart re-used music from the *Ascanio in Alba* overture as a symphony, and at some point in 1774 (or so the evidence of writing and paper suggests) he did the same with the overture to *Il sogno di Scipione*, which, two years after the sole performance, was unlikely to be remembered by the audience. The overture was originally in two movements, a light, Italianate Allegro moderato which led directly into a triple-metre slow movement, prettily scored with oboes and flutes. That movement had led straight into a recitative; now Mozart supplied a Presto finale (K.163) in sonata form, to make up a three-movement symphony (K.161/141*a*)—a spirited and witty piece that makes a virtue out of the necessity of beginning on a dissonance (dictated by the harmonic context at the end of the slow movement), which he ingeniously uses in a different way in the movement's secondary material.

Standing slightly apart from this sequence of symphonies is Mozart's contribution to the Salzburg summer festivities. His Serenade in D K.203/189*b* is dated August 1774 and, like the other multi-movement serenades composed at that time of year, served as university Finalmusik. There is no Salzburg documentation to prove that the 1774 Finalmusik was composed by Mozart, and it was long supposed that this particular work had been written for the archbishop's nameday (it is still sometimes called the 'Colloredo Serenade'). It is anyway unlikely that Mozart would have written a work for performance on 30 September as early as August. But the true origins of the work are established by a reference in a letter Leopold wrote four years later, when he refers to a performance of Wolfgang's Finalmusik-symphony with oboe solos in the Andante and Trio: K.203 is the only Finalmusik to answer that description.

With eight movements and a march, this is the longest of the Finalmusiken. It follows the usual pattern, with what is in effect a three-movement violin concerto within a symphony (this time a five-movement one, with two minuets)—Mozart later detached the first movement and the last three for use as a symphony. It begins with Mozart's first slow introduction, a seven-bar Andante maestoso, which presumably had some particular function, if only to quieten the festive audience. Compared with symphonies of the same period, serenades tend to be lighter and more direct in manner, to eschew counterpoint and other features that call for close listening, and to move at a rather slow harmonic tempo. The general approach is less refined. Mozart's handling of sonata-form recapitulations is symptomatic: while in his symphonies and chamber works he almost always adjusts the tonal balance after the restatement of the principal theme with a shift towards the subdominant, to adjust the listener's tonal expectation for the tonic return of the secondary material, in this serenade (and the same is true in K.185, the 1773 Finalmusik) the recapitulations of both the first movement and the finale display no such subtlety. This represents a clear distinction in Mozart's thinking between what will serve the casual listener and what will satisfy the attentive one. As in K.185, the 'violin concerto', which here forms the second, third and fourth movements, is in a foreign key, this time B flat. Perhaps this implies that the work was not intended to be performed without at least short breaks. It takes the form Andante–Menuetto–Allegro. Musically it has few complexities, but the Andante gives the soloist ample time to draw a graceful line, with expressive appoggiaturas and some high-lying cantilena, while the cheerful Allegro allows scope for effective bravura writing. Both are in sonata-ritornello forms. In the orchestral movements, Mozart as usual provides variety of colour: the minuets have solos for flute and bassoon in one trio and for oboe in the other. Between the minuets lies the heart of the work, the soft-toned, sensuous Andante (not so marked, in fact), with gentle accompanying textures for muted strings and warmly graceful lines that typify his serenade manner. Yet here too Mozart took less trouble than usual over the actual composition, again leaving recapitulated material unaltered. This is the Andante with oboe solos referred to in Leopold's 1778 letter. The concerto movements may well be the 'violin concerto' that Mozart was reported as playing in August 1774 at a ceremonial High Mass at Maria Plain, a well-known pilgrimage church in a village just outside Salzburg (he also played an 'organ concerto', probably one of the church sonatas).[20]

There is however one aspect of composition to which Mozart

seems to have given special attention. The march, K.237/189*c*, designed to introduce the serenade, proclaims a pair of descending arpeggios, in D and in A:

A similar figure provides the bass of the opening of the slow introduction:

and appears again in the Allegro of the concerto section:

It recurs in the Andante, given extra prominence by the keying of one horn in G and the other in D, but now to the same melodic line as in the slow introduction. The use of material from one movement as slow introduction to another—or the use of material from a slow introduction within another movement—is surely without precedent. It would be misguided to read too much into it, as an artistic or unifying device, but clearly Mozart was, lightheartedly, setting up some sort of beacon.

Among the other instrumental works from about this time are a set of sixteen minuets (K.176), written in December 1773, and two sonatas for keyboard duet. Mozart and his sister had played duets as children (see Chapter 4) and may well have continued to do so domestically. Possibly the composition of these two duets, K.381/123a and K.358/186c, is evidence of that, unless they were intended for teaching. The autographs are on paper of a type that Mozart seems first to have used for the K.167 mass, in the late spring of 1773, but the handwriting is believed to indicate a date about a year earlier for K.381 and the turn of 1773–4 for K.358.[21] These pieces, familiar to all piano duettists, are certainly a good deal easier than Mozart and his sister needed. They draw on the symphonic style in their first movements, with their gestures, lyrical secondary themes, and implied Mannheim crescendos and scrubbing strings, but the interplay between Primo and Secondo (especially the dialogues and the alternating solos) is of a kind unique to the piano duet and in some sense actually inaugurated by these works, which are very much *sui generis*. The heavy bass textures, inevitable with the small keyboard for which Mozart was writing, suffer on a modern instrument but sound clear and gently percussive on a period one. The two duets were published together in Vienna as Mozart's op.3 in 1783.

The only other keyboard work from this time is a set of variations on a theme by Johann Christian Fischer, an oboist and composer whom the Mozarts had met in the Netherlands; he had held posts in Dresden, Potsdam and London, and was married for a time to Gainsborough's daughter. The theme Mozart chose, from the rondo of one of his oboe concertos, was enormously popular and often used for variations. Mozart's set of twelve grow steadily in brilliance as they progress, while remaining wedded to the concept of the figurative variation: each one exploits some particular pattern or technique. There is no *minore* variation, nor any that departs metrically from the

Fischer theme, but the penultimate one is an elaborate Adagio with the repeats written out with further elaboration. The set was published in Paris in 1778.

INSTRUMENTAL MUSIC WAS not Mozart's main occupation during the spring and summer of 1774. Although, as we have seen, the composition of new music was not obligatory for him in his employment as a composer to the archbishop's Kapelle, he either wanted to compose sacred music or was persuaded to do so. Four substantial works and probably some shorter ones date from this time.

To judge from its scale, his setting of the Litany of Loreto, completed in May, seems likely to have been intended for the cathedral rather than for a celebration in Schloss Mirabell, as K.109 may have been. The litany, K.195/186*d*, is set for the full forces available at Salzburg—four-part strings, oboes and horns, with the usual trombones. The gentle supplicatory tone is still there, for example in the slow introduction to the Kyrie, but the main part of that movement is a substantial sonata-form chorus with solo sections in a free semi-contrapuntal style. That is followed by a 'Sancta Maria' setting, an expressive Andante initially for soprano, with some fioritura in the solo part, with the other soloists intervening and the chorus joining in the 'ora pro nobis' responses. After a brief but sombre 'Salus infirmorum', with some striking and adventurous choral writing, the 'Regina angelorum' is a lively and ingeniously constructed tenor aria, in a sonata-ritornello pattern with the choral responses 'ora pro nobis' built into the tuttis. The work ends with an eloquent 'Agnus Dei' setting for soprano, with wide leaps and chromaticisms, and choral involvement, including a highly original ending with a chromatic descent ('miserere nobis') and a *decrescendo* to silence.

Two mass settings come from the summer of 1774: K.192/186*f* in F, dated 24 June, and K.194/186*h* in D, of 8 August. These belong firmly in the 'missa brevis' tradition, like the 1768–9 settings K.49 and

65. In a famous letter of 1776 to Padre Martini, Mozart—or perhaps Leopold, for the letter is in his hand although signed by Wolfgang—was to write:[22]

> Our church music is very different from that of Italy, since a Mass with everything—the Kyrie, Gloria, Credo, the epistle sonata, the offertory or motet, Sanctus and Agnus Dei, even the most solemn when said by the Prince himself, must not last more than three-quarters of an hour. So you see that special study is required for this kind of composition.

Mozart's letter is not an attack upon archbishop Colloredo or his reformist tendencies, nor a criticism, as it has sometimes been represented. Nothing he writes indicates that the policy he describes is new, and indeed K.65, written in Schrattenbach's time, typifies the short mass setting as favoured in Salzburg. Nor does he say that Colloredo banned fugal treatment, as Jahn and others have suggested, although of course the extended fugal sections in 'Cum Sancto Spiritu' and 'Et vitam venturi', which traditionally ended the Gloria and Credo respectively in the Austrian mass, had to be abandoned as time did not permit.

The two 1774 settings are prime examples of the style of which Mozart is speaking. They fall just short of the perfunctory: each is about twenty minutes long, and there is rarely time to dwell on the text in a way that would allow the music to engage with it more than superficially. Both settings are, however, attractive and ingenious on their own level, and the F major K.192, set with a pair of trumpets as well as the three-part Salzburg strings (no independent violas) and trombones doubling the men's voices, has particularly noteworthy features. The Kyrie, after a *galant* orchestral ritornello, uses short, closely imitative choral treatment, with brief solos, in what is in effect a miniature sonata-form movement (the 'Christe' forms the development). In the Gloria, where so many words need to be accommodated and appropriately set, Mozart follows no particular formal framework although he observes the rule of recapitulating in the home key music stated first in another; and there is a fugal exposition, but no more than that, to 'Cum Sancto Spiritu'. The Credo, however, is of unusual interest. It belongs in an Austrian tradition of 'Credo masses'[23] in which the word 'Credo' is reiterated throughout the section. Here Mozart sets the word in the opening bars, which he would not otherwise have done, for the opening words of the Gloria and Credo are normally intoned in mass settings of this kind, with the sung text beginning at 'Patrem omnipotentem':

This four-note tag is of course one that has become famous from the finale of Mozart's 'Jupiter' Symphony, and we shall find it elsewhere in his music (as we did in the K.16 symphony). In the context of the mass it becomes, as in the models, a powerful assertion of belief. It breaks in, in all four voices, after eight bars, then does so repeatedly from bar 27, in a contrapuntal context:

from the soloists in turn a little later:

and chorally after 'descendit de caelis', heralding the 'Et incarnatus', which is marked off not as it most commonly is by a slower tempo but by the use of the soloists and the minor mode. The four-note phrase returns as if a fugue theme, and again to punctuate the ensuing sections. Lastly, it forms the basis of a fugal exposition on 'Et vitam venturi' and a close stretto for 'Amen':

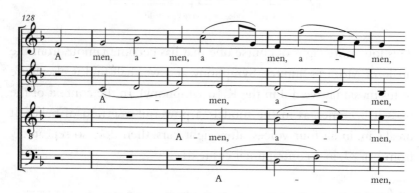

and there is a *piano* and more conclusively harmonized statement of it to end the movement. The origins of the phrase itself have been much explored, both for historical reasons and in order to enlarge our understanding of its significance for Mozart, its relationship to plain-chant and its use as a theoretical model.[24] The Sanctus is imposing, the basses descending grandly by step for nearly an octave. The 'Hosanna' is a fugal exposition, the Benedictus (as often, for four solo voices) gentle and minuet-like. If the Credo hints at the 'Jupiter', the Agnus Dei hints at that of the Requiem with its sombre flowing passages in D minor. Solo voices sing the first line, chorus the chromatically harmonized 'miserere nobis', and the music then turns optimistically to F major and 3/8 for a cheerfully homophonic 'Dona nobis pacem'.

The D major work K.194 is even shorter. Its Kyrie uses essentially the same technique of intermittent, short-phrase imitative writing, though with a lesser role for the strings, and is little more than half the length. The Gloria is a direct homophonic four-part setting with short solo passages; there is no fugal writing, even at the end. The Credo, however, is more extended than that of K.192, a triple-metre Allegro with busy violin parts and homophonic choral writing that allows the long text to be speedily despatched. Nine bars of Andante accommodate the 'Et incarnatus', with a brief soprano solo in B minor, and then the Allegro returns, with a short imitative treatment of 'Et resurrexit' (to be echoed at the 'Amen'). There is again a change of texture for a tenor solo at 'Et in spiritum sanctum'. 'Et vitam venturi' is set to the music of the opening bars, but there is no formal structure to the movement. Both the Sanctus and the 'Hosanna' are built from short points of imitation, and the Benedictus is again for the soloists, with a characteristic sweetness of flavour from its graceful line and its chromatic appoggiaturas. As in K.192, Mozart begins the Agnus Dei sombrely, in the relative minor, with the same alternation of solo and chorus, and this continues through a quite full setting, in a modest-sized sonata-form movement, of 'Dona nobis pacem'.

Two of Mozart's epistle sonatas, K.144/124a and 145/124b, can be dependably dated, on grounds of handwriting, to 1774. Since these are in D and F, there is every reason to think that they were intended for use with the masses in those keys, K.145 with K.192 and K.144 with K.194. The former is a triple-metre sonata-form piece with an urbanely witty ending, the latter a busier, more demonstrative movement in a symphonic manner. Its striking opening clearly precluded full recapitulation, which would be excessively dramatic in so short a work: Mozart accordingly short-circuited the 'double return' and then expanded the repetition of the secondary material.

His other substantial sacred work of June 1774 was a pair of psalm settings for vespers, *Dixit Dominus* and *Magnificat*, the opening and concluding psalms of the vesper service. Presumably music by other composers, or plainchant, was used for the four intervening psalms on the occasion for which these two were written. The music itself, at least in the *Dixit*, is in the same manner as the mass settings of the time—chiefly in a straightforward chordal style for the chorus, against a fabric of busy violins, but with a few passages using a short-breathed imitative technique, particularly in the doxology in the slower final section. There is little solo vocal music. Trumpets and drums provide a festive colouring. The *Magnificat* is musically more interesting and better held together because Mozart uses a phrase of *Magnificat* plain-chant—a simple three-note rising pattern, identical with the first three notes of the Credo theme referred to above. It appears, in one voice or more, and sometimes in all four, in the setting of each passage of text except the one given to solo voices. Again, the metre changes for the doxology setting, but here there is a formal fugue to 'et in saecula saeculorum', complete with a series of strettos that have little of the schoolroom atmosphere that belongs to some of Mozart's earlier examples.

There are a number of shorter sacred works of this period. A solo motet, *Ergo interest* K.143/73a, probably belongs to the end of 1773. As the Köchel numbers indicate, it was first assigned to the end of Mozart's last Milan visit (when he is thought to have written some motets that are lost), then to a rather earlier date. The paper is in fact Italian, but Mozart is known to have continued using it in Salzburg, and the handwriting indicates a later date. The motet takes the form of a recitative and an expressive aria ('Quaere superna'), high in tessitura and including some fioritura writing, with a simple string accompaniment. Of a setting for two sopranos, *Sub tuum praesidium* K.198/158b/C3.08, no verifiable source survives; although the work finds a place in the NMA, its general style is very uncharacteristic and its authenticity must be at best suspect. Two choral settings of the *Tantum ergo* survive, in B flat K.142/186*d*/C3.04 and in D K.197/Anh.186*e*/C3.05, in sources that have some claim to authenticity. There is evidence that the B flat work is by the Bohemian composer Jan Zach. The setting in D, a short, jubilant piece for chorus with trumpets and drums (the work is probably occasioned by Ascension Day), could well be Mozart's own, although it must be risky to give full credence to the authenticity of any work that is always coupled in its sources with another known to be doubtful.

15

Operas, Sonatas, Serenades, Concertos

A T SOME POINT during the spring or summer of 1774, Mozart received an invitation to compose an opera for Munich the following season: the second new opera for the carnival season at the end of the year, traditionally an *opera buffa*. The principal carnival opera, an *opera seria*, was to be a fresh setting of *Orfeo ed Euridice*, by Antonio Tozzi (Gluck's setting had aroused little interest in Munich when given there in revised form two years before). Mozart's work would be given not in the recently built Residenztheater (or Cuvilliéstheater, as it is now known, after its original architect), which was reserved for serious opera and ballet, but in the old court theatre, the Opernhaus am Salvatorplatz, converted long before from a granary and used for entertainments for a wider, middle-class audience. His commission will have come from the intendant of the Munich theatres, Count Joseph Anton von Seeau. Possibly friends at court, including Count Waldburg-Zeil, now Bishop of Chiemsee, formerly the Dean at Salzburg and one of Colloredo's rivals for the archbishopric, could have influenced the choice. The approval of the Elector, Maximilian III Joseph, would also have been needed. His interest in the young Mozart will have helped secure the necessary leave of absence from Salzburg.

The subject of the new opera was to be *La finta giardiniera* ('The feigned garden-girl'), using a libretto set for the Teatro delle Dame in Rome by Pasquale Anfossi during the previous year's carnival season. The librettist is unknown: the name of Giuseppe Petrosellini, probably author of the original *Il barbiere di Siviglia*, has been suggested. The longstanding notion that the text was by Ranieri de' Calzabigi, modified by Marco Coltellini (reviser of *La finta semplice*), is mistaken, no doubt the result of confusion between this opera and Tozzi's, for which those writers were indeed responsible. Some passing points of similarity have been taken to imply that Mozart knew Anfossi's setting, but these are *opera buffa* clichés, and it would be surprising if he ever had sight of the score.[1]

An *opera buffa* did not need the careful tailoring to the voices that was obligatory for an *opera seria*. In comic opera, casting was more by type and by comic aptitude than by voice. It is likely, then, that when Mozart and his father left for Salzburg, on 6 December 1774, less than three weeks before the scheduled date of the première, at least part of the opera (probably including much of the recitative) was already written.[2] They broke their journey with only a single overnight stop, at Wasserburg, and reached Munich the next evening, where they took small but 'quite comfortable' lodgings with Johann Nepomuk Pernat, a canon at a Munich church and son of the city mayor. Leopold's second letter casts some light on Munich operatic practices. As the public had to pay (in many cities the public was admitted free to performances at a court opera house), an opera could not be given more than twice in succession, or attendances would fall; accordingly, several operas had to be kept in repertory. The singers were thus so busy that Wolfgang's new work could not be quickly prepared, and it would not be given until 29 December. That turned out to be optimistic.

Meanwhile, Leopold was looking for other opportunities, and he evidently found some. Maria Anna was asked to send copies of settings of the sacramental litany by Wolfgang (K.125, the one modelled on one of his own,[3] with an extra sheet indicating cuts in the lengthy

'Pignus' fugue) for performance on New Year's Day. Leopold already had with him two of Wolfgang's short masses, probably K.192 and 194, which he directed in the court chapel during February. It was agreed that Nannerl would come for the performance and the carnival festivities, although Leopold was slow, perhaps reluctant, to set in train the arrangements for her—clearly he had some anxieties about the family's making a general exodus for Munich in case doing so sent the wrong message to their Salzburg colleagues and employers (that is surely why Maria Anna stayed behind). There were instructions for Nannerl to bring music—sonatas by Bach (probably meaning J.C.), Paradisi and any others she wanted, Wolfgang's sonatas and his variations (K.179 and 180) and, among concertos, not his for keyboard (K.175), which they already had, but 'a few others', presumably the J.C. Bach arrangements, K.107.

The enigma here is 'Wolfgang's sonatas'. Mozart had composed a group of sonatas in the mid-1760s, the lost K.33d–g, but he would hardly have wanted to produce what would now seem childish pieces, especially as he and Leopold were eager to impress the Munich court. It was suggested by Einstein, in his edition of Köchel, that the group beginning with K.279/189d, which Köchel himself had dated far too late, to 1778, were the works in question. But Wolfgang Plath's close analysis of features of the script seems to indicate that they were written only at the start of 1775, in Munich, and that dating has been generally accepted.[4]

The particular feature on which that argument hangs is the form of Mozart's letter p, his abbreviation (usually in the form *pia:* or *p:*) for *piano*. We saw in Chapter 13 that in scores written up to late 1774 there is a straight prefatory downward stroke to the foot of the p, but that in later scores Mozart began the prefatory stroke with an upward hook. Upward hooks predominate in the autograph manuscript of the sonatas, of which all leaves but one survive. Mozart's writing habits, as we have seen, are broadly very consistent; yet there are some p marks in the sonatas that lack an upward hook, and he still sometimes used the simple wedge shape in *La finta giardiniera* (as the facsimile page reproduced in the NMA volume, p. xxii, shows: only five of the 16 *p* marks on that page have the hook). In any case, the possibility cannot be ruled out that Mozart composed the sonatas in Salzburg—where they would have been played exclusively by Mozart or by a member of his family, obviating the need for dynamic marks—and then added the dynamic indications in Munich for performances there.

Another possibility is that the autograph that has come down to us was copied in Munich from a lost original (it is known that the Mozart family had another copy), with some recomposition—the final sonata apart, it shows very few changes or corrections and could be a copy rather than a working manuscript. It may also be argued that Mozart would not have written sonatas with so much dynamic gradation without having a fortepiano to hand (as he would have had Munich) or in mind. But a clavichord, whose loudness is controlled by the player and which certainly was available to Mozart in Salzburg, could also have occasioned the dynamic marks.[5] Finally, although the first movement of the first sonata is missing from this autograph, we know from Johann André's description of it that it was written on Salzburg paper different from the rest of the manuscript (which may explain how it got lost), supporting the idea that some or several of the six sonatas may have been written in Salzburg and that the autograph we have is a (possibly revised) fair copy.

Thus, while the findings of the *Schriftchronologie* are a valuable and important tool in the dating of many works, it may be unwise to depend too heavily on its rather rigid and schematic conclusions when they conflict, as they do here, with other factors. The balance of probabilities must be taken to suggest that the sonatas were at least begun in Salzburg, although (as we shall see) the last of them was certainly written in Munich. The paper evidence is inconclusive: they are on a typical ten-stave Salzburg paper of the same type as most of *La finta giardiniera*, begun in Salzburg and completed in Munich. It bears the K. number 196.

During December Mozart was busy finishing his opera and teaching it to the singers, although he had to spend nearly a week in his rooms with a swollen face. At first Leopold described it as toothache but he later put it down to the extreme cold they had suffered on the journey—he recommended to Nannerl not only footbags but warmed fur-lined boots and hay round the feet, as well as a rug and a well-wrapped head. Mozart was able to add his usual humorous and cryptic notes to his sister, one of them in Latin, one a reminder to call on an unnamed girl with a tender message. At the first rehearsal, Leopold reports, the opera had been so well received that the performance would be postponed until 5 January—in order, he writes, that the singers could learn it more thoroughly and thus act it better. This reads unconvincingly, but it would not be surprising if the singers found *La finta giardiniera* longer and more difficult than they had expected. Leopold also reports, with crocodile tears, that people were saying it would eclipse Tozzi's serious opera, just as, the previous year, a comic opera by Tozzi had done its serious rival: shades of Hasse in Milan in 1771! The orchestra told him that all the arias were beautiful and there was no finer composition. The singers' reactions are unreported. Wolfgang, he said, was likely to be commissioned to write the serious opera next year. That did not in fact happen.

The performance was in fact even further postponed, this time until Friday 13 January; Mozart told his mother not to worry about the bad omen of the date. Apparently circumstances during carnival decreed that performances could be given at the Salvatortheater only on Fridays. But 20 January was impossible, as the anniversary of the death (even as long ago as in 1745) of the preceding Elector, and the performance planned for 27 January, Mozart's nineteenth birthday, was cancelled as a member of the cast was ill (probably Teresa Manservisi, a 'miserable' singer, according to Leopold). So the opera did not have its second hearing until Thursday 2 February, now in the Redoutensaal and shortened in the continued absence of the ill singer, and the final one was on 2 March. Three performances, one of them incomplete, may not seem to reflect a true success. But, writing to his mother, Mozart reports his triumph at the première: there was much applause, with cries of 'Viva maestro' and 'Bravo', and the Elector and Electress were gracious. Curiously, Mozart apologizes for having to prolong his stay in Munich to attend (or direct) later performances, as otherwise his work would 'be quite unrecognizable—for very strange things happen here'. There must have been undercurrents that neither father nor son wanted to report in their letters, which might be intercepted by the Salzburg authorities. Leopold commented on what he saw as the embarrassed reaction of the archbishop, who visited Munich during the carnival but missed the opera, at his employee's success, and Mozart had his own dig at Salzburg provincialism in criticizing the naive reactions of one of their friends.

As no libretto was printed, exact details of the cast remain unknown. Some of the names listed below are inferred from what is known of the singers in the company, but only Rosa Manservisi can be identified with certainty:

Don Anchise, *podestà (mayor) of Lagonero, in love with Sandrina*	Augustin Proper Sutor (*tenor*)
Sandrina, *a gardener: actually the disguised Marchesa Violante in love with Belfiore, who supposes her dead*	Rosa Manservisi (*soprano*)
Il Contino Belfiore, *formerly in love with Violante and now with Arminda*	Johann Baptist Walleshauser (*tenor*)
Arminda, *Milanese gentlewoman, at first in love with Ramiro, now betrothed to Belfiore*	[Unknown] (*soprano*)
Il Cavalier Ramiro, *in love with Arminda and abandoned by her*	Tommaso Consoli (*soprano castrato*)
Serpetta, *the podestà's maidservant, in love with him*	Teresa Manservisi (*soprano*)

Nardo, *a gardener, Sandrina's cousin:*   Giovanni Rossi or
   actually Violante's servant Roberto   Giovanni Paris (*bass*)
   in disguise, in love with Serpetta

In its original Roman libretto *La finta giardiniera* is described as a *dramma giocoso*, the term later used in the librettos of *Don Giovanni* and *Così fan tutte*. It had often been applied to literary texts, since the time of Goldoni, less often by composers to musical ones (Mozart called his later operas *opere buffe*), and tended to be favoured for those that made a clear distinction between *parti serie* (the serious roles, usually lovers and members of the nobility), *parti di mezzo carattere* (intermediate roles, serious people in comic situations or vice versa) and *parti buffe* (comic roles, generally servants or foolish old men). Here Arminda and Ramiro are largely *seria*, Belfiore and Sandrina (Violante) are *mezzo carattere*, and the Podestà, Serpetta and Roberto are *buffa*. The plot is absurd, and the libretto is verbose and poorly constructed, with feeble motivation and too many arias (and too few ensembles)—precisely the kind of comic opera text that Mozart was later at pains to avoid. He must have found, even at the age of eighteen, that it challenged him only on a modest plane.

Before the action of the opera, Belfiore has struck his beloved, Violante, during a lovers' tiff and believes her to be dead, but she, disguised as a gardener, and her servant Nardo are trying to seek him out. Essentially the plot deals, first, with the resolution of their dilemma (achieved only by having them both go mad) and the consequent dilemmas of the other characters, and then with class and love, especially with love's inability to override class barriers and the foolishness of those who try to make it do so. Mozart's music, then, even if it embodies no wider view, is a response to a series of situations among a group of highly diverse characters. It deals effectively with these, in established ways, but the repetitiveness of the situations contrived by the librettist means that the music is inclined to make the same gestures several times over: there are too many frivolous arias about love, and too many outbursts of anger that give rise to the same kinds of aria. Further, Mozart's inclination to write longish and well-developed arias led inevitably to an opera lengthier than its plot and characters can readily justify.

After a two-movement overture, the opera begins with an *intro-duzione*, an opening ensemble designed to introduce the characters but not normally involving action. This is an early example of the *introduzione*, which came to be used quite frequently in early nineteenth-century Italian opera. It seems to have been intended ironically, beginning and ending 'Che lieto giorno, che contentezza' ('What a happy day, what contentment'), but between those bland professions each of the five characters on the stage tells of his or her cause for unhappiness.

The purely *buffo* numbers lie in the tradition extending from Pergolesi to Donizetti: standard comic sentiments conveyed in rapid music, with light orchestral textures and short, sometimes repetitious vocal phrases, often in 6/8 metre. They incorporate various standard comic devices. In his first aria, for example, the Podestà sings about the effects of music upon him, closely illustrated in the score with flourishes for flute and oboes when they are referred to and changes of key at 'si cangia l'armonia'. His pomposity and self-importance are captured in his blustery second aria, his confusion in his third. Serpetta is introduced in a cavatina shared, a verse apiece, with Nardo. Her first aria is a typical utterance of a sexually knowing maidservant, a brisk 6/8 piece—a type to come to maturity with Despina in *Così fan tutte*. Her second carries the same message, initially a wheedling Andantino grazioso before more 6/8 Allegro high spirits. Nardo begins with a standard cynical servant's aria, another 6/8 Allegro, about woman's intractability and the foolishness of the pursuit, and in Act 2 he woos Serpetta, vainly, in Italian, French and English styles. Mozart handles these situations with aplomb, but the scope they offer is limited.

The *seria* characters, Ramiro and Arminda, each begin with an aria that might have found a place in an *opera seria*. Virtually all the arias here are in sonata-ritornello form, less extended than those in *Mitri-*

date or *Lucio Silla* that have middle sections and *dal segno*. Mozart did not have to go far from his *Lucio Silla* style in writing a simile aria for Ramiro, who parallels his escape from a love affair with a bird's flight from its cage, 'Se l'augellin sen fugge', or in setting Arminda's disquisition on man's fickleness, 'Si promette facilmente'. Each is a smoothly written, spacious aria, with no particular characterization of the text except for some imagery of the bird's wings in the violin figuration. But Arminda's impassioned G minor aria at the beginning of Act 2, in outrage at her new lover's inconstancy (Belfiore has seen Sandrina and is distracted), makes effective use of the traditional expressive repertory for rage—tremolando strings, sharp accents, dotted rhythms and syncopations. Ramiro's Larghetto aria in Act 2 as he rediscovers his love for Arminda is one of the score's most exquisite numbers, with its graceful line and its unusual setting with strings and prominent bassoons. A castrato role in a comic opera is rare, since the realism of *opera buffa* consorts uneasily with the implied convention. Mozart's music for Ramiro is judged accordingly, and it is he who is assigned possibly the opera's most powerful aria, 'Va pure ad altre in braccio', his dismissal of the faithless Arminda in a stormy C minor denunciation. The three-bar phrases in these two arias, which result from setting seven-syllable lines in triple metre, impart a tension to Ramiro's music, as if he were at odds with the world.

The music for these characters, comic and serious, indicates the range of Mozart's score and his capacity to reproduce the manner of contemporary opera, *seria* as well as *buffa*. The most inventive and varied musical treatment however goes to the central characters, the lovers. Their quarrel, and its initial outcome (Belfiore's imagined freedom from the ties of love, Violante's disguise and its consequences), in some way motivate every episode in the opera. Violante is at once set apart from the other characters by her seriousness of tone in the *introduzione*, but her first aria, sung in her guise as Sandrina the garden-girl, is servant's music, a manner she adopts again in Act 2 when the Podestà tries to woo her. Alone, she can be herself: in her cavatina at the end of the first act, though to a cliché verse about the mournful turtle-dove ('Gema la tortorella'), she has an exquisite line against muted or pizzicato strings, weaving her counterpoint to the first-violin melody against soft triplets from the seconds. This is one of a family of Mozart arias that goes back to *Apollo et Hyacinthus*. Her climactic scene comes at the end of the second act, when she has been abandoned at night in a wild place (at the instigation of Arminda and with the connivance of Serpetta, who both see her as a threat to their marital plans). There are in effect two arias, a C minor outburst of terror, 'Crudeli, fermate, crudeli', with breathless, detached phrases in voice and orchestra alike, which leads directly into an accompanied recitative and an A minor cavatina of despair with solo oboe and bassoon, breaking into further orchestral recitative as madness sets in, and then directly into the act finale.

Belfiore begins with an aria in extravagant praise of Arminda's beauty, with a hint of the pompous and the mock-majestic, as if *opera seria* parody. There is certainly parody in his 'Da Scirocco a Tramontana', as he reels off details of his ancestry; this is pure *buffa*. (In the German version of the opera this aria was plausibly reassigned to the Podestà.) Belfiore's character deepens, musically speaking, when he re-encounters Violante: half-recognizing her in Sandrina, he sings a touching aria in F major, 'Care pupille', lent soft colouring by the flutes. His counterpart to Sandrina's mad scene, immediately preceding it, is a recitative and aria where he too loses his senses, first believing that Sandrina is indeed Violante, then that it was a pretence. A dramatic and expressive accompanied recitative, worthy of any serious opera, leads into an *arioso* which, as he fades into delusion, becomes a minuet: a mad scene culminating in a dance was a long-established tradition. The situation is resolved in a long scene at the end of the opera. As they come back to the real world, a recitative, delicately scored with disconnected orchestral texture to provide an eloquent metaphor for the state of their minds and of their relationship, is followed by a duet in three sections—an Adagio in B flat for Belfiore's eloquent pleas of love and their sad farewells, a brief C minor Andantino as they falter and hesitate, and an Allegro in B flat where dialogue turns to true duet singing, symbolizing their reconciliation. The flux of emotion is happily mirrored in the music, and it remains only for the other pairs of lovers to come to terms and for all to sing a D major chorus.

The other act finales are extended action ensembles in the usual *opera buffa* tradition. The first begins, in C major, with Sandrina fainting on discovering Belfiore's plan to marry Arminda, and he is led to wonder whether Violante is still living. The initial group, these two with Arminda and Ramiro, are stunned by the turn of events as the Podestà enters, and the music moves from a C major Allegro (ending in E minor) to an E flat Adagio (similarly, ending in G minor). The Podestà, left alone for an outburst, in D, is joined by Serpetta and Nardo; the music moves to G major, and all seven characters join in a lively ensemble, of dialogue, recrimination and confusion. The mood changes, as Arminda denounces Belfiore for his interest in Sandrina: the key moves to D major, the metre to triple, as each in turn expresses her or his predominant reaction to events, and finally to A major as they all sing together at the curtain. The key sequence is unexpected, no doubt intended to tauten the drama by moving successively to dominant keys, though without the internal tonal logic that was later to govern and underpin Mozart's *buffo* finales. But the basic method—with change of key, metre and sometimes tempo to mark decisive points in the action—is effectively carried through.

The second-act finale begins in E flat, a key associated with Belfiore throughout: it is the key of his first aria, his madness aria, the first Act 3 duet and the orchestral recitative of the reconciliation scene. He introduces this finale, set in 'a deserted and rocky spot in a partly ruined ancient aqueduct, with a practicable dark grotto', where Sandrina has been abandoned and the other characters, surprisingly, have also turned up. The darkness and confusion, as they wander around trying to identify one another, parallels their state of mind. The modulation to G major and switch to triple metre are motivated by Ramiro's taking the initiative and eventually bringing lights, to discover that their identifications are mistaken. In a C major Allegro there is a series of angry denunciations, and all but the principal couple express their rage. It is left to Sandrina and Belfiore to conduct a pathetic mad scene, in G major and 3/4 Andantino, where they think themselves, in the traditional way, characters from classical myth and pastoral—Thyrsis and Chloris, Orpheus (pizzicato strings represent his lyre), Medusa and Hercules. The C major music resumes as the crazed couple express joy and the others horror. Again, the tonal scheme here has no discernible broader logic but serves the immediate need, as may equally be said of the schemes of the opera as a whole. Few opera composers by this date, and not very many in the 1780s, used tonality functionally.

After its limping initial run, *La finta giardiniera* was probably never again heard in Mozart's lifetime in Italian. But it had some circulation in a German translation, *Die verstellte Gärtnerin*, made at the end of the 1770s for the travelling company of Johann Böhm, who gave it in Augsburg, Frankfurt and elsewhere, and for which Mozart made some modifications to accommodate the German words and also some cuts. It has been given as *Die Gärtnerin aus Liebe* and *Die schöne Gärtnerin* and under various other titles. German versions follow the Singspiel pattern, using spoken dialogue rather than simple recitative. Mozart's autograph of the first act has long been lost, and for a long time no accurate Italian text for the complete opera was available (although some of it could be reconstructed from surviving copies of the Anfossi libretto), but in the 1970s a copy of the original was discovered in a Brno library, in time for it to be included in the NMA printing and at last making it possible to hear the work as it was given in Munich.

THE MOZARTS, FATHER, son and daughter, had to remain in Munich (and no doubt wanted to) until the end of the carnival, as the final performance of the opera was on the day after Ash Wednesday. They left for home the following Monday. The Munich carnival was an event that attracted visitors, from Salzburg as elsewhere (Nannerl had in fact been brought to the city by a friend from Salzburg, Frau Robinig, going to the carnival), and the three of them went, with at least Nannerl in fancy dress, to most of the balls in the Redoutensaal. A Munich correspondent to the *Deutsche Chronik* reports hearing Mozart play for Franz Joseph Albert, landlord of Zum schwarzen Adler and a noted connoisseur:[6]

> In Munich last winter I heard two of the greatest keyboard players, Mr Mozart and Captain von Beecke; my host Mr Albert . . . has an excellent fortepiano in his house. There I heard these two giants in contest. Mozart played very strongly and read at sight everything that was put before him. But no more than that; Beecke far surpasses him. Winged agility, grace, melting sweetness and an entirely individual, self-formed taste and the clubs that no-one is likely to wrest from this Hercules.

The Mozarts had previously met Beecke in Paris. He was now in his early forties and music director to the Prince of Oettingen-Wallerstein, and much more experienced a fortepianist.

Mozart also spent some of his time composing. Besides the masses that were performed in the electoral chapel, a new offertory motet, *Misericordias Domini* K.222/205a, was given on the first Sunday in Lent. He wrote this piece with great care and valued it highly. Clearly it was intended to impress the Elector who, Mozart later told Padre Martini, had asked to hear some of his contrapuntal compositions and to whom he presented a copy. Later he sent a copy to Martini, and he took the work with him on his travels. For chorus and strings, it contrasts simple harmonized settings of the words 'Misericordias Domini' with a series of different, increasingly elaborate and often chromatic four-voice settings of 'cantabo in æternum', in vigorous counterpoint (based on a theme from a *Benedixisti Domine* by Eberlin which Mozart had recently copied out) involving close imitation of various kinds, sometimes inverted and ingeniously overlapping.

Martini, predictably, admired it, saying that it had all the qualities that music today demands.[7]

Another composition thought to belong to the weeks in Munich is the little sonata K.292/196c for bassoon, with an unspecified bass part that can be played on a cello, another bassoon or even as a keyboard continuo accompaniment. It is generally taken to have been written for Thaddäus von Dürnitz, the bassoon-playing baron from Munich who (as noted earlier) was long supposed to be the dedicatee of the K.191 concerto, although Mozart and he were unacquainted when the concerto was composed. There is no firm evidence that this sonata was written for him, or indeed that it was written by Mozart at all. No autograph survives, nor is there any documentary reference to it, and the only source is a published edition of about 1800. But musically it is perfectly plausible as a work of Mozart's, with its touches of wit in the bassoon writing in the opening movement closely akin to those in the concerto, its eloquent Andante and a number of characteristic compositional features. These include, in the first and second movement, the use of an idea from the last bars of the exposition to launch the development, and, in the finale, the varied final appearance of the rondo theme, much as at the equivalent point in the concerto.

Dürnitz, who held a post at the Munich court, was a pianist as well as a bassoonist, and it was for him that Mozart wrote the last of the group of six piano sonatas discussed at the beginning of this chapter. K.284/205b in D is referred to in several letters as his 'Dürnitz sonata' and stands somewhat apart from the others, as Mozart's decision many years on to publish it with later works implicitly acknowledges. It nevertheless completes the key sequence of the group, C–F–B flat–E flat–G–D, using six of the seven major keys with minimum sharps or flats. Mozart may well have composed the set with a view to publication as a whole, although Dürnitz's ownership of one of the sonatas might have precluded publication for an agreed period, probably a year or two. In fact Dürnitz never paid for the sonata, or did so very late; Leopold reminded Wolfgang to try to collect what was due to him when he was in Munich in 1777.[8] Late in 1775, Leopold wrote to the publisher Breitkopf in Leipzig offering him a selection of music, including piano sonatas 'in the same style as those of Carl Philipp Emanuel Bach "mit veränderten Reprisen" '. Although Mozart's sonatas do not have varied reprises nor many other points of resemblance to Bach's, these can be the only sonatas he had in mind unless, improbably, he intended Mozart to compose another set in the C.P.E. Bach manner. When he was in Paris in 1778, Mozart considered selling the set to a publisher there.[9] But apart from K.284 the sonatas remained unpublished in his lifetime. Breitkopf rejected Leopold's offers, but ironically it was his firm that first published the five sonatas in their collected edition of Mozart's music in 1799.

Mozart would certainly have been acquainted with the C.P.E. Bach sonatas, but one has to look elsewhere for influences or models, and they are not obvious or easy to find. This was not a case where Mozart was eager to emulate some other composer. He would have come across the rather slight and by then old-fashioned sonatas by Leopold and his Salzburg contemporaries, such as Eberlin and Adlgasser, some of which had been published in anthologies, as well as sonatas by the leading Austrian keyboard composer, Wagenseil, whose music he had played in childhood and on his visits to Vienna. We know, of course, from his concerto adaptations that he was familiar with the sonatas of the 'Parisian Germans', Schobert, Raupach, Eckard and Honauer, and also J.C. Bach. The family letters make reference to a number of Italian composers' keyboard pieces: Leopold once recommended sonatas by Rutini and he asked Nannerl to bring to Munich sonatas by Paradisi. Some of the sonatas of Joseph Haydn, H.XIV:21–6, had recently been published in Vienna and Amsterdam, and it is likely that Leopold, always eager to keep up with the latest music by leading composers, would have had a copy.

It is easy enough, looking at these various sonatas, to find points of resemblance with Mozart's set of six, whether it be a theme or a phrase or a formal feature. In general, diagnoses of 'influence' would be misguided. All these composers, and dozens more, wrote in the same basic idiom and used the same musical forms. To none can any particular innovation be ascribed that Mozart copied. Most of them, especially the Italians and Haydn, wrote music that is substantially easier to play and simpler and less varied in texture than Mozart's. Mozart himself regarded his sonatas as 'difficult', alluding to them as such in a letter. Referring to Aloysia Weber, he wrote 'Can you believe it? she played my difficult sonatas at sight, *slowly* but without missing a single note!', and Leopold told him that he and Nannerl, in practising, 'always choose the most difficult ones and particularly the works in C major and F major'.[10]

The work in C (K.279) is the first of the set—the autograph manuscript is laid out in sequence, with the sonatas numbered. The particular difficulty to which Leopold was referring was surely to do with the left-hand part, which is exceptionally active and participates in the musical argument much more fully than is usual in the keyboard music of the time, where the left hand is so often relegated to long spells of Alberti bass accompaniment. Its opening movement is arresting for its ready command of the brilliant keyboard manner of the day, with its spread chords, arpeggio patterns and sprightly acciaccaturas. There is Alberti bass here too, where there is melodic matter in the right hand, but that is only brief, as the movement has little melody but much figurative writing shared between the hands and is held together by derivatives of the exclamatory four-note phrase heard in the left hand at the opening. In the finale too the left-hand participation represents an important part of the musical argument; there are hints from the start that counterpoint is in the offing, and more than that in the brief development of this sonata-form movement. The central Andante gives Mozart scope to show his singing keyboard style—graceful triple-time music with a flowing triplet accompaniment. But there are striking dynamic effects, remarkable bearing in mind his comparative unfamiliarity with the fortepiano, as well as chromatic writing in the secondary material, intensified by throbbing left-hand chords towards the major cadences.

The F major sonata (K.280) too involves a good deal of interplay between the hands in the fast movements, but its slow movement, an F minor Adagio in *siciliano* rhythm is its remarkable feature, and here there are points in common in rhythm, line and harmony with the slow movement of the K.488 piano concerto, more than a long decade ahead. This, the only minor-key movement in the set, has been compared with the F minor Adagio of Haydn's F major sonata HXVI:23, chiefly because of the similarity of its opening phrase, but its sustained line, its harmonic surprises, its changes of texture and its chromaticisms inhabit a very different world from Haydn's rather more formally couched movement, with its consistent accompaniment patterns and its decorous cadences. Haydn's is a binary movement, Mozart's a sonata-form miniature, with a characteristic twist where the secondary theme holds to the minor key.

If, as he may well have done, Mozart planned these sonatas with thoughts of their use as teaching pieces, then the B flat work K.281 would surely have been composed with a view to neat and precise fingerwork, with the trills and the rapid but not too demanding scales and filigree passage-work of its first movement. The Andante amoroso middle movement—an indication very rare in Mozart—has a leisured sensuousness that hints at the world of the wind serenade, in its traditional key of E flat. The finale is the only rondo in the series, a fully worked out sonata-rondo, with a tonic recapitulation of its first, dominant-key episode and two passages (one just before the first return, the other preceding the recapitulated episode) that suggest cadenzas, an idea Mozart pursued in some of his later piano sonatas. This finale, weightier than the sonata-form finales of the other sonatas, counterbalances the slighter opening movement. For the next sonata, K.282 in E flat, however, Mozart tried a different pattern, starting with an Adagio, a movement of refined invention and a rather intimate and personal character. In rounded binary rather than sonata form, it recalls its opening at the start of the development but not again until the slightly plaintive coda. A cheerful minuet follows, much in the manner once more of a wind serenade, and a lively sonata-form finale. The first two movements make particular play with dynamic contrasts, often with alternate phrases *piano* and *forte*: perhaps Mozart was relishing the opportunities the Munich forte-pianos opened up for him. It is however true that the music makes no less sense, even if a slightly different sense, without these dynamic extravagances.

The last of the five sonatas, the popular K.283 in G, is the most polished and confident in its workmanship. In the first movement the elegant sequence of ideas, the carefully constructed phrase repetitions, the witty interludial 'development' and the careful foreshortening of the primary material in the recapitulation to provide an ingenious adjustment of the tonal balance—all these show a new degree of control over the material. The Andante is equally deft, with similarly graceful management of the recapitulation and a tiny coda, like that in the first movement of K.282, nostalgically echoing the opening. The finale is a rapid, extended sonata-form Presto, quite a virtuoso piece, with a very exact recapitulation, unusual for Mozart.

The sixth sonata, K.284 in D, stands apart from the other five. Written for Dürnitz, it can only have been written in Munich during the run of *La finta giardiniera*. The autograph—and it is clear that Mozart actually composed the work on to this manuscript, which contains all six sonatas—shows a rejected version of part of the first movement, which offers a rare glimpse into Mozart's compositional workshop.[11] He wrote an entire exposition and 19 bars of development, then abandoned it. He had built his development, as in the K.292 duet for bassoon and cello (probably also intended for Dürnitz), from an idea heard in the last bars of the exposition, but found himself unable to carry it off with the wit that this procedure requires if it is to be convincing, or to find the right tonal direction for it. There is an ineffective piece of imitative writing, an attempt to change the pace, and then the music sticks uncomfortably in B minor—at which point Mozart gave up and crossed the development through. Rather than write a new development to the same exposition, he then crossed out the exposition too and began the sonata again. The music as finally written is still the same kind of piece, energetic and in a bold range of styles, starting with a motivic phrase and a *piano* continuation in the manner of a symphonic opening and including (for the first time in his music) a pseudo-orchestral manner that a number of other piano composers were currently using. The primary material, once past the opening flourish, is new, but the linking and secondary material is virtually identical in the two versions, and the new development section is again thematically independent of the exposition. There are several conclusions to be drawn here about Mozart's composition processes: he did not (as was often supposed) conceive movements in their entirety before setting pen to paper; when he allowed his fancy free rein, it could carry him astray; he did not necessarily require the material of one section to determine the material of another; and he could decide on the character of a movement without making specific decisions about its actual material.

The forthright, outgoing nature of this movement is paralleled by the rest of the sonata. Its Andante is a *rondeau en polonaise*, in which the polonaise theme is decorated on its two returns. The finale is a set of variations on a gavotte-like theme, by far Mozart's most elaborate set of variations to date. He had often played variations, sometimes impromptu, on his early travels, and two works written in the Netherlands, K.24 and 25, remain as formalized records of such occasions. He had written two further sets recently, one (K.180/173*c*) on a Salieri aria when he was in Vienna in 1773, and another (K.179/189*a*) the following summer on a popular minuet from a concerto by the oboist Johann Christian Fischer. A much admired player, except by Mozart, whose later comments on him are highly critical, Fischer was active mainly in London. The K.179 variations are essentially melodic ones in which the outline of the theme and mostly its bass are preserved, while increasingly rapid and rhythmically inventive music is woven from it. There is usually a minor-key variation, a penultimate slow variation and a final one in changed metre. This pattern, which Mozart used throughout his career, is broadly followed in the finale of the sonata K.284, but on a far more ambitious scale: the early variations elaborate on the theme, but the later ones develop figures derived from it, and several use such techniques as hand-crossing, canon and orchestral effects. The manuscript shows that, after he had composed the eleventh variation, an Adagio, and had begun the twelfth, Mozart decided that instead of simple repeats to each half (as in the earlier variations) he would write out the repeats in elaborated form. This is the earliest example of the 'double variation' that he used in many later works.

Clearly Mozart perceived this sonata, with its larger scale and its bolder invention, as a different kind of work from the other five. In 1784, when he evidently needed a third work to make up a set for publication, along with a recent sonata (K.333) and one with violin (K.454), this was the sonata he chose. He or his editors made some small changes in the dynamics and articulation and more substantial ones to the melodic line of the Adagio variation, sometimes simply to clarify the notation but more often to elaborate the music further.

In the course of composing these six sonatas, Mozart moved from writing polished but fairly conventional music to pieces of much greater individuality in which his invention has far freer rein. The extraordinary strides he made, over a period of perhaps four months or possibly much less, had a parallel shortly after in another group of works, his violin concertos. He and his father were back in Salzburg on 7 March 1775. Mozart's immediate task was the composition and performance of *Il rè pastore* in April. The sequence of violin concertos—assuming that K.207, the first, belongs to 1773 rather than 1775 (see p. 306)—began in June, continued in September and October and finished in December. The only other significant instrumental works of 1775 are the first of a group of wind divertimentos, K.213, and the Finalmusik K.204/213a, which like Mozart's other serenades of the period incorporates a violin concerto.

There are four works of the serenade or Finalmusik type with violin concertos, all dating from around the time of the violin concertos proper. The chronological sequence of all these works is as follows: the first violin concerto (K.207) dates most probably from April

1773; the serenade K.185 from August 1773; the serenade K.203 from August 1774; the second concerto K.211 from April 1775; the serenade K.204 from August 1775; the next three violin concertos K.216, 218 and 219 from September, October and December 1775; and the final serenade, the 'Haffner', from August 1776. Each of the serenades has an Andante and an Allegro (in that order) in concerto style and each also has a minuet, either centrally or finally (in the case of K.185 after several other movements), with a solo violin part in its trio. Taking account of the serenades and their relation to the concertos puts Mozart's development in the concertos in a slightly different perspective, and comparison between the two genres offers hints about his attitudes to them. Leaving aside the 'Haffner', the two types of work are on much the same scale—the concertos proper are only marginally longer—but Mozart's handling of the musical forms in the serenade concertos is more direct; their relation to the concertos proper is analogous to that between the serenades' symphonic movements and the symphonies of the time. The textures are less elaborate, the thematic structure is simpler, and in the concertos, ritornello material is used in more complex ways, there is more thematic development, and heavier technical demands are made on the soloist. All these differences speak of the requirements of music designed to be attentively listened to rather than casually heard.

The first concerto, K. 207, is closest to the serenade pattern in its violin writing. K.211, presumably the first of the 1775 sequence, begins with an uncharacteristic movement, by Mozart's own standards almost clumsily written, and of a curiously old-fashioned cast with its early *galant*-style triplets and its short phrases. It seems akin in style to the rather conservative Italian concertos of Pietro Nardini, whose music Mozart had encountered in Florence in 1770 (at the time of his friendship with Nardini's pupil Thomas Linley), and indeed those of Boccherini, although there can be no certainty that Mozart had ever come across them. Its finale is more characteristic, a *menuet en rondeau* of a similar cast to those in the bassoon concerto and the two-violin concertone, and it sets the tone for the dance-rhythm finales of the next three concertos. It has a formal oddity: Mozart chose to use the second episode (in the subdominant) rather than the first as the subject of the recapitulatory episode later in the movement.

When, five months later, he came to write K.216, he was thinking on a different scale. The first movement, 100 bars longer (226 as against 126), is the first of his concerto movements in which Mozart introduced new thematic material for the soloist and often exclusive to him, a procedure he normally followed in the mature piano concertos. Whereas previously, in nearly all his concerto Allegros and in most of his arias he had included both primary and secondary material (in the tonic key) in the opening ritornello, now he provided an additional secondary theme, conceived for solo violin and unsuitable for transfer to the orchestra. Here the extra theme has an intermediate role, more as part of the linking material than as a principal idea, but it is significant in that it shows Mozart already on the way towards expanding the musical framework. The expressive canvas of the slow movement is enlarged too. This is an Adagio, not an Andante, with muted upper and pizzicato lower strings, and soft flutes to replace the oboes, and with throbbing triplets accompanying the soaring violin line, which flowers with increasing expressive detail as the music proceeds. The finale is a lengthy Rondo in, for the most part, a lively 3/8. But for its third episode the tempo changes to Andante, the metre to 2/2, the key to G minor for a gavotte-like section of 13 bars, and then to G major and Allegretto for a new theme of a 'folky' nature. This has been identified as one marked 'à la mélodie de Strassbourger' in a collection assembled in 1813, which explains references in Mozart family letters to his 'Strassburg concerto'.[12]

Until the discovery in 1956 of the 'Strassburg' theme, the next concerto, K.218, was generally supposed to be the 'Strassburger', for it too has an episode in the finale with a derived theme of a folk character. This episode is in musette style, with a drone bass, on the open G string, and both these features are clearly in some way allusive. Here the quoted theme is treated as greater length than previously and is integrated more fully into the fabric of the music. The finale is basically a 6/8 Allegro ma non troppo, but with a graceful little 2/4 refrain, Andante grazioso, recurring halfway through, and twice more (varied and shortened) later in the movement. The first movement follows the formal pattern of K.216, with a new theme for the soloist in the linking material: Mozart evidently saw this as an effective way of setting the soloist apart as well as increasing the scale of the music. Again, too, there is a distinctive slow movement, marked Andante cantabile, allowing the violin an outpouring of singing melody, which at times is echoed by the oboe.

Almost as if, once having embarked on violin concertos, he could not break off until he had carried the genre a stage further, Mozart completed yet another before the end of the year. K.219 in A does indeed break new ground, even with its opening bars: a vigorous, arresting gesture of rising arpeggio figures against tremolandos. What can a solo violin make of this? The answer is, first, that before engaging on the Allegro the soloist has a rapt six bars of solo, Adagio, above a soft, shimmering accompaniment: and then the orchestra repeats its original opening, counterpointed by the solo violin in a buoyant, striding theme across its entire compass. This is music that defines a new relationship between soloist and orchestra. Thereafter the movement continues along regular patterns, with an extra solo theme, as in the preceding works. The Adagio is a richly detailed movement in the rare key of E major (in each of these concertos the slow movement is in the dominant rather than the more usual subdominant). Longer than those of K.216 or 218, it has a full ritornello with a statement of the secondary theme, while in the other two works only the primary material is heard. Mozart supplements this after the soloist's entry with an additional new solo theme.

The finale begins as a graceful Tempo di Menuetto and is in an expanded sonata-rondo form, *A-B-A-C-A-D-A-B-A*. But episode *D* introduces a new rhythm and foreign, indeed exotic material. This is Mozart's first use of the 'alla turca' style. Turkish music had entered Viennese consciousness during the various wars of recent times with the Ottoman Empire, including the siege of Vienna in 1683 (and further wars were to come). Gluck, Haydn and Dittersdorf were among the composers to have imported the exotic effects of 'janissary music' into their own works. In this long episode (131 bars of 2/4) Mozart drew on a passage in the finale of *Le gelosie del serraglio*, the ballet given three years before in Milan after Act 1 of *Lucio Silla* (probably by another composer). After this colourful and rousing episode, the minuet returns, with more decoration each time, and the movement reaches a quiet, epigrammatic end.

This flurry of violin concertos might seem to suggest that Mozart had found some particular reason for exploring and developing the genre, or at least a particular exponent who spurred him to do so. Neither a reason nor an exponent is known. As we have seen, it is unlikely, in view of Leopold's reference to 'the concerto' that Wolfgang wrote for Kolb, that anything other than the one written separately, K.207, was designed for him. We know of no other violinist in Salzburg at this time for whom the others are likely to have been intended—though the possibility of some connection with the amateur violinist Count Johann Rudolph Czernin, a friend and nephew of the archbishop, cannot be wholly ruled out—and there is no information on the subject in the family letters. Mozart himself, of course, led the violins in the orchestra, but had he written the concertos to play them himself he would surely have given them on other occasions, during his travels, and there would be some reference in the correspondence. Later they were performed by Antonio Brunetti, the Neapolitan violinist who was appointed to the court music early in 1776 as Hofviolinist and 'Hofmusikdirektor, Hofkonzertgeiger und Hofkonzertmeister', although he did not use the title Konzertmeister until the next year, when Mozart left.[13] Brunetti was not much admired personally by the Mozarts, who found him coarse and deplored his womanizing (he made Michael Haydn's sister-in-law pregnant, and later married her, but apparently had also been involved with another local woman). Leopold once reported favourably on his playing of K.216, and he must also have played K.207 and 219. It was at his request that in 1776 Mozart wrote a replacement slow movement for K.219, the Adagio K.261, because Brunetti found the original 'too artificial'.[14] Whether the new movement satisfied Brunetti is not recorded. This too has a melodic line full of artifice, but at least it is shorter and more obvious in its charm and appeal than the earlier one, and the use of flutes in place of oboes lends it an additional softness and transparency of texture. There is no documentary proof that the Rondo K.269/261a, also composed at Brunetti's request, was a replacement for the finale of K.207, but that seems overwhelmingly likely. It is a full-length sonata-rondo, in 6/8 metre and gigue-like rhythm, of no particular originality apart from some deft touches of wit and some unusual three-bar phrases which prevent its falling into excessive regularity. The original finale of K.207 is a sonata-form movement; it is worth noting that Mozart also replaced his only other sonata-form finale in a concerto, that of the piano concerto K.175.

Three further violin concertos have been attributed to Mozart. One, in E flat K.268, is now believed to be by Friedrich Johann Eck, a violinist and composer with Mannheim and Munich connections. Mozart met him in 1780 and was said to have written the concerto for him, and it was published as Mozart's in 1799. Mozart's authorship is hardly plausible, and it has been suggested, improbably, that Eck based the work on a sketchy original.[15] Another, K.271a/271i in D, published in the NMA as a doubtful work, has a curious history. It first appeared in print in 1907, when it was greeted with scepticism on account of its style, its musical quality and its questionable sources. One of the source manuscripts, claimed as a copy of an autograph lost in the 1830s by the Parisian violinist and conductor F.-A. Habeneck, is annotated 'concerto per il violino di W.A. Mozart, Salisburgo, li 16 di Luglio 1777'. Mozart did in fact play a violin concerto in Salzburg on 25 July 1777, at a nameday celebration for his sister, but there is no evidence, nor any likelihood, that it was a new work. It has been argued that the concerto as we have it could be a revision of Mozart's original, incorporating his ideas and following his structural outline

but with the solo part rewritten to accommodate French violin techniques of the 1830s (one copy belonged to a pupil of the violinist
Pierre Baillot). But there is little in this consistently banal and repetitive music to suggest more than an amateurish attempt to compose
in a vaguely Mozartian manner.[16] A work called the Adelaïde Concerto, in D, enjoyed a brief currency as a rediscovered Mozart work
after its publication in 1933 but is actually one of a group of works
ascribed to eighteenth-century composers but written by Marius
Casadesus (1892–1981) and his brothers (cadenzas were supplied by
Hindemith). Finally, there is some scholarly literature, including contributions by Alfred Einstein and Hans Keller, in which the indebtedness of K.218 to a concerto supposedly by Boccherini is discussed.
The violin concerto concerned is however by the violinist Samuel
Dushkin (1891–1976), friend of Stravinsky and pupil of Kreisler
among others; he modelled the work closely on K.218 and published
it with a false attribution to Boccherini.

PROBABLY THE COMMISSION, from his own archbishop, for the
composition of *Il re pastore* had been issued to Mozart before he went
to Munich in December. The occasion that called for it was a visit to
Salzburg by the Archduke Maximilian, Maria Theresa's youngest son,
who needed to be feted in the city when he paused there on a journey from Vienna to Italy. That was to be in April 1775. Two works
were planned, both of them serenatas and both to texts by Metastasio: *Gli orti esperidi*, by Fischietti, the Kapellmeister, which was given
on 22 April, and Mozart's work, given the next day. On his third
evening there was a concert, given by members of the Salzburg nobility, in which the archbishop took part, at the end of which 'the
famous young Mozart was heard on the keyboard and played various
pieces out of his head with as much art as pleasantness'.[17]

The text of *Il re pastore* had been written as a three-act *opera seria*
libretto in 1751, when it was set by the Viennese Kapellmeister

Giuseppe Bonno. It had been set at least twenty times since then by (among others) Hasse, Gluck, Lampugnani, Piccinni, Jommelli and Tozzi. Mozart could have seen the setting by Felice Giardini given in London in 1765. Pietro Alessandro Guglielmi had set it in Venice in 1767, and in 1774 his version was revived in Munich, in two-act form, with the second and third acts compressed into one. It was this version in two acts, the normal length for a serenata, that Mozart set, although some passages from the Metastasio original are restored, and a few new lines of recitative are added;[18] these changes were presumably specified in the commission, as would be normal for a court entertainment. It was given on 23 April at the archbishop's Residenz. It is unlikely that it was fully staged. Archduke Maximilian's own travel diaries refer to it as a 'cantata', and the only Salzburg source—the diaries of the councillor Joachim Ferdinand von Schiedenhofen, a friend and near neighbour of the Mozart family—mentions it only as a 'serenada'.[19] As there were no castratos in Salzburg, Tommaso Consoli was brought in from Munich for the occasion (and a flute player, J.B. Becke). Consoli, the Ramiro of La finta giardiniera, is the only member of the cast who can be firmly identified. The other roles were taken by members of the local establishment; Maria Magdalena Lipp, Michael Haydn's wife, was probably one of the sopranos. This is the cast:

Alessandro [Alexander the Great], king of Macedonia	(tenor)
Aminta [Amyntas], *shepherd, in love with Elisa, but unknown to himself*	Tommaso Consoli (soprano castrato)
Abdalomino [Abdalomynus], *rightful heir to the kingdom of Sidon*	
Elisa, *Phoenician lady, descendant of Cadmus, in love with Amyntas*	(soprano)
Tamiri [Tamyris], *daughter of Strato, the tyrant ruler (now dead) of Sidon, in love with Agenor, disguised as a shepherdess*	(soprano)

Agenore [Agenor], *Sidonian nobleman, friend*   (*tenor*)
  of Alexander, in love with Tamyris

Like most of the Habsburg serenatas, *Il rè pastore* tells an allegorical
tale, superficially about Alexander the Great and his restoration of the
true heir to the Sidonian throne, but in reality about the usual topic—
virtue, and its rewards from a benevolent ruler and a benevolent deity.
Here it is Amyntas, the shepherd king of the title, who loves Elisa, and
is rewarded for his humility and his steadfastness by being united with
her and restored to the throne. After various misunderstandings
(because of Alexander's initial intention of marrying Amyntas to
Tamyris, daughter of a previous ruler), and some examples of virtuous behaviour, other characters too end up with the right partner.

The serenata follows the usual Metastasian pattern of alternating
recitative and arias: there are twelve arias altogether, with a duet to
end the first part and a 'chorus' ensemble with all the singers to end
the second. Most of the arias follow the standard sonata-ritornello
pattern, but not, for a domestic Salzburg entertainment, on the
expansive scale that Mozart had used in Italy for the opera-house
singers. Amyntas, naturally, is specially favoured. He has a short arietta
following directly from the overture, setting with its gentle 6/8
rhythm the atmosphere of the pastoral world. Of his two full-length
arias, the first is 'Aer tranquillo', the longest aria in the work, with a
contrasting, minuet-like *grazioso* middle section, and it demands
strong virtuoso singing. It is of particular interest too for Mozart's
handling of the tuttis, in which different material is used interchangeably—this is an early example of a technique of 'open-ended' themes
that Mozart was to develop in the mature piano concertos. He drew
on the opening phrase of this aria for the opening of the K.216 violin concerto a few weeks later. Amyntas's final aria is the exquisite
'L'amerò, sarò costante', with an obbligato for solo violin and an
accompanying texture for flutes, English horns and bassoons. It is a
rondo, its form reflecting the constancy of which he speaks, its

melody the depth of his sincerity, all reinforced by the key of E flat major, traditional to the most serious and heartfelt expression.

Alexander's music speaks in appropriately regal tones. He too has three arias, two of them set with trumpets, and the central one—the longest and the most demanding—with florid music for flutes and oboes. Mozart was to use this combination again to majestic effect in *Idomeneo*. The unusually elaborate flute part was no doubt intended for the visiting flautist from Munich. Musical invention is closely matched to character in Elisa's music, too, with the blithe, carefree phrases of her first aria, when she is lauding simple rural bliss and innocence, and the tortuous lines and exclamatory gestures of her second, two-tempo aria, when she is separated from Amyntas. The secondary characters, Tamyris and Agenor, each have one small-scale aria accompanied only by strings and one larger aria, of which Agenor's, sung when he believes himself deprived of his beloved, is comparable to Elisa's in its passion, with its broken vocal line, its urgent tremolandos and syncopations, and its minor key.

The opportunities offered by this rather contrived libretto are limited, especially the shortened version, with the unnaturally speedy resolution of its dilemmas, but Mozart still succeeded in producing a varied work with some appealing music. It had only the single hearing. Nevertheless, Mozart clearly thought well of it. In October 1777 he gave a copy to Josef Myslivecek after meeting him in Munich (it is, incidentally, curious that he had a spare copy with him on his travels). The following spring, in Mannheim, he had Aloysia Weber sing four arias from it, including 'Aer tranquillo', and he also performed the overture there.[20] Like that of *La finta giardiniera*, to which he added a finale (K.121/207a) at some point in 1775 to make a three-movement symphony, he adapted this one (K.102/213c), leaving the first movement as it stands, turning the first arietta into an oboe solo (with the orchestral oboe parts going to flutes), then adding a seven-bar link and a new finale, a very spirited and surprisingly long *contredanse en rondeau*. A March in C K.214, dated 20

August 1775, is likely to have been intended for use with this work as a small-scale serenade.

It was not until the time of *Idomeneo*, in 1780–81, that Mozart had an opportunity to return to opera. But he had some tangential contact with it in Salzburg during 1775 and 1776 when an Italian *opera buffa* company was playing in the city. The Mozarts, avid theatregoers and close neighbours of the theatre, evidently established friendly contact with the company, and Mozart was asked to compose additional music for their performances, presumably for singers to whom the existing arias were poorly suited, whether new members of the company or local substitutes. He supplied five in all, two for tenor in May 1775, one for soprano that autumn and two the following autumn for alto castrato and tenor.

No source is known for the text of the first of these arias, 'Si mostra la sorte' K.209, but it may well have been intended, like the second, 'Con ossequio, con rispetto' K.210, as an insertion or substitute aria for Piccinni's *L'astratto ovvero Il giocator fortunato* (1772). The first is a gracefully amorous piece, the second a rapid, mock-pompous one with comic asides (it is sung by Capitan Faccenda, disguised as Doctor Testa Secca, asking Don Timoteo for his daughter's hand). The aria of autumn 1775, 'Voi avete un cor fedele' K.217, was for *Le nozze di Dorina*, to a Goldoni libretto. It is unclear whether the opera was Baldassare Galuppi's of 1755, called simply *Le nozze*, or Gioacchino Cocchi's of 1762, *Le nozze di Dorina* (the text was later the basis of Sarti's popular opera *Fra i due litiganti*, quoted in *Don Giovanni*). The aria, substantial with ironic overtones, set in alternating slow and fast sections, shows a remarkable advance in comic aptitude in its gestures and its timing as compared with anything in *La finta giardiniera*. One of the two arias of the following year, 'Clarice cara mia sposa' K.256, is a further substitute piece for a tenor, Antonio Palmini, in *L'astratto*, a very fast-moving patter-song marked 'In tempo comodo d'un gran ciarlone' (' . . . a great chatterbox'). The other, 'Ombra felice . . . Io ti lascio' K.255, is Mozart's only aria for the alto voice. It was written for Francesco Fortini, a castrato from the Bavarian court, currently in Salzburg to sing with the visiting opera troupe, and was intended not for inclusion in an opera but as a concert piece. The text, from an opera libretto by Giovanni de Gamerra originally called *Medonte, rè d'Epiro* or in some settings *Arsace*, is a lover's farewell, with an impassioned orchestral recitative followed by what Mozart called an 'Aria en rondeau'. A traditional rondo of the *A-B-A-C-A-D-A* pattern, with the *A* theme an Andante moderato (in gavotte rhythm) and the episodes mainly Allegro assai, it has the effect of alternating sorrow and 'barbaro tormento'. Mozart thought well enough of it to ask his father to send it to him in Vienna in 1783, but it may not actually have been performed there.[21] At some point in 1776 Mozart was involved in composing music for the Gebler drama *Thamos, König in Ägypten,* for which he had written two choruses in 1774. He returned to it in 1779, and it will be discussed in Chapter 19.

16

Frustration

THE TWO-AND-A-HALF YEARS that Mozart spent in Salzburg between his return from Munich after *La finta giardiniera* in March 1775 and his departure in September 1777 make up the longest spell he had had in his native city since his infancy. The Mozart family did not set foot out of Salzburg during those 30 months except for occasional brief excursions to visit nearby friends. That this period was for the Mozarts an unhappy and increasingly frustrating one is abundantly clear. The family had been told they could expect no professional advancement in Salzburg. Leopold was still a vice-Kapellmeister, with arduous duties. The Kapellmeister, Fischietti, had left in 1775 and had not been replaced (he went briefly to Italy, had no success there, and came back to Salzburg, where he taught for a time at the cathedral choir school). Some of his responsibilities had devolved on to Leopold, who had neither extra reward nor any likelihood of the succession, for the archbishop favoured appointing an outsider, preferably from Italy: the idea that it is preferable to bring in fresh blood at the top, rather than promote and so maintain existing situations and rivalries, is not a new one. Wolfgang was still employed as a Konzertmeister on a modest annual salary of 150 gulden. Neither, it seems, exerted himself unduly in the archbishop's service. Leopold had composed little or nothing since the early 1760s. Wolfgang wrote several masses and other liturgical works during these years, but his instrumental music was directed towards other patrons, not the court. The prospects were nil. The Mozarts had looked for employment elsewhere but had repeatedly failed. They knew that Wolfgang's gifts were of an order to merit a lucrative and artistically rewarding position at a large court, but he had no means of attaining anything of the kind. It is not difficult to imagine the feelings of Mozart himself, fed on the compliments of princes since childhood and now working in a secondary post at a third-rate court.

Understandably, posterity has taken the Mozarts' view and has judged Hieronymus Colloredo harshly for his failure to nurture his resident genius. But he had a point of view too, and priorities of his own. The management of his diocese was more important than any one person in it. He was a reformist churchman, in tune with the Enlightenment ideas that Joseph II was currently trying to propagate in Vienna. He instituted in Salzburg a simplified liturgy, with shorter, more readily comprehensible services, terminated the use of instrumental music in the smaller, local churches, and required that hymns be sung in German. He closed the university theatre and abolished the tradition of Benedictine schooldrama, but also had a new town theatre opened (very close to the Mozarts' house, in the Hannibal-Platz, where the present Landestheater stands). He opposed excessive idolatry and superstition, he reformed the local schools, and he maintained the tradition of evening concerts in the Residenz, but shortened them to about one-and-a-quarter hours (often taking part in them himself). The musical establishment at Salzburg was not the first among his concerns, but its smooth and efficient running was to him more important than the welfare of the Mozarts—the devious, scheming father, whose resentment towards the court was ill-concealed and whose ambitions for his son governed his life, and the unruly, talented young man, very conscious of his own abilities, apt to annoy his colleagues through his awareness of his superior gifts, and regularly wanting leave to compose and perform elsewhere (also, as Colloredo is likely to have heard through his Habsburg connections, constantly seeking new positions). Such views as these are not of course recorded but they are readily inferable from Colloredo's actions. He had the reputation of being a difficult man, dictatorial and autocratic, with few friends, and he seems to have been generally disliked, not only among the musical establishment and the cathedral chapter but also more generally in Salzburg.

This two-and-a-half-year period was probably one of growing discontent and tension in the Mozart family. As they were together all through this period, there are of course no family letters. Our solitary sources for information on their activities are Schiedenhofen's diary, Nannerl's occasional notes in her diary and a handful of references in Salzburg records. Schiedenhofen notes a number of events in Salzburg at which Mozart's music was played, such as the annual Finalmusik in 1775. He mentions a litany and a mass at the cathedral at Easter 1776, as well as music for Countess Lodron and for the Haffner family wedding celebrations that summer, and he refers to visits to the Mozart family and walks taken with them.[1] Only some of the pages of Nannerl's diary, in which some of the entries are made by Wolfgang, survive; they cover, very patchily, the period from 1775 to 1780 and 1783. Most are simple reports of everyday events—marriages, deaths, music performed in the cathedral, visits to the hairdresser, arrivals and departures (among them the passage of an elephant through the city in May 1776). As far as letters are concerned, there are just two. Leopold wrote late in 1775 to the publisher Breitkopf, offering music by his son and asking for a list of works by C.P.E. Bach. No reply has survived, but Breitkopf did not publish any of Mozart's music. On 4 September 1776 Mozart (ostensibly—the handwriting is his father's, the signature his) wrote the letter to Padre Martini already alluded to. Martini replied at the end of the year, with a request for portraits of Mozart and Leopold. Leopold had Wolfgang painted by a local artist during 1777, a rather sombre representation of him in black, wearing his Order of the Golden Spur (see illustration on the facing page), and sent the portrait to Martini in Bologna late in 1777.[2]

The September letter is the one in which Mozart referred to the need to write short mass settings because of the time restrictions in Salzburg. In it he mentions that his father's service at the cathedral 'gives me an opportunity to write as much church music as I like'. Six settings belong to these months: K.220/196*b*, K.262/246*a*, K.257, K.258, K.259 and K.275/272*b*. All but the last are in C major, the key Mozart was evidently obliged to use for Salzburg Cathedral settings that included parts for trumpets, no doubt because of the type of instrument played by the archbishop's trumpeters. All his Salzburg masses with trumpets, but only those, are in C.

Not all are short masses. One of them, possibly the earliest, K.262, is in fact among Mozart's longest settings. Evidence based on the paper he used suggests that it was composed in the early summer of 1775.[3] The festive nature of this *missa longa*, with oboes and horns as well as trumpets, is unmistakable. The Kyrie, after a flourish from 'rushing violins', begins as an ebullient double fugue with a striding main theme. It is, however, an orthodox sonata-ritornello movement, with the 'Christe eleison' (sung by the soloists) as its secondary material and with graceful motivic work for the violins running through it. The words of the Gloria are shared between choir and soloists. Its spirited mood is interrupted for a minor-key Andante at 'Qui tollis peccata mundi', briefly recapitulating at the 'Quoniam', and the movement ends with a triple fugue, fully developed with ingenious strettos. Although each of the six parts of the mass is set in a single continuous movement in all six of these works, the Credo here is exceptional in its sectional structure. After the usual change of tempo for the 'Et incarnatus' and 'Crucifixus' (here Adagio ma non troppo), there is a brief, vigorous 'Resurrexit' and a lyrical G major section for 'Et in spiritum sanctum'. The opening music is then briefly recapitulated, and the movement ends with what is in effect a sixth section, a closely argued 'Et vitam venturi' fugue of 124 bars, with an elabo-

Mozart wearing the Order of the Golden Spur: anonymous oil painting, 1777 (*Civico Museo Bibliografico Musicale, Bologna*)

rate series of progressively more complex strettos. Another exceptional feature is a Benedictus in which the choir's Hosannas are heard throughout as a background to the soloists' 'Benedictus qui venit'. This is a mass setting designed to make a strong and original impression. Some scholars have conjectured that its scale indicates composition for a special occasion presided over by the archbishop, others that it must have been intended for a different celebrant, since the archbishop would countenance only short settings, and still others that it may have been written for St Peter's rather than the cathedral. It has to be a serious candidate for consideration as the new Mozart mass given in the cathedral, with the archbishop as celebrant, on Easter Sunday 1776 (7 April), as reported by Schiedenhofen,[4] although that casts doubt on the dating to the previous summer.

By contrast, K.220—impossible to date with any precision, with the autograph lost and no evidence of the date of any performance—reverts to the modest scale of K.192 and 194 and is considerably shorter than either of them. The work is known as the *Spatzenmesse* ('Sparrow Mass') because of the violins' repeated chirping acciaccatura figure in the Sanctus. The text is economically set, with dialogue (sometimes overlapping) among the soloists to expedite its delivery, and the Credo, characterized by its busy violin writing, has a mere ten-bar Andante interlude for 'Et incarnatus' and 'Crucifixus'. There are no final fugues in the Gloria or Credo. As in K.262 the Kyrie is a miniature sonata-form movement, without development, in just 38 bars; its material is re-used for the end of the mass, the 'Dona nobis pacem', a procedure Mozart had not followed before.[5]

The autograph scores of the three masses K.257, 258 and 259 were all dated by Leopold, but as with several other autographs of these years the dates have been tampered with and cannot be trusted. As they now stand, K.257 shows November 1776, 258 and 259 December 1776. The months are not in question, but the last figure of the year, the 6, has been heavily written over. Paper studies show that K.258 includes sheets of a paper-type used otherwise only in the K.219 violin concerto and an aria, K.217, both of which belong to the end of 1775, and sketches for K.257 are found on a sheet bearing sketches from another aria, K.256, of September 1775. This does not irrefutably prove that the two masses belong to that year, but it is overwhelmingly probable that they do. The paper used for K.259 is also found in several works over a longer period, so paper studies offer no help in determining its date.

The three masses are all of the *missa brevis* type, but their inclusion of trumpets (K.257 also requires oboes) brings them into the category sometimes called *missa brevis et solemnis*. When Mozart told Padre Martini in his letter that 'special study' was needed for this style of composition, he may have meant that he had developed a method of setting the liturgical text that gave it due weight and allowed him adequate scope for its expression, without infringing the severe time limitation prescribed in Salzburg. He achieved this with careful handling of musical forms and judicious distribution of the text between soloists and choir. Most of the Kyries, for example, follow the miniature 'sonata-form' pattern already noted in K.220, that is, with a gesture towards a tonic appearance of material first heard in the dominant; usually this is the setting of 'Christe eleison', for the soloists, with a choral 'Kyrie eleison'. In the Gloria, the soloists normally take over at 'Laudamus te' or 'Domine Deus' or both, with the chorus returning for collective statements, for example at 'Qui tollis', and there is generally a sense of recapitulation at 'Quoniam' (or in K.259 at 'Cum Sancto Spiritu'). In each mass the Credo begins as a vigorous choral affirmation, followed by an 'Et incarnatus' in slower tempo for the soloists, in a minor key (or the subdominant), with the choir re-entering at 'Crucifixus' and the fast tempo resuming at 'Et resurrexit', often again with a semblance or reality of recapitulation. The traditional concluding fugues of the Gloria and Credo are absent, but Mozart often includes some kind of contrapuntal passage at or near these points, supplying a little extra weight to round off a lengthy section. The Sanctus settings are, of course, firmly choral, the Benedictus settings usually lyrical in style and for solo voices. There is regular use of word-painting: 'resurrexit' customarily has a rising phrase, but more particularly such phrases as 'miserere nobis' use a minor key and chromatic harmony. There is, in the usual Austrian way, much lively violin writing in the quick movements, not simply passages of rapid notes but often a repeated figure that lends unity and continuity to a section. As in K.262, Mozart sometimes recalls the opening of a work at the end, not directly but with a clear allusion— in K.257 an echo, partial and inexact yet unmistakable, of the Kyrie appears at 'Dona nobis pacem', and a clear reminiscence (though in a different metre) at the equivalent point in K.259.

Each of the three masses has other particular points of interest. K.257 is sometimes known as the 'Credo' mass because throughout that section the word 'Credo' is reiterated, to a brief motif, lending the music force and unity; the procedure is similar to that in K.192, but rather differently executed. K.257, its larger scale implied by the solemn, Andante maestoso introduction to the Kyrie, is substantially the longest of the three. In K.258 there are unusual antiphonal exchanges between soloists and choir in the Benedictus. This is sometimes known as the Spaur mass: Leopold refers in a letter[6] to the mass Mozart wrote for the consecration of Count Ignaz Joseph von Spaur, late in 1776, as administrator of Brixen diocese and titular Bishop of Chrysopel, but there is no evidence that this was the work referred to. K.259, the shortest of the three and known as the 'Organ solo' mass because of the obbligato for the organ in the Benedictus, has other imaginative touches of scoring, notably the use of pizzicato second violins and basses, with oboes, in the Agnus Dei. None of these masses, following the Salzburg tradition, has a part for violas, and probably the bass part was assigned only to double-basses, without cellos. In all of them the presence of three trombones, alto, tenor and bass, supporting those voices in the choir, is taken for granted.

A pendant to the series is the *Missa brevis* K.275/272b, in B flat, which, without trumpets or other wind, is in a more intimate style, recalling older Salzburg traditions. Here the Benedictus is a gracefully written solo for soprano, and there are no final fugues to the Gloria or the Credo (though there is a gesture towards counterpoint in the Gloria). The work is, however, oddly proportioned, with the Agnus Dei by far the longest movement with a prolonged setting for soloists and choir of 'Dona nobis pacem', ending *piano*. The autograph is lost and the date of composition uncertain, but we know that the work was performed, possibly for the first time, on 21 December 1777, in which 'the castrato sang excellently', presumably in the Benedictus (this was Francesco Ceccarelli, then new to the Salzburg Kapelle).[7]

The epistle sonatas were, of course, adjuncts to the mass settings, and it is tempting to try to work out which ones belong with which settings, if such associations exist. We saw (p. 349) that there is good reason to think that K.144 and 145 may be linked with the masses K.192 and 194. Seven sonatas—K.212 in B flat, 241 in G, 244 in F, 245 in D, 263 in C, 274 in G and 278 in C—belong to the years of the six masses; three of them (K.212, 241 and 263) are written on the papers that Mozart predominantly used for the masses (and many other works), and two (K.274 and 278) on a paper used for K.257. But the keys do not tally as one might expect them to. The B flat sonata is dated July 1775, probably two years earlier than the B flat mass, although the date of the mass is only a *terminus ante quem* and it could have been written two years earlier. Two of the sonatas, K.263 and 278, are in C; more then half of the epistle sonatas are for strings and continuo organ only, but K.263 calls for trumpets and timpani and has a solo organ part, while K.278 requires trumpets and oboes. This might suggest a link between K.263, written late in 1776, and the 'Organ solo' mass K.259, probably of similar date. The autograph of K.278, one of the longest and most ceremonial in manner of the sonatas, could in the same way be associated with any of the masses; Mozart headed this work 'Sonata pro festis palii'—for one of the high church festivals—and its composition date of March–April 1777 suggests Easter. There is, however, no simple one-to-one relationship between the epistle sonatas and the masses: the sonatas were indeed often intended for use in mass settings other than Mozart's own.

Mozart did not allow the constraints of the form to shackle his invention unduly. In K.212 he finds scope for some imitative writing and a brief development with lively contrapuntal dialogue. K.241 is a bustling little symphonic movement, with a development that takes up the rhythm of the secondary material in dramatic fashion. The next two sonatas are his first with obbligato organ, which in K.244 invites a hint of concerto procedures as the organ echoes the opening theme, and there are some moments of dialogue, although generally the organ is used in both sonatas and in K.263 for colour, sustained notes and reinforcement. The organ reverts to a continuo role in the playful and spirited K.274, and in the much grander and more formal K.278. This sonata is the only one of this group in a rounded binary form, as the arresting nature of the opening almost predicates, and in fact the opening figure is heard again only in the final five bars, as a rhetorical gesture rather than a reversed recapitulation.

Three smaller liturgical works probably come from these years.

One is the 'offertorium de venerabili sacramento' *Venite, populi* K.260/248*a*, dated 1776 and generally believed to have been composed for Ascension Day, a vigorous setting for double choir. The two groups are often in opposition, and if sung from the spaced galleries in Salzburg Cathedral the piece would make a fine effect, with its interwoven strands of four-part counterpoint and its dramatic antiphonal writing. Its first modern edition was prepared by Brahms, who conducted a performance in Vienna in 1872. An *Alma Dei creatoris* K.277/272*a* was probably composed in the summer of 1777. Mozart's autograph is lost, but a copy survives in Salzburg with his annotations, and this seems likely to be the work that Leopold referred to in a letter as an *Alma redemptoris mater* in F, a Marian offertory just performed in Salzburg. It is in an antiphonal style, with the choir responding to each line of text sung by the soprano or alto—a graceful and neatly constructed piece on a sonata-form pattern, if harmonically unadventurous for Mozart. Similar in mood, but altogether more personal in cast, is a Marian gradual, *Sancta Maria, mater Dei* K.273, dated 9 September 1777, two weeks before Mozart's departure. It has often been suggested that the piece was a votive offering. It was not, however, intended for use in the cathedral: it calls for violas, rarely used there, and is a straightforward choral setting without soloists, who in cathedral works were normally given a voice. The original performing parts, dated 1777, are at St Peter's, which must be taken to indicate that it was written for use there. It is tempting to see this appealing piece—perhaps in two senses—as representing something more personal than most of the Salzburg liturgical music.

There is one further substantial sacred work of these years, the *Litaniae de venerabili altaris sacramento* K.243, written in March 1776, first given on Palm Sunday, 31 March, and repeated at the Mirabell Palace on Ascension Day, 23 May.[8] Mozart had set this text before, in his K.125, which was closely modelled on a setting of his father's. K.243, altogether more original, is a virtual compendium of Salzburg church styles of the time. The text for the veneration of the sacrament is a long one, interspersed repeatedly with pleas of 'miserere nobis', and makes a work in ten movements, some of them linked and performed without breaks. It is set with oboes (doubling flutes), bassoons and horns as well as the usual trombones and strings—exceptionally, with divided violas.

Some of the choruses are of a quite conventional cast, for example the reflective opening 'Kyrie' and the closing 'Miserere', which use the same material. But others broach new territory for Mozart, notably the group beginning with the 'Verbum caro factum', a sombre G minor movement with chromatic writing and restless violin figuration, continuing with the 'Hostia sancta', with its forceful choral exclamations and its expressively pleading cries of 'miserere nobis', and finally the 'Tremendum', with its representation of terror that would not seem out of place in the Verdi Requiem. The 'Viaticum' also breaks new ground, with the choral sopranos singing a line of plainsong against a soft orchestral texture of sustaining wind and violas, with pizzicato violins and basses. The choral climax however is the extended fugue, 'Pignus futurae gloriae'. Mozart's setting of this text in K.125 had also been a full-blown fugue, on a lengthy, nine-bar subject (the Mozarts later cut 50 of its 230 bars). The new one is shorter but more elaborate and more dramatic in conception. The fugue's progress is constantly interrupted by outbursts of 'miserere nobis', set in double counterpoint that works in conjunction with the fugue subject. Soon a second fugue subject is added, and the two worked together and jointly in stretto. This is no mere exercise in technique but music whose shifting patterns and dramatic effects are designed, successfully, to intrigue the ear and impress the senses. Of the three aria-like movements, the tenor 'Panis vivus' has much the manner of a heroic opera aria; Mozart remembered its opening 15 years later when writing the 'Tuba mirum' of his Requiem. All three have demanding *fioritura* writing. The others are for soprano—a 'Dulcissimum convivium', gracefully set as an Andantino with flutes, bassoons and muted strings, and an exquisitely scored 'Agnus Dei' with obbligato parts for oboe, flute and (exceptionally) cello. Clearly this

Salzburg Cathedral interior, showing the four raised galleries used by the musicians: engraving by M. Küsell, *c1680* (*Museum Carolino Augusteum, Salzburg*)

work drew a special effort from Mozart, and it makes a fitting climax to his middle-period Salzburg liturgical music. In 1777 he suggested that Leopold should send a copy to their friends at the Heiligkreuz monastery in Augsburg, and it was performed there the following May. It was also given in Salzburg at Easter 1778.

HIS LITURGICAL MUSIC represents Mozart's principal contribution to court musical activities in these years, but not his only one. Another was a group of wind divertimentos, for pairs of oboes, bassoons and horns, which seems likely to have been intended for the archbishop's diversion—not, probably, for his concerts, where strings were used and the tone was more serious, but as background music or *Tafelmusik*, to accompany his meals. It was long thought that there were six of these, a conventional number for a set of works, but the lack of an authentic source for K.289/271*g*, as well as the marked lack of an authentic tone to the music itself, has led to the expulsion of that work from the canon.

These slight but fetching pieces, neatly and wittily written, were composed between the summer of 1775 and the beginning of 1777. Most have sonata-form opening movements. K.252/240*a* however opens with an Andante, followed by a minuet and then a polonaise with a charming swing to its rhythms before the Presto finale— where the horns are sent up to their top register in the coda. K.253 is the only one in three movements: it begins with a set of variations, ingeniously written to exploit the ensemble's textural possibilities, and includes an Adagio (as usual the penultimate variation), so making a separate slow movement inappropriate. Here the minuet, with a *ländlerisch* trio, follows. Giving the horns something showy to play towards the end is one of Mozart's favourite pranks: he does it too in the last two movements of K.213, of which the finale is a *contredanse en rondeau*. In the B flat divertimentos, K.240 and 270, where the horns are high-pitched and execution is difficult and strenuous, he is more careful, leaving them to vitalize the tuttis with their ring. K.240

begins and ends with sonata-form movements (the first of them again saves the opening bars, though not the main part of the principal material, for a final gesture—a unique compromise), and its minuet entertainingly exploits a dotted figure within the accompanying texture. K.270 is on a different scale from the others, with first-movement themes of a symphonic character, a more serious if brief development and a neatly extended codetta. The gavotte-style Andantino, another *ländler*-style trio to the minuet and a busily scurrying Presto finale elevate this piece beyond its supper-music function.

These divertimentos and a single serenade probably represent Mozart's only contributions to the court instrumental music during the period 1775–7. The serenade, K.204/213*a*, is the Finalmusik of 1775. Mozart completed it on 5 August. Schiedenhofen reported four days later: 'After dinner to the Finalmusik, which Mr Mozart had composed. I went first to the Mirabell, then the University . . . met the Barisanis, the Loeses and the Robinigs', and again, two weeks later: 'After dinner to the Finalmusik, which was by Mozart. There I saw the Robinigs, Barisanis, Daubrawas and Mozarts'. There is no reason to doubt that K.204 in D was the work given, on all three occasions, or perhaps four. It follows much the same pattern as K.203, also in D. It is in seven movements with the usual march (K.215/213*b*), and a three-movement violin concerto follows the first 'symphony' movement. Here the concerto is in A, marking it off much less sharply from the rest of the work than in K.203, where it was in B flat. It is notable for the eloquent and high-lying solo violin part, as much in the Allegro as in the Andante. Among other features are a slow movement with prominent solo writing for the flute, oboe and bassoon, a trio to the minuet in which the second flute is singled out as soloist, and a finale with a teasing Andantino introduction which recurs, briefly, three times within the finale. Mozart himself detached the 'symphony' movements from the 'concerto' ones, for separate use, and in 1783 asked his father to send them to Vienna along with several other symphonies (K.182, 183, 201 and 385). That gives some indication of his own valuation of the work.

Two other serenade-like works of this period might be imagined as happy choices for a summer evening's entertainment were it not that they were both composed in January, the *Serenata notturna* K.239 in 1776 and the *Notturno* K.286/269a in 1777. No performance of either is documented. But this was of course the time of carnival, and it is not hard to imagine that these works, both embodying comic elements, might have been intended for an associated event. We know from Schiedenhofen that the Mozarts played a part in such events in 1776.[9] The title 'notturno', or 'Nachtmusik', implied an entertainment work, generally of a relaxed character and suitable for outdoor performance, bearing no relation to the later, Romantic nocturne. The *Serenata notturna* resembles in its instrumentation—though not in its form or content—the Baroque concerto grosso, with a 'concertino' of two violins, viola and violone (as Mozart wrote, or double-bass) set against a 'ripieno' of two violins, violas and cellos, with timpani. The gruffly supported solo group in contrast with the tutti, reinforced by timpani, gives the work an entirely individual and uniquely evocative sound. Usually the tutti strings, when playing, double the solo, but occasionally Mozart enriches the sound by having them an octave apart. The piece consists simply of a march, a minuet and a rondo finale. Both the march and the main part of the minuet, in regular two- and four-bar phrases, depend almost wholly on statement by the soloists and response by the 'ripieno' or a tutti. Mozart's invention is carefully designed in short phrases of a question-and-answer kind, or perhaps more like a conversation in which one group caps what the other suggests. The finale exploits the ensemble's sonorous possibilities a little further. It is a simple ternary movement, with an opening section, then a brief, mock-dramatic, recitative-like Adagio for the solo group, and a middle section (mainly in the subdominant), which leads back to a full reprise and a coda, with middle-section material now in the tonic. Curiously, it begins Allegretto, but the middle section is marked Allegro, and that is never contradicted: did Mozart intend the reprise to be faster, or the tempo to adjust itself, or was it an oversight?

The other *Notturno*, a year later, is also an experimental piece. It is composed for four orchestras, each of two violins, viola and bass, with two horns. Mozart labelled the second, third and fourth orchestras 'l'echo 1mo', 'l'echo 2do' and 'l'echo 3o': the work is in fact a study in echoes, heard at a variety of decreasing time-lapses. Thus the opening four-bar phrase of the first movement is repeated three bars later by the second group, its final two bars are repeated two bars later by the third group, and its final bar one bar later by the fourth. The pattern is constantly shifting, and although the actual invention is cliché, and of necessity very limited in harmonic variety because of the overlaps, the effect is charming, as long as the music is heard either from different angles or at different distances. This means that the third group rarely play more than two bars, or the fourth more than one, at a time. The final movement, a minuet, is artfully contrived to allow some of the echoes to fall at different parts of the bar. Only in the trio is the echo principle abandoned; Mozart will surely have felt that it had been taken far enough.

Another, smaller 'Nachtmusik' dates from these years. That was the term used by Nannerl Mozart in a letter written in 1800 to Breitkopf & Härtel in the course of correspondence about her brother's *Nach-lass*. 'I have a very small Nachtmusick set for two violins and bass, but this is a very simple composition which he made in his early years, so I would venture that it is not such as I should send, as it seems to me too unimportant'.[10] This is the Trio in B flat K.266/271f. She no doubt called it 'Nachtmusik' because it followed the common *galant* two-movement form (slow–minuet or slow–rondo) of the trio-sonata *notturno*, as used by J.C. Bach and others of his generation. It is a strange piece, unadventurous in invention and conservative in style (the equality of interest between the two violin parts recalls the trio-sonata tradition), and composed at an elementary technical level as compared with Mozart's other music of the time, but the date of early 1777 is borne out by the handwriting and the paper-type. There must be some explanation of why he should have written this piece, in a manner closer to his father's style than his own.

'Nachtmusik' was the term often applied in Mozart's circle to the large-scale divertimentos he wrote in 1776 and 1777 for Countess Lodron. Maria Antonia Lodron, daughter of the Oberstkämmerer Count Arco, was the wife of Count Ernst Maria Lodron (known privately among the Mozarts as Count Potbelly), who held the position of Erbmarschall or hereditary Oberst-Landmarschall. She was an influential member of the old Salzburg nobility—there were former archbishops in both his and her families—and she was close to the present archbishop. Their Primogenitur Palace lay on the northern side of the Hannibal-Platz, very close to the Mozarts' house. To judge by a remark in one of Leopold's letters,[11] the Mozarts did not like or trust her, but her goodwill was important. Later her daughters were pupils of the Mozarts. Her nameday, St Antony, fell on 13 June and needed to be celebrated musically within the 'Octave' or week following. For the 1776 and 1777 events Mozart wrote two of his finest divertimentos. These will have been played beneath her window, by a band organized by the Mozarts, and probably with Wolfgang playing the first violin. We know, from an account in a later letter of Leopold's describing the farcical failure of an attempt to serenade her in 1778 (when Wolfgang was away), what the procedure and the protocol were on such occasions.[12]

The two works are K.247 in F, with its attendant march K.248, and K.287/271b/271H. Both are set for two violins, viola and bass, with two horns (in the Salzburg tradition 'basso' here means double-bass and no cello—Mozart's heading for K.247, 'Divertimento à 6 strom:', and the static style of the bass part bear this out). There is good reason to think that when he had first embarked on a divertimento he had in mind a work for only one violin, with viola, bass and horns: that is the instrumentation of a 77-bar draft, in F, K.288/271h/246e. The music has limited melodic interest and seems structurally unpromising, as well as thin in texture, but Mozart re-used a phrase from it in

One of the Lodron palaces in Salzburg (on the right): watercolour by
H. Sattler, 1833 (*Museum Carolino Augusteum, Salzburg*)

K.247 (first movement, bars 20–24), a sure indicator that he had by
then abandoned it. K.247 is decidedly a divertimento for violin with
accompaniment—high-spirited, carefree music with an abundance of
fluent melody and fanciful flights into the violin's topmost register as
its points of climax. In the first movement Mozart uses his new

device of a recapitulation that begins part-way through the primary material, reserving the arresting opening statement for a flourish in the closing bars. There are two slow movements and two minuets, the first slow movement a brief and graceful rondo, the second a tender, flowing Adagio in sonata form where the violin's additional embellishment in the recapitulation heightens the expression. The lengthy finale—the trend towards assigning greater weight to finales is already noticeable—is a kind of double sonata-rondo, with an extra central episode, yet this is perhaps the most sophisticatedly witty movement of Mozart's to date. If his feelings towards Countess Lodron were ambiguous he certainly managed to conceal them here.

He did so again a year later in the 'Zweite Lodronische Nachtmusik' K.287. This follows exactly the same pattern, down to the formal quirk in the first movement—here the effect of the recapitulation being in progress without ever having announced its arrival is particularly marked. Again, the first violin part is of a strongly concertante character. The first of the slow movements is an elaborately worked set of variations, the second a heartfelt Adagio with inner accompanying parts (for muted violin and viola) of a true chamber-music richness of detail. The finale of K.247 has a brief, straightforward slow introduction; here the introduction takes the form of a pseudo-recitative, and it recurs before the final appearance of the main theme of the sonata-rondo (which is said to be based on an Austrian folktune). Mozart set considerable store by these two works and took them with him on his travels in 1777–8. He reported to his father on performances in Munich, where 'I played as though I were the finest fiddler in the whole of Europe' (which encourages the supposition that he had played them himself in the Salzburg performances). Later, in 1781, he asked for them to be sent to Vienna. In 1778 one or both were given twice by Kolb in Salzburg.[13]

Between these two, in July 1776, Mozart composed two other substantial works of a similar kind. One is the divertimento in D K.251. It has long been thought that he composed it in honour of Nannerl's nameday, 26 July, although it seems strange, however great his brotherly devotion, that he should have exercised himself professionally to such an extent for a domestic celebration (and there is no record of his having done so for any other relative on any other occasion). However, in 1778, when he was in Paris, he wrote in his gratulatory letter to Nannerl: 'I am sorry not to be able to send you a present of a musical composition, such as I did a few years ago'.[14] We can only conjecture as to whether such a present would have been a full-scale divertimento, but we know of no other likely purpose for this work. It was not a Finalmusik: works by the local composer Joseph Hafeneder and by Joseph Haydn were given that year, according to Schiedenhofen.[15] But Schiedenhofen records no such event as a musical performance for Nannerl, as he would surely have done, and as indeed he did the following year when Mozart organized a concert in her honour—which could have been the occasion referred to in his letter from Paris.

K.251 is rather shorter and less demonstrative than the Lodron divertimento. Although the work was clearly intended for solo performance, the first violin part is here fully integrated into the string texture, which at times has an orchestral character with tremolandos, accompanying figuration and use of the oboe (which has few solos). The work is also much less generous in its musical material: as compared with the plethora of themes in K.247 and 287, the first movement here is monothematic, its secondary theme a transposition of the principal one, worked with a touch of contrapuntal repartee, and its rhythm and shape provide the source of the entire movement's material. The development is more purposeful and symphonic, for in the violin-dominated works the needs of the solo line, as in a concerto, tend to dictate the patterns and argue against textural interplay. There is a minuet, an Andantino and—instead of both a minuet and a set of variations—a second minuet, which itself has three simple melodic variations and a *da capo*. Again the finale is an extended sonata-rondo, and its final episode (which recurs within the return of the secondary material) is of popular character, giving an impression of a theme quoted allusively. A 'Marcia alla francese' is part of the work, presumably intended to preface it and conclude it.

This work was written immediately after another large-scale summer serenade, not a Finalmusik but an equally large-scale work, composed to a commission from the younger Sigmund Haffner 'per la sposalizio del Sigr. Spath colla Sig^ra: Elisabetta Haffner', to quote Leopold's heading to the score. The marriage of Marie Elisabeth Haffner, daughter of the elder Sigmund (a prominent merchant in Salzburg and a former mayor), to Franz Xaver Späth, took place on 22 July. The serenade was given the previous evening in the summer-house in their garden in the Paris-Lodrongasse, near the Loreto church, close to the Mozarts' house.

No-one could wish for a more splendid wedding present nor more lasting a memorial, for in his Haffner Serenade in D K.250/248*b* Mozart truly excelled himself and carried the Salzburg serenading tradition into a new creative realm. After a more than usually lively, even perky march, the introduction, Allegro maestoso, is not a conventional slow introduction but effectively a 35-bar fanfare—clearly a statement to establish the grandeur of the occasion. At the same time it prefigures the main thematic idea of the movement. The Allegro is largely based on busy unison passages and forceful tutti writing, with a little flourish from the introduction as the chief idea in the development. It is hard to understand how a movement of such nobility can be built of material of no real distinction or individuality. Following the standard Finalmusik pattern, as the one that Salzburg audiences would recognize for a festal occasion, the second, third and fourth movements form the violin concerto, in G. Here it takes a rather different pattern from the one Mozart used in the 1773–5 Finalmusiken. First is an Andante, in sonata form, then second a minuet—in a fiery G minor, with a G major trio for solo violin and flutes, bassoons and horns—and then a rondo. The 'Rondeau', as Mozart headed it, is an extended piece (455 bars), another sonata-rondo with an extra episode, with generous and constantly witty involvement of the effervescent and bewitching rondo theme in the episodic and linking material. The four-note figure of that theme corresponds, by design, chance or subconscious connection, with the emphatic four-note figure reiterated by the violins in the *maestoso* introduction.

Then the 'symphony' resumes, with a movement headed 'Menuetto galante': Mozart's use of that adjective must refer to the particular swagger of its rhythms. The Andante that follows, in A major, and—aptly for a wedding serenade—with all the expressive sense of the traditional key for a love duet, has an unusually elaborate structure, basically sonata-rondo. But it is complicated first by the way Mozart treats the particularly alluring second part of the principal theme as a kind of refrain, reintroducing it several times quite unexpectedly; secondly by his division of the secondary theme into two, and recapitulating them separately and in opposite sequence; and thirdly by the way he playfully varies the principal theme on each recurrence. A third minuet follows, this one with two trios. The finale has an Adagio introduction, only 16 bars, but it is music of true gravity and nobility. It is as if Mozart felt a need to make some comment on the occasion that went beyond the splendour, the gaiety and the vivacity, a need we may recognize, for example, a decade hence in *Le nozze di Figaro*. But not for long—the exuberant yet closely argued gigue-finale, in sonata form and with both halves repeated, will have sent the Haffner guests home in high spirits.

Mozart later used the five orchestral movements as a symphony, with some significant changes. The first movement repeat was omitted, and a moment of silence at the end was filled in with a fanfare (silence in a concert hall would have invited premature applause). The trio of the Menuetto galante was rewritten, with the second violin switched from arpeggio figuration to repeated triplets (hinting at a faster tempo for concert performance), and new sustaining parts were added for flutes and bassoon. Further, he added a timpani part throughout the work. It is slightly surprising that he had not included timpani originally, as they are almost invariable companions of trumpets, and there was a spare staff in the score. Perhaps there was no room for them in the Haffner summer-house, or possibly a timpanist played from the trumpet part. Mozart played the 'Finalmusik with the Rondo' in Munich in September 1777, which surely refers to K.250 (using the term 'Finalmusik' out of habit). He directed an open-air performance in the Kollegien-Platz, near the university, in September 1779, and gave the symphony section the following March at the Salzburg theatre.[16]

Mozart's remaining instrumental works from this period nearly all involve the keyboard. His only true chamber music of these years is the Piano Trio in B flat K.254, dated August 1776. He himself headed it 'Divertimento à 3', and when it was published, in Paris shortly after his visit in 1778, it was as 'Divertimento pour le clavecin ou forte piano a compagnement violino è violoncello'. The choice of title is not significant; Mozart himself referred to it as a trio, and later he used the title 'terzett' for piano trios. Written in Salzburg, with its reported absence of pianos, it should perhaps be regarded as harpsichord music, but the generous sprinkling of dynamic markings throughout the keyboard part, as well as their placing, must indicate that he had in mind not the harpsichord but the piano. Conceivably one of his Salzburg patrons or friends owned a piano, unknown to us, or perhaps, though it seems improbable as early as summer 1776, he was thinking of using the trio on tour, as he indeed did in late 1777. It is not impossible that the dynamic indications were added later, although their close relation to the actual invention makes that seem unlikely.

The trio K.254 is primarily a keyboard work, very much in the manner of an accompanied sonata, with long stretches of music where the string parts are scarcely obbligato. The opening movement has the vigorous momentum characteristic of a 3/4 Allegro, with repeated notes and sharp accents, and is in clear-cut sonata form with a strongly argued development based on the primary themes. There is some interchange of material between piano and violin, but much more in the Adagio, where the sustained theme and its murmuring rapid-note accompaniment pass back and forth. The finely detailed writing here evidently baffled the violinist with whom Mozart played the work in Munich: 'indeed I had a fine accompaniment! I had to play his part for six bars'.[17] The finale is a graceful extended minuet headed 'Rondeau: Tempo di menuetto', a sonata-rondo in its shortest form (*A-B-A-C-B-A*), with the recapitulation beginning with the secondary material—analogous in its relation to the fuller form with rounded binary to sonata.

Mozart's second piano concerto, K.238 in B flat, dates from the beginning of 1776. He wrote it, apparently, for himself rather than a patron. It represents a considerable advance on its predecessor of 1773, K.175, in its management of the solo-tutti relationship, especially in the sharing of material and the handling of accompanying textures, the integration of bravura passages into the fabric of the work, and in its thematic character, although it still lacks an individual thematic profile of the kind that Mozart had developed in his last three violin concertos, K.216, 218 and 219. The essentials of the later concerto first-movement form are there, too, although the soloist's additional secondary idea has no more than a transitional character. The main secondary theme, a kind of rhythmic dialogue, has a curious consequent, which gives the impression of going melodically into reverse: the notes are echoed backwards in altered rhythm. The Andante un poco adagio, a sonata-form movement with no development section, has flutes replacing oboes and the violins muted. Here the interchange between tutti and solo takes on the character of dialogue in which the soloist is spurred on by the orchestra to greater depths and increasing elaboration. The finale is a full-scale sonata-rondo with episodes of some brilliance. There are no dynamic indications in the keyboard part in the first two movements, but the rondo has passages with rapid alternations of *piano* and *forte*. Although in Salzburg Mozart can only have played the work on the harpsichord, he must also have had in mind the possibilities that the new fortepiano would offer, to the extent that, as in K.254, they affected the actual musical invention. He wrote out cadenzas for all three movements, which survive separately from the autograph; only the one for the Andante refers thematically to the movement it belongs to. The existence of separate cadenzas implies that someone other than Mozart performed the concerto (he would expect to improvise them afresh at any performance), most probably Nannerl or a pupil. He must surely have played it in Salzburg himself. It is one of the works he gave several times during his travels in 1777–8, but there is no record of his playing it in Vienna.

Another solo concerto, K.246 in C, followed in April 1776. It was written for Countess Antonie von Lützow, a niece of the archbishop, sister of Count Czernin and wife of the Commandant of the old Salzburg fortress on the hill (Hohensalzburg) overlooking the city. The solo part, intended for an amateur, is accordingly considerably easier than that of K.238, with limited bravura writing and the left hand rarely assigned anything more than Alberti bass patterns, and the relationship between soloist and orchestra is generally simpler and less subtly managed. In its form, the first movement closely follows the pattern seen in K.238, but the actual musical ideas are direct, even commonplace, and while the Andante, a sonata-form movement with a melodic interlude in place of development, shows a melodic line of some refinement, its charm is essentially superficial. The finale is a sonata-rondo in minuet rhythm. No other work of Mozart's touches the lightweight, *galant* manner of the time quite so closely as K.246. The Mozarts, however, valued the work: Wolfgang performed it on tour, along with K.238, and he and Nannerl used it as a teaching piece for their pupils. This use of the work is reflected in the survival, uniquely, of a continuo realization in Mozart's own hand for the solo pianist in the tutti sections—an invaluable guide as to what he expected to be played, at least by a beginner—and of three pairs of cadenzas, for the first two movements, again all in Mozart's own hand. One set (listed as 'A' in the NMA), jotted down on empty staves in the solo part of a set of a copyist's performing material in a Salzburg library and no doubt originally used locally in Salzburg, are no more than brief flourishes, clearly intended for a soloist of fairly

modest pretension. Another pair ('B'), written out together on a separate, larger sheet probably just after the concerto was composed, are
again little more than flourishes but slightly longer; these were also
copied out by Leopold, which implies that they were originally
regarded as belonging with the work. The third set ('C'), written on
a paper-type that Mozart used only from 1779, are much longer and
incorporate thematic material from the movements: these, if the most
interesting, might be thought disproportionate to the concerto.

Between K.238 and K.246, in February 1776, Mozart composed
another concerto, for three keyboards. It was written for Countess
Lodron and two of her daughters, Aloysia and Josepha, who were
respectively 15 and 11 and pupils of the Mozarts' colleague Adlgasser.
Mozart made due allowance in the keyboard parts. The countess is
entrusted with most of the main musical ideas, on their first appearance, and the most demanding of the bravura writing, but Aloysia's
part is almost on the same level. Josepha is allowed her moments,
most of them in the first movement, but generally her role is much
simpler, and in the ensemble writing the third instrument chiefly adds
fullness and sometimes an extra glitter to the textures. Mozart's chief
way of maintaining the interest here, and in late comparable works, is
to use themes that are susceptible, on repetition, to being turned in a
different direction, so that when the second soloist takes up an idea
just heard there is often a sense of discourse, even contradiction, or
capping a point just made—often with the assistance in a new counterpoint of the player who made it. With three soloists, that would
anyway lead to otiose repetition, and here the subsidiary role of the
third precludes that. But sometimes Mozart has the third player lead
off in a different direction after dialogue between the first two, as if
intervening in their discussion with a new thought—a typical example of how closely keyed is Mozart's invention to the medium for
which he is composing. The formal pattern followed in the first
movement of K.238 serves again here, with the development section,
though quite brief, happily managed for its climax of textural complexity, which is echoed in the cadenza (fully composed, of course,

not left for improvisation *a 3*). The Adagio takes the same formal pattern but here the secondary solo theme is more clearly defined, playing a structural role rather than merely serving as transitional material. Bearing in mind the limitations of the medium and the social purpose of the work, the strongly expressive character of this movement, with its melodic warmth, its chromaticisms and its textural richness and originality, is remarkable. The graceful and tuneful minuet-rondo finale is a sonata-rondo; there is an improvisatory 'lead-in' (or *Eingang*) each for the first and second soloist, and finally one for the two of them an octave apart.

Concertos for three keyboard instruments are not the kind of work one can expect to perform very often. Mozart gave at least two performances outside Salzburg in the ensuing years, playing with the piano manufacturer J.A. Stein and the local organist in Augsburg in 1777 and organizing a performance by three young ladies in Mannheim the following spring.[18] The first of these, and probably both, will have been on fortepianos. Countess Lodron had only harpsichords, yet Mozart's autograph score includes frequent dynamic indications, among them 'cresc.', which could not be executed on the instrument. Here at least he must have been thinking ahead towards later use of the work. In about 1779 he opened up more opportunities for its performance by arranging the solo music for just two instruments, which, considering the nature of the third part, presented no difficulties and involved little more than the transfer to one of the other parts anything that was essential in the third. In this more useful form he probably played it in Salzburg and he later had Leopold send it to him in Vienna, though it is not known whether he performed it there.

THESE KEYBOARD CONCERTOS are accomplished music, by any standard, yet in comparison with the last three violin concertos, the Lodron divertimentos and the Haffner Serenade, and indeed the finest of the symphonies of 1773–4, they seem like prentice works, lacking the easy command of the idiom that allowed Mozart the individuality of voice that in those other pieces is so very much more apparent. There are perhaps hints of it in the slow movement of K.238. It seems as if he needed the experience of wrestling with a genre before he had full mastery of it, which perhaps is unsurprising, but the non-simultaneity of his maturing is marked at this period.

Before he left Salzburg in the autumn of 1777, however, Mozart had taken a large further step with the piano concerto. In January that year, the month of his twenty-first birthday, he composed K.271 in E flat, the so-called 'Jeunehomme Concerto', supposedly written for a French pianist of that name. No 'Mlle Jeunehomme' ever existed; she was invented—and described, absurdly, as 'une des plus célèbres virtuoses du temps'—by Mozart's French biographers Wyzewa and Saint-Foix, as their interpretation of Wolfgang's references to 'Jenomy' or 'Jenomè' and Leopold's to 'Genomai'.[19] The pianist for whom the concerto was written was correctly identified only in 2005, as Louise Victoire Jenamy (daughter of the distinguished French choreographer and dancer Jean-Georges Noverre), who in 1774 had married Joseph Jenamy, a member of an old mercantile family from Savoy.[20] The Mozarts had become acquainted with Noverre in Vienna in 1773 and may have met her then.[21] Was her pianism, or her personality, a particular stimulant to Mozart? or is it simply that he had reached a stage of maturity in relation to the piano concerto that merely needed a pretext for its expression?

Whatever the case, this concerto, beyond dispute his greatest work to date, establishes the style and manner of the piano concertos to come. It starts with an unorthodox stroke, a fanfare-like theme from the orchestra, to which the soloist responds with an answering phrase. This early entry does not of itself affect the actual form of the movement, but it does, first, establish very strongly the concept of dialogue between soloist and orchestra. It sets a precedent of exchanging material, which Mozart pursues in the piano's similar interruptions to later orchestral ritornellos, where the piano makes free with the orchestra's music, and it gives an opportunity for a witty swap at the recapitulation, where the piano plays the fanfare phrase, the orchestra the response—and the piano goes on to further development arising from the orchestra's phrase. Equally significant is Mozart's handling of the ritornello material here. As usual, the main secondary theme—in fact, a linked pair of themes—is heard from the orchestra in the opening ritornello, but the tutti passages around it are sharply defined, in their material and their function, and they are designed as 'open-ended' or modular—that is, they can be fitted to other themes and fulfil a similar formal function.

The piano's main entry, after the opening ritornello, breaks new ground too. Analogous to a singer's entry on a long note, in a *messa di voce* or a long crescendo—a time-honoured expressive device—the piano's entry is on a long trill, which steals upon the ear as the orchestra fades away. The soloist is left with a shy, tentative new phrase before the orchestra returns with the fanfare of the opening, and the soloist now pursues a response into bravura and modulation. The interchange of material continues as the piano takes up the second limb of the secondary theme, heard first with a string accompaniment figure (of a marked character), then taken up by the oboe as the piano moves briefly into accompaniment before carrying the theme and the musical argument forward. The sequence of events in the development begins with the piano's assuming ownership of another of the figures from the opening ritornello, and then moving on, with another 'tentative' phrase, to develop the primary theme—development that continues into the recapitulation, as we have seen. Even in the closing ritornello, after the cadenza, the piano intervenes, with a long trill as before; this time it leads to the soloist's final assertion, with a series of arpeggios, of his place in the scheme of things.

The Andantino—the term indicates a movement slower than an Andante—is even more remarkable, with its strong elegiac character established by the minor key, the dark opening for muted violins where the firsts and seconds are in close canon on their G string, the sombre octaves from oboes and horns, the rise and fall of the string phrases, the Neapolitan harmony and the subdued ending of the opening ritornello, akin to operatic recitative at a tragic moment. The dark violins' sonorities then turn out to be the accompaniment to a declaimed, dramatic melodic line from the piano. The pattern of interchange continues. The piano assumes a voice in the secondary material (heard in the opening ritornello), pursues it with a florid continuation, and takes over the recitative-like figure. The poignant character of the music is underlined further when, in the recapitulation, the music first stated in E flat major is reheard in C minor, so acquiring an increasingly tragic slant. And again, after the cadenza, the close is unorthodox: the cadenza ends with three bars of piano solo, the orchestra's Neapolitan harmony is forcefully recalled (the strings unmuted for these final bars), and the piano signs off with a version of the tragic 'recitative' phrases.

A substantial finale was clearly needed and, predictably, Mozart answered the need in a number of novel ways. Its basic pattern is the usual sonata-rondo one, with a main theme whose bustling piano figuration gives the effect of a scurrying 'moto perpetuo'. Almost the entire movement is run through with busy, restless piano texture. But the second episode is a courtly cantabile minuet, in two strains, each heard first on the piano and repeated with rich elaboration and a string accompaniment (outer strings pizzicato, inner ones muted). That is followed by a brief and almost atmospheric passage, for soft strings underlaid with a haze of rapid arpeggios from the piano, leading back to the recapitulation. Here Mozart found a way of bringing additional weight to the finale—almost analogous to the minuet and finale of a symphony—to counterbalance the earlier movements, as well as a way of breaking up what would otherwise have had to be too prolonged a fast movement. At any rate, the movement is remarkable equally for the new level of virtuosity that it demands and for the numerous bold, witty and adventurous routes along which it takes in its course.

As with K.246, alternative cadenzas survive: two sets for the first two movements and three lead-ins for the finale. The earlier cadenzas, written at the time the concerto was composed, are short—20 bars for the first movement, 12 for the second. The later set, written on a paper-type Mozart was using in 1784, the year of six of his Viennese piano concertos, are of respectively 32 and 26 bars and exploit more of the movements' thematic material. They show a different conception of the cadenza—no longer an extended flourish that may or may not incorporate material from the movement but rather a new and expressive development of the material. These later cadenzas are thus in a sense at odds with the rest of the work, extending its expressive character in a way that can seem inappropriate to its manner and its scale. The three sets of lead-ins for the finale show an analogous change. The earliest ('A' in the NMA), which survive only in copies by Leopold and Nannerl, are florid and brilliant passages of pianistic display, improvisatory in nature and unconnected thematically with the movement. The next set ('C'), written in 1783 and sent to Nannerl, are also simple flourishes but rather shorter and less demonstrative, and perhaps written for Nannerl as better suited to her style of playing.[22] The latest set ('B'), written at the same time as the second set of cadenzas, are both slightly longer and take material from the movement as their starting-point. The direction of Mozart's thinking about the concerto cadenza in the early-middle 1780s is clear.

The stride that Mozart had taken towards maturity between K.238 and 246 on the one hand, and K.271 on the other, is unmistakable. It may be seen too in his oboe concerto in C K.271k, composed in the spring or summer for the young Italian oboist Giuseppe Ferlendis, who joined the Salzburg Kapelle in April 1777 (and left in summer 1778). Structurally the oboe concerto follows quite closely the pattern of the violin concertos. But its conception in terms of the specific expressive and virtuoso capacities of the oboe are clear in the nature of its thematic material, which offers opportunities for crisp articulation and neat melodic shaping, and in the particular eloquence of the Adagio, with its chromatic lines and telling passages of dialogue with the violins. (The concerto is rather better known in its incarnation for flute, K.314: see Chapter 17.)

There is a parallel here in Mozart's secular vocal music. A visitor to

Salzburg during the summer of 1777 was the soprano Josepha Dusek (or Duschek, née Hambacher) from Prague, who had recently married the Czech composer F.X. Dusek. Her grandfather was the Salzburg merchant and until 1775 mayor of the city, Ignaz Anton von Weiser, author of the libretto of *Die Schuldigkeit des ersten Gebotes* and an old friend of the Mozarts, and Josepha's mother lived in Salzburg. The friendship between Mozart and Josepha was to last all his life. His first aria for her was 'Ah, lo previdi . . . Ah, t'invola . . . Deh, non varcar' K.272, a scena to words by Cigna-Santi, the librettist of *Mitridate*, taken from his libretto *Andromeda* and originally written in 1755 (probably Mozart or Dusek had found the text in a more recent source, such as Paisiello's setting of 1774 or Gazzaniga's of 1775). Andromeda believes her beloved, Perseus, has killed himself in a fit of madness, and first rails at Eurystheus for not preventing it, then welcomes reunion with Perseus in death. The Allegro of this two-part aria, a furious outburst in C minor, is followed by an orchestral recitative and a cavatina, with poignant oboe writing. The powerful emotional character of the music, perhaps especially in the central recitative with its intense chromatic writing and wilful changes of tempo, offers a clear foretaste of the world of *Idomeneo*. Mozart had outgrown Salzburg.

17

Mannheim

URING 1777 THE Mozart family's discontent with their
situation in Salzburg reached a point at which action had to
be taken. In March, Leopold had petitioned the archbishop:
neither the original document nor Colloredo's reply survives, but the
response was negative. In his petition Leopold is likely to have sought
some kind of promotion, for himself, for Wolfgang or for both, or at
least an increase in salary, for he was nursing the injustice of having
to perform some of the Kapellmeister's duties since Fischietti's departure, without additional reward. Probably he knew by then that the
archbishop was seeking a new Kapellmeister from Italy, for in June
the appointment was announced of Giacomo Rust, Roman born,
Neapolitan trained, active and moderately successful in the operatic
world of Venice. Fischietti had received 800 gulden per annum; Rust
was to be paid 1000. Moreover, the family was smarting under a comment from the archbishop to the effect that Wolfgang knew nothing
of composition and should go to Naples to study at a conservatory.[1]
Leopold had planned to petition the archbishop again, in June, this
time for several months' leave of absence for himself and Wolfgang,
but an imperial visit to Salzburg was imminent at the time and the
orchestra was needed at full strength. When he later made that

request, he was turned down, but the archbishop evidently added that Wolfgang, as only a part-time employee, could be released to travel alone. Leopold evidently accepted the offer of Wolfgang's release, but then the archbishop 'made some gracious objections'.

Most of this information comes from the petition that Mozart sent to Colloredo in August 1777, written out (and no doubt actually drafted) by his father, in which he formally applied for his release.[2] The Mozarts couched the request in language, perhaps not without a hint of irony, that they thought suitable for a prince of the church: they talk of Wolfgang's gratitude for his father's loving and attentive upbringing, of making the most of God's gift of talent, and of Wolfgang's putting himself in a position to repay his debt by caring for his father in the years to come, as the gospel required of a son, and safeguarding too the future of his sister. Accordingly, he wished to be released from service in order to travel. A reference to an earlier rebuff—'when I begged for permission to travel to Vienna, Your Highness was graciously pleased to declare that I had nothing to hope for and would do better to seek my fortune elsewhere'—would, had the archbishop been affected by such comments, have made it still harder for him to refuse Mozart's request.

Colloredo did now consent to Mozart's release, with an ironic response: 'father and son have permission to seek their fortune elsewhere, according to the gospel'. Leopold, always anxious about his situation at Salzburg, was shocked at what seemed like his dismissal and was indeed ill with worry, according to Schiedenhofen.[3] But Colloredo, while offering Leopold the chance to go too, was not actually dismissing him, and gave no instruction to stop his salary except 'in the event of his leaving service'. Leopold evidently made it clear that he was intending to stay. There was no possible way that he could afford to forgo his Salzburg salary and travel with his son.

This however raised grave difficulties. For a start, father and son had never before been apart. Leopold had always managed Wolfgang's day-to-day activities, in every detail. Although Mozart was now 21,

every significant decision about his life had been made on his behalf
by his father. Could Leopold now be confident that his son had the
requisite judgment, knowledge and diplomatic, financial and personal
skills to negotiate travel to the courts of southern and western Germany (where their chief hopes lay) and seek positions there? Would
a young man travelling by himself be taken seriously? would he be in
the right places at the right times, and seeing the right people? In the
past, Leopold had dealt with all the troublesome minutiae of their
journeys: planning the routes, choosing the mode of travel and book-
ing the coaches, finding inns or monasteries for their lodging, seeking out and meeting the local musicians to determine whether a
concert could profitably be arranged and then arranging it, organizing the actual music from which they would play (which often had
to be copied locally), ensuring that the right potential patrons were
approached and in the right way with the appropriate letters of introduction, and dealing with countless other difficult issues. On their
previous travels Mozart himself had been free to concentrate on
composing and performing music; now these would be only two of
many tasks. There was another important difference too. On their
previous travels Mozart, and often Nannerl too, were famous as child
prodigies and their reputation had travelled before them. Now
Mozart was simply a young professional musician among many. He
could not expect to arouse the same degree of curiosity or interest
among patrons or the public, nor, probably, the same degree of ready
support from other musicians. And all these were critical, in the new
situation of Mozart's career and the family finances. Leopold had
taken a loan of 300 gulden from a young Jesuit-trained clergyman,
Joseph Bullinger, a good friend of the family, to help them meet the
initial costs (although the total of his debts was about half as much
again; his annual salary was 354 gulden),[4] and it was essential that the
journey be at worst self-supporting. Mozart would have to give concerts that would make a profit, simply to cover his expenses, and, so
as not to waste money, would have to move on speedily from any-

where that looked unpromising in terms of rewards or a court position. That was not always easy when local rulers could at whim keep him waiting for weeks for a hearing.

It is also legitimate to wonder, as Leopold must have done (and certainly did before long), whether Mozart was capable of taking the degree of responsibility that he would now have to shoulder. The risks of releasing into the world a 21-year-old who had never before moved from under his parents' watchful eye need no emphasis. Further, he had always been the object of high praise, even idolatry, and this had had its effect on him. Although we may reasonably feel, as he did, that his extraordinary gifts entitled him to extraordinary treatment—only a Kapellmeister's post would be good enough, he wrote more than once (doubtless echoing remarks of Leopold's)[5]—that is hardly a view that would have been widely shared at the time, nor one that would have endeared him to his potential colleagues, still less his potential employers.

It is not surprising, then, that Leopold felt it would be unwise for him to allow Mozart to travel by himself. He accordingly decided that he should be accompanied by his mother. Maria Anna could not perform any of the tasks to do with music-making or dealings with patrons, but she could cope with some of the domestic matters, such as his clothes, lodging and food, and could keep a general eye on his behaviour. Her presence might also, in some degree, ensure that Mozart would keep the family's priorities firmly in view and report accurately and regularly to his father in his letters home, and indeed she could do some of the letter-writing herself. In the event the decision to send Maria Anna, and not to recall her to Salzburg part-way through the travels, turned out to be not merely of doubtful benefit but, ultimately, tragic.

Clearly the primary intention of this journey was that Mozart should obtain a rewarding court appointment, at one of the courts of southern or western Germany, of which those at Munich and Mannheim seemed the most promising as they had the largest and most active musical establishments. Beyond them lay Paris, where the

Mozarts had met several German musicians of quite modest talents (at least compared with Wolfgang's) who made a good living and where Mozart surely could. Whether the ultimate aim was a move for the entire Mozart family, to be maintained by Wolfgang and, as long as he also held an appointment, by Leopold, or that simply Wolfgang would take a position and the family would stay in Salzburg, remains uncertain. Some authorities firmly believe that the former was the intention, although there is little in the correspondence to suggest as much. Writing from Munich during the early stages of his journey, Mozart put forward a scheme for staying there on a freelance basis, and added, as an afterthought: 'should you ... feel inclined (as I heartily wish that you may) to leave Salzburg and end your days in Munich, it would be quite simple to arrange it'.[6] Then, in a letter Mozart wrote from Paris in summer 1778—the letter in which he relates to Leopold and Nannerl the full circumstances of his mother's last illness and death—he refers to his looking forward to the family's reunion and being able to 'live somewhere together (which is my sole ambition)'.[7]

To read that as a considered statement of his or the family's aims places altogether too heavy a construction on a remark made under great emotional pressure. Nothing that he wrote elsewhere suggests that either he or Leopold had any serious thoughts of a position for Leopold as well as one for himself, and indeed Leopold wrote in one of his letters to Wolfgang in Mannheim 'you know how I have pointed out that it would be impossible for us all to leave'.[8] When, in a later letter to Paris, Leopold sketched a scenario for the whole family to be there together, it is clear that he was postulating a situation that he considered ideal but unlikely.[9] And when Wolfgang expressed such pious hopes, it is all too clear that he was doing so largely to impress his father with a show of filial loyalty and devotion.

MOTHER AND SON set out from Salzburg at 6.00 in the morning of 23 September 1777, after a few frenzied days of preparation. Leopold, although still unwell, was up until 2.00 the night before dealing with the packing. Speaking hurt his chest, affected by catarrh, and he was unable to give all the verbal instructions he had intended to. But it was anyway perhaps safer to pass them on in writing, and his extensive letters are a mine of information about travel and society in southern Germany at the time. In the period of nearly 16 months before the family—depleted—was reunited, 131 letters passed between the travellers and father and daughter at home, 69 from Leopold and Nannerl, 62 from Maria Anna and Wolfgang. During the early months of the journey each pair of correspondents wrote twice weekly; the number decreased later (except in the turbulent period of February 1778), and from the spring of 1778 letters were less regular, for various reasons, though generally about fortnightly. Happily for posterity, all the letters are preserved, thanks primarily to Leopold's sense of history and of his son's importance, and many of them are very long and detailed. We accordingly have a full account of the events of Mozart's journeys and musical doings (or at least as full as he chose to report), a great deal of gossip about Salzburg events of the time, and an intimate picture of the personal concerns of a family which, in spite of the many tensions that developed over these months, remained a very close and loving one.[10]

Mozart and his mother travelled in a chaise that Leopold had recently bought for about 80 gulden; horses would be hired at inns in the usual way. Their first call was to be Munich. He wrote home on their first evening a high-spirited letter, reporting from Wasserburg on a lopsided cow that he had seen, on his confidence in dealing with the postillions and the porters, and celebrating his freedom from 'H.C. ein schwanz' ('that prick Hieronymus Colloredo'). In his reply Leopold tells the travellers of his dismay when he realized that he had forgotten to give Wolfgang a father's blessing and how on their departure he and Nannerl both slept from emotional exhaustion. But in the main the letter is divided between instructions, particularly about what they should do on reaching Augsburg (who they should call on, that Wolfgang should wear his papal cross there and in any city where there is no ruling lord, that they should remember to get the servant to use boot-trees—in short, advice at many different levels), and news from Salzburg (about his and Nannerl's social activities, the court musicians, the music performed).

On 24 September they reached Munich, where they stayed at Zum schwarzen Adler, the inn owned by their friend the musical connoisseur Franz Joseph Albert. Two days later Mozart was able to meet Count Seeau, who had charge of all court entertainments, and tell him of his situation and availability. Seeau agreed that a good composer was needed at the court and suggested he ask for an audience with the Elector, Maximilian III Joseph. All this was duly reported to Leopold, whose advice came back by return of post: tell the Elector about your contrapuntal music (this was evidently his particular interest—witness the K.222 motet Mozart had written to impress him at the time of *La finta giardiniera*) and show him your diplomas from Bologna and Verona and Padre Martini's testimonial of 1770 (he did in fact later show them to Seeau). But before Mozart received that letter he had seen Count Waldburg-Zeil, the Bishop of Chiemsee, who was pessimistic; the Elector had said that it was too soon and that Mozart needed to travel to Italy and make his name there. The exaggerated prestige 'these great lords' attached to Italy understandably irritated him. The next day he managed to meet the Elector, who questioned him about his relationship to the Salzburg court. He told the Elector that Salzburg was no place for him, that he had three times been to Italy and written three operas there, and that he was eager to serve the Bavarian court . . . 'Yes, my dear boy, but I have no vacancy. I am sorry. If only there were a vacancy'—and he walked off. It is not hard to imagine that some word may have been uttered in ruling circles about the Mozarts being difficult employees, but if, as Leopold wrote, there simply was no vacancy, there was little that even the Elector could do.

Mozart had not quite given up hope of Munich. Albert and he devised a scheme under which ten connoisseurs would pay him five gulden each a month to live there and compose and perform new music, providing 600 gulden a year, which could be augmented by occasional earnings through Seeau to, say, 800. After a year or two, if he won honour and prestige through his work, he thought, he might be sought after by the court. A later letter proposes an alternative scheme, involving the composition of a regular supply of German operas for Seeau. Leopold's response, predictably, was sceptical: where are these philanthropists to come from who will dependably pay five gulden a month, and what would they expect in return? what sort of routine work would Seeau demand of him? how long would he have to wait in Munich to see if these schemes were practicable? 'You can live that way anywhere, not just in Munich. You must not make yourself so cheap and throw yourself away in this manner, for indeed we have not yet come to that'. These schemes would do him no honour—and how the archbishop would laugh! Nannerl echoed his views. They clearly felt that Mozart should set his sights higher, and he seems to have agreed fairly readily. His idea of opera as a basis had come partly through his contact with Count Joseph von Salern, intendant of the opera, at whose house he played several of his recent divertimentos. This was music-making for its own sake, not the kind of concert that Leopold was hoping he would give to recoup some of his expenses. A programme of concertos and chamber works given at Albert's on 4 October was also an informal affair (this is the event at which Mozart said he played, in his K.287 divertimento, as if he were 'the finest fiddler in all Europe'). An attempt by Albert to organize a more formal academy, on which Maria Anna reported and which would have produced some revenue, seems to have come to nothing. There is no indication, in fact, that Mozart earned any money at all in Munich.

While he was in the city Mozart renewed acquaintance with the Bohemian composer Josef Myslivecek, a friend since the time of the first Italian journey. He was in hospital, his face appallingly disfigured by the medical treatment he had there, apparently radical cauterization of his nose—almost certainly for syphilis, although he himself attributed it to a carriage accident. Mozart reluctantly visited him and found the experience deeply distressing, but he returned, with his mother, just before they left Munich. Myslivecek talked of handing on to Mozart a commission for an opera at Naples. Mozart was enthusiastic at the prospect ('I have an inexpressible longing to compose another opera'), and Leopold too welcomed the idea. Myslivecek and Leopold corresponded extensively on this subject and on others (including the securing of payment from Colloredo for some music Myslivecek had written for him, which required a good deal of negotiation), but the plan never materialized, and Leopold finally came to doubt his sincerity.

Serious composition was, of course, at a standstill during these weeks of travel. All Mozart produced at Munich was a set of four keyboard preambula, which apparently were exercises in modulation for Nannerl. Sadly, they do not survive; Leopold thought them 'superlatively beautiful'. He was of course playing, and as usual he was looking out for interesting music by other composers. He came across a set of sonatas for keyboard and violin by the Dresden composer Joseph Schuster, his recent *VI divertimenti da camera*, of which he wrote: 'I've often played them here. They aren't bad. If I stay here I shall write six in this same style, as they are very popular here'. He sent a copy to Nannerl for her and Leopold to divert themselves.

On 11 October Mozart and his mother finally left for Augsburg—high time, said Leopold, irritated that they had spent almost three weeks in a place where they could not hope to make any money. They had on the whole enjoyed themselves there. They saw many friends, including singers and others who had taken part in *La finta giardiniera*, went three times to the theatre (where Mozart was very taken with a new young singer, Margarethe Kaiser, and tried to meet her), and had some agreeable music-making. And above all they felt free of the shadow of Colloredo. The journey on to Augsburg was short, a mere nine hours on the road, and they reached Leopold's native city the same evening, lodging, as Leopold had directed, at the inn Zum weissen Lamm. Mozart's first call, the next morning, was on his uncle, Leopold's younger brother the bookbinder Franz Alois Mozart, who took him to see the chief magistrate, Jakob Wilhelm von

Langenmantel, in effect the highest official in this 'free city'. Mozart played for him on the clavichord and met his son, who took him in the afternoon to meet the eminent maker of keyboard instruments Johann Andreas Stein. Mozart tried out the Stein fortepianos, then and in further visits, reporting that they delighted him for their even tone, clean damping and the effectiveness of their escapement action. It was after his final visit, and in the light of the playing of Stein's daughter Nanette (a clumsy pianist, Mozart thought, but later a noted piano manufacturer and a staunch friend of Beethoven's), that he made his famous pronouncement about rubato: 'What these people fail to grasp is that in tempo rubato in an Adagio the left hand should play in strict time; with them the left hand always follows suit'.

The next day Mozart and his uncle paid a visit to the Augustine monastery of Heiligkreuz, where they returned several times. At a long musical session there Mozart played a Vanhal violin concerto, his own concerto K.216, a symphony, a sonata, a set of variations K.179 and a series of improvisations on the organ, chiefly of fugues. Before he left he presented copies of two of his masses to the monastery. He had a less pleasant experience with Langenmantel's son. First he promised to arrange a concert for Mozart, exclusive to members of the Akademie der Augsburger Patrizier, and then withdrew as they had insufficient money for a decent fee. But they invited him to come to their own concert a few days later. Then, after a day of music-making and a visit to the theatre, the young man and his friends twitted Mozart mercilessly about the papal order that he was wearing, to the point where Mozart forcibly expressed his disgust and walked out. But the next morning Stein, the local composer and music director Friedrich Graf and others determined to arrange an appropriate concert. In the event Mozart was prevailed upon to go to the patricians' concert, held in the 'Stube' at the Rathaus, where one of his symphonies was given (in which he played the violin), and he played a keyboard or violin concerto, as well as the K.283 piano sonata. He was paid ten gulden. But the main musical event in Augsburg was the concert that Stein and his friends arranged in the Fugger hall. The programme included the K.238 piano concerto, the three-piano concerto (with the local organist and Stein), the piano sonata K.284 and several improvisations, including 'a magnificent sonata in C major out of my head, with a rondo finale'. The concert was a success in Leopold's terms, too: the takings amounted to 90 gulden and the expenses were small. Mozart reckoned, as they were leaving Augsburg, that they were about 27 gulden out of pocket on the journey so far. (Maria Anna later wrote that they had enclosed, in response to Leopold's repeated requests, Albert's bill from Munich, but Leopold said that he had never received it.)

During their fortnight in Augsburg Mozart struck up a playful friendship with the 19-year-old daughter of Franz Alois, Maria Anna Thekla Mozart, his 'Bäsle' (little girl cousin, the diminutive of *Base*). The letters he sent her during the ensuing months, with their bawdy humour, conjured surprise, embarrassment and alarm from early Mozart biographers and a variety of conjecture about sexual relationships from more recent ones. There is no particular reason to suppose that Leopold's brother's family should have had very different ideas about humour from Leopold's own, or that the typically Bavarian and Austrian kind of 'joke' about bodily functions and their products should not have been part of the Augsburg family's life as much as the Salzburg family's. In the very first letter of this journey, Maria Anna had written to her husband: 'Adio ben mio leb gesund, Reck den arsch zum mund, ich winsch ein guete nacht, scheiss ins beth das Kracht' ('Farewell, my love, keep well, Stick your arse in your mouth, I wish you a good night, Shit in your bed with a crash'). If such rhymes were part of the daily family dialogue, as clearly they were, it is scarcely surprising that Mozart employed humour of this kind with his cousin. His first letter to her, written a few days after their parting, is very brief, with a reminder about some music to be sent. Six days later a longer one followed, full of preposterous, jokey rhymes and with plenty of dashes of coarse bodily humour. Another, written soon after, and probably very short, does not survive. The fourth is in the same mode as the second (it also carries a remark on the cover, quoting what are evidently Maria Anna's comments, beginning 'Now do send her a sensible letter for once . . .'). A fifth followed three weeks later. Mozart wrote to his cousin twice in 1778 and once in each of the next three years. While there are a number of nonsense remarks in the earlier letters that might, with sufficient eagerness and imagination, be thought to carry heavily coded sexual meanings, there is nothing even faintly amorous in the tone or the content of any of them and certainly nothing to imply that the cousins had become lovers (even if they had the opportunity, in the Bäsle's father's

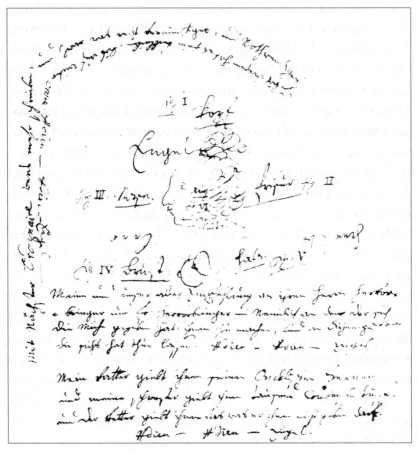

Part of a letter from Mozart to Maria Anna Thekla Mozart ('Bäsle'), 10 May 1779 (*British Library, Stefan Zweig Collection*)

house).[11] A comparison between the tone of these letters and the solitary one he wrote to Aloysia Weber, whom we know he loved, speaks for itself.[12]

LEOPOLD HAD CAREFULLY mapped a route for the travellers' journey on to Mannheim, allowing for them to pause at several potential sources of patronage. He knew that Wolfgang would be eager to reach Mannheim by 4 November, St Charles's Day, when the nameday of the Elector Carl Theodor would be celebrated with a new opera, but he knew too that the opera would be repeated and that Mozart could go to a later performance. That route would have taken them first to Dischingen, a seat of the Prince of Thurn and Taxis, to the monastery at Kaysersheim (now Kaisheim), where the abbot was said to be a generous patron, then to Wallerstein or Hohenaltheim, at one of which Prince Ernst Kraft of Oettingen-Wallerstein would be resident. Then they would go to Würzburg, passing through Ansbach (where the Margrave might provide work) and Mergentheim (where the Commandant might). In the event, they went to Hohenaltheim and met the Prince, who was however in mourning for his wife and in no mood to listen to music. Mozart met his director of music, his old acquaintance Ignaz von Beecke, who seems to have behaved in a friendly and generous way to him, not reciprocated in the harsh remarks Mozart made to Leopold about his musical talents. They remained there an extra day, as Mozart had a heavy cold, and then went on a more direct route to Mannheim, ignoring Leopold's plans for calls at Kaysersheim, Ansbach and Würzburg but travelling by a shorter, more southerly route through Ellwangen, Cannstatt (now a suburb of Stuttgart) and Bruchsal. Beecke had suggested a route, but this proved impossible for carriages, and a diversion was necessary. Possibly Mozart had learnt in Augsburg that some of the calls Leopold had proposed would be pointless as the potential patrons were away, though had he done so he would surely have told Leopold. But the result was that he earned nothing on the journey and failed to secure some of the letters of recommendation that would have served him at Mannheim and elsewhere.

The Mozarts arrived at Mannheim on 30 October and, on a friend's recommendation, took rooms at the Pfälzischer Hof. The next day Mozart called on the director of instrumental music and Konzertmeister, Christian Cannabich, a gifted composer with a reputation extending to Paris and beyond through his symphonies and concertante symphonies (the multiple concerto or sinfonia concertante was a genre much favoured in Mannheim, as well as Paris, as one might expect when there were so many virtuoso players to hand). The orchestra that the Elector Carl Theodor had assembled there since the 1750s, under Johann Stamitz and his successors, many of them from Bohemia, was everywhere regarded as outstanding, and moreover there was an opera house that was adventurous in its new commissions and German opera was coming into favour. There could be no better place, Mozart must have felt, for him to be. Leopold had cautiously advised him not to disclose his ambitions to the other

View of Mannheim: engraving by [Johann Anton?] Riedel, 1779 (*Mozart-Gedenkstätte, Augsburg*)

musicians, and to judge by Mozart's report on that first morning he was probably right:

> [Cannabich and I] went together to the rehearsal. I thought I should not be able to stop myself from laughing when I was introduced to the people there. Some, who knew me by repute, were very polite and highly respectful, but others, who had knew nothing of me, stared at me wide-eyed, and certainly in a rather sneering manner. They seemed to think, because I am small and young, that nothing great or mature can come out of me, but I'll soon show them.

Mozart quickly made a good friend of Cannabich and cemented the friendship by writing, for his daughter Rosa, a girl of thirteen 'who plays the piano quite nicely', a new sonata, whose first two movements were finished within five days of his arrival. He also made a present to Friedrich Ramm, the principal Mannheim oboist, of the oboe concerto he had composed shortly before he left Salzburg. Ramm was 'crazy with delight' and played it at least five times in the next few months.

Cannabich took Mozart to meet the Kapellmeister, Ignaz Holzbauer, who suggested to the intendant, Count Savioli, that the Elector should give Mozart a hearing. Although Mozart made it clear to Cannabich at an early stage that he would like to stay in Mannheim for the winter (at this time of the year travelling would soon be difficult), it was not until 18 November that the question of a permanent position there came up, and then (or so Mozart reported) it was raised by Cannabich himself. Meanwhile he reported to his father on the music there, the excellence and size of the orchestra, the feebleness of the choir and the wretched playing of the two court organists. He also expressed forcibly his view of the deputy Kapellmeister, the theorist and composer G.J. Vogler, whom he thought 'conceited and incompetent' and whose sneering criticism of J.C. Bach's *Lucio Silla*, written for performance at Mannheim in 1775 on the libretto Mozart had set in Milan, he found offensive. Later, in January, Vogler was keen to know Mozart better and to play his music; they played together, and Vogler performed the K.246 piano concerto at sight, although, Mozart wrote, much too fast.

But it seems that Mozart found a place for himself in the Mannheim musical community during his first few days there. His mother could report on his meeting with the Electress, their attendance during the nameday festivities at a court banquet and reception, then an opera—this was Holzbauer's *Günther von Schwarzburg*, a serious opera in German, justly described as 'very beautiful, the music incomparably fine'—and on the third day a concert at which Mozart played a concerto, a sonata and an improvisation. She also writes of Mozart's being asked to hear the Elector's natural children play the piano and comment on their progress. Mozart himself reported a brief conversation with the Elector during which he mentioned his readiness to write an opera, and on another occasion he improvised before the Elector, who sat close by and 'kept on asking for more'. For this he later had his reward, not money (as he had hoped) but a fine gold watch ('I now have five watches. I am therefore seriously considering having an additional watch pocket on each leg of my trousers so that, when I visit some great lord, I shall wear both watches . . . so that it will not occur to him to present me with another'). There was private music-making with the Cannabich family and that of Johann Baptist Wendling, the flautist.

Leopold responded with encouragement and advice—Mozart should show what he can do on the organ and in composition, and should cultivate influential people at court—and with news about music in Salzburg, as well as the occasional irritated rebuke about the lack of clarity and precision in his and Maria Anna's letters or their frequency. One of Mozart's letters described, at Leopold's request, his meeting with Beecke at Hohenaltheim during the journey—how Beecke had received him respectfully and courteously, had offered him advice about going to Paris, had tried to arrange an audience with the Prince and applauded Mozart's playing—but Mozart always seems to have felt bound to add deprecatory comment about Beecke and his abilities. This critical vein, always offered from his own stand-point of casually (and correctly) assumed superior perception, and applied most of all to potential rivals—Beecke was a virtuoso pianist, Vogler a deputy Kapellmeister—makes all too clear his arrogance towards his fellow musicians and makes the reader wonder how effec-tively it was concealed in his day-to-day social contact with them. It is clear that he and his father had long been exchanging such thoughts about their colleagues and rivals, and his father's readiness to do so, and to assume that other people's actions were often motivated by base emotions of some sort, did nothing to help Mozart in his social, or in some ways his personal, development. Leopold certainly passed on to his son some of his own misanthropy and cynicism, typ-ified in his remark: 'Mark it well, my son, *if there is just one man in a 1000* who with no element of self-interest is your true friend, *he is one of the greatest wonders of this world*'.[13]

It is sobering to compare the tone of Mozart's letters home with that of Leopold's to him and Maria Anna. Clearly Mozart, in spite of his anxieties, was enjoying life on the edge of the Mannheim group of musicians. He lunched and dined with one or another most days. He made music with them in the evenings. He went to parties. He does not say so, of course, but it is obvious that he relished the free-dom from his father no less than his freedom from Colloredo. His high spirits break through time and again in his letters. He could joke about the fifth gold watch, but it must have seemed less funny to Leopold when it compelled him to borrow still more money to meet their expenses. He could joke about the name, Schmalz (meaning 'fat'), of the Mannheim banker who was not in a position to give him cash, but the remarks about Mr Butter, Mr Cheese and Mr Milk may not have amused Leopold when he had to explain that the credits had been arranged through a banker in Augsburg and had to be extended. Nor will Leopold have taken much pleasure in a story of a party with Mannheim musicians at the Cannabichs' where Mozart 'perpetrated . . . rhymes . . . on such subjects as muck, shitting and arse-licking', or even at his painstakingly assembled list, carefully set out in alphabetical order, of friends in Salzburg to whom he wanted to send greetings. And a sudden proposal to visit Princess Caroline of Nassau-Weilburg at Kirchheimbolanden to play to her, where he expected a fee equivalent to 66 gulden, and where they would stay 'as long as the officers' table was to our taste', seemed to Leopold like a madman's ravings, particularly as it took no account of the fact that a journey to Kirchheimbolanden would be much better combined with one to other nearby centres or even whether the Princess was at home.

Mozart's insensitivity in the treatment of his father, and his inability to handle the situation with even a modest degree of tact, seem extraordinary. He must have known of the acute anxieties that possessed Leopold, at home in Salzburg, out of control of the situation, as his actions ran the family into ever-mounting debt. He was so occupied with his own doings and thoughts that he rarely troubled himself to keep his father properly informed or even to present his thoughts in ways that Leopold was likely to find acceptable. Many of Leopold's letters of these months embody an assumption that the travellers would quickly move on—as he had directed—if Mannheim proved unpromising, but Mozart never made his intentions clear, except that he would wait for a decision from the Elector, who might ask him to stay for the winter, if not indefinitely. If he did not know when, or in what direction, they might travel, Leopold could not arrange for them to have money to pay for their lodging. The slowness of communication made the situation worse—a letter usually took five days between Salzburg and Mannheim, which allowing for twice-weekly post days generally gave a response time of twelve days. Wolfgang's naive homilies on the inevitability of God's will, doubtless echoing ones he had heard at home, left Leopold unimpressed, as they seemed too like excuses for inaction. Nearly all Leopold's letters of these weeks are in some degree concerned with possible onward routes, to Mainz and its vicinity, to the Austrian Netherlands (present-day Belgium), to Paris, always with an eye to the courts and noble homes en route where a concert might be given and money earned.

But the normal family correspondence and exchange of information continues, often quite massively as Leopold tells Maria Anna and Wolfgang in almost every letter about the musical activities at court, the personal lives of their numerous friends and the court musicians, visitors to the city and the activities of their little shooting group that met every weekend (the travellers still participating, in their absence, with someone else shooting on their behalf; sometimes Wolfgang designed the week's targets *in absentia*). The family remained as close as ever, if on one level relations were under strain.

The long wait for a decision from the Elector had raised Mozart's hopes: if he had been kept six weeks in Mannheim, and had such close contact with the Elector's children, surely he could expect some level of patronage beyond a gold watch. But on 8 December he finally heard that there was no appointment to be had. Travelling on at this time of year, with his mother, was out of the question. His friends rallied round. He could be accommodated at the house of the Court Chamberlain, Serrarius; his mother could be found cheap lodging for two months and then go home. A pupil of Wendling's would commission some flute quartets and concertos from him for 200 gulden. Cannabich would find him a couple of pupils. He could compose some sonatas for piano and violin and publish them by subscription. At the end of the winter he would go, as had been suggested earlier, to Paris in the company of a group of Mannheim musicians familiar with the city, including Wendling and Ramm, who had told him of the tempting opportunities open to him there. Wendling promised Maria Anna that he would watch over Mozart like a father.

Leopold had already prepared himself for the disappointing news and took it calmly. He broadly accepted the scheme, except that he insisted that Maria Anna and Wolfgang should not live apart. In fact they were quickly able to arrange for a large room to accommodate them both at the Serrarius family house, where Maria Anna was kindly treated, in return for piano lessons for the stepdaughter, Therese Pierron (the wife's daughter by a previous marriage: Mozart referred to her as the 'house nymph'). This arrangement was both cheaper and far more comfortable than life at the inn, where Maria Anna had often been bitterly cold during the daytime, as the payment for a fire covered warmth only in the morning and evening. She now took her meals with some old friends, the Danner family, and Mozart ate with the Wendlings. This would now be their regime for the remainder of their stay in Mannheim. In mid-December Maria Anna at last managed to provide a cogent account of their finances: the innkeeper's bill in Mannheim amounted to 111 gulden; they had 72 gulden from their original capital (the original calculation from Augsburg had not taken account of all the concert expenses) and had drawn 150 from Schmalz. With 200 gulden to come from the flute music—commissioned by a German surgeon, Ferdinand Dejean, who worked for the Dutch East India Company and is called variously a Dutchman and an Indian in Mozart's letters[14]—Leopold could feel more comfortable, although he asked for reassurance that the sum would actually be forthcoming.

ONCE THE DECISION to remain in Mannheim for several weeks had been made, the tone of the correspondence became calmer. It seemed, in the early days of January, that the Mozart family was in a state of relative equilibrium: life in Mannheim was under control, with some money being earned, and plans for the next months were sensibly and even promisingly formed. Mozart had heard that in Vienna Joseph II was to start a German opera company and asked his father to make enquiries about opportunities there. Leopold began to consider Maria Anna's homeward journey, and whether the family chaise should be sold in Mannheim or perhaps in Augsburg. He also provided detailed instructions about which clothes Mozart would need in Paris; nothing should be left in Mannheim.

Maria Anna and Wolfgang were shocked to learn of the sudden death at the end of December of the court organist at Salzburg, their close family friend and colleague Cajetan Adlgasser, who was only 48;

he had some kind of seizure while playing the organ in the cathedral. Leopold, rather unwillingly, took over the teaching of the Lodron daughters. A new organist would be required, and as Rust was unwell and wanting to return to Italy the Kapellmeistership was also likely to fall vacant soon. On 31 December they heard too of the sudden death, from smallpox, of the Elector of Bavaria. This had a far-reaching effect on employment prospects in both Munich and Mannheim. Maximilian III Joseph was the last of the Wittelsbachs, and the succession now passed to the Sulzbach line, which meant that Carl Theodor, Elector of the Palatinate, was heir. Carl Theodor left Mannheim for Munich immediately on hearing the news. He initially ceded much of Lower Bavaria to Joseph II of Austria, but that was unacceptable to Prussia and Saxony and provoked the War of the Bavarian Succession. There was an invasion, but little fighting (it is sometimes called the Potato War, as the Prussian army's chief role was picking potatoes), and in 1779 Lower Bavaria was largely restored. Nevertheless, the situation posed a considerable threat to the inhabitants of the region during 1778, with armies on the move and danger from rampaging groups of deserters, and discussion of the situation occupies large tracts of Leopold's letters. This proved to be the end of Mannheim as a powerful court: Carl Theodor moved to Munich, and during 1778 most of the musicians followed. It must soon have been clear to the Mozarts that henceforth fewer musicians would be employed at these centres and that the prospects of a position for Wolfgang were considerably diminished.

It was about this time that Mozart came into contact with the Weber family—Fridolin Weber, a bass singer in the Kapelle and a copyist, and his wife Marie Cäcilia, who had four daughters, Josepha (b 1758), Aloysia (b c1760), Constanze (b 1762) and Sophie (b 1763). The first we hear of them is in a letter of 17 January 1778 in which Mozart tells his father of the revival of his plan to visit the Princess of Nassau-Weilburg at Kirchheimbolanden, about 60 km north of Mannheim, a ten-hour drive, but now in the company of Weber ('a thoroughly honest German who is bringing up his children well') and his second daughter, Aloysia, who 'sings most admirably and has a lovely, pure voice . . . she sings most excellently my aria written for De Amicis with its horribly difficult passages . . . accompanies herself well and also plays galanteries quite decently'.[15] What is more, 'she can go to the Electress whenever she likes, because of her good behaviour'. It is plain that Mozart was eager to convince his father of the merits of the Weber family.

This letter began what can only be described as an attempt at manipulation, and an inept one. The time for departure to Paris was approaching, with the coming of the Lent season. Mozart, privately enamoured with Aloysia Weber, was now not so eager to leave Mannheim or indeed to go to Paris. In his long, carefully written but deeply misguided letter of 4 February, he first describes the visit to Kirchheimbolanden, during which he gave several concerts, with Aloysia singing and playing. They were paid only seven louis d'or in all (he had hoped for eight each), and the profit, allowing for travel, lodging and the meals they preferred to take at the inn instead of free ones at court, was 42 gulden. He had felt bound to pay half the expenses for the party of three. On the way home they spent five days

Aloysia Weber [Lange]:
anonymous oil painting,
c1780s (*Internationale
Stiftung Mozarteum,
Salburg*)

at Worms, staying with Weber's brother-in-law. But the main point of the letter was that he no longer wanted to travel with Wendling and Ramm. On this, Mozart knew how to win Leopold over:

> Wendling is a basically honest and very good man, but sadly he has no religion whatever, and the whole family are the same. I need only say that his daughter has been someone's mistress [the Elector's]. Ramm is a decent fellow, but a libertine. I know myself, and am certain that I have enough religion never to do anything that I could not do openly before the whole world; but the very idea of being . . . in the society of people whose way of thinking is so entirely different from my own appals me.[16]

The alternative scheme he now proposed was that he should remain at Mannheim to finish the Dejean flute music at leisure, while Weber arranged concert engagements for him. He feels at home in the Weber family; the father is just like Leopold in his character and his way of thinking. His dearest wish, he continues, is to make this family happy and prosperous. He has advised them to go to Italy. Would Leopold write to their friends there and help him arrange a tour, for himself and Aloysia, with Fridolin Weber in attendance and the eldest daughter as cook? He would gladly write an opera for Italy at half-price in order to make Aloysia's name. He would also take her to Switzerland and perhaps the Netherlands. Maria Anna added a surreptitious postscript while Wolfgang was at dinner. She begins: 'You will have seen from this letter that when Wolfgang makes new friends he immediately wants to give his life and property for them'; he will not listen to her and objects if she remonstrates with him. She did however support his reservations about Wendling and Ramm and, fatefully, she offered to accompany him to Paris herself.

On the same day, thinking Mozart's departure for Paris imminent, Leopold addressed a sombre and heartfelt letter to his son, provoked by the prospect of his son's going still further distant from Salzburg.

He looks back over his own life and his career, discusses the hard times he has been through supporting the family (including his impoverished mother-in-law) on a tiny income, and the debt—the first of his life—of 700 gulden that he has now run up, and he gently sounds some warnings about Paris and the dangers he might find himself drawn into there from companions and from women. Another letter a few days later is concerned with more banal dangers, such as slippery paving-stones and leaving sums of money lying around, and he also lists people Mozart should call on in Paris. He further names some of the Parisian musicians, several of them men and women of fame and distinction, who as a class Mozart should generally avoid—'you will gain nothing by associating with these people, and to be intimate with them may even do you harm'. Except with people of high rank he advises aloofness: *'please behave like an Englishman'.*

It is not hard to imagine Leopold's dismay on receiving Wolfgang's letter overturning the plan. He read the new proposal 'with amazement and horror', but the letter he wrote was not so much angry as despairing—despair at Wolfgang's fecklessness and his slender grasp of the realities of life. It is a long letter, carefully and temperately argued. Leopold recalls the objectives of Wolfgang's journey and the importance of keeping them clearly in focus; he reminds his son of the risky Munich scheme he had espoused; he recapitulates the various whims and fancies to which Wolfgang has given rein since he left Salzburg; he painstakingly explains (with several examples) how even the most famed German sopranos have never ventured to Italy, and how hopeless it would be for a girl of sixteen who has never before appeared on a stage; he points out how damaging such a venture would be to Wolfgang's reputation and how humiliating for himself; he reproaches Wolfgang for his tardiness in producing the flute music, for which the payment is so urgently needed; and he ends with kindly and constructive advice about Aloysia Weber—let Anton Raaff, the aging but distinguished international tenor at Mannheim listen to her and give an opinion. And he exhorts Wolfgang to do justice to himself and his great gifts: '*Off with you to Paris!* and that soon! find your place among great people. *Aut Caesar aut nihil.*' If at the end of the letter he permits himself a little self-pity that is not hard to understand.

Mozart's irresponsible behaviour had a further consequence. In this letter, or more exactly in a postscript written on the cover, Leopold ordered that Maria Anna should not come home as had been planned but should go on to Paris with him, as she had recently offered.

The delays attendant on postal communication meant that Mozart wrote twice more to his father before he had this reaction to the letter of 4 February. Both make a bad situation worse. One refers to his unwillingness to undertake teaching in Paris, which would involve the tiresome business of going to pupils' houses and waiting around for them; he had just given up a pupil in Mannheim because she was out when he called. He had no objection to giving lessons as a favour but felt himself above calling on his pupils, as all other teachers did. The other concerns Maria Anna's planned homeward journey, and his flute compositions. He had composed, he writes, two concertos and three quartets, but had been paid only 96 gulden, a little under half the agreed sum, as the commission was not yet finished ('as you know, I become quite powerless when obliged to write for an instrument I cannot bear'). He also refers to a concert that included three of his concertos (he played K.175, Rosa Cannabich played K.238 and Ramm the K.271*k* oboe concerto) and arias sung by Aloysia as well as improvisations.

He could hardly have irritated Leopold more if he had been trying. Leopold began a letter on 15 February, then set it aside to write a rather warmer one, thanking Wolfgang for the French song he had sent (K.307/284*d*) and offering general advice about his time in Paris. He completed the one he had put aside, much sharper in tone, and sent it on 23 February. As he pointed out, he was now forced into the position of having to attend pupils at their houses, which Wolfgang loftily declined to do; and he had been urging Wolfgang to complete the flute commission weeks ago, a commission he had earlier, apparently untruthfully, said was for three short and easy concertos and two quartets. Was it three and two, or two and three? To that, one might add that perhaps it was one and four; in a doggerel verse letter sent to his mother when he was in Worms, Mozart had written:[17]

Wendling, no doubt, is in a rage
That I haven't composed a single page;
But when I cross the Rhine once more,
I'll surely dash home through the door
And, lest he call me mean and petty,
I'll finish off his four quartetti.
The concerto for Paris I'll keep, 'tis more fitting,
I'll scribble it there some day when I'm shitting.

The other issue that rankled with Leopold was that neither Mozart nor Maria Anna had come to realize sooner that Wendling was no fit travelling companion, when they had spent so much time in his company and become so friendly with his family. It does not seem to have occurred at this point to Leopold, with his reflex anxiety about godless people, that perhaps Wendling was not really so dangerous and that Mozart's growing attachment to Aloysia Weber and his hopes of spending more time with her might have led him into exaggeration and a plausible excuse for a change of plan. In a further letter, three days later, Leopold tells Wolfgang that he is sending arias suitable for Aloysia, some of them specially recopied. Here he also writes in some detail (and not without a hint of self-pity) about the shabby state of his clothes, which he cannot afford to replace, and mentions too that he has been working at music with Nannerl, who has made great progress, improving her command of harmony, modulation, improvisation and accompaniment. The example of the Adlgasser family, and the poverty into which they had been plunged by Cajetan's death, provided a sobering reminder of what awaited Nannerl if her own father died and she could not pursue a professional career: domestic service was the only possibility.

Mozart's response to Leopold's letters was a trifle sheepish. He had not really expected his father to agree to the Weber scheme, he now says, but had promised the Webers that he would broach the matter; he was hurt about the reproaches for his frivolous behaviour, which he denied (news had reached Leopold of Mozart's clowning one evening at Wallerstein); and he protested his awareness of the preparation that Aloysia would need before public appearances could be contemplated. He must surely have found the stream of reproaches tiresome and difficult to answer (particularly as they were substantially justified), and the even more voluble stream of advice, however necessary, must surely have wearied him too. But in these last letters from Mannheim he also wrote about his recent music, with obvious pleasure and excitement, in particular about some arias he had been composing for Aloysia, Raaff and Wendling's wife Dorothea, who was the leading soprano in Mannheim. And at last he seemed to be warming to the opportunities open to him in Paris. He was especially pleased to learn from Leopold, at the beginning of March, that their old friend Baron Grimm would be in the city, which meant that many doors would be open to him (Grimm had in fact been at Mozart's concert in Augsburg, but the Mozarts missed him there). Mozart's final letter from Mannheim, sent on 11 March, announces that they have at last been able to sell the chaise, for 40 gulden, to the coachman who would drive them in it to Paris, reducing the cost of the journey accordingly. On 12 March there was a farewell concert at Cannabich's house, at which the three-piano concerto was played by Rosa, Aloysia Weber and Therese Pierron, and Aloysia sang two arias. On 14 March they set out.

MOZART WAS IN Mannheim for four-and-a-half months. They were not unproductive. Sadly, he wrote nothing for the famous orchestra: composing for this 'army of generals' would have provided a challenge to which he would surely have risen. Nor, as yet, did he compose in the characteristic Mannheim genre, the sinfonia concertante. He had begun to write a mass, probably in mid-December, when he

thought that presenting one to the Elector might help his employment prospects. He wrote about 20 bars of a Kyrie, up to the beginning of the 'Christe eleison', in quite an elaborate style (K.322/296a),
but there was little point in continuing when the likelihood of
employment faded, although he did refer to working on it in February. Some sketches in the same key, E flat, for a Sanctus were no doubt
also intended for this work. Otherwise his Mannheim output consists
of the three arias already mentioned, two French *ariettes*, the piano
sonata for Rosa Cannabich and another piano sonata (curiously,
never mentioned in the correspondence with Leopold—it could be
the work referred to briefly in a letter to Mozart's cousin) and five
accompanied sonatas. Four of these were intended for the set of six
that Mozart went on to complete and publish in Paris; the other—
again, nowhere referred to in the correspondence—was composed
for Therese Pierron.

In Augsburg, Mozart had improvised 'a magnificent sonata in C,
with a rondo finale'. Possibly something of that improvisation found
its way into the K.309 piano sonata, the one he composed for Rosa
Cannabich. When Leopold saw the sonata, which Mozart sent home
for copying, he wrote that it was 'a strange composition. It has something in it of the *rather artificial* Mannheim style, but so very little that
your own good style is not spoilt'. Nannerl later added that 'one can
see from the style that you wrote it in Mannheim'. Perhaps Leopold
had in mind the vigorous pseudo-orchestral gestures of the first
movement: its forthright opening statement is of a kind that the
Mannheimers used in their symphonies, and some of the *forte* passages
have the air of a tutti. The irregular phrase structure is also unusual,
at least in the context of a piano sonata. But it is the slow movement,
Andante un poco adagio, that is exceptional, and more likely to have
seemed to Leopold artificial in its style. Mozart wrote that 'it is full of
expression and must be played accurately and with the exact shades
of *forte* and *piano*, precisely as they are marked', and he later told a
friend that he 'would make it fit closely the character of Mlle Rosa
. . . she is exactly like the Andante'.[18] This movement, as far as we

know his only one designed to portray a specific person, is a kind of double-variation movement, not unlike the form that Haydn later cultivated. It is essentially ternary, *A-B-A*, but first the *A* section and then the *B-A* section is repeated, each time with increasing elaboration. The principal theme is halting in character, with dotted rhythms and rests and restlessly alternating *piano* and *forte*, but it seems to flower with its layers of decoration, and the music has a delicate expressive nature of its own, one that Mozart never tapped again. The Rondeau finale, which has some passages suggesting Mannheim-style violin tremolandos, is a sturdier piece but still graceful in character.

The other piano sonata's origins are mysterious. It seems, from remarks in two of Mozart's letters to his cousin in Augsburg, that he may have committed himself to sending a sonata to Josepha Freysinger, one of two sisters, 'beautiful young ladies' whom he had met in Munich and whose father had been a student with Leopold. Evidently they were friends of Maria Anna Thekla, whom he asked to convey greetings and apologies 'for not yet having sent the sonata'. He planned to send it to his cousin to forward. Later, 'she must possess herself in patience a little longer'.[19] Whether a sonata was ever written for Josepha Freysinger, or, if it was, whether it was sent, remains uncertain. Mozart, usually so communicative about his compositions and so excited about them that he always wanted to tell his father what he was writing, nowhere mentioned composing another sonata. He might have been hesitant to tell him that he had promised a sonata, for nothing, to a 'beautiful young lady'.

Whatever the case, Mozart had written K.311 in D before he reached Paris. The autograph is headed 'No. 7', so it may well have been reckoned the next in sequence after the first group of six, which are also numbered. In style, K.311 is close to K.284 in its outgoing D major brilliance, with almost unceasing rapid notes in the first movement, and like K.284 in Mozart's first, abortive attempt, it takes the main idea for its development from the cadence figure that ends the exposition, this time successfully. Uniquely among his piano sonatas, this movement has a 'reversed recapitulation', a type much favoured by Mannheim composers. It was preferred here partly at least because the opening gesture would have required an awkward break in the momentum of the development had it occurred at the conventional point; in the event, it provides a culminating rhetorical flourish to a spirited movement. A comparison between the slow movement, Andante con espressione, and that of K.309 may clarify Leopold's remark about artificiality. Here the more flowing and continuous line, the simpler decoration of the principal theme when it recurs (the movement is a sonata rondo) and the more stable dynamics provide music no less expressive but without the aura of high, perhaps exaggerated, sensibility. K.311 has an extended and ebullient 6/8 finale, a richly developed sonata rondo, which is substantially Mozart's longest movement to date for solo piano. A brief cadenza heralds the recapitulation; and unusually placed and differentiated dynamic markings indicate the care that he must have taken in the performance of such movements. If this sonata was truly for Fräulein Freysinger, she must have been an exceptionally fine pianist. The work's virtuoso character can leave little doubt that Mozart, to whomever he may have sent it, wrote it principally in order to play it himself.

When, probably in mid-December 1777 or early January 1778, Mozart decided to take up Wendling's suggestion that he should write a set of accompanied sonatas for publication, he is likely to have recalled that only shortly before, in Munich, he had expressed interest in writing precisely such a set, provoked by the example of Schuster's popular works, which he had sent to Salzburg for Leopold and Nannerl to see and play. Schuster wrote two sets of works for keyboard and violin in the 1770s, and it is the set called *Divertimenti da camera* that was circulating in Munich at this time.[20] Mozart thought them worth playing, and worth emulating—his characteristic reaction on coming across something new, to show himself and the world that he could do better. Schuster's music is slender and its ideas are mostly conventional and sometimes banal. But the pieces do show some quite ingenious and novel handling of the relationship between the keyboard and the 'accompanying' violin. In Mozart's childhood sonatas (he had written none since), the violin was rarely required to do more than sustain harmonic notes, supply accompanying figuration, support a melody a third or a sixth below or reinforce it in a loud passage, and occasionally partake in a scrap of dialogue. Schuster goes beyond that, with more extended dialogues and interchanges of material, and he often assigns the main melodic material to the violin or involves it in contrapuntal writing.

Mozart did not have the Schuster sonatas by him as he wrote his own (he had sent them to Nannerl and told her she need not return them), but clearly his own ideas about the medium had been stimulated, and a few of Schuster's phrases had lodged in his memory. The beginning of his first sonata, K.301/293a in G, has a faint but unmistakable echo of the first movement of Schuster's third, and its finale has phrases in common with Schuster's. The busy, vigorous D major manner of Mozart's sixth is found in Schuster's fifth. Mozart's ideas on piano and violin textures may well have been opened up by the Schuster works, but his actual handling goes far beyond them in its imaginative scope and, characteristically, his feeling for the possibilities of the medium drew him into devising kinds of musical invention that allowed for new modes of dialogue and interplay. The one point in which Mozart was clearly indebted to Schuster is in the form of the first movement of his third sonata, K.303/293c. Schuster's third divertimento begins with a nine-bar Adagio, in G minor, followed by an Allegro in B flat major. The Adagio recurs, as if a first-subject 'recapitulation', to be followed by a G minor recapitulation of the material of the Allegro. The movement can thus be seen as a kind of sonata-form pattern, with the primary material slow and the secondary fast. Mozart had used this scheme before, in the K.171 string quartet, but his revival of it in K.303 points to Schuster's model. Other novel features, which Mozart did not pursue in his sonatas, is a movement (the first of no. 5) that ends with a passage of recitative, leading directly into the ensuing Adagio, and one (in no. 4) with passages offering a credible imitation of a late Baroque keyboard style.

These sonatas are among Mozart's most original works to date and

of very diverse character. All except the last of the eventual set of six
(two, composed later, will be discussed in the next chapter) are in the
two-movement form widely preferred for domestic music in the
galant era, a form Mozart otherwise never used. Usually these comprise a sonata-allegro followed by a rondo or a minuet. He began the
first sonata, the autograph shows, offering the option of violin or flute
for the accompanying part—perhaps he had in mind the possibility
of offering it to his flautist patron—but he soon removed the alternative, and after a dozen bars the music of K.301 is beyond the flute's
range. The sonata begins with the main melodic line on the violin,
but for most of the movement the keyboard predominates, although
there is much dialogue and division of material, rhythmic as well as
melodic, and the poetic colour of a high violin line, sustained or
momentarily melodic, above a busy and active piano part, is exploited
in new ways. The finale, a brisk 3/8, has the atmosphere of a rondo
but the form of a minuet and trio.

The character of Mozart's keyboard writing is influenced in these
sonatas, to a greater extent than in his solo sonatas, by the sound of
the piano: he still had the ring of Stein's instruments in his ears. The
repeated soft chords at the opening of K.302/293*b*, and the extended
Mannheim-style crescendo soon after, could not have been conceived in terms of harpsichord sound. This, with its opening flourish,
is music typical of Mozart's E flat style, as too is the rondo finale, an
Andante grazioso whose gentle sentiment reflects Mannheim taste.
Here Mozart achieves some attractive variety of texture with his
ingenious octave doublings, the violin sometimes above the keyboard
and sometimes below. Schuster's example had stimulated him into
discovering a new range of textural devices, which in turn led to an
enlarging of his expressive canvas. In K.303, the first movement is
divided, along the Schuster model, between Adagio and Molto
Allegro, sharply contrasted in style, the former with a decorated line
of some intensity, the latter in a brilliant style with dashing triplets for
the piano. The finale is an expansive binary-form minuet in a courtly,
elegant style. The last of these four works, K.305/293*d* in A, starts

with a lively movement in the 6/8 rhythm of a gigue (like the late sonata in A, K.526), with some ingenious misplacing of musical patterns—four-note phrases in a metre with units of three—to keep the ear alert. At the beginning of the development Mozart uses the Baroque device of inversion of the opening theme (there is a parallel to this in K.301). The finale is a set of variations.

The sonata written for Therese Pierron stands somewhat apart from these. It is unclear why Mozart excluded it from the published set, composing an extra sonata instead: perhaps its presentation to Therese precluded its inclusion in a set that was to bear another dedication (to the Mannheim, or later Bavarian, Electress). Probably Mozart never intended it for this set: like K.303, it is in C major, and two sonatas in the same key would be unusual. It is in three movements and rather different in manner from the other sonatas, more public and outgoing, more susceptible to effective performance. The violin part is less prominent, less nearly equal in status to the piano's, and the keyboard writing in the outer movements, no doubt tailored to Therese's technique, calls for particularly crisp and nimble fingerwork. As in the other sonata written in Mannheim for a girl pupil, the aura of feminine sensibility pervades the graceful Andante.

The other body of instrumental works from the Mannheim months is the flute music. We do not know exactly what Mozart gave Dejean for his 96 gulden. There are two flute concertos, K.313/285*c* in G and K.314/285*d* in D, of which the latter was not a new work but a transposed and slightly altered version of the K.271*k* oboe concerto. There is also a separate Andante in C K.315/285*e*, which could have been intended as an independent piece, or as one movement of another concerto that was otherwise unwritten, or as a replacement for the slow movement of K.313 if Dejean had not liked it. Of the promised flute quartets, one was certainly completed, K.285; the autograph survives, dated 25 December 1777. There can be little doubt that Mozart wrote a second quartet for Dejean at some point—during the summer of 1778 Mozart wrote to Leopold that he would send two flute quartets, with a batch of other music—though whether he had written it in Mannheim or in Paris is uncertain. The second quartet is almost certainly K.285*a*, a two-movement work in G; its sole contemporary source is a Viennese edition of 1792, where it appears as the second and third movements of a quartet beginning with the first movement of K.285. There is no reason to question its authenticity, although the possibility of its originally having another movement cannot be excluded. Mozart produced one other flute quartet, K.298 in A, which dates from 1786–87 and therefore cannot have been written to round out Dejean's commission.

A two-movement work in C, K.Anh.171/285*b*, published in Speyer in 1788, is a forgery that was sometimes reckoned to be the third of the Dejean works. Its first movement begins attractively, but its later material is uncharacteristic of Mozart, and its second movement is demonstrably an arrangement of the variation movement from Mozart's serenade for 13 instruments of the early 1780s (K.361/370*a*).[21] This puzzling work also includes ten bars that correspond with a Mozart sketch of 1781, although the music is unrelated to the remainder of the movement. The sketch may be from Mozart's workings for the quartet, but its music was 'borrowed' by someone else for insertion here. The piece was apparently assembled, using some Mozart material—perhaps including the beginning of a third Dejean quartet that was never completed—by an opportunist hack working for a none-too-scrupulous publisher.

There is little in Mozart's works for flute to betray his erroneously supposed lack of sympathy for the instrument.[22] The K.314 concerto is a virtually exact transposition of the oboe work, with some changes in articulation and in a few details of the figuration to accommodate the flute's different capacities. The first movement of the K.313 concerto is unexceptional, deftly and often felicitously written for the instrument, making particular use of its topmost register, but not showing the kinds of boldness in which the K.271 piano concerto or the last of the violin concertos abound. But this was, of course, not only his first venture (and in fact his last), but it was also intended for an amateur player. It is the more surprising, then, that the slow movement, Adagio ma non troppo, is music of considerable intensity, with much eloquent detail in the flute writing. If the manner and the softly flowing accompanying textures (with flutes replacing oboes in the orchestra) are akin to those of some of the serenades, the shaping of the long solo section has a force that would not belong in a serenade context. Whether this movement proved too much for Dejean and resulted in the composition of the much lighter and charming Andante in C K.315, we cannot know. For the finale Mozart turned to the *menuet en rondeau* style of the finales of the bassoon concerto and the two-violin concertone, but this is a more spirited and more mature example, longer and more fully worked out. Justifying his tardiness over the flute music, Mozart had written to Leopold: 'I could, to be sure, scribble off things the whole day long, but this kind of composition goes out into the world and I naturally do not want cause to be ashamed of my name on the title-page'. K.313 no doubt cost him effort, and repaid it.

So too did the first—or the one always assumed to be the first—of the flute quartets, K.285 in D. The flute quartet was a popular genre in the 1770s because of the flute's prime position as the gentleman amateur's instrument. Mozart surpasses his models in his happy management of the relationship between a concertante part and the strings, using the string trio sometimes in accompaniment but often in various kinds of dialogue, as when, after the statement of the opening theme, the strings embark on a new idea to which the flute's response provides a new twist. Mozart's skill in writing music for the middle voices of the ensemble, in both the first movement and the ebullient sonata-rondo finale, keeps the listener's ear alert. For the Adagio he supplied an enchantingly pathetic song for the flute, accompanied pizzicato, in B minor, which has been described as 'of the sweetest melancholy, perhaps the most beautiful accompanied solo ever written for the flute'.[23] It is not great music, but it could have been written only by a composer of the greatest mastery. K.285a, the (supposedly) second, is in two movements, a neatly written but more ordinary Andante (with a miniature reversed recapitulation) and a minuet. Dejean may have had cause to complain about the quantity of music that Mozart supplied for him, but could not grumble at the quality of the best of it, which has lent a measure of immortality to his name.

It is not perhaps surprising, however, that of all the music Mozart wrote at Mannheim the most personal and most profoundly expressive is the aria 'Non so d'onde viene' K.294. He told his father:

> For practice I have . . . set to music the aria 'Non so d'onde viene', which was so beautifully composed by [J.C.] Bach. Simply because I know Bach's setting so well and like it so much, and as it is always ringing in my ears, I wanted to try to see whether, despite this, I could not write an aria totally unlike his. . . . At first I had intended it for Raaff, but the beginning seemed to me too high for his voice. But I liked it so much that I didn't want to alter it; and from the orchestral accompaniment too it seemed to me better suited to a soprano. So I decided to write it for Mlle Weber.

This dual inspiration—reinforced by the words, which begin 'I do not know from where this tender emotion comes'—drew from him an aria of quite exceptional tenderness of emotion, beautifully scored with flutes, clarinets, bassoons and horns, in the unfailingly expressive key of E flat, with some faint echoes of the J.C. Bach setting.[24] It is formally ingenious too, with a faster middle section and, when the slower music returns, what is in effect a partial recapitulation and extended coda rather than the more usual simple repetition. It speaks unmistakably of his feelings for Aloysia Weber. For part of the aria Mozart later supplied a decorated text, which shows how closely the original line is followed and which passages are left as they stand. This was the first of many arias that he was to write for Aloysia. Several years later, he reset the text, this time for a bass voice; the words, from Metastasio's L'Olimpiade, were not intended for a lover but a father who is drawn to a young man who later turns out to be his son.

The other Mannheim arias were for members of the musical establishment there. Composing an aria for the elderly tenor Anton Raaff probably began as a diplomatic exercise, but the result is another exquisite piece, perfectly tailored to the voice. Raaff was a product of the Bernacchi school of singing, with its emphasis on smooth lines and gentle portamentos. Mozart gave him exactly the kind of music he sang most comfortably, to words he already knew ('Se al labbro mio non credi', taken from an aria in Hasse's *Artaserse*, a Metastasio opera, although these words were originally written by Antonio Salvi and were carried across into *Artaserse* from his *Arminio*). He shortened the aria and made other adjustments to suit Raaff, whose sustaining ability was now limited. The aria 'Ah non lasciarmi, no' K.486*a*/295*a*, for Dorothea Wendling, a Metastasio setting from *Didone abbandonata*, is a slighter piece, but carefully written for her voice and to exploit her admired pathetic characterization and expressive phrasing. Possibly it was only begun at Mannheim and finished rather later.[25] These gestures towards his Mannheim acquaintances would later turn out to be useful investments.

18

'Off with you to Paris!'

N 14 MARCH 1778, Mozart and his mother left Mannheim. There were fond farewells with the Webers— Aloysia had knitted some mittens for Wolfgang, and Fridolin gave him the comedies of Molière (in German)—but a curiously cool parting from Cannabich, with neither gift nor thanks for the sonata immortalizing his daughter; perhaps he felt his support and hospitality had been enough. Although it was little more than 500 kilometres, their journey to Paris, through Metz, Clermont-en-Argonne and Reims, took them nine-and-a-half uncomfortable and boring days. In Paris, they lodged at first in rue Bourg L'Abbé, with a Herr Mayer, where a previous Salzburg visitor had stayed.[1]

Here was Mozart's opportunity. Paris was the greatest city of the European continent, a leading musical centre, with many music-loving amateurs, a large music-publishing industry, a busy operatic life and a good deal of concert activity by the standards of the times. Much of the music-making took place in large private houses, but there was also the Concert des Amateurs, which held weekly events in its winter season, and the Concert Spirituel, so called because its concerts, unrivalled in prestige, were given on certain days in the church calendar (about 25 in the year) when the Opéra was closed, with the Opéra orchestra, and its programmes usually included sacred works. In the 1778 Easter season Mannheim musicians were playing a prominent part, with Wendling, Ramm and the bassoonist Heinrich Ritter playing concertos (along with the well-known hornist Jan Václav Stich, also known as Giovanni Punto) and Raaff singing several arias.

The Mozart family letters are in effect the only source we have for Mozart's activities in Paris; there is virtually no reference in any Parisian document to him during his months in the city. Fortunately, Mozart and his mother's letters are full and very informative, although their number is small by comparison with those from Mannheim and the other German cities. Post from (and to) Paris was costly, and letters between there and Salzburg took longer, generally nine or ten days. Allowing for twice-weekly post days, this meant that it could take close to a month for an exchange of views or for a question to be answered.

MOZART SOON CALLED on Baron Grimm and Mme d'Épinay, who were his principal links with Parisian musical and cultural life, and on Noverre and his daughter Mme Jenamy. In his first few days he also saw his Mannheim friends, including Raaff, and the Palatinate ambassador in Paris, Count Sickingen, to whom he had letters of introduction from Cannabich and Baron von Gemmingen-Homberg, author and Mannheim government official. Maria Anna's first substantial letter home, sent on 5 April, must have been heartening to Leopold, with its news of Wolfgang's energetic pursuit of contacts and of his industry. He has been asked, she writes, by Joseph Legros, director of the Concert Spirituel (a distinguished high tenor who created several Gluck roles), to write a *Miserere*, he is composing two concertos, one for the flute and one for the harp, and an act of an opera, and he has a pupil at a high rate of pay. She however feels as if in prison, sitting in a small, dark room by herself all day (Wolfgang goes out to compose as there is no space for a piano there, and he lunches with friends), and the French food is unspeakable and costly. Mozart added a note, explaining that the *Miserere* was in fact a series of replacement movements for a work by Holzbauer to make it better suited to the Concert Spirituel chorus, that there was to be a sinfonia concertante for wind instruments, and the opera was to be an entire one, called *Alexandre et Roxane*. He also mentioned that they were shortly moving to a lodging in the rue Gros Chenêt (now the rue du Sentier, 2e *arrondissement*), which Mme d'Épinay, Grimm's mistress, had found for them. This letter crossed with Leopold's response to their first from Paris, advising them to trust Grimm and take him into their confidence, and commenting too on Wolfgang's recent request, in his last letter, that Leopold write more cheerfully. This gave occasion for a reminder of the debts Leopold had got himself into for Wolfgang's sake, with thoughts on his habit of considering situations carefully and his hopes that Wolfgang would now be in a position to make him more cheerful. His next letter is largely about music-making in Salzburg, especially the activities of a new amateur orchestra led by Count Johann Rudolph Czernin, a young nephew of the archbishop's, in which Nannerl was to be the harpsichord continuo player. He received Wolfgang's latest letter while he was writing and responded to the news of the compositions under way—it is clear, here and in many other letters, that his chief delight lay in hearing (and in hearing about) his son's new works—and he urged Wolfgang to be sure to accommodate French taste, however much he might deplore it, in the music he was writing.

But Wolfgang's resistance to the French, the actual people, their language, their singing, their musical taste, was deep-rooted, and events during the next weeks strengthened it. Grimm had given him an introduction to the Duchesse de Bourbon, and at her request he called on her.

> I had to wait for half an hour in a large, ice-cold, unheated room, which didn't even have a fireplace. Eventually the Duchesse de Chabot entered, with the greatest politeness,

and asked me to do my best with the clavier in the room, as none of hers was in good order; would I try it? I said I would be happy to play something, but at the moment it was impossible, as I couldn't feel my fingers for the cold; could I at least be taken to a room where there was a fire? O oui Monsieur, vous avez raison. That was all she replied. Then she sat down and began to draw, and went on doing so for a whole hour, in the company of some gentlemen, all sitting in a circle around a large table. I had the honour of waiting for a whole hour. Not only my hands but my whole body and feet were cold, and my head too began to ache. There was also utter silence. I didn't know what to do for cold, headache and boredom. I often thought, if it weren't for M Grimm I'd be out of here like a shot. Finally, to cut a long story short, I played, on that wretched, miserable pianoforte. But what was worst is that Madame and her gentlemen never for a moment broke off their drawing, always concentrating on it, so I was playing to the table, chairs and walls.[2]

He later recovered his spirits somewhat, playing to the Duchesse's husband, who listened attentively. But he went on to explain to Leopold the difficulty of calling on potential patrons—the muddy roads, the long distances, the cost of a carriage, the fact that the French politely praise his playing but consider their applause sufficient reward.

At the Concert Spirituel things were not much better. Of the four choruses he had written for Holzbauer's *Miserere*, only two were performed, as the work turned out to be too long—and few people even knew that he had composed the pieces. An aria of Mozart's (listed as by 'Mezart') was given a few days later, on 21 April. But, he reports, there has been a 'Hickl–hackl' over the sinfonia concertante he had written for the Mannheim wind players. This had been commissioned by 5 April, when he referred to it in a letter. He took his score to Legros for copying but discovered it a few days later, hidden away among the music in Legros's office, and Legros claimed he had for-gotten about it. To the irritation of the wind players as well as Mozart, it was taken off the programme and never performed. It is unclear whether it had been intended for the concert on 12 April, when a new sinfonia concertante by the Italian composer Giuseppe Cam-bini, for the same instruments and the same players, was given (and repeated a week later)—in which case he would have been expected to write it rather quickly—or for a later one. Mozart thought its sup-pression was Cambini's doing. In front of other musicians, Mozart had played a piece of Cambini's from memory and then, egged on by Ramm and the others and perhaps too eager to score off Cambini, improvised what he could not remember, evidently to the composer's discomfiture.[3] The incident itself illustrates all too plainly why Mozart was liable to be unpopular with at least some of his fellow musicians. Leopold, responding in his next letter,[4] warns Mozart of the jealousy of other musicians but is silent on the unwisdom of alienating them.

By mid-May, however, Mozart and his mother seemed reasonably settled in Paris. She writes of renting rooms and buying their own furniture in the autumn. He now had three pupils. One was the daughter of Adrien-Louis Bonnières de Souastre, Comte de Guines, a former diplomat who had worked in Berlin and London but had been recalled because of financial irregularities, who plays the flute 'extremely well'. The daughter 'plays the harp *magnifique*' and is greatly talented, Mozart says, with an extraordinary memory, but is no composer—his account of provoking her into composing as much as four bars of a minuet is hilarious. He had written a concerto for father and daughter (not one each, as Maria Anna had earlier thought). He expects to receive the libretto of his planned opera quite soon, and meanwhile is to write a ballet for Noverre. He then tells Leopold that he has been offered the post of organist at Versailles, at 2000 livres per annum, for which he would have to spend six months of the year at Versailles and the remainder in Paris or else-where. That was the equivalent of 915 gulden 45 kreuzer in Salzburg currency, more than double Leopold's annual salary for half a year's employment. This, it might seem, could have been the end of Mozart's quest, and an assurance of prosperity and perhaps even reunion for the family. 'I do not think I shall accept it', he wrote, although he would ask the advice of friends. Paris, as he pointed out, was an expensive place to live. Leopold, perhaps surprisingly, wrote only briefly on the matter in his long next letter, reminding Mozart that this would be a salaried appointment (he would be paid even when he was ill), that he would be constantly in the presence of the royal family and other influential people, and that he could teach and compose for the theatre and the Concert Spirituel. In a later letter, he expresses doubt as to whether the offer was a real one or simply a pious hope on the part of one of Mozart's friends. Mozart responded by saying that Grimm had echoed his reservations, and he had never thought seriously about it; he did not want an organist's position— only a Kapellmeistership, and a well-paid one, would do. Whether or not the offer was a firm one, Mozart had set his sights higher, and in different directions.

   Leopold, however, was now thinking along rather different lines, which may account for his rather mild encouragement of Wolfgang over the Versailles position. In his letter of 11 June he first referred to the possibility of Wolfgang's returning to Salzburg. It was in fact the Versailles position that made it possible for the issue to be raised in Salzburg where, with Adlgasser dead, a new Konzertmeister-organist was needed. At a chance encounter early in June, Countess Lodron[5] had enquired about Mozart's progress; Leopold was able to tell her of the Versailles offer. It was soon reported back to Leopold that the countess, who was at least ostensibly a friend of the Mozart family and seems to have served as chief emissary between them and the archbishop, regretted her absence from Salzburg when Mozart decided to leave and wanted to know whether Leopold was eager to have him back. Further, she indicated that were he to return Mozart would be paid 600 gulden as Konzertmeister-organist with a prom-ise of eventually becoming Kapellmeister. Michael Haydn's candidature for promotion was now ruled out, partly because of his drinking habits (according to Leopold, who once referred to a performance affected by 'a slight tipsiness which made his head and his hands refuse to agree'), but also because his wife's sister had sullied the family's reputation by giving birth to a child by Brunetti. Meanwhile, the archbishop was writing to Italy for a new Kapellmeister to succeed Fischietti and was trying to recruit Luigi Gatti of Mantua, whom the Mozarts had met there in 1770 when he copied out a mass of Wolfgang's. Along with this information is much more news of Salzburg musical life, in particular about Count Czernin's amateur orchestra.

Mozart's next letter, sent with Maria Anna's last on 12 June, is largely about Raaff, with whom he and his mother had struck up a warm friendship. Raaff and his wife were regular visitors to the Mozarts, and Raaff was singing at the Concert Spirituel, where Mozart had come increasingly to admire the beauty of his voice, his bravura singing and his diction, and especially his interpretation of short pieces, although Raaff's Bernacchi-influenced style of singing, with a tendency to lapse too readily into a smooth cantabile, was not really to Mozart's taste. There are some fascinating comments on singing in this letter, including one on vocal vibrato—Mozart found a heavy vibrato 'detestable' and liked only a natural trembling of the voice. He also mentions here the new symphony he had written for the Concert Spirituel, to be given at the Corpus Christi concert on 18 June. Leopold's response contains more news about the Czernin orchestra (especially about a disastrous breach of etiquette, when Czernin gave his sister, Countess Lützow, precedence in serenading over the higher-ranking Countess Lodron), with queries about the musicians and others Mozart had met in Paris and about the projected opera, and a further report on his dealings with the court. Count Starhemberg had been sent to sound him out, rather obliquely, about Mozart, whom he warmly praised, but Leopold was evidently guarded and non-committal while giving his views on other aspects of the court music. He adds: 'I am not writing all this with the purpose, my dear Wolfgang, of persuading you to come back to Salzburg—for I would not depend in the slightest degree on the word of the archbishop'.

Before that letter was received, however, events in Paris had taken a tragic turn for the Mozart family. Leopold had reminded Maria Anna that she should be bled, a traditional medical procedure at this time of year. The task was duly done, on 11 June. Five or six days later she was unwell, with diarrhœa, and she was unable to go on 18 June to hear Mozart's new symphony at the Concert Spirituel. On 19 June, with severe headache, she retired to bed, and the next day a fever began. They carried a number of medical remedies with them, and Mozart gave her an anti-spasmodic powder (they had none left of their favourite home medicine, black powder or *pulvis epilepticus*). On 23 June her hearing failed. She was reluctant to see a French doctor; on 24 June an elderly German one came and administered rhubarb powder in wine. When, two days later, he returned, he made the gravity of the situation clear to Mozart. Grimm sent his doctor, but it was too late. She made her final confession and took extreme unction on 30 June. She was delirious during the next three days, and died on the evening of 3 July. (Not far away, at Ermenonville, Jean-Jacques Rousseau had died the day before.) She was buried the next day at St Eustache; the churchyard no longer exists but there is a memorial tablet to her in the church. François-Joseph Heina, a Czech-born hornist, trumpeter and music publisher, who with his wife Gertrude had befriended the Mozarts, was present at the interment. Maria Anna was 57 years old. The nature of her final illness is unknown; typhoid and typhus fever have been suggested.[6]

Mozart had not written to his father to tell him of his mother's illness. He will have realized that there was little point in doing so. It could only cause painful anxiety, and there was no prospect of Leopold's coming to Paris to be with Maria Anna: his financial situation, with heavy debts and no cash to hand, precluded his leaving Salzburg. In any case, if she was in mortal danger he would almost certainly have been too late. So Mozart had now to tell his father and his sister of the tragedy. He decided to write to Leopold to tell him

St Eustache, Paris, where Mozart's mother was buried: engraving (*Internationale Stiftung Mozarteum, Salzburg*)

at first only that Maria Anna was seriously ill, and at the same time to write to the family friend and priest, Abbé Bullinger, to tell him the true state of affairs. This thoughtful procedure may perhaps have softened the blow. Leopold's next letter, begun on 12 July, starts by offering his wife congratulations on her nameday. The following morning, however, Wolfgang's letter, dated 3 July and presumably posted the next day, reached him. Leopold immediately realized that by this time she had probably died. Nannerl 'wept copiously' and suffered sickness and headache. The day was one on which there was a shooting game at the Mozarts', which Leopold could not cancel. After it, when their friends, all very sad, left, Bullinger stayed behind and 'acted his part well', gently intimating to Leopold that Maria Anna was indeed dead. Leopold then finished his letter to his son, with many enquiries about the events surrounding her death and the aftermath, many injunctions to care for his own health, many expressions of his love for his wife and of his acceptance of God's will.

It is not easy to understand fully the undercurrents in the family correspondence at the best of times, and at the worst it is all the more difficult. Wolfgang repeatedly urges Leopold to resign himself to God's will, to accept that his mother is now enjoying the blessings of heaven, that all things have their appropriate time, that one day they will all be reunited, that no doctor or other man or chance or misfortune can give or take away life when God has decided otherwise. Is there a hidden plea here for exculpation, an anxious desire to persuade Leopold that, whatever he might have done when in charge of her during her illness, it would have made no difference, since it was God's unalterable will that she should die when she did? Leopold too wrote of submission to the will of God, but he also wondered, understandably, whether Wolfgang had waited too long before calling for a doctor, although his criticism is at least partly directed at Maria Anna herself and her excessive confidence in her strength and health (no doubt, too, she was reluctant to run up doctors' bills). Clearly Leopold felt that events might have had another outcome had he himself been present, with his greater experience of tending illness, but each time he touches on that theme he comes back to seeing Maria Anna's death as pre-ordained by God. He does however permit himself to remark that, had Wolfgang gone to Paris with Wendling and his colleagues as originally planned, Maria Anna would have been able to return home, and would not have died: accordingly, Wolfgang had to act as he did to enable the will of God—that she die on 3 July—to be fulfilled. The conflict between his almost fatalistic religious stance and his sense that Wolfgang and his actions were ultimately to blame for his wife's death lends a certain ambiguity, not to say convoluted logic, to much of what he writes in his letters of July and August, and that is surely a true reflection of his state of mind in the first weeks after his bereavement. Wolfgang must have felt, reading his father's letters, and especially when Leopold divulged to him the confidential postscript Maria Anna had written in Mannheim on 5 February, that in some degree Leopold saw him as responsible for her death, but it would be surprising if that added substantially to the guilt he already harboured.

As he pointed out in a letter at the end of July,[7] Mozart had no experience of death. He did not know that, to come to terms with it, it is important for many people who are bereaved to rehearse in their minds the circumstances, and in his first letters he gave Leopold and Nannerl little concrete information about his mother's final illness, her death or her burial, concentrating instead on religious consolation and exhortations to acceptance and prayer. Leopold asked him for more, and in that letter he gave a fairly detailed account of events up to 27 June, but then broke off: 'as I have more urgent matters to write about, I shall continue this story in my next letter'. In the event he never did so. He did not mention until much later, when his mother's effects had been returned to Salzburg, that he had given her amethyst ring (a gift from Madame d'Épinay on their previous visit) to the nurse, who would otherwise have taken her wedding ring, and had pawned her gold watch. He did include in the two crucial letters—the one telling Leopold of her mortal illness, the next announcing her death—a great deal of other material about his musical activities and the performance of his new symphony at the Concert Spirituel. Some writers have thought this insensitive; yet Leopold was always desperately anxious to know of such matters and would certainly have wanted and expected to hear any news as soon as possible, irrespective of the wider context.

During those last days of his mother's life Mozart wrote a number of other letters, three of which were to Fridolin Weber in Mannheim. None of these, written on 27 and 29 June and 3 July, survives but they are alluded to in a later letter,[8] from which it is clear that Mozart had been trying to work out ways of bringing Aloysia, her father and possibly the entire Weber family to Paris. He had tried, without success, to obtain an engagement for Aloysia at the Concert Spirituel for winter 1778–9. Rather surprisingly, he told Weber that the journey, food, lodging, wood and light would cost nothing, and they would surely find work for Aloysia in the concert seasons. Weber must have mentioned to Mozart the possibility of Aloysia's joining a travelling theatre group, the Seyler company, based in Mainz, a prospect to which

Mozart reacted (as no doubt he was intended to) with some degree of alarm: this was not a respectable profession, and the musical opportunities would be poor. His letter is a strange document, full of financial and career advice to a much older family man from a young man who had failed to establish his own position and succeeded only in inflating the family debts. It has to be seen as reflecting the image of himself that Mozart wanted to convey to the Webers. At the same time he wrote to Aloysia, a dignified, fairly formal but warm letter, largely on musical matters. Its tone makes it clear that the relationship between them had never been very close.

What is also clear, in the light of these letters, is that Mozart had been hatching a number of alternative plans that would enable him to be close to the Weber family, whether in Paris, Mannheim or Mainz. He learnt from Weber late in July that the Elector had decided to take up residence in Munich, which meant that Mannheim would lose its importance. The musicians had been offered the option of staying or moving with the main court establishment to Munich. Weber wanted to move, as Aloysia might obtain employment at the court theatre, but (like Leopold) could not do so without clearing his local debts. Mozart's cultivation of the company of Raaff and Sickingen (who had a brother connected with the Mainz court) during his time in Paris, rather than that of influential Frenchmen, seems likely to have been related to a possible move to one of the German courts. He was increasingly negative about staying in Paris: two of his pupils were away in the country and the third, the Guines girl, was to marry and discontinue lessons. He was prepared to write only a grand opera, as a short one would not be worth while, and if the French did not like it 'all would be over—I would never get another commission'. He mentioned 'other plans' but was not yet ready to disclose them, which must have enraged Leopold, although it is clear that he easily guessed that they had to do with being close to Aloysia.

Leopold's response was also pessimistic about Paris, though for different reasons. He had now received a frank letter from Grimm, in whose house Mozart had lived since his mother's death, about prospects there. Grimm doubted whether Mozart could even earn a bare living there for himself.

> He is too good-natured, too little active, too easily caught out, too little concerned with ways of advancing his career. Here, to make an impression, one must be crafty, enterprising and bold. I would wish him, for success, half the talent and double the savoir faire ... I give you this faithful account not to grieve you but so that you can take the best possible course of action.[9]

Grimm also explained the problems of earning a living as a piano teacher in Paris and the difficulty of making any impact in the operatic world when opinions were so strongly polarized between the adherents of Piccinni and those of Gluck. It was clear that Grimm, for all his goodwill, was despairing of Mozart's success in Paris and was keen to see him leave. Leopold urged Mozart to use his time profitably: if he could not teach, then he should compose—something 'short, easy and popular' that would be suitable for publication, perhaps string quartets.

> Do you perhaps believe that you would be lowering yourself by writing such pieces? By no means! Did [J.C.] Bach, in London, publish nothing but similar trifles? What is small can still be great, when it is written in a natural, fluent and easy manner, and at the same time is soundly composed. . . . Did Bach lower himself in this way?—Not at all! good composition and form, il filo[10]—that's what distinguishes the master from the bungler, even in trifles.

Leopold is often criticized for remarks such as these: is he trying to subvert his son's creative genius for sordid commercial reasons? To us, aware of the later Mozart and of Romantic notions of the artist fulfilling his destiny, it may seem so. But Leopold belonged to an age—

and so, marginally, did Wolfgang—when the composer was still more functionary than visionary and it was his role to supply what his employers or his public required of him.

Leopold's anxieties about the state of Mozart's finances were warranted. He goes on to warn his son that he should not expect to be housed and fed by Grimm and Madame d'Épinay, whose own circumstances were by no means easy. Mozart's expenses, including his mother's medical and burial costs, must have been considerable. He had received only partial payment for the Guines lessons and the concerto and nothing as yet from the publishers with whom he was dealing (for the publication of the set of six piano and violin sonatas, including four written in Mannheim), and his later assertion that he had been paid by Legros for two symphonies and the sinfonia concertante is dubious. Leopold knew that he had taken up a sum deposited with a banker and correctly guessed that he had also had to borrow from Grimm. Yet in his next letter[11] Leopold emphasizes that all Mozart's planning 'must be directed solely towards making [his] way successfully in Paris' and that he should only wait and see whether anything might transpire at Mannheim or Munich, Mainz or Salzburg—and any position at Mannheim or Munich would last no longer than the Elector himself, as there was no true heir, while the music at Mainz was poor by comparison with Salzburg, which had the further advantage of being closer to Italy. In this very long letter he also gives vent to his feelings about Wolfgang's concern for the Webers. While he is happy to assist Aloysia as far as possible, he asks:

> . . . but are our resources sufficient to give help to a family with six [actually four] children? who can do that?—me?— you?—you, who have not yet been able to help your own family? You write—'*dearest father! I commend them to you with all my heart. If they could only enjoy an income of 1000 gulden for a few years.* My beloved son! when I read that, how could I not fear for your sanity? For God's sake! I am to help them to get 1000 gulden for a few years! If I could, I would first

help *you* and *myself* and *your dear sister*, already 27 *and not provided for, and I grow older.*

Mozart wrote to his father on the same day, a short letter, sent from
St Germain, where he was a guest for just over a week at the
Maréchal de Noailles' chateau. There he met Bach, over from London to hear the Opéra singers before writing a new opera for them:
'you can imagine his delight and mine at meeting again; perhaps his
delight may not have been quite as sincere as mine—but one must
admit that he is an honourable man'. It is curious that Mozart so
often felt the need to sound a critical note, even of a man whose
kindness and goodwill were generally acknowledged—the price of
knowing the superiority of your gifts and the envy they aroused, and
of being the misanthropic Leopold's son. He also met the admired
castrato Giustino Ferdinando Tenducci, a friend of Bach's, and composed for him a scena, K.315*b*, with piano, oboe, bassoon and horn,
now presumed lost.[12]

A few days later, however, Leopold had changed his mind about his
son's future. Wolfgang must come back to Salzburg.[13] On the morning of 31 August he secured, he says, the archbishop's agreement to
new terms: a salary of 500 gulden and leave to travel for composing
operas, with an apology for not appointing him Kapellmeister—
impossible for someone who had just resigned. The archbishop
excused himself for his recent refusal by saying that he deplored people going about the world begging—shades of Maria Theresa, whose
views on the Mozarts he may have heard. If Leopold were ill or tired
Wolfgang would take on his duties. He was to have the title of Konzertmeister and would be relieved by a deputy of most of the routine
church services. Essentially, this was Adlgasser's position. Leopold had
also secured an additional 100 gulden for himself, as money recently
had been freed by the death of the retired Kapellmeister Giuseppe
Lolli. So although Mozart's own salary had slipped by 100, the family income would still be close to 1000.

Leopold's anxiety for Wolfgang's acceptance of these terms

induced him to write again four days later, assuring him that he could remain in touch with Aloysia by post—and that he was happy for Mozart to conduct such a correspondence privately, without his (Leopold's) even knowing, still less seeing. He also suggested that he mention in Munich that he is going back to Salzburg with a salary of 700 or 800, but would be open to a competitive offer and would welcome an opera commission. There is also a reminder of how strongly Mozart had written about his desire to see and embrace his father again, and of the beggary to which they might be reduced if he did not return.[14] Another letter a week later includes a list of the Mannheim musicians moving to Munich, among whom, he points out, there is no organist or clavier player, nor a Kapellmeister, which could mean that there might be a vacancy. So, unless he is still planning to stay in Paris, Mozart should travel through Munich. Leopold promised to write again in a week, when the archbishop's formal notice of appointment should have arrived. The archbishop 'has great respect' for Mozart and wants him to direct performances from the harpsichord.

It is hard to know whether Leopold was telling nothing but the truth when he conveyed the archbishop's proposals to Mozart. The final offer, when it finally came, was less attractive and less unambiguous than he had implied: that may be because he had gilded the lily somewhat to put pressure on Wolfgang, or because the archbishop and his advisers decided to be less generous than they had earlier indicated, or because some of the promises made verbally could not be reproduced in a formal, written agreement. Probably it was a mixture of all three. At any rate, when Mozart received the 31 August letter, his feelings were mixed. He had so many times, and so warmly, professed his longing to be back with his family that, although he still hated the attitude of the archbishop towards the musicians in Salzburg, he could scarcely refuse the position offered to him, and he made it clear that that was his chief reason for returning. In his reply,[15] his last letter from Paris, he lays down conditions: that he be allowed to travel every other year, and that he refuses to be kept to the violin ('I will no longer be a fiddler. I want to conduct at the clavier and accompany arias'); and he wanted the authoritative role of director, not the secondary one of leading violinist. He further wished there could be a written agreement that he would eventually be Kapellmeister, but recognized the impossibility of that. Meanwhile, his situation in Paris was improving, and he would have liked to stay on to write an opera were it not for the fact that if, when an opera is completed and rehearsed, the 'stupid Frenchmen' do not like it, it could simply be dropped and the composer left unpaid—and that was something he did not care to risk.

He could not, however, leave Paris at once. He explained to his father that he needed to collect money due to him from Guines and Legros, that he had still to compose six trios (these, 'for which', he wrote, 'I will be well paid', never materialized), and he had a number of plans for publishing his music (he wanted to take advantage of being in the largest music publishing centre in Europe) and thus to raise money for the homeward journey. He would like to sell his three piano concertos (K.238, 246 and 271), his 'six difficult sonatas' (K.279–84) and perhaps his violin concertos, which he would shorten ('in Germany we rather like length, but after all it is better to be short and good'). He had symphonies with him, but most were not, he said, in the Parisian taste. In fact, none of these plans materialized. The six piano and violin sonatas were being engraved and were soon to be printed, by the Sieber firm; he planned to collect a set hot off the press so that he could present a bound copy to their dedicatee, the former Mannheim Electress, now in Munich, which might produce a reward. None of the works mentioned was published, except, rather later, the Concert Spirituel symphony, the Paris K.297/300a, which was the property of Legros and the Concert Spirituel—and they rather than Mozart would have sold it to Sieber. His friends the Heinas, however, published three sets of piano variations (K.180/173c, K.179/189a and a new set, written in Paris, K.354/299a). It seems likely that he also left in Paris copies of three piano sonatas, the two he had composed in Mannheim (K.309/284*b* and 311/284*c*) and a third, written in Paris, K.310/300*d*. These too were published, though not until 1782 and in a wretchedly inaccurate edition, by Heina, who also issued the K.254 piano trio about that date. It is more likely that he sold these to the Heinas when he was in Paris than that he sent them at a later date from Salzburg or Vienna. Possibly he gave them one or other of these groups of works out of friendship—they had been particularly kind to him at the time of Maria Anna's death—or perhaps in discharge of a debt, which may be why he left the matter discreetly unmentioned in his letters home.

Much of this letter, however, is given over to an attack on Grimm. Having learnt that 'this upstart Baron' had been critical of him in his letter to Leopold, and now finding that Grimm was eager to see him leave Paris as speedily as possible, Mozart was unforgiving. Grimm is of the Italian faction and is doing him down; he doubts whether Mozart could compose a French opera; he casts all his kindnesses in your teeth; he may be afraid of losing the money he advanced during Maria Anna's illness. The room Mozart was using in Mme Épinay's house is simply four bare walls; the food he consumes costs nothing and the only money Grimm has spent on him is on candles. Now Grimm tells him he must leave in a week, although Leopold expects him to await a letter with instructions for the return journey. Mozart asked Leopold to reply immediately so that he could leave on 6 October; and he wanted to take a slightly longer route, via Mannheim, if the Webers were still there rather than in Munich.

Grimm did in fact do his best to speed the parting guest. Clearly his patience with Mozart had worn thin. He arranged the return journey, with a view to economy rather than comfort or rapidity, so that Mozart left Paris on 26 September 1778, before Leopold's response to his letter, sent two days before, had arrived. When he picked it up *en route* he must have been delighted to learn that the Webers had been taken on in Munich, Aloysia at 600 gulden and her father at 400, so they would have the 1000 he so much wanted on their behalf. The proposed visit to Mannheim was now pointless. Leopold also tells of his own dealings with Grimm, in which his generosity and friendliness seemed to belie Mozart's own experiences.

IN A LETTER sent from Nancy after a slow week of travel, Mozart told Leopold that he was bringing back, of his own finished compositions, only his sonatas. He did not have the two symphonies or the sinfonia concertante that he had written for the Concert Spirituel, as Legros had bought them from him. 'He thinks that only he has them, but he is wrong, for they are still fresh in my memory and as soon as I get home I shall write them down again.'[16] There are several puzzles here. The sonatas have usually been identified as those for piano and violin, K.301–306, but a later letter makes it clear the engraved edition is still under preparation. Unless another copy had been made, that means that the manuscripts must still have been in the engraver's hands. Possibly he was referring to the piano sonatas K.309–311. As to the 'two symphonies' for the Concert Spirituel, one is the Paris Symphony, the other the 'new symphony' billed for performance on 8 September; in fact there is every reason to believe that this was not a new work but one of the old symphonies that Mozart had in his baggage.[17] It is plain that he felt it necessary to lead his father into thinking that he had been more industrious than he actually was, for his output in the Paris months was, by Mozart's standard, quite modest: three orchestral works (the Paris Symphony, the Concerto for Flute and Harp and the Sinfonia Concertante), a gavotte, the ballet for Noverre, the choruses for Holzbauer's *Miserere*, two piano and violin sonatas, one sonata and two sets of variations for piano, and an aria for Aloysia Weber.

Of the orchestral works, the Sinfonia Concertante K.Anh.9/297*B* for flute, oboe, bassoon and horn is lost. The Concert Spirituel library was distributed and much of it apparently destroyed after the demise of the organization in 1792. Mozart had intended to write out afresh this and the other works that he had sold to Legros, but it seems that he never did so, at least with this and the non-existent second symphony. The sinfonia concertante was composed for a team of virtuosos and there were no soloists capable of performing it in Salzburg. It has however been suggested that the Sinfonia Concertante for oboe, clarinet, bassoon and horn in E flat K.297*b*/Anh.C14.01 is an arrangement of it. This work was found by the Mozart scholar Otto Jahn, probably in the 1860s, and a copy, without ascription, was discovered in his library after his death in 1869 and auctioned as a work by Mozart. It was taken into the first complete edition and widely assumed to be his later transcription of the Paris work. Many Mozart scholars, however, questioned the attribution for a range of reasons—the quality of the invention, the general style and the relation of its figuration to that of other works of the same date, the handling of key structure, the repetitiveness and other features that seem untypical. Some scholars have proposed that the work incorporates Mozart's original solo parts, transcribed for different upper instruments and provided with a new and later orchestral setting, but this is at best farfetched.[18] Köchel and the NMA place it among dubious and spurious works, and the latter category is surely where it belongs.

The Concerto for Flute and Harp K.299/297*c*, written for the Guines family in April 1778, is often described as a salon piece, but it carries that style to new levels of wit, elegance and expressiveness. It is more concerto than sinfonia concertante (Mozart gave it no heading but referred to it as a concerto) in that the soloists are exhibited much more as a complementary pair, used in combination, than as soloists or rivals in virtuosity. The special nature of the solo instruments predicated delicate, transparent orchestral textures, and these Mozart provided by letting in plenty of air, with rests and detached writing. The first movement follows one of his usual concerto patterns, with the soloists taking up and extending the ritornello material and moving into the dominant for new secondary themes. These are designed for dual presentation, with characteristic writing for both instruments, before the original secondary and cadential material is brought back in extended and more soloistic form. The 'development' section introduces a note of gentle pathos, with the flute offering a new minor-key theme. After a regular recapitulation and a cadenza (which Mozart did not supply), the arpeggio call that opens the movement is used to round it off—a new and witty usage of the rhetorical device that Mozart had used in so many of his symphonies.

The Andantino is one of Mozart's most exquisitely sensuous creations. The violas are divided, the oboes and horns silent. The flute's thematic matter has an air of yearning, with phrases constantly aspiring upward only to fall back, and the harp has rich, spread chords in the final bars. Nothing could be more appropriate for a French concerto than a gavotte-rondeau finale. This example is usual in form for Mozart: *A-B-A-C-B-A*, with the second *B* a tonic recapitulation of the first. Its special charm derives from the delightful procession of melodic ideas in the first episode, ingeniously varied later. Writing a concerto for flute and harp, neither of them instruments for which Mozart had any particular affinity, and keeping it within the reach of good amateurs, poses all sorts of problems of balance and proportion, but Mozart handles the combination as if he had been writing flute and harp concertos from the cradle.

The only major orchestral work of the Paris months is of course the Paris Symphony K.297, no. 31 in the traditional numbering. It came into being because of the suppression of the sinfonia concertante. After a period of avoiding Legros, Mozart met him while calling on Raaff. He reported the whole encounter to Leopold.

> It is really a miracle to have the pleasure of seeing you again—Yes, I have a great deal to do—Will you stay and join us at our table today?—I must ask to be excused as I am already engaged—M Mozart, we must spend a day together again soon—That would give me great pleasure—a long pause—eventually, A propos. Will you not write a grand symphony for me for Corpus Christi?—Why not?—Can I then rely on this?—Oh yes; if I may rely with certainty on its

being performed—and that it will not go the same way as my sinfonia concertante—then the dance began . . .

Mozart had the symphony finished by 12 June; the performance was to be on 18 June. He wrote to his father that he was 'quite pleased' with it, but professed to care little about whether it pleased the audience. 'I can answer for its pleasing the *few* intelligent French people there; the stupid ones—I don't see it as a great misfortune if they don't like it . . . and I have been careful not to leave out the *premier coup d'archet*—and that is enough. What a fuss the oxen here make of this!' He is alluding here to the pride this virtuoso orchestra took in its powerful tutti opening. He reports more fully in his next letter (3 July):

At the rehearsal I was very worried, as I had never in my life heard a worse performance; you can't imagine how, twice over, they scraped and scrambled through it.—I was truly most upset—I was eager to rehearse it again, but there were so many other pieces to rehearse and no time left; so it was with a heavy heart, and in a restless, angry mood, that I went to bed. The next morning I decided not to go to the concert at all; but by evening the weather was fine and I decided to go, and that if it was going badly, as at the rehearsal, I would go up on the platform and take the violin right out of the hands of M Lahoussaye, *first violin*, and direct it myself . . . Right in the middle of the first Allegro, there was a passage that I knew must please, all the hearers were quite carried away—and there was a great burst of applause—but I had known when I wrote it what kind of effect it would make, so I brought it back again at the close—when there were shouts of Da Capo. The Andante also pleased, but above all the last Allegro—as I had heard that all the last Allegros here, like the first, begin with all the instruments, usually in unison, I began mine with the two violins alone, *piano* for the first eight bars—after which came a *forte*—this made the audience, as I expected, say 'ssh' at the *piano*—and then came the *forte*—when they heard the *forte* they at once began to clap their hands—I went as soon as the symphony was over to the Palais Royal—I had a large ice—and I said the Rosary as I had vowed.

The Paris Symphony is, predictably, in D major, the key *par excellence* for brilliant orchestral writing. It is for a larger orchestra than Mozart had ever used before, with a pair of clarinets along with flutes, oboes, bassoons, horns, trumpets and timpani, with some 22 violins, five violas, eight cellos and five double-basses (probably the bassoons and possibly the brass were doubled). He relished the sound of the clarinets in the orchestral tutti, as a later letter makes clear. Leopold remarked that, to judge by the Parisian symphonies he had seen, the French must like noisy symphonies. Mozart's Paris Symphony is quite noisy. It has vigorous, stirring tuttis, with a lively violin line and an active line for the basses, lending the music extra animation. The actual thematic matter is relatively conventional, more a matter of figures than melodies, but there is no development as such, and most of the working-out of ideas comes at their presentation. The one idea that pervades the first movement is that of the *premier coup d'archet*, which consists of no more than four repeated D major chords and an upward scale. It is all a part of Mozart's irony about the French that he then cocks a snook at the idea by following it with a *piano* phrase for the violins alone. But he does turn the concept to musical advantage, using the *coup d'archet* phrase at several critical junctures in the music: to herald the secondary material, to underpin the tutti that closes the exposition, to initiate the development section and to carry through its main modulation, to bring in the recapitulation (inevitably), to mark the point—always critical in his music—where the recapitulation diverges from the exposition, and of course to close the movement.

What was the idea that Mozart 'knew must please'? It may well be the continuation of the main secondary idea, the passage (at bar 65) where the upper strings play in three octaves above pizzicato basses and changing wind harmonies, and which after a brief tutti resumes and moves in a new direction, presented with a different twist each time:

But the movement is full of phrases to charm the Parisians' ears. In no other work did he plan his effects so carefully.

'The Andante also pleased', wrote Mozart, but evidently not so much. In his 9 July letter he wrote:

> [Legros] said it had too much modulation—and was too long—but all this was because the audience forgot to make as much noise or as long a noise as they did for the first or last movements—but the Andante has given the greatest pleasure *to me*, to all connoisseurs, music-lovers and most of the audience—it is just the opposite of what Legros says—it is entirely natural—and short.—But to satisfy him (and, he says, several others), I have written another one—each is appropriate in its own way—for each has its own character . . .

The new movement was given in the repeat performance at the Assumption concert, on 15 August. It has been generally supposed that the familiar 6/8 Andante, surviving in the autograph, is the original slow movement and the shorter 3/4 Andante in the first edition, published as 'Du Repertoire du Concert Spirituel', the replacement. That has however been questioned in the light of the existence of a manuscript sheet showing, on one side, the complete melodic outline of the 3/4 movement and on the other sketch material for the finale.[19] The case would be strong if it could be shown that Mozart wrote on both sides at about the same time, but it is no less likely that he would have picked up a part-used sketch sheet to set down his thoughts for a replacement movement when he heard Legros' comments. His leaving the 3/4 movement in Paris for Legros and taking the 6/8 one home must support the traditional view. The 6/8 is in fact the longer and more elaborately worked movement so would be an unlikely substitute for one that Legros considered too long. In its original conception, the 6/8 Andante was even longer, with an additional episode that Mozart rejected to leave it as a sonata-form movement without development. He revised the movement during his journey home. One detail concerns the two-bar phrase that is echoed in the minor in the exposition, which originally he duplicated in the recapitulation before deciding to adjust the expressive sense by presenting it, instead, first in the minor with the echo in the major. The 3/4 Andante is simpler in style and scoring (with only a single flute, oboe and bassoon) and is in rounded binary form, music of the grace and sensibility that one might expect in a serenade more than a symphony.

Parisian symphonies rarely have minuets, and Mozart's is in three movements. For the finale, with its hushed opening, Mozart wrote a helter-skelter piece, designed to show off the Paris violins and to tease the ears of the audience, including some playful counterpoint in the development section. Listening to this work, one is conscious, as in no other of Mozart's, of his keen awareness of his audience, his eagerness to manipulate them and win them, his readiness to feed their collective foibles of taste and the irony, even cynicism, with which he did so. That does not make it an inferior work, but certainly one that occupies a special place in his output.

Just a week before the Paris Symphony had its première, Noverre's ballet *Les petits riens* had the first of its seven performances at the Opéra, following Piccinni's opera *Le finte gemelle*. Mozart wrote that Noverre needed only half a ballet 'and for this I composed the music. Six pieces in it are composed by others and are made up wholly of wretched old French airs, while the overture and contredanses, about twelve pieces in all, are contributed by me'. The music was initially lost, but in 1872 a copy was found in the Opéra archives. It is in three parts, the first purely anacreontic (to a tale about the capture of Cupid in a cage), the second a game of blind man's buff, the third a story about two shepherdesses competing for the love of a shepherd who in the end turns out to be a shepherdess in disguise (as she proves by baring her breast). The composers, unfortunately, are not identified, and there is no way of relating the score to the events of the plot. There is an overture followed by 20 dances, six of which are music of high quality. A number of the others are technically so poorly written that it is inconceivable that Mozart could have had anything to do with them, but there are two or three of which his authorship cannot be ruled out. The overture is a spirited little piece, of a processional character, just over 100 bars, which curiously never wanders from C major. The pieces that seem sure to be Mozart's are nos. 9, possibly 10, 11–12, 15–16 and 19. These, deftly and delicately written, include an echo piece for two flutes and two violins, a Pantomime of exquisite charm and elegance and a variety of gavottes, among them a rustic piece and a hauntingly graceful slow one. There is also a 6/8 movement called 'Gavotte gracieuse'. While he was in Paris Mozart also wrote an orchestral piece headed Gavotte (K.300, in B flat), which survives in a separate manuscript; it is not in fact a gavotte but a bourrée. There is no way of determining whether it is linked, as would seem likely, with Noverre or with *Les petits riens*.

In Mannheim, Mozart had composed four of the piano and violin sonatas of the set of six that he planned to dedicate to the Palatinate Electress. As he does not refer to them in his letters and did not date the manuscripts, we do not know precisely when he wrote the last two. He noted 'à Paris' at the head of K.304/300c, and for the last of them, K.306/300*l*, he used a different batch of manuscript paper, of French manufacture; this and the handwriting suggest early summer for K.304 and later summer for K.306.[20] K.304, Mozart's solitary work in the key of E minor, is the most individual of the sonatas in the set. It begins austerely, with a sombre theme, *piano*, in bare octaves, and a sharper response, *forte*, still in unison. Its later presentation with different, sometimes pungent harmonies and even in canon, enlarging its expressive potentialities, and the use of figures drawn from it in a variety of contexts, show Mozart exploring the possibilities of his themes in a new range of ways. The theme, although already recapitulated at the orthodox point, makes an extra appearance as a coda: not with the rhetorical effect of a reversed recapitulation or a climactic gesture but rather with what seems like a nostalgic farewell. This atmosphere of high sensibility permeates the second movement too, a Tempo di Menuetto of a wistful character with the balmy effect of soft, repeated major-key chords and gentle chromaticisms in its warm, *dolce*, E major trio section.

The final sonata, K.306, is of an altogether different stamp—an expansive, vivacious work, with some hints of the brilliant Mannheim (and Paris) orchestral manner, for the pianist especially, with his cascades of rapid notes. This movement has a genuine reversed recapitulation of a highly dramatic character. The sonata is the only one of the set in three movements: there is a central Andantino, its expressive content shared equally between the instruments, and then a finale, substantially the longest movement in the set. This is a two-tempo movement, recalling some of the violin concerto finales. Following a graceful 2/4 Allegretto opening, which twice recurs, the main section, in 6/8, consists of a sonata-form exposition and, after a recurrence of the 2/4 material, a recapitulation, which then leads into a cadenza for the piano with violin support. A draft of 76 bars of this movement, and of the exposition of the first movement, show the music as it was first conceived, different only in details of the texture and precision of the notation. These sonatas, as a set, show once more Mozart's way of gaining freedom in a form simply by composing a few examples. The new adventurousness he discovered on the journey from K.301 to K.306, in the treatment of form, in the subtle handling of the piano–violin relationship, in the boldness of his material, is palpable.

Biographers of Mozart have understandably been ready to relate the composition of two minor-key works, the E minor piano and violin sonata and the A minor piano sonata K.310/300d (his only instrumental work in A minor), to his mother's death. To do this is perhaps to look at Mozart through Romantic eyes. There is no real reason to imagine that he used his music as vehicle for the expression of his own personal feelings: at this period, at least, there is certainly no evidence that he did so—no statement in a letter about the significance of any work to life events. Later, the composition of the intense minuet of the D minor string quartet K.421 when his wife was in labour with their first child might be cited, as too could the black emotions he described at a time when he might have been writing the G minor Symphony K.550. He in fact wrote to Leopold that in the days of his mother's illness he 'had ample leisure for composing, but could not have written a single note'. His letters written on the day of her death and in the ensuing days do not suggest that the emotions he was experiencing were of a kind that he would want to express in music, or that he would have wished to express his grief and his turmoil through the creation of music such as that of K.310. Possibly the bleak qualities of the E minor work and the immediacy of its emotional character could more reasonably be read in this sense. Less so the A minor sonata, in which the sustained urgency and agitation of the first movement seem almost to embody anger and frustration—both of them emotions he is known to have felt, directed variously, towards his father and the archbishop, Salzburg and its inhabitants, Grimm and Legros, the Parisians and the French nation in general. It would surely be unwise to seek interpretations of too specific a nature.

The much-reproduced autograph (in the Berlin Preussische Staatsbibliothek before World War II, since then in New York) does seem to suggest some heat of creativity, with its tight-packed notes, its overflowing staves and its heavy abbreviation—an analogue to the urgent dotted rhythms, the purposeful flow of shorter notes and the music's remarkably strong sense of direction, in the tonal plan of the development in particular. If the second-subject music, in C major, seems to allow a little relief, its recurrence at the end of the movement, now firmly locked in A minor, is all the more uncompromising, with no extra coda but three bars interpolated to heighten the drama of the close. The Andante, with its florid and expressively intense melodic line, seems at first to be in a world similar to that of K.309 (in the same key, F major), but it is a sonata-form movement and takes a different direction. It has at its centre a powerful development section with agitated triplets and suspensions carrying the music through a sequence of keys, to arrive back at the dominant of F and thus to the recapitulation with a characteristic sense of inevitability and just timing. The finale, a sonata rondo of restless rhythmic energy, has a major-mode central episode but ends with a fiery and vigorous assertion of the minor.

Mozart wrote two sets of piano variations in Paris. One, on 'Je suis Lindor' K.354/299a, was probably composed in the earlier part of his stay and was published by Heina during 1778, along with the Fischer variations K.179 and the Salieri set K.180. The theme—it represents Mozart's first contact with Beaumarchais—comes from Antoine-Laurent Baudron's setting of a Romanze in Act 1 of *Le barbier de Seville*. It follows a typical pattern, initially with simple figuration in the right hand and then the left, then more playful melodic ideas and increasing brilliance leading to rapid scale passages. There is a minuet variation, with a cadenza leading to a minor-mode one, and an artfully managed pair of variations with the effect of shimmering pedal notes, first right hand then left. The twelfth variation, an Adagio with a broadly sweeping right-hand line, leads to a final *da capo* of the theme. On 20 August *Julie*, a *comédie mêlée d'ariettes* dating from 1772 by Nicolas Dezède, was revived. Mozart presumably heard it. His variations on its rather trite air 'Lison dormait' again follow his customary scheme, with a minor-mode variation, an Adagio and a final (ninth) variation in altered metre, leading to a brief cadenza and *da capo*. The work was not published until 1786. Other sets of variations on French themes, sometimes suspected of originating when Mozart was in Paris, were written later.

The only other piece of Mozart's from his Paris months is the aria he composed for Aloysia Weber, 'Popoli di Tessaglia . . . Io no chiedo' K.316/300*b*: 'I have written it *only* for you—so I seek no other praise than yours;—I can only say that of my compositions of this kind—I must confess that it is the best I have written in all my life'.[21] Here is certainly a work coloured by his emotional involvement. This setting of words from Ranieri de' Calzabigi's libretto for Gluck's *Alceste*, sung in Act 1 when Alcestis believes her husband King Admetus has to die, is a noble *scena*. It starts with an elaborately scored, chromatic accompanied recitative followed by a two-tempo aria. First there is an Andantino with prominent oboe and bassoon parts and a smoothly flowing cantabile vocal line, set unusually high to accommodate Aloysia's voice and culminating in a coloratura passage rising to top D and E. This is a plea for pity from the gods. What follows is a fiery Allegro assai which, if not wholly motivated by the text (referring to her terror and her love), gives the voice plenty of opportunity for strong, forthright tone in the upper register and a couple of flights far beyond normal soprano range to a top G.

MOZART LEFT PARIS on 26 September, booked by Grimm on a slow coach to Strasbourg, one that would take ten or twelve days— no economy, he points out, as there were more overnight stops at inns. At Nancy ('a charming place, with handsome houses, fine, broad streets and superb squares') he wrote to his father saying he had changed to a faster coach, to leave the next morning; but he must have stayed there for a time, waiting for the fast coach, as the journey took 18 or 19 days. Leopold was alarmed: he knew when Mozart had left, and had heard through the Strasbourg bankers with whom he had arranged credit that he had not arrived and was afraid he had been waylaid on the journey. Mozart was in Strasbourg for 18 days, and wrote from there, principally to acknowledge three letters that he had received and to tell his father that he would have liked to stay longer in Paris, where he knew he could have 'gained honour, reputation and wealth', and was returning to 'the bitterness of Salzburg' only for the joy of embracing his father. In Strasbourg, however, he gave a solo concert. This was something entirely unknown at the time—it is usually reckoned that the solo recital was invented by Liszt, 60 years later. Mozart was anxious not to risk money by engaging an orchestra. The audience was modest and his profit was three louis d'or (or 33 gulden). He was then advised to give a concert in the theatre, with an orchestra, but again it was a small audience and like 'a table laid for eighty with only three for dinner'. Nevertheless, he writes, 'I played for a very long time for my own amusement, giving one more concerto than I had promised—and in the end extemporizing for quite a while'. He played two Silbermann organs in the Lutheran churches, and met the elderly Kapellmeister, F.X. Richter, a composer who had formerly been at Mannheim, who now 'lives very economically, for instead of 40 bottles of wine a day he now swills only 20'. Floods on the route home delayed his departure until 3 November, gave him time to arrange a third concert, and compelled him to take a different route. Experienced local travellers advised him to go via Mannheim.

So Mozart was after all able to visit 'his beloved Mannheim', as he wrote to his father. He arrived there on 6 November, to be greeted by Madame Cannabich, with whom he stayed (her husband was now in Munich), and who told him the latest news of the Mannheim and Munich musicians—including a report that Aloysia Weber was now receiving 1000 gulden a year and her father, who taken on the additional post of prompter, 600. The Seyler theatrical company was visiting Mannheim and, he tells Leopold, will not let him go until he has written a duodrama, a melodrama with two characters: that is, a work in which 'there is no singing, only declamation, to which the music is like a sort of obbligato accompaniment to a recitative' (in Mozart's own words). He was, he reports, greatly taken with the genre when he heard two examples, *Medea* and *Ariadne auf Naxos* (both 1775), by Georg Benda, the Czech-born composer who was its leading practitioner and, he said, 'always my favourite among the Lutheran Kapellmeisters'. In his enthusiasm Mozart expressed the view that 'most operatic recitative should be treated in this way' (he writes as though the genre were entirely new to him, although he had in fact written an entr'acte in this style for *Thamos, König in Ägypten*: see Chapter 19). He would need six or eight weeks in Mannheim and might be paid 40 louis d'or.

So deep was Mozart's emotional involvement with Mannheim, his friends there and this new project that he seems to have been unable to foresee Leopold's reaction. It duly came:[22]

> I don't know what I must write to you—I shall either lose my senses or go into a decline and die. It is impossible for me to recall all the projects that you have had in your head and written about to me since your departure from Salzburg without my losing my sanity. All of them have been proposals, empty words and in the end they come to *nothing whatever.*

He complains of Mozart's sitting around in Nancy frittering away money and his long stay in Strasbourg (Leopold had told him not to linger unless money could be made), and now he is planning two months at Mannheim, with no court and no prospects there. He lists all the money drawn, spent on the journey and added to Leopold's debts, amounting to 863 gulden, over 14 months: their finances could only be restored by his returning promptly. Were he to write about this to Madame Cannabich, he says, in an implicit threat, she and their friends would do less to persuade him to remain in Mannheim. Another, more conciliatory letter followed four days later, saying that Mozart's judgment was askew because of his love for Aloysia and his hatred of the idea of re-entering the archbishop's service. Leopold assures Mozart that he was in no way opposed to his love for Aloysia, which all Mannheim (and seemingly all the south German musical world) knew about by now; and in Salzburg he would be only a short distance from Munich. He was clearly pleased to be able to report that a colleague had been telling the archbishop of Mozart's successes in Mannheim earlier in the year. As late as 24 November Mozart was cherishing hopes of writing a melodrama, when he wrote a formal letter to Baron Dalberg, head of the Seyler company, with an undertaking to compose the work for a fee of 25 louis d'or (275 gulden). In his response to Leopold, Mozart says that he has already begun work on the melodrama, on the drama *Semiramis* by Gemmingen. Nothing survives, however, and if he did compose any music it is either lost or was only in his head. But he did start work in Mannheim on a concerto for violin and piano (K.Anh.56/315*f*), which he contemplated playing with the violinist Ignaz Fränzl, leader of a new 'accademie des amateurs' there, but then broke off after 120 bars.[23]

Mozart left Mannheim on 9 December, after five weeks, travelling with the Abbot of Kaysersheim and so taking, again, a rather different route from the one, lined with potential patrons, that Leopold had recommended. He was in Kaysersheim, presumably as a guest of the Abbot (he refers to his 'cloistered life'), from 13 to 24 December, during which time the package from Grimm with his newly published sonatas caught up with him. He had expected to travel on through Augsburg and see his Bäsle again, but as he had been offered transport direct to Munich by the Abbot he wrote to her from Kaysersheim, a frivolous rhyming letter, suggesting that she should meet him in Munich, 'where she might have a large role to play': this mysterious remark must surely refer in some way to the reunion he was contemplating with Aloysia. He arrived in Munich on 25 December, where he was hoping to stay with the Webers. Aloysia was now an established court singer, with a handsome salary, equal to Leopold and Wolfgang Mozart's together if the latest rumour was true. Her father too was comfortably placed. Mozart could be of no help to them. Whether or not such matters are material, Mozart found Aloysia changed. There is in fact little evidence that she was ever emotionally involved with him; we know that they spent time and made music together but (as we have seen) the relationship was fairly formal and Mozart may have given it greater weight than Aloysia did. At any rate, she received him coolly. His next letter to his father does not spell this out: he merely says 'for today I can only weep ... my heart is full of tears'. But there is another witness, Constanze Weber, later Constanze Mozart, the third of the four Weber sisters, who was of course present in Munich at the time. Her second husband Georg Nikolaus Nissen was later Mozart's biographer; his account of the occasion inevitably comes to us through the prism of Constanze's memory:[24]

> ... on his way back from Paris, Mozart appeared, in mourning for his mother in the French style in a red jacket with black buttons, and he found that Aloysia's feelings for him had altered. She who previously had wept for him seemed no longer to know him when he came in.

Nissen adds that Mozart went to the piano and sang 'Ich lass das Mädel gern, das mich nicht will' ('I readily give up the girl who doesn't want me', or possibly he sang a coarser version). The hopes that had dominated his life and his thoughts during the months in Paris had been banished in an instant.

Mozart had a gift for Aloysia. In 1788, he presented Aloysia Lange (her married name), the Viennese soprano, with the aria 'Ah se in ciel, benigne stelle' K.538, probably the last of several pieces that he composed for her. It was always assumed that it was composed only in 1788, as that is the date on the finished score. But there also exists a *particella*—a working short score, giving just the voice and the bass part, from which the singer could learn the aria. This is written, in Mozart's handwriting of 1778–9, on paper of a type he otherwise used exclusively for the late stages of *Idomeneo* and for the oboe quartet K.370, music that he wrote in Munich in the last weeks of 1780 and the first of 1781, but the two sheets here are unique in having ten stave lines (the others have 12 or 14). It must therefore have been obtained separately. The paper was manufactured in Kandern, near Basle; he could have bought it during the journey or on arrival in Munich. It is impossible to say whether he arrived with the intention of presenting it to her, or whether he wrote it during his few days in the city, and there are no means of knowing whether it was complete or simply a vocal line and bass. Perhaps the likeliest scenario is that he composed it in outline *en route* and then, discouraged, put it aside, and went back to complete it ten years later. Whether Aloysia or he was in possession of the *particella* during those years is a matter for conjecture.

If Mozart had still entertained hopes of an appointment in Munich, he will have abandoned them a few days later when he received Leopold's letter of 28 December.[25] The political situation in Bavaria and the state of the court made employment there an uncertain prospect. In a severely worded letter Leopold angrily summons him home ('I command you to leave at once . . . your conduct is disgraceful'). Two or three days later Leopold received Wolfgang's letter, written after his rejection by Aloysia, and with it a letter from their Munich friend, the flautist Johann Baptist Becke,[26] telling him that Mozart was distressed and anxious about the reception he would receive at home. Leopold appears to have misunderstood the grief expressed in Wolfgang's letter; he writes:[27]

> If your tears, your sadness and your heartfelt anxiety have no other reason but that you doubt my love and tenderness for you, then you may sleep peacefully—eat and drink peacefully and return home still more peacefully. I see that you don't really know your father. It is clear from our friend's letter this seems to be the main cause of your sadness: oh, I hope there is no other!

Mozart may not have known his father, but nor did Leopold know his son. And in fact, in his reply, Mozart said that he exaggerated, though he did not explain that his distress was primarily caused by Aloysia. He still refused to come at once, insisting on staying to present bound copies of the sonatas to the Electress, which he did on 7 January 1779, and he would then remain to see the carnival opera, Schweitzer's *Alceste* (Aloysia was singing in it, as too was the bass Ludwig Fischer for whom he was later to write), to be given on 12 January. He would need too to wait for the present or cash that he could expect in response to the dedication of the sonatas. Meanwhile, Maria Anna Thekla arrived in Munich, and Mozart asked if she could accompany him home. Leopold had arranged for Mozart to travel with a friend, the Salzburg businessman F.X. Gschwendtner; he should not wait in Munich for the Bäsle's father's permission, but if she came on the mail coach a few days later she would be welcome. Mozart arrived home about 16 January; we do not know whether the Bäsle followed.

MOZART HAD BEEN away from home for nearly 16 months. He had been 21 years old when he left; now he was nearly 23. He had not secured the hoped-for court position, nor had he shown himself able to sustain a freelance life on his own. Years of having every decision made on his behalf had left him poorly equipped to make them himself. Leopold's over-management of the family over many years and his unwillingness to cultivate independence and responsibility in his son, if understandable in that he had always wanted to give precedence to Wolfgang's development as a musician, had their inevitable outcome. Mozart had shown no real understanding of the value of money, nor, apparently, of any obligation to consider loyalty to his family as a proper motive for his actions and decisions. He preferred to do what he felt to be appropriate to his very special talents, an attitude that posterity may approve in the case of a remarkable genius but not one that necessarily served the best interests of his career. It would be unfair to lay at his own door all the blame for what may be seen as his selfishness and his disinclination to behave like a normal member of society. But all his life Wolfgang had been made aware by his father of how exceptional he was, and it is scarcely to be wondered at if he became self-centred and arrogant. The patterns laid down in his childhood would prove to be lasting.

Mozart biographers, naturally enough, have sided with Wolfgang in his running disputes with his father during the period of his absence from home in Mannheim and Paris, sometimes to an absurd degree. Yet the arguments in Leopold's letters—assuming that he was honest in his statements about the family finances[28]—are hard to counter. He could not responsibly carry heavy debts, run up in order to give Wolfgang the opportunities he asked for, that threatened the family's reputation and jeopardized its future. His only means of rectifying the situation, when it became painfully clear that Wolfgang could not make a living for himself in Paris, a city he anyway loathed, was a position in Germany or in Salzburg, and political events ruled out the best German possibilities (Wolfgang had neglected to investigate others when he had the opportunity to do so). Leopold has been charged too with jealousy of Wolfgang's other attachments, especially those to women. Looked at more soberly, and in the light of Wolfgang's own impetuous behaviour patterns, he was justified; as Maria Anna had said in her secret postscript earlier in the year, Wolfgang was ready to give his life and property for new acquaintances. Leopold did not in fact discourage his interest in women, but noted them and commented occasionally on Wolfgang's fickleness: when he understood the seriousness of his attachment for Aloysia he sent arias for her, made suggestions for the furtherance of her career and offered Wolfgang opportunities to be close to her. And over the complex issue of blame in respect of Maria Anna's death he was remarkably restrained, doing little more than wondering, as anyone might, whether the best possible care was exercised and always providing the shelter of the will of God.

All these actions have to be seen within the broad context of Salzburg society, the Mozarts' religious faith and eighteenth-century family life. The expressions of love and care and shared emotions and interests that recur time and again in their letters are not routine or ritual but genuine and deeply felt, even where anger and frustration are expressed and half-truths are being told, as they were in both directions. And Leopold repeatedly wrote of his longing to hear his son's latest music, which clearly was a central concern of his existence. The dilemma he faced, in nurturing an abnormally gifted son, was a familiar one—how to develop the great gifts to their maximum and at the same time to bring him to some kind of normal maturity. In the first he succeeded, and, as far as posterity is concerned, that is probably the more important. For the second, Mozart himself would ultimately have to take responsibility.

19

Salzburg Concertmaster-Organist

WHATEVER THE RECRIMINATIONS, there was surely plenty of fatted calf for the prodigal son on his return to Salzburg—or more exactly, there were capons, to go by Leopold's earlier report on the preparations for celebrating the homecoming. Mozart soon submitted his formal petition for the post of court organist, in the place of Cajetan Adlgasser, which was duly accepted. He was to carry out his duties 'with diligent assiduity and irreproachably, in the Cathedral as well as in the Court and in the Chapel, and shall as far as possible serve the Court and Chapel with new compositions made by him'. He was to perform the same duties and receive the same salary as Adlgasser, 450 gulden, not the 600 or the 500 that Leopold had reported when Mozart was pondering whether to return (Leopold had said he told Starhemberg that 450 would not be acceptable). Although there was an assistant, modestly paid, the promise that Wolfgang would be relieved of routine cathedral duties seems to have been forgotten, if indeed it was ever made. He was also required to take over the teaching of the boys in the Kapellhaus, which had been done since Adlgasser's death by the court tenor, Spitzeder.

With the family again together, there is of course no correspondence to inform us of events over the next 22 months. There were not in fact very many events. The surviving fragments of Nannerl's diary provide a glimpse into the family's domestic life, at least as Nannerl viewed it; about 15 weeks of entries survive from 1779 and four weeks and odd days from 1780.[1] Occasionally her brother wrote the entries for her. Her notes for the early months of 1779 are brief and record what she sees as the day's principal activities, or at least those that she might want to recall (presumably the loss of her mother left her with increased domestic responsibilities, although some might have fallen to servants). These are attendance at Mass, almost every morning, often at the cathedral or Holy Trinity, and visiting or being visited by friends. Katherina Gilowsky von Urazowa (or 'Catherl', a member of a medical family at the court) was clearly her closest friend, and they exchanged visits almost daily. They had friends among the other young women of roughly their age, such as the daughters of the Mayr and Mölk families. Many of their circle were, of course, court officials and court musicians. There is the castrato Francesco Ceccarelli, who had been recruited for the court when Mozart was away and had quickly become a good friend to Leopold and Nannerl, often making music with them; the new court oboist Joseph Fiala, also a composer and cellist, who now occupied the Getreidegasse flat in which the Mozarts had lived; the court hornist and violinist Johann Georg Bauer; the assistant organist Anton Paris; the court paymaster Franz Vinzenz Lankmayr; and the Weyrothers (the father had charge of the stables and stud, the son was an amateur violinist). Adlgasser's widow and daughter sometimes appear. There are such old friends as Bullinger, the Hagenauers and Schachtner, and members of other Salzburg families such as the Antretters and occasionally even the Lodrons and Firmians. On one occasion, 15 June 1779, their visitors included the Bishop of Königgrätz (a member of the Arco family) and the Counts Starhemberg and Czernin.

It was a busy and lively social life. There is scarcely a day when there was no visitor to the Mozarts' house, sometimes for a meal, and on many days Nannerl visited friends. Sometimes they played family games, usually card games. Card-playing was a central part of their family activities and they played a variety of games (brandeln, schmieren, tarock, tresette and several others are mentioned).[2] For a particular circle of friends there was a session at home each Sunday, and occasionally on a weekday, of their favourite *Bölzschiessen* (airgun shooting at home-painted targets). The week's *Bestgeber*, who designed the targets and provided the prizes, is always named, as too is the week's winner. Nannerl often records visits to the theatre, after which they sometimes went for a stroll with friends. Once she wept so much at the 'comedie' that she had a headache. The theatre played an important part in their lives, and the family went to most of the performances (about four a week). There was no resident company but a stream of visiting ones, of up to 30 or 40 members, which gave a variety of operas, plays and ballets and with whom the Mozarts often made friends. On Good Friday Nannerl and Catherl made a pilgrimage to 16 churches in Salzburg and then went to the cathedral in the evening. Sometimes she noted the weather—fine days, snow, thunderstorms.

Relatively little is said in the diary about domestic music-making, though once there were quintets with strings and horns. Occasionally Nannerl reported the composer of a major piece given in the cathedral, such as Adlgasser or Michael Haydn, and once Mozart himself—a litany, on 30 March 1779, probably K.243 (at Easter, when a new mass of his was almost certainly given, she mentions only being at a rehearsal on the Saturday and on Sunday 4 April, 'auf dem grossen Chor'). Sometimes she identified a work heard at the theatre, for example when Johannes Heinrich Böhm's company was visiting Salzburg in the winter of 1779–80. Several members of the company were on visiting terms with the Mozarts. Böhm's musicians took part in a concert ('Schlackademie') in the Tanzmeisterhaus on 18 February 1780, for which a kind of parody programme was listed by Mozart (with numerous puns) in Nannerl's diary;[3] the programme included a symphony drawn from the Haffner Serenade. During the summer of 1780 the entries are in Mozart's own hand, but worded as if written in the first person by Nannerl, often including puns, word-plays on the names of their friends, interpolations of words in other languages and various jocular remarks. It was in that summer or the autumn that the Mozarts commissioned the well-known family portrait, attributed to Johann Nepomuk della Croce, showing Nannerl and Wolfgang at the keyboard and Leopold behind, with Maria Anna's portrait hanging on the wall. Sittings for it were completed at the end of the year. It now hangs in the Tanzmeistersaal in the family house in Salzburg.

The diary is informative about the Mozarts' social circle, but tells us virtually nothing about the family's professional life. During this time Nannerl was doing some teaching and so visited her pupils each morning. Presumably Mozart and his father were in attendance at court, or in the Kapellhaus (Leopold's duties included supervising the teaching there), at least in the mornings, and they will have been

The Mozart family: oil painting, 1780–81, probably by Johann Nepomuk della Croce (*Internationale Stiftung Mozarteum, Salzburg*)

required to attend three evenings a week (Tuesday, Thursday and Saturday) for the regular court concerts. These, according to a letter of Leopold's,[4] were now reduced to about 75 minutes' music, a symphony, an aria, another symphony or a concerto and a final aria. In 1780 the orchestra establishment was slightly larger than it had been in 1773 (see pp. 326–7), with probably 23 violin and viola players, two cellists, four violone players, five oboists doubling flute, three bassoonists, two each of hornists and trumpeters and a timpanist.[5] Probably the Mozarts sometimes made music with the amateur orchestra founded by Count Czernin, which as originally listed by Leopold was rather differently balanced, with 15 violins, two violas, five cellos and two basses, and a minimal wind section of just two oboes and two horns.

THE DECREE CONFIRMING Mozart's appointment was issued on 17 January 1779 and the order for his salary to be paid followed on 26 February. Clearly he took the requirement of producing new music seriously, at least to start with. On 23 March he completed a new mass, the one known as the 'Coronation' Mass in C K.317, and this was surely the one performed at the cathedral on 4 April. The word 'Coronation' that became attached to the work early in its history has caused a good deal of confusion. A speculation that the work was intended for use at a ceremony of the coronation of an image of the virgin at the church at Maria Plain—a village and pilgrimage site about five kilometres north of Salzburg, which Mozart and his sister visited on the morning of 15 April—was put forward in the early years of the twentieth century with no basis of evidence and is wholly fictional. Probably the work acquired its name in 1791 as a result of its performance, under the direction of Salieri, in the course of the coronation ceremonies in Prague of Leopold II as king of Bohemia.[6]

The inventiveness and the vigour of K.317, Mozart's first work for Salzburg Cathedral after his return, might be seen as a token of his readiness to exert himself in his new role—although it should perhaps be said that he might have begun the work in Munich, where he had planned to compose a mass, presumably with the idea of winning favour and employment there.[7] He composed it on the small oblong manuscript paper from a batch that he had used while he was away, but also before he left and after he came back. It is written to conform with the Salzburg liturgical requirement for brevity, but is more substantial in its material and better unified than any previous mass or indeed any subsequent one, and is generally acknowledged to be the finest of his complete mass settings. The arresting dotted rhythms at the opening, and the use of trumpets as well as horns, bring a ceremonious character to the music and are happily set off against the soloists' ample phrases at 'Kyrie eleison' and, in the minor, 'Christe eleison': it is as though Mozart had Aloysia's soprano still resonating in his ears. The Gloria is a lively sonata-form setting, with text and music more closely linked than usual, in that the musical logic reinforces certain exclamations, such as 'Laudamus te', 'Glorificamus te' or 'gloriam tuam'. The soloists present the secondary material ('Domine Deus'), and the music then moves to the minor for 'Qui tollis' and the soloists' 'miserere nobis'. The recapitulation is at 'Quoniam', with the softer music previously heard at 'bonae voluntatis' now serving for 'Jesu Christe'. There is no 'Cum Sancto Spiritu' fugue, which Salzburg time would not allow, but at least a small gesture of imitation at 'Amen'.

The violins are kept busy throughout the Gloria, but it is the Credo that better exemplifies the Austrian 'rauschende violinen', with its rapid running notes virtually unbroken except for the 'Et incarnatus' (Adagio, muted strings, minor-key, set for the soloists). The form is rondo-like, and again there is no closing fugue, but this time the 'Amen' setting involves at least a brief contrapuntal passage, to descending phrases (as in the Gloria). At the end, the words 'Credo in unum Deum' recur, as if provoked by the final recurrence of the violin figuration heard at the beginning. There is another such unorthodoxy when the Benedictus, a gentle setting for the soloists, briefly returns during the final 'Hosanna'. The soprano solo that begins the Agnus Dei is however the expressive highpoint of the work, an exquisite setting that anticipates 'Dove sono' in *Le nozze di Figaro*, as has often been pointed out. It leads directly into the 'Dona nobis pacem', which begins as a recapitulation of the solo music of the Kyrie, but then moves from Andante to Allegro con spirito and from solo to choral (the choir heralded by a reminder of the dotted rhythms of the opening), and the music is developed afresh to provide a vigorous ending.

While there can be no certainty about the linking of mass settings and epistle sonatas, it is overwhelmingly likely that the sonata K.329/317*a* was intended for use with K.317; it is in the same key, uses precisely the same instrumental forces and was written on the same type of paper. In these last sonatas Mozart, as court organist, would have been at the organ himself, and accordingly they all have solo organ parts. K.329 is a large-scale piece, with energetic tuttis and much playful dialogue between the strings and the oboes, to which the organ here and there adds an extra voice as well as filling out and brightening the orchestral sound. The written-out part in the tuttis probably represents the kind of continuo accompaniment Mozart would have expected from the organ in a sacred work. Another sonata, K.328/317*c*, also in C, is on the more usual chamber-music scale, scored only for strings. Here again the solo music for the organ is no more than the occasional sally, with a sudden moment of prominence in the closing bars.

The final epistle sonata, K.336/336*d*, is dated March 1780 and written on the same paper-type as the Mass in C K.337 of the same date, and there is every reason to think, though no way to prove, that they were intended for use in the cathedral at Easter. This sonata, scored only for strings, has a solo organ part like no other and is in effect a miniature concerto movement, in normal concerto form with an opening ritornello of only ten bars and a 'development' of just eight. It is tempting to diagnose from the mass to which it evidently belongs—Mozart's last complete setting—a diminishing interest in providing music of high quality for the cathedral. On the same scale as K.317, and without the trumpets (though there are independent bassoon parts), it has little distinctive music and few of the felicities of its sister work. There are again no final fugues for the Gloria or Credo, though a more extended and contrapuntal 'Amen' to the former. There are two unusual features: a lengthy choral setting, in a strict *a capella* fugal style and austere manner, of the Benedictus, a section Mozart usually set with more obvious affection; and an Agnus Dei for solo soprano with obbligato parts for oboe, bassoon and organ, creating with the violins an appealing and constantly changing fabric of sound. The main theme of this last movement is of the 'Porgi Amor' family, and its key is the traditionally expressive E flat. Mozart left a partial setting of the Credo, a substantial fragment of 136 bars, going up to the words—aptly enough—'non erit finis' ('there will be no end'). Its tempo marking, unconventional for church music, is 'Tempo di Ciacconna', and it has something of the swagger of the French operatic final dances that are similarly marked. It is not easy to see why he abandoned this quite colourful piece in favour of the eventual one.

Mozart also wrote two settings of the vesper psalms: *Vesperae solennes de Domenica* K.321 in 1779, and the next year *Vesperae solennes de Confessore* K.339 (written for a saint's day). These are in fact identical texts; the psalms sung on Sunday, 109 to 113 in the Vulgate, are also used when saints' days fall on certain days of the week, as evidently did the one, unknown to us, for which K.339 was intended. Vesper settings, like those of the litanies, are not unified by key as mass settings are. Mozart's general pattern here, in the outer movements (the 'Dixit' and the Magnificat) and the second and third psalms, the 'Confitebor' and the 'Beatus vir', is to move fairly rapidly through the long texts, with little or no verbal repetition, with the music alternating between sections in four-part homophony and sections that are either solos or loosely contrapuntal (mostly assigned to the soloists). Behind the homophonic sections the violins maintain a generally busy line, while in the others they support, elaborate or enrich the musical texture. The key schemes are quite limited, with a modulation to the dominant and ventures into the close minor keys, and there is usually some kind of recapitulation shortly before the setting of the doxology. Sometimes there is a hint of musical punning with a recapitulatory gesture at 'Sicut erat in principio' ('as it was in the beginning'), but this may simply be a consequence of the exigencies of musical form.

The other two psalms follow a different pattern. The 'Laudate pueri' is set for the most part in *a capella* fashion. Much of the K.321 setting is canonic, sometimes in two parts and occasionally in all four, and sometimes by inversion. The K.339 setting maintains the style more consistently and uses stretto and inversion, and in the doxology, where the orchestral writing becomes free instead of doubling the voices, there are 'mirror' passages, with one voice singing simultaneously the inversion of another. The 'Laudate Dominum' is set for soprano each time, in K.321 a charming aria with organ obbligato and passages of coloratura writing, in K.339 the famous 6/8 setting where the voice floats gracefully and movingly against soft string textures and sustaining bassoon, finally to be echoed by the choir in the doxology. Throughout K.339 the level of invention is high: the 'Dixit' and the 'Beatus vir', both in 3/4, move spiritedly and purposefully, and there is effective and unusual choral writing in the 'Confitebor'. In his early Vienna days Mozart asked his father to send these pieces and some masses so that he could show them to Baron van Swieten;[8] it would have been the 'Laudate pueri' settings that would have interested Van Swieten, who had a taste for older, contrapuntal music.

One further, shorter sacred work is likely to belong to this period, a setting of the Marian antiphon *Regina coeli* K.276/321b. No autograph survives and nothing is known of its performance, but its general style, broadly similar to that of the vesper psalm settings, suggests that it belongs to these years. It is a bright, festive piece in C major, in tune with the text, with a moment of reflection at the sustained solo setting of 'Ora pro nobis Deum', which is accompanied by twittering figures in the violins akin to those in the 'Sparrow' Mass.

Required 'as far as possible to serve the Court and Chapel with new compositions made by him', Mozart seems to have set limits as to what 'possible' really meant. If 1779 saw the composition of a mass and a vespers setting for the cathedral, that is probably all, unless the two new symphonies of the spring and summer were intended for the court concerts. The first of these is K.318 in G, no. 32. Its unorthodox one-movement form has often led to this symphony's being suspected of having theatrical origins, although it does not follow the traditional Italian overture pattern. It has been coupled with the music Mozart wrote for *Thamos, König in Ägypten* and with the incomplete Singspiel known as *Zaide*. But for either of those its date, 26 April 1779, is wrong: the 1773 version of *Thamos* was years back, the final version months ahead, and *Zaide* was almost certainly not yet even a gleam in his eye. Another possibility is that it was intended for the Böhm company. Böhm visited the Mozarts on 3 April and, conceivably, could have invited Mozart to write an overture for use in his Salzburg season, which began in June. K.318 is sometimes called 'Ouverture', but the original heading on the score, not in Mozart's own hand, is 'Sinfonia'. Whatever its origins, Mozart acknowledged its aptness as an operatic overture when in 1785 he provided it to preface a Viennese production of Bianchi's *La villanella rapita*, for which he also composed two vocal numbers. The interchange of symphonies and overtures was commonplace at the time: works written as overtures were often published as symphonies, and works written as symphonies were often used as overtures.

The traditional Italian overture was a true three-movement piece. K.318 is a single movement in binary form, or sonata form with a reversed recapitulation, with a complete slow movement, a miniature sonata-rondo, folded into it. It is written for an unusually large orchestra for Salzburg, calling for flutes as well as oboes, with bassoons and four horns, a pair each in G and D. (Later, in Vienna,

Mozart added trumpet and possibly timpani parts, unusual in a work in G, as trumpets keyed in C had to be used, which limits their role even more severely than usual.) The theatrical quality of K.318 is not merely a matter of its form. It starts with an arresting gesture:

quickly moving on to vigorous tuttis, often in the Mannheim manner, with busy tremolando violins and active, virile bass lines. After the secondary theme, in a lighter, *opera buffa* manner, there is a protracted Mannheim crescendo, with tremolando strings in a rising pattern and the rest of the orchestra gradually entering above a repeated-note bass. At its climax the inner and lower voices take up the above theme. The development has that phrase in the inner voices, taking over the whole texture. When it comes to a halt, a slow movement follows, a 3/8 Andante of nearly 100 bars. In this miniature rondo Mozart extracts an unusual range of colour from his enlarged wind palette, demonstrating in its pendant 'horn-call' phrases just why he needed pairs of horns in two keys. After it, the 'Primo tempo' returns, for a recapitulation of the secondary material with a return of the opening gesture (above) at its climax, but enhanced and sharply dramatized by an extra step upwards, with a *fortissimo* horn fanfare and a sudden hush before the movement, and the symphony, is rounded off in orderly fashion. It is natural to suppose that in this work Mozart was showing his Salzburg audiences something of the sophistication he had picked up in the wider orchestral worlds of Mannheim and Paris.

But the next symphony, no. 33 in B flat K.319, which followed in the summer, is more conservative in style. It has no demonstrative tuttis, and in the first movement especially there is a good deal of almost string-quartet-like writing, sometimes with delicate woodwind echoes. The musical ideas are argued through to some extent in the exposition, so it is not surprising when it comes to the 'development' that Mozart elects to use new material, principally a four-note theme:

which carries the music through a variety of keys while counterpoints are woven around it. The Andante moderato, quietly heartfelt in a manner characteristic of its key of E flat, is again in sonata form but, exceptionally for a slow movement, it has a reversed recapitulation: here the final return is less a dramatic event than a happy coincidence of homecoming and finality. Again the very brief 'development' is on new material:

which happens to be identical (apart from an octave displacement) with the four-note theme above.

Mozart had used this theme before, notably to the words 'Credo, credo', and he was to use it again in the great finale of his last symphony. A very similar idea, essentially the same with a single note altered, appears at the corresponding point in the finale of this symphony, with countersubjects that invert or outline it, again supplying the entire material for the development:

Clearly the gambit is an intentional one: a 'development' section in each movement based on new material, with the material thematically linked. Mozart could hardly have done this by accident. Was he trying to bring some kind of unity to the work? If so, does the fact that he never repeated the procedure, or anything like it, indicate that he thought it unsuccessful, or unnecessary? Some scholars have carried the point further and spotted the four notes within the melodic lines of the minuet and the trio that Mozart added to the symphony in Vienna, but that is far-fetched. That new movement, in very much the same expressive mode as the rest of the work, was probably written about 1785 (to judge by the paper-type), no doubt to make the symphony more suitable for use in a Viennese concert.

No. 33 is lightly scored, with just pairs of oboes, bassoons and horns (in high B flat) besides strings. The next Salzburg symphony, the last Mozart was to compose there, is dated 29 August 1780. It was no doubt written for the court concerts on 2 and 4 September in which, Nannerl's diary tells us, Mozart took part. No. 34 in C K.338, calling for trumpets and drums, moves to the world of C major martial brilliance with its pompous opening, triad figures and fanfare rhythms—although the *piano* echo suggests, as in the Paris Symphony, a hint of mockery, and the minor-key echo a moment later makes it clear that this is not to be exclusively a brilliant piece. In fact the minor mode intrudes again in the tutti that follows, and there are implications of it in the chromatic bassoon and oboe counterpoints to the main secondary theme. Here again there is no development but a freely modulating interlude leading to a condensed recapitulation—the echo passages and a Mannheim crescendo heard in the exposition are jettisoned, but the opening material returns climactically at the end. This is both a straight recapitulation and a reversed one, providing a strong, rhetorical conclusion.

Next—as second movement, rather than third, where he normally placed it—Mozart began a minuet. He may even have finished it. But he evidently decided against including it in the symphony, and the pages it occupied are torn out, most probably by Mozart himself. The beginning, however, was written on the back of the last page of the first movement, so the first 14 bars of what looks to be a pleasant, unexceptional minuet survive. Another minuet in C, K.409/383f, which exists as an independent movement, was thought by Einstein to have been written for this symphony.The autograph is on the same paper-type as the additional trumpet parts for K.318, and it was probably written in 1782–3. Most scholars reject the idea of a link with the symphony: K.409 calls for flutes, not otherwise used in K.338, and its expansive style, with much concertante writing in the trio for flute and oboe, matches it poorly with the rest of the work. But neither of those arguments is conclusive. Mozart may have wanted to take advantage of the availability of flutes, and there are other examples in his output of added or substituted movements uncertainly matched to their context. Further, the opening idea of the rejected minuet has echoes in K.409. Finally, it is difficult to imagine any other purpose for this extended, symphonic minuet.There is no doubt that to modern ears it falls uncomfortably into the symphony, but we should not rule out the possibility that this is what Mozart intended.

The first movement was originally headed 'Allegro', to which Mozart later added 'vivace'. The slow movement was headed 'Andante di molto', but here too he seems to have moved towards a faster tempo, for when he sold a set of parts to the Prince of Fürstenberg in 1786, he qualified it 'più tosto Allegretto'. Scored only for strings, with bassoons adding definition to the bass line and the violas divided to permit a richer texture, it is music of delicate sensibility rather than depth of expression, with many subtleties in its five-part writing and in the imitative dialogue between the violins. The finale is Mozart's last and most brilliant essay in the rumbustious 6/8 style, with dashing scale passages, twisting little phrases from the oboes, witty *piano* passages, and a hint of fire in the development section—a happy reconciliation between traditional high-spirited jig and symphonic vigour.

One other substantial orchestral work belongs to these two years in Salzburg, the serenade in D K.320. It is dated 3 August 1779 and clearly it was written for the year's university Finalmusik ceremony.

According to Mozart's early biographer F.X. Niemetschek, it was intended for the celebration of Colloredo's nameday on 30 September, but as with K.203[9] that cannot be the case, and in fact Mozart referred to this work in a letter as his 'latest Final musique' when he performed part of it at a concert in Vienna in 1783.[10] It is in seven movements:

1 Adagio maestoso—Allegro con spirito (D)
2 Menuetto: Allegretto [trio with solo flute and bassoon] (D)
3 Concertante: Andante grazioso (G)
4 Rondeau: Allegro ma non troppo (G)
5 Andantino (d)
6 Menuetto [second trio with solo posthorn] (D)
7 Finale: Presto (D)

This work, the 'Posthorn Serenade', crowns Mozart's contributions to the genre, going beyond the Haffner work of 1776 in its symphonic character and its expressive scope. The tuttis of the first movement, with their insistent figuration, powerful dialogue between violins and basses and bold, Mannheim-influenced orchestral writing, have a new grandeur, and allow Mozart to construct a strong movement made up of deftly managed figures with virtually nothing that could be called a theme. One unusual feature is the recurrence of the slow introduction, written in the main tempo in notes of double the original length (whether this gives an indication of relative tempos is a moot point). Another is the secondary theme, which is interrupted every four bars by an abrupt *forte* interjection: one is bound to wonder whether this gesture had some external significance. The finale too has more substance than that of the Haffner. A clear sonata-form movement with a playful secondary theme, it is delightfully garnished by the oboes and has touches of counterpoint in the development. When he presented the 'symphony' as a separate work—no performance is documented, but a set of parts with autograph annotations survives—it was as a three-movement work, with the D minor

Andantino as the middle movement. Its main theme is of the same family as that of the C minor Andantino of the K.271 piano concerto. This is the darkest movement he wrote in a serenade, with its sombrely scored opening for the strings and the poignantly chromatic lines and intense harmonies that follow.

In the 1783 performance, the third and fourth movements were presented together as a separate work, which survives as an authentic manuscript. Mozart could also have included the first minuet where, analogous to the minuets with violin solos in earlier serenades, the flute and bassoon are prominent in the trio. The concertante group however is larger, consisting of pairs of flutes, oboes and bassoons. Mozart's recent experience in the twin homes of the sinfonia concertante, Mannheim and Paris, must surely have affected his choice. The exquisite Andante grazioso is formally a curious amalgam of ritornello and sonata, with a constantly shifting texture as material is freely shared between soloists and orchestra. Its beguiling nature recalls the sensuousness of J.C. Bach, with its mellifluous woodwind thirds and the echoes and imitations between and among the flutes and the oboes that allow the texture to luxuriate. And when the soloists embark on a cadenza the orchestra twice intervenes, to support them and to offer a recapitulation of its own, before the cadenza is completed. The Rondeau is in a similar vein, with much interplay between the first flute and first oboe. It is the second minuet of K.320 that gives the work its name: here the *corno di posta* plays postal calls in the second trio. The suggestion that Mozart wrote it to indicate his eagerness to travel away from Salzburg is not to be taken seriously, for its use is simply a summer frolic, in keeping with the occasion. It would be alien to Mozart's thinking to intrude his private anxieties into a public work, and in any case he had been in Salzburg only six months when he composed it. He wrote two marches for this serenade; the first includes a rare instance in his music of 'col legno' playing, used to accompany a sprightly oboe echo of a pompous phrase just heard on unison strings.

It was probably during the summer of 1780 that Mozart wrote the last of his Salzburg divertimentos, K.334/320*b* in D. He later referred to it in a letter as the 'Musique vom Robinig'.[11] In the summer of 1780, Georg Sigmund Robinig, who played the violin and had been a boyhood friend of Mozart's, graduated at the university. It was probably for a celebration of that event that the work was commissioned by his family, the Robinig von Rottenfelds, who were manufacturers of scythes and chemicals in factories near Salzburg and had an iron-monger's shop in the Getreidegasse. The autograph of K.334 is lost—the Mozarts lent it to the Munich violinist J.F. Eck at some point and he evidently failed to return it—but the associated march, K.445/320*c*, survives and has been dated by its paper-type and hand-writing to the summer of 1780.[12]

K.334 is a six-movement work for strings (two violins, viola, double-bass) and a pair of horns, on the same pattern as the Lodron divertimentos of 1776–7, K.247 and 287. Like those works, it is composed in a spacious, relaxed fashion, calling for considerable agility from the first violinist, and falling easily on the ear. The musical ideas are handled with touches of wit, heard in the first movement, for example, in the way the first violin decorates the secondary theme presented by the second violin, or in the way the opening theme is used to close the exposition. The rather protracted and mechanical development here is not one of Mozart's most appealing, however. The movement that follows, a fairly straightforward set of figurative variations, has a few surprises (as when the humble horns are briefly given a leading voice), and the well-known first minuet is a piece with a delicious charm akin to the world of Boccherini. The Adagio offers the first violin a good deal of expressive scope, although it is more classically austere in manner than the richly elaborate Adagio of K.287. After a further minuet, with two trios, there is an extended rondo in 6/8, of nearly 400 bars, that has much ingenuity and wit. A large-scale sonata-rondo structure, it has many close links in the the-matic material between its sections, and the first-violin bravura writ-ing (rising to a *d''''*) gives it a concerto-like air.

There are two further substantial instrumental works from this final spell in Salzburg, both double concertos, both in E flat, both obscure in their early history. These are the sinfonia concertante for violin and viola K.364/320*d*, and the two-piano concerto K.365/316*a*. No occasion is known for which they are likely to have been intended, although there could have been court concerts or other events for which no documentary record survives. K.364 could have been played by Brunetti and Mozart, who is known to have played the viola, at least in his later years.

The want of background material for the string concerto is particularly striking. There is no reference to it whatever in any document of Mozart's time, or in the family correspondence. The autograph score is lost; all that survives are a few leaves with texts and sketches for the cadenzas and an early draft of the close of the first movement. Mozart had of course written a two-violin concerto, or concertone, not long before; it would be reasonable to suppose that his renewed interest in the genre had been provoked by his months in Mannheim and Paris, the two great orchestral centres of Europe where the multiple concerto particularly flourished because of the aggregation of virtuoso instrumentalists. Among the Mannheim composers, Carl Stamitz (1745–1801), who was not himself at the Palatine court during Mozart's visit (he was working in London at the time), in particular, had composed a considerable number of works for two strings—two violins, violin and viola, violin and cello—which Mozart is likely to have come across. Of these, violin and viola must surely have been the most appealing combination to him: two equal instruments offered no contrast (and he had done it before), violin and cello differed too much in pitch and technical capacity. The violin would shine more readily through the orchestral texture than the viola would, but for this he had a remedy, which others had applied in the past: he required the violist to tune his strings a semitone high, and by setting the concerto in E flat gave him both tauter strings, and so a brighter and clearer sound, and an easier and more resonant key (D) to play in.

When he wrote the two-violin Concertone, Mozart set aside the usual relationship between orchestral tutti and solo entry, partly because of the varied material that the multiplicity of soloists predicated. But the principal secondary theme there is duly taken up by the violins. In the first movement here—marked Allegro maestoso—there is no relationship whatever between the ritornello and the solo material. The ritornello starts with one of Mozart's typical affirmations of the sound of E flat major chords, moves on to dialogue between the violins and the violas (they are divided throughout—part of the symmetrical patterning that characterizes the work); then another brief tutti, followed by a brief dialogue, now between oboes and horns; and then a long Mannheim crescendo leads to a tutti from which, as it fades, the solo violin and viola emerge from the orchestral texture on sustained high notes, with an eloquent descending phrase. Now the interplay between soloists begins, and across the movement it takes numerous forms: in this opening paragraph, for example, a phrase copied a couple of bars later; a phrase imitated canonically after a bar, leading to parallel movement in tenths or sixths; a phrase echoed four bars on and then freshly turned, at different pitch, to lead the music in a new direction. Then the soloists take turns at bravura—there is always a sense of their pursuing each other's ideas in friendly, collaborative conversation—leading to the main secondary theme, an arresting, even assertive four-bar phrase left open by the violin, and carried to its cadence by the viola: from which more bravura writing (five bars each) leads to their playing in parallel, and a climax of joint bravura brings in the central ritornello. The variety of device, and the way Mozart uses it to tease, surprise and delight the ear and the mind, continues through the development, which begins with a new theme but mainly consists of imitation between violin and viola, sometimes against dialogue between oboes and horns and usually to symmetrical accompanying patterns in the orchestral strings. In the recapitulation, more exact than most of Mozart's, the roles of violin and viola are reversed, so that the gloss each places on the other's music takes on fresh shades of meaning.

The Andante, in C minor, is another belonging to the family of the

K.271 Andantino. Its opening orchestral statement of eight bars, against a softly sombre orchestral texture, is immediately taken up and elaborated by the violin, turning it into a richly expressive line, then by the viola, which, starting in its veiled lower register, carries the music in a different direction, to E flat major, for the secondary material: and there a dialogue begins, between violin and viola of an eloquence Mozart was rarely (perhaps in the K.515 quintet) if ever to surpass; each phrase from one instrument seems to draw something richer and more passionate from the other. This is its first section, which leads to the central tutti; it is in two-bar, then one-bar phrases, before the orchestra intervenes and with the soloists leads to the central tutti. The brief second limb follows, but dialogue soon gives way to the soloists' joining together in rhythm, with chromatic unison accompaniment from the orchestra to guide the music firmly to C minor: where the third follows, an intensified recapitulation of the first, leading in turn to a climactic, almost disorderly few bars before the closing tutti, in which, as in the first movement, a cadenza relieves the generated intensity. The final Presto, in a spirited contredanse rhythm, is on a large scale, nearly 500 bars: formally it is a rondo, with a single episode that is transposed and adjusted to provide a second one, but Mozart also applies his technique of open-ended themes so that much of the subsidiary material can be shifted and used in different contexts to different effect.

Clearly the concept of the multiple concerto was of particular interest to Mozart about this time: there is the Paris wind concertante, the flute and harp concerto K.299 and the wind concertante in K.320 as well as K.364 and 365 (K.299, admittedly, was not written from choice). There might have been two more. One is the concerto in D for violin and piano that he had begun at Mannheim in November 1778, of which he wrote a complete, 74-bar opening ritornello, in a broad, spacious style, using an orchestra with trumpets and drums.[13] Thereafter he wrote a 'continuity draft' of 45 bars, giving, in his usual way when he was composing, the main line of the music and sometimes more; this one begins with 11 bars for violin and 11 for piano (the orchestral accompaniment would have been added later), then a three-bar tutti, and a 20-bar section for violin and piano together. He remained in Mannheim for a further four weeks, and (unless he was fully occupied with the melodrama *Semiramide*, which seems unlikely), would have had the time to complete it had he wanted to; but the occasion for such a piece disappeared when he had to leave Mannheim and that, rather than dissatisfaction with what he had written, may explain why he broke off. Composing a concerto for two instruments of such different potential does pose awkward questions. He also embarked, back in Salzburg, on a triple concerto for violin, viola and cello, K.Anh.104/320*e*, in A (the viola is again required to tune up, this time by a whole tone). Here too he completed the opening ritornello, of 51 bars, and the main line of a further 84 bars, mainly solo material but with three brief tuttis. There is some characteristic invention in the ritornello, and the solo parts, as far as they go, indicate that Mozart had a spacious and brilliant piece in mind; but the music, and the point at which he broke off, suggest that when he came to grapple with the problems of writing for three instruments on equal terms—which, in Mozart's language, could often involve repeating ideas three times over—he found them intractable and inhibiting. But this too may have been abandoned because of poor prospects of a performance, bearing in mind the lack in Salzburg of a cellist of the necessary virtuoso quality.

The Two-Piano Concerto K.365 has traditionally been assigned to the beginning of 1779, but such evidence as there is suggests a much later date.[14] Mozart used the same papers as he did for all but the earliest of the other works of these two years, and for *Idomeneo*. There is no record of any performance. It is however worth noting that on 3 September 1780, between the two court concerts already mentioned, Mozart and his sister played at the Mirabell—as it happens, Mozart's entry for that date in Nannerl's diary is the only one he wrote in the first person—when he noted: 'Concert auf 2 klavier aus dem f gespiellt' (they also played the four-hand sonata in D K.381 and Mozart sightread two sonatas by Cambini).[15] The concerto in F is

K.242, the three-piano concerto, in its two-piano version. Does the choice of the early work imply that the new one was not yet written? or perhaps the reference to the key indicates that there was in fact a choice. But Mozart often named keys, even when unnecessary, and the former inference seems the likelier: in which case K.365 would have been written in September or October 1780.

K.365 uses many of the dialogue devices of the string work, but it conforms more closely to the standard formal pattern that Mozart was now using for his piano concertos, with the soloists' initial entry echoing the orchestral opening. But most of the ideas, unlike those in the single piano concertos, depend for their meaning on the concept of statement and response, so that when one piano plays a phrase the other usually has an immediate answering one—which may seem to cap the argument, or to pursue it, or to turn it in a new direction. Here it is done in a way that does not depend on differences in timbre. Sometimes the soloists seem to interrupt each other, as when one piano seems to approaching a cadenza and the other heads it off with a new diversion, a new elaboration or a new modulation. In the development the soloists tussle over which theme should be developed or by reshaping or presenting at different pitch each other's phrases. Curiously, ideas that might seem banal if played in succession on one piano are transformed into interesting conversation on two. In the Andante Mozart uses to poetic effect the possibilities of enriching the melodic lines with dialogue and overlap, and in providing filigree accompaniment by the pianos to the orchestral oboes, along with a central section of more impassioned dialogue. In the finale, a lively sonata-rondo, Mozart is freer in his use of two-piano textures for their own sake, particularly in the main (and recurring) episode, and there is a good deal of light-hearted interplay especially in the cadenza, which culminates in a rollicking restatement of the main theme, with the wind instruments gradually joining in until the orchestral takes over. The work was originally written with only oboes and horns, but early bassoon parts with Mozart's annotations survive in Salzburg and may have been part of the original conception. Parts for clarinets, trumpets and timpani that survive for the outer movements were probably supplied by Mozart when, in 1781 and 1782, he played the work in Vienna with his pupil Josepha Auernhammer.

One further instrumental work belongs to this period, the piano and violin sonata K.378/317d in B flat. This is in fact his only accompanied sonata composed in Salzburg, at least since his infancy, and it is hard to imagine to what it owes its existence. Mozart and Brunetti could have played it at court, but sonatas were not normal court fare. Nannerl and he might certainly have played it at some unrecorded event but had it been their practice to play accompanied sonatas there would surely be many more of the kind. K.378 was later to be published along with the sonata left over from Mannheim, K.296, and four others written in Vienna. There is no doubt over its belonging to these months: paper and handwriting are consistent with dates of 1779 or 80, and when Mozart later referred to the work in a letter to Nannerl from Vienna he made it clear that it was a work she already knew.[16] It represents a substantial step beyond the Mannheim–Paris sonatas, the group dedicated to the Palatine Electress, in its scale and the fluidity of its writing. Piano and violin now exchange material freely and Mozart permits himself to plan some of his themes, in what is melodically an unusually abundant movement, in terms primarily of the violin, for example the one that begins the secondary material. The music is carefully composed: the first movement provides an excellent instance of Mozart's adjusting the listener's tonal expectation in the recapitulation by hinting at the subdominant key in the bridging material, so that when the music halts at a cadence on the dominant its resumption in the tonic (where previously it had resumed in the dominant) has a particular logic. The Andantino, in E flat, with its opening melody characteristically arching up to a top G and down again, shows a novel formal feature, applying Mozart's use of the 'open-ended' theme: a simple ternary movement, it re-uses the expressive second strain of the middle section within the reprise of the first, now giving the music a new and stronger emotional twist.

A vigorous 3/8 rondo finale is further enlivened by an episode in 4/4 with scurrying triplets.

MOZART'S EAGERNESS TO write dramatic music found outlets too during 1779–80. Back in 1773, he had composed two choruses for a Viennese production of a play by Tobias Philipp Baron von Gebler, vice-chancellor at the Habsburg court in Vienna. The choruses for *Thamos, König in Ägypten*, which Gebler had originally hoped would be written by Gluck, were apparently written by a minor composer, Johann Tobias Sattler, and found unsatisfactory at the première, given by the Karl Wahr company, in Pressburg (Bratislava) in December 1773. When the play was given at the Kärntnerthortheater on 4 April 1774, the *Historisch-kritische Theaterchronik von Wien* reported: 'the music by *Herr Karl Mozzart* is artfully and beautifully written'.[17] The report alludes only to choruses. The play was given again, with Mozart's music, at the Laxenburg Palace, south of Vienna, on 4 May. In January 1776 *Thamos* was performed at the theatre in Salzburg during a visit by the Wahr troupe. Probably it was then that Mozart composed an additional chorus for the final act; the reference by the local critic to choruses and repetition implies that the additional chorus (no.7 in the NMA) was given then. Extra text was provided, anonymously, but generally thought to be by the local poet and friend of the Mozarts, Johann Andreas Schachtner. The four entr'actes and a brief 'Schlußmusik', which may be an alternative to the final chorus, may date from then too; they are written on papers of types he used almost exclusively in 1775–77. However, although his handwriting for the entr'actes can be reliably dated to around 1777, the handwriting of the choruses is markedly later and indicates a date around 1779.[18] No wonder Wolfgang Plath described *Thamos* as, of all Mozart's works, perhaps the one with 'the most complicated and obscure genesis'. What seems most likely, then, is that Mozart's work on *Thamos* (K.345/336a) was done in three spells: in 1773–74, when he wrote two choruses, in 1775–77, when he wrote a further chorus and the instrumental pieces, and in about 1779, when he apparently rewrote the earlier choruses (using paper set aside for the purpose before he left Salzburg in 1777). This sounds improbable, but at least it conforms with such evidence as we have. There must have been some involvement with a production by a visiting company, Böhm's in winter 1779–80 or Emanuel Schikaneder's, which was in Salzburg later in 1780.

The play itself, a heroic drama about dynastic struggles in Heliopolis, in ancient Egypt, did not stay long in favour; Mozart briefly had hopes of using the music for a revival in Vienna in 1783 but finally had to tell his father that it was no longer performed.[19] The choruses are substantial pieces. The first, a song of praise to the sun from the temple virgins and priests, is cast in a brilliant C major with an orchestra including pairs of flutes, oboes, bassoons, horn, trumpets and drums as well as three trombones and strings. Its second version is much more richly written and imaginatively elaborated: the orchestral setting has greater variety and vitality and the contrasting middle section for the solo priests and sun-maidens is freshly set in a more vivid style with livelier accompaniment. The final chorus, whose earlier version survives only in incomplete form, was in effect rewritten, using some of the same material, to make a big ternary movement with a middle section with solos for the priests and the sun-maidens, where the new text offers opportunities for graphic orchestral writing. The exalted, triumphal tone, together with the Egyptian setting and the texts involving 'sanfter Flöten Zauberklang' and 'Tempel Hallen', has invited analogies with *Die Zauberflöte*, but there is no particular reason to think that Mozart recalled *Thamos* when writing the later work. Mozart's contribution also includes a third chorus, prefaced with solo music for the High Priest: this carries the music, at the dénouement, from a dark, mysterious D minor into jubilant D major.

The entr'actes are quite brief pieces, the length of short symphony movements, and mostly on a high level of dramatic intensity. Leopold Mozart noted in the score the stage action represented in the music:

broadly, each is designed to capture in music the mood of the act just finished and prepare to the one to follow. The restless C minor Allegro at the end of the first act represents the conspirators' decision to seize the throne, with its sharp accents and its anxious chromaticisms. Second is an E flat Andante, where different passages stand for characteristics of the *dramatis personae*—the good character of Thamos, evident at the close of Act 2, is cited opposite the warm opening theme, and the Act 3 conflict between Pheron's 'false character' and the honourable Thamos gives rise to a contrast between an uneasy, detached, minor-key passage and a flowing, major-key oboe melody. The conspirators' traitorous discussion ends Act 3, reflected in Mozart's impassioned G minor Allegro, with strong offbeat accents; but one of the characters now enters and declaims the opening speech of Act 4 against the music, which provides expressive commentary (much along the lines of the melodrama that Mozart was to encounter in Mannheim in autumn 1778). Leopold's only annotation for the fourth entr'acte is that Act 4 ends in general confusion: the entr'acte is another stormy and agitated Allegro vivace assai, in D minor, sombre and chromatic but resolving for a happy ending in D major. This heralds the second chorus. A further D minor one, representing Pheron's despair, blasphemy and death, must have been replaced by the third choral piece.

There is some fine music in *Thamos*, music unlike anything else that Mozart wrote, both in its noble choruses and its graphic entr'actes. It is, however, condemned by its close links with its original context—a play that is no longer viable—to be heard only in a detachment that divorces it from its real function and limits its expressive potency.

Similar questions attend Mozart's other dramatic work of these months, the unfinished and nameless opera, K.344/336*b*, generally called *Zaide*. This is the only work of any substance that Mozart composed 'on spec'. It is sometimes suggested that Mozart intended *Zaide* for a visiting troupe in Salzburg, but that is not the case. His correspondence with Leopold, before and after its composition, makes it clear that it had always been viewed as a means of entry into the Viennese operatic world. At the beginning of 1778, from Mannheim, Mozart had written to tell his father of the plans of which he had heard for the establishment of a German opera company in Vienna, and had asked him to enquire of their friends in the capital about the position of Kapellmeister or the possibility of securing a commission.[20] Leopold immediately wrote to Franz von Heufeld, a dramatist and a court auditor in Vienna, who replied at some length, explaining the situation in Vienna (no composer would be taken on, with Gluck and Salieri already court employees) and suggesting that Mozart should compose a German comic opera and submit it to the emperor.[21] Leopold forwarded the letter to Wolfgang, who—his mind full of plans embracing Aloysia Weber—dismissed with some irritation the idea of writing a comic opera rather than a serious one, and, moreover, with no certainty of payment. 'Don't forget my wish to write an opera . . . but Italian, not German, serious, not buffa', he wrote; and again, in his next letter, 'To write opera is at the forefront of my mind; French rather than German, and Italian rather than French or German'.[22]

Back in the sober atmosphere of Salzburg, however, a year and more later, with Aloysia out of the picture, his stage ambitions unabated and any prospect of escape from Salzburg worth pursuing, he evidently had second thoughts. For a libretto, he approached Schachtner. The standard procedure, when an opera was not being commissioned afresh, was to find an existing libretto that could be used, or adapted, or at least could serve as a model. They chose one on a story—of three west Europeans who meet as slaves of a Sultan, and try to escape—that had been popular in southern Germany over several decades. Probably the libretto from which Schachtner worked was that of *Das Serail, oder Die unvermuthete Zusammenkunft in der Sclaverey zwischen Vater, Tochter, und Sohn* ('The Seraglio; or The Unexpected Reunion in Slavery of Father, Daughter and Son'), by Franz Josef Sebastiani. It was originally set by Joseph Friebert, probably in the mid-1760s; Alfred Einstein discovered a copy of the libretto from a 1779 revival at Passau, where Friebert was Kapellmeister.[23] No complete text survives of Mozart's work; all we have is his score, which of course includes the words for its 15 numbers along with a brief libretto cue preceding each of them. Mozart and his father, as we shall see from the *Idomeneo* correspondence, had clear ideas about the putting together of an opera, and they were no doubt deeply involved in the planning of *Zaide*. We cannot know how much of the dialogue was altered, of course, as we do not have Schachtner's, although it is clear that he rewrote much of it.[24] He also did a great deal of rewriting of the aria texts, to give them the verse structures that Mozart wanted and to improve their often uncomfortable diction; he dropped one character, a female slave, whose folkish texts were alien to Mozart, and added another, the slave dealer Osmin; he changed the Sultan's role from a spoken part to a sung one; and he may have created a three-act version from the two-act original.

Zaide survives as 15 musical numbers in two acts. There is no overture (Mozart would have composed that last, in his usual way), nor is there a dénouement. When the opera breaks off, the three westerners who tried to escape from their Muslim captor—in the original the father, Renegat, his daughter Zaide, spotless jewel of the harem, and her brother Comatz—are awaiting torture and death; but this is the eighteenth-century stage, and a discovery is surely to be made (in the original, it is that Renegat long ago saved the Sultan's life) that will permit the ruler to be merciful and lead to their being freed. This is the cast as adjusted for the opera:

Zaide, *the sultan's favourite*	(*soprano*)
Gomatz, *a European nobleman, now a prisoner*	(*tenor*)
Allazim, *captain of the slaves*	(*bass*)
Sultan Soliman	(*tenor*)
Osmin, *slave dealer*	(*bass*)
Four slaves	(*tenors*)
Zaram, *chief janissary*	(*spoken part*)

It was at the end of 1778 that Mozart had encountered the melodramas of Georg Benda and had written to his father that 'most operatic recitative should be treated in this way'. Here he had a chance to put his thoughts into effect. After a brief opening chorus for a group of slaves breaking stones, Gomatz bemoans his situation in a melodrama ('Unerforschliche Fügung!'). Winding and falling violin phrases instantly capture his despair and sense of oppression and his lapsing wearily into sleep, as the music's energy dissipates, its tempo slows and its melodic spans contract. This movement is in fact Mozart's solitary essay in the expressive use of melodrama; its only other appearance in *Zaide* is at the beginning of Act 2, when Soliman discovers that Zaide has fled, and there it is used for little more than the punctuation of exclamations of rage. The first act of *Zaide* is concerned solely with the emotions of the three Europeans. Zaide chances upon the sleeping Gomatz, and sings 'Ruhe sanft, mein holdes Leben', one of Mozart's most exquisitely graceful arias, in the style of a minuet and much in the manner of J.C. Bach. At the end of the act, Gomatz and Zaide, aided by Allazim, set sail for freedom with him, in a terzet in E major (the key Mozart favoured for music concerned with travel by sea), in which the gently swaying 6/8 Andantino to which they embark gives way to a triumphant *alla breve*. The triumph of course is brief. In Act 2, Soliman fulminates in a typical D major vengeance aria, with trumpets and drums, paralleling himself with the savage lion who has been dishonoured, and on their recapture threatens them in an elaborate, richly scored aria in a heroic style. This pairing of arias—the two for Gomatz are separated only by a duet in Act 1, the two for Soliman by a short aria for Osmin in Act 2—continues with two arias in immediate succession for Zaide herself, a delicately pathetic rondo in the traditionally gentle key of A major bewailing her lost freedom, and a raging aria in G minor, 'Tiger! Wetze nur die Klauen', challenging and reproaching Soliman for his savagery. The act ends with a quartet in which Zaide and Gomatz, supported by Allazim, each beg Soliman to spare the other. The music accommodates their pleas along with his stern

refusals, in its contrasts of tone and in the way that his decisive inter-
ventions force their phrases towards cadences and carry their chromaticisms back to clear-cut tonality.

In some modern revivals this, for want of any further music, has
been treated as the finale of the opera. But there can be no question
that a *lieto fine* was intended: a tragic ending would have been entirely
out of keeping with eighteenth-century theatrical custom and aesthetic principle. This has been recognized in many revivals, and sometimes the opening chorus has been used to form a finale, although it
is inappropriate and lacks the necessary weight. It is reasonable, however, to imagine that Mozart and Schachtner would have devised
some twist in the plot analogous to that of Sebastiani and Friebert in
Das Serail (and indeed to what happens in the finale of *Die Entführung
aus dem Serail*, of 1782): that is, to invent some circumstance that

Folio 3^r from the autograph score of 'Zaide', showing the opening of the
first melodrama (*Staatsbibliothek, Preussischer Kulturbesitz, Berlin*)

would justify an act of magnanimity on Soliman's part. If *Zaide* was to have been a two-act work, a dialogue and a final ensemble might have served for the dénouement. But if it were a normal three-act opera, the additional plot event would have had to be of sufficient complexity to give scope for, perhaps, two or three arias, and probably a duet and a closing ensemble. We may be sure that Schachtner and Mozart had abandoned the idea of Gomatz and Zaide as brother and sister, or Allazim as their father, since there is no mention of blood relationships in the text we have, and the tone of both words and music makes it abundantly clear that they were to be perceived as lovers.

As it stands, then, *Zaide* is only part of an opera. Even so, it represents a substantial advance in maturity and in technique as compared with Mozart's preceding operatic works, those of his Italian years or *La finta giardiniera* and *Il rè pastore*. It came after an operatic hiatus of five years, years in which Mozart had been parted from his father, had seen his mother die and had fallen in love. He had seen aspects of the world hitherto shielded from him. He had moved from the age of 19 to the age of 24. He was setting a text, for the first time since childhood, in his native tongue, not in the Italian that symbolized operatic convention. He could, and surely did, plan with his librettist the kinds of verse he wanted for each character, and this gave him better control over the kinds of music he could assign to each. It is no coincidence that the two arias for Soliman, the old-fashioned despot, are the longest, and the only ones with lengthy opening ritornellos and extended working-out: that is because they are intentionally formal statements of a traditional situation by an older character. The arias for the lovers have an altogether more natural and more direct mode of utterance than their counterparts in his earlier operas, and relatively simple structures to match. Accordingly, the characters in *Zaide* begin to assume something closer to the individuality of those in his mature operas.

Clearly Mozart thought well of *Zaide*: he asked Leopold to bring it to Munich for his friends there to hear, and later took it to Vienna. There he showed it to Gottlieb Stephanie, one of the managers of the new German opera company, and wrote:[25]

> ... as for Schachtner's operetta, there is nothing to be done—for the reason I have often mentioned. Stephanie is going to give me a new libretto, a good one, he says ... I could not contradict Stephanie. I merely said that except for the long dialogues, which could easily be changed, the piece was very good, but not suitable for Vienna, where people prefer comic pieces.

The reason he had often mentioned must be the Viennese preference for comedy. He had known about this when he began work on *Zaide*, but must initially have hoped it would turn out to be sufficiently comic. Osmin's Act 2 aria is wholly comic, no less so than those of his *Entführung* namesake (*Entführung* was of course the libretto that Stephanie was to provide for him), but Mozart had pursued his inclination when he made the choice, no doubt because he was looking for something that would be more receptive to the kind of music he was eager to write than the ordinary, trivial comedy of the time. In his succeeding works, *Idomeneo* and especially *Die Entführung*, whose plot has much in common with *Zaide* (as for example do Gluck's *La rencontre imprévue* and Haydn's *L'incontro improvviso*), he carried further the lessons he had learnt during the composition of *Zaide*, and he occasionally echoed its actual music. The manuscript of *Zaide* was found in Mozart's library after his death; his widow was unable to identify it. It was among those sold to Johann Anton André, the publisher and composer in Offenbach, who catalogued, edited and published many of them. He gave *Zaide* its name (preferring it to *Das Serail*, to avoid confusion), commissioned a new text, and supplied an overture and finale (not Symphony no. 32 K.318, which Einstein proposed, and which has no connection with the work). The music had its first hearing in the theatre in 1866, when it was given in Frankfurt on Mozart's birthday. There have been further attempts to bring it plausibly to the stage, including one with additional material by Italo Calvino, but the want of a convincing musical ending tells against it. Apart from the occasions on which he played it over to friends, Mozart never heard a note of the work.

20

Idomeneo at Munich

IDOMENEO IS MOZART'S Mannheim opera. 'My dearest wish', he told the Palatine Elector in November 1777, 'is to write an opera here'. It took three years for his wish to be fulfilled, and by that time 'here' was somewhere else. What he had wanted was to write an opera that drew on the intellectual commitment of the Mannheim court coupled with the expressive resource of the splendid Mannheim orchestra. But now, of course, the Munich and Mannheim courts were amalgamated, the Elector Palatine was the Elector of Bavaria, and most of the members of the former orchestra were in Munich, where they formed the basis of the Bavarian court orchestra. So it was from Munich that the commission came in 1780. Mozart had his connections there too, including the opera intendant Count Seeau, to whom he will surely have spoken when in 1779 he was in the city and went to the carnival opera. His friends from Mannheim, Raaff and Cannabich in particular (Cannabich was close to Countess Paumgarten, the Elector's current favourite), are likely to have supported his claims for consideration. The fee he was paid is unknown. Leopold referred in a letter to its modesty;[1] it may have been as little as the 125 gulden he had talked of, back in 1777, for a

German opera in Munich, though more probably it was nearer 200. The librettist received 90 gulden and the translator 45.

The choice of topic for a new opera, especially one as important as the carnival opera, lay with the ruler himself, in consultation with his literary advisers and the opera intendant. The Mannheim court had long been progressive in its operatic outlook.[2] Operas given there had often used texts based on French models, and there had been experiments, as in Schweitzer's works, with opera in German. The 1780 carnival opera, *Telemaco*, was by a Mannheim composer, Franz Paul Grua, primarily a writer of church music, and this was his only opera. Its main source was François de la Motte-Fénelon's influential didactic romance *Les aventures de Télémaque* (1696), in which a version of the mythological story of Idomeneus, king of Crete at the time of the Trojan War, is related. Fénelon was an admired Enlightenment figure: the Mozarts had visited his tomb at Cambrai in 1766, and Wolfgang read at least part of *Télémaque* at Bologna during the summer of 1770.[3]

The text for Mozart's opera was to be based on the libretto that Antoine Danchet had written for André Campra's *Idomenée*, given at the Paris Opéra in 1712, drawn from Fénelon and a drama of 1705 by Prosper Jolyot de Crébillon. The five-act *tragédie en musique* now had to be translated and rearranged in three acts. An Italian librettist was needed. Clearly it would be convenient to engage someone resident in Salzburg who could work closely with Mozart. One of the chaplains at the court there was Giovanni Battista (or Gianbattista) Varesco, born in Trento in 1735 and trained in the classics by the Jesuits. Presumably Mozart and his father put his name to Seeau when the commission was agreed, during the late spring or the summer of 1780. There is a note in Nannerl's diary, in Mozart's hand, of a visit by Varesco to the Mozarts' house (his only recorded one during the summer) on 22 August.

We have no means of knowing whether the 22 August meeting was an initial approach, a discussion of progress to date or, least likely, the handing-over of a draft text. Most probably it was about that time that a plan for the opera, referred to several times in the correspondence, was drawn up: it will have constituted a list of the scenes, indicating the placing of the lyrical musical numbers (arias, ensembles, choruses) and probably also where the recitative was to be orchestrally accompanied as opposed to simple recitative with continuo. The plan was submitted for agreement with Count Seeau and others at Munich, probably including Cannabich (as orchestra director), the ballet master, the scene designer and even the senior singers.

Varesco's task was a complicated and difficult one. Mozart, and his father too, probably played a considerable part, not as regards the actual wording but in determining the structure. Varesco had not only to translate the text—he used about two-thirds of Danchet's actual lines in direct translation—and to adjust the plot, but also in effect to change the genre. It had to be given the happy ending that by this date was obligatory, politically and philosophically, and it had to be imbued with some of the moral force that had become part of serious opera in the Metastasian era—human beings must be less the playthings of the gods and more in control of their own fates, and thus made responsible for their bad deeds and worthy of reward for their good ones.[4] Varesco reduced the number of characters, taking out most of Danchet's confidants (allowing for soliloquy, as opposed to the dialogue so beloved of French *tragédie*) as well as the now outdated allegorical or supernatural figures (Jealousy, Nemesis and Venus). He needed to eliminate or adapt the *divertissements*, the spectacular dance and choral scenes important in French opera. He had to adjust Danchet's scene structure to some degree so that arias represented an emotional culmination, as in normal Metastasian *opera seria*, but—and this was surely at Mozart's specific request—he often kept characters on stage, even after their own arias, to maintain continuity by eliding scenes, so that the action would be as if in 'real time'.

Writing for the Munich company, Mozart had no need to defer composition until he met the singers. He knew all but one of them already and had composed for Raaff and Dorothea Wendling in the past. (Aloysia Weber was no longer in the company: she and her family had left in 1779 when she took up a position in Vienna, and on 31 October 1780 she had married the court painter and actor Joseph Lange. Her father had died in Vienna in October 1779.) He could start at the beginning and write most of the opera straight through, if he wanted to. But he would of course need to be in Munich, to be sure that the singers were happy with their arias (and to adjust or rewrite them if not), to teach them to those singers who needed it, to complete the work in collaboration with the intendant and his colleagues, to rehearse the opera and to direct the early performances. There is no record of his application to the archbishop for permission to travel to Munich, nor of the archbishop's reply, but a later reference in the correspondence implies that he was granted only six weeks' leave, scarcely sufficient for a full-scale serious opera—and that despite the promises that Leopold had originally secured, or claimed to have secured, about leave of absence to compose operas. (Leopold later decided to interpret this as six weeks to compose and another six to rehearse and perform; the archbishop was preoccupied with other matters and raised no objection.) [5]

During the composition of well over half of *Idomeneo*, Varesco was in Salzburg and Mozart was in Munich. Their collaboration was conducted by post, with Leopold Mozart serving as intermediary, and a very active intermediary with plenty of opinions of his own. This, happily for posterity, means that we have access to a unique and extraordinarily revealing correspondence, which illuminates every aspect of the work's genesis—its planning, its composition and the theatrical and other practical factors affecting its performance—and above all Mozart's thinking about the relationship of words and drama to music. It also sheds light on the role Leopold continued to play at this point in his son's composing.[6]

IDOMENEO DEALS WITH the dilemma of the father called upon to sacrifice his child, a tale familiar in eastern Mediterranean mythology (as in the biblical story of Jephtha and his daughter Iphis, and the *Iliad* story of Agamemnon and Iphigeneia). Idomeneo, king of Crete, beset by a ferocious storm at sea on his arrival home from the Trojan War, promises Neptune the sacrifice of the first human being he meets if he is spared. He meets a young man who, to his horror, identifies himself as his son Idamante. He flees and tries to circumvent the obligations of his vow, concealing his obligation until he is compelled to reveal it, when a monster ravages the land. Idamante, who is loved by both Ilia (whom he loves) and Electra, prepares himself for sacrifice but is spared by the god, speaking through his oracle, when Ilia offers herself in his stead. This is the cast:

Idomeneus [Idomeneo], *king of Crete*	Anton Raaff (*tenor*)
Idamantes [Idamante], *his son*	Vincenzo dal Prato (*castrato soprano*)
Ilia, *Trojan princess*	Dorothea Wendling (*soprano*)
Electra [Elettra], *Greek princess*	Elisabeth Wendling (*soprano*)
Arbaces [Arbace], *Idomeneus's confidant*	Domenico de' Panzacchi (*tenor*)
High Priest	Giovanni Valesi (*tenor*)
Oracle	[Unknown] (*bass*)
Chorus of Cretans, Trojan prisoners, sailors	

Mozart left Salzburg on 5 November 1780, travelling overnight by the mail coach. It was an uncomfortable journey: ' . . . I really never thought I should bring my behind to Munich intact!—it became quite sore—and no doubt a fiery red—for two whole stages I sat with my hands dug into the upholstery and my behind in mid-air'. He was soon in contact with Seeau and on 8 November sent instructions to Varesco about the preparation of the libretto for printing. Mozart warned him that alterations would be needed, including cuts in the recitative, but reassured him that his whole text would be printed in the libretto for sale in the opera house (this was the customary procedure: unset passages were normally distinguished by quotation marks, as 'versi virgolati', or with brackets, although here they are unmarked). He also asked Varesco to modify the text of Ilia's Act 2 aria, 'Se il padre perdei', to remove an aside—admissible in dialogue, but not in an aria, where words have to be repeated. He notes that 'we have agreed' that the aria would be an Andantino with obbligato flute, oboe, bassoon and horn. This statement indicates a limit to the composer's autonomy: Seeau and Cannabich, and perhaps Dorothea Wendling (who would be singing the aria), partook in the decision, although the idea will surely have come from Mozart himself, thinking of Wendling, Ramm and his other friends in the orchestra.

That aria falls early in Act 2. It seems likely that Act 1 was by then nearly complete and Mozart may have been quite advanced with Act 2, as on 15 November he could report that Elisabeth Wendling (always 'Lisel' in his letters) was delighted with her two arias and had sung them half-a-dozen times (the second falls halfway through Act 2). The Wendling sisters-in-law were typically cast, Dorothea in the *prima donna* role, calling for pathetic singing, Lisel in the fiery *seconda donna* one.[7] Dorothea too was 'arcicontentissima' with the opening scene. Mozart wrote Idomeneo's Act 1 aria within a few days of reaching Munich; he showed it to Raaff on 14 November. No doubt he felt he should postpone composing for the elderly tenor, now 66, until he had heard him again. (The aria is written on different paper, a type otherwise used only in Act 3, so probably bought in Munich, and Mozart's letter of 27 December anyway makes it clear that Leopold had not heard it.) Mozart had misgivings about Raaff's acting ('like a statue') and feared for the crucial recognition scene where father and son meet and which demanded particular sensitivity, especially as he had heard that the castrato had never before appeared on the stage (that was not in fact true) and was apt to run out of breath in the middle of an aria. When Mozart came to work with his 'molto amato castrato dal Prato' he realized that he would have to teach him the opera note by note.

That ironic phrase comes in Mozart's letter of 15 November, by which date discussion had begun of the general shape of the drama as it was developing. From this point onwards, two themes run through everything Mozart had to say on the subject: brevity and naturalness. It had become plain to him that the libretto was far too long and could not be set in full. Varesco had to be told that a duet planned for the sacrifice scene, where Idamante and Ilia vie for the right to die so that the other may live, must go, 'and indeed with more profit than loss to the opera; for when you read it you realize that it becomes limp and cold . . . and the noble struggle between Ilia and Idamante is prolonged and loses its force'. Varesco resisted, but Leopold persuaded him, and went on to advise Mozart how the scene should be set: 'a few words of recitative, interrupted by a subterranean rumbling, and then the utterance of a subterranean voice. This voice and its accompaniment must be moving, terrifying and out of the ordinary; and it can be a masterpiece of harmony'. Leopold makes suggestions too about the staging. There was no single stage director or producer in charge of such matters. Mozart's letter of 13 November refers to a working lunch at Seeau's with Cannabich, the stage designer Lorenzo Quaglio and the ballet-master Le Grand on the subject, and in a later letter he refers to the 'action and groupings' being settled with Le Grand. It generally fell to the librettist, as creator of the drama, to control the staging, but the composer, the designer and the ballet-master would also contribute their ideas, and so too would the singers, especially the senior ones, in their own arias. Stage etiquette was so standardized and stage comportment so well understood that there was little scope for disagreement.

Effective musical drama was one thing, plausibility another. The text had specified that Idomeneo, a king, should be all alone on a ship at his first entry. That would not do, Mozart said; a king must have a retinue. Leopold remarked that he had made this point before in a letter to Munich but had been overruled, as thunderstorms and the sea pay no attention to the laws of etiquette. But now Quaglio himself raised the point. A suitable modification would be made. Then, Mozart asked, could the short aria for Idomeneo within the Act 2 finale be dropped and a recitative substituted, at the point where a thunderstorm has frustrated the departure of Idamante and Electra? 'There will be such noise and confusion that an aria at this point would cut a feeble figure . . . and the thunderstorm is hardly likely to subside just for Mr Raaff to sing an aria, is it?' The vain Raaff, wanting more opportunities than his earlier arias allowed to show off his cantabile, asked for an extra aria at the end of Act 3, where a quartet had been planned, which Mozart thought a good idea—'thus', he wrote, 'a useless piece will be got rid of—and Act 3 will be far more effective'.

In his first two weeks in Munich Mozart, it seems, was doing almost as much planning and working with the singers as actual composing. He did write one piece beside Raaff's aria. Before he left Salzburg he had promised to provide a song for use in a play, Gozzi's *Le due notti affannose*, being given (in German, probably as *Peter der Grausame*) by Emanuel Schikaneder's company, who were playing at the theatre. Leopold had to send him a couple of reminders. The piece, 'Die neugeborne Ros' entzückt' K.315*a*, was wholly lost until 1996, when one sheet (probably of four or five) came to light. But by 24 November—when he told his father about a scandalous incident at a court concert, when the husband of the famous soprano Madame Mara had tried to oust the orchestra's cellist and practically came to blows with Cannabich—he was planning the embarkation scene at the end of Act 2. The original libretto here had four appearances of the choral refrain, with three solo sections in between, and these were reduced to two and a single solo. Five days later Mozart had received a text for the new Raaff aria, but neither he nor Raaff liked it, particularly since the way the sense fell across the lines precluded a normal musical treatment of the verse; would Varesco try again? Also, he commented on the oracle scene:

Tell me, do you not find the speech of the subterranean voice too long? Consider it carefully.—Imagine yourself in the theatre, and that the voice must be terrifying—it must be penetrating—and one must believe that it is real—how can this be believed, when the speech is so long, for during this time the hearer will become increasingly sure that it is meaningless?— If the Ghost's speech in *Hamlet* were not so long it would have a better effect.

Just before then, Mozart had lunched with Panzacchi. One result—there being no such thing as a free lunch—was a request that Arbace's Act 3 recitative be extended; 'we must do what we can to oblige this worthy old fellow', who was a good actor. Raaff had now seen his Act 2 aria and 'is as excited by it as a passionate young man with his beloved, for he sings it at night before he goes to sleep and again in the morning when he wakes up'. At the first rehearsal, at Seeau's house with a reduced band, Ramm had told Mozart that no music had ever impressed him so deeply. 'I cannot tell you', Mozart wrote to Leopold, 'how delighted and astonished they all were.' Most of the family correspondence during December is concerned with local news and gossip, with reports on musical events and, from Nannerl to Wolfgang, on theatre activities in Salzburg. In only one letter, written on 16 December when the six-week leave was due to expire, does Mozart refer to his discontent with Salzburg, in particular the archbishop and his nobility. He clearly had hopes that a Munich position might be available. On 29 November 1780, Maria Theresa had died in Vienna. With Munich outside the Habsburg domains this fortunately did not involve closure of the theatres, but it did make it necessary for Mozart to ask Leopold to send his black suit (in which Leopold could conveniently wrap a pair of trumpet mutes, not available in Munich and needed in the march in Act 2).

But a few days later more anxieties surfaced. On 19 December, when Mozart had only three arias, a chorus, the overture and the ballet music still to write, the first two acts were to be rehearsed with full orchestra, the third (as far as it went) with a small group. This must have shown that the opera was running far too long. Mozart demanded cuts in several places, including the recognition scene in Act 1 and at the opening of Act 2. Leopold summoned Varesco for an emergency meeting. They 'saw no reason to shorten' the recitative; he explains why every line is significant, and ends with proposals of cuts of about a minute in Act 1 and a half-minute and two-and-a-half minutes in Act 2. In his next letter Mozart described further tussles with Raaff, who objected to the quartet in Act 3—no opportunity to open up the voice—and complained about the new Act 3 aria, with its awkward syllables ('vien mi a rinvigorir'). Leopold argued the point, but by 1 January 1781 Varesco had written another new text, and Mozart had it two days later and immediately set it. The oracle's utterance came up for discussion and drew suggestions from Leopold:[8]

> I imagine you will choose low wind instruments to accom-
> pany the subterranean voice. How would it be if, after the
> *slight* subterranean rumble, the instruments *sustained, or rather
> began to sustain*, their notes, softly, and then make a *crescendo
> such as might inspire terror*, and during the *decrescendo the voice
> would begin to sing*? And there might be a terrifying crescendo
> at *each phrase uttered by the voice*.

To this Mozart responded on 3 January: the accompaniment was for just three trombones and two horns, behind the stage. That however was only the beginning of a saga. A week later he reported a 'desper-ate fight' with Seeau over the trombones; clearly the hire of three extra players for a few moments' music did not please the intendant. Another week later, after rehearsal of Act 3, the opera was still run-ning far too long. The aria for Idamante, as he goes to his (supposed) death, had to go; 'in any case, it is out of place there', Mozart wrote on 18 January, not without justification. And finally the new aria for Raaff, which had caused so much trouble, had to go too: 'we must make a virtue of necessity'. This surely was problematic, since it meant that after the oracle's pronouncement (which Mozart had shortened yet again) there was only Electra's stormy aria, a brief recitative and the chorus and ballet to end the opera.

At this point the family correspondence ends. Leopold and Nannerl left for Munich, arriving there on 26 January 1781. It must have been shortly after Mozart's final letter that the libretto was reprinted. Like most librettists, Varesco took his work very seriously in its own right and required that his drama be printed in full, and in the correspondence Leopold often stressed the importance of respecting his wishes. He had sent the text, with a German translation by J.A. Schachtner, and it had already been typeset and printed, including all the items and the recitative to be cut, with the Italian text on the left-hand pages and the German on the right. But now there were so many changes that it would be useless for its primary purpose, that is, to enable a member of the audience to follow the text in the opera house. So a revised edition was rushed into print, in Italian only (it was too late now for a translation). Reflecting the intentions of Mozart and his colleagues as they were, probably on or about 20 January, it shows the cuts he had detailed in his letters and more. Electra's final aria, 'D'Oreste, d'Aiace', is excised, replaced by a fiery exit recitative, and there are cuts in the earlier public scenes too. The text of the oracle's pronouncement in the original libretto is the lengthy one that Mozart first set, before he protested about it; he had in fact produced two more settings with trombones, one fairly short and another a perfunctory nine bars, but the text in the second libretto corresponds with a further, fourth setting, without trombones, presumably under pressure from Seeau. Economy had prevailed.

In the edition of *Idomeneo* published in the NMA in 1972, the primary text corresponds broadly to that of the second libretto;[9] all the remaining music, including many stretches of recitative, is consigned to an appendix. But in 1981 the original performing score, prepared by a court copyist, belatedly came to light in the Bavarian State Library. This makes it clear that the battles over the text persisted up to the last moment.[10] There are two further layers of changes, made in pencil and red crayon (there are corresponding red crayon marks in the autograph score). In Acts 1 and 2 there are some small cuts, mainly in recitative, and of singers' cadenzas. In Act 3 two more entire

numbers disappear, the love duet for Ilia and Idamante at the beginning of the act and Arbace's scene, with his finely sombre orchestral
recitative and his aria, soon after. There are also clear indications that
Idamante's 'No, la morte' was restored, although it may seem the least
significant and dramaturgically the weakest of the last three arias as
well as being the one Mozart was least reluctant to part with.

  Idomeneo had its first performance on 29 January 1781, at the new
electoral theatre, now known, after its architect, as the Cuvilliès-
Theatre: it still stands (although in a slightly different position since
its destruction in World War II). The opera was repeated on 5 and 12
February and had been scheduled for two further performances, on
19 and 26 February, but gave way to a banquet in honour of the
Duke Karl August Christian of Zweibrücken and in favour of a
fancy-dress ball. The 12 February performance was followed by a ball.
Possibly some of the marked cuts may have been made only on nights
when an early finish was necessary; or perhaps there were changes,
one way or another, between performances in the light of the opera's
length. There are no records whatever of its reception. Mozart himself reported the Elector's pleasure after one of the rehearsals. Newspaper reports merely mention the event, that Quaglio was the
designer and that text and music came from Salzburg.

JUST AFTER THE beginning of Act 2 of *Idomeneo*, Ilia sings her aria
with four obbligato wind instruments, 'Se il padre perdei', the E flat
aria d'affetto that is traditionally the emotional centrepiece of the
prima donna's contribution. It is tenderly written and exquisitely
scored. In it she tells Idomeneo that although she has lost her father
(King Priam) and her Trojan homeland, she has found new kindness
here in Crete and he is as a second father to her. She goes off, leaving him alone to muse, in his ensuing recitative, on the cruel fate that
his oath has brought about, for her as well as for himself and
Idamante. The first part of his recitative is run through with excerpts
from the orchestral accompaniment to her aria, now darkened by

transposition to the minor key, a lower register and different scoring. This is a unique example, showing Mozart using thematic material in a new way, to comment on the relation between Ilia's hopes and Idomeneo's gloomy thoughts. He is recalling her expression of happiness which, as the music is telling us, is illusory.

Within the confines of the operatic idiom of Mozart and his contemporaries, this is something that can be done only in what is usually called 'accompanied recitative' or 'orchestral recitative', of which there is far more, and of a far more varied character, in *Idomeneo* than in any of Mozart's earlier operas (and, broadly speaking, his later ones too). Here he uses orchestral recitative not, as he generally does elsewhere, primarily for representation of a character *in extremis*, leading to an aria in which the extreme emotion is given vent, but to play a much more active role in the depiction of character and feeling. This is of course not unrelated to what Gluck had been doing in his recent 'reform operas'. Mozart and his father knew Gluck's *Orfeo ed Euridice* and *Alceste*, and comparisons have been drawn between the oracle scenes in *Alceste* and *Idomeneo*. It is however clear from the family correspondence that, even though Leopold's ideas here were not unlike Gluck's, he thought when writing that he was making original suggestions; he would otherwise surely have referred to a model familiar to both of them. But Gluck was not the only 'reformer' in this sense. Other composers, such as Tommaso Traetta and Niccolò Jommelli, and librettists (notably Mattia Verazi) had been working to very similar ends, and several of them had been closely associated with Mannheim. Munich too had links with this reform movement during the 1760s and early 70s.[11] The central point, historically and aesthetically, is that from the outset *Idomeneo* was projected as an Italian opera on a French-style libretto, and that Mozart's opportunity to control the revision of the Danchet libretto allowed him, in his aim to write a powerful and effective *dramma per musica*, to expand his armoury and go far beyond the relatively simple succession of arias and recitatives that he had taken for granted as part of the genre when he was writing *Mitridate* and *Lucio Silla* in Italy.

The result is an opera in which the musical pull on the emotions very rarely relaxes. It begins in the eighth bar. The overture starts with a formal, conventional, fanfare-like phrase, to which the lower strings then respond, against a menacing tremolando, with a lowering chromatic phrase that at once hints at the dark events to come. The woodwind downward flick ending with repeated notes occurs at several points in the opera and seems to stand for Idamante:

It appears in Ilia's opening aria, when she expresses her guilt at falling in love with a Greek:

and most poignantly where Idomeneo finally discloses, in Act 3, the identity of the sacrifice victim (see the example following). The form it takes at the end of this last example (shown at *x*), incorporating chromatic falling fourths with some of the intermediate notes omitted, also occurs elsewhere, notably at the end of the overture and at the fateful moment where Idomeneo recognizes his son. Other phrases in the opera also seem to be used allusively, notably a short one that appears numerous times (for example in the closing three bars of the overture) and has been identified as referring to reconciliation.[12] These are not leitmotifs in the Wagnerian sense; Wagner's

leitmotifs have a different function. It is highly unlikely that Mozart
used such devices with any thought that they would be perceptible
as specific indicators of meaning to the opera-house listener, but they
provide a particular kind of expressive coherence, and certainly held
additional meaning for him as the creator of the work. Their persistent presence heightens the effect of the recitative. It is also likely that
Mozart had the allusive use of key in his mind: there are several points
at which striking or unconventional modulations seem in some sense
portentous, or at least suggestive. The use of key in Mozart's operas is
however a large topic and one better discussed in conjunction with
the Da Ponte operas of the later 1780s.

Orchestral recitative is used in the opera in many other ways, often to more conventional and straightforward dramatic effect. At the moment where father and son recognize each other, simple recitative (with only continuo accompaniment) gives way to an orchestral outburst as Idomeneo sees the horror of the situation, and the orchestra plunges in as he exclaims 'Spietatissimi dei!' ('Pitiless gods!'). At the point in the final act when Ilia and Idamante come to perceive that their love is mutual, the strings steal softly in, lending the music a gentle flood of warmth as the couple move towards their duet. Orchestral recitative used a number of standard devices, of which Mozart had established his command in childhood and demonstrated in Milan in 1770. Here that repertory is extended, partly through a new kind of statuesque grandeur or formality of musical diction. Examples include the three sombre, martial wind calls heard at the end of the recognition scene when Idomeneo flees from Idamante and commands his son not to pursue him, and the six chilling chromatic wind flourishes that follow. And there are many examples where Mozart uses contrapuntal, often imitative writing for the strings to establish an almost ritual-like character to the utterance and give it due weight and moment: a good case is the last one in the opera, when Idomeneo addresses the people of Sidon as he hands on the throne. It is this sense of the hieratic that permeates the opera, and it is felt the most powerfully in the orchestral recitatives, which inhabit an exalted world into which Mozart never again ventured.

The role assigned to orchestral recitative is of course intimately connected with the mode of approach to, and departure from, the individual arias. The opera as conceived has fourteen arias, three for each principal and two for Arbace. Only four of them are preceded by simple recitative, the remainder by orchestral ones. Even more significant, just two end with a clear break and a resumption of recitative, although others have natural end-of-scene breaks. With several, Mozart ensures a sense of continuity by writing a brief orchestral phrase to lead directly into the resumption of recitative, so circumventing applause and avoiding any sense of a break in time and continuity. The opportunity for this enhanced continuity was provided by the French libretto, and we may be sure that Mozart had encouraged Varesco to preserve what he clearly saw as opportunities for sustaining the dramatic tension.

The planning of the arias to suit the voices available to him remained, in spite of any higher objectives, a central part of Mozart's task. No opera would be a success if the singers could not sing it effectively and with conviction. Mozart had little trouble with his cast. The *prima donna*, Dorothea Wendling, singing Ilia, had a sympathetic voice and musical personality; here, exceptionally, she has an aria close to the beginning of each of the three acts. Only the first is preceded by an orchestral recitative, which sets the tone of the opera, with its wide and strongly expressed series of emotions, before leading to her G minor aria with its complex of emotions, sorrow, guilt and love. This aria leads directly into simple recitative: Mozart is both symbolizing her emergence from her inner thoughts to the realities around her and at the same time ensuring dramatic continuity. In just the same way, her second aria leads directly into Idomeneo's recitative where its motifs are echoed, and her third at the opening of Act 3 gives way to Idamante's entry and her alarmed exclamation in orchestral recitative (she had thought him departed for Argos with Electra). The range of her arias is narrow, essentially three different expressions of tenderness: she is emotionally a fixed, stable point in the opera.

Electra's arias, which are all seamlessly linked to the items around them, take advantage of Lisel Wendling's passionate manner. Her Act 1 outburst on learning that Idomeneo is apparently drowned is coloured by swooping orchestral figuration hinting at the waves, and is marked by a curious tonal twist: it is in D minor but its recapitulation begins in C minor, giving a sense of the music unhinged or, to the listener, in some way awry or out of kilter. It soon returns to D minor, but then finally reverts to C minor with a violent turn as the aria leads directly into the next scene—the storm that strikes Idomeneo's ship as it approaches Crete. (Ilia's reaction makes better sense in

Danchet's version than in Varesco's, since there Idomeneo has amorous designs on her, and his death would leave her free for Idamante.) Ilia's gentler Act 2 aria again follows an orchestral recitative, motifs from which find a place in the secondary material of the aria, and it leads into the ceremonial march to the harbour. Her Act 3 aria, omitted as we have seen at the première, is the furious, crazed 'D'Oreste, d'Aiace', arising from an accompanied recitative of the same character but ending as she storms off and the last scene begins.

It was cutting the suit to fit Anton Raaff's difficult figure that was most problematic to Mozart. Raaff was anxious to deploy his smooth cantabile but eager too to show that he was still capable of dealing with virtuoso *fioritura*. The words of Idomeneo's first aria, as he contemplates the terrible consequences of his vow, offer no scope for either, but the Act 2 'Fuor del mar, ho un mar in seno' is a noble *tour de force*, a brilliant D major piece with trumpets and drums and military rhythms, music fit for a king. It duly portrays both the raging of the seas and the storm within his breast, with its agitated, tremolo-like writing for the strings, its long vocal roulades and its burbling wind passages all adding up to a noble expression of the agonies of mind he has created for himself. This aria ends with a formal cadence—Raaff had to be able to acknowledge his applause—but when, five years later, Mozart revised the opera he provided not only a simplified version for a less sturdy tenor but also adjusted the ending to make the music flow continuously into the next orchestral recitative. Raaff's last aria, 'Torna la pace', bows to his demands, allowing for his old-fashioned *portamento* singing in the manner of his favourite composer, Hasse. It is carefully placed in his best register and never covered by the quite rich orchestration: it is a pity that it was never sung.[13] It is a three-part aria, *A* (ending in the dominant), *B* (in a contrasting metre) and *A'* (modified to end in the tonic). This sonata-form-like pattern, though usually with no contrast in metre and sometimes no 'development' area at all, predominates in *Idomeneo* and allows for arias more succinct and more purposefully shaped than the expansive scheme of the earlier operas required.

The music for Idamante, most of which Mozart evidently composed before he had met Dal Prato (two of his three arias are in Act 1), is no less carefully composed than that for the singers he knew. The first, 'Non ho colpa', responding to Ilia's reproach at his words of love, emerges from a quickening simple recitative into a slow introductory section, then moves on to an Allegro with several brief Larghetto moments. Its main section is distinguished by the rich expressive detail of its scoring and those shifts between major and minor that cast shadows so strongly over much of the music of *Idomeneo*—including Idamante's second aria, sung after his encounter and apparent rejection by his father. Compared with the music for the principals, the two arias for Arbace are slender. Mozart's professed desire to do well by the singer, Panzacchi, could not override his incapacity to supply strong music for words that carry no effective message. The supreme moment for Arbace is the orchestral recitative 'Sventurata Sidon!', preceding his Act 3 aria, in which he bewails the unhappy fate of his nation, but this was cut before the first night.

That recitative follows what is perhaps the most emotionally charged item in the opera, the quartet 'Andrò ramingo e solo': Idamante, told by his father to leave, resolves to seek death alone elsewhere. There ensues an ensemble like no other in Mozart's operas, as the lovers express their suffering, Electra calls for vengeance and Idomeneo himself rails at Neptune, all in music that is highly chromatic, constantly shifting between major and minor and modulating to distant flat keys. The voices sing sometimes singly or in pairs, often in successive imitations that build up a full and harmonically rich texture, heavy with dissonance and of almost unbearable poignancy. The quartet ends with Idamante repeating his opening line, 'I go to wander alone', his last phrase tailing off unresolved as the orchestra draws to a hushed E flat cadence.[14] A later anecdote refers to this quartet. When Mozart and his wife were visiting Leopold and Nannerl in Salzburg in 1783, the quartet was sung: Mozart 'was so overcome that he burst into tears and quitted the chamber'.[15] Mozart valued it at the time of its composition too. When Raaff had questioned it, as it

gave his voice no scope, Mozart replied: ' . . . if I knew of one single
note that should be changed in this quartet, I should alter it at once.
But there is nothing so far in my opera with which I am as pleased
. . . '.[16] There are two other ensemble items. The love duet for
Idamante and Ilia in Act 3 which immediately precedes the quartet is
an appealing, sensitively written two-tempo piece, moving from an
Andante to a gentle Allegretto as their love is fully owned; it was
omitted in the original performances. There is also a terzet, which in
effect is part of the Act 2 finale.

That and the other great public scenes represent another part of
the French legacy to *Idomeneo*. French opera of the post-Lully period
normally included extended and spectacular *divertissements*, often one
in each of the five acts, embodying dance and choral singing and
sometimes only quite loosely related to the *tragédie* itself. The ending
of Act 1 of *Idomeneo* is typical, as the original libretto acknowledges.
There the words 'Fine dell'Atto Primo' follow Idamante's aria, there
is a new heading 'Intermezzo' for a scene in which Idomeneo's
homecoming is celebrated, and at the end the words 'Fine dell'Atto
Primo, e dell'Intermezzo' appear. The Act 2 finale is heralded by a
formal march as the Cretans arrive to see Idamante embark for Argos
with Electra, and a chorus (in E major, Mozart's favoured key for gentle breezes) 'Placido è il mar' follows, in a gently rocking metre, with
one solo verse from Electra (not the three Varesco had contemplated).
After Idomeneo has charged his son to heroic deeds to fit him for
kingship, the three join in a terzet, for Electra a formal farewell, for
Idamante a heartbreaking parting from Ilia, for Idomeneo a fearful
evasion of his vow. The music touches on all these emotions. When
Idamante and Electra move to embark, it turns from major to minor
and accelerates as the sky blackens and a fierce storm breaks—'Qual
nuovo terrore!' ('What new terror!') cry the chorus, as the music tears
into shooting scales and wailing chromatics and a fearsome monster
emerges from the sea. The people of Crete will suffer for the failings
of their king: who, they ask, in a demand twice repeated and punc-
tuated by harsh, disruptive wind chords, is to blame? In a tense, frag-

mented recitative (this is the point where Mozart wisely ruled out an aria) Idomeneo confesses that he is the guilty one. The storm rages on to turbulent music, and the terror-struck Cretans flee the monster, leaving a desolate scene.

That scene drew from Mozart the boldest music he had yet composed, in its range of expression and its novelty of techniques, both harmonic and orchestral. The great scenes of Act 3 surpass it in grandeur and majesty. After the quartet and Arbace's scene, a flurry of allusive themes of strongly contrasting character and abrupt changes of key warn us that great events are afoot. The High Priest calls Idomeneo to account in the great square before the palace for the blood, death and devastation that have beset Sidon: 'Al tempio, Signore!' ('To the temple, Sire!'). Who is the victim? Idomeneo can no longer conceal the truth. 'Oh voto tremendo!' ('Oh terrible vow!'), sing the people of Sidon, as the music settles in the fateful key of C

Design for the Temple of Neptune in *Idomeneo*: watercolour by Lorenzo Quaglio; it is not known whether this design was in fact used in the production (*Theater-Museum, Munich*, Inv. IX Slg. Q. Nr. 44/30)

minor, to the anxiously muttering triplets of the muted violins, the chromatic wails of the woodwind and the sombre fanfares of the muted trumpets. The choral utterance possesses a gravity learnt in Salzburg Cathedral but far beyond anything Mozart had written for the church. The music softens, to C major, through a passage laden with familiar motivic allusion, into a solemn march in F as they move to the temple. There Idomeneo, echoed by the priests, prays to Neptune in a 'Cavatina con coro' of extraordinary originality and compelling hieratic force. The violins, *pizzicato*, are in fast-moving arpeggio patterns, the flutes and oboes in echoing, overlapping three-note phrases that lend the texture a curious glacial quality, and at the end an ascending, aspiring oboe phrase falls back on a sombre cadence, unmistakable symbol of a prayer unanswered.

The dénouement follows, with Idamante's entry and the long, intense dialogue between father and son before the sacrifice. Idamante's aria 'No, la morte io non pavento' ('No, I do not fear death') belongs within it, but it is easy to sympathize with Mozart's doubts about its dramatic propriety, and still easier to agree that a further duet with Ilia at this point would have been damaging. Such movements at this point belong in an earlier concept of serious opera, and *Idomeneo* has gone beyond them. The same cannot be said of Electra's aria. Its excision makes her role seem, if not trivial, at least supernumerary (which in a sense it anyway is, since she has no real involvement in the main action of the opera). But the closing scenes do demand something further from Idomeneo himself—an expression of his setting right his relationship with the world—and that is exactly what Mozart's noble accompanied recitative and his beautiful, lyrical and exquisitely scored setting of 'Torna la pace al core' does perfectly (making prominent use of clarinets, available in Munich but used surprisingly little in the opera). It is, however, very long for its situation in the opera, as Mozart must have realized when he composed it and then speedily agreed to omit it. The work ends with a chorus and a ballet, including a splendid and expansive French-style Chaconne.

MOZART WAS 25 years old two days before the opera's première. *Idomeneo* is, however, a fully mature work, and it represents the peak of his achievement in serious opera, the field of music that mattered to him most of all. Not until the very end of his life, more than ten years later, did he have the opportunity to return to serious opera, and by then the genre was a different one. Some writers have sought to explain the depth of his involvement in the work with some pseudo-Freudian explanation: it is an opera about father and son, Idomeneo and Idamante, and so struck a special chord in a composer whose relationship with his father was so central. This is specious and unnecessary, and in any case the opera is unconcerned with the father–son relationship, which is normal, uncomplicated and predictable. The crucial relationship, the one that governs Idomeneo's actions, is that between himself and the gods, or more broadly between the society of ancient Crete and its gods. *Idomeneo* stands as a masterpiece because Mozart was able to forge what is essentially a new language, in which he could portray so strongly in his music the stark inevitabilities of Greek tragedy while at the same time drawing us deeply into the predicaments and the fates of its principal characters.

Mozart was understandably eager to present *Idomeneo* in Vienna during the next phase of his life. But serious Italian opera was not performed in Vienna except on special court occasions. He had hopes of its use during a state visit and played it over to a group of influential Viennese in May 1781, but Gluck's music was preferred. He was ready to adapt the work to the different conditions there: 'I would have altered Idomeneo's role completely and made it a bass part for Fischer. I would have made several other changes and arranged it more in the French style', he wrote.[17] As in a French opera, the king would have been a bass and Idamante a tenor. His friends advised him to include music from it in his concerts, and he did so at least once, when 'Se il padre perdei' was sung, by Aloysia Lange, on 23 March 1783.[18]

Not until 1786 did he have an opportunity for anything more

extensive, when he organized a performance in the theatre at the Auersperg Palace in Vienna, with amateur singers. The part of Arbace was dropped, and Idamante was cast as a tenor. This occasioned a number of changes. The Act 2 trio and the Act 3 quartet were adjusted to accommodate a tenor voice: simply singing Idamante's part an octave lower would have blurred the texture, and other modifications were needed.[19] Mozart made a shorter and simpler version of 'Fuor del mar', and adjusted the ending so that it led without a break into Electra's recitative. (It was long supposed that this version was made because Raaff balked at its demands, or Mozart could not trust him to meet them, but it is in fact on a paper-type that Mozart used only in Vienna in the period 1785–9 and there is no sign of it in the Munich performing material.) He wrote a new duet, 'Spiegarti non poss'io' (K.489), to replace the one for Ilia and Idamante in Act 3, which had never been performed; the new one is slower (in a single tempo, Larghetto) and substantially shorter.[20] Here Mozart made a rare clerical error, writing a soprano clef sign against Idamante's part but notating the music as if he had written a tenor clef. This would not be worth mentioning were it not that there is a greater enigma surrounding the other alteration, the addition of a new, extended aria for Idamante at the beginning of Act 2, to replace Arbace's scene. Mozart wrote an orchestral recitative, 'Non più, tutto ascoltai', and an aria, 'Non temer, amato bene' (K.490), but he notated them in the soprano clef, and this time at soprano pitch. Whether this was simply an error—it would be a highly uncharacteristic one, for to him sound and symbol were one—or whether it signifies some other intention it is impossible to say. The aria itself is an appealing piece, cast in the new, now fashionable rondò form (a slow section followed by a fast one), and with an elaborate obbligato violin part, written for Mozart's friend Count Hatzfeld. But it can only be damaging to include it in a performance of the opera, for several reasons. In general style (and this applies equally to the orchestral recitative) it is markedly different from, and distinctly later than, the parent work, and the virtuoso violin writing and its interplay with the voice are out of keeping with it. It is excessively long for the opera, and the outright declaration of love on Idamante's part that it embodies is incompatible with what follows. The author of the words of the two new numbers is unknown, but it is unlikely to be Varesco. At the time Mozart was working closely with Lorenzo da Ponte.

THE MOZARTS WERE in no hurry to return to Salzburg. They were presumably obliged to remain in Munich for the first three performances, that is, until 12 February. At that point further performances may still have been in prospect, although none took place. The archbishop was in any case now away. He had left Salzburg about 20 January for Vienna, where there would be various festivities on the full succession of Joseph II after the death of his mother Maria Theresa. Some of the archbishop's retinue, Leopold had reported to his son,[21] had already left, and others, including the castrato Ceccarelli and the violinist Brunetti, were preparing to follow; it must have occurred to them that Mozart, as the principal court keyboard player, was likely to be required too. The postponement of the *Idomeneo* première meant that Leopold could not seek permission for his journey from Colloredo, who had already left, and that meant too that he would not be drawing attention to Mozart's prolonged absence (Mozart had made it very clear, in his letter when the six weeks had expired, that but for Leopold's feelings he would welcome dismissal and a freelance life in Munich).

No doubt all three of the Mozarts took advantage of the social pleasures available to them in Munich during the carnival weeks. Wolfgang also did some composing. Traditionally, the *Kyrie* K.341 has been assigned to this period, and so until quite recently was the Serenade for 13 instruments K.361/370a, but the former probably, and the latter certainly, belong to rather later dates. He did however compose the Oboe Quartet K.370/368b in Munich, for Friedrich Ramm, a small masterpiece that artfully exploits the sweet tone and crisp articulation of the instrument. The central Adagio in D minor touches on real depth of feeling, and the finale is a frolic in which, for a time, the oboe has a different time-signature from the strings, leading to a witty contradiction of rhythms—clearly a jocular challenge from Mozart to Ramm. The only other certain product of the Munich weeks is a *scena*, written for the Elector's favourite, Countess Josepha von Paumgarten—a Metastasio setting: 'Misero, dove son! ... Ah! non son' io che parlo' K.369. In its original context it is sung by a woman whose father's betrayal has led to her lover's imprisonment. It begins with an orchestral recitative, whose repeating string figuration has an almost *Idomeneo*-like character, followed by a two-part aria, a lyrical Andante and an Allegro, making no virtuoso demands. Mozart later had it sent to him in Vienna, where it was sung by the tenor Valentin Adamberger in the concert during Lent 1783 when Aloysia sang 'Se il padre perdei'.

The aria is dated 8 March 1781. Between 7 and 10 March the Mozarts visited the Augsburg area. Whether they called on Leopold's brother and Mozart's Bäsle in the city itself is unknown, but a letter survives reporting their visit to the Heiligkreuz monastery nearby: 'In the last few days we have had the honour and pleasure of the company of Herr Kapellmeister Mozart of Salzburg, whose two children, from Wednesday until today have continuously entertained us with almost more than heavenly music on two fortepianos'.[22] On 12 March the family broke up: Leopold and Nannerl returned to Salzburg, but Wolfgang had been summoned to Vienna to attend the archbishop. On 14 March he arrived in the imperial capital, where the next and the most dramatic chapters in his relations with the Salzburg court were to be conducted and where he was to spend the rest of his life.

NOTES

Bibliographic Abbreviations

AcMoz *Acta Mozartiana*

K.   number in Ludwig von Köchel: *Chronologisch-thematisches Verzeich-nis sämtlicher Tonwerke Wolfgang Amadé Mozarts* (Leipzig, 1862)

K.³   number in Ludwig von Köchel: *Chronologisch-thematisches Verzeich-nis sämtlicher Tonwerke Wolfgang Amadé Mozarts*, ed. Alfred Einstein (Leipzig, 3/1937; with supplement, Ann Arbor, 1947)

K.⁶   number in Ludwig von Köchel: *Chronologisch-thematisches Verzeich-nis sämtlicher Tonwerke Wolfgang Amadé Mozarts*, ed. Franz Giegling, Alexander Weinmann and Gerd Sievers (Wiesbaden, 6/1964)

LMF   *Letters of Mozart and his Family*, ed. Emily Anderson, rev. after Alec Hyatt King and Monica Carolan by Stanley Sadie and Fiona Smart (London, 1985, rev. 1988) [references indicate Letter numbers]

MBA   *Mozart: Briefe und Aufzeichnungen*, ed. Wilhelm A. Bauer and Otto Erich Deutsch with Joseph Heinz Eibl (Kassel, 1962–75) [refer-ences indicate Letter numbers]

MDB   *Mozart: A Documentary Biography*, ed. Otto Erich Deutsch, trans. Eric Blom, Peter Branscombe and Jeremy Noble (London, 1965, 2/1966)

MDL   *Mozart: Die Dokumente seines Lebens, gesammelt und erläutert*, ed. Otto Erich Deutsch (Kassel, 1961)

MDLA   *Mozart: Die Dokumente seines Lebens: Addenda, Neue Folge*, ed. Cliff Eisen (Kassel, 1997)

MISM   *Mitteilungen der Internationalen Stiftung Mozarteum*

MJb   *Mozart-Jahrbuch* (1950–)

NMA   *Wolfgang Amadeus Mozart: Neue Ausgabe sämtlicher Werke* [Neue Mozart-Ausgabe], ed. Internationale Stiftung Mozarteum Salzburg (Kassel etc., 1955–)

NMD   *New Mozart Documents: A Supplement to O.E. Deutsch's Documentary Biography*, ed. Cliff Eisen (London, 1991)

Preface

1 See Neal Zaslaw, 'Mozart as a Working Stiff', *On Mozart*, ed. J. M. Morris (New York, 1994), 102–12.

2 Robert Spaethling's *Mozart's Letters, Mozart's Life: Selected Letters* (New York, 2000), which includes translations of more than 275 letters, proved helpful in this task.

Chapter 1

1 For an account of Salzburg musical traditions see Constantin Schneider: *Geschichte der Musik in Salzburg* (Salzburg, 1935); Ernst Hintermaier: *Die Salzburger Hofkapelle von 1700 bis 1806: Organisation und Personal* (diss., Salzburg University, 1972); Cliff Eisen: 'Salzburg under Church Rule', *Man and Music: The Classical Era*, ed. Neal Zaslaw (London, 1989), 166–87; Neal Zaslaw: *Mozart's Symphonies: Context, Performance Practice, Reception* (Oxford, 1989), Chapter 1 and Appendix C; and Ruth Halliwell: *The Mozart Family* (Oxford, 1998).

Much frank discussion of the Salzburg musical establishment in Mozart's day is, of course, to be found in the family letters: *The Letters of Mozart and his Family*, trans. and ed. Emily Anderson (London, 1938;

rev. Alexander Hyatt King and Monica Carolan, 2/1966; rev. Stanley Sadie and Fiona Smart, 3/1985, rev. 1988) [*LMF*]; this, the most complete edition of the family correspondence when it was first published, contains only shortened versions of many of Leopold's letters and does not include his or Nannerl's travel notes, which are to be found in the complete critical edition, *Mozart: Briefe und Aufzeichnungen*, ed. Wilhelm A. Bauer, Otto Erich Deutsch and Joseph Heinz Eibl (Kassel, 1962–75) [*MBA*].

2 Admirably summarized by Zaslaw: 'from the west (French dance music), from the north (Germanic counterpoint, Italian-inspired Mannheim orchestral devices, touches of *Empfindsamkeit*), from the east (Bohemian and Viennese four-movement concert symphonies with repeats, brilliant wind-writing), and from the south (Italianate cantabile melodies, "orchestral noises", three-movement overture-symphonies without repeats)': *Mozart's Symphonies*, 14.

3 For a fuller account of this genre, see Chapter 8.

4 *Historisch-Kritische Beyträge zur Aufnahme der Musik*, iii, 183–98: 'Nachricht von dem gegenwärtigen Zustande der Musik Sr. Hochfürstl. Gnaden des Erzbischoffs zu Salzburg im Jahr 1757'; for a translation, see Zaslaw, *Mozart's Symphonies*, Appendix C.

5 For Leopold Mozart, see Max Seiffert: 'Vorwort', *Ausgewählte Werke von Leopold Mozart*, Denkmäler der Tonkunst in Bayern, xvii, Jg. ix/2 (1908); Ludwig Wegele, ed.: *Leopold Mozart, 1719–1787: Bild einer Persönlichkeit* (Augsburg, 1969); Wolfgang Plath: 'Mozart, (1) Leopold', *The New Grove Dictionary of Music and Musicians*, ed. Stanley Sadie (London, 1980); Cliff Eisen: 'Mozart, (1) Leopold', *The New Grove Dictionary of Music and Musicians*, ed. Stanley Sadie (London, 2/2001); Cliff Eisen: 'The Symphonies of Leopold Mozart: Their Chronology, their Style and Importance for the Study of Mozart's Early Symphonies', *MJb 1987–8*, 181–93; Maynard Solomon: *Mozart: A Life* (New York, 1995); and, for a particularly full and well-balanced account of the man and the family, Halliwell: *The Mozart Family*.

6 See J. Mančal: 'Vom "Orden der geflickten Hosen": Leopold Mozarts Heirat und Bürgerrecht', *Leopold Mozart und Augsburg* (Augsburg, 1987), 31–54 (discussed in Halliwell: *The Mozart Family*, 18).

7 Research on Mozart's ancestry, much of it the work of local histori-

ans in southern Germany and Austria, and consisting largely of individual investigations of the families of his ancestors, is published in a variety of periodicals and collections. A family tree and a discussion of the family's background is to be found at the end of vol. i and on pp. 511–12 of Arthur Schurig: *Wolfgang Amadeus Mozart: Sein Leben und sein Werk* (Leipzig, 1913), but more recent research is drawn together by Heinz Schuler in his typescript studies, with genealogical charts, *Die Vorfahren Wolfgang Mozarts* (Essen, 1972) and *Die Gesamtverwandtschaft Wolfgang Amadeus Mozarts* (Essen, n.d.), and his *Wolfgang Amadeus Mozart: Vorfahren und Verwandte* (Neustadt an der Aisch, 1980). See also Adolf Layer: *Die Augsburger Künstlerfamilie Mozart* (Augsburg, 1970) and Ludwig Wegele: *Der Augsburger Maler Anton Mozart* (Augsburg, 1969).

8 See Adolf Layer: 'Der Augsburger Buchbinder Johann Georg Mozart', *Archiv für Geschichte des Buchwesens*, xi (1970), 873–84.

Chapter 2

1 Letter of 21 November 1772: *LMF* 162, *MBA* 267.

2 Albert von Mölk, in his supplementary remarks to Nannerl's letter sent to the obituarist F.X. Schlichtegroll, written in spring 1792, now in the Mozarteum, Salzburg: *MDB* 454–62, and *MDL* 398–405.

3 For a full account of Nannerl's dealings with Mölk and Schlichtegroll, see Bruce Cooper Clarke: 'Albert von Mölk: Mozart Myth-Maker? Study of an 18th Century Correspondence', *MJb 1995*, 155–91.

4 Now in the Mozarteum, Salzburg; published in NMA, IX:27, i.

5 His letter (formerly in the Albi Rosenthal collection, Oxford, now in the Bodleian Library) is reproduced in *MDB* 451–3, *MDL* 395–8.

6 Letter of 21 June 1763: *LMF* 11, *MBA* 50.

7 Letters of 3, 16, 19, 30 October, 6, 10 and 24 November and 10 and 29 December 1762: *LMF* 1–9, *MBA* 32, 34–6, 40–42, 45–6. For Hagenauer, and a discussion of these letters, see Otto Erich Deutsch and Wilhelm A. Bauer: 'Leopold Mozarts Briefe an Hagenauer', *MISM*, viii (1959), 8–9.

8 See Josef Saam: 'Mozart in Passau', *AcMoz*, xiii/1 (1962), 7–15.

9 Letter of 16 October 1762: *LMF* 2, *MBA* 34.

10 The diaries, in the Vienna Staatsarchiv, consist of 57 manuscript volumes, in French. They have not been fully transcribed or edited but a number of the musical references are reproduced in Otto Erich Deutsch: 'Mozart in Zinzendorfs Tagebüchern', *Schweizerische Musikzeitung*, cii (1962), 211–18, and they are substantially surveyed in Dorothea Link: *The National Court Theatre in Mozart's Vienna* (Oxford, 1998); see also Dexter Edge: 'Mozart Reception in Vienna, 1787–91', *Wolfgang Amadè Mozart: Essays on his Life and Works*, ed. Stanley Sadie (Oxford, 1996), 66–117.

11 This anecdote, from Schlichtegroll's *Nekrolog auf das Jahr 1791* (Gotha, 1793), comes from Nannerl's draft response to the second series of questions from Schlichtegroll; see *MBA* 1213.

12 See Franz Martin: 'Das "Nannerl Mozart in Galakleid"', *MJb 1950*, 49–61.

13 See Anton Neumayr: *Music and Medicine*, i (Bloomington, IN, 1994), 105, and Peter J. Davies: *Mozart in Person: His Character and Health* (London, 1989), 12. These two studies provide modern accounts of Mozart's medical history but sometimes differ in their interpretation of described symptoms.

14 See Wolfgang Plath: 'Leopold Mozarts Notenbuch für Wolfgang (1762)—eine Fälschung?', *MJb 1971–2*, 337–41. The 'Wolfgang Notenbuch' was exhaustively discussed by Hermann Abert (*W.A. Mozart*, Leipzig, 1919–21, Chapter 1) to demonstrate Leopold's methodical teaching and the profound influence of the north German style on Mozart.

15 The illness is described in Leopold's letter of 15 November 1766, when Mozart had a similar complaint: *LMF* 45, *MBA* 113. See also Davies, *Mozart in Person*, 14–15.

16 See *MBA* 1210.

Chapter 3

1 Letter of 30 July 1768: *LMF* 62, *MBA* 135.

2 Letter of 8 June 1764: *LMF* 28, *MBA* 89.

3 The letters drawn upon in the first part of this chapter, up to the family's departure from Germany, are of 11 June (Wasserburg) and 21 June

(Munich), 11 July (Ludwigsburg) and 19 July (Schwetzingen), 3 August (Mainz), 13 and 20 August (both Frankfurt) and 26 September (Coblenz) 1763: *LMF* 10–17, *MBA* 49, 50, 53, 56, 59, 62–64. Harrison James Wignall: *In Mozart's Footsteps* (New York, 1991) provides much information about the cities the Mozarts passed through and the buildings and other sites they visited.

4 Letter of 27 November 1777: *LMF* 250, *MBA* 380.

5 *MBA* 52.

6 He refers to it in a letter from Frankfurt, 20 August 1763: *LMF* 16, *MBA* 63. See György Gaby: 'Das Reiseklavichord W.A. Mozarts', *Studia Musicologica Academiae Scientiarum Hungaricae*, x (1968), 153–62.

7 *The Present State of Music in Germany, the Netherlands, and United Provinces* (London, 1773), reproduced in P.A. Scholes, ed.: *Dr. Burney's Musical Tours in Europe* (London, 1959), ii, 34–5. There are several studies in German of music at the Mannheim court; the best in English is Eugene K. Wolf: 'The Mannheim Court', in *Man and Music: The Classical Era*, ed. Zaslaw, 213–39.

8 For Mozart's visit to Mainz, see Adam Gottron: *Mozart und Mainz* (Mainz, 1951).

9 Letter of 4 December 1777: *LMF* 255, *MBA* 385.

10 Letter of 7 December 1780: *LMF* 371, *MBA* 556.

11 *Ordentliche Wochentliche Franckfurter Frag- und Anzeigungs-Nachrichten*, 30 August 1763: *MDB* 25, *MDL* 26.

12 Letter of 27 November 1777: *LMF* 250, *MBA* 380.

13 The visit to Paris is covered by letters from Leopold Mozart to Lorenz Hagenauer of 8 December and end of December 1763, 1–3 and 22 February, 4 March and 1 April 1764: *LMF* 19–20, 22–5, *MBA* 73, 75, 80–83.

14 *MBA* 74.

15 Letter of 9 February 1778: *LMF* 284b, *MBA* 420.

16 Quoted in *MDB* 26–7, *MDL* 27–8; the *Correspondance* was published complete, ed. Maurice Tourneux, in 1877–82 (see vol. v, 410–12).

17 *MBA* 84.

18 The book is published in full in the NMA, IX:27, i, ed. Wolfgang Plath, with introduction and commentary; its structure and history are discussed by Alan Tyson: 'A Reconstruction of Nannerl Mozart's

Music Book (Notenbuch)', *Music & Letters*, lx (1979), 389–400. The numberings used here follow the NMA, with 1–52 following the sequence in the book as it survives and 53–64 representing the pieces either surviving on detached leaves, identified as part of the book in its original form, or known to have been a part of it.

19 Georg Nikolaus Nissen: *Biographie W.A. Mozart's: Nach Originalbriefen, Sammlungen alles über ihn Geschriebenen, mit vielen neuen Beylagen, Steindrücken, Musikblättern und einem Fac-simile* (Leipzig, 1828). Nissen was the second husband of Mozart's widow, Constanze. His musical supplement, of twenty early keyboard pieces that Mozart learnt or composed as a child, is the only surviving source for K.2 and K.5 and for their dating; Nissen's text and information almost certainly come from leaves removed from the Nannerl Music Book (see Tyson: 'A Reconstruction', note 16). Other early pieces not included by Nissen were presumably removed from the Music Book before he had access to it.

20 See NMA IX:27, i, Appendix I, 171–2.

21 See Eduard Reeser: *De klaviersonate mit vioolbegleiding in het parijsche muziekleven ten tijde van Mozart* (Rotterdam, 1939); William S. Newman: *The Sonata in the Classic Era* (Chapel Hill, 1963; New York, 3/1983); Ronald R. Kidd: *The Sonata for Keyboard with Violin Accompaniment in England (1750–1790)* (diss., Yale U., 1967); and Stanley Sadie: 'Music in the Home II', *The Blackwell History of Music in Britain: The Eighteenth Century*, ed. H. Diack Johnstone and Roger Fiske (Oxford, 1990), 313–54.

22 See Eduard Reeser: preface to NMA VIII:23, i.

23 Letter of 13 August 1778: *LMF* 323, *MBA* 476.

24 Letter of 3 December 1764: *LMF* 33, *MBA* 94.

Chapter 4

1 The letters from Leopold Mozart to Lorenz Hagenauer covering the period the Mozarts spent in London are *LMF* 26–37, *MBA* 86, 88–98.

2 Letter of 28 May 1764: *LMF* 27, *MBA* 88.

3 The tale is related in her diary; see *Thraliana: The Diary of Hester Lynch Thrale (later Mrs Piozzi) 1776–1809*, ed. Katharine C. Balderston (Oxford, 1942), i, 141; it seems to be based on a passage hazily remem-

bered from Daines Barrington's report on Mozart to the Royal Society (see note 28). See Cliff Eisen: 'Mozart Apocrypha', *Musical Times*, cxxvii (1986), 685, and *NMD*, no. 122.

4 *The Public Advertiser*, 9 May 1764, 21 May 1764: *MDB* 33–4, *MDL* 34–5.

5 See Simon McVeigh: *Concert Life in London from Mozart to Haydn* (Cambridge, 1993), 56–7; the dimensions are given in *Survey of London*, xx, 68.

6 *The Public Advertiser*, 26 June 1764: *MDB* 36, *MDL* 37.

7 The first excerpt is from 'Noch einige Anecdoten aus Mozarts Kinderjahren', *Allgemeine musikalische Zeitung*, ii/17 (22 January 1800), col. 300–301: *MDB* 494, *MDL* 426. The second is from her recollections as sent to Schlichtegroll, though little used by him; see Chapter 2, note 2, and *MBA* 1212.

8 See *Survey of London*, xxxiii: St Anne, Soho (London, 1966), 160–61.

9 Published in *The Leisure Hour* (London, 1882), 274; faulty punctuation in the transcription for the printed version is corrected here. For Nannerl's recollection see *MBA* 1212.

10 For an account of the music (not just by Handel) heard in London during the Mozarts' time in the city, see Donald Burrows: 'Performances of Handel's Music during Mozart's Visit to London in 1764–5', *Händel-Jahrbuch*, xxxviii (1992), 16–32.

11 'Either Caesar or nothing': i.e. only a high ambition justifies the effort.

12 *MDB* 38, *MDL* 39.

13 Grimm reported this in a letter of 13 December to Ludwig of Saxe-Gotha, asking him to exercise his influence through his family connections with the English royal family: see *MDB*, pp. 37–8; *MDL*, p. 38.

14 Beda Hübner, librarian of St Peter's Abbey, in his diary, 'Diarium Patris Bedae Hübner ordinis sanctissimi patris benedicti in antiquissimo monasterio ad sanctum Petrum apostolum Salisburgi professo ac sacerdote indignissimo', in the library of St Peter's Abbey, Salzburg: *MDB* 68–9, *MDL* 64.

15 From his advertisement in the *Public Advertiser*, 15 February 1765 (and *The Gazetteer*, 16 February): *MDB* 41, *MDL* 41.

16 Letter of 19 March 1766: *LMF* 35, *MBA* 96.

17 Nissen, *Biographie W.A. Mozarts*, 102. We do know, from Nannerl's later correspondence, that Wolfgang wrote some small four-hand pieces in

London; they are referred to in her letters to Breitkopf & Härtel of 23 March 1800, 1 October 1800, 30 April 1804, 15 May 1805 and 30 April 1807: *MBA* 1293, 1313, 1365, 1369 and 1377.

18 For an analysis of the 1768 list, see Neal Zaslaw: 'Leopold Mozart's List of his Son's Works', *Music in the Classic Period: Essays in Honor of Barry S. Brook*, ed. Allan W. Atlas (New York, 1985), 323–58.

19 See Cliff Eisen: 'Mozart and the Four-Hand Sonata K. 19d', *Haydn, Mozart, and Beethoven: Studies in Music of the Classical Period, Essays in Honour of Alan Tyson*, ed. Sieghard Brandenburg (Oxford, 1998), 91–9; for the publishing history of the work, see Alan Tyson: 'The Earliest Editions of Mozart's Duet-Sonata K.19d', *Music Review*, xxx (1969), 98–105.

20 June issue, p. 452, in a review of a duet arrangement of Piccinni's overture to *La buona figliuola*; see *NMD*, no. 7.

21 Advertised in *The Public Advertiser*, 9 April and 30 May (Thrift Street), 8, 9, 10 and 11 July (Swan and Hoop) and elsewhere: *MDB* 44–6, *MDL* 43–5. The Swan and Hoop is sometimes, as in *MDB* and *MDL*, incorrectly named as Swan and Harp. The name was correctly translated by C.F. Pohl (*Mozart und Haydn in London*, Vienna, 1867, p. 134) as 'Schwan und Reifen'.

22 Issue of 6 August 1765. No copy of the original is known: see *MDB* 48, *MDL* 47–8. Nissen cites the report as appearing in the *Salzburger Zeitung* and prints a further sentence referring to the British Museum and its request for Mozart items; see below.

23 See Cecil B. Oldman: 'Beckford and Mozart', *Music & Letters*, xlvii (1966), 110–15.

24 See Ian Woodfield: 'New Light on the Mozarts' London Visit: A Private Concert with Manzuoli', *Music & Letters*, lxxvi (1995), 187–207; the excerpt from Lady Clive's letter, in the Clive papers in the India Office Library, London, is quoted from Woodfield.

25 Woodfield: 'New Light', 202.

26 In a letter to Fanny Burney, 13 December 1790, reprinted in Kerry S. Grant: *Dr Burney as Critic and Historian of Music* (Ann Arbor, 1983): *NMD*, no. 5. For Burney and Mozart, see Cecil B. Oldman: 'Dr. Burney and Mozart', *MJb 1962–3*, 75–81, and *MJb 1964*, 109–10.

27 In his musical notebook, reprinted in *Memoirs of Dr Charles Burney*

1726–1769, ed. Slava Klima, Garry Bowers and Kerry S. Grant (Lincoln, NE, and London, 1987), 164: *NMD*, no. 4.

28 Barrington's report was delivered to the Secretary of the Royal Society, Dr Mathew Maty, on 28 September 1769, and read on 15 February 1770; it was published in the *Philosophical Transactions*, lx (1771), 54–64, and reprinted in Barrington's *Miscellanies* (London, 1781), 279. It is also reprinted in *MDB* 95–100.

29 For a full account of the Mozarts and the British Museum, see Alec Hyatt King: 'The Mozarts at the British Museum', *Musical Pursuits: Selected Essays*, British Museum Occasional Papers, ix (London, 1987), 52–72.

30 See Christopher Roscoe: 'Two 18th-Century Non-Events', *Musical Times*, cxii (1971), 18–19. The references to the family's last few days in England are in a letter sent from The Hague on 19 September: *LMF* 38, *MBA* 102.

31 Neal Zaslaw (*Mozart's Symphonies*, 18–20) suggests a symphony made up of K.15*kk* (E flat), 15*dd* (A flat) and 15*cc* and 15*ee* (E flat, a minuet and trio). K.15*kk* however would seem more likely to be a slow movement, to fall between two B flat outer movements, K.15*ii* and K.15*ll*, in a three-movement work; while K.15*cc* has the scale and manner of a first movement and could well precede K.15*dd* and a minuet-and-trio pairing of K.15*ee* and 15*ff*. The suggestion that any such schemes represent Mozart's original intentions is of course purely conjectural.

32 See Cliff Eisen: 'Contributions to a New Mozart Documentary Biography', *Journal of the American Musicological Society*, xxxix (1986), 620–23.

33 The *Thematisches Verzeichnis der sämtlichen Werke von W.A. Mozart* was a manuscript catalogue of Mozart's works made by the Breitkopf & Härtel publishing firm in Leipzig early in the nineteenth century and kept in their archive; it recorded Mozart's works, as known to its compilers, by genre. It was destroyed in World War II but a copy owned by Köchel survives, in the library of the Gesellschaft der Musikfreunde, Vienna. The Breitkopf Manuscript Catalogue (as it is usually known, to distinguish it from the printed catalogues issued by the firm and published as *The Breitkopf Thematic Catalogues*; facsimile edited by

Barry S. Brook, New York, 1968) is the sole source of information about several works attributed to Mozart, but it was uncritically assembled and an entry does not serve as a guarantee of a work's authenticity; indeed a number of the incipits in it are known to belong to works by other composers. For a discussion of the catalogue, see Zaslaw, *Mozart's Symphonies*, 130–33.

34 See Neal Zaslaw and Cliff Eisen: 'Signor Mozart's Symphony in A minor, K. Anhang 220 = 16a', *Journal of Musicology*, iv (1986), 191–206; and Jens Peter Larsen and Kamma Wedin, eds.: *Die Sinfonie KV 16a 'del Sigr. Mozart': Bericht über das Symposium in Odense . . . Dezember 1984* (Odense, 1987).

35 All information on the paper-types used by Mozart comes from Alan Tyson, in particular his *Mozart: Studies of the Autograph Scores* (Cambridge, MA, and London, 1987), his volume on paper-types published as NMA XX:33 and numerous generously informative personal communications over many years.

36 See Robert Münster: 'Neue Funde zu Mozarts symphonischen Jugendwerk', *MISM*, xxx/1–2 (1982), 2–11.

37 See Eisen: 'The Symphonies of Leopold Mozart', 186.

38 The sheet was offered for sale at Sotheby's in December 1993 but not sold.

39 See King: 'The Mozarts at the British Museum', and Burrows: 'Performances of Handel's Music'.

Chapter 5

1 The letters drawn upon in this chapter are those of 19 September, 5 November and 12 December 1765, written from The Hague; 16 May and 9 June 1766, from Paris; and 10, 15 and 22 November 1766, from Munich: *LMF* 38–46, *MBA* 102–4, 107–9 and 112–14. Leopold's travel diaries for this period are *MBA* 99–101, 105 and 110, and Nannerl's are *MBA* 100 and 106.

2 Identified by Wignall (*In Mozart's Footsteps*, 62) as the present Baudelo Chapel, formerly of the order of St Bernard of Clairvaux; the organ, restored, still exists, in the Dutch Reformed Church, Vlaardingen, near Rotterdam.

3 For the Mozarts' sojourn in the Netherlands, see Daniel François Scheurleer: *Mozart's verblijf in Nederland* (The Hague, 1883) and *Het muziekleven in Nederland in de tweede helft der 18e eeuw in verband met Mozart's verblijf aldaar* (The Hague, 1903).

4 For Mozart's appearances before Prince William and at the British ambassador's residence, see *NMD*, nos. 11, 12 and 13.

5 See Neumayr: *Music & Medicine*, 110–14, and Davies: *Mozart in Person*, 22–3.

6 Wolfgang Plath, 'Vorwort', NMA IX: 27, i, pp. ix–xxvii; reprinted in Plath, *Mozart-Schriften: Ausgewählte Aufsätze*, ed. Marianne Danckwardt (Kassel, 1991), 349–74.

7 This has only recently been established: see *MDLA* 8–9.

8 *Correspondance littéraire*, vii, 81f: *MDB* 56–7, *MDL* 54–5.

9 For Mozart at Dijon, see Eugène Fyot: 'Mozart à Dijon', *Mémoires de l'Académie des sciences, arts et belles-lettres de Dijon: année 1937* (Dijon, 1938), 23–41, and R. Thiblot: 'Le séjour de Mozart à Dijon en 1766', ibid., 139–43; also *MDB* 57–8, *MDL* 55–6, *NMD*, no. 21.

10 From a letter from Johann Rudolf Forcart to Isaac Iselin, Basle (Staatsarchiv, Basle); see Lucas A. Staehelin: 'Neues zu Mozarts Aufenthalten in Lyon, Genf und Bern', *Schweizerische Muzikzeitung*, xcvi (1956), 46–8: *MDB* 58, *MDL* 56.

11 See postscript to letter of 30 November 1771: *LMF* 154a, *MBA* 258.

12 Letter of 16 August 1766: *LMF* 43, *MBA* 111.

13 For the Mozarts' stay in Switzerland see Lucas A. Staehelin: *Die Reise der Familie Mozart durch die Schweiz* (Berne, 1968); Staehelin 'Neues zu Mozarts Aufenthalten'; and Max Fehr and Leonhard Calfisch: *Der junge Mozart in Zürich* (Zürich, 1952).

14 His letters (in *Oeuvres*, ed. Garnier, xliv, 452–3 and 493) are cited in *MDB* 59 and 66, *MDL* 57 and 62.

15 Quoted in Staehelin, *Die Reise*, 93–4: *NMD*, no. 23.

16 Staehelin, 'Neues zu Mozarts Aufenthalten', p. 46: *MDL*, p. 57, *MDB*, p. 59.

17 *Mémoires ou essais sur la musique* (Paris, 1795), i, 84–5; see Henri Kling: 'Mozart et Grétry à Genève 1766–1767', *Journal de Genève* (28 July 1866): *MDB* 477, *MDL* 415–16.

18 Letter of 10 November 1766: *LMF* 44, *MBA* 112.

19 The manuscript journal of Jean-Henri Polier and Salomon de Sévery's *Livre des comptes pour la dépense commencé le 17 mars 1766*, in Staehelin: *Die Reise*, 95 and 31: *NMD*, nos. 24 and 25. Authorities differ as to the precise dates of the stay in Lausanne, but the concert dates (15 and 18 September) and Leopold's statement that they were there for five days leave little room for ambiguity.

20 *Post- und Ordinarii Schaffhauser Samstags Zeitung* (11 October 1766); see Staehelin: *Die Reise*, 75–6: *NMD*, no. 26.

21 The event was reported 24 years later in a letter referring to Sixt Bachmann (as he was then called), in *Musikalische Korrespondenz der Teutschen Filarmonischen Gesellschaft* (Speyer, 24 November 1790): *MDB* 379, *MDL* 333.

22 See the preface to NMA, IV:12, i (by Wolfgang Plath) and the Kritischer Bericht, where the sources are noted; see also Zaslaw: *Mozart's Symphonies*, 52–5.

23 See Münster: 'Neue Funde'.

24 To Breitkopf & Härtel, 18 June 1801: *MBA* 1336.

25 See in particular Wolfgang Plath: 'Beiträge zur Mozart-Autographie II: Schriftchronologie 1770–1780', *MJb 1976–7*, 131–73, esp. 138–9. See also *Mozart: Studies of the Autograph Scroes*, ed. Alan Tyson, 2 vols., in NMA X:33, 1 and 2 (Wasserzeichen-Katalog).

Chapter 6

1 *Allgemeine musikalische Zeitung*, ii/17 (Leipzig, 22 January 1800), col. 300: *MDB* 493, *MDL* 426.

2 See Hübner, 'Diarium', and Herbert Klein: 'Unbekannte Mozartiana von 1766/67', *MJb 1957*, 168–85: *MDB* 55, 67–76, *MDL* 53–4, 63–71.

3 See Neal Zaslaw: *Mozart's Symphonies*, Chapter 4, 'The *Sinfonia da Chiesa*, and Salzburg (1766–1767)', pp. 71–98, in which references to the late eighteenth-century use of symphonies and other instrumental music in ecclesiastical contexts are drawn together.

4 Hübner, entries for 12 March and 19 March; Minutes of the Salzburg Gymnasium, 12 March and 2 April: *MDB* 68–70, *MDL* 72–4.

5 His report on Mozart to the Royal Society, 1769: see Chapter 4 note 28.

6 The background to the work is discussed particularly fully and informatively by Alfred Orel in his preface to NMA II:5/1.

7 From the minutes of the Salzburg Gymnasium, 13 May 1767: *MDB* 75, *MDL* 70.

8 There are useful discussions of these works by Edwin J. Simon: 'Sonata into Concerto', *Acta musicologica*, xxxi (1959), 170–85, and John Irving: *Mozart's Piano Concertos* (Aldershot, 2003), Chapter 2; the preface to NMA X:28, Abt. 2, by Eduard Reeser, is also valuable.

9 As Wyzewa and Saint-Foix argue on stylistic grounds; see Théodore Wyzewa and Georges Saint-Foix: *Wolfgang Amédée Mozart: Sa vie musicale et son oeuvre* (Paris, 1912–46), i, 189–90.

Chapter 7

1 The letters drawn upon in the first part of this chapter are those of 22 and 29 September, 7, 14 and 17 October, and 10 and 29 November 1767, and 12, 23 and 30 January and 13 February 1768: *LMF* 47–56 (that of 7 October 1767 is not in *LMF*), *MBA* 116–26.

2 City names in this part of Europe are given here in the form used by the Mozarts themselves, and indeed normally by (Austrian) government at the time, rather than in modern Czech or Slovak forms. Brünn is modern Brno, Olmütz is Olomouc, Pressburg is Bratislava (or in Hungarian Poszony), Wischkau is Vyškov.

3 Letter of 28 May 1778: *LMF* 306, *MBA* 450. The song was thought by Einstein, writing in K³, to be *An die Freude* K.53/47e, but that is unlikely (see p. 158); see Karl Pfannhauser: 'Zu Mozarts Kirchenwerken von 1768', *MJb 1954*, 150–68, esp. 163.

4 Nannerl's memoirs, published in the *Allgemeine musikaliche Zeitung*, ii/17 (Leipzig, 28 January 1800), col. 300: *MDB* 494, *MDL* 426.

5 In a letter to Breitkopf & Härtel, 24 November 1799, enclosing her memoirs for publication in the *Allgemeine musikalische Zeitung*: *MDB* 493, *MDL* 425–6.

6 From the diary of the Prior of Sternberg, Aurelius Augustinus, 30 December 1767: *MDB* 77, *MDL* 72.

7 The original, dated 21 September 1768, is in the University Library, Glasgow (Zavertal Collection); it was printed by Nissen, *Biographie*

W.A. Mozart's, 145–52, and in Henry George Farmer and Herbert Smith: *New Mozartiana* (Glasgow, 1935), 113–19: *MDB* 80–84, *MDL* 74–8; also *MBA* 139. This is the principal source for much of the information in the ensuing paragraphs.

8 Letter of 30 July 1768: *LMF* 62, *MBA* 135.

9 The issue of the garden is discussed by Alfred Orel: 'Der Mesmerische Garten', *MJb 1962–3*, 82–95; the letter is that of 21 July 1773, *LMF* 177, *MBA* 288.

10 *MDB* 84–5, *MDL* 78.

11 *MDB* 85, *MDL* 78–9.

12 It has been published several times, with varying degrees of accuracy, notably in Nissen, *Biographie W.A. Mozart's*, Appendix, 3–5; K^6, pp. xxv–xxvi; and *MBA* 144. It is fully and perceptively discussed, with a complete facsimile, by Zaslaw in 'Leopold Mozart's List'; see also Münster: 'Neue Funde'.

13 Köchel suggested 1769, as the K^1 number 76 indicates; Otto Jahn, in *W.A. Mozart*, i (Leipzig, 1856), 701, gives '177?'; Einstein proposed autumn 1767, hence the K^3 number; Wyzewa and Saint-Foix, in *Wolfgang Amédée Mozart*, i,178, give reasons for December 1766 of which Zaslaw, in *Mozart's Symphonies*, 103, justly observes: 'To call this speculation is too generous; it is sheer fantasy'.

14 Wyzewa and Saint-Foix: *Wolfgang Amédée Mozart*, i, 179–80.

15 See Cliff Eisen: 'Problems of Authenticity among Mozart's Early Symphonies: The Examples of K. Anh. 220 (16a) and 76 (42a)', *Music & Letters*, lxx (1989), 505–13, and *The Symphonies of Leopold Mozart and their Relationship to the Early Symphonies of Wolfgang Amadeus Mozart: A Bibliographical and Stylistic Study* (diss., Cornell University, 1986).

16 For a comprehensive and authoritative discussion of the background, the libretto and the work itself, see Linda L. Tyler: '*Bastien und Bastienne*: The Libretto, Its Derivation, and Mozart's Text-Setting', *Journal of Musicology*, viii (1990), 520–52.

17 Edited by Robert Haas, Camillo Schoenbaum and Herbert Zeman in *Denkmäler der Tonkunst in Österreich*, lxiv, Jg. 33/i (Vienna, 1926) and cxxi (Vienna, 1971).

18 See Linda L. Tyler: '*Bastien und Bastienne* and the Viennese Volkskomödie', *MJb 1991*, 576–9.

19 The relationship of music and metric structure is perceptively discussed by Tyler in '*Bastien und Bastienne*: The Libretto', esp. 542–52.

20 See Rudolph Angermüller: 'Johann Andreas Schachtners "Bastienne"-Libretto', *MISM*, xxii/1–2 (1974), 4–28. The autograph is in the Biblioteka Jagiellońska, Kraków, and the early copy in the Bibliothèque Royale Albert Ier, Brussels.

21 See Tyson: *Mozart: Studies of the Autograph Scores*, 96, 99, 224 and 336.

Chapter 8

1 A recommendation from J.A. Hasse, written at Leopold's request to a friend in Venice (*MDB* 92–3, *MDL* 84–5), and dated 30 September, mentions that they were planning to leave Salzburg on 24 October.

2 *MDB* 88–9, *MDL* 81–2.

3 Noted in Hagenauer's diary: *MDB* 86, *MDL* 79. According to Walter Senn, K.65, as a *missa brevis*, would have been inappropriate for this occasion (Preface, NMA I:1, i, pp. xii–xiii).

4 A full account of the Salzburg serenade traditions and repertory is given in Andrew Kearns: 'The Orchestral Serenade in Eighteenth-Century Salzburg', *Journal of Musicological Research*, xvi (1997), 163–97.

5 *MDB* 91, *MDL* 83.

6 See Wolfgang Plath, 'Beiträge zur Mozart-Autographie, II: Schriftchronologie 1770–1780', *MJb 1976–7*, 135, n.7.

7 Letter of 18 August 1771: *LMF* 139, *MBA* 241.

8 *MDB* 93–4, *MDL* 85–6.

9 No formal record survives of Mozart's (honorary) appointment at this date but Hagenauer mentions it in his diary (*MDB* 94–5, *MDL* 86). Mozart's letter of 11 September 1778, when he declared 'I will no longer be a fiddler' (*LMF* 331, *MBA* 487), implies that that is what he had been until then. For the listing in the *Hochfürstlich-Salzburger Kirchen- und Hof Kalendar* of 1770, see *MDB* 102, *MDL* 93.

10 4 September 1776: *LMF* 205, *MBA* 325.

11 They are printed in the appendix to NMA I:1, i, 320–21.

12 See Tyson: *Mozart: Studies of the Autograph Scores*, 333–4.

13 See Wilhelm Kurthen: 'Studien zu W.A. Mozarts kirchenmusikalischen Jugendwerke', *Zeitschrift für Musikwissenschaft*, iii (1921), 194–222.

14 The principal fruits of Plath's research appear in two densely detailed but elegantly argued articles, 'Beiträge zur Mozart-Autographie I: Die Handschrift Leopold Mozarts', *MJb 1960–61*, 82–117, and 'Beiträge zur Mozart-Autographie II: Schriftchronologie 1770–1780', *MJb 1976–7*, 131–73.

15 Tyson's essays on Mozart's papers, which include a full discussion of the implications and the limitations of paper research in establishing a chronology, are collected in his *Mozart: Studies of the Autograph Scores*; his detailed analyses of individual watermarks and paper-types appear in NMA X:33, 1–2 (*Wasserzeichen-Katalog*).

Chapter 9

1 See, for example, Leopold's responses to his wife's remarks in his letters, written during the second Italian journey, of 5 and 12 October 1771: *LMF* 146–7, *MBA* 248–9.

2 *MDB* 92–3, *MDL* 84–5.

3 Letter of 26 January 1770: *MBA* 157.

4 The letters drawn upon in this chapter, up to the Mozarts' arrival in Bologna in July–August, are those of 14, 15, 17 and 22 December 1769, 7, 11 and 16 January, 3, 10, 17 and 27 February, 3, 13, 24 and 27–8 March, 3, 14, 21, 25 and 28 April, 2, 19, 22, 26 and 29 May, 5, 9, 16, 27 and 30 June, 4, 7, 21 and 28 July and 4 August 1770: *LMF* 71–106, *MBA* 147–50, 152–3, 155, 157–65, 168, 170–71, 173, 176–9, 181–2, 184–6, 189–91, 193–5, 197, 199–202. A useful guide to Mozart's activities in Italy is Guglielmo Barblan and Andrea Della Corte: *Mozart in Italia: I viaggi e le lettere* (Milan, 1956).

5 The *Innsbrucker Montägige Ordinari Zeitung* (18 December 1769): *MDB* 101, *MDL* 92.

6 These are reprinted in *MBA*, for this journey as nos. 151, 154, 156, 166, 172, 174, 183, 192, 229 and 235.

7 Letter of 7 January 1770: *LMF* 75, *MBA* 152.

8 *MDB* 105, *MDL* 95–6; facsimile in Barblan and Della Corte: *Mozart in Italia*, opposite p. 49 (wrongly dated).

9 The composer, not mentioned by Mozart, is unknown. There were numerous settings of the *Demetrio* text, of which the most recent were

by Pampani (1768,Venice), Monza (1769, Rome) and Piccinni (1769, Naples), but none of those composers is known to have had any connection with Mantua.There is no basis for the identification in *LMF* of the work as Hasse's, which dates back to 1730 (with revivals and possibly revisions in 1732, 1734, 1740 and 1747) and is very unlikely to have been revived as late as 1770. The list of musicians the Mozarts met in Mantua, as shown in their travel notes (*MBA* 156), offers no clues.

10 The manuscript programme is in the AccademiaVirgiliana (successor to the original Accademia), Mantua, as is the printed one; the invitation is in the collection of Marchese Arco, Mantua.The two last are reproduced in Otto Erich Deutsch: *Mozart und seine Welt in zeitgenössischen Bildern*, NMA X:32 (1961).

11 *Gazzetta di Mantova* (19 January 1770), facsimile in Barblan and Della Corte: *Mozart in Italia*, opposite p. 64: *MDB* 107–8, *MDL* 97–8.

12 *Gazzetta di Mantova* (26 January 1770): *MDB* 109–10, *MDL* 99–100.

13 The *Ergo interest . . . Quaere superna* K.143/73a has been suggested as one of them, but it almost certainly belongs some three years later; see p. 350.

14 Established by Anthony Pryer in a closely argued article, 'Mozart's Operatic Audition: The Milan Concert', *Eighteenth-Century Music, ii* (2005).

15 Letter of 21 April 1770: *LMF* 88a, *MBA* 177.

16 *MDB* 111, *MDL* 101.

17 Letter of 24 March 1770: *LMF* 84a, *MBA* 168.

18 Letter of 24 March 1770: *LMF* 84, *MBA* 170.

19 Letter of 27 March 1770: *LMF* 85, *MBA* 171.

20 Noted in orders of payment and Leopold's receipt: *MDB* 114–15, *MDL* 104.

21 Letter of 3 April 1770: *LMF* 86, *MBA* 173.

22 Letter of 14 April 1770: *LMF* 87, *MBA* 176.The Mozarts' sojourn in Rome is discussed in Barblan and Della Corte: *Mozart in Italia* and in Elisabeth J. Luin:'Mozarts Aufenthalt in Rom', *Neues Mozart-Jahrbuch*, iii (1943), 45–62.

23 Mölk was later a canon at Salzburg Cathedral and a hospital inspector in the city; it was he who supplied information to Schlichtegroll for Mozart's obituary; see p. 17.

24 Letter of 19 May 1770: *LMF* 92, *MBA* 184.

25 In the Bologna State Archives; they are reprinted in *MDB* and *MDL*.

26 Letter of 19 May 1770: *LMF* 92, *MBA* 184.

27 Noted by Giovanni Xavier Biringucci, minister at the College, in his diary: *NMD* no. 30.

28 Letter of 28 March 1770: *MDB* 113–14, *MDL* 102.

29 Letter of 19 May 1770: *LMF* 92a, *MBA* 184.

30 See Leopold's letter of 14 April 1770: *LMF* 87, *MBA* 176, and Wolfgang's of 25 April 1770: *LMF* 89, *MBA* 179.

31 Saverio Mattei: *Saggio di poesie latine, ed italiane*, ii (Naples, 1774), 268–79; English translation in Charles Burney: *A General History of Music* (London, 1776–89), ed. Frank Mercer (1935), ii, 932.

32 In her reminiscences sent to Schlichtegroll: see *MDB* 459, *MDL* 403 and *MBA* 1212. This incident is not mentioned in any surviving letter from Leopold.

33 Letter of 21 July 1770: *MBA* 199 (*LMF* 103 lacks the material about travel).

34 See Leopold's letter of 30 June 1770: *LMF* 100, *MBA* 194.

35 Personal communication from Dr Wolfgang Plath (28 October 1985), written after he had examined the autograph in Kraków.

36 See Jan LaRue: 'Mozart or Dittersdorf—KV 83/73q', *MJb 1971–2*, 40–49.

37 See Zaslaw: *Mozart's Symphonies*, 95ff, esp. 97–8.

38 Letter of 22 September 1770: *LMF* 114a, *MBA* 210.

39 By Einstein, in K^3, pp. 126 (K.97/73*m*) and 127 (K.95/73*n*); also on p. 168 for K.96/111*b*, of which by the time of *Mozart: His Character, his Work* (London, 1946), 'one can say with certainty that the minuet was inserted later'. This is pure speculation and highly unlikely. For none of these symphonies does an autograph, or other firm authentication, survive.

40 He referred to it in his letter of 24 March 1778: *LMF* 299, *MBA* 439.

41 For a full discussion of its style see Ludwig Finscher: 'Mozarts erstes Streichquartett: Lodi, 15. März 1770', *Analecta musicologica*, no. 18 (1978), 246–70.

Chapter 10

1 The letters drawn upon in this chapter are those of 11, 21 and 25 August, 1, 8, 10, 18, 22 and 29 September, 6, 20 and 27 October, 3, 10, 17 and 24 November and 1, 8, 15, 22 and 29 December 1770, and 12 January, 13 and 20 February and 1, 6, 14/18 and 25 March: *LMF* 107–37, *MBA* 203–11, 213–14, 216–29, 230–34, 236 and 238.

2 From Burney's travel notes, British Library, Add. 35122, ed. in H.E. Poole: notes in *Music, Men and Manners in France and Italy, 1770: Being a Journal . . . Written during a Tour through those Countries . . . transcribed from . . . British Museum Additional Manuscript 35122*, ed. H. Edmund Poole (London, 1969), 98. See also Charles Burney: *The Present State of Music in France and Italy* (London, 1771, 2/1773), 228: *MDB* 140, *MDL* 126. Burney's later version, in the Osborn Collection, 73.1, Yale University, provides the basis of the text in Percy Scholes: *Dr. Burney's Musical Tours in Europe* (Oxford, 1959), i, 161–2: *MDB* 125, *MDL* 113.

3 Letter of 29 September 1770: *LMF* 115, *MBA* 211.

4 Burney: *The Present State of Music in France and Italy*, 81–2.

5 Singers' fees are discussed in Kathleen K. Hansell: *Opera and Ballet and the Regio Ducal Teatro of Milan 1771–1776: A Musical and Social History* (diss., University of California at Berkeley, 1979), 214–19.

6 It is described in Daniel Heartz: 'Constructing *Le nozze di Figaro*', *Journal of the Royal Musical Association*, cxii (1987), 77–98.

7 See his letter of 24 November 1770: *LMF* 122, *MBA* 220.

8 Letter of 6–10 May 1778: *LMF* 304, *MBA* 448.

9 For a discussion of these versions see Harrison James Wignall: 'The Genesis of "Se di lauri": Mozart's Drafts and Final Version of Guglielmo Ettore's Entrance Aria from *Mitridate*', *Mozart-Studien*, v (1995), 45–100, and his *Mozart, Guglielmo d'Ettore and the Composition of 'Mitridate'* (diss., Brandeis University, 1995).

10 This is no. 20, 'Vado incontro al fato estremo'. Rita Peiretti of Turin discovered in 1991 that the aria beginning on p. 213 is a version of the setting by Gasparini in the Accademia Filarmonica, Turin (the source was missing at the time of preparation of the NMA text); it is one of the numbers lacking in the score in the Bibliothèque Nationale, Paris

(Conservatoire collection, D 4342–4). Mozart's own original setting begins on p. 337 in the NMA appendix.

11 Letter of 5 January 1771: *LMF* 129, *MBA* 227.

12 2 January 1771: *MDB* 130–31, *MDL* 117.

13 See Luigi Ferdinando Tagliavini: 'Quirino Gasparini and Mozart', *New Looks at Italian Opera in Honor of Donald J. Grout*, ed. William W. Austin (Ithaca, NY, 1968), 151–71, and Mercedes Viale Ferrero: *La scenografia del '700 e i fratelli Galliari* (Turin, 1963). Some of the sketches for the Galliari sets for Gasparini's *Mitridate* survive in the Pinacoteca Nazionale, Bologna; three are reproduced in Tagliavini, 163–5.

14 Mozart's use of these aria forms is discussed in Helga Lühning: 'Mozarts Auseinandersetzung mit der da capo-Arie in *Mitridate, Rè di Ponto*', *MJb 2001*, 427–61.

15 Established by Daniel Freeman and discussed by Wignall in *Mozart, Guglielmo d'Ettore*, 173ff.

16 Letter of 11 September 1778: *LMF* 331, *MBA* 487.

17 See letters of 27 October 1770: *LMF* 118, *MBA* 216, and 13 February 1771: *LMF* 132, *MBA* 231.

18 Their correspondence is in the Museo Correr, Venice; see *MDB* 132 and 134, *MDL* 119 and 120–21.

Chapter 11

1 See Leopold's letter of 20 February 1771: *LMF* 123 (the relevant passage is not in *LMF*), *MBA* 232.

2 Letter of 19 July 1771: *MBA* 239 (not in *LMF*). The letters referred to in this chapter are those of 16, 18, 24 and 31 August, 7, 13, 21 and 28 September, 5, 12, 19 and 26 October, 2, 9, 16, 23 and 30 November, and 8 and 11 December 1771: *LMF* 139–56, *MBA* 240–51 and 254–60.

3 According to a statement in a libretto of a later setting of the text, given in Lisbon in 1785 (see Eric Blom: 'Mozart, (3) Wolfgang Amadeus Mozart', *Grove's Dictionary of Music and Musicians*, London, 1954, v, 958–9), the libretto was arranged by Parini after a libretto by a poet formerly active in the Milan theatre, Claudio Nicolò Stampa; but Parini's autograph text, with sketch material, survives, and there is no evidence of Stampa's involvement.

4 For fuller discussion of Mozart's litany settings see the preface to NMA I:2/i, by Hellmut Federhofer and Renate Federhofer-Königs; see also Renate Federhofer-Königs: 'Mozarts "Lauretanische Litaneien" KV109 (74e) und 195 (189d)', *MJb 1967*, 111–20; Karl Gustav Fellerer: 'Mozarts Litaneien', *Bericht über die musikwis-senschaftliche Tagung der Internationalen Stiftung Mozarteum in Salzburg 1931* (Leipzig, 1932), 136–41; and Karl August Rosenthal: 'Mozart's Sacramental Litanies and their Forerunners', *Musical Quarterly*, xxvii (1941), 433–55.

5 Letter of 18 August 1771: *LMF* 139, *MBA* 241.

6 Paper studies bear out Leopold's statement. Apart from the large-scale movements demanding 12-staff paper, the score is written on paper of one type (Tyson 27), but the paper used for the overture, choruses and recitatives has slightly different dimensions to the rulings from that used for the arias; clearly he used up one batch before moving to the other. See Tyson: NMA X:33/2, pp. 10 and 53.

7 The dates, not firmly established from local reports, are corroborated in documents in the Vienna Hof-, Haus- und Staats-Archiv, Lombard Collection, 103.

8 See *NMD*, no. 35.

9 For a discussion of the genre and the place within it of *Ascanio in Alba*, see Klaus Hortschansky: 'Mozarts *Ascanio in Alba* und der Typus der Serenata', *Analecta musicologica*, no. 18 (1978), 148–59.

10 *MBA* 252; the contract for the planned Venice opera had been issued the previous August though the Mozarts must have left Salzburg before its arrival; see *MDB* 135, *MDL* 121.

11 See his letter of 9 November: *LMF* 151, *MBA* 255.

12 Letter of December 8: *LMF* 155, *MBA* 259.

13 Staats-Archiv, Vienna; facsimile in Barblan and Della Corte: *Mozart in Italia*, Plate XXXI, opposite p. 168, reprinted in *MDB* 138, *MDL* 124.

14 *MDB* 137–8, *MDL* 123.

15 Letter of 21 July 1784: *LMF* 516, *MBA* 799.

16 For a full account of the background to the Paduan oratorio tradition in Mozart's time, see Paolo Pinamonti, ed.: *La Betulia liberata* (n.p., 1989), a booklet, incorporating a facsimile of a libretto to a setting ascribed to Mysliveček, issued in conjunction with a performance of

Mozart's work in Padua in September 1989. It includes: Paolo Cattelan: 'Mozart e la "religio" musicale padovana', 7–40; Giorgio Mangini: 'I trionfi di Giuditta', 41–80; and Bruno Brizi: 'Nota al testo', 82–8.

17 For a description, see pp. 224–5.

18 It is the only work of any substance omitted from the Philips 'complete' recording of Mozart's works issued for the bicentenary. Its situation is discussed by Gerhard Allroggen: 'Zur Frage der Echtheit der Sinfonie KV Anh.216 = 74g', *Analecta musicologica*, no. 18 (1978), 237–45.

19 See Einstein, in K³, p. 151, and Zaslaw: *Mozart's Symphonies*, 151–5.

20 See *Mozart's Symphonies*, 186–8.

21 This is suggested by the *MBA* editors: Leopold refers to 'eine starke Musik bey H: von Mayer' the previous day; Albert von Mayr, court treasurer to the Archduke Ferdinand, was a son of a Viennese court treasurer who had befriended the Mozarts. See letter of 23 or 24 November 1771: *LMF* 153, *MBA* 257.

22 See Dwight Blazin: 'The Two Versions of Mozart's Divertimento K.113', *Music & Letters*, lxxiii (1992), 32–47; see also Albert R. Rice, ibid., lxxiv (1993), 485–7.

Chapter 12

1 Hagenauer had become Abbot of St Peter's Monastery in 1786; the obituary is in his diary (i, 246f.), in the monastery archives; see *MDL*, p. 258, *MDB*, p. 293.

2 See Joseph Heinz Eibl: 'Die Mozarts und der Erzbischof', *Österreichische Musikzeitschrift*, xxx (1975), 329–41; Heinz Schuler: 'Fürsterzbischof Hieronymus von Colloredo: Herkunft und Ahnenerbe', 'Mozart und die Colloredos: Genealogische Miszellen zur Biographie des Fürsterzbischofs Hieronymus von Salzburg', *MISM*, xxxiv (1986), 1–17, 18–30.

3 *NMD*, no. 38; see C.B. Oldman: 'Charles Burney and Louis de Visme', *Music Review*, xxvii (1966), 95–6.

4 By Alfred Einstein; see *Mozart: His Character, His Work*, 172–3.

5 James Webster, in 'The Scoring of Mozart's Chamber Music for Strings', *Music in the Classic Period: Essays in Honor of Barry S. Brook*, ed.

Atlas, 259–96, esp. 269–70 and 278, argues in favour of regarding these works as true string quartets, possibly of an informal kind.

6 *MBA* 263, *LMF* 158.

7 Published as a supplement to the NMA, X:28, Abt. 3–5, i.

8 Letters of 14 and 21 December 1774: *LMF* 190 and 192, *MBA* 301 and 305.

9 Letter of 29 June 1778: *LMF* 310, *MBA* 457.

10 Letter of 12 April 1778: *MBA* 446, *LMF* 302.

11 For the dating of these works on the basis of handwriting, and discussion of Leopold's contribution, see Plath: 'Beiträge zur Mozart Autographie I', 96, and 'Beiträge zur Mozart Autographie II', 151.

12 See Plath: 'Beiträge zur Mozart-Autographie II', 145.

13 Cliff Eisen points out (preface to *Orchestral Music in Salzburg, 1750–1780*, Recent Researches in the Music of the Classical Era, xl, Madison, WI, 1994, p. xvii) that the Salzburg parade band, according to a 1769 inventory, included two small E flat horns pitched an octave higher than normal: these would seem to be the instruments Mozart calls for here. According to Zaslaw (*Mozart's Symphonies*, 232), a high E flat horn can sometimes be produced by using a high B flat crook and eliminating the normal tuning-piece.

14 Zaslaw, *Mozart's Symphonies*, 23–6, quotes various versions of the Christmas song; for a discussion of the significance of the use of chant in symphonies see Zaslaw, Chapter 4.

15 See Cliff Eisen: 'The Salzburg Symphonies: A Biographical Interpretation', *Wolfgang Amadè Mozart: Essays on his Life and his Music*, ed. Stanley Sadie (Oxford, 1996), 178–212.

16 The letters covering their five-month absence from Salzburg, and drawn upon in the ensuing pages, are those of 28 October, 7, 14, 21 and 18 November, 5, 12, 18 and 26 December 1772, 2, 9, 16, 23 and 30 January, and 6, 13, 20 and 27 February: *LMF* 159–76, *MBA* 264–72, 275, 277, 279, 281–4 and 286–7.

17 Folchino Schizzi: *Elogio storico di Wolfgango Amadeo Mozart* (Cremona, 1817), 25–8: *NMD*, no. 39.

18 The background to the opera and its performance, and the sources, are exhaustively discussed by Kathleen K. Hansell in the preface to her edition of the work, NMA II:5/7.

19 In the Pinacoteca Brera, Milan, and Pinacoteca Nazionale, Bologna;
    two are reproduced in NMA II:5/7 and in Rudolph Angermüller:
    Mozart's Operas (New York, 1988), and two others (one a different ver-
    sion of the same scene) in Carolyn Gianturco: *Mozart's Early Operas*
    (London, 1981).

20 See Walter Senn: 'Mozarts Skizze der Ballettmusik "Le gelosie del ser-
    raglio" (KV Anh.109/135a), *Acta musicologica*, xxxii (1961), 168–82;
    Gerhard   Croll: 'Bemerkungen   zum   "Ballo   Primo"   (KV
    Anh.109/135a) in Mozarts Mailänder "Lucio Silla"', *Analecta musico-
    logica*, no. 18 (1974), 160–65; and Kathleen K. Hansell, preface to
    NMA II:5/7, pp. xxviii–xxix.

21 Hansell (preface to the NMA II:5/7, p. xxi) states that the arias are 50
    per cent longer than those written for Milan by Paisiello at this date.

22 See his letters of 24 March and 22 September 1770: *LMF* 84a and
    114a, *MBA* 168 and 210. In the former he remarks that Italian min-
    uets are played slowly, have plenty of notes, and have many bars—for
    example the first part 16 bars, the second 20 or 24; in the latter he says
    they would have liked to introduce German-style minuets into Italy
    where the minuets last nearly as long as a whole symphony. The
    lengths of the sections of the main part of the minuets in K.156 are
    14 and 22 bars, in K.158 20 and 44. See also Chapter 9, p. 205.

Chapter 13

1 See Roger Hellyer: 'Mozart's Harmoniemusik', *Music Review*, xxxiv
   (1973), 146–56.

2 For a discussion of these papers see Alan Tyson: 'The Dates of Mozart's
   Missa brevis K. 258 and *Missa longa* K. 262 (246a): An Investigation into
   his *Klein-Querformat* Papers', *Mozart: Studies of the Autograph Scores*,
   162–76.

3 See Eisen: preface to *Orchestral Music in Salzburg*, p. xvii.

4 This was discovered by A. M. Stoneham; see his letter to *The Musical
   Times*, cxxv (1984), 75. Rudolph Angermüller has noted that it also
   appears in the ballet *Annette et Lubin*, by Louis Granier, given in Paris
   when Mozart was there in 1778; see *W.A. Mozarts musikalische Umwelt
   in Paris* (Munich and Salzburg, 1982).

5   See Ernst Fritz Schmid: 'Gluck—Starzer—Mozart', *Zeitschrift für Musik*, civ (1937), 1198.

6   The paper evidence is inconclusive: they are written on the same paper as K.166 but Mozart continued to use this paper all through 1774 and 1775. Plath, however, states that the handwriting indicates a date of about mid-1773; see 'Beiträge zur Mozart-Autographie II', 167.

7   See Neal Zaslaw: 'Mozart's Orchestral Flutes and Oboes', *Mozart Studies*, ed. Cliff Eisen (Oxford, 1991).

8   The handwriting of the violin concertos may readily be examined in the facsimile score, ed. Gabriel Banat (New York, 1986). For Plath's comments, see 'Beiträge zur Mozart-Autographie II', 166–7; see also Tyson: *Mozart: Studies of the Autograph Scores*, 163, and Christoph-Hellmut Mahling: introduction to NMA V:14/1, p. xi.

9   3 August 1778: *LMF* 320, *MBA* 473.

10 Details of the Kolb family are given in the *MBA* notes. For discussion of Kolb and other violinists, see Boris Schwarz: 'Violinists around Mozart', *Music in the Classic Period: Essays in Honor of Barry Brook*, ed. Atlas, 233–48.

11 *LMF* 177 and 178, *MBA* 288 and 289.

12 Letter of 25 September 1777: *LMF* 208, *MBA* 331.

13 See Wolfgang Plath: 'Beiträge zur Mozart-Autographie II: Schrift-chronologie 1770–1780', *MJb 1976–7*, 131–73, esp.152.

14 See Carl Bär: 'Die "Antretterin-Musik"', *Acta mozartiana*, x (1963), 30–37, and 'Zur Andretter-Serenade KV185', *MISM*, ix/1–2 (1960), 7–9.

15 Now, shamefully, dispersed among a variety of collections, private and public, by a greedy purchaser who promptly split it up and sold off the pages piecemeal; fortunately there exist photocopies.

16 Einstein: *Mozart: His Character, His Work*, 210.

17 Letter of 23 January 1773: *LMF* 171, *MBA* 281.

18 August 1777: *LMF* 206, *MBA* 328; *MDB* 162–3, *MDL* 145–6.

19 Letter of 4 September 1773: *LMF* 183, *MBA* 294.

20 The letters drawn upon in the ensuing discussion are those of 21 July, 12, 14, 21, 25 and 28 August, and 4, 8, 11, 15, 18 and 22 September 1773: *LMF* 177–88, *MBA* 288–99.

21 See Alan Tyson: *Mozart: Studies of the Autograph Scores* (Cambridge, MA, and London, 1987), 24; according to Wolfgang Plath, 'Among all of Mozart's works it probably [has] the most complex and most obscure composition history', 'Beiträge zur Mozart-Autographie II: Schriftchronologie 1770–1780', *MJb 1976–7*, 131–73, esp.172.

22 *MDB* 146, *MDL* 131.

23 *MDB* 148–9, *MDL* 133–4.

24 The relationship of K.168–173 to Haydn's quartets, and its assessment by recent scholars, is discussed by Peter A. Brown: 'Haydn and Mozart's 1773 Stay in Vienna: Weeding a Musicological Garden', *Journal of Musicology*, x (1992), 192–230.

25 Einstein (*Mozart: His Character, His Work*), pp.176–7, makes this comparison, among others, misnumbering op.17 no.2 as no.3, in which he is followed by A. Hyatt King: *Mozart Chamber Music* (London, 1968), p. 13.

26 See Warren Kirkendale: *Fugue and Fugato in Rococo and Classical Chamber Music* (Durham, NC, 2/1979), esp. Appendix I.

27 Brown cites several examples in 'Haydn and Mozart's 1773 Stay in Vienna', 213.

Chapter 14

1 See Leopold's letter to Hagenauer, 12 December 1765: *MBA* 104, and his letter to his wife, 20 February 1771: *MBA* 232 (the relevant portions of both letters are absent from *LMF*).

2 *MBA* 283 (the relevant portion is not in *LMF*).

3 For a full account of the history of the house see Rudolph Angermüller:' "Können Sie denn noch ein paar Zimmer anbauen lassen?": Zur Geschichte des Mozart-Wohnhauses', *MISM*, xliv/1–2 (1996), 1–83.

4 This manuscript, at one time owned by Leopold von Sonnleithner, then by August Cranz, of Hamburg, who became a music publisher in Leipzig, passed into a private Viennese collection and was sold at Sotheby's in 1987 for £2.3m; the purchaser placed it on deposit in the Pierpont Morgan Library, New York.

5 See Cliff Eisen: 'Mozart's Salzburg Orchestras', *Early Music*, xx (1992),

89–103, and Zaslaw: *Mozart's Symphonies*, 205, both after Hintermaier: *Die Salzburger Hofkapelle*, 543.

6 Einstein: *Mozart: His Character, His Work*, 223.

7 Théodore de Wyzewa and Georges de Saint-Foix: *Wolfgang Amédée Mozart: Sa vie musicale et son oeuvre* (Paris, 1912–46), ii, 120–25.

8 H.C. Robbins Landon: 'La crise romantique dans la musique autrichienne vers 1770: Quelques précurseurs inconnus de la symphonie en sol mineur (KV 183) de Mozart', *Les influences étrangères dans l'oeuvre de W.A. Mozart*, ed. André Verchaly (Paris, 1958), 27–46.

9 See Jens Peter Larsen: 'The Symphonies', *The Mozart Companion*, ed. H.C. Robbins Landon and Donald Mitchell (London, 1956), 156–98, esp. 173–4.

10 See Brown: 'Haydn and Mozart's 1773 Stay in Vienna', 225–30.

11 See Cliff Eisen: 'Mozart and the Viennese String Quintet', *Mozarts Streichquintette*, ed. Cliff Eisen and Wolf-Dietrich Seiffert (Stuttgart, 1994), 127–51, esp. pp.132–3.

12 See Lothar Herbert Perger: 'Thematisches Verzeichnis der Instrumentalwerke von Michael Haydn', *Denkmäler der Tonkunst in Österreich*, xxix, Jg. xiv/2 (Vienna, 1907), nos. 108 and 109; see also Marius Flothuis: 'Quintette für Streichinstrumente von Michael Haydn', *MJb 1987–8* (Kassel, 1988), 49–57.

13 See Mozart's letter of 23 March 1782 (*MBA* 665, *LMF* 445), in which he refers to the replacement finale K.382 that he had just composed for it.

14 See Cliff Eisen: 'The Mozarts' Salzburg Copyists: Aspects of Attribution, Chronology, Text, Style and Performance Practice', *Mozart Studies*, ed. Cliff Eisen (Oxford, 1991), 253–307, esp. 286–7.

15 K.175 was written for harpsichord, as were most, if not all, of Mozart's Salzburg keyboard concertos. It would however be pedantic to avoid the standard appellation for this group of works, and the term 'piano concerto' will henceforth be used in this volume.

16 Letters of 13 November 1777, *LMF* 240, *MBA* 369, and 12 January 1778, *LMF* 272, *MBA* 403.

17 Mozart's father urged him (letter of 11 December 1777, *LMF* 259, *MBA* 389) to perform it in Mannheim. He must in fact have played it to Wendling and Bagge before his father's letter reached him (see his letter of 14 December, *LMF* 260, *MBA* 390).

18 See Chapter 9, note 35.

19 The incipit for the concerto in F is in K^6. For the concerto K.Anh.230a/C14.03, in B flat, see Ernst Hess: 'Ist das Fagottkonzert KV.Anhang 230a von Mozart?', *MJb 1957* (Salzburg, 1958), 223–32.

20 Reported by Beda Hübner: see *NMD*, no. 41.

21 See Plath: 'Beiträge zur Mozart-Autographie II', 151 (K.381), 153 (K.358).

22 Letter of 4 September 1776, *LMF* 205, *MBA* 323.

23 See Georg Reichert: 'Mozarts "Credo-Messen" und ihre Vorläufer', *MJb 1955*, 117–44.

24 See for example Alec Hyatt King: *Mozart in Retrospect* (London, 1955), Appendix 2 (noting use of the figure by Mozart and other composers from Palestrina to Brahms and D'Indy); Susan Wollenberg: 'The Jupiter Theme: New Light on its Creation', *Musical Times*, cxvi (1975), 781–3; and Ellwood Derr: 'A Deeper Examination of Mozart's 1–2–4–3 Theme and its Strategic Deployment', *In Theory Only*, viii (1985), 5–43.

Chapter 15

1 See Hermann Abert: *W.A. Mozart* (Leipzig, 6/1923), i, 463, and Volker Mattern: *Das Dramma giocoso 'La finta giardiniera': Ein Vergleich der Vertonungen von Pasquale Anfossi und Wolfgang Amadeus Mozart* (Laaber, 1989).

2 The letters drawn upon in the first part of this chapter are those of 9, 14, 16, 21, 28 and 30 December 1774 and 5, 11, 14, 18, 21 January, 8, 15 and 21 February and 1 March 1775: *LMF* 189–203, *MBA* 300–18.

3 See Chapter 12.

4 See Wolfgang Plath: 'Zur Datierung der Klaviersonaten KV 279–284', *AcMoz*, xxi (1974), 26–30.

5 For a full discussion of the keyboard instruments used by Mozart, see Richard Maunder: 'Mozart's Keyboard Instruments', *Early Music*, xx (1992), 207–19.

6 *Deutsche Chronik*, Jg. 2/34, p. 267 (Augsburg, 27 April 1775): *MDB* 153, *MDL* 138.

7 See his letter of 18 December 1776, *MBA* 325, in response to Mozart's of 4 September 1776: *LMF* 205, *MBA* 323.

8 See his letters of 15 October and 1 December 1777: *LMF* 222 and 252, *MBA* 350 and 382.

9 Letter of 11 September 1778: *LMF* 331, *MBA* 487.

10 See letters of 17 November 1777 and 4 February 1778: *LMF* 244 and 281, *MBA* 374 and 416.

11 The autograph of all six sonatas, lacking the original first folio (with the first movement of K.279), is in the Biblioteka Jagiellońska, Kraków. Facsimiles of the first two pages of the autograph of K.284 and a transcription of much of the movement are published in László Somfai: 'Mozart's First Thoughts: The Two Versions of the Sonata in D major, K284', *Early Music*, xix (1991), 601–13.

12 Letters from Leopold Mozart, 6 October 1777, and Wolfgang, 23 October 1777: *LMF* 216 and 228b, *MBA* 344 and 355. See Dénes Bartha, 'Mozart et le folklore musical de l'Europe centrale', *Les influences étrangères*, ed. Verchaly, 157–81, esp. 'Note', 178–80.

13 Hintermaier: *Die Salzburger Hofkapelle.*

14 See letters of 25 September 1777 and 9 October 1777: *LMF* 208 and 218, *MBA* 331 and 346; for personal comments on Brunetti see letters of 6 October 1777, 22 and 25–6 February and 11 June 1778 and 24 March and 8 and 11 April 1781: *LMF* 216, 289, 291, 308, 395, 397 and 398, *MBA* 344, 428, 430, 452, 585, 587 and 588.

15 See Walter Lebermann: 'Mozart—Eck—André: Ein Beitrag zu KV 268 (365b)(C.14.04)', *Die Musikforschung*, xxxi (1978), 452–65.

16 See Christoph-Hellmut Mahling: 'Bemerkungen zum Violinkonzert KV 271i', *MJb 1978–9*, 252–7, and 'Nochmals Bemerkungen zum Violinkonzert D-dur KV 271a (271i)', *MJb 2001*, 101–8.

17 Reported in the travel journal of the Archduke; see *MDB* 151–2, *MDL* 137.

18 See Sergio Durante: 'Considerations on Mozart's Changing Approach to Recitatives and on other Choices of Dramaturgical Significance', *MJb 2001*, 231–44, and Klaus Hortschansky: ' "Il Re Pastore": Zur Rezeption eines Librettos in der Mozart-Zeit', *MJb 1978–9*, 61–70. There is no evidence that the Salzburg court chaplain and poet, Gio-

vanni Battista Varesco, was involved in the shortening of the text or any other aspect of its preparation, as is sometimes suggested.

19 See *MDB* 151–3, *MDL* 136–7.

20 See letters of 11 October 1777, 7 and 14 February 1778: *LMF* 219, 283a and 286a, *MBA* 347, 419 and 423.

21 Letter of 12 April 1783: *LMF* 486, *MBA* 739.

Chapter 16

1 See Otto Erich Deutsch: 'Aus Schiedenhofens Tagebuch', *MJb 1957*, 15–24.

2 Letter to Padre Martini, 22 December 1777: *LMF* 266, *MBA* 396.

3 See Alan Tyson: 'The Dates of Mozart's *Missa brevis* K.258 and *Missa longa* K.262 (246a)'.

4 *MDB* 156, *MDL* 140.

5 A version of K.220, with added parts for toy instruments, was made by Paul Wranitsky for Empress Marie Therese at the end of the century; see John A. Rice: 'Adding Birds to Mozart's "Sparrow Mass"', *Mozart Society of America Newsletter*, vii/2 (2004), 8–9.

6 Letter of 28 May 1778: *LMF* 306, *MBA* 450.

7 See Leopold Mozart's letter of 21–22 December 1777: *LMF* 265, *MBA* 395.

8 Noted respectively by Schiedenhofen and Nannerl Mozart in their diaries: see *MDB* 156, *MDL* 140.

9 See *MDB* 155–6, *MDL* 140.

10 Letter of 8 February 1800: *MBA* 1280.

11 He refers to 'her usual insincere friendliness': letter of 5 January 1778: *LMF* 270, *MBA* 401.

12 Letter of 29 June 1778: *MBA* 457 (the relevant passage is omitted from *LMF* 310).

13 See Wolfgang's letters of 2 and 6 October 1777, Leopold's of 12 April and 3 August 1778, and Wolfgang's of 4 July 1781: *LMF* 214, 217b, 302, 320 and 414, *MBA* 342, 345, 526, 590 and 609.

14 Letter of 20 July 1778: *LMF* 315b, *MBA* 466.

15 See Deutsch: 'Aus Schiedenhofens Tagebuch', 21.

16 Letter of 2 October 1777: *LMF* 214, *MBA* 342; the Salzburg performances were recorded by Mozart in Nannerl's diary, *MBA* 527 and 529.

17 Letter of 6 October 1777: *LMF* 217b, *MBA* 345. Later, however, Leopold could report a more satisfactory performance, in which Nannerl was accompanied 'most excellently' by two musicians from Wallerstein (letter of 26 January 1778: *LMF* 276, *MBA* 410).

18 See his letters of 23 October 1777 and 24 March 1778: *LMF* 228b and 299, *MBA* 355 and 439.

19 See Wyzewa and Saint-Foix: *Wolfgang Amédée Mozart*, iii, 362.

20 This discovery was made by Michael Lorenz; see his 'The Jenamy Concerto', *Newsletter of the Mozart Society of America*, x/1 (27 January 2005), 1–3. Mozart's references to her are in his letters of 5 April and 11 September 1778: *LMF* 300a and 331, *MBA* 440 and 487, Leopold's in his of 12–20 April 1778: *LMF* 302, *MBA* 446.

21 They had lunch with him on 29 August (letter of 28 August: *LMF* 182, *MBA* 293).

22 See Mozart's letter of 15 February 1783: *LMF* 481, *MBA* 728.

Chapter 17

1 See Leopold's letter to Padre Martini, 22 December 1777: *LMF* 266, *MBA* 396; a number of remarks in Wolfgang's letters (such as that of 4 November 1777: *LMF* 235, *MBA* 363) indicate his outrage.

2 For the full text see *MDB* 162, *MDL* 145; also *LMF* 206, *MBA* 328.

3 See his diary entries, *MDB* 164, *MDL* 146–7.

4 In his letter of 20 November 1777 (*LMF* 246, *MBA* 375) he itemizes his debts: 300 gulden to Bullinger, more than 100 to Weiser and about 40 to Kerschbaumer (one of a Salzburg family with a shop close to the Mozarts' house). In the next letter (24 November) he mentions that he had overlooked a 'rather large' debt to Hagenauer.

5 Letters of 7 February and 3 July 1778: *LMF* 283a and 311, *MBA* 419 and 458.

6 Letter of 29–30 September 1777: *LMF* 212a, *MBA* 339.

7 Letter of 31 July 1778: *LMF* 319, *MBA* 471.

8 Letter of 18 December 1777: *LMF* 262, *MBA* 392.

9 Letter of 6 April 1778: *LMF* 301, *MBA* 444.

10 The letters drawn upon in the present chapter cover the periods from 23 September to 12 October 1777 (Munich): *LMF* 207–20, *MBA* 329–48; 14 to 29 October 1777 (Augsburg): *LMF* 221–31, *MBA* 349–59, and 31 October 1777 to 11 March 1778 (Mannheim): *LMF* 232–97, *MBA* 360–436.

11 For the opposite view, see Solomon: *Mozart*, 163–6; Solomon follows Wolfgang Hildesheimer: *Mozart* (Frankfurt, 1977). Solomon's surprising suggestion that the remark 'Whoever doesn't believe me may lick me world without end . . . for I fear that my muck will soon dry up' is a 'rollicking reference to oral sex' needs to be read in the light of the countless references to muck and arse-licking in the rest of the family correspondence.

12 Letter of 30 July 1778: *LMF* 318, *MBA* 470.

13 Letter of 4 December: *LMF* 255, *MBA* 385.

14 See Frank Lequin: 'Mozarts " . . . rarer Mann" ', *MISM*, xxix/1–2 (1981), 3–19.

15 'Ah, se il crudel periglio', from *Lucio Silla*. 'Galanteries', in this context, signifies short keyboard pieces.

16 Letter of 4 February 1778: *LMF* 281, *MBA* 416.

17 Letter of 31 January 1778: *LMF* 278, *MBA* 412. I quote Emily Anderson's translation, which is far from literal although it fairly captures the spirit. The original lines read: Herr Wendling wird wohl böse seyn, / Daß ich kaum nichts geschrieben fein, / Doch wenn ich komm' über d'Rheinbrücke / So kom ich ganz gewiß zurücke / Und schreib die 4 Quartetti ganz / Damit er mich nicht heißt ein Schwantz. / Und das Concert spar ich mich nach Paris, / Dort schmier ichs her gleich auf den ersten Schiß.

18 See Leopold's letter of 11 December, Nannerl's postscript to Leopold's of 8 December, and Mozart's letters of 14 November and 6 December 1777: *LMF* 258, 257a, 243a and 256, *MBA* 388, 387, 373 and 386.

19 Letters of 5 November and 3 December 1777: *LMF* 236 and 254, *MBA* 364 and 384.

20 They are available in a modern edition, ed. W. Plath, Nagels Musik-Archiv nos. 229, 232 and 233 (Kassel, 1971–3).

21 This is argued by Roger Lustig: 'On the Flute Quartet, K.285b (Anh.171)', *MJb 1997*, 157–79, and Daniel N. Leeson: 'A Revisit:

Mozart's Serenade for Thirteen Instruments, K.361 (370a), the "Gran Partitta"', *MJb 1997*, 181–223.

22 Neal Zaslaw has pointed out in a private communication that the error comes from a misreading in a letter Mozart wrote to Leopold dated Mannheim, 14 February 1778. The German word *ein* can mean either 'one' or 'an'. Mozart originally wrote 'I also quickly become disgusted as soon as I must write continually for *ein* [meaning *one*, not *an*] instrument'; the phrase 'which I cannot bear' he added only later. So, it was not the flute that he could not bear, but a lack of timbral variety.

23 Einstein: *Mozart: His Character, His Work*, 178.

24 See Stephan Kunze: 'Die Vertonungen der Aria "Non so d'onde viene" von J.C. Bach und Mozart', *Analecta musicologica*, no. 2 (1965), 85–110.

25 See Paul Corneilson: 'An Intimate Vocal Portrait of Dorothea Wendling: Mozart's "Basta, vincesti . . . Ah non lasciarmi, no" K.295a', *MJb 2000*, 29–45.

Chapter 18

1 The letters drawn upon in the present chapter cover from 16 March 1778 to 11 January 1779: *LMF* 298–352, *MBA* 438–521.

2 Letter of 1 May 1778, *LMF* 303, *MBA* 447.

3 This incident is presumably the model for the very similar one, with Salieri as the composer, in Peter Shaffer's play and the film *Amadeus*.

4 Letter written between 29 April and 11 May 1778: *LMF* 304, *MBA* 448. Less than one-third of this long letter (much of it devoted to the mental problems of their lodger, Sandl Auer, and to the current war preparations) is included in *LMF*; similarly with Leopold's letters of 28 May and 29 June 1778: *LMF* 306 and 310, *MBA* 450 and 457.

5 He refers to her simply as 'the Countess'; some commentators have taken this to mean Countess Wallis, the Archbishop's sister, but the context and the evidence favour Countess Lodron, who was the Archbishop's close confidante.

6 See Neumayr: *Music and Medicine*, 125, and Davies: *Mozart in Person*, 49. Pneumonia and tuberculosis have also been suggested.

7   Letter of 31 July 1778: *LMF* 319, *MBA* 471.

8   Letter of 29 July 1778: *LMF* 317, *MBA* 469.

9   Quoted (in French) by Leopold in his letter of 13 August 1778: *LMF* 323, *MBA* 476.

10 'Il filo': literally, 'the thread', by which Leopold means the line, the logical continuity of the music.

11 27 August 1778: *LMF* 326 (much shortened), *MBA* 478.

12 See C.B. Oldman: 'Mozart's Scena for Tenducci', *Music & Letters*, xlii (1961), 44–52. Charles Burney mentioned the work to Daines Barrington, who referred to it in his *Miscellanies* (London, 1781), with his 'Account of a very Remarkable Young Musician' (see Chapter 4, note 27); Burney however names the accompanying instruments as five-part strings, oboe, two clarinets, chromatic horn, piano and two horns.

13 Letter, sent as an enclosure to one to Grimm, of 31 August 1778: *LMF* 328, *MBA* 480.

14 Letter of 3 September 1778: *LMF* 329 (large sections omitted), *MBA* 482.

15 Letter of 11 September 1778: *LMF* 331, *MBA* 487.

16 Letter of 3 October 1778: *LMF* 335, *MBA* 494.

17 See Neal Zaslaw: 'Mozart's Paris Symphonies', *MT*, cxix (1978), 753–7. For a time a two-movement work in B flat found in a Paris archive in 1901, in an edition of about 1805 with an ascription to Mozart, was supposed to be the 'new symphony', $K^3.311a$/Anh.C11.05. It has no stylistic affinities with Mozart's music.

18 This theory was originally put forward by Samuel Baron and Barry S. Brook and exhaustively argued in Daniel N. Leeson and Robert D. Levin: 'On the Authenticity of K. Anh. C14.01 (297b), a Symphonia Concertante for Four Winds and Orchestra', *MJb 1976–7*, 70–96, and Robert D. Levin: *Who Wrote the Mozart Four-Wind Concertante?* (Stuyvesant, NY, 1988); these tendentious studies are convincingly dispatched by Richard Maunder in his review of Levin's book, *Journal of the Royal Musical Association*, cxvi (1991), 136–9.

19 See Alan Tyson: 'The Two Slow Movements of Mozart's "Paris" Symphony, K.297', *Mozart: Studies of the Autograph Scores*, 106–13.

20 See Plath: 'Beiträge zur Mozart-Autographie II', 170.

21 Letter (in Italian) to Aloysia Weber, 30 July 1778: *LMF* 318, *MBA* 470.

22 Letter of 19 November 1778: *LMF* 340, *MBA* 505.

23 See Chapter 19, pp. 509–10.

24 Nissen: *Biographie W.A. Mozart's*, 414–15.

25 *LMF* 347 (less than a quarter of the letter is included), *MBA* 512.

26 *MBA* 514.

27 Letter of 31 December 1778: *LMF* 349, *MBA* 515.

28 Maynard Solomon, in *Mozart*, does not believe he was, but there is no firm evidence to support his theories.

Chapter 19

1 It is included in *MBA*, and published separately, with facsimiles and extensive and valuable annotation, in *Marie Anne Mozart: 'meine tag Ordnungen'*, ed. Geneviève Geffray with Rudolph Angermüller (Bad Honnef, 1998).

2 See Günther G. Bauer: *Mozart: Glück, Spiel und Leidenschaft* (Bad Honnef, 2003).

3 Because of the cutting and pasting of the pages by Constanze Mozart, the dating of this event has long been confused (as in *MBA* 529) and given as 18 March; see Halliwell: *The Mozart Family*, Appendix I, 643–8, where the analysis of the material sets the record straight and firmly establishes the correct date.

4 17 September 1778: *MBA* 482 (the relevant passage is omitted in *LMF* 332).

5 See Eisen: 'Mozart's Salzburg Orchestras', and Zaslaw: *Mozart's Symphonies*, 338, both after Hintermaier: *Die Salzburger Hofkapelle*, 544.

6 See H.C. Robbins Landon: *Mozart: The Golden Years, 1781–1791* (London, 1989) and Landon: *1791: Mozart's Last Year* (London, 1988).

7 Letter of 29 December 1778: *LMF* 348, *MBA* 513.

8 Letter of 12 March 1783: *LMF* 483, *MBA* 731.

9 See Chapter 14.

10 Letter of 29 March 1783: *LMF* 484, *MBA* 734.

11 Letter of 8 May 1782: *LMF* 450, *MBA* 673.

12 See Plath: 'Beiträge zur Mozart-Autographie II', 172.

13 See his letter of 12 November 1778: *LMF* 339, *MBA* 504; for discussion of the work see Robert D. Levin: 'Das Konzert für Klavier und

Violine D-dur KV Anh.56/315f und das Klarinettenquintett B-dur, KV Anh.91/516c: Ein Ergänzungsversuch', *MJb 1968–70*, 304–26 [in English].

14 See Ulrich Konrad: 'Mozarts "Gruppenkonzerte" aus den letzten Salzburger Jahren: Probleme der Chronologie und Deutung', *Beiträge zur Geschichte des Konzerts: Festschrift Siegfried Kross zum 60. Geburtstag*, ed. Reinmar Emens and Matthias Wendt (Bonn, 1990), 141–57.

15 *Marie Anne Mozart: 'meine tag Ordnungen'*, 92.

16 Letter of 4 July 1781: *LMF* 415, *MBA* 610.

17 See Alfred Orel: 'Zu Mozarts Sommerreise nach Wien im Jahre 1773', *MJb* 1951, 34-49; *MDB* 148, *MDL* 133.

18 See Tyson: *Mozart: Studies of the Autograph Scores*, 24-5; and Plath, 'Beiträge zur Mozart-Autographie II', 172-3.

19 See his letter of 15 February 1783: *LMF* 481, *MBA* 728.

20 Letter of 11 January 1778: *LMF* 271c, *MBA* 402.

21 Reprinted in *MDB* 169-72, *MDL* 152-4; also *MBA* 407.

22 Letters of 4 and 7 February 1778: *LMF* 281 and 283a, *MBA* 416 and 419.

23 Alfred Einstein: 'Die Text-Vorlage zu Mozarts Zaide', *Acta musicologica*, ix (1936), 30-37; the libretto's background is discussed by Friedrich-Heinrich Neumann: 'Zur Vorgeschichte der Zaide', *MJb* 1962-3, 216-47. A facsimile of the Sebastiani text as set by Friebert is included in the NMA Kritische Bericht, II/5:10 (1963). A later article by Andreas Kroeper demonstrates, however, that Mozart's and Schachter's model was the libretto printed for a production in Bozen (Bolzano) in 1779; see Andreas Kröper-Hoffmann: '*Zaide*—bühnenreif! Zur Adaption der Texte Sebastianis auf Mozart/Schachtner', *Hudební Veda*, xl (2003), nos. 2–3, pp. 135–54, and Thomas Betzwieser: ' "Seine teutsche Oper ohne Titel, großtentheils vollendet"—die Rätzel um Mozarts Zaide', *Almanach der Mozart-Woche Salzburg 2005*.

24 The structures of the original and Schachtner's revision are clearly laid out in Linda L. Tyler: ' "Zaide" in the Development of Mozart's Operatic Language', *Music & Letters*, lxxii (1991), 214-35; this valuable article also includes a detailed analysis of the arias.

25 Letter of 18 April 1781: *LMF* 399, *MBA* 590.

Chapter 20

1 Letter of 11 December: *LMF* 373, *MBA* 558.

2 See Marita McClymonds: 'Mannheim, *Idomeneo* and the Franco-Italian Synthesis in Opera Seria', *Mozart und Mannheim*, ed. Ludwig Finscher, Bärbel Pelker and Jochen Reutter (Frankfurt, 1994), 187–96.

3 See letters of 16 May 1766: *LMF* 41, *MBA* 108, and 8 September 1770: *LMF* 111a, *MBA* 207.

4 For an account of the transformation of the libretto, see Lois Rosow: '*Idomeneo* and *Idoménée*: The French Disconnection', paper read at the American Musicological Society, Chicago, 1991, and Julian Rushton and Don Neville: 'From Myth to Libretto', in *Idomeneo*, ed. Julian Rushton (Cambridge, 1993), 69–82.

5 See Mozart's letter to his father, 16 December 1780, *LMF* 376, *MBA* 563, and Leopold's reply of 25 December, *LMF* 380, *MBA* 569.

6 The letters drawn upon in this chapter are those written between 8 November 1780 and 22 January 1781: *LMF* 356–91, *MBA* 535–81.

7 See Paul Corneilson: 'Mozart's Ilia and Electra: New Perspectives on *Idomeneo*', *Mozarts Idomeneo und die Musik in München zur Zeit Karl Theodors*, ed. Theodore Göllner and Stephan Hörner (Munich, 2001), 97–113; and Corneilson: 'An Intimate Vocal Portrait'.

8 Letter of 29 December 1780: *LMF* 382, *MBA* 572.

9 Exceptions are made for the choral scenes in Act 3, which are printed in full with 'Vi—de' markings to indicate the cuts.

10 See Robert Münster: 'Neues zum Münchner "Idomeneo" 1781', *AcMoz*, xxv (1982), 10–20.

11 See Karl Böhmer: *W.A. Mozarts Idomeneo und die Tradition der Karnevalsopern in München* (Tutzing, 1999).

12 See Daniel Heartz: 'Tonality and Motif in *Idomeneo*', *Musical Times*, cxv (1974), 382–6; Julian Rushton: ' "La vittima è Idamante": Did Mozart have a Motive?', *Cambridge Opera Journal*, iii (1991), 1–21; Julian Rushton: 'Tonality and Motive', *Idomeneo*, ed. Rushton, 129–39; and Rushton: 'A Reconciliation Motif in *Idomeneo*', *Words about Mozart: Essays in Honour of Stanley Sadie*, ed. Dorothea Link and Judith Nagley (Woodbridge, 2005), 21–32.

13 See Daniel Heartz: 'Raaff's Last Aria: a Mozartian Idyll in the Spirit of Hasse', *Musical Quarterly*, lx (1974), 517–43.

14 For discussion of the quartet, see Daniel Heartz: 'The Great Quartet in Mozart's *Idomeneo*', *Music Forum*, v (1980), 233–56, and Marita McClymonds: 'The Great Quartet in *Idomeneo* and the Italian *opera seria* Tradition', *Wolfgang Amadè Mozart: Essays on his Life and Music*, ed. Sadie, 449–76.

15 Rosemary Hughes and Nerina Medici di Marignano, eds.: *A Mozart Pilgrimage: Being the Travel Diaries of Vincent & Mary Novello in the Year 1829* (London, 1955), 114–15.

16 Letter of 27 December 1780, *LMF* 381, *MBA* 570.

17 See his letter of 12 September 1781: *LMF* 424, *MBA* 624.

18 Letter of 29 March 1783: *LMF* 484, *MBA* 734.

19 The two versions are printed in parallel in the NMA score.

20 There also survives a 22-bar sketch, Sk1785i in Ulrich Konrad: *Mozarts Schaffensweise* (Göttingen, 1992), 259, for a soprano–tenor duet in A major, which Konrad cannot place. It belongs to the period of the revision of *Idomeneo* and could be linked with the Act 3 duet, although the text Mozart ultimately used and the rhythms of the sketch do not match. See Ulrich Konrad: 'Mozart's Sketches', *Early Music*, xx (1992), 119–30.

21 Letter of 11 January 1781: *MBA* 578 (also *LMF* 388, but the relevant sections are omitted).

22 Letter from D.B. Strobl, treasurer of the monastery, to H. Lech: *MDB* 193, *MDL* 171.

BIBLIOGRAPHY

Works Cited

NOTE: For a list of bibliographic abbreviations, see pp. 549–50.

Abert, Hermann: *W.A. Mozart* (Leipzig, 1919–21; 6/1923).

Allroggen, Gerhard: 'Zur Frage der Echtheit der Sinfonie KV Anh.216 = 74g', *Analecta musicologica*, no. 18 (1978), 237–45.

Angermüller, Rudolph: 'Johann Andreas Schachtners "Bastienne"-Libretto', *MISM*, xxii/1–2 (1974), 4–28.

————: '"Können Sie denn noch ein paar Zimmer anbauen lassen?"': Zur Geschichte des Mozart-Wohnhauses', *MISM*, xliv/1–2 (1996), 1–83.

————: *Mozart's Operas* (New York, 1988).

————: *W.A. Mozarts musikalische Umwelt in Paris* (Munich and Salzburg, 1982).

Atlas, Allan W., ed. *Music in the Classic Period: Essays in Honor of Barry S. Brook* (New York, 1985).

Bär, Carl: 'Die "Antretterin-Musik"', *Acta mozartiana*, x (1963), 30–37.

————: 'Zur Andretter-Serenade KV185', *MISM*, ix/1–2 (1960), 7–9.

Barblan, Guglielmo, and Andrea Della Corte: *Mozart in Italia: I viaggi e le lettere* (Milan, 1956).

Barrington, Daines: 'Account of Mozart, Mr. Charles Wesley, Master Samuel Wesley, little Crotch, the Earl of Mornington,' *Philosophical Transactions*, lx (1771), 54–64, reprinted in Barrington's *Miscellanies* (London, 1781) and *MDB* 95–100.

Bartha, Dénes: 'Mozart et le folklore musical de l'Europe centrale', *Les influences étrangères*, ed. André Verchaly (Paris, 1958), 157–81.

Bauer, Günther G.: *Mozart: Glück, Spiel und Leidenschaft* (Bad Honnef, 2003).

Betzwieser, Thomas: ' "Seine teutsche Oper ohne Titel, größentheils vollendet"—die Rätsel um Mozarts Zaide', *Almanach der Mozart-Woche Salzburg 2005*.

Blazin, Dwight: 'The Two Versions of Mozart's Divertimento K.113', *Music & Letters*, lxxiii (1992), 32–47.

Blom, Eric: 'Mozart, (3) Wolfgang Amadeus', *Grove's Dictionary of Music and Musicians*, London, 1954, v, 923–83.

Böhmer, Karl: *W.A. Mozarts Idomeneo und die Tradition der Karnevalsopern in München* (Tutzing, 1999).

Breitkopf & Härtel: *The Breitkopf Thematic Catalogues*; facsimile, ed. Barry S. Brook (New York, 1968).

——: 'Thematisches Verzeichnis der sämtlichen Werke von W.A. Mozart' (manuscript compiled Leipzig, early 19th c.).

Brown, Peter A.: 'Haydn and Mozart's 1773 Stay in Vienna: Weeding a Musicological Garden', *Journal of Musicology*, x (1992), 192–230.

Burney, Charles: *Memoirs of Dr Charles Burney, 1726–1769*, ed. Slava Klima, Garry Bowers and Kerry S. Grant (Lincoln, NE, and London, 1987).

——: *Music, Men and Manners in France and Italy, 1770: Being the Journal . . . Written during a Tour through those Countries . . . transcribed from . . . British Museum Additional Manuscript 35122*, ed. H. Edmund Poole (London, 1969).

——: *The Present State of Music in France and Italy* (London, 1771, 2/1773).

——: *The Present State of Music in Germany, the Netherlands, and United Provinces* (London, 1773), reproduced in *Dr. Burney's Musical Tours in Europe*, ed. Percy A. Scholes (London, 1959).

Burrows, Donald: 'Performances of Handel's Music during Mozart's Visit to London in 1764–5', *Händel-Jahrbuch*, xxxviii (1992), 16–32.

Clarke, Bruce Cooper: 'Albert von Mölk: Mozart Myth-Maker? Study of an 18th Century Correspondence', *MJb 1995*, 155–91.

Corneilson, Paul: 'An Intimate Vocal Portrait of Dorothea Wendling: Mozart's "Basta, vincesti . . . Ah non lasciarmi, no" K.295a', *MJb 2000*, 29–45.

————: 'Mozart's Ilia and Electra: New Perspectives on *Idomeneo*', *Mozarts Idomeneo und die Musik in München zur Zeit Karl Theodors*, ed. Theodore Göllner and Stephan Hörner (Munich, 2001), 97–113.

Croll, Gerhard: 'Bemerkungen zum "Ballo Primo" (KV Anh.109/135a) in Mozarts Mailänder "Lucio Silla"', *Analecta musicologica*, no. 18 (1974), 160–65.

Davies, Peter J.: *Mozart in Person: His Character and Health* (London, 1989).

Derr, Ellwood: 'A Deeper Examination of Mozart's 1–2–4–3 Theme and its Strategic Deployment', *In Theory Only*, viii (1985), 5–43.

Deutsch, Otto Erich: 'Aus Schiedenhofens Tagebuch', *MJb 1957*, 15–24.

————: 'Mozart in Zinzendorfs Tagebüchern', *Schweizerische Musikzeitung*, cii (1962), 211–18.

————: *Mozart und seine Welt in zeitgenössischen Bildern*, NMA X:32 (1961).

Deutsch, Otto Erich, and Wilhelm A. Bauer: 'Leopold Mozarts Briefe an Hagenauer', *MISM*, viii (1959), 8–9.

Durante, Sergio: 'Considerations on Mozart's Changing Approach to Recitatives and on Other Choices of Dramaturgical Significance', *MJb 2001*, 231–44.

Edge, Dexter: 'Mozart Reception in Vienna, 1787–91', *Wolfgang Amadè Mozart,* ed. S. Sadie, 66–117.

Eibl, Joseph Heinz: 'Die Mozarts und der Erzbischof', *Österreichische Musikzeitschrift*, xxx (1975), 329–41.

Einstein, Alfred: *Mozart: His Character, His Work* (London, 1946).

————: 'Die Text-Vorlage zu Mozarts Zaide', *Acta musicologica*, ix (1936), 30–37.

Eisen, Cliff: 'Contributions to a New Mozart Documentary Biography', *Journal of the American Musicological Society*, xxxix (1986), 620–23.

————: 'Mozart and the Four-Hand Sonata K. 19d', *Haydn, Mozart, and Beethoven: Studies in Music of the Classical Period, Essays in Honour of Alan Tyson*, ed. Sieghard Brandenburg (Oxford, 1998), 91–9.

————: 'Mozart and the Viennese String Quintet', *Mozarts Streichquintette*, ed. Cliff Eisen and Wolf-Dietrich Seiffert (Stuttgart, 1994), 127–51.

————: 'Mozart Apocrypha', *Musical Times*, cxxvii (1986), 685.

————: 'Mozart, (1) Leopold', *The New Grove Dictionary of Music and Musicians*, ed. Stanley Sadie (London, 2/2001).

————: 'The Mozarts' Salzburg Copyists: Aspects of Attribution, Chronology, Text, Style and Performance Practice', *Mozart Studies*, ed. Cliff Eisen (Oxford, 1991), 253–307.

——: 'Mozart's Salzburg Orchestras', *Early Music*, xx (1992), 89–103.

——: *Orchestral Music in Salzburg, 1750–1780*, Recent Researches in the Music of the Classical Era, xl (Madison, WI, 1994).

——: 'Problems of Authenticity among Mozart's Early Symphonies: The Examples of K. Anh. 220 (16a) and 76 (42a)', *Music & Letters*, lxx (1989), 505–13.

——: 'The Salzburg Symphonies: A Biographical Interpretation', *Wolfgang Amadè Mozart*, ed. S. Sadie, 178–212.

——: 'Salzburg under Church Rule', *Man and Music: The Classical Era*, ed. Neal Zaslaw (London, 1989), 166–87.

——: *The Symphonies of Leopold Mozart and their Relationship to the Early Symphonies of Wolfgang Amadeus Mozart: A Bibliographical and Stylistic Study* (diss., Cornell University, 1986).

——: 'The Symphonies of Leopold Mozart: Their Chronology, Their Style and Importance for the Study of Mozart's Early Symphonies', *MJb 1987–8*, 181–93.

Farmer, Henry George, and Herbert Smith: *New Mozartiana* (Glasgow, 1935).

Federhofer-Königs, Renate: 'Mozarts "Lauretanische Litaneien" KV109 (74e) und 195 (189d)', *MJb 1967*, 111–20.

Fehr, Max, and Leonhard Calfisch: *Der junge Mozart in Zürich* (Zürich, 1952).

Fellerer, Karl Gustav: 'Mozarts Litaneien', *Bericht über die musikwissenschaftliche Tagung der Internationalen Stiftung Mozarteum in Salzburg 1931* (Leipzig, 1932), 136–41.

Finscher, Ludwig: 'Mozarts erstes Streichquartett: Lodi, 15. März 1770', *Analecta musicologica*, no. 18 (1978), 246–70.

Flothuis, Marius: 'Quintette für Streichinstrumente von Michael Haydn', *MJb 1987–8* (Kassel, 1988), 49–57.

Fyot, Eugène: 'Mozart à Dijon', *Mémoires de l'Académie des sciences, arts et belles-lettres de Dijon: année 1937* (Dijon, 1938), 23–41.

Gaby, György: 'Das Reiseklavichord W.A. Mozarts', *Studia Musicologica Academiae Scientiarum Hungaricae*, x (1968), 153–62.

Gianturco, Carolyn: *Mozart's Early Operas* (London, 1981).

Gottron, Adam: *Mozart und Mainz* (Mainz, 1951).

Grant, Kerry S.: *Dr Burney as Critic and Historian of Music* (Ann Arbor, 1983).

Haas, Robert, Camillo Schoenbaum and Herbert Zeman, eds.: *Teutsche Comoedie Arien,* in Denkmäler der Tonkunst in Österreich, lxiv, Jg. 33/i (Vienna, 1926) and cxxi (Vienna, 1971).

Halliwell, Ruth: *The Mozart Family* (Oxford, 1998).

Hansell, Kathleen K.: *Opera and Ballet and the Regio Ducal Teatro of Milan 1771–1776: A Musical and Social History* (diss., University of California at Berkeley, 1979).

Heartz, Daniel: 'Constructing *Le nozze di Figaro*', *Journal of the Royal Musical Association*, cxii (1987), 77–98.

———: 'The Great Quartet in Mozart's *Idomeneo*', *Music Forum*, v (1980), 233–56.

———: 'Raaff's Last Aria: a Mozartian Idyll in the Spirit of Hasse', *Musical Quarterly*, lx (1974), 517–43.

———: 'Tonality and Motif in *Idomeneo*', *Musical Times*, cxv (1974), 382–6.

Hellyer, Roger: 'Mozart's Harmoniemusik', *Music Review*, xxxiv (1973), 146–56.

Hess, Ernst: 'Ist das Fagottkonzert KV.Anhang 230a von Mozart?', *MJb 1957* (Salzburg, 1958), 223–32.

Hildesheimer, Wolfgang: *Mozart* (Frankfurt, 1977).

Hintermaier, Ernst: *Die Salzburger Hofkapelle von 1700 bis 1806: Organisation und Personal* (diss., Salzburg University, 1972).

Hortschansky, Klaus: 'Mozarts *Ascanio in Alba* und der Typus der Serenata', *Analecta musicologica*, no. 18 (1978), 148–59.

———: ' "Il Re Pastore": Zur Rezeption eines Librettos in der Mozart-Zeit', *MJb 1978–9*, 61–70.

Hübner, Beda: 'Diarium Patris Bedae Hubner ordinis sanctissi patris benedicti in antiquissimo monasterio ad anctum Petrum apostolum Salisburgi professo ac sacerdote indignissimo', manuscript, library of St Peter's Abbey, Salzburg.

Irving, John: *Mozart's Piano Concertos* (Aldershot, 2003).

Jahn, Otto: *W.A. Mozart* (Leipzig, 1856–9).

Kearns, Andrew: 'The Orchestral Serenade in Eighteenth-Century Salzburg', *Journal of Musicological Research*, xvi (1997), 163–97.

Kidd, Ronald R.: *The Sonata for Keyboard with Violin Accompaniment in England (1750–1790)* (diss., Yale U., 1967).

King, A. Hyatt: *Mozart Chamber Music* (London, 1968).

———: *Mozart in Retrospect: Studies in Criticism and Bibliography* (London, 1955).

———: 'The Mozarts at the British Museum', *Musical Pursuits: Selected Essays*, British Museum Occasional Papers, ix (London, 1987), 52–72.

Kirkendale, Warren: *Fugue and Fugato in Rococo and Classical Chamber Music* (Durham, NC, 2/1979).

Klein, Herbert: 'Unbekannte Mozartiana von 1766/67', *MJb 1957*, 168–85.

Kling, Henri: 'Mozart et Grétry à Genève 1766–1767', *Journal de Genève* (28 July 1866).

Konrad, Ulrich: 'Mozarts "Gruppenkonzerte" aus den letzten Salzburger Jahren: Probleme der Chronologie und Deutung', *Beiträge zur Geschichte des Konzerts: Festschrift Siegfried Kross zum 60. Geburtstag*, ed. Reinmar Emens and Matthias Wendt (Bonn, 1990), 141–57.

———: *Mozarts Schaffensweise: Studien zu den Werkautographen, Skizzen und Entwürfen* (Göttingen, 1992).

———: 'Mozart's Sketches', *Early Music*, xx (1992), 119–30.

Kröper-Hoffmann, Andreas: '*Zaide*—bühnenreif! Zur Adaption der Texte Sebastianis auf Mozart/Schachtner', *Hudební Veda*, xl (2003), nos. 2–3, pp. 135–54.

Kunze, Stephan: 'Die Vertonungen der Aria "Non so d'onde viene" von J.C. Bach und Mozart', *Analecta musicologica*, no. 2 (1965), 85–110.

Kurthen, Wilhelm: 'Studien zu W.A. Mozarts kirchenmusikalischen Jugendwerke', *Zeitschrift für Musikwissenschaft*, iii (1921), 194–222.

Landon, H.C. Robbins: 'La crise romantique dans la musique autrichienne vers 1770: Quelques précurseurs inconnus de la symphonie en sol mineur (KV 183) de Mozart', *Les influences étrangères dans l'oeuvre de W.A. Mozart*, ed. André Verchaly (Paris, 1958).

———: *Mozart: The Golden Years, 1781–1791* (London, 1989).

———: *1791: Mozart's Last Year* (London, 1988).

Larsen, Jens Peter: 'The Symphonies', *The Mozart Companion*, ed. H.C. Robbins Landon and Donald Mitchell (London, 1956), 156–98.

Larsen, Jens Peter, and Kamma Wedin, eds.: *Die Sinfonie KV 16a 'del Sigr. Mozart'*: *Bericht über das Symposium in Odense . . . Dezember 1984* (Odense, 1987).

Layer, Adolf: 'Der Augsburger Buchbinder Johann Georg Mozart', *Archiv für Geschichte des Buchwesens*, xi (1970), 873–84.

———: *Die Augsburger Künstlerfamilie Mozart* (Augsburg, 1971).

Lebermann, Walter: 'Mozart—Eck—André: Ein Beitrag zu KV 268 (365b)(C.14.04)', *Die Musikforschung*, xxxi (1978), 452–65.

Leeson, Daniel N.: 'A Revisit: Mozart's Serenade for Thirteen Instruments, K.361 (370a), the "Gran Partitta"', *MJb 1997*, 181–223.

Leeson, Daniel N., and Robert D. Levin: 'On the Authenticity of K. Anh. C14.01 (297b), a Symphonia Concertante for Four Winds and Orchestra', *MJb 1976–7*, 70–96.

Lequin, Frank: 'Mozarts " . . . rarer Mann" ', *MISM*, xxix/1–2 (1981), 3–19.

Levin, Robert D.: 'Das Konzert für Klavier und Violine D-dur KV Anh.56/315f und das Klarinettenquintett B-dur, KV Anh.91/516c: Ein Ergänzungsversuch', *MJb 1968–70*, 304–26 [in English].

———: *Who Wrote the Mozart Four-Wind Concertante?* (Stuyvesant, NY, 1988).

Link, Dorothea: *The National Court Theatre in Mozart's Vienna* (Oxford, 1998).

Lorenz, Michael: 'The Jenamy Concerto', *Newsletter of the Mozart Society of America*, x/1 (27 January 2005), 1–3.

Lühning, Helga: 'Mozarts Auseinandersetzung mit der da capo-Arie in *Mitridate, Rè di Ponto*', *MJb 2001*, 427–61.

Luin, Elisabeth J.: 'Mozarts Aufenthalt in Rom', *Neues Mozart-Jahrbuch*, iii (1943), 45–62.

Lustig, Roger: 'On the Flute Quartet, K.285b (Anh.171)', *MJb 1997*, 157–79.

Mahling, Christoph-Hellmut: 'Bemerkungen zum Violinkonzert KV 271i', *MJb 1978–9*, 252–7.

———: 'Nochmals Bemerkungen zum Violinkonzert D-dur KV 271a (271i)', *MJb 2001*, 101–8.

Mančal, Josef: 'Vom "Orden der geflickten Hosen", Leopold Mozarts Heirat und Bürgerrecht', *Leopold Mozart und Augsburg. 200. Todestag von Leopold Mozart. 50 Jahre Gedenkstätte "Mozarthaus". 50 Jahre Mozart-gemeinde Augsburg*, ed Ottmar F.W. Beck (Augsburg, 1987), 31–54.

Martin, Franz: 'Das "Nannerl Mozart in Galakleid"', *MJb 1950*, 49–61.

Mattei, Saverio: [Excerpt from] *Saggio di poesie latine, ed italiane*, ii (Naples,

1774), 268–79; English translation in Charles Burney: *A General History of Music* (London, 1776–89), ed. Frank Mercer (1935), ii, 932.

Mattern, Volker: *Das Dramma giocoso 'La finta giardiniera': Ein Vergleich der Vertonungen von Pasquale Anfossi und Wolfgang Amadeus Mozart* (Laaber, 1989).

Maunder, Richard: 'Mozart's Keyboard Instruments', *Early Music*, xx (1992), 207–19.

———: Review of *Who Wrote the Mozart Four-Wind Concertante?* by Robert D. Levin, *Journal of the Royal Musical Association*, cxvi (1991), 136–9.

McClymonds, Marita: 'The Great Quartet in *Idomeneo* and the Italian *opera seria* Tradition', *Wolfgang Amadè Mozart*, ed. S. Sadie, 449–76.

———: 'Mannheim, *Idomeneo* and the Franco-Italian Synthesis in Opera Seria', *Mozart und Mannheim: Kongressbericht Mannheim 1991*, ed. Ludwig Finscher, Bärbel Pelker and Jochen Reutter (Frankfurt, 1994), 187–96.

McVeigh, Simon: *Concert Life in London from Mozart to Haydn* (Cambridge, 1993).

Mozart, Leopold: *Ausgewählte Werke*, ed. Max Seiffert. Denkmäler der Tonkunst in Bayern, xvii, Jg. ix/2 (1908).

[Mozart, Leopold]: 'Nachricht von dem gegenwärtigen Zustande der Musik Sr. Hochfürstl. Gnaden des Erzbischoffs zu Salzburg im Jahr 1757', *Historisch-Kritische Beyträge zur Aufnahme der Musik*, iii, 183–98; for a translation, see Zaslaw, *Mozart's Symphonies*, Appendix C.

Mozart, Maria Anna. *Meine tag Ordnungen: Nannerl Mozarts Tagebuchblatter 1775–1783*, ed. Geneviève Geffray with Rudolph Angermüller (Bad Honnef, 1998).

———: 'Noch einige Anecdoten aus Mozarts Kinderjahren', *Allgemeine musikaliche Zeitung*, ii/17 (Leipzig, January 1800), cols. 300-301.

Mozart, Wolfgang Amadeus: *Mozart's Letters, Mozart's Life*, ed. & tr. Robert Spaethling (New York, 2000).

Münster, Robert: 'Neue Funde zu Mozarts symphonischen Jugendwerk', *MISM*, xxx/1–2 (1982), 2–11.

———: 'Neues zum Münchner "Idomeneo" 1781', *AcMoz*, xxv (1982), 10–20.

Musikalische Korrespondenz der Teutschen Filarmonischen Gesellschaft (Speyer, 24 November 1790).

Neumann, Friedrich-Heinrich: 'Zur Vorgeschichte der Zaide', *MJb 1962–3*, 216–47.

Neumayr, Anton: *Music and Medicine* (Bloomington, IN, 1994).

Newman, William S.: *The Sonata in the Classic Era* (Chapel Hill, 1963; New York, 3/1983).

Nissen, Georg Nikolaus: *Biographie W.A. Mozart's: Nach Originalbriefen, Sammlungen alles über ihn Geschriebenen, mit vielen neuen Beylagen, Steindrücken, Musikblättern und einem Fac-simile* (Leipzig, 1828).

Novello, Vincent, and Mary Novello: *A Mozart Pilgrimage: Being the Travel Diaries of Vincent & Mary Novello in the Year 1829*, ed. Rosemary Hughes and Nerina Medici di Marignano (London, 1955).

Oldman, Cecil B.: 'Beckford and Mozart', *Music & Letters*, xlvii (1966), 110–15.

———: 'Charles Burney and Louis de Visme', *Music Review*, xxvii (1966), 95–6.

———: 'Dr. Burney and Mozart', *MJb 1962–3*, 75–81 and *MJb 1964*, 109–10.

———: 'Mozart's Scena for Tenducci', *Music & Letters*, xlii (1961), 44–52.

Orel, Alfred: 'Der Mesmerische Garten', *MJb 1962–3*, 82–95.

———: 'Zu Mozarts Sommerreise nach Wien im Jahre 1773', *MJb 1951*, 34–49.

Perger, Lothar Herbert: 'Thematisches Verzeichnis der Instrumentalwerke von Michael Haydn', *Denkmäler der Tonkunst in Österreich*, xxix, Jg. xiv/2 (Vienna, 1907), nos. 108 and 109.

Pfannhauser, Karl: 'Zu Mozarts Kirchenwerken von 1768', *MJb 1954*, 150–68.

Pinamonti, Paolo, ed.: *La Betulia liberata* (n.p., 1989); includes Paolo Cattelan: 'Mozart e la "religio" musicale padovana', 7–40; Giorgio Mangini: 'I trionfi di Giuditta', 41–80; and Bruno Brizi: 'Nota al testo', 82–8.

Piozzi, Hester Lynch: *Thraliana: The Diary of Hester Lynch Thrale (later Mrs Piozzi) 1776–1809*, ed. Katharine C. Balderston (Oxford, 1942).

Plath, Wolfgang: 'Beiträge zur Mozart-Autographie I: Die Handschrift Leopold Mozarts', *MJb 1960–61*, 82–117.

———: 'Beiträge zur Mozart-Autographie II: Schriftchronologie 1770–1780', *MJb 1976–7*, 131–73.

———: 'Leopold Mozarts Notenbuch für Wolfgang (1762)—eine Fälschung?', *MJb 1971–2*, 337–41.

————: 'Mozart, (1) Leopold', *The New Grove Dictionary of Music and Musicians*, ed. Stanley Sadie (London, 1980).

————: 'Vorwort', NMA IX: 27, i, pp. ix–xxvii; reprinted in Plath, *Mozart-Schriften: Ausgewählte Aufsätze,* ed. Marianne Danckwardt (Kassel, 1991), 349–74.

————: 'Zur Datierung der Klaviersonaten KV 279–284', *AcMoz*, xxi (1974), 26–30.

Pohl, C.F.: *Mozart und Haydn in London* (Vienna, 1867).

Pryer, Anthony: 'Mozart's Operatic Audition: The Milan Concert', *Eighteenth-Century Music*, ii (2005).

Reeser, Eduard: *De klaviersonate mit vioolbegleiding in het parijsche muziekleven ten tijde van Mozart* (Rotterdam, 1939).

Reichert, Georg: 'Mozarts "Credo-Messen" und ihre Vorläufer', *MJb 1955*, 117–44.

Rice, Albert R.: 'The Two Versions of Mozart's Divertimento K.113', *Music & Letters*, lxxiv (1993), 485–7.

Rice, John A.: 'Adding Birds to Mozart's "Sparrow Mass"', *Mozart Society of America Newsletter*, vii/2 (2004), 8–9.

Roscoe, Christopher: 'Two 18th-Century Non-Events', *Musical Times*, cxii (1971), 18–19.

Rosenthal, Karl August: 'Mozart's Sacramental Litanies and their Forerunners', *Musical Quarterly*, xxvii (1941), 433–55.

Rosow, Lois: '*Idomeneo* and *Idomenée*: The French Disconnection', paper read at the American Musicological Society, Chicago, 1991.

Rushton, Julian: 'A Reconciliation Motif in *Idomeneo*', *Words about Mozart: Essays in Honour of Stanley Sadie*, ed. Dorothea Link and Judith Nagley (Woodbridge, 2005), 21–32.

————: 'Tonality and Motive', *Idomeneo*, ed. Rushton, 129–39.

————: '"La vittima è Idamante": Did Mozart have a Motive?', *Cambridge Opera Journal*, iii (1991), 1–21.

Rushton, Julian, and Don Neville: 'From Myth to Libretto', in *Idomeneo*, ed. Julian Rushton (Cambridge, 1993), 69–82.

Saam, Josef: 'Mozart in Passau', *AcMoz*, xiii/1 (1962), 7–15.

Sadie, Stanley: 'Music in the Home II', *The Blackwell History of Music in Britain: The Eighteenth Century*, ed. H. Diack Johnstone and Roger Fiske (Oxford, 1990), 313–54.

Sadie, Stanley, ed.: *Wolfgang Amadè Mozart: Essays on his Life and Works* (Oxford, 1996).

Scheurleer, Daniel François: *Mozart's verblijf in Nederland* (The Hague, 1883).

———: *Het muziekleven in Nederland in de tweede helft der 18ᵉ eeuw in verband met Mozart's verblijf aldaar* (The Hague, 1903).

Schizzi, Folchino: *Elogio storico di Wolfgango Amadeo Mozart* (Cremona, 1817).

Schlichtegroll, Friedrich: *Nekrolog auf das Jahr 1791* (Gotha, 1793).

Schmid, Ernst Fritz: 'Gluck—Starzer—Mozart', *Zeitschrift für Musik*, civ (1937), 1198.

Schneider, Constantin: *Geschichte der Musik in Salzburg* (Salzburg, 1935).

Scholes, Percy: *Dr. Burney's Musical Tours in Europe* (Oxford, 1959).

Schuler, Heinz: 'Fürsterzbischof Hieronymus von Colloredo: Herkunft und Ahnenerbe', 'Mozart und die Colloredos: Genealogische Miszellen zur Biographie des Fürsterzbischofs Hieronymus von Salzburg', *MISM*, xxxiv (1986), 1–17, 18–30.

———: *Die Gesamtverwandtschaft Wolfgang Amadeus Mozarts* (Essen, n.d.).

———: *Die Vorfahren Wolfgang Mozarts* (Essen, 1972).

———: *Wolfgang Amadeus: Vorfahren und Verwandte* (Neustadt an der Aisch, 1980).

Schurig, Arthur: *Wolfgang Amadeus Mozart: Sein Leben und sein Werk* (Leipzig, 1913).

Schwarz, Boris: 'Violinists around Mozart', *Music in the Classic Period*, ed. A. W. Atlas, 233–48.

Senn, Walter: 'Mozarts Skizze der Ballettmusik "Le gelosie del serraglio" (KV Anh.109/135a), *Acta musicologica*, xxxii (1961), 168–82.

Simon, Edwin J.: 'Sonata into Concerto', *Acta musicologica*, xxxi (1959), 170–85.

Solomon, Maynard: *Mozart: A Life* (New York, 1995).

Somfai, László: 'Mozart's First Thoughts: The Two Versions of the Sonata in D major, K284', *Early Music*, xix (1991), 601–13.

Staehelin, Lucas A.: 'Neues zu Mozarts Aufenthalten in Lyon, Genf und Bern', *Schweizerische Muzikzeitung*, xcvi (1956), 46–8.

———: *Die Reise der Familie Mozart durch die Schweiz* (Berne, 1968).

Stoneham, A.M.: letter to *The Musical Times*, cxxv (1984), 75.

Tagliavini, Luigi Ferdinando: 'Quirino Gasparini and Mozart', *New Looks at Italian Opera in Honor of Donald J. Grout*, ed. William W. Austin (Ithaca, NY, 1968), 151–71.

Thiblot, R.: 'Le séjour de Mozart à Dijon en 1766', *Mémoires de l'Académie des sciences, arts et belles-lettres de Dijon: année 1937* (Dijon, 1938), 139–43.

Tyler, Linda L.: '*Bastien und Bastienne* and the Viennese Volkskomödie', *MJb 1991*, 576–9.

———: '*Bastien und Bastienne*: The Libretto, Its Derivation, and Mozart's Text-Setting', *Journal of Musicology*, viii (1990), 520–52.

———: ' "Zaide" in the Development of Mozart's Operatic Language', *Music & Letters*, lxxii (1991), 214–35.

Tyson, Alan: 'The Dates of Mozart's *Missa brevis* K. 258 and *Missa longa* K. 262 (246a): An Investigation into his *Klein-Querformat* Papers', *Mozart: Studies of the Autograph Scores*, ed. Tyson, 162–76.

———: 'The Earliest Editions of Mozart's Duet-Sonata K.19d', *Music Review*, xxx (1969), 98–105.

———: *Mozart: Studies of the Autograph Scores* (Cambridge, MA, and London, 1987).

———: 'A Reconstruction of Nannerl Mozart's Music Book (Notenbuch)', *Music & Letters*, lx (1979), 389–400.

———: 'The Two Slow Movements of Mozart's "Paris" Symphony, K.297', *Mozart: Studies of the Autograph Scores*, ed. Tyson, 106–13.

Viale Ferrero, Mercedes: *La scenografia del '700 e i fratelli Galliari* (Turin, 1963).

Webster, James: 'The Scoring of Mozart's Chamber Music for Strings', *Music in the Classic Period,* ed. A. W. Atlas, 259–96.

Wegele, Ludwig: *Der Augsburger Maler Anton Mozart* (Augsburg, 1969).

Wegele, Ludwig, ed.: *Leopold Mozart, 1719–1787: Bild einer Persönlichkeit* (Augsburg, 1969),

Wignall, Harrison James: *In Mozart's Footsteps* (New York, 1991).

———: 'The Genesis of "Se di lauri": Mozart's Drafts and Final Version of Guglielmo Ettore's Entrance Aria from *Mitridate*', *Mozart-Studien*, v (1995).

Wolf, Eugene K.: 'The Mannheim Court', *Man and Music: The Classical Era*, ed. Neal Zaslaw, 213–39.

Wollenberg, Susan: 'The Jupiter Theme: New Light on its Creation', *Musical Times*, cxvi (1975), 781–3.

Woodfield, Ian: 'New Light on the Mozarts' London Visit: A Private Concert with Manzuoli', *Music & Letters*, lxxvi (1995), 187–207.

Wyzewa, Théodore de, and Georges de Saint-Foix: *Wolfgang Amédée Mozart: Sa vie musicale et son oeuvre* (Paris, 1912–46).

Zaslaw, Neal: 'Leopold Mozart's List of his Son's Works', *Music in the Classic Period,* ed. A. W. Atlas, 323–58.

——: 'Mozart as a Working Stiff," *On Mozart,* ed. J.M. Morris (New York, 1994), 102–12.

——: Neal Zaslaw, 'Mozart's Orchestral Flutes and Oboes,' *Mozart Studies,* ed. Cliff Eisen (Oxford, 1991).

——: 'Mozart's Paris Symphonies', *MT,* cxix (1978), 753–7.

——: *Mozart's Symphonies: Context, Performance Practice, Reception* (Oxford, 1989).

Zaslaw, Neil, and Cliff Eisen: 'Signor Mozart's Symphony in A minor, K. Anhang 220 = 16a', *Journal of Musicology,* iv (1986), 191–206.

CLASSIFIED INDEX OF MOZART'S WORKS

(including lost, attributed, doubtful, and spurious works)

Note: For detailed indexing, please refer to Köchel number index.

SACRED MUSIC: MASSES, MASS MOVEMENTS, REQUIEM

Kyrie fragment in E flat, K.322/296a: 441–42
Kyrie in D minor, K.341: 547–48
Kyrie in F, K.33: 96, 103, 107
Mass in C, K.66 *(Dominicus-Messe)*: 166–67, 168–69, 315
Mass in C, K.139/47a *(Waisenhaus-Messe)*: 142, 143, 159–61, 163
Mass in C, K.167: 307–9, 344
Mass in C, K.257 ('Credo' mass): 147, 386, 388–90
Mass in C, K.262/246a: 386–87, 388, 389
Mass in C, K.317 ('Coronation'): 494–96, 497
Mass in C, K.337: 496–97
Missa brevis in B flat, K.275/272b: 386, 390, 391
Missa brevis in C, K.220/196b *(Spatzenmesse)*: 386, 387–88, 389, 499, 579n5
Missa brevis in C, K.258 ('Spaur' mass): 386, 388–90
Missa brevis in C, K.259 ('Organ solo' mass): 386, 388–90, 391
Missa brevis in D, K.194/186h: 345–46, 349, 354, 388, 390
Missa brevis in D minor, K.65/61a: 162–63, 167–68, 346
Missa brevis in F, K.192/186f: 147, 345–49, 354, 388, 389, 390
Missa brevis in G, K.49/47d: 143, 159, 160, 167, 345
Requiem in D minor, K.626: 169, 393

SACRED MUSIC: LITANIES, VESPERS, VESPER PSALMS

Dixit Dominus and *Magnificat,* K.193/186g: 350
Litaniae de venerabili altaris sacramento, K.125: 266–67, 353–54, 392, 393

SACRED MUSIC: SHORT WORKS

SACRED MUSIC: CHURCH (EPISTLE) SONATAS

SACRED MUSIC: ORATORIOS, SACRED DRAMAS, CANTATAS

THEATRE MUSIC: OPERAS, MUSICAL PLAYS, DRAMATIC CANTATAS

THEATRE MUSIC: BALLETS

VOCAL MUSIC: DUETS

VOCAL MUSIC: FUGUE

VOCAL MUSIC: ARIAS AND SCENES FOR VOICE AND ORCHESTRA

VOCAL MUSIC: SONGS

VOCAL MUSIC: CANONS

CONCERTED INSTRUMENTAL ENSEMBLES:
SYMPHONIES, SYMPHONY MOVEMENTS

CONCERTED INSTRUMENTAL ENSEMBLES:

CASSATIONS, SERENADES, DIVERTIMENTOS, MISC. WORKS

CONCERTED INSTRUMENTAL ENSEMBLES: MARCHES

CONCERTED INSTRUMENTAL ENSEMBLES: DANCE MUSIC

Contredanse in B flat, K.123/73g: 195, 206
Minuet in C, K.409/383f: 503
Minuet in E flat, K.122/73t: 206
minuets, K.41d (lost): 143
minuets, K.65a/61b: 173
minuets, K.103/61d: 202, 277
minuets, K.164/130a: 277
minuets, K.176: 344

CONCERTED INSTRUMENTAL ENSEMBLES: CONCERTOS, KEYBOARD

Concerto in A, K.488: 368
Concerto in B flat, K.238: 406–7, 408, 410, 425, 439, 468
Concerto in C, K.246: 407–8, 412, 430, 468
Concerto in D, K.175: 326, 332–34, 376, 406, 439
Concerto in E flat, K.271 ('Jeunehomme Concerto'): 410–13, 448, 468, 505, 509
Concerto in E flat for two keyboards, K.365/316a: 507, 509, 510–12
Concerto in F for three keyboards, K.242: 408–9, 425, 441, 510–11
pasticcio concerto in B flat, K.39: 124–25, 127, 269
pasticcio concerto in D, K.40: 125, 127, 269
pasticcio concerto in F, K.37: 124–27, 269
pasticcio concerto in G, K.41: 125, 127, 269
pasticcio concertos, K.107: 269–70, 354
Rondo in D for keyboard and orchestra, K.382: 333, 576n13
Violin and Piano Concerto in D, K.Anh.56/351f: 484, 509–10

CONCERTED INSTRUMENTAL ENSEMBLES: CONCERTOS, STRING

Adagio in E for violin and orchestra, K.261: 376
'Adelaide Concerto,' K.Anh.294a/C14.05: 377
Concertone in C for two violins, K.190/186E: 326, 334–35, 337, 372, 507–8
Rondo in B flat for violin and orchestra, K.269/261a: 376
Sinfonia Concertante in E flat for Violin and Viola, K.364/329d: 507–9
Triple Concerto fragment in A for violin, viola and cello, K.Anh.104/320e: 510
Violin Concerto in A, K.219: 306, 372, 374–76, 388, 406
Violin Concerto in B flat, K.207: 306–7, 315, 371–72, 375, 376
Violin Concerto in D, K.211: 306, 372–73
Violin Concerto in D, K.218: 306, 372, 373–74, 377, 406
Violin Concerto in D, K.271a/271i: 376–77
Violin Concerto in E flat, K.268: 376
Violin Concerto in G, K.216 ('Strassburg' concerto): 306, 372, 373, 375, 379, 406, 424

CONCERTED INSTRUMENTAL ENSEMBLES:

CONCERTOS, WIND INSTRUMENTS

Andante in C for flute, K.315/285e: 447, 449
Bassoon Concerto in B flat, K.191/186e: 335–37, 365, 372

CHAMBER MUSIC: KEYBOARD AND
VIOLIN SONATAS (ACCOMPANIED SONATAS)

Sonata in A, K.305/293d: 442, 445, 446–47, 465, 470, 477, 484, 487
Sonata in A, K.526: 447
Sonata in B flat, K.378/317d: 512–13
Sonata in B flat, K.454: 371
Sonata in C, K.296: 442, 447, 512
Sonata in C, K.303/293c: 442, 445, 446, 465, 470, 477, 484, 487
Sonata in D, K.306/300l: 465, 470, 478–79, 484, 487
Sonata in E flat, K.302/293b: 442, 446, 465, 470, 477, 484, 487
Sonata in E minor, K.304/300c: 445, 465, 470, 477–78, 479, 484, 487
Sonata in G, K.301/293a: 442, 445, 446, 447, 465, 470, 477, 487
Sonata in G, K.379/373a: 81, 295
Sonatas, K.6–9: 46, 50, 54–57, 68, 86, 143, 444–45
Sonatas, K.10–15: 68, 74, 86–87, 143, 444–45
Sonatas, K.26–31: 94, 106–7, 143, 444–45

CHAMBER MUSIC: WIND

flute pieces, K.33a (lost): 101, 143
Sonata in B flat for bassoon, K.292/196c: 365, 369

KEYBOARD MUSIC: SONATAS

Sonata in A minor, K.310/300d: 469, 470, 479–80
Sonata in B flat, K.333/315c: 371
Sonata in B flat for keyboard duet, K.358/186c: 344
Sonata in C, K.309/284b: 429, 442–43, 444, 469, 470, 480
Sonata in C for four hands, K.19d: 71–72
Sonata in D, K.284/205b: 365–66, 369–71, 425, 443, 468, 578n11
Sonata in D, K.311/284c: 442, 443–44, 469, 470
Sonata in D for keyboard duet, K.381/123a: 277, 344, 510
Sonatas, K.33d–g (lost): 112, 354
Sonatas, K.279–283/189d–h: 326, 354–55, 365–69, 424, 468, 578n11

KEYBOARD MUSIC: VARIATIONS

Variations on a theme by Fischer, K.179/189a: 344–45, 354, 370–71, 424, 468, 480
Variations on 'Je suis Lindor,' K.354/299a: 468, 470, 480
Variations on 'Laat ons juichen, Batavieren!' by Graaf, K.24: 94, 103–4, 143, 370
Variations on 'Lison dormait,' K.264/315d: 470, 480–81
Variations on Salieri's 'Mio caro Adone,' K.180/173c: 316, 317, 354, 370, 468, 480
Variations on 'Willem van Nassau,' K.25: 94, 103–4, 143, 370

KEYBOARD MUSIC: MISCELLANEOUS

INDEX OF MOZART'S WORKS
BY KÖCHEL NUMBER
(includes lost, attributed, doubtful, and spurious works with Köchel numbers)

GENERAL INDEX

Note: Numbers in *italics* indicate illustrations. For Mozart's works, please see the indexes listed by Köchel number and by genre.